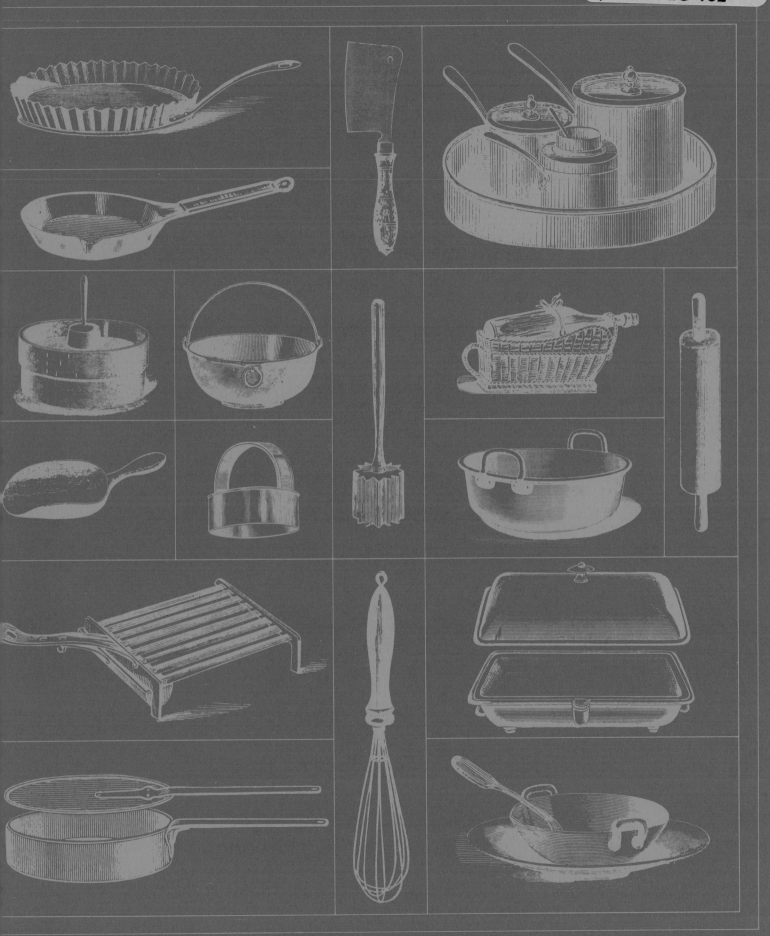

# Great Cooking
## The Best Recipes from TIME-LIFE BOOKS

*The recipes anthologized in this volume were taken from the following TIME-LIFE books:*

# Great Cooking

## The Best Recipes from TIME-LIFE BOOKS

HENRY HOLT AND COMPANY · NEW YORK

Time-Life Books Inc.
is a wholly owned subsidiary of
**TIME INCORPORATED**

*Founder:* Henry R. Luce 1898–1967

*Editor-in-Chief:* Henry Anatole Grunwald
*President:* J. Richard Munro
*Chairman of the Board:* Ralph P. Davidson
*Corporate Editor:* Ray Cave
*Group Vice President, Books:* Reginald K. Brack Jr.
*Vice President, Books:* George Artandi

**TIME-LIFE BOOKS INC.**

*Editor:* George Constable
*Executive Editor:* George Daniels
*Director of Design:* Louis Klein
*Director of Editorial Resources:* Phyllis K. Wise
*Acting Text Director:* Ellen Phillips
*Editorial Board:* Russell B. Adams Jr., Dale M. Brown,
Roberta Conlan, Thomas H. Flaherty, Donia Ann Steele,
Rosalind Stubenberg, Kit van Tulleken, Henry Woodhead
*Director of Photography and Research:* John Conrad Weiser

*President:* Reginald K. Brack Jr.
*Executive Vice Presidents:* John M. Fahey Jr., Christopher T. Linen
*Senior Vice Presidents:* James L. Mercer, Leopoldo Toralballa
*Vice Presidents:* Stephen L. Bair, Ralph Cuomo, Juanita T. James,
Hallett Johnson III, Robert H. Smith, Paul R. Stewart
*Director of Production Services:* Robert J. Passantino
*Quality Control:* James J. Cox (director)

*Great Cooking* was created
for TIME-LIFE BOOKS
by Sheldon Cotler + Associates Inc.

**SHELDON COTLER + ASSOCIATES INC.**

*Director:* Sheldon Cotler
*Editor:* Gerry Schremp
*Text Research Director:* Eleanore W. Karsten
*Designers:* Sheldon Cotler, Leonard Vigliarolo
*Editorial Manager:* Felice R. Lerner
*Art Studio:* Laura Jane Bernay, Ian Cotler,
Frances Fifield, Linda Fiordilino,
Janice Hogan
*Researcher:* Suzanne Odette Khuri
*Copy Staff:* Charles Rizzuto, Jane B. Whipple

**PHOTOGRAPHY: ARIE deZANGER**

*Chef and Food Stylist:* Wilma deZanger
*Props:* Ann Pratt
*Photography Assistant:* Peggy Spinelli

Published by Henry Holt and Company, Inc.,
521 Fifth Avenue, New York, New York 10175.

Distributed in Canada by Fitzhenry & Whiteside,
195 Allstate Parkway, Markham, Ontario L3R 4T8.

Library of Congress Cataloging-in-Publication Data
Great cooking.
    Includes index.
    1. Cookery.    I. Time-Life Books.
TX652.G724 1986      641.5      86-11947
ISBN 0-8050-0147-6
First Edition
Printed in the United States of America
10 9 8 7 6 5 4 3 2 1

ISBN 0-8050-0147-6

# Contents

COVER: SCAMPI WITH GARLIC BUTTER (RECIPE, PAGE 174)

# Introduction

The great 19th Century French gastronome Anthelme Brillat-Savarin once wrote that "the discovery of a new dish does more for human happiness than the discovery of a new star." He can be forgiven a bit of hyperbole; he was then at the apogee of a life devoted to sumptuous dining, in an age when French cuisine was approaching dazzling heights of invention.

Yet his point remains as true as ever. Food is sustenance, but great food is art, with all its infinite possibilities and challenges.

Over the past two decades, Time-Life Books has published upward of 80 cookbooks containing more than 10,000 recipes of every imaginable sort. All but one of these volumes were published in series, the first of which was The Foods of the World—27 volumes exploring a multitude of cuisines from that of provincial France and Germany to the far reaches of Asia and the islands of the Caribbean. The Good Cook, in 28 volumes, undertook to explain cooking techniques for everything from hearty stews to sublime sauces. Great Meals in Minutes focused its 22 volumes on menu planning and dishes that could be prepared in less than one hour—but with no compromise in excitement or quality. Yet another series, Healthy Home Cooking, set for itself the goal of providing dishes that were at once within nutritional guidelines for sodium, cholesterol, caloric content and the like. In addition, Time-Life Books has published a classic single volume, *Great Dinners from Life,* which brought together the finest recipes from *Life* magazine's highly acclaimed series of articles on food.

In one way or another, all of these volumes were dedicated to the art of cooking, to freshness and innovation, to excellence. Many of the 10,000 recipes were original, invented for the occasion by Time-Life's cooks and consultants. Some were modern incarnations of centuries-old instructions. Still others were amended versions of exotic recipes with arcane techniques and difficult-to-procure ingredients.

This volume is a celebration of those recipes, a compendium of the best and most interesting dishes published by Time-Life Books. They range from the perfectly simple—an omelet, for example—to the marvelously elaborate, such as a Viennese sachertorte. And they represent the entire spectrum of dining well—commencing with hors d'oeuvre and finishing with a flourish of fruits and desserts. □ The Editors

# Hors d'Oeuvre

# Hors d'Oeuvre

FRONTISPIECE: BLINY

L ike a welcoming smile, an hors d'oeuvre holds out a promise of good things and happy times to come. The food may be as simple as crackers and a spread such as Liptauer cheese, or as demanding as a homemade pâté. Caviar—displayed at left in one of the buckwheat pancakes the Russians call *bliny*—is the most regal way to start a meal. As with so many hors d'oeuvre, *bliny* may be presented as a formal first course or on a buffet table along with other choice morsels.

Whatever the hors d'oeuvre, they should be served in small helpings to stimulate, not satisfy, the appetite. And they should complement the meal (the work, or *oeuvre*) that follows by contrasting with it. When, for example, the main course is to be heavily sauced, the hors d'oeuvre should be light, and vice versa. A hot main course benefits from a cold first course, a cold main course from a hot appetizer. A main course of crisp and chewy foods is set off best by a satiny smooth hors d'oeuvre; a soft and unctuous main course is dramatized by something crunchy; raw vegetables, or *crudités,* are an obvious choice and can be given distinction with the addition of unexpected varieties such as sunchokes or jícama.

To introduce a meal with a flourish, hors d'oeuvre should be put together artfully. The ideal is achieved, according to the English food writer Elizabeth David, when "each dish looks as if it had been freshly imagined, prepared for the first time, especially for you."

## Herbed Cheese Pastry

**To serve 4 to 6**

| | |
|---|---|
| **One 5-ounce container cream cheese with herbs and garlic** | **fresh parsley leaves** |
| **⅓ cup ricotta cheese** | **½ teaspoon salt** |
| **1 egg** | **Freshly ground black pepper** |
| **1 tablespoon finely chopped** | **5 tablespoons butter, melted** |
| | **6 sheets phyllo pastry, defrosted if frozen** |

Preheat the oven to 375°F. Combine the herbed cream cheese, ricotta, egg, parsley, salt and pepper in a blender or food processor, and blend until smooth. Scrape down the sides of the bowl if necessary.

Using a pastry brush, brush the bottom and sides of a shallow round 8-inch baking pan with melted butter. Keeping the remaining sheets of phyllo covered with a damp cloth as you work, line the pan with one sheet. Let the edges of the phyllo hang over the sides, but fit and press the sheet neatly inside the pan. Brush the sheet with melted butter. Place four more sheets in the pan, buttering each one as you add it. When you are done, there should be no spaces where the pan shows through.

Spread the cheese mixture over the phyllo. Place one-half sheet of phyllo over the cheese. Brush the phyllo with butter. Loosely fold up the overhanging phyllo to enclose the cheese—a rough, rustic surface will look best.

Brush the other half sheet of phyllo with butter and roll it up. Twist it into a rough rosette and center it on top. Brush the pastry with butter. Bake it for 20 minutes or until it is golden brown. To serve, run a knife around the edge of the pan; carefully lift the pastry out with a metal spatula, and place it on a serving dish. Cut it into wedges and serve it hot as a first course.

■ CHICKEN AND GAME HEN MENUS

## Skewered Cheese and Toast Fans

**To serve 6**

| | |
|---|---|
| **Three 3-ounce or two 4-ounce individual loaves Italian white bread** | ANCHOVY SAUCE |
| **One ½-pound ball mozzarella cheese** | **8 flat anchovy fillets** |
| **¼ cup butter, melted** | **1 clove garlic, chopped fine** |
| | **½ cup butter, cut into bits** |

Preheat the oven to 375°F. Prepare the sauce by mashing the anchovies with a fork in a small bowl, then mix in the garlic. Melt the ½ cup of butter in a small skillet over low heat. Add the anchovy-and-garlic mixture and stir until smooth. Cover the skillet to keep the sauce warm, and set the skillet aside.

Trim the crusts and ends from the bread; cut the small loaves in half crosswise and the larger ones into thirds. You should have six stubby sticks about 1½ inches high, 1½ inches wide and 2½ inches long. Starting at one end of each piece, cut four slits ½ inch apart; cut just to within about ¼ inch of the bottom so that the piece will stay together and form a kind of fan. Cut the ball of mozzarella into thirds, then cut each third in half. Cut each piece of cheese into four slices ¼ inch thick and about 1 inch square. Fit the cheese slices into the slits in each stick of bread neatly. Thread the bread and cheese onto skewers. Holding the skewers upright, brush the bread with the ¼ cup of melted butter.

Arrange the skewers on a foil-covered baking sheet. Bake for five minutes, or until the cheese melts. The bread will be a light golden color. To toast it to a deeper brown, run the skewers under the broiler for 30 to 40 seconds, watching them carefully. To serve, slide the fans off the skewers onto small plates, and pour anchovy sauce over them.

■ GREAT DINNERS FROM LIFE

## Liptauer Cheese

**To make about 2 cups**

| | |
|---|---|
| **1 cup cottage cheese** | **1 teaspoon dry mustard** |
| **½ cup unsalted butter, softened** | **1 teaspoon chopped capers** |
| **1 tablespoon sweet Hungarian paprika** | **1 tablespoon finely chopped onion** |
| **Freshly ground black pepper** | **½ cup sour cream** |
| **Salt** | **3 tablespoons finely cut fresh chives** |
| **2 teaspoons caraway seeds** | |

With a wooden spoon rub the cottage cheese through a sieve into a mixing bowl. Cream the butter in another bowl by beating it against the side. Beat in the cheese, paprika, a generous grinding of pepper, salt to taste, caraway seeds, mustard, capers, onion and sour cream.

Shape the cheese into a mound and decorate it with the chives, or form it into a ball and roll it in the chives. Refrigerate it for two hours or until firm.

■ THE COOKING OF VIENNA'S EMPIRE

## Fruit Crudités with Roquefort Spread

**To serve 4**

| | |
|---|---|
| **¼ pound Roquefort cheese, softened** | **2 large ripe pears** |
| **½ cup sour cream** | **2 large Red Delicious apples** |
| **½ to ¾ cup chopped pecans or walnuts** | **Lettuce leaves, washed and spun or patted dry** |

In a mixing bowl, mash the Roquefort with a fork. Stir in the sour cream and ½ cup chopped nuts. Cover the cheese until you are ready to serve it.

Just before serving, quarter and core the pears and apples; do not peel them. Cut each quarter into three or four slices. Line a serving plate with the lettuce leaves. Arrange the fruit slices and cheese spread on the leaves. Garnish the top with more nuts.

■ BRUNCH MENUS

## Artichokes Stuffed with Shrimp

**To serve 4**

| | |
|---|---|
| **4 large artichokes, each 4 to 5 inches in diameter, stems and tops trimmed, leaf tips removed** | **parsley leaves, preferably flatleaf parsley** |
| **1 lemon, halved crosswise** | **2 teaspoons finely grated fresh lemon peel** |
| **Salt** | |
| **1 pound uncooked shrimp, shelled and deveined** | CREOLE VINAIGRETTE SAUCE |
| **1¼ cups butter, cut into bits** | **2 tablespoons tarragon vinegar** |
| **6 cups fresh bread crumbs** | **1 teaspoon paprika** |
| **1 cup finely chopped onions** | **½ teaspoon Creole mustard or other pungent, dark prepared mustard** |
| **4 teaspoons finely chopped garlic** | **¼ teaspoon cayenne pepper** |
| **2 cups freshly grated Romano or Parmesan cheese** | **½ teaspoon salt** |
| **½ cup finely chopped fresh** | **6 to 8 tablespoons olive oil** |

In a 10- to 12-quart enameled or other nonreactive pot, bring 5 quarts of water to a boil over high heat. Drop in the artichokes, 2 tablespoons of salt and one lemon half, and return the water to a boil. Cook briskly, uncovered, for 15 to 20 minutes or until the bases of the artichokes show no resistance when pierced with the point of a small, sharp knife. Using tongs, invert the artichokes in a colander to drain. Discard the lemon and all but about 1 inch of the cooking liquid. Set the pot aside.

Meanwhile, drop the shrimp into enough lightly salted boiling water to cover them. Cook, uncovered, for three to five minutes, until the shrimp are pink and firm to the touch. Drain the shrimp; reserve four for garnish and chop the rest fine. Set them all aside.

Melt 1 cup of the butter bits in a heavy 12-inch skillet set over moderate heat, stirring so that the butter does not brown. When the foam begins to subside, add the bread crumbs and stir until they are crisp and golden. With a rubber spatula, scrape the crumbs into a bowl; set aside.

In the same skillet, melt the remaining ¼ cup of butter. Add the onions and garlic, and stir for about five minutes, until they are soft and translucent but not brown. Scrape the onion mixture over the bread crumbs, add the chopped shrimp, grated cheese, parsley and lemon peel, and toss the ingredients together gently but thoroughly with a spoon; taste for seasoning. Divide the shrimp mixture into four equal portions.

To stuff one artichoke, start near the base, gently ease back the top of one leaf, and spoon about a teaspoonful of one portion of the shrimp mixture into the opening. Push the shrimp mixture down between the leaf and the artichoke, then press the leaf into place. Repeat until all of the large green outer leaves have been stuffed, then stand the artichoke upright on a large piece of heavy-duty aluminum foil. Fold the foil tightly up and around the artichoke, and twist the ends securely together at the top. To keep the stuffing in place, tie a short length of kitchen cord around the width of the foil package. Stuff and wrap the remaining artichokes in the same way.

Stand the artichokes upright in the reserved pot and bring the

**ARTICHOKES STUFFED WITH SHRIMP**

liquid to a boil over high heat. Cover tightly and steam the artichokes for 20 minutes. Meanwhile prepare the sauce by combining the vinegar, paprika, mustard, cayenne and salt in a deep bowl and beating them vigorously with a wire whisk to dissolve the salt. Whisking constantly, dribble in the oil a few drops at a time until no more oil is absorbed. Taste for seasoning, and add more salt and pepper if desired.

Cut the four reserved shrimp into fan shapes, slicing through the shrimp lengthwise four or five times without cutting through the tails. Spread each shrimp into a fan shape. With tongs, transfer the artichokes to a cutting board and remove the strings and foil. Arrange the artichokes attractively on individual plates, and place a shrimp fan on top of each one. Serve the vinaigrette sauce separately as an accompaniment to the artichokes' inner leaves and bottoms.

■ AMERICAN COOKING: CREOLE AND ACADIAN

heat for about two minutes, then turn them over and fry for another minute or two, until they are lightly browned. Remove them from the heat.

Fill the mushroom caps with the ricotta mixture, and top each one with bits of mozzarella. Arrange the caps side by side in a shallow baking dish or pan, and bake them in the center of the oven for eight minutes or until the filling begins to bubble. Slide the caps under a hot broiler for 30 seconds to brown the mozzarella topping. Serve them at once as an accompaniment to drinks or as part of an antipasto.

■ AMERICAN COOKING: THE MELTING POT

## Baked Stuffed Tomatoes Sicilian Style

**To serve 4**

| | |
|---|---|
| 4 tomatoes, 3 to 4 inches in diameter | ably Italian-style, packed in olive oil), drained and broken into small pieces |
| Salt | |
| 2 to 3 tablespoons olive oil | 2 tablespoons capers, rinsed and drained |
| ¼ cup finely chopped onions | |
| ½ teaspoon finely chopped garlic | 6 black olives (preferably Mediterranean style), pitted and chopped fine |
| 1 cup fresh bread crumbs | |
| 4 flat anchovy fillets, drained, soaked in cold water for 10 minutes, dried and chopped fine | 4 tablespoons finely chopped fresh parsley leaves, preferably flatleaf parsley |
| One 7-ounce can tuna (prefer- | 1 tablespoon freshly grated Parmesan cheese |

Preheat the oven to 375°F. Slice about ¼ inch off the top of each tomato. Using your index finger or a teaspoon, scoop out all the pulp and seeds from the tomatoes, leaving hollow shells about ¼ inch thick. Sprinkle the insides of the shells lightly with salt and invert them over paper towels to drain.

Meanwhile, heat 2 tablespoons of olive oil in a heavy 8- to 10-inch skillet, and in it cook the onions and garlic, stirring frequently, until the onions are transparent but not brown—about five minutes. Stir in the bread crumbs, anchovies and tuna; stirring constantly, cook for one to two minutes. Remove the skillet from the heat and add the capers, olives and 3 tablespoons of the parsley. If the mixture looks dry and crumbly, add 1 or 2 teaspoons of olive oil. Spoon the stuffing mixture into the hollowed tomatoes; sprinkle them with the grated cheese and a few drops of olive oil.

Arrange the stuffed tomatoes in one layer in a lightly oiled 8- or 9-inch baking dish, and bake them for 20 to 30 minutes or until they are tender but not limp and the crumbs on top are brown and crisp. Serve the tomatoes hot or cold, sprinkled with the remaining parsley.

■ THE COOKING OF ITALY

## Stuffed Mushrooms

**To make 1½ dozen**

| | |
|---|---|
| 1 cup ricotta cheese | 1 tablespoon fresh lemon juice |
| ¼ cup finely chopped fresh parsley leaves | ¼ cup olive oil |
| | 18 mushroom caps |
| ¼ pound prosciutto, chopped fine | 2½ ounces mozzarella cheese, cut into ¼-inch bits (about ½ cup) |
| 2 teaspoons salt | |
| Freshly ground black pepper | |

Preheat the oven to 400°F. Place the ricotta in a large mixing bowl and, with a wooden spoon, beat in the parsley, prosciutto, salt, a few grindings of black pepper and the lemon juice. Beat vigorously until the mixture is smooth. Set aside.

In a 10- or 12-inch stainless-steel or enameled skillet, heat the oil. Drop in the mushroom caps, and fry them over moderate

## Imam Bayildi

*It is told of this delectable Middle Eastern eggplant dish that a certain holy man once swooned after simply inhaling its fragrance, and it has ever since been known as imam bayildi, or "the priest fainted."* ❧

**To serve 6**

| | |
|---|---|
| 3 small eggplants | Freshly ground black pepper |
| 6 tablespoons olive oil | 4 tomatoes, peeled, seeded |
| 2 onions, sliced thin | and cut into chunks |
| 1 green pepper, halved, | 2 tablespoons fresh lemon |
| seeded, deribbed and cut | juice |
| into thin julienne strips | 2 tablespoons chopped fresh |
| 1 garlic clove, chopped fine | parsley leaves, preferably |
| 1½ teaspoons salt | flatleaf parsley |
| ½ teaspoon sugar | ¼ cup pine nuts (pignolia) |
| ¼ teaspoon dried oregano | |

Place the eggplants in a large pot and cover them with boiling water. (To avoid bruising them, you may need to cook them one at a time.) Cook them, uncovered, over high heat for five minutes. Turn them often, using a wooden spoon to prevent puncturing the skin. Transfer the eggplants to cold water to cool them quickly.

With a large, sharp knife, cut the cooled eggplants in half lengthwise. To remove the eggplant pulp without piercing the skin, first cut around the inside of each half about ½ inch from the edge. Next, cut squares into the pulp, being careful to leave ½ inch of shell. Scoop out the pulp—a serrated grapefruit knife is ideal for this. Measure and reserve 4 cups of pulp; discard the rest or use it for another purpose. Place the eggplant shells, skin side up, on a paper-towel-lined tray, and refrigerate them until you are ready to serve them.

Heat 3 tablespoons of the olive oil in a large skillet over moderate heat, and in it sauté the onions and pepper until they are just wilted—about five minutes. Add the garlic and the cut-up eggplant pulp; cover the skillet and cook, stirring occasionally, for seven minutes or until the eggplant is very tender. Add the salt, sugar, oregano and a generous grinding of black pepper. Stir, then cook for about two minutes.

Transfer the vegetable mixture to a large bowl. Gently stir in the cut-up tomatoes; add the remaining olive oil and the lemon juice. Cover the mixture and refrigerate it for at least four hours. Just before serving, pat the insides of the eggplant shells with paper towels and, using a slotted spoon, heap the vegetable mixture into the shells. Sprinkle the eggplants with the parsley and pine nuts.

■ GREAT DINNERS FROM LIFE

IMAM BAYILDI

## Benne-Seed Biscuits

*Slaves who arrived in Charleston in the 1600s brought benne (sesame) seeds to America. The name persists.* ❧

**To make about 8 dozen**

| | |
|---|---|
| ½ cup sesame seeds | ½ cup butter, chilled and cut |
| 2 cups all-purpose flour | into ¼-inch bits |
| 1 teaspoon double-acting | ¼ cup milk |
| baking powder | Coarse (kosher) salt |
| ½ teaspoon salt | |

Preheat the oven to 350°F. Spread the sesame seeds evenly in a shallow baking dish and, stirring occasionally, toast them until golden brown. Set the seeds aside.

Combine the flour, baking powder and salt, and sift them into a large, chilled bowl. Add the butter bits and, with your fingertips, rub the fat and flour together until the mixture resembles flakes of coarse meal. Pour in the milk and mix with your hands or a spoon. Then blend in the sesame seeds, wrap the dough in wax paper, and refrigerate it for at least one hour.

Preheat the oven to 350°F. Cut the chilled dough in half and shape each half into a rectangle. Place one-half at a time between two sheets of lightly floured wax paper and roll out the dough paper thin. Gently peel off the top sheet of wax paper and, with a 1½-inch biscuit cutter, cut the dough into rounds. Use a metal spatula to transfer the rounds to ungreased baking sheets. Gather the scraps, shape, roll and cut them.

Bake the biscuits for 10 to 12 minutes or until they are a pale golden color. Slide them onto wire racks and immediately sprinkle the tops lightly with coarse salt. The biscuits can be kept for two to three weeks in a tightly covered jar or tin.

■ AMERICAN COOKING: SOUTHERN STYLE

## Bagna Cauda

*Raw vegetables served with dip are often called by their French name, crudités. You may substitute almost any raw vegetable you like for those listed: fennel strips, white turnip wedges, jicama strips, cauliflower or broccoli flowerets, red or white radishes. If the butter and cream separate as the sauce stands, beat them together with a whisk.* ◆●

### To serve 6

| | |
|---|---|
| 1 cucumber, peeled, seeded and cut into 2-by-½-inch strips | leaves separated, washed and spun or patted dry |
| 2 carrots, peeled and cut into 2-by-½-inch strips | 12 cherry tomatoes |
| 1 sweet red pepper, seeded, deribbed and cut into 2-by-½-inch strips | ¼ pound mushrooms, whole if small, quartered if large |
| 1 green pepper, seeded, deribbed and cut into 2-by-½-inch strips | Italian bread sticks |
| | DIP |
| 4 stalks celery, cut into 2-by-½-inch strips | 2 cups heavy cream |
| | ¼ cup butter |
| 1 bunch scallions, trimmed and cut into 2-inch lengths | 8 flat anchovy fillets, drained, rinsed and chopped fine |
| 1 small head romaine lettuce, | 1 teaspoon finely chopped garlic |
| | 1 canned white truffle, chopped fine (optional) |

Soak the vegetable strips in a bowl of ice cubes and water for an hour to crisp them. Pat them dry with paper towels, and arrange them on a platter with the romaine leaves, tomatoes and mushrooms. Cover them with plastic wrap and refrigerate them. Arrange the bread sticks separately.

In a heavy 1-quart enameled or stainless-steel saucepan, bring the cream to a boil and cook it, stirring frequently, for 15 minutes or until it has reduced to about 1 cup.

Choose a 3- to 4-cup enameled or flameproof earthenware casserole that fits over a candle warmer, spirit lamp or electric hot tray. On the stove, melt the butter in the casserole over low heat; do not let it brown. Add the anchovies and garlic, then the reduced cream and optional truffle, and bring the sauce to a simmer, stirring constantly; do not let it boil. Serve the *bagna cauda* at once, accompanied by the cold vegetables and bread sticks.

■ THE COOKING OF ITALY

## Guacamole

*Guacamole can be presented at room temperature or chilled as a dip for fried tortillas, a sauce for tacos and tostados or a salad. For a salad, mound the guacamole on leafy cups of crisp lettuce and garnish it with wedges of tomato.* ◆●

### To make about 2 cups

| | |
|---|---|
| 2 large avocados | and chopped coarse |
| 1 tablespoon finely chopped onion | 1 tablespoon finely chopped fresh coriander leaves |
| 1 tablespoon rinsed, finely chopped canned serrano chili | ½ teaspoon salt |
| | ⅛ teaspoon freshly ground black pepper |
| 1 tomato, peeled, seeded | |

Cut each avocado in half. With the tip of a small knife, loosen the seed and lift it out. Remove any brown tissue-like fibers clinging to the flesh. Strip off the skin with your fingers, starting at the narrow, or stem, end (the dark-skinned variety often does not peel easily; you may need to use a knife to pull the skin away). Coarsely chop the avocados; then, in a large mixing bowl, mash them with a fork to a smooth purée. Add the chopped onion, chili, tomato, coriander, salt, and a few grindings of black pepper, and stir the mixture together gently but thoroughly. Taste for seasoning. To prevent the guacamole from darkening, cover with plastic wrap and refrigerate. Stir the guacamole before serving.

■ LATIN AMERICAN COOKING

## Asparagus Wrapped in Prosciutto

### To serve 4

| | |
|---|---|
| 12 large spears asparagus (about 1 pound), ends trimmed and bottom ⅓ of stalks peeled | 2 tablespoons finely chopped shallots |
| | 2 tablespoons raspberry vinegar or red-wine vinegar |
| 12 thin slices prosciutto (about ½ pound) | 1 tablespoon Dijon mustard |
| ½ teaspoon finely chopped garlic | 2 tablespoons finely chopped fresh parsley leaves |
| | 6 tablespoons olive oil |

Bring 1 quart of lightly salted water to a boil in a large skillet over high heat. Put in the asparagus in a single layer. Cover the skillet and cook the asparagus for about six minutes or until it is barely tender when pierced with the tip of a small knife. Drain the cooked asparagus in a colander, and immediately refresh it by running cold water over it for a few seconds.

Pat the asparagus dry with paper towels. Wrap each piece from the stem to just below the tip with a slice of prosciutto. Divide the asparagus among four plates; set aside.

For the dressing, combine the garlic, shallots, vinegar, mustard and parsley in a small bowl. Whisking continuously, add the olive oil in a slow, steady stream; stir until the dressing is well blended and creamy. Spoon the dressing over the asparagus and serve.

■ SALAD MENUS

17

## Chicken-Liver Pâté

### To make about 4 cups

| | |
|---|---|
| ¼ cup plus 1 teaspoon butter, softened | ½ teaspoon ground ginger |
| 1 onion, cut into chunks | ½ teaspoon ground allspice |
| 1 garlic clove, halved | 1 teaspoon salt |
| 2 eggs | 1 teaspoon freshly ground white pepper |
| 1 pound chicken livers, trimmed | 1 cup heavy cream |
| ¼ cup all-purpose flour | Pumpernickel bread |

Preheat the oven to 325°F. Use the teaspoon of butter to coat the bottom and sides of a 1-quart baking dish. Combine the onion, garlic and eggs in a blender or food processor and blend for a minute. Add the livers and blend for two minutes longer. Add the flour, spices, salt, pepper, remaining butter and the cream; blend until smooth. Pour the mixture into the baking dish and cover it with foil.

Set the dish in a pan of hot water, and bake the pâté for three hours. Remove the foil and cool the pâté. Re-cover the dish and chill the pâté for at least four hours. To serve, spread the pâté on squares of pumpernickel.

■ GREAT DINNERS FROM LIFE

## Spiced Pork Spread

### To make about 4 cups

| | |
|---|---|
| 1½ pounds lard, cut into 2 inch pieces or 1½ pounds pork kidney fat, sliced thin | thick (about 4 cups) |
| 2 pounds lean boneless pork shoulder, cut into 2-inch chunks | 1 tablespoon mixed pickling spice, tied in cheesecloth |
| 4 large onions, sliced ⅛ inch | 2 tablespoons salt |
| | ½ teaspoon freshly ground black pepper |
| | Toast points or crackers |

Spread half of the lard over the bottom of a heavy 4- to 5-quart casserole. Scatter half of the pork chunks and all of the onions over the lard. Add the pickling spice, and sprinkle with the salt and pepper. Place the rest of the pork on top. Then scatter the remaining pieces of lard over it. With the flat of your hand, firmly press down the layers of lard, pork and onions.

Cover the casserole tightly and set it over the lowest possible heat. Simmer, undisturbed, for three hours or until the pork is tender enough to be mashed against the sides of the casserole with a spoon. Keep the heat low enough to prevent the pork from browning. Remove the casserole from the heat, discard the pickling spice, and let the pork mixture cool to room temperature. Put the contents of the casserole successively through the coarsest, then the finest, blades of a food grinder. Return the pork mixture to the casserole and, stirring constantly, simmer over moderate heat for about 15 to 20 minutes.

Pack the mixture tightly into a 1-quart bowl or eight 4-ounce individual earthenware crocks, and push it down with a spoon.

Let the mixture cool to room temperature; then refrigerate for four to six hours or until thoroughly chilled and completely firm. Serve on toast points or crackers.

The pork spread may be sealed with a layer of melted fat and safely kept in the refrigerator for several weeks: Chill the crocks until the spread is firm. Then melt additional lard or some butter, and pour a ¼-inch layer of fat over the surface of the spread.

■ AMERICAN COOKING: NEW ENGLAND

## Country Pâté

### To make about 3 pounds

| | |
|---|---|
| 1½ pounds boneless pork, ground fine twice | Salt |
| 1 pound boneless veal, ground fine twice | Freshly ground black pepper |
| | 2 large onions, sliced thin |
| ¾ cup dry white wine | 2 small cloves garlic, halved |
| 2 tablespoons brandy | 1 pound fresh pork fatback, sliced thin |
| 2 tablespoons oil | 1 cornichon pickle for garnish |

In a large bowl, combine the pork and veal. Mix the wine, brandy and oil with salt and pepper to taste, and pour the mixture over the meats. Scatter the onions and garlic on top. Cover the bowl tightly and refrigerate it for at least 24 hours.

Preheat the oven to 375°F. Discard the onions, but put the garlic through a press and knead it into the meats together with the wine mixture. Break off a small piece of meat and fry it in a lightly oiled skillet over moderate heat for three or four minutes, or until its juices run clear, without a trace of pink. Taste the piece and, if you like, add more garlic, salt and pepper. (Pork is unsafe to eat uncooked; do not taste the meats raw.)

Slightly overlapping the slices, line the bottom and sides of a 2-quart terrine mold or a 7½-by-3½-by-2½-inch loaf pan with the fatback. Pack the meat mixture into the mold, and arrange the remaining slices of fatback on top of it. Fit foil over the mold, or cover the meat mixture with foil and a lid. To let steam escape, pierce a hole in the foil with a skewer. If you are using a lid, insert the skewer through its hole to puncture the foil.

Set the mold on a rack in a large pan or dish. Place them all in the oven, and pour enough almost-boiling water into the pan to cover two-thirds of the mold. Bake for two hours or until the pâté shrinks slightly from the sides of the mold and the surrounding fat and juices are a clear yellowish white with no traces of pink. Or insert a meat thermometer; it should register 160°F. when the pâté is done.

Take the pâté from the oven, but leave the foil in place. Set the pâté on a rack to cool to room temperature. Then put another pan with a heavy can or weights inside it, or even a brick, on top of the pâté, to compact the meats. Chill the pâté thoroughly (overnight is best) with the weights in place. Before serving, cut the cornichon into a fan shape, slicing lengthwise through the pickle four or five times to within ½ inch of one end. Spread the slices into a fan, and garnish the pâté with it.

■ GREAT DINNERS FROM LIFE

## Potted Shrimp

**To serve 6**

| | |
|---|---|
| ¾ cup butter, cut into small bits, plus ½ cup clarified butter, melted | Salt |
| ½ teaspoon ground mace | 1 pound shelled cooked tiny fresh shrimp (60 or more) or 2 cups drained canned tiny shrimp |
| ½ teaspoon freshly grated nutmeg | Toast points |
| ⅛ teaspoon cayenne pepper | |

Melt the ¾ cup of butter over moderate heat in a heavy saucepan. Stir in the mace, nutmeg, cayenne and enough salt to taste. Add the shrimp to the butter mixture, turning them about with a spoon to coat them evenly.

Spoon the mixture into six 4-ounce ramekins or individual baking dishes, dividing the shrimp equally among them. Seal each portion by pouring in a thin layer of the clarified butter. Refrigerate the shrimp for at least six hours.

Potted shrimp are traditionally served with toast points as a first course, or with tea.

■ THE COOKING OF THE BRITISH ISLES

## Mussel and Caper Spread

**To make about 3 cups**

| | |
|---|---|
| 6 dozen large mussels in their shells, scrubbed and debearded | MAYONNAISE |
| | 2 egg yolks |
| 2 hard-boiled eggs, chopped fine | 1 tablespoon white-wine vinegar |
| ¼ cup capers, drained, rinsed in a sieve and patted dry with paper towels | 1½ teaspoons dry mustard |
| | Salt |
| | Freshly ground white pepper |
| ¼ cup finely cut fresh chives | 1 cup vegetable oil |
| ¼ cup finely chopped fresh parsley leaves | 2 tablespoons fresh lemon juice |
| Toast points | 1 teaspoon finely chopped garlic |

Combine the mussels and 1 cup of water in a heavy 4- to 6-quart casserole and bring to a boil over high heat. Cover tightly, reduce the heat to low and let the mussels steam for 10 minutes, turning them once or twice with a slotted spoon.

Using tongs or a slotted spoon, transfer the mussels to a large platter. All of the shells should open; discard any mussels that remain shut. Remove and discard the shells. Then chop the mussels and let them cool to room temperature.

Meanwhile, prepare the mayonnaise by first dropping the egg yolks into a small bowl. Beat them vigorously with a whisk or rotary or electric beater for about two minutes, until they thicken and cling to the beater when it is lifted from the bowl. Stir in the vinegar, mustard, and salt and white pepper to taste. Then beat in ½ cup of the oil, ½ teaspoon at a time; make sure each addition is absorbed before adding more. The mayonnaise now should have the consistency of thick cream. Beating constantly, pour in the

remaining oil in a slow, thin stream. Stir in the lemon juice and garlic and taste for seasoning. Refrigerate the mayonnaise until you are ready to use it.

When the mussels are cool, combine them gently but thoroughly with the chopped eggs, capers, chives and parsley. Stir in the mayonnaise. Serve the spread with toast points, as a first course or an accompaniment to drinks.

■ AMERICAN COOKING: NEW ENGLAND

## Creamed Oysters and Shrimp in Shells

**To serve 4**

| | |
|---|---|
| 6 tablespoons butter | 3 tablespoons all-purpose flour |
| ½ pound medium-sized uncooked shrimp, shelled, deveined and coarsely chopped | 1 egg yolk |
| | ¼ teaspoon freshly ground white pepper |
| 2 dozen oysters, shucked, with the oyster liquor and the deeper half shell of each oyster reserved | 1 teaspoon salt |
| | Rock salt or coarse (kosher) salt |
| | ¼ cup fresh bread crumbs |
| ½ to 1 cup milk | ½ cup freshly grated Gruyère or Emmentaler cheese |
| 2 tablespoons dry white wine | |

Preheat the oven to 450° F. Melt 2 tablespoons of the butter in a small skillet. Drop in the shrimp and, stirring constantly, cook over moderate heat for two to three minutes, until they begin to turn pink. Set them aside.

Measure the oyster liquor, and add enough milk to make 1¾ cups. Stir in the wine. In a heavy 8- to 10-inch skillet, melt the remaining 4 tablespoons of butter over moderate heat, but do not let it brown. Then stir in the flour and mix them thoroughly. Pour in the oyster-liquor mixture and, stirring constantly with a whisk, cook over high heat until the sauce boils and thickens lightly. Reduce the heat to low and simmer for about three minutes. Then beat the egg yolk lightly in a bowl, add about ¼ cup of sauce, and whisk the egg-yolk mixture into the sauce in the pan. Season with white pepper and salt. Remove the skillet from the heat and stir in the reserved shrimp.

Fill a large shallow baking dish to a depth of about ¼ inch with rock salt. (The salt will not only act as a bed for the oysters, but will also help keep them hot after they have cooked.) Spoon about 1 tablespoon of the shrimp sauce into each oyster shell, top with an oyster, and blanket the oyster with a second tablespoonful of the shrimp sauce. Arrange the filled shells side by side in the salt-lined baking dish. Bake the oysters in the top third of the oven for about eight minutes or until the sauce has begun to bubble. Sprinkle the oysters evenly with the bread crumbs and the cheese. Return them to the oven for another three or four minutes or until the cheese melts and the crumbs brown lightly. You may then, if you like, slide the dish under the broiler—about 3 inches from the heat—for a minute or two to brown the tops further. Serve at once.

■ A QUINTET OF CUISINES

## Oysters and Bacon en Brochette

**To serve 6**

| | |
|---|---|
| 10 to 14 tablespoons butter | into 1-inch pieces |
| 6 slices homemade-type white bread, trimmed of crusts and cut diagonally into triangles | 3 dozen shucked oysters, drained |
| | 1 teaspoon salt |
| 2 tablespoons chopped fresh parsley leaves, preferably flatleaf parsley | ½ teaspoon freshly ground black pepper |
| | 2 cups unsifted corn flour or all-purpose flour |
| Vegetable oil for deep-frying | 1 lemon, cut lengthwise into 6 wedges |
| 8 slices bacon, cut crosswise | |

Preheat the oven to its lowest setting. Line two baking sheets with a double thickness of paper towels, and place them in the middle of the oven.

In a heavy 8- to 10-inch skillet, melt 4 tablespoons of the butter over moderate heat. When the foam begins to subside, add four or five of the bread triangles and, turning them frequently with tongs, fry them until they are crisp and golden brown on both sides. Transfer the browned triangles to a paper-lined tray to keep them warm. Then fry the rest of the triangles in a similar manner, adding up to 4 tablespoons more butter to the skillet as needed.

Add the remaining 6 tablespoons of butter to the same skillet, and stir so that it melts evenly without browning. Off the heat, stir the parsley into the butter; set this sauce aside. Pour vegetable oil to a depth of 2 to 3 inches into a deep fryer or heavy saucepan at least 8 inches in diameter, and heat the oil to a temperature of 350° F. on a deep-frying thermometer.

Place the bacon in a heavy 12-inch skillet over moderate heat; stir frequently until the pieces are translucent but not brown.

Drain the bacon on paper towels. Pat the oysters completely dry with paper towels, and season them on both sides with salt and pepper. One at a time, roll the oysters in the flour to coat them evenly. Vigorously shake off the excess flour. String the pieces of bacon and the oysters alternately on six 6-inch-long metal skewers, pressing them tightly together.

With tongs, carefully place two of the skewers in the hot oil. Turning the skewers frequently, deep-fry the bacon and oysters for four to five minutes or until the oysters are plump and delicately browned. As they finish cooking, transfer the oysters and bacon on their skewers to the second paper-lined pan, and keep them warm in the oven while you deep-fry the rest.

While the oysters are still hot, arrange two of the toast triangles on each of six heated serving plates and lay one skewer across them. Dribble the butter-and-parsley sauce over the oysters, garnish the plates with the lemon wedges, and serve at once.

■ AMERICAN COOKING: CREOLE AND ACADIAN

## Gravlax

*Layered with salt and herbs, fillets of raw fish acquire a firm, but still tender, texture and a fragrant taste. Traditionally, gravlax is served as part of a smorgasbord or alone as an hors d'oeuvre, accompanied by mustard sauce.* ❧

**To serve 8 to 10**

| | |
|---|---|
| 3 to 3½ pounds center-cut fresh salmon, cleaned and scaled | MUSTARD SAUCE |
| | ¼ cup dark, highly seasoned prepared mustard |
| 1 large bunch fresh dill | 1 tablespoon powdered mustard |
| ¼ cup coarse (kosher) salt or regular salt | |
| | 3 tablespoons sugar |
| ¼ cup sugar | 2 tablespoons white vinegar |
| 2 tablespoons white or black peppercorns, crushed | ⅓ cup vegetable oil |
| | 3 tablespoons finely cut dill |

Ask the fish dealer to cut the salmon in half lengthwise and to remove the backbone and the small bones as well.

Wash the fish under cold running water and pat it dry with paper towels. Place half of the fish, skin side down, in a deep glass, enamel or stainless-steel baking dish or casserole. Wash and then shake dry the bunch of dill, and place it on the fish. (If the dill is of the hothouse variety and not very pungent, chop it coarsely to release its flavor and sprinkle it over the fish instead.) In a separate bowl, combine the coarse salt, sugar and crushed white peppercorns. Sprinkle this mixture evenly over the dill. Top with the other half of the fish, set skin side up. Cover the container with aluminum foil, and on it set a heavy platter slightly larger than the salmon. Pile the platter with several cans of food; cans make convenient weights that are easy to distribute evenly.

Refrigerate the salmon for 48 hours or up to three days. Turn the fish over every 12 hours, basting with the liquid marinade that accumulates and separating the halves a little to baste the salmon inside. Replace the platter and weights each time.

Remove the *gravlax* from its marinade, scrape away the dill

GRAVLAX

and seasonings, and pat the salmon dry with paper towels. Place the separated halves, skin side down, on a carving board and slice them thin on the diagonal, detaching each slice from the skin.

To prepare the mustard sauce, mix the two mustards, sugar, and vinegar in a small bowl. With a wire whisk, slowly beat in the oil until the mixture forms a thick mayonnaise-like emulsion. Stir in the dill. The sauce may be kept refrigerated in a tightly covered jar for several days, but it will need to be whisked before serving.

NOTE: For the impressive presentation shown above, cut one or more English hothouse cucumbers into 4-inch sections; carve 1-inch-deep triangles around one end of each quarter to form a crown shape, then use a melon baller or teaspoon to scoop out the flesh from inside each quarter, leaving ¼ inch at the base of the crown. Loosely roll up two slices of salmon, stand them in a cup, and top them with a teaspoonful of rinsed, drained capers. Serve the cups on Bibb lettuce leaves, garnished with additional salmon slices rolled into cone shapes, fresh dill sprigs and twisted lemon slices.

■ THE COOKING OF SCANDINAVIA

## Bliny

*Bliny have a distinctive taste, mainly because they are made with a yeast batter. Their preparation should start about six hours before serving time. When the batter is complete, the pancakes must be cooked and served at once.* ❧

**To make about 1 dozen**

| | |
|---|---|
| ½ cup lukewarm water (110°F. to 115°F.) | 1 teaspoon sugar |
| 1½ packages active dry yeast | 1 cup butter, melted and cooled |
| ½ cup buckwheat flour | 2 cups sour cream (1 pint) |
| 2 cups all-purpose flour | 3 egg whites |
| 2 cups lukewarm milk (110°F. to 115°F.) | ½ pound red or black caviar or 1 pound thinly sliced smoked salmon, sturgeon or herring fillets |
| 3 egg yolks, lightly beaten | |
| ½ teaspoon salt | |

Pour the lukewarm water into a small, shallow bowl, and sprinkle the yeast over it. Let the yeast stand for two or three minutes, then stir to dissolve it completely. Set in a warm, draft-free place for three to five minutes or until the mixture almost doubles.

In a large mixing bowl, combine ¼ cup of the buckwheat flour and the 2 cups of all-purpose flour. Make a well in the center, and pour in the yeast mixture and 1 cup of the lukewarm milk. Slowly stir the flour into the liquid ingredients with a large wooden spoon, then beat vigorously until the mixture is smooth. Cover the bowl loosely with a towel, and set it aside in the warm, draft-free spot for three hours, or until the mixture doubles in volume.

Stir the batter thoroughly and vigorously beat in the remaining ¼ cup of buckwheat flour. Cover with a towel and let the batter rest in the warm draft-free spot for another two hours. Again stir the batter and gradually beat in the remaining cup of lukewarm milk and the 3 egg yolks, salt, sugar, 3 tablespoons of the melted butter and 3 tablespoons of the sour cream.

Beat the egg whites until they form stiff peaks on the beater when lifted from the bowl. With a rubber spatula, fold the whites gently but thoroughly into the batter, cover loosely with a towel, and let rest in the warm draft-free place for 30 minutes.

Preheat the oven to 200°F. With a pastry brush, lightly coat the bottom of a 10- to 12-inch skillet (preferably with a nonstick surface) with melted butter. Set the pan over high heat until a drop of water flicked across its surface evaporates instantly. Pour in about 3 tablespoons of the batter for each pancake; you should be able to make about three at a time, each 3 to 4 inches wide. Fry the pancakes for two to three minutes, then brush the tops lightly with butter. With a spatula or your fingers, turn the pancakes over and cook for another two minutes or until golden brown. Transfer the pancakes to an ovenproof dish, and keep them warm in the oven while you fry the remaining pancakes similarly.

Serve the *bliny* hot, accompanied by bowls of the remaining butter and sour cream. Traditionally, *bliny* are spread with melted butter, then a spoonful of sour cream and are topped with a mound of red caviar or smoked fish. If you are serving black caviar, omit the sour cream.

■ RUSSIAN COOKING

SHRIMP AND SCALLOP SEVICHE

## Shrimp and Scallop Seviche

*This Latin American method of "cooking" fish by pickling it in citrus juice is similar to the European method of pickling raw herring in vinegar. Here, the shrimp are cooked briefly—no more than three minutes—to give them color—before they are pickled with the scallops.* ❧

**To serve 6**

| | |
|---|---|
| 2 pounds shrimp, poached just until firm, shelled deveined and cut into thirds | 2 tablespoons finely chopped green pepper |
| 1 pound uncooked bay scallops, left whole, or sea scallops, sliced thin | ½ cup olive oil |
| | ½ teaspoon dried oregano |
| | Tabasco sauce |
| 1 cup fresh lime juice | Salt |
| 6 tablespoons finely chopped red onion | Freshly ground black pepper |
| | 2 avocados, halved, pitted, peeled and sliced |
| ¼ cup chopped fresh parsley leaves | Purple kale leaves for garnish |
| | Curly-leaf lettuce for garnish |

Combine the shrimp, scallops and lime juice in a nonreactive bowl. Cover the bowl and let the shellfish marinate for three to four hours at room temperature, stirring occasionally.

Drain and discard the juice, then add the onion, parsley, green pepper, olive oil, oregano, a dash of Tabasco, and salt and pepper to taste. Toss the ingredients together lightly. Refrigerate the *seviche* for an hour. Transfer the *seviche* to a serving dish; add the avocado slices; garnish with kale leaves and curly-leaf lettuce.

■ GREAT DINNERS FROM LIFE

## Snails in Burgundy-Wine Sauce

**To serve 4**

| | |
|---|---|
| 4 slices homemade-type white bread | Salt |
| 2 slices bacon, diced | Freshly ground black pepper |
| 1 small onion, chopped fine | Two 7½-ounce cans giant snails without shells |
| 1 large clove garlic, chopped fine | 2 tablespoons unsalted butter |
| 1 cup red Burgundy wine | 2 tablespoons all-purpose flour |
| ½ cup chicken stock | 4 parsley sprigs for garnish |
| 1 tablespoon brandy | |

Preheat the oven to 350° F. With a biscuit cutter or small knife, cut out a 3-inch round from each slice of bread. Set the rounds on a baking sheet and toast them in the oven for five minutes or until they are lightly browned. Place the croutons in four small soup bowls or on salad plates.

In a medium-sized saucepan, cook the bacon over moderate heat, stirring frequently, for three to five minutes or until it browns. Add the onion and garlic, and cook for three to five minutes or until the onion is translucent. Add the wine, stock, brandy, and salt and pepper to taste, and bring this sauce to a boil. Add the snails to the sauce; reduce the heat to low and simmer for five minutes. With metal tongs, transfer the snails to a bowl, and cover it with foil to keep them warm.

In a small bowl, blend the butter with the flour until smooth. Add this butter-flour mixture to the sauce all at once. Whisk until the ingredients are blended, and cook the sauce, still whisking frequently, for about three minutes or until it thickens and is smooth. Spoon the snails over the croutons, cover each portion with sauce, and serve, garnished with a parsley sprig if desired.

■ FRENCH REGIONAL MENUS

## Hot Crab-Meat Canapés

**To make 2 dozen**

| | |
|---|---|
| ½ pound fresh, frozen or canned crab meat, drained, picked clean of shell and cartilage, and flaked | 1 tablespoon finely cut fresh dill |
| | 1 tablespoon butter |
| | 1 tablespoon all-purpose flour |
| 1 tablespoon dry sherry | 1 egg yolk |
| 1 teaspoon salt | 1 cup light cream |
| ⅛ teaspoon freshly ground white pepper | 6 slices homemade-type white bread |

In a large mixing bowl, combine the crab meat, sherry, salt, pepper and dill; set aside. Melt the butter, without browning it, in a small, heavy saucepan; remove the pan from the heat and stir in the flour. In a small bowl, mix the egg yolk and cream with a whisk, and briskly whisk this mixture into the butter-flour roux. Return the pan to the heat, and cook slowly, whisking constantly for a minute or two, until the sauce thickens; do not let it boil. Pour the sauce over the crab-meat mixture in the bowl, and stir them together with a spoon. Taste for seasoning.

Cut four rounds from each slice of bread, using a small biscuit cutter or a glass. Toast the bread rounds on one side under a moderately hot broiler. Spread the untoasted side of each round generously with the crab-meat mixture, mounding it slightly. Refrigerate the canapés until ready to serve them.

Just before serving, place the canapés under a hot broiler for a minute or so to brown the crab-meat mixture lightly. Serve very hot.

■ THE COOKING OF SCANDINAVIA

# Soups

# Soups

FRONTISPIECE: CHICKEN AND AVOCADO SOUP

For as far back as anyone can remember, the steaming soup pot has symbolized a well-ordered home and a contented family. Indeed, in the early 19th century, the French epicure, Anthelme Brillat-Savarin went so far as to declare that a woman who could not make a soup should not be allowed to marry, for she was doomed to failure. But there is remarkably little risk of heartbreak. Given even a modicum of care, soup is wonderfully easy to concoct.

Fundamental to many soups are stocks produced from meats, poultry, seafood or vegetables simmered in water. Alone, a stock constitutes a soup usually called "broth" or by its French name "bouillon." Meat stock as clear as glass and so rich that it jells naturally when chilled is "consommé."

Starting with stock, a cook can quickly assemble a refreshing cooler for a hot day or a warming brew for a chilly one. The delicate chicken and avocado soup at left represents clear stock with light embellishment; a robust Italian fish soup contains more fish than stock.

Not all soups call for stock. Plain water, vinegar and oil liquefy the delicious Iberian invention known as gazpacho. Milk—or milk and cream—ensures the luxuriousness of chowder. And vegetables especially lend themselves to purées. Whether prepared for a first course or a meal in itself, soup making invites experiment. The principles are simple, and the ingredients may be arranged to suit a season—or a whim.

## Cold Cucumber and Yogurt Soup

**To serve 4**

| | |
|---|---|
| 1 medium-sized or 2 small cucumbers, peeled, halved, seeded and cut into 1/4-inch dice | 1 tablespoon finely cut fresh dill |
| 1 teaspoon salt | 1/2 teaspoon finely chopped garlic |
| 2 cups plain yogurt | 2 tablespoons sunflower oil or olive oil |
| 1/3 cup chopped walnuts | 1 cup crushed ice cubes |

Place the cucumber dice in a small bowl, and sprinkle them evenly with 1/2 teaspoon of the salt; set aside at room temperature for about 15 minutes. Then put the dice in a sieve, rinse briefly under cold running water, and drain. Spread the cucumber out on paper towels and pat the dice thoroughly dry.

Combine the cucumber, yogurt, walnuts, dill, garlic and the remaining 1/2 teaspoon salt in a deep bowl, tossing them about with a spoon until thoroughly mixed. Stir in the sunflower oil by the teaspoonful, making sure each addition is absorbed before adding more.

Ladle the soup into a bowl and refrigerate it for one hour or until it is thoroughly chilled. Stir 1 cup of crushed ice cubes into the bowl immediately before serving.

■ A QUINTET OF CUISINES

## Cold Greek Lemon Soup

*This version of the classic Greek avgolemono is designed to be served cold. If you prefer, serve it hot—as soon as you season the frothy, lemon-scented stock and egg mixture.* ❖●

**To serve 4**

| | |
|---|---|
| 4 cups chicken stock | 2 eggs |
| 4 mint sprigs, tied in cheesecloth, plus 1 teaspoon chopped fresh mint leaves | 1/3 cup fresh lemon juice |
| | Salt |
| 1/3 cup long-grain white rice | Freshly ground black pepper |
| | 4 thin lemon slices |

In a 3- to 4-quart saucepan, bring the stock to a boil over high heat. Add the cheesecloth-wrapped mint and the rice to the stock. Reduce the heat to moderately low, cover the pan, and cook the rice for 15 to 20 minutes or until it is tender. Discard the cheesecloth packet.

In a large nonreactive bowl, beat the eggs with a whisk until light and frothy. Whisking constantly, add the hot stock and rice mixture very slowly so that the eggs will not curdle. Stir in the lemon juice, and add salt and black pepper to taste. Cover the bowl with foil or plastic wrap, and refrigerate the soup for several hours to chill it thoroughly. Divide the soup among four chilled bowls and garnish each serving with a lemon slice and 1/4 teaspoon chopped mint.

■ MAKE-AHEAD MENUS

## Gazpacho

**To serve 6 to 8**

| | |
|---|---|
| 5 tomatoes, peeled, cored and chopped coarse | 4 teaspoons salt |
| 2 cucumbers, peeled and chopped coarse | 1/4 cup olive oil |
| | 1 tablespoon tomato paste |
| 1 large onion, chopped coarse | |
| 1 green pepper, halved, seeded, deribbed and chopped coarse | GARNISH |
| | 1 cup 1/4-inch bread cubes, cut from French or Italian bread trimmed of crusts |
| 1 garlic clove, chopped | |
| 2 to 3 cups coarsely crumbled French or Italian bread, trimmed of crusts | 1/2 cup finely chopped onion |
| | 1/2 cup finely chopped peeled cucumber |
| 4 cups cold water | 1/2 cup finely chopped green pepper |
| 1/4 cup red-wine vinegar | |

In a deep bowl, combine the coarsely chopped tomatoes, cucumbers, onion and green pepper with the garlic and crumbled bread, and mix them thoroughly. Then stir in the water, vinegar and salt. Ladle the mixture, about 2 cups at a time, into the jar of a blender, and blend at high speed for one minute or until reduced to a smooth purée. Pour the purée into a bowl and, with a whisk, beat in the olive oil and tomato paste.

(To make the soup by hand, purée the vegetable and bread mixture in a food mill or, with the back of a large spoon, rub it through a sieve set over a bowl. Discard any pulp left in the mill or sieve. Beat the olive oil and tomato paste into the purée.)

Cover the bowl tightly with foil or plastic wrap and refrigerate it for at least two hours or until thoroughly chilled. Just before serving, whisk or stir the soup lightly to recombine it. Then ladle it into a chilled tureen or individual soup bowls. Accompany the *gazpacho* with the bread-cube and vegetable garnishes, presented in separate serving bowls.

NOTE: If you prefer crisp croutons for the garnish, fry the bread cubes. Heat 1/4 cup of olive oil over moderate heat in a small skillet. Drop in the bread cubes and, turning them frequently, cook them until they are golden brown on all sides. Drain them on paper towels and cool.

■ THE COOKING OF SPAIN AND PORTUGAL

## Cold Beet Soup with Shrimp

**To serve 6 to 8**

| | |
|---|---|
| 1 pound firm young beets, peeled and grated coarse | 4 scallions, including 2 inches of green tops, sliced ¼ inch thick |
| 6½ cups cold water | 4 red radishes, sliced thin |
| 3 tablespoons red-wine vinegar | ¼ cup finely cut fresh dill |
| Salt | 3 tablespoons fresh lemon juice |
| 1½ teaspoons sugar | Freshly ground white pepper |
| 1 pound shrimp, peeled and deveined | 1 lemon, sliced thin, for garnish |
| 1 cup sour cream | 3 eggs, hard-boiled, chilled and chopped fine, for garnish |
| 2 cucumbers, peeled, halved lengthwise, seeded and cut into ¼-inch dice | |

In a 3- to 4-quart enameled or stainless-steel saucepan, bring the grated beets and cold water to a boil over high heat. Reduce the heat to moderate, and cook uncovered for 10 minutes, then reduce the heat to low. Stir in 2 tablespoons of the vinegar, 1 teaspoon salt and 1 teaspoon of the sugar, and simmer, partially covered, for 30 minutes. Drain the beets in a fine sieve set over a large bowl. Set the beets and the cooking liquid aside to cool to room temperature.

Bring 1 quart of water to a boil in a small pan, drop in the shrimp and cook them, uncovered, for three minutes or until they turn pink and are firm to the touch. Drain and coarsely chop the shrimp. Set them aside to cool.

When the beet cooking liquid is completely cooled, stir in the sour cream with a whisk. Then stir in the beets, shrimp, cucumbers, scallions, radishes, 2 tablespoons of the dill, the lemon juice, the remaining tablespoon of vinegar, ½ teaspoon of sugar and a grinding of white pepper. Taste for seasoning, cover the bowl with plastic wrap, and refrigerate for at least two hours or until the soup is thoroughly chilled.

To serve, ladle the soup into a chilled tureen or individual soup bowls. Sprinkle the remaining dill on top and, if you like, garnish the soup with lemon slices and chopped hard-boiled eggs.

■ A QUINTET OF CUISINES

## Sugar Snap Pea Soup

**To serve 4**

| | |
|---|---|
| 2 tablespoons unsalted butter | Salt |
| 4½ cups water | White-wine vinegar |
| 1 bunch scallions | 2 tablespoons finely cut fresh chives |
| 1 pound Sugar Snap peas or snow peas, chopped coarse | Freshly ground black pepper |

In a heavy 3- to 4-quart saucepan over moderate heat, melt the butter in ½ cup of the water. Meanwhile, rinse the scallions and pat them dry with paper towels. Trim the ends and remove any bruised greens. Slice enough of the scallions ½ inch thick to measure about 1¼ cups.

COLD BEET SOUP WITH SHRIMP

Add the scallions to the pan and, stirring occasionally, cook for about five minutes or until they are soft but not browned. Add the peas and continue cooking, stirring from time to time, for about two minutes. Stir in the remaining 4 cups of water and 1 teaspoon of salt. Slowly bring the soup to a boil, uncovered, over moderate heat. As soon as the soup comes to a boil, reduce the heat and simmer it gently for five minutes. Remove the soup from the heat and set it aside to cool slightly.

Transfer the soup to a blender and purée it for at least one minute at the highest speed. Or purée it in batches in a food processor. Pour the soup through a fine sieve set over a bowl, pressing with the back of a large spoon to force any remaining solid bits through. Return the soup to the saucepan. Just before serving, place the pan over low heat. Warm the soup, but do not let it boil. Taste the soup and adjust its seasoning by adding a few drops of vinegar or some salt.

Divide the soup among four warmed individual bowls, and serve it garnished with chives and generous grindings of pepper.

■ SALAD MENUS

While the soup simmers, preheat the oven to 325°F. Spread the slices of bread in one layer on a baking sheet, and bake for 15 minutes. With a pastry brush, lightly coat each slice with olive oil. Then turn the slices over and bake for another 15 minutes or until the bread is completely dry and lightly browned. Rub each slice with a cut side of the garlic clove and set the *croûtes* aside.

To serve, place the *croûtes* in a warmed tureen or individual soup bowls and ladle the soup over them. Pass the grated cheese separately.

ALTERNATIVE: For onion soup *gratinée*, preheat the oven to 375°F. Ladle the soup into an ovenproof tureen or soup bowls, top it with *croûtes,* and spread the grated cheese on top. Sprinkle the cheese with a little melted butter or olive oil. Bake for 10 to 20 minutes, or until the cheese melts; if desired, slide the soup under a hot broiler for a minute or two to brown the top.

■ THE COOKING OF PROVINCIAL FRANCE

## Vegetable Soup

**To serve 6**

| | |
|---|---|
| **8 cups beef stock** | **¹/₂ cup shelled peas** |
| **Salt** | **¹/₂ cup unpeeled zucchini** |
| **Freshly ground black pepper** | **slices** |
| **12 baby carrots, or plain carrots cut into twelve 2-inch ovals** | **¹/₂ cup peeled, cubed white turnip** |
| **2 small onions, sliced** | **2 tomatoes, peeled, seeded and cut into large chunks** |
| **1 leek, sliced** | **1 small garlic clove, chopped fine** |
| **¹/₂ cup sliced celery** | |
| **¹/₂ cup cut green beans** | **¹/₄ cup chopped fresh parsley leaves** |
| **¹/₂ cup julienne strips green and red pepper** | **¹/₂ teaspoon crumbled dried basil** |
| **¹/₂ cup fresh corn kernels cut from 2 ears of corn** | **¹/₂ teaspoon crumbled dried oregano** |
| **¹/₂ cup shelled lima beans** | |

Measure the stock into a 4- to 5-quart saucepan. Warm the stock and season it to taste with salt and pepper. Add all of the vegetables and herbs, and stir very gently to mix them.

Bring the soup to a boil, cover the pot, and reduce the heat. Simmer the soup without stirring—which may break up the more fragile vegetables—for 30 minutes or until the large pieces, especially the carrots, are tender and cooked through. Taste for seasoning, and serve in a heated tureen or individual soup bowls.

■ GREAT DINNERS FROM LIFE

## French Onion Soup

**To serve 6 to 8**

| | |
|---|---|
| **¹/₄ cup butter** | CROÛTES |
| **2 tablespoons vegetable oil** | **12 to 16 slices French or Italian bread, each cut 1 inch thick** |
| **6 to 8 cups thinly sliced onions** | **2 teaspoons olive oil** |
| **Salt** | **1 garlic clove, halved** |
| **3 tablespoons flour** | **1 cup grated Gruyère cheese or Gruyère and Parmesan** |
| **8 cups beef stock or beef and chicken stock combined** | |

In a heavy 4- to 5-quart saucepan or a soup kettle, melt the butter with the oil over moderate heat. Stir in the onions and 1 teaspoon salt. Cook over low heat, stirring occasionally, for 20 to 30 minutes, or until the onions are a rich golden brown. Sprinkle flour over the onions and cook, stirring, for two to three minutes. Remove the pan from the heat. In a separate saucepan, bring the stock to a simmer, then stir the hot stock into the onions. Return the soup to low heat and simmer, partially covered, for another 30 to 40 minutes, skimming off the fat. Taste for seasoning.

## Creamy Carrot-Orange Soup

**To serve 4**

| | |
|---|---|
| **3 tablespoons unsalted butter** | **white rice** |
| **1 cup coarsely chopped** | **1 orange** |
| **onions** | **4 cups chicken stock** |
| **1½ cups thinly sliced carrots** | **8 parsley sprigs** |
| **1 small garlic clove, halved** | **¼ teaspoon sugar** |
| **2 tablespoons long-grain** | **½ cup heavy cream** |

In a heavy 3- to 4-quart saucepan, melt the butter over low heat. Add the onions, carrots, garlic and rice. Stirring occasionally with a wooden spoon, cook the mixture for about five minutes or until the vegetables are soft but not browned.

Meanwhile, rinse and dry the orange. Cut it in half crosswise. Using a zester or a paring knife, remove the peel from one half, and then squeeze the juice of that half into a small bowl. Cut four ¼-inch-thick slices from the remaining half. Set the juice and orange slices aside.

Add the orange peel, stock, 4 parsley sprigs and the sugar to the vegetables, and bring the mixture to a boil. Reduce the heat to low, cover the pan, and simmer the vegetables for 25 to 30 minutes or until they are tender. Remove the parsley sprigs from the soup and discard them; set the soup aside to cool.

Pour the cooled soup into a blender and purée it; or purée it in batches in a food processor. Just before serving, return the soup to a pan, stir in the reserved orange juice and the cream, and heat the soup briefly over moderately low heat; do not let it boil. Serve the soup from a warmed bowl or divide it among four individual soup bowls, and garnish each serving with an orange slice topped with a parsley sprig.

■ SALAD MENUS

## Fresh Tomato and Fennel Soup

**To serve 4**

| | |
|---|---|
| **¼ cup unsalted butter** | **reserved** |
| **1 large onion, sliced** | **1 cup chicken stock** |
| **6 tomatoes, peeled, seeded** | **Salt** |
| **and chopped coarse** | **Freshly ground black pepper** |
| **1 small fennel bulb, sliced** | **½ cup milk** |
| **thin, with leafy sprigs** | |

In a 3- to 4-quart saucepan, melt the butter over moderate heat. Add the onion and cook, stirring with a wooden spatula, until the onion is soft—about five minutes. Add the tomatoes, fennel slices, stock, 1 teaspoon of salt and a few grindings of pepper to taste. Cover and bring the mixture to a boil over high heat. Reduce the heat and simmer for 20 minutes or until the fennel slices are tender. Pour the mixture into a bowl, and let it cool for at least five minutes. Rinse the saucepan and set it aside.

Using a ladle, transfer the mixture in batches to a food processor or blender; process the mixture until smooth, and pour it into another bowl. Place a sieve over the original saucepan and, using

the back of a spoon, push the soup mixture through the sieve into the pan. Add the milk to the soup and bring it to a simmer over moderately high heat. Taste and correct the seasoning. Ladle the soup into a tureen and garnish it with fennel sprigs; serve at once.

NOTE: When fresh fennel is not available, you can substitute a heaping tablespoonful of fennel seeds. Wrap the seeds in cheesecloth and tie the package with a long piece of string so that you can conveniently add the seeds with the tomatoes and remove them when the tomatoes have cooked.

■ FISH AND SHELLFISH MENUS

## Peanut Soup

*Undeniably, this exotic soup calls for some ingredients that may require special shopping trips. The dried hot chilies and the jalapeños will be available where Latin American or Asian foods are sold. Both chilies must be handled cautiously. The coconut milk used may be homemade (Index/Glossary) or bought canned from a store selling Latin American or Asian products. The tahini required is a paste made from ground hulled sesame seeds; it is popular in Middle Eastern cooking.* ◆

**To serve 4**

| | |
|---|---|
| **3 tablespoons vegetable oil** | **1 cup creamy peanut butter** |
| **3 dried hot chilies or 1 tea-** | **½ cup coconut milk** |
| **spoon hot-red-pepper flakes** | |
| **3 garlic cloves, chopped fine** | GARNISHES |
| **1 onion, chopped fine** | **4 dried red chilies** |
| **1 tablespoon flour** | **1 tomato, peeled, seeded and** |
| **¼ teaspoon ground cumin** | **cut into ½-inch cubes** |
| **Freshly ground black pepper** | **4 scallions, sliced thin** |
| **¼ teaspoon ground coriander** | **2 fresh or canned jalapeño** |
| **¼ teaspoon turmeric** | **chilies, halved, seeded and** |
| **4 cups vegetable stock** | **chopped coarse** |
| **2 tablespoons *tahini*** | **½ cup dry-roasted peanuts** |

In a 3- to 4-quart nonreactive saucepan, heat the oil and cook the dried chilies over moderately high heat for one minute; remove the chilies and discard them. Add the garlic and onion. Stirring frequently, cook them for about five minutes or until they are golden but not dry. Add the flour, cumin, ¼ teaspoon pepper, coriander and turmeric, and stir constantly for one minute. Stir in the vegetable stock and bring it to a boil.

Add the *tahini,* then the peanut butter, and stir until both dissolve. Let the mixture return to a boil. Stir in the coconut milk and boil the soup until it is smooth, about one minute. Taste, and correct the seasonings. If necessary, keep the soup warm over low heat. To serve, ladle the soup into four warmed soup bowls. Decorate each serving with a dried red chili; present the garnishes separately in small bowls.

■ MEATLESS MENUS

## Philadelphia Pepper Pot

**To serve 6**

| | |
|---|---|
| 1 pound tripe, cut into ½-inch squares | 1 cup finely chopped onions |
| 1 meaty veal shank (about 1 pound), sawed into 2 or 3 pieces | ½ cup finely chopped celery |
| | ½ cup finely chopped green pepper |
| 8 cups water | 3 tablespoons flour |
| 6 whole black peppercorns | 2 potatoes, peeled and cut into ¼-inch dice |
| Salt | Crushed dried hot red pepper |
| ¼ cup butter | Freshly ground black pepper |

Combine the tripe, veal shank and water in a heavy 4- to 5-quart casserole. The water should cover the meats by at least 2 inches; if necessary add more. Bring to a boil over high heat, skimming off the foam and scum as they rise to the surface. Add the peppercorns and 1 teaspoon salt, reduce the heat to low, and simmer, partially covered, for two hours or until the tripe is tender.

With a slotted spoon, transfer the tripe and pieces of veal shank to a platter or cutting board. Remove the veal from the shank, discard the bones and cut the meat into ½-inch pieces. Strain the cooking liquid through a fine sieve set over a bowl; measure and reserve 6 cups. If there is less, add enough water to make that amount.

In the same casserole, melt the butter over moderate heat. When the foam subsides, add the onions, celery and green pepper, and stir for about five minutes. When the vegetables are soft but not browned, add the flour and mix well. Stirring constantly, pour in the reserved cooking liquid in a slow, thin stream, and cook over high heat until the soup thickens lightly, comes to a boil and is smooth. Add the potatoes, tripe and veal, reduce the heat to low, and simmer for one hour, partially covered.

Taste the soup for seasoning. Add more salt if needed and enough crushed red pepper and freshly ground black pepper to give the soup a distinctly peppery flavor. Serve at once directly from the casserole.

■ AMERICAN COOKING: THE EASTERN HEARTLAND

## Oxtail Soup

**To serve 4**

| | |
|---|---|
| 3 tablespoons butter | 1 leek, tied together |
| 1 tablespoon vegetable oil | 1 teaspoon crumbled dried thyme |
| 2 pounds oxtail, cut into 1-inch sections | 5 whole black peppercorns |
| 1 onion, sliced thin | Salt |
| 1 carrot, sliced thin | Freshly ground black pepper |
| 2 tablespoons flour | ½ cup finely diced carrot |
| 8 cups beef stock | ½ cup finely diced turnip |
| Bouquet garni made of 2 parsley sprigs, 2 celery ribs and | 1 to 2 tablespoons dry Madeira or port wine |

In a heavy 4- to 5-quart saucepan or casserole, melt 1 tablespoon of the butter with the oil over moderate heat. Add the oxtail and

PHILADELPHIA PEPPER POT

cook, turning frequently, until the pieces are golden brown on all sides. Using kitchen tongs, transfer the oxtail pieces to a plate. Cook the sliced onion and carrot in the fat remaining in the pan for eight to 10 minutes, or until they are soft and lightly browned. Add the flour and stir until browned. Remove the pan from the heat and let it cool slightly. Whisking vigorously, beat in the beef stock a little at a time. Still whisking, bring the soup to a boil and cook it until it is smooth and begins to thicken.

Return the oxtail to the pan together with the bouquet garni, thyme and peppercorns, and bring the soup to a boil over high heat. Skim the fat from the surface, reduce the heat, and simmer the soup, partially covered, for three and a half hours, skimming it frequently. Lift out the oxtail with a slotted spoon, and strain the soup through a fine sieve into a large mixing bowl. Let it settle for a few minutes, then skim off the surface fat. Taste the soup, season it with salt and pepper, and return it to the pan.

Melt the remaining 2 tablespoons of butter in a 6- to 8-inch skillet and in it cook the diced carrot and turnip, stirring frequently, for one or two minutes to coat them with butter. Add the carrot, turnip and oxtail to the soup, and simmer for 30 minutes, skimming the fat from the surface as necessary. To serve, ladle the soup into a warmed tureen and stir in the wine.

■ THE COOKING OF PROVINCIAL FRANCE

## Latin American Chicken and Ham Soup

**To serve 10 to 12**

| | |
|---|---|
| One 3½- to 4-pound chicken, cut into 6 or 8 serving pieces | and chopped coarse |
| 1 onion, halved | 1 cup finely diced carrots |
| 4 cups chicken stock | 1 cup long-grain white rice |
| 8 cups cold water | Freshly ground black pepper |
| 6 tomatoes, peeled, seeded | 1 cup finely diced cooked ham |
| | 1 tablespoon finely chopped fresh parsley leaves |

In a 5- to 6-quart flameproof casserole, combine the chicken, onion, chicken stock and water. Bring to a boil over high heat, skimming off the foam and scum as they rise to the surface. Reduce the heat to low, cover the casserole, and cook the chicken, undisturbed, for 20 to 30 minutes or until it is tender but not falling apart. Transfer the chicken to a plate to cool.

Strain the stock through a fine sieve into a bowl, and discard the onion. Clean the casserole. Skim the stock of as much surface fat as you can, and return the stock to the casserole. Add the tomatoes, carrots, rice and a few grindings of pepper, and bring the mixture to a boil over high heat. Reduce the heat to low, cover the casserole and, stirring occasionally, simmer for 30 minutes.

Remove the skin from the chicken with a small, sharp knife or your fingers. Cut or pull the meat away from the bones. Cut the meat into julienne strips about ⅛ inch wide and 1 to 1½ inches long. Add the chicken meat and the ham to the simmering soup, and cook for four or five minutes to heat them through. Stir in the parsley, taste for seasoning, and serve at once, directly from the casserole or from a warmed tureen.

■ LATIN AMERICAN COOKING

## Chicken and Avocado Soup

**To serve 6**

| | |
|---|---|
| 6 cups chicken stock | oregano |
| 1 whole chicken breast | ½ teaspoon salt |
| 2 onions, sliced | ¼ teaspoon freshly ground black pepper |
| ½ teaspoon ground coriander | 1 avocado |
| ½ teaspoon crumbled dried | |

Pour the chicken stock into a large saucepan. Add the chicken breast, onions, coriander, oregano, salt and pepper. Bring the stock to a boil, reduce the heat, cover the pan, and poach the breast in the simmering stock for 20 minutes. Remove the chicken breast and let it cool. Strain the stock into another saucepan, and set it aside. Discard the cooked onions. When the chicken is cool and firm to the touch, peel off the skin. Then, with a large, sharp knife, cut the chicken into julienne strips. Just before serving, stir the strips into the soup and heat it. Cut the avocado in half, remove the pit, slip off the skin, and cut the avocado into thin slices. Ladle the soup into warmed individual soup bowls. Add the avocado; the slices will float.

■ GREAT DINNERS FROM LIFE

## Chicken Soup with Poached Eggs

**To serve 4**

| | |
|---|---|
| ¼ cup butter | 3 cups chicken stock |
| 4 slices Italian bread, each cut ½ inch thick | 2 tablespoons freshly grated Parmesan cheese |
| 4 very fresh eggs | |

In a heavy 8- to 10-inch skillet, melt the butter over moderately low heat and in it cook the bread, turning the slices frequently, for four or five minutes or until they are golden brown on both sides. Place one slice of bread in each of four individual soup bowls.

Bring 2 inches of water to a simmer in a 10- to 12-inch skillet. Break one egg into a saucer. Holding the saucer as close to the water as possible, slide the egg into the skillet. Gently lift the white over the yolk with a wooden spoon. Following the same procedure and keeping the water at a slow simmer, break the remaining eggs into the saucer one at a time and slide them into the water. Try to keep them separate. Poach the eggs for three to five minutes, depending on how firm you want them. Then remove them from the water with a slotted spatula or spoon and place one egg on top of the fried bread in each soup bowl. Heat the chicken stock to a simmer in a small saucepan, sprinkle the eggs with grated Parmesan cheese and pour the stock around it. Serve the soup at once.

■ THE COOKING OF ITALY

## Scotch Broth

**To serve 6 to 8**

| | |
|---|---|
| 2 pounds lamb neck or shoulder with bones, cut into 6 pieces | ½ cup finely chopped carrot |
| | ½ cup finely chopped turnip |
| 8 cups cold water | ½ cup finely chopped onion |
| 2 tablespoons pearl barley, soaked in water for 2 hours | ½ cup finely chopped leek, including 2 inches of the green top |
| 1 teaspoon salt | ½ cup finely chopped celery |
| ⅛ teaspoon freshly ground black pepper | 1 tablespoon finely chopped fresh parsley leaves |

Place the lamb in a heavy 4- to 5-quart casserole and add the water. Bring to a boil over high heat, skimming off the foam and scum as they rise to the surface. Drain the barley and add it with the salt and pepper, reduce the heat to low, partially cover the casserole, and simmer the mixture for one hour. Add the carrot, turnip, onion, leek and celery, partially cover again, and cook for one hour longer. With a slotted spoon, transfer the lamb to a plate, and pull or cut the meat away from the bones. Cut the meat into ½-inch cubes. Return the meat to the soup, and simmer for two or three minutes to heat it through. Taste for seasoning. Serve the soup from a warmed tureen or in individual soup bowls; sprinkle it with parsley just before serving.

■ THE COOKING OF THE BRITISH ISLES

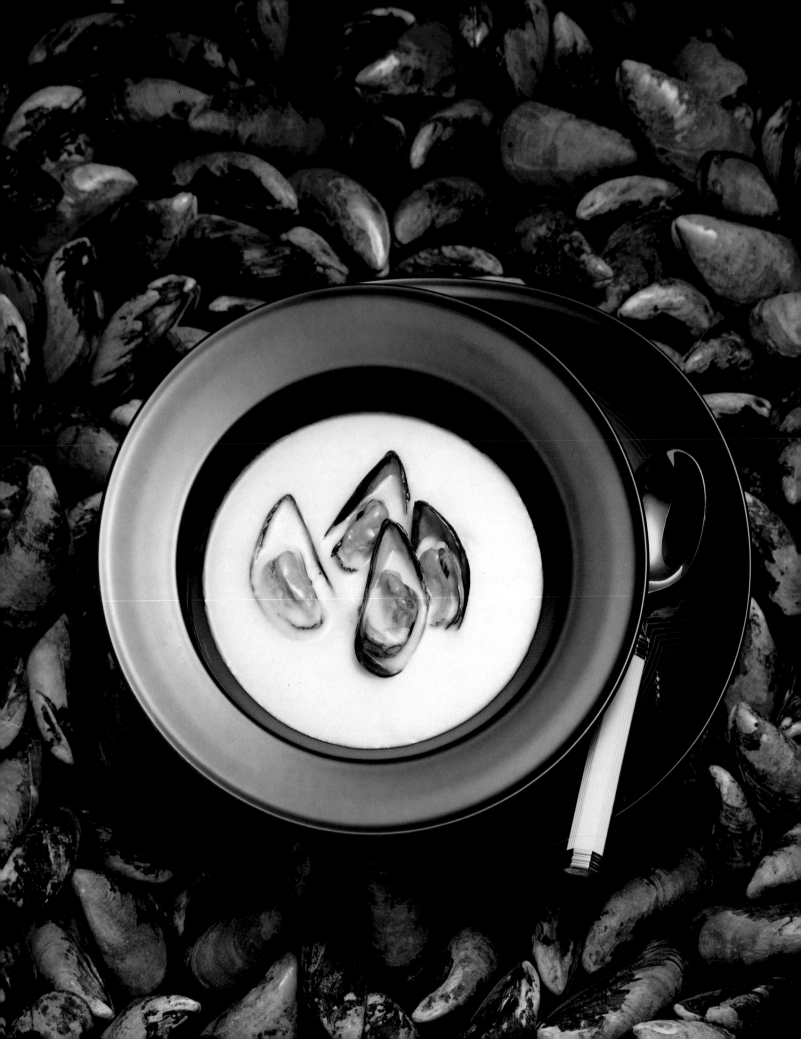

## Nantucket Scallop Chowder

**To serve 4**

| | |
|---|---|
| 6 tablespoons plus 1 teaspoon butter | Salt |
| 2 onions, sliced ¼ inch thick | 1 pound bay scallops, left whole, or sea scallops, cut against the grain into ¼-inch slices |
| 4 cups milk or 2 cups milk and 2 cups cream | Paprika |
| 1 potato, peeled and cut into ½-inch dice (about 1 cup) | |

In a heavy 2- to 3-quart saucepan, melt 3 tablespoons of the butter over moderate heat. When the foam begins to subside, add the onions and cook, stirring frequently, for about five minutes or until they are soft and translucent but not browned. Pour in the milk and bring the mixture to a simmer. Reduce the heat to low and simmer, partially covered, for 15 minutes.

Meanwhile, drop the potato dice into enough lightly salted boiling water to cover them by at least 1 inch and cook briskly until tender. Drain thoroughly and set aside in a bowl.

Melt 2 tablespoons of the butter in a heavy 10- to 12-inch skillet. Drop in the scallops. Turning them about almost constantly with a slotted spoon, fry over high heat for two or three minutes, until they are opaque on all sides. Set the scallops aside with the potato dice.

Strain the onion-and-milk mixture through a fine sieve into a bowl; discard the onions and return the liquid to the saucepan. Add the scallops and potato dice, and simmer for two or three minutes to heat them through. Taste the chowder for seasoning, and ladle it into warmed individual soup bowls. Place 1 teaspoon of butter in each bowl, sprinkle the chowder with a little paprika, and serve at once.

■ AMERICAN COOKING: NEW ENGLAND

## Italian Fish Soup

**To serve 6 to 8**

| | |
|---|---|
| ½ cup olive oil | tomatoes, peeled, seeded and cut up) |
| 2 pounds each fillets or steaks of 3 kinds of white fish— such as haddock, flounder, cod, perch, pollack, snapper, mackerel, bass, or rockfish—cut into 2-inch serving pieces | 3 tablespoons chopped fresh parsley leaves |
| | 1 teaspoon finely chopped garlic |
| | ½ teaspoon crumbled dried oregano |
| ¼ teaspoon powdered saffron or crumbled saffron threads | Salt |
| 4 cups fish stock | Freshly ground black pepper |
| 1 cup coarsely chopped fresh tomato pulp (about 1 pound | 1 tablespoon grated lemon peel |

Heat the olive oil over moderate heat in a heavy 4- to 5-quart flameproof serving casserole. Brown the fish pieces in the oil for two or three minutes on each side. Tip the casserole slightly and, with a bulb baster, remove all but 2 or 3 tablespoons of the oil. Stir the saffron into the fish stock to dissolve it. Then add the stock along with the tomatoes, 1 tablespoon of the parsley, the garlic, oregano, 1 teaspoon salt and a few grindings of black pepper to the casserole.

Stirring gently, bring the soup to a simmer. Reduce the heat to low, cover the casserole and cook the soup for five minutes or until the fish flakes easily when prodded with a fork. Be careful not to overcook it. Taste, and season the soup with more salt and pepper, if needed. Sprinkle the top with the remaining parsley and the lemon peel. Serve the soup directly from the casserole.

■ THE COOKING OF ITALY

## Mussel Brose

**To serve 4 to 6**

| | |
|---|---|
| 36 live mussels in their shells | or dry white wine |
| 1 cup finely chopped leeks, including 2 inches of the green | 3 tablespoons butter |
| | 3 tablespoons flour |
| ½ cup finely chopped celery | 2 cups milk |
| ½ cup finely chopped onion | 2 tablespoons heavy cream |
| 3 parsley sprigs | Salt |
| 1 cup dry hard cider, preferably imported English cider, | Freshly ground black pepper |
| | Freshly grated nutmeg |

Scrub the mussels thoroughly under cold running water with a stiff brush or soapless steel-mesh scouring pad. With a small, sharp knife scrape or pull the black ropelike tufts off the shells and discard them.

In a 6- to 8-quart enameled or stainless-steel pot, combine the leeks, celery, onion, parsley and cider. Drop in the mussels, cover, and bring to a boil over high heat. Reduce the heat to low. Shaking the pot from time to time, simmer for about five minutes or until the mussels open; discard those that remain closed. With a slotted spoon, transfer the mussels to a plate. Strain the stock through a fine sieve lined with a double thickness of cheesecloth, and return it to the pot. Traditionally, the mussels are left in the half shell. To serve the soup in that way, remove and discard the upper halves of the shells. Or you may remove the mussels from their shells entirely. In either case, cover the mussels with foil to keep them warm and set them aside.

In a heavy 2- to 3-quart saucepan, melt the butter over moderate heat. Add the flour and mix together thoroughly. Pour in the milk and, stirring constantly with a whisk, bring to a boil over high heat. Reduce the heat to moderate and continue to cook, stirring, until the sauce is smooth and thick. Pour it into the strained stock, stir in the cream, and season lightly with salt and a few grindings of pepper and some grated nutmeg. Bring the soup to a simmer over low heat, stirring frequently. Then add the mussels and cook only long enough to heat them through; taste for seasoning. Serve the soup in heated individual soup plates.

■ THE COOKING OF THE BRITISH ISLES

# Salads

# Salads

FRONTISPIECE: KIWI AND SPINACH SALAD

When John Gerard, the noted 16th century English writer, penned his *Herball,* extolling the "vertues" of plants, he suggested that "lettuce maketh a pleasant sallad, being eaten raw with vinegar, oile and a little salt." Salad then meant salted greens, from the Latin *herba salada,* and it probably was intended to cure some ailment. Today, the meaning of "salad" has been expanded to encompass robust concoctions as well as the refreshing kiwi and spinach at left.

Greens moistened with a sauce or dressing remain fundamental. However, the greens may be red, and the familiar iceberg lettuce is often replaced by crisp leaf lettuce or soft, faintly sweet butterhead, Bibb and Boston lettuces. Along with these are crunchy, almost-pungent Romaine, musky spinach, mildly bitter Belgian endive, tangy dandelions, tart arugula, strongly flavored escarole and chicory, and lemony sorrel.

In the lexicon of garnishes are tomatoes, avocados, cucumbers, and the edible flower buds of calendulas, day lilies, nasturtiums, roses and violets.

Beyond the basic salads are the plenitude of combinations made from raw and cooked vegetables, fruits, meats, fish and shellfish, pasta, rice and other grains. Some are as highly structured as cucumber mousse, but most are in the improvisational spirit of the French salade niçoise—a beneficent blend of ingredients at hand. These salads may constitute a first course or complement the main course. Or, they may become the main course itself.

## Radicchio and Arugula Salad with Warm Mushroom Dressing

*Both of the leafy vegetables for this salad are identified here by their commonly used Italian names. Radicchio is also known as "red chicory"; arugula is widely cultivated as "rocket."* ◆●

**To serve 4**

| | |
|---|---|
| ¼ **cup pine nuts (optional)** | 2 **tablespoons olive oil** |
| ¼ **cup red-wine vinegar** | ½ **pound fresh mushrooms,** |
| ¼ **cup water** | **wiped clean, trimmed and** |
| 1 **teaspoon fresh lemon juice** | **sliced thin** |
| 1 **teaspoon Worcestershire** | 1 **small head radicchio, leaves** |
| **sauce** | **separated, washed, spun or** |
| 2 **teaspoons sugar** | **patted dry, and torn into** |
| 2 **teaspoons Dijon mustard** | **bite-sized pieces** |
| 1 **small garlic clove, chopped** | 2 **bunches arugula, stems** |
| **fine** | **trimmed, washed, spun or** |
| ¼ **teaspoon salt** | **patted dry, and torn into** |
| ⅛ **teaspoon freshly ground** | **bite-sized pieces** |
| **black pepper** | |

Preheat the oven to 350°F. Spread the pine nuts in a pie pan, if you are using them, and toast them in the oven for five minutes, or until lightly browned. Let the pine nuts cool.

To prepare the dressing, combine the vinegar, water, lemon juice, Worcestershire, sugar, mustard, garlic, salt and pepper in a screw-top jar with a tight-fitting lid. Add the olive oil, close the jar, and shake it vigorously.

At serving time, pour the dressing into an 8- to 10-inch nonreactive saucepan, and set it over moderately high heat. When the dressing is hot, add the mushrooms. Stirring occasionally, cook for five minutes or until the mushrooms are tender. Divide the radicchio leaves among four salad plates and top them with the arugula. Spoon the mushrooms and dressing evenly over the leaves and sprinkle each salad with toasted pine nuts.

■ MEATLESS MENUS

## Green Salad with Fried Goat Cheese

**To serve 4**

| | |
|---|---|
| 1 **egg** | 1 **teaspoon Dijon mustard** |
| 1 **teaspoon water** | **Salt** |
| ¼ **cup dry bread crumbs** | **Freshly ground black pepper** |
| 5 **ounces goat cheese, chilled** | **Vegetable oil for frying** |
| **and cut into 8 slices, each ¼** | 1 **head romaine lettuce, leaves** |
| **to ½ inch thick** | **separated, washed, spun or** |
| 2 **tablespoons vegetable oil** | **patted dry, and torn into** |
| 2 **tablespoons olive oil** | **bite-sized pieces** |
| 2 **tablespoons red-wine vinegar** | |

In a small bowl, beat together the egg and water. Spread the bread crumbs onto a small, flat plate. Dip one cheese slice at a time into the beaten egg, then coat it with bread crumbs. Place the coated slices in a pie pan, cover with foil, and set it in the freezer; let the slices freeze for at least 30 minutes.

To prepare the dressing, combine the vegetable oil, olive oil, vinegar, mustard, and salt and pepper to taste in a large bowl; whisk the ingredients until blended. Set the dressing aside.

At serving time, pour vegetable oil to a depth of ¼ inch into a large skillet, and heat the oil over moderate heat until a cube of bread dropped into the skillet browns lightly in 40 seconds. Fry the cheese slices for about three minutes on each side or until they are crisp and evenly browned. Drain on paper towels.

Whisk the dressing to recombine it, drop the lettuce pieces into the bowl, and toss them with the dressing. Divide the greens among four salad plates, and top each serving with two slices of the fried goat cheese.

NOTE: Because of its soft texture, goat cheese tends to be crumbly. Chilling it well ahead of time makes slicing it easier; freezing the slices for even 30 minutes helps them to hold their shape when fried.

■ VEGETABLE MENUS

## Caesar Salad

*This salad is believed to have been created in Mexico or California in the 1920s. The inventive chef, it is said, was named Caesar.* ◆●

**To serve 4 to 6**

| | |
|---|---|
| 1 **loaf French or Italian bread,** | **Salt** |
| **trimmed of crusts and cut** | **Freshly ground black** |
| **into 1-inch cubes** | **pepper** |
| ¼ **to ½ cup vegetable oil** | ½ **cup olive oil** |
| 1 **teaspoon finely chopped** | ¼ **cup fresh lemon juice** |
| **garlic** | 1 **cup freshly grated** |
| 2 **eggs at room temperature** | **Parmesan cheese** |
| 2 **heads romaine lettuce,** | 6 **to 8 flat anchovy fillets,** |
| **leaves separated, washed,** | **drained and cut fine** |
| **spun or patted dry, and** | **(optional)** |
| **chilled thoroughly** | |

In a heavy skillet large enough to hold all of the bread cubes in one layer, heat ¼ cup of vegetable oil over high heat. Add the cubes and brown them on all sides, shaking the pan to turn them; if necessary, add up to ¼ cup more vegetable oil. Remove the skillet from the heat, then add the garlic and toss the croutons about in the hot oil. Remove the croutons to paper towels to drain until cool and crisp.

Plunge the eggs into rapidly boiling water, cover the pan, and cook the eggs for one minute to set them slightly; lift them out of the pan with a slotted spoon and set aside. Break the chilled romaine into serving-sized pieces and scatter it in the bottom of a large salad bowl, preferably of glass or porcelain. Add salt and pepper to taste and the olive oil, and toss the lettuce with two large spoons or, better still, with your hands. Then break the eggs on top of the salad, add the lemon juice, and mix again until the lettuce is thoroughly coated. Add the cheese and the anchovies, if you are using them, and mix once more. Scatter the croutons over the top, and serve at once on chilled salad plates.

■ AMERICAN COOKING

## Green Bean Salad

**To serve 4 to 6**

| | |
|---|---|
| 1 pound green beans, ends trimmed | Freshly ground black pepper |
| 3 tablespoons red-wine vinegar | ½ cup olive oil |
| ½ teaspoon dry mustard | 12 cherry tomatoes |
| Salt | 1 red onion, cut into ⅛-inch slices and separated into rings |

Bring 3 quarts of lightly salted water to a boil in a large nonreactive pan. Drop in the beans and boil them, uncovered, for five to 10 minutes, until tender but still slightly resistant to the bite—*al dente*. Drain the beans and transfer them to a serving bowl.

With a wire whisk, beat the vinegar, mustard, and salt and pepper to taste together in a small bowl. Still whisking, slowly pour in the oil; continue to whisk until the mixture is smooth. Pour the dressing over the beans, and add the tomatoes and onion. Toss the ingredients together lightly with a wooden spoon. Cover the bowl with foil or plastic wrap, and refrigerate the salad for at least two hours before serving.

■ AMERICAN COOKING: THE NORTHWEST

## Celery Slaw

**To serve 4 to 6**

| | |
|---|---|
| 1 bunch celery | ½ cup sour cream |
| ¼ cup wine vinegar | 1 onion, cut into ⅛-inch slices and separated into rings |
| 1 tablespoon sugar | |
| ¼ teaspoon paprika | 1 pimiento, cut into strips about 1 inch long and ⅛ inch wide |
| 1 teaspoon salt | |
| Freshly ground black pepper | |
| ⅔ cup vegetable oil | |

With a small, sharp knife, remove the celery leaves. Separate the bunch into individual ribs, trim the roots ends with the knife, and scrape off the heavy outside strings and any brown blemished areas. Wash the ribs under cold running water, and pat them dry with paper towels. Then, holding the knife on the diagonal, cut the ribs crosswise into slices ⅛ inch thick and drop them into a large bowl; set aside.

Combine the vinegar, sugar, paprika, salt and a few grindings of pepper in a small, deep bowl, and beat with a wire whisk until the sugar dissolves. Whisking the mixture constantly, pour in the vegetable oil in a very slow, thin stream. When the sauce thickens and is smooth, beat in the sour cream with the whisk. Taste for seasoning.

Pour the sauce over the celery, add the onion rings, and toss together gently but thoroughly. Cover the slaw with foil or plastic wrap, refrigerate it, and marinate the celery in the sauce for about three hours. Just before serving, taste the slaw for seasoning again, and gently stir in the pimiento strips.

■ AMERICAN COOKING: THE EASTERN HEARTLAND

## Summertime Vegetable Aspic

**To serve 4**

| | |
|---|---|
| 9 tomatoes, cored and chopped coarse | 2 teaspoons salt |
| 2 onions, chopped coarse | Freshly ground black pepper |
| ½ cup coarsely chopped celery leaves | 1 cup thinly sliced cabbage |
| | ½ cup coarsely chopped celery |
| 2 parsley sprigs plus 2 tablespoons chopped fresh parsley leaves | ⅓ cup finely chopped green pepper |
| 1 small bay leaf | 1 carrot, cut into ⅛-inch slices |
| ½ cup cold water | |
| 4 teaspoons unflavored gelatin | 1 tablespoon finely chopped pimiento |
| 1 tablespoon fresh lemon juice | |

Combine the tomatoes, onions, celery leaves, parsley sprigs, bay leaf and ¼ cup of cold water in a 3- to 4-quart nonreactive saucepan, and bring to a boil over high heat, stirring from time to time. Reduce the heat to low and simmer, partially covered, for 30 minutes or until the vegetables are very soft. Strain the mixture through a fine sieve set over a bowl, pressing down on the vegetables with the back of a spoon to extract as much of their juices as

GREEN BEAN SALAD

## Jícama Salad

*Native to Mexico, jícama is a crunchy tuber that looks somewhat like a turnip, but tastes like a cross between an apple and a water chestnut. Whole or cut-up jícama is available at many supermarkets and wherever Mexican foods are sold. Store it refrigerated—in a plastic bag or sliced and submerged in water in a covered container.* ◆●

**To serve 4**

| | |
|---|---|
| 1 pound jícama | leaves separated, washed, |
| 1/4 cup fresh orange juice | and spun or patted dry |
| 2 tablespoons walnut oil | 1/2 cup walnut halves for |
| 1 teaspoon chili powder | garnish |
| 1 tablespoon grated orange | 12 whole black olives for |
| peel (optional) | garnish |
| 1 small head red leaf lettuce, | |

Peel the jícama and cut enough julienne strips to measure ³/₄ cup. For the dressing, combine the orange juice, walnut oil and chili powder; add grated orange peel, if desired. Add the jícama and turn with a spoon to coat the strips evenly. Line four salad plates with the lettuce. Divide the jícama salad among the plates; garnish with walnut halves and black olives, if you like.

■ MEXICAN MENUS

## Cucumber, Beet and Onion Salad

**To serve 4**

| | |
|---|---|
| 3 young beets | 1 red onion, cut into 1/8-inch |
| 3/4 cup raspberry vinegar | slices |
| 2 tablespoons plus 1/4 cup | 1 large bunch watercress, |
| fresh lemon juice | trimmed, washed, and spun |
| 2 1/2 teaspoons salt | or patted dry |
| Freshly ground black pepper | 2 tablespoons olive oil |
| 1 or 2 tablespoons sugar | 1 small bunch chives, |
| 1 large cucumber, peeled, | trimmed, washed, patted dry |
| halved, seeded and cut | and chopped coarse |
| diagonally into 1/8-inch slices | |

With a vegetable peeler or small knife, peel the beets. Grate them in a food processor fitted with a metal blade or grater. In a small, nonreactive bowl, combine the beets with 1/2 cup of the vinegar, 2 tablespoons of lemon juice, 1 teaspoon of salt, and pepper to taste. Check the seasoning; if the beets are not sweet, add 1 tablespoon of sugar.

In another small nonreactive bowl, combine the cucumber with 1/4 cup of lemon juice, 1 1/2 teaspoons of salt, pepper to taste and 1 tablespoon of sugar. Place the onion slices in another small nonreactive bowl, add 2 cups of cold water and the remaining 1/4 cup of raspberry vinegar.

Just before serving, drop the watercress into a bowl and toss it with the olive oil. Drain the vegetables and pat them dry with paper towels. Arrange the beets, cucumber slices, onion slices and watercress in concentric circles on salad plates and sprinkle them with chives.

■ FRENCH REGIONAL MENUS

possible before discarding them.

Pour the remaining ¹/₄ cup of cold water into a small heatproof bowl and sprinkle the gelatin over it. When the gelatin has softened for two to three minutes, set the bowl in a skillet of simmering water, and cook over low heat, stirring constantly, until the gelatin dissolves completely.

Stir the dissolved gelatin into the vegetable juices, add the lemon juice, salt and a few grindings of black pepper, and taste for seasoning. Refrigerate until the mixture begins to thicken and is syrupy. Then stir in the cabbage, celery, green pepper, carrot, chopped parsley and pimiento.

Rinse a 3-cup mold under cold running water, and invert it to drain. Pour the vegetable aspic mixture into the mold, cover with foil or plastic wrap, and refrigerate for at least two hours or until firm to the touch.

To unmold and serve the aspic, run a thin-bladed knife around the edges of the mold to loosen the sides and dip the bottom briefly in hot water. Invert a serving plate over the mold and, grasping plate and mold together, turn them over. Rap the plate sharply on a table: The vegetable aspic should slide out easily.

■ AMERICAN COOKING: SOUTHERN STYLE

## Zucchini and Yogurt Salad

*In Indian cookery, this cooling mixture of vegetables and yogurt is called a "raita" and is served to balance the heat of curries.* ❧

**To serve 4**

| | |
|---|---|
| 1 small zucchini | ⅓ cup chopped fresh mint |
| 1⅓ cups plain yogurt | leaves plus 4 mint sprigs |
| ⅓ cup sour cream | ⅓ cup chopped fresh |
| 1½ teaspoons sugar | coriander leaves |
| ¾ teaspoon salt | 2 tablespoons light |
| 2 large scallions, white parts | vegetable oil |
| only, cut into ⅛-inch slices | ¾ teaspoon ground cumin |
| 2 slices fresh ginger root, diced | |

Rinse the zucchini and dry it with paper towels; trim off the ends. Using the coarse side of a grater, grate the zucchini. Blot it with paper towels and set aside in a colander. In a medium-sized bowl, combine the yogurt, sour cream, sugar and salt. Mix in the scallions, ginger, mint and coriander.

Heat the oil in a 6- to 8-inch skillet over high heat until it is very hot but not smoking. Turn off the heat, sprinkle the oil with the cumin, and immediately add the zucchini. Toss the zucchini in the hot oil until it is barely cooked. Add the zucchini to the yogurt mixture and blend them well. To serve, divide the salad among four plates, and garnish it with mint sprigs.

■ **MEATLESS MENUS**

## Tomato and Celery Root Salad

*The chèvre, or French goat cheese, used to flavor the dressing for this salad has a distinctive, tangy taste. It comes in many shapes (often logs), either plain or rolled in powdered ash, which gives the cheese a slight saltiness.* ❧

**To serve 4**

| | |
|---|---|
| ¼ pound mild *chèvre,* | dried basil |
| preferably Montrachet, or | 1 large garlic clove, peeled |
| feta cheese cut into small | and halved |
| pieces | ¾ cup olive or light |
| 1 small bunch arugula or | vegetable oil |
| watercress, trimmed, with | ¼ cup balsamic, red-wine, or |
| 4 stems set aside for garnish | tarragon vinegar |
| 2 or 3 large fresh basil leaves, | 4 tomatoes |
| or 1 teaspoon crumbled | 1 large celery root |

In a food processor or blender, combine the cheese with the arugula, basil, garlic, oil and vinegar. Purée until the dressing is smooth, about one minute.

Core each tomato and cut it crosswise into four slices. Peel the celery root and coarsely grate it, or cut it into ⅛-inch-thick julienne strips. Divide the tomato slices equally among four salad plates. Mound the celery root beside the tomatoes, and garnish each serving with a stem of arugula. Just before serving, process the dressing to recombine it, then spoon it over the salad.

■ **FRENCH REGIONAL MENUS**

FLORENTINE TOMATO AND BREAD SALAD

## Tomato Salad with Tarragon

**To serve 4**

| | |
|---|---|
| 1 tablespoon chopped fresh tarragon leaves, plus 20 sprigs for garnish, or 1 teaspoon crumbled dried tarragon | dried tomatoes or ¼ cup olive oil |
| ¼ cup fresh orange juice | 1 tablespoon finely chopped drained oil-packed sun-dried tomato |
| 1 tablespoon fresh lemon juice | Salt |
| ¼ cup oil drained from sun- | 4 large tomatoes, cored and cut into ¼-inch slices |

For the dressing, combine the chopped tarragon, orange juice, lemon juice, oil, sun-dried tomato and a pinch of salt in a small bowl. With a fork, beat the dressing until well blended. Divide the sliced tomatoes among four salad plates, and pour the dressing over them. Garnish the salad, if you like, with tarragon sprigs.

■ TURKEY AND DUCK MENUS

## Florentine Tomato and Bread Salad

*In its native land, this classic salad is called "panzanella" from the Italian word "pane," meaning bread. The tomatoes for the salad should be freshly picked, if possible, and the bread be of the highest quality. Allow the bread cubes to dry out completely so that they will hold their shape when soaked.* ❧

**To serve 4**

| | |
|---|---|
| 2 cups ½-inch cubes cut from stale whole-wheat Italian bread | basil leaves |
| | 5 tablespoons olive oil |
| 1 cucumber | 2 tablespoons red-wine vinegar |
| 4 to 6 tomatoes, peeled, seeded and cut into 1-inch pieces | Salt |
| | Freshly ground black pepper |
| ¾ cup chopped red onion | 1 small head romaine lettuce, leaves separated, washed, and spun or patted dry |
| 3 tablespoons chopped fresh | |

Place the bread cubes in a mixing bowl, and add enough cold water to cover them. Let the cubes soak for five minutes. Meanwhile, halve the cucumber lengthwise and cut off the ends, but do not peel it. Scrape out the cucumber seeds with a teaspoon. Cut enough cucumber into ¼-inch dice to measure 1½ cups. Drain the bread, gently squeezing out as much of the moisture as you can with your hands.

Drop the bread cubes into a large salad bowl, and mix in the cucumber, tomatoes, onion, basil, 4 tablespoons of the olive oil, 1 tablespoon of the vinegar, about 1 teaspoon of salt and about ¼ teaspoon of pepper. Cover the bowl and let the mixture stand at room temperature for at least two hours.

To serve the salad, add the remaining spoonfuls of olive oil and vinegar, and additional salt and pepper to taste. Line a platter with romaine leaves, and spoon the salad onto the center of the leaves, or serve directly from the salad bowl.

■ MAKE-AHEAD MENUS

## Sunchokes Vinaigrette

*A native American, the sunchoke—or "Jerusalem artichoke" as it is also called—is the knobby root of the perennial sunflower.* ❧●

**To serve 4**

| | |
|---|---|
| 2 lemons | chives or scallion tops |
| 1 pound sunchokes | Salt |
| 1 teaspoon Dijon mustard | Freshly ground white pepper |
| 2 tablespoons white-wine vinegar | Lettuce leaves, washed and spun or patted dry |
| 2 tablespoons walnut oil | 4 to 6 cherry tomatoes, |
| 4 tablespoons safflower oil | halved, or 1 tomato, sliced, |
| 2 tablespoons finely cut fresh | for garnish |

In a 4- to 5-quart saucepan, bring 2 quarts of lightly salted water to a boil. Squeeze in 2 or 3 tablespoonfuls of lemon juice. Scrub the sunchokes with a brush under cold running water. Trim off the tips of protruding knobs and, without peeling the sunchokes, cut them into ⅛-inch slices. As you work, place the slices in a bowl; sprinkle with lemon juice to prevent discoloration.

Blanche the sunchoke slices in the boiling water until they are barely tender, about five minutes. Drain them in a colander, refresh them immediately in cold water, and drain again.

With a wire whisk, combine the mustard and vinegar in a large mixing bowl. Add the walnut and safflower oils in a slow, steady stream, whisking constantly. Add the chives, and salt and pepper to taste. When the sunchokes cool slightly, add them to the bowl and toss them with the dressing.

To serve, line a platter with the lettuce leaves. Using a slotted spoon, place the sunchokes on the lettuce. Garnish the salad with tomatoes, if desired.

■ AMERICAN REGIONAL MENUS

## Cucumber and Tomato Salad

**To serve 4**

| | |
|---|---|
| 1 cucumber, peeled, halved, seeded, and cut lengthwise into ⅛-inch slices, then crosswise into ½-inch pieces | ½-inch dice |
| | 1 tablespoon finely chopped fresh coriander leaves |
| | 1 cup plain yogurt |
| 1 tablespoon finely chopped onion | 1 teaspoon ground cumin, toasted over low heat for 30 seconds |
| 1 tablespoon salt | |
| 1 small tomato, cut into | |

Combine the cucumber, onion and salt in a small bowl, and mix thoroughly. Let the mixture rest at room temperature for five minutes, then squeeze the cucumbers gently to remove the excess liquid. Drop the cucumber pieces into a deep bowl, add the tomato and coriander, and toss together gently.

Combine the yogurt and cumin, and pour it over the vegetables, tossing them to coat them evenly. Taste for seasoning, cover tightly, and refrigerate until completely chilled before serving.

■ THE COOKING OF INDIA

CUCUMBER MOUSSE WITH GAZPACHO SAUCE

## Cucumber Mousse with Gazpacho Sauce

**To serve 8**

2 tablespoons unflavored
   powdered gelatin
¾ cup chicken or vegetable
   stock
2 cucumbers, peeled, halved,
   seeded, and cut into 2-inch
   strips
1 cup plain yogurt
2 scallions, white bottoms
   only, chopped
1 jalapeño pepper, halved
   and seeded
1 tablespoon chopped fresh
   coriander leaves

1 tablespoon fresh lime juice
6 drops Tabasco sauce

GAZPACHO SAUCE

6 tomatoes, peeled, seeded
   and chopped fine
2 scallions, green tops only,
   cut up
1 tablespoon chopped fresh
   coriander leaves
1 garlic clove, chopped fine
1 tablespoon olive oil
1 tablespoon fresh lime juice
4 drops Tabasco sauce

In a small bowl, soften the gelatin in ¼ cup of the stock until spongy. In a small saucepan, bring the remaining ½ cup of stock to a boil; add the gelatin mixture, and stir to dissolve the gelatin thoroughly. Set the gelatin mixture aside.

Purée the cucumbers, yogurt, scallion white bottoms, jalapeño pepper and 1 tablespoon of coriander with 1 tablespoon of lime juice and 6 drops of Tabasco in a food processor or blender. Add the gelatin mixture. Pour this mousse mixture into a 2-quart mold, and chill until firm to the touch, at least two hours.

To make the sauce, combine the tomatoes, green scallion tops, 1 tablespoon of coriander and the garlic with the oil, 1 tablespoon of lime juice and 4 drops of Tabasco. Refrigerate the mixture.

At serving time, run a blade along the edge of the mold to loosen the mousse. Set the mold in shallow hot water for 30 seconds, then place an inverted serving platter over the mold and, grasping plate and mold together, turn them over. Rap the plate sharply on a table. The mousse should slide out easily. Spoon the sauce on top of the mousse and around its sides.

■ FRESH WAYS WITH VEGETABLES

## Sweet-and-Sour Carrots

**To serve 4**

½ cup fresh lemon juice
2 tablespoons sugar
¼ teaspoon freshly ground
   black pepper
6 cups coarsely grated carrots
1 small head Bibb lettuce,

leaves separated, washed,
   and patted or spun dry
1 tablespoon chopped fresh
   parsley leaves
1 tablespoon chopped filberts
   for garnish

Mix the lemon juice, sugar and pepper in a medium-sized bowl, stirring until the sugar dissolves. Add the carrots and stir to coat them well. Cover the bowl and refrigerate until ready to serve, stirring the carrots once or twice. To serve, line a platter with the lettuce leaves, mound the carrots on top and sprinkle the salad with the parsley and the filberts, if you are using them.

■ EGG AND CHEESE MENUS

## Indian Mixed-Bean Salad

**To serve 6 to 8**

| | |
|---|---|
| 1½ cups cooked chickpeas | of green tops |
| 1½ cups cooked black-eyed peas | 3 tablespoons finely chopped fresh coriander leaves |
| 1½ cups cooked red kidney beans | 1 fresh hot green chili, about 3 inches long, washed, seeded and chopped fine |
| 1 large garlic clove, peeled and flattened with side of heavy knife or mallet | ¼ teaspoon ground cumin |
| 1 tablespoon olive oil | ½ teaspoon salt |
| ½ cup finely chopped scallions, including 1 inch | Freshly ground black pepper |
| | 3 tablespoons fresh lemon juice |

Drain freshly cooked chickpeas, black-eyed peas and kidney beans in a sieve or colander, and cool them to room temperature before using them. (If you are using canned peas and beans, drain them, rinse and pat dry with paper towels.)

Combine the garlic and olive oil in a small cup, and steep at room temperature for 15 minutes.

To assemble the salad, combine the scallions, coriander, chili, cumin, salt and a few grindings of black pepper in a small bowl. When they are well mixed, stir in the lemon juice. Add the peas and beans; toss together gently and sprinkle the olive oil on top.

Stir the peas and beans together again, then push the garlic clove underneath the surface and cover the bowl with foil or plastic wrap. Refrigerate the salad for at least two hours, until it is well chilled. Remove the garlic before serving the salad.

■ THE COOKING OF INDIA

## Yankee Potato Salad

**To make 8 cups**

| | |
|---|---|
| 3 pounds new potatoes, washed | 1½ cups finely chopped green pepper |
| 1 teaspoon salt | 4 tablespoons chopped fresh parsley leaves |
| 2 tablespoons white-wine vinegar | 2 cups mayonnaise, preferably homemade |
| ¾ cup finely chopped celery | 3 hard-boiled eggs, sliced |
| ¾ cup finely chopped onion | |

Fill a 6- to 8-quart pot halfway with water and bring the water to a boil over high heat. Add the potatoes, bring the water to a boil again, then reduce the heat to moderately high—the water should continue boiling. Cook the potatoes for seven to 15 minutes or until they are barely tender when pierced with the tip of a small knife. Drain the potatoes in a colander.

When the potatoes are cool enough to handle, peel them and cut them into ½- to ¾-inch dice. Place the potatoes in a large bowl and gently stir in the salt, vinegar, celery, onion, green pepper and 2 tablespoons of the parsley. Fold in the mayonnaise. Taste the salad and adjust the seasoning. Serve the salad garnished with the egg slices and the remaining chopped parsley.

■ AMERICAN COOKING

## Bulgur Wheat Salad

*This unusual dish comes from the Middle East where it is called "tabbouli." Its basis is the crushed wheat called "bulgur," which becomes fluffy with a chewy texture when cooked. If your grocer does not have it, try a health-food store. In this recipe, the wheat is cooked by steeping— the ancient Levantine technique. To cook it on the stove as you would other cereals, follow the package instructions.*

**To serve 8**

| | |
|---|---|
| 2 cups bulgur wheat | 2 tomatoes, peeled, seeded and finely chopped |
| 1 cup finely chopped fresh parsley leaves | ½ cup fresh lemon juice |
| ½ cup finely chopped fresh mint leaves, plus whole mint leaves for garnish | ½ cup olive oil |
| | Salt |
| ½ cup finely chopped scallions, including 2 inches of the green tops | Freshly ground black pepper |
| | Curly-leaf lettuce |
| | 8 thin lemon slices for garnish |

Put the wheat into a large pot or mixing bowl, and pour about 2 quarts of boiling water over it. Cover and let it stand for two to three hours, until the wheat is light and fluffy; drain in a strainer, shaking it until the wheat is very dry.

In a mixing bowl, combine the wheat with the parsley, mint, scallions, tomatoes, lemon juice, olive oil, and salt and pepper to taste, and stir gently until mixed. Chill the salad for at least one hour. To serve, line a serving bowl with lettuce, mound the salad on top, and garnish with lemon slices and mint leaves.

■ GREAT DINNERS FROM LIFE

BULGUR WHEAT SALAD

## Caviar Potato Salad

**To serve 6**

| | |
|---|---|
| 6 boiling potatoes, peeled | ¹/₂ cup sour cream |
| ¹/₄ cup cider vinegar | 2 tablespoons finely cut fresh |
| ¹/₂ cup finely chopped onions | dill, plus dill sprigs for |
| One 2-ounce jar red caviar | garnish |
| 1 cup mayonnaise, | Freshly ground black pepper |
| preferably homemade | |

Drop the potatoes into enough boiling water to cover them completely. Cook briskly, uncovered, until the potatoes are tender and show no resistance when pierced deeply with the point of a small, sharp knife, after about 10 minutes.

Drain the potatoes in a sieve or colander and, while they are still warm, peel and cut them into ¹/₂-inch-thick slices. Place the slices in a bowl, add the vinegar and onions, and toss together gently but thoroughly with a spoon.

Reserve about 1 teaspoon of caviar to garnish the salad, and place the rest in a small bowl. With a rubber spatula, stir in the mayonnaise, sour cream, dill and a few grindings of pepper; taste for seasoning. Pour the mixture over the potatoes and use the spatula to toss the slices gently until they are evenly coated.

Mound the salad in a serving bowl, spread the reserved teaspoon of caviar on top, and garnish the salad with sprigs of dill if desired. Serve at once.

■ AMERICAN COOKING: THE GREAT WEST

## Tangy Rice Salad

**To serve 4**

| | |
|---|---|
| 1¹/₂ cups freshly cooked long-grain white rice, cooled | 2 tablespoons red-wine vinegar |
| One 6-ounce can flat anchovy fillets, drained and chopped coarse | ¹/₂ teaspoon dry mustard |
| | Salt |
| ¹/₂ cup chopped scallions | Freshly ground black pepper |
| ¹/₂ cup chopped pimiento | 6 tablespoons olive oil |
| 1 tomato, cored and cut into ¹/₄-inch dice | Chilled crisp lettuce leaves |

Place the rice, anchovies, scallions, pimiento and tomato in a serving bowl, and toss together thoroughly with a fork.

With a wire whisk, beat the vinegar, mustard, a pinch of salt and a few grindings of pepper in a small bowl until the salt dissolves. Add the oil gradually and continue beating until the dressing is smooth and thick. Taste for seasoning, then pour the dressing over the rice mixture and stir well.

For each serving, arrange several lettuce leaves to form a cup on a chilled plate, and spoon the salad into the cup. Alternatively, pack the salad into a 2- to 3-cup mold, cover it with plastic wrap, and refrigerate for two hours or until thoroughly chilled. Before serving, remove the plastic, and place an inverted plate over the mold. Grasping plate and mold together firmly, quickly turn them over; the salad will slide out. Surround it with lettuce and serve at once.

■ AMERICAN COOKING: THE NORTHWEST

## French Potato Salad

**To serve 6 to 8**

| | |
|---|---|
| 2 pounds unpeeled new red potatoes, washed | including 2 inches of green tops |
| ¹/₂ cup olive oil | 2 tablespoons chopped fresh |
| ¹/₄ cup tarragon vinegar | parsley leaves |
| ¹/₄ cup beef stock | Salt |
| ¹/₄ cup chopped scallions, | Freshly ground black pepper |

Drop the potatoes into a 4- to 5-quart saucepan half filled with lightly salted boiling water. Bring the water to a second boil, cover the pan, reduce the heat, and cook the potatoes for seven to 15 minutes or until tender but still firm.

Meanwhile, combine the oil, vinegar, stock, scallions, parsley, and salt and pepper to taste; mix well. When the potatoes are cooked, drain and slice them. Immediately put them into a large bowl; pour the oil and vinegar mixture over the warm potato slices, and mix them gently but thoroughly together. All of the liquid should be absorbed by the potatoes. Cover the salad and keep it at room temperature until ready to serve it, or chill it.

■ GREAT DINNERS FROM LIFE

## Mango Salad

**To serve 4**

| | |
|---|---|
| 6 to 8 leaves red or green leaf lettuce or Boston lettuce, washed and patted or spun dry | chopped walnuts |
| | 2 tablespoons grated fresh coconut or dried, unsweetened coconut |
| 2 mangoes, peeled, halved, pitted, and cut into long slices ¹/₂ inch thick | ¹/₄ cup fresh lime juice |
| | ¹/₄ cup fresh lemon juice |
| 2 tablespoons pine nuts or | 1 tablespoon honey |

Line a platter with the lettuce leaves. Arrange the mango slices on the lettuce, and sprinkle the pine nuts or walnuts on top. In a small bowl, combine the coconut, lime and lemon juices, and honey; beat with a fork to blend them. Pour this dressing over the salad.

■ MEXICAN MENUS

## Mediterranean Orange Salad

**To serve 4**

| | |
|---|---|
| 1 head romaine lettuce, leaves separated, washed, and spun or patted dry | Freshly ground black pepper |
| | 4 large navel oranges |
| ¹/₂ cup walnut or olive oil | 8 Mediterranean-style black olives, preferably Kalamata olives, pitted and quartered lengthwise |
| 2 tablespoons fresh lemon juice | |
| 1 garlic clove, chopped fine | |
| Salt | 2 tablespoons chopped fresh parsley leaves |

Line a serving platter with the lettuce. Combine the oil, lemon juice, garlic, and salt and pepper to taste in a small bowl; stir the dressing with a fork to blend it. With a small, sharp knife, peel the oranges, removing as much of the white pith as possible. Cut the oranges crosswise into slices ¹/₂ inch thick. Arrange the oranges on the lettuce, overlapping the slices slightly. Sprinkle the salad with olives. Pour the dressing over the salad and sprinkle parsley over the top.

■ ITALIAN MENUS

## Bibb Lettuce and Sliced Pears with Walnut Vinaigrette

**To serve 4**

| | |
|---|---|
| ¹/₄ cup walnut oil | 1 large pear |
| 2 tablespoons white-wine vinegar | 2 heads Bibb lettuce, leaves separated, washed, and patted or spun dry |
| Salt | |
| Freshly ground black or white pepper | ¹/₄ cup walnut pieces |

Combine the oil, vinegar, and salt and pepper to taste in a small bowl. Whisk until the ingredients are blended. Set the vinaigrette dressing aside.

Wash the pear and pat it dry. With a small, sharp knife cut the pear into quarters and remove the core. Cut each quarter lengthwise into five slices. Place the slices in a bowl, add about 2 tablespoonfuls of the vinaigrette, and stir gently to coat the slices, thus preventing them from turning brown. Cover the bowl with plastic wrap and refrigerate.

Just before serving, arrange the lettuce leaves on individual plates and top them with the pear slices. Whisk the vinaigrette to blend it again, then pour over the salad. Sprinkle each portion with walnut pieces.

■ EGG AND CHEESE MENUS

## Waldorf Salad

*Oscar Tschirky, who was known as Oscar of the Waldorf and was the maître d'hôtel of the famous Manhattan establishment from 1893 to 1943, invented Waldorf salad. Walnuts have become an indispensable ingredient, but they were not part of the original salad.* ✦●

**To serve 6 to 8**

| | |
|---|---|
| 3 large apples, cored and cut into ¹/₂-inch pieces | 1 cup mayonnaise, preferably homemade |
| 2 tablespoons fresh lemon juice | ¹/₂ cup heavy cream |
| 3 celery ribs, trimmed and cut into ¹/₄-inch dice | 1 or 2 heads Boston or Bibb lettuce, leaves separated, washed, patted or spun dry, and chilled |
| 1 cup coarsely chopped walnuts | |

Combine the apples and lemon juice in a deep bowl, and turn the apple pieces about gently with a spoon to moisten them evenly. Stir in the celery and walnuts.

In a small bowl, mix the mayonnaise and cream and, when the mixture is smooth, pour it over the apples. Toss all the ingredients together.

Shape the lettuce leaves into cups on six to eight chilled individual serving plates. Mound the Waldorf salad in the cups, dividing it evenly among them. Or, if you prefer, you can line a serving bowl with the lettuce leaves, and then mound the salad in it. Serve at once.

■ AMERICAN COOKING: THE EASTERN HEARTLAND

BIBB LETTUCE AND SLICED PEARS WITH WALNUT VINAIGRETTE

## Apple and Celery Root Salad

**To serve 4**

| | |
|---|---|
| ¹/₂ cup mayonnaise, preferably homemade | ¹/₂ teaspoon salt |
| ¹/₄ cup sour cream | Freshly ground black pepper |
| 1 tablespoon finely cut fresh dill | 1 large tart cooking apple, peeled, cored and cut into ¹/₄-inch slices |
| 1 tablespoon finely chopped fresh parsley leaves | 1¹/₄ to 1¹/₂ pounds celery root |

In a large mixing bowl, beat together the mayonnaise, sour cream, dill, parsley, salt and a few grindings of pepper. Gently stir in the apple slices, cover the bowl, and set aside. With a small, sharp knife, peel the celery root and cut it crosswise into ¹/₈-inch slices. Drop the slices into enough lightly salted boiling water to cover them completely, and cook, uncovered, over moderate heat, for 20 to 25 minutes, or until the root shows only the slightest resistance when pierced with the tip of a small, sharp knife. Drain thoroughly and pat the slices dry with paper towels. Add the celery root to the mayonnaise mixture, and stir gently to coat the slices well. Taste for seasoning and serve at once.

■ THE COOKING OF GERMANY

## Kiwi and Spinach Salad

**To serve 4**

| | |
|---|---|
| 3 cups spinach | 1 garlic clove, slivered |
| 2 cups red-leaf lettuce | Salt |
| 1 cup arugula, dandelion or mustard greens | Freshly ground white pepper |
| 3 tablespoons safflower oil | 1 large kiwi, peeled and sliced |
| 3 tablespoons fresh lemon juice | 1 small red onion, sliced thin and separated into rings |
| 2 tablespoons honey | |

Remove any thick stems from the spinach, lettuce and arugula. Wash all of the greens, and dry them in a salad spinner or pat them dry with paper towels. Tear the greens into bite-sized pieces and place them in a salad bowl; cover with plastic wrap and refrigerate. In a small bowl, combine the oil, lemon juice, honey and garlic; season to taste with salt and white pepper. Set this dressing aside.

Just before serving, remove the garlic from the dressing. Toss the greens with the dressing, divide them among four individual salad bowls, and garnish them with the kiwi and onion.

■ FISH AND SHELLFISH MENUS

## Vermicelli Salad with Sliced Pork

**To serve 6**

8 ounces vermicelli
1/2 tablespoon safflower oil
1/4 pound pork loin, cut into
   julienne strips
2 garlic cloves, chopped fine
2 cups julienne carrot strips
2 cups julienne celery strips

2 teaspoons dark sesame oil
1/4 teaspoon salt
Freshly ground black pepper
6 drops Tabasco sauce
2 tablespoons rice vinegar
1 teaspoon cream sherry

Bring 3 quarts of lightly salted water to a boil in a large, covered pot. Add a dollop of vegetable oil to keep the pasta from sticking or boiling over. Break the vermicelli strands into thirds and drop them into the pot. Cook the pasta for five minutes or until it is slightly resistant to the bite—*al dente*.

Meanwhile, heat the safflower oil in a wok or large skillet over moderately high heat. Stir-fry the pork in the oil for two minutes. Add the garlic and cook for 30 seconds, stirring constantly. Add the carrots and celery, and stir-fry for two minutes more; remove from the heat.

Drain the pasta, and toss it in a large bowl with the pork and vegetables. Drizzle the sesame oil over it, then sprinkle with the salt, some black pepper and the Tabasco. Toss the salad thoroughly. Pour the vinegar and sherry over the salad and toss it again. Let the salad cool; serve it at room temperature or chilled.

■ FRESH WAYS WITH PASTA

## Turkey Salad with Yogurt-Buttermilk Dressing

**To serve 6**

1 1/4 pounds small unpeeled
   new potatoes, cooked and
   cubed
2 tablespoons olive oil
1 cup fresh mushrooms, wiped
   clean and quartered
1/8 teaspoon salt
1 green pepper, seeded,
   deribbed and cut into
   chunks
2 tablespoons dry white wine
2 1/2 cups cooked cubed turkey
   breast meat
1/2 cup watercress leaves
1/2 cup chopped scallions
1 head Bibb lettuce, leaves
   separated, washed, and
   spun or patted dry

2 tomatoes, cored and sliced
1 small cucumber, sliced thin
1 red onion, sliced thin

YOGURT-BUTTERMILK
DRESSING
1 scallion, chopped
2 tablespoons red-wine
   vinegar
1 tablespoon fresh lemon juice
1/2 teaspoon celery seeds
4 drops Tabasco sauce
1/4 teaspoon salt
Freshly ground black pepper
3 tablespoons olive oil
1/4 cup buttermilk
1/4 cup plain yogurt
1 garlic clove, chopped

Heat the 2 tablespoons of olive oil in a heavy, nonreactive 1-quart saucepan over moderate heat. Add the mushrooms and salt, and cook for about one minute. Add the green pepper and wine, and continue cooking for five minutes, stirring occasionally. In a large bowl, combine the potatoes, turkey, watercress and scallions. Toss in the mushroom mixture. Set aside.

To prepare the dressing, place all of the ingredients in a screw-top jar with a tight-fitting lid and shake vigorously until thoroughly blended, about 30 seconds. Add the dressing to the turkey mixture and toss lightly.

Arrange lettuce on six individual plates, and place a generous portion of salad on each one. Garnish with slices of tomato, cucumber and red onion.

■ FRESH WAYS WITH POULTRY

## Beef Salad with Caper Sauce

**To serve 4**

2 pounds beef tenderloin
1 tablespoon Cognac
1 shallot, chopped fine
Salt
Coarsely ground black pepper
1 tablespoon olive oil
1/2 pound green beans, ends
   trimmed
1 bunch arugula, trimmed,
   washed, and spun or
   patted dry
1 tomato, cut into 1/4-inch
   slices
1 red onion, cut into 1/4-inch
   slices
French potato salad (page 53)

CAPER SAUCE
2 tablespoons sherry vinegar
1 teaspoon Dijon mustard
1/4 teaspoon salt
1/4 teaspoon coarsely ground
   black pepper
1/2 cup olive oil
1 tablespoon capers, drained
1 large shallot, chopped fine
2 tablespoons chopped fresh
   parsley leaves
1 tablespoon chopped fresh
   tarragon leaves or
1/2 teaspoon crumbled
   dried tarragon

Rub the beef with the Cognac and place in a small flameproof roasting pan. Sprinkle the beef with one chopped shallot, 1/4 teaspoon of salt and 1/2 teaspoon of pepper, and rub it with 1 tablespoon of olive oil. Set the beef aside for 30 minutes.

Meanwhile, boil the beans, uncovered, in 1 quart of lightly salted water for three minutes, until barely tender. Drain the beans and refresh them for a few moments under cold running water. Drain them again, then refrigerate them.

Preheat the oven to 450° F. Place the beef over high heat and sear it on all sides, turning the meat with tongs, for five minutes. Roast the meat in the oven for 15 to 20 minutes, until a meat thermometer, in the thickest part, registers 125° to 130° F. The meat will be rare. Cover and refrigerate the meat. About 30 minutes before serving, remove the beef and beans from the refrigerator.

For the sauce, whisk the vinegar, mustard, and the 1/4 teaspoon each of salt and pepper in a nonreactive bowl. Add the 1/2 cup of oil in a slow, steady stream, whisking constantly until well blended. Stir in the capers, one chopped shallot, parsley and tarragon.

Add 2 tablespoonfuls of the sauce to the beans, and toss them together. Cut the beef into 1/2-inch slices. Mound the French potato salad and the green beans on a large platter. Arrange the beef, onion and tomato slices decoratively, adding the arugula. Drizzle a few spoonfuls of sauce over the beef. Serve the remaining sauce separately.

■ MAKE-AHEAD MENUS

## Chicken Liver and Lettuce Salad

**To serve 4**

| | |
|---|---|
| 1 small head Bibb or Boston lettuce, leaves separated | ½ pound chicken livers, trimmed and cut into 1-inch pieces |
| 8 to 10 large romaine lettuce leaves | 2 teaspoons sugar |
| 4 bacon slices, cut into 1-inch squares | 1 tablespoon Dijon mustard |
| 1 yellow onion, chopped | 2 tablespoons red-wine vinegar |

Wash the Bibb and romaine lettuce under cold running water; dry it in a salad spinner or pat dry with paper towels. Tear the leaves into bite-sized pieces. Arrange the lettuce on four individual salad plates.

In a heavy 10- to 12-inch skillet, cook the bacon for about three minutes. Add the onion and chicken livers. Stirring often, cook until the livers are browned but still tender, about four minutes. Stir in the sugar and mustard. Add the vinegar, pouring it down the side of the skillet to avoid splattering; stir the mixture for two minutes, until bubbly. Place the livers on the plates; top them with the pan sauce. Serve at once.

■ FRENCH REGIONAL MENUS

## Southern Chicken Salad with Boiled Dressing

**To serve 6 to 8**

| | |
|---|---|
| Two 3- to 3½-pound chickens, cut up | ¼ cup fresh lemon juice |
| 1 onion, sliced | |
| 1 carrot, sliced | BOILED DRESSING |
| ½ cup chopped celery leaves | 3 tablespoons sugar |
| 3 parsley sprigs | 1 tablespoon flour |
| 2 teaspoons salt | 1 teaspoon dry mustard |
| 10 whole black peppercorns | 1 teaspoon salt |
| 4 hard-boiled eggs, chopped | ½ cup distilled white vinegar |
| 1 cup finely chopped celery | ½ cup water |
| ½ cup chopped scallions | 1 tablespoon butter |
| | 2 eggs |

Combine the chicken, onion, carrot, celery leaves, parsley, salt and peppercorns in a heavy 4- to 5-quart casserole, and add enough water to cover the chicken. Bring to a boil over high heat, reduce the heat to low and simmer, partially covered, for 30 minutes, until the chicken is tender. Transfer the chicken to a platter or cutting board. (Strain the stock and reserve it for another use.)

Remove the skin and bones. Cut the meat into 1-inch pieces and place in a serving bowl. Add the hard-boiled eggs, celery, scallions and lemon juice. With a wooden spoon, toss the ingredients together gently.

To prepare the boiled dressing, in a small bowl, beat the eggs lightly. In a small, nonreactive saucepan, combine the sugar, flour, mustard and 1 teaspoon of salt. Whisking constantly, stir in the vinegar, water and butter, and cook over moderate heat until the mixture comes to a boil and thickens lightly. Stir 1 or 2 tablespoonfuls of the simmering liquid into the beaten eggs, then pour

the heated eggs into the saucepan and whisk until the dressing is smooth. With a rubber spatula, transfer the dressing to a bowl. Let it cool to room temperature.

To serve, pour the dressing over the chicken and stir until the chicken and vegetables are moistened.

■ AMERICAN COOKING: SOUTHERN STYLE

## Black Bean and Turkey Salad

**To serve 10**

| | |
|---|---|
| 1⅔ cups dried black beans, washed, picked over, soaked overnight and drained | coarsely chopped and drained |
| | 1 small green pepper, seeded, deribbed and chopped |
| 1 onion, chopped coarse | 3½ cups julienne cooked turkey breast meat |
| 2 garlic cloves, chopped | |
| One 3-inch cinnamon stick, halved | 1 head red-leaf or Bibb lettuce, leaves separated, washed, and spun or patted dry |
| 1½ teaspoons chopped fresh thyme leaves or ½ teaspoon crumbled dried thyme | |
| | CORIANDER DRESSING |
| 1 small dried hot red chili with seeds removed or ¼ teaspoon cayenne pepper | 5 tablespoons chopped coriander leaves |
| | 2 garlic cloves, chopped |
| 1 bay leaf | ¾ cup red-wine vinegar |
| ½ teaspoon salt | 1 tablespoon fresh lemon or lime juice |
| ½ pound snow peas, strings removed, sliced into julienne strips | 2 tablespoons Dijon mustard |
| | 2 tablespoons honey |
| 1 small cantaloupe, seeded, peeled and cut into small chunks | 10 to 15 drops Tabasco sauce |
| | ¼ teaspoon salt |
| | Freshly ground black pepper |
| 6 scallions, trimmed and sliced thin | ⅓ cup safflower oil |
| | ¼ cup olive oil |
| 3 tomatoes, peeled, seeded, | |

Put the beans in a heavy 4-quart casserole with the onion, garlic, cinnamon, thyme, chili, bay leaf and salt. Add enough water to cover the beans by 2 inches, bring it to a boil, and boil for 10 minutes. Reduce the heat and skim off the foam that rises to the surface. Cover and simmer just until the beans are tender—one to one and a half hours. Drain the beans and rinse under cold running water. Remove the chili, cinnamon and bay leaf, and drain the beans again.

Blanch the snow peas in boiling water for 15 seconds, and refresh them under cold running water for a few moments; drain and place on paper towels to dry.

Put all of the dressing ingredients, except the oils, in a food processor or blender and process for 15 seconds. Add the oil slowly and process until smooth, about 30 seconds.

In a large bowl, combine the cantaloupe, scallions, tomatoes, green pepper, turkey, snow peas and beans. Pour 1 cup of the dressing over the salad and toss lightly. To serve, mound the salad on lettuce leaves arranged on individual plates or on a platter, and pass the remaining dressing separately.

■ FRESH WAYS WITH POULTRY

## Salade Niçoise

**To serve 4 to 6**

| | |
|---|---|
| 1 large head Boston or romaine lettuce, leaves separated, washed, and spun or patted dry | ½ cup black olives, preferably Mediterranean-style, halved and pitted |
| 1 to 2 cups French potato salad (page 53) | 8 to 12 flat anchovy fillets, drained |
| 4 large tomatoes, quartered | 2 cups cooled, cooked green beans |
| 3 hard-boiled eggs, quartered | ½ cup vinaigrette sauce (Index/Glossary) |
| 1 seven-ounce can tuna, preferably Italian tuna packed in olive oil, drained and broken into chunks | 3 tablespoons finely chopped fresh parsley leaves |

Line a large, chilled salad bowl with the lettuce, and spread the potato salad in the bottom of the bowl. Arrange the tomatoes, eggs, tuna, olives, anchovies and green beans on top in an attractive pattern—concentric circles, wedges or strips. Spoon the vinaigrette over the salad, sprinkle the salad with parsley, and serve it immediately. Toss the ingredients together gently at the table.

■ THE COOKING OF PROVINCIAL FRANCE

## Herring Salad with Sour-Cream Sauce

**To serve 8 to 10**

| | |
|---|---|
| ¼ pound chopped herring such as *matjes,* pickled or Bismarck, plus ¼ pound herring cut into 1-inch squares for garnish | Salt<br>Freshly ground black pepper |
| ½ pound chopped cooked tongue or veal (optional) | DRESSING |
| ½ cup diced cold boiled potatoes | 3 chilled hard-boiled eggs, halved and the whites finely chopped |
| 3 cups diced cold cooked beets plus 3 tablespoons beet juice reserved for the sauce | 1 tablespoon prepared mustard |
| | 2 tablespoons white-wine vinegar |
| ½ cup peeled, cored, chopped apple | ¼ cup vegetable oil |
| | 2 to 4 tablespoons heavy cream |
| ⅓ cup chopped onion | |
| ½ cup chopped dill pickle | SAUCE |
| 4 tablespoons finely cut fresh dill | 3 tablespoons reserved beet juice |
| 2 tablespoons white-wine vinegar | ½ teaspoon fresh lemon juice |
| | 1 cup sour cream |

In a large mixing bowl, combine the herring, tongue, if you are using it, potatoes, beets, apple, onion and pickle. Mix 3 tablespoons of the dill with the vinegar, and add salt and pepper to taste. Pour this flavoring over the salad ingredients and toss them together gently with a wooden spoon.

HERRING SALAD WITH SOUR-CREAM SAUCE

To prepare the dressing for the salad, force the egg yolks through a sieve into a small bowl with the back of a large spoon, and mash them to a paste with the prepared mustard. Gradually beat in the vinegar and oil. Add the cream, 1 tablespoon at a time, beating after each addition, until the dressing has the consistency of heavy cream. Pour the dressing over the salad, mix it in lightly but thoroughly, cover the bowl, and chill the salad for at least two hours.

Just before serving, transfer the salad to salad plates or a large serving bowl or platter and sprinkle it with the chopped egg whites and the remaining chopped dill. Garnish with the herring squares. Stir the reserved beet juice and the lemon juice into the sour cream until the mixture is smooth and well blended. Pass this sauce separately.

■ THE COOKING OF SCANDINAVIA

## White Bean and Tuna Salad

**To serve 4 to 6**

4 cups canned *cannellini* or
 other white beans (two 1-
 pound cans), drained,
 rinsed and drained again, or
 2 cups dried white kidney,
 marrow, Great Northern or
 navy beans, washed and
 picked over, soaked
 overnight and drained
¼ cup olive oil
1 tablespoon fresh lemon
 juice

½ teaspoon salt
Freshly ground black pepper
¼ cup finely chopped
 scallions
2 tablespoons chopped fresh
 parsley leaves, preferably
 flatleaf parsley
1 seven-ounce can tuna,
 preferably Italian tuna
 packed in olive oil, drained
 and broken into chunks

If you are using canned beans, spread them on paper towels to dry before putting them into a serving bowl. If you are using soaked dried beans, put them in a heavy 4-quart saucepan, and add enough water to cover them by 2 inches. Bring the water to a boil and boil for 10 minutes. Reduce the heat and skim off the foam that rises to the surface. Cover and simmer just until the beans are tender—one to one and a half hours. Drain the beans in a colander, rinse them under cold running water, and drain them again. Transfer the beans to a serving bowl to cool.

To assemble the salad, combine the olive oil, lemon juice, salt and a few grindings of pepper, and pour them over the beans. Add the scallions and parsley, and gently mix all of the ingredients together. Transfer the bean mixture to a platter, and arrange the chunks of tuna on top.

■ **THE COOKING OF ITALY**

# Crayfish Salad with Fresh Dill

*A court bouillon, like the one in which these crayfish are poached, usually combines water with wine or vinegar and aromatic vegetables and herbs. The proportion of wine or vinegar to water may be varied to taste, as may the quantities and types of vegetables and herbs.* ❖●

**To serve 4**

| | |
|---|---|
| 36 large live crayfish, rinsed | COURT BOUILLON |
| 1 cup heavy cream | 2 cups dry white wine |
| 3 teaspoons finely cut fresh dill | 2 cups water |
| 3 tablespoons fresh lemon juice | 1 tablespoon coarse salt |
| Salt | Cayenne pepper |
| Freshly ground white pepper | ½ teaspoon mixed dried herbs |
| 1 head curly-leaf lettuce, separated into leaves, washed, and spun or patted dry | 1 bay leaf |
| | 1 bouquet garni, including fresh parsley and dill |
| | 1 large onion, sliced thin |
| | 1 carrot, sliced thin |
| | 8 to 10 peppercorns |

For the *court bouillon,* bring the wine and water to a boil in a large nonreactive pot. Add the salt, a pinch of cayenne, the mixed herbs, bay leaf, bouquet garni, onion and carrot. Cover and simmer the *court bouillon* over medium heat for 30 minutes; add the peppercorns after 20 minutes.

Add half of the crayfish to the *court bouillon,* cover the pot tightly, and cook the crayfish for five minutes, shaking occasionally. With a skimmer, remove the crayfish to a bowl. Cook the remaining crayfish similarly. Combine the two batches and let them cool in the *court bouillon.*

Reserve the eight largest crayfish for garnish. Pull off the tails of the rest, shell them, and set the tail meat aside in the *court bouillon* with the whole crayfish.

In a mortar, pound the heads, claws, legs and coral of the crayfish, a small batch at a time. Purée each pounded batch through the medium disk of a food mill and discard the shells. Press the purée a little at a time through a fine-meshed sieve.

Mix the cream with 2 teaspoons of the dill and the lemon juice. Whisk in the crayfish purée. Add salt and white pepper to taste. Arrange the lettuce leaves on individual plates and divide the purée among them. Drain the reserved crayfish tail meat and distribute it over the purée. Place two unshelled crayfish on each plate, and sprinkle with the remaining dill.

■ THE GOOD COOK: WINE

# Pasta Salad with Lobster and Snow Peas

*The radiatori called for in this recipe is a pasta with ridges that resemble the heating coils of a radiator. Cooking the pasta in the lobster water infuses it with the flavor of the shellfish.* ❖●

**To serve 4**

| | |
|---|---|
| One 1½-pound live lobster | 2 tablespoons fresh lemon juice |
| ¼ cup very thinly sliced shallots | ½ pound *radiatori* or medium-sized pasta shells |
| 1 tablespoon red-wine vinegar | ½ pound snow peas, stems and strings removed, halved diagonally |
| 3 tablespoons olive oil | 1 tablespoon chopped fresh basil or flatleaf parsley leaves |
| 2 garlic cloves, lightly crushed | |
| ¼ teaspoon salt | |
| Freshly ground black pepper | |

Pour enough water into an 8- to 10-quart pot to fill it about 1 inch deep. Bring the water to a boil and add the lobster. Cover the pot tightly and steam the lobster until it turns a bright reddish orange—about 12 minutes.

Meanwhile, put half of the shallots in a nonreactive bowl with the vinegar, and let them stand for five minutes. Whisk in 2 tablespoons of the oil, then stir in the garlic, ⅛ teaspoon of the salt and some pepper. Set this vinaigrette aside.

Remove the lobster from the pot, and set it on a dish to catch the juices. Pour 2 quarts of water into the pot along with 1 tablespoon of the lemon juice, and bring the liquid to a boil.

When the lobster has cooled enough to handle, pour the juices from its dish into the pot. Twist off the tail and claws from the body; crack the shells and remove the meat from the tail and claws. Add these shells along with the body to the boiling liquid and cook for 10 minutes. Cut the meat into ½-inch pieces, and set it aside in a bowl.

Use a slotted spoon to remove the lobster shells from the boiling liquid; then add the pasta. Start testing after about 13 minutes and cook the pasta until it is only slightly resistant to the bite—*al dente.*

While the pasta is cooking, pour the remaining tablespoon of oil into an 8- to 10-inch skillet, and heat it over moderately high heat. Add the snow peas along with the remaining 2 tablespoons of shallots and ⅛ teaspoon of salt. Stirring constantly, cook until the snow peas turn bright green, about one and a half minutes. Scrape the contents of the skillet into the bowl with the lobster.

When the pasta finishes cooking, drain it and rinse it briefly under cold running water to remove surface starches and prevent the pieces from sticking together. Remove the garlic from the vinaigrette, then combine the vinaigrette with the pasta. Add the lobster mixture, the basil, the remaining tablespoon of lemon juice and some more pepper, and toss well.

The salad may be served immediately, although allowing it to stand for 30 minutes will meld the flavors. If you like, chill the salad before serving it.

■ FRESH WAYS WITH PASTA

Poultry

# Poultry

FRONTISPIECE: CHICKEN TANDOORI

Benjamin Franklin campaigned to have the turkey, the "true, original native fowl," declared the national bird. On Thanksgiving Day, it most certainly is. But the rest of the year, the bald eagle decorates the Great Seal of the United States and the chicken dominates the American dinner table.

Every cuisine has made its own the mild-flavored, all-purpose chicken, of which the 16th century Italian ornithologist Ulisse Aldrovani said, "If there is a need for an elegant and groaning board, you have in the chicken the most praiseworthy meat." The old birdman was being just a trifle generous; in his day, chicken was really a pretty tough fowl—nothing like today's pampered and tender specimens.

By comparison with chickens, ducks and geese are assertive in taste and their layers of fat considerably more generous. Yet cooked properly, these birds have a rare, rich succulence and a skin that becomes crackly crisp. A Chinese feast is not worthy of the name without duck, nor a German or Scandinavian holiday complete without goose.

Besides these farmyard familiars, cooks now enjoy Rock Cornish hens—a tiny form of chicken—and equally tiny squab, or domesticated pigeons, which have only dark meat with a faintly gamy quality. And such huntsmen's birds as pheasant and quail are raised in captivity, extending further still the pantheon of poultry.

# Chicken Tandoori

*In India, the chicken is roasted in a tandoor—a deep clay-lined pit with hot coals at the bottom. You can get a similar smoky flavor by roasting the birds on a roasting spit in a hooded charcoal grill. Fresh mixed vegetables, called a "salat," provide a base for serving the chicken. Traditionally the salat includes tomatoes and radishes as well as onions, lemons and hot chilies.* ❖●

### To serve 6 to 8

| | |
|---|---|
| Two 3-pound chickens, rinsed and patted dry | ¹/₂ teaspoon red food coloring |
| ¹/₂ cup fresh lemon juice | ¹/₄ teaspoon cayenne pepper |
| 4 teaspoons salt | 2 tablespoons *ghee* or clarified butter |
| 1 teaspoon saffron threads soaked in 3 tablespoons boiling water for 5 minutes | 2 large onions, cut lengthwise into thin slivers |
| 2 teaspoons coriander seeds | 1 cucumber, unpeeled and diced |
| 1 teaspoon cumin seeds | 3 small fresh hot green chilies, halved lengthwise and seeded |
| One 1-inch slice fresh ginger root, chopped coarse | Lime slices for garnish |
| 2 garlic cloves, chopped coarse | |
| 1 cup plain yogurt | |

Truss the birds securely. With a small knife, cut two slits about ¹/₂ inch deep and 1 inch long in both thighs and breasts of each bird. Mix the lemon juice with the salt and rub them over the chickens, pressing the mixture into the slits. Place the chickens in a large, deep casserole, pour the saffron and its soaking water over them, and marinate them at room temperature for about 30 minutes.

Sprinkle the coriander and cumin seeds into a small ungreased skillet and, shaking the pan constantly, toast them over moderate heat for a minute or so. Then drop the seeds into a blender or food processor, add the ginger, garlic and 2 tablespoons of the yogurt, and blend at high speed until the mixture is reduced to a smooth paste. With a rubber spatula, scrape the paste into a mixing bowl. Stir in the remaining yogurt, the food coloring and the cayenne. Spread this paste evenly over the chickens, cover the casserole, and marinate for 12 hours or overnight at room temperature, or for at least 24 hours in the refrigerator.

Preheat the oven to 400°F. Arrange the chickens side by side on a rack in a shallow roasting pan large enough to hold them easily. Pour any liquid that has accumulated in the casserole over the chickens and rub each one with 1 tablespoon of the *ghee*. Roast, uncovered, in the middle of the oven for 15 minutes, then reduce the heat to 350°F., and continue roasting the birds, undisturbed, for 1 hour more. To test for doneness, pierce a thigh with the point of a knife: The juice that runs out should be clear. A meat thermometer inserted in the thigh should register 180°F.

Meanwhile, prepare the *salat*. Spread the onion slivers over a large platter and decorate them with the cucumber and chilies.

Remove the birds from the oven, cut away the trussing strings, and let the chickens rest for five or 10 minutes for easier carving. Just before serving, cut each chicken into six or eight serving pieces and arrange them on the *salat*. Garnish with lime slices.

■ THE COOKING OF INDIA

# Casserole-roasted Chicken with Vegetables

### To serve 4

| | |
|---|---|
| ¹/₄ cup butter, softened, plus 5 tablespoons butter, cut into bits | 16 white onions, 1 inch across |
| ¹/₄ teaspoon finely chopped garlic | 6 carrots, cut into ovals 2 inches long |
| ¹/₂ teaspoon crumbled dried thyme | 16 potato balls, 1 inch across, or ovals, 2 inches across |
| One 4-pound roasting chicken, rinsed and patted dry | Salt |
| | Freshly ground black pepper |
| ¹/₄ pound salt pork, diced | 1 bouquet garni made of 4 parsley sprigs and 1 bay leaf, tied together |

Preheat the oven to 350°F. Beat 2 tablespoons of softened butter together with the garlic and thyme. Spread the butter inside the chicken. Truss the chicken and rub the outside with the remaining softened butter. Simmer the salt pork dice in 2 cups of water for five minutes; drain them and dry them with paper towels.

In a heavy oval casserole just large enough to hold the chicken, melt 1 tablespoon of the butter bits over moderate heat, and in it brown the pork dice, stirring frequently, until they are crisp and golden. With a slotted spoon, remove the dice and set them on paper towels to drain. In the rendered pork fat, brown the chicken on all sides. Lift it out and pour off all but a thin film of fat from the casserole. Return the chicken and browned pork dice to it.

In a heavy 10- to 12-inch skillet, melt the remaining butter bits over moderate heat. Stirring frequently, cook the onions, carrots and potatoes for five minutes or until lightly colored. Arrange the vegetables around the chicken. Season with salt and pepper, add the parsley and bay leaf, and cover the casserole. If the lid is not snug, drape foil over the chicken before putting the lid on.

On top of the stove, heat the casserole until the fat begins to sputter. Cook the chicken in the middle of the oven, basting it every 20 minutes with pan juices, for one hour or until the juices that run from the chicken are yellow when it is lifted with a wooden spoon inserted in its tail opening. A meat thermometer inserted into a thigh will register 180°F.

To serve, transfer the chicken to a heated platter and arrange the vegetables around it. Let the chicken rest for five to 10 minutes before carving it. Discard the herbs and skim all possible surface fat from the sauce left in the casserole. Taste the sauce and correct the seasoning. Serve the sauce separately.

■ THE COOKING OF PROVINCIAL FRANCE

SPATCHCOCK CHICKEN WITH BASIL-YOGURT SAUCE

## Spatchcock Chicken with Basil-Yogurt Sauce

*The word "spatchcock" comes from the Irish term "dispatch cock," a dish for a sudden occasion. A quickly prepared accompaniment might be sautéed yellow squash slices and sweet red pepper strips sprinkled with chopped parsley.* ❧

**To serve 4**

| | |
|---|---|
| One 3-pound chicken, rinsed and patted dry | 3 scallions, chopped |
| 1 cup plain yogurt | 2 garlic cloves, chopped fine |
| 1 cup fresh basil leaves, chopped, or 2 cups fresh spinach leaves, lightly steamed and squeezed dry, plus 1 basil sprig for garnish | 1 tablespoon olive oil |
| | ⅓ cup freshly grated Parmesan or Romano cheese |
| | ⅛ teaspoon salt |
| | Freshly ground black pepper |

Preheat the oven to 400°F. Pour a 1-inch layer of water into a large pot. Set a metal steamer or rack in the pot, and bring the water to a boil. Remove the backbone of the chicken by cutting along both sides. Turn the bird over and press it with your hand to flatten it for even cooking. Place the chicken, skin side up, on the steamer. Cover the pot tightly and steam the chicken for 15 minutes over high heat.

Meanwhile, combine the yogurt, chopped basil, scallions, garlic, oil and half of the Parmesan cheese in a food processor or blender. Process until smooth, then transfer this sauce to a sauceboat, and set it aside at room temperature.

Set the steamed chicken on a rack in a roasting pan. Sprinkle it with the salt and a few grindings of pepper. Roast for about 25 minutes or until the skin is crisp and light brown.

Remove the bird from the oven and sprinkle the remaining cheese over it. Roast the chicken for eight to 10 minutes more or until the cheese is golden brown and the bird's juices run clear when a thigh is pierced with a knife tip. Let the chicken rest for five to 10 minutes, garnish it with the basil sprig, and then carve it at the table. Pass the sauce separately.

■ FRESH WAYS WITH POULTRY

## Roast Chicken with Chicken-Liver Stuffing

**To serve 4**

| | |
|---|---|
| 2 tablespoons butter, cut into bits, plus 2 tablespoons butter, softened | 1 tablespoon finely cut fresh dill |
| 2 tablespoons finely chopped onion | 1 cup bread crumbs |
| | 1 egg, lightly beaten |
| 3 chicken livers, trimmed | Salt |
| 2 tablespoons chopped fresh parsley leaves | Freshly ground black pepper |
| | One 2½- to 3-pound chicken, rinsed and patted dry |

In a heavy 6- to 8-inch skillet, melt the butter bits over moderate heat. Stir in the onions and cook, stirring frequently, for five minutes, or until soft and translucent. Add the livers and, stirring constantly, cook for three minutes, until they stiffen and brown lightly. Remove the pan from the heat, chop the livers coarse, and place them in a mixing bowl with the onions. Add the parsley, dill, bread crumbs and egg, season to taste with salt and pepper, and set aside.

Preheat the oven to 450°F. Stuff the breast and neck cavities of the chicken with the liver mixture, and secure the openings with skewers, or sew them closed with kitchen string. Truss the chicken securely and place it on its back on a rack in a shallow roasting pan. Spread the softened butter over the chicken, and season the bird with salt and a few grindings of pepper. Roast the chicken for 10 minutes, then reduce the heat to 350°F. Basting the chicken from time to time with pan juices, roast it for 50 minutes longer or until the juices run clear when a thigh is pierced with the tip of a knife. A meat thermometer inserted in the thigh should register 180°F.

Transfer the chicken to a heated serving platter and let it rest for five to 10 minutes before carving it.

■ AMERICAN COOKING: THE MELTING POT

# Chicken Kiev

*A classic Ukrainian dish, chicken Kiev is internationally famed. The traditional recipe calls for pounded boned chicken cutlets rolled around fingers of plain butter. Herb seasonings add zest to a relatively simple dish.* ❧

**To serve 4**

| | |
|---|---|
| Two 1-pound whole chicken breasts, skinned, boned and halved | Vegetable oil for deep frying Radish sprouts for garnish |
| ¾ cup unsalted butter | |
| Salt | OPTIONAL SEASONINGS |
| Freshly ground black pepper | 1 teaspoon fresh lemon juice |
| 2 eggs | 1 teaspoon finely cut fresh chives |
| Flour | |
| 2 cups fine dry white-bread crumbs | 1 tablespoon finely chopped fresh parsley leaves |

Place the halved breasts, smooth side down, on a cutting board. With a small knife and your fingers, remove the fillet from each half. Lay the halves and fillets, one pair at a time, between sheets of wax paper. With the flat side of a cleaver or a meat pounder, pound them ⅛ inch thick. If holes appear in the flesh, overlap the edges of the tear slightly and pound gently to join them. Set these cutlets aside.

Cut the butter into eight equal pieces. Shape each piece into a cylinder about ½ inch thick and 3 inches long. Wrap the cylinders in wax paper and chill until firm. (Or, cream the butter by mashing it against the side of a bowl with a wooden spoon. Beat into it any or all of the optional seasonings. Divide the butter and shape it into eight cylinders. Chill until firm.)

To assemble the cutlets, gently peel off the wax paper and sprinkle the chicken lightly with salt and freshly ground black pepper. Center a cylinder of butter lengthwise on a breast, fold one long side of the breast over it. Then fold over the short ends and cover them with the other long side.

In a small bowl, beat the eggs just long enough to combine them. Spread flour and the bread crumbs on two separate strips of wax paper. One at a time, dip each cutlet into the flour. Tap off the excess flour and, cradling it in your palms, pat the cutlet into a long cylinder tapered at each end. Now dip the cutlet into the eggs, making sure its entire surface is coated, and roll it in the bread crumbs, again making sure it is thoroughly coated.

Arrange the cutlets, side by side, on a platter and refrigerate them for one to two hours; the coating should be set before they are fried.

About 30 minutes before serving time, preheat the oven to 200°F. Line a shallow baking dish with a double thickness of paper towels and place it in the oven. Pour a layer of oil 3 or 4 inches deep into a deep fryer or a heavy saucepan into which a frying basket will fit. Set the pan over high heat until the oil registers 360°F. on a deep-frying thermometer.

Fry four of the cutlets in the basket for five minutes or until golden brown, then transfer them with tongs to the lined baking dish. Fry the remaining cutlets similarly. The finished cutlets may remain in the oven for up to 10 minutes before serving without losing freshness and letting their butter escape. If you like, they may be garnished with radish sprouts.

■ RUSSIAN COOKING

# Roast Capon with Sage Corn-Bread Stuffing

**To serve 8**

| | |
|---|---|
| 1 tablespoon butter | 1 cup flour |
| 4 large onions, sliced thin | 1 tablespoon baking powder |
| 1 tablespoon safflower oil | ¼ teaspoon salt |
| One 9- to 10-pound capon, rinsed and patted dry | ¼ teaspoon freshly ground black pepper |
| ½ teaspoon salt | 1 cup buttermilk |
| ¼ cup diced boiled ham | 1 egg, beaten |
| ½ cup chicken stock | 2 tablespoons safflower oil |
| | 2 tablespoons chopped fresh sage leaves or 1½ teaspoons crumbled dried sage |
| SAGE CORN BREAD | |
| 1 cup yellow cornmeal | |

For the corn bread, first preheat the oven to 425°F. With a pastry brush, lightly coat the bottom and sides of an 8-inch square baking pan with oil. In a mixing bowl, combine the cornmeal, flour, baking powder, ¼ teaspoon of salt and the pepper. Stir in the buttermilk, egg, 2 tablespoons of oil and the sage. Pour the batter into the pan, and bake until golden brown—20 to 25 minutes.

To make the stuffing, melt the butter in a heavy-bottomed saucepan over moderately low heat. Add the onions and cook for 20 minutes, stirring occasionally. Add the tablespoon of safflower oil, and cook for about 40 minutes more, or until the onions are caramelized. Scrape the bottom frequently to avoid sticking and burning.

While the onions cook, prepare the capon. Tuck the wings behind the shoulder, and tie the ends of the drumsticks together with kitchen cord. Set a metal steamer or rack in the bottom of a large stockpot, and pour in enough water to cover the bottom by 1 inch. Bring the water to a boil, then place the bird in the pot and cover it tight. Steam it for 20 minutes over high heat. Remove the capon, sprinkle at once with ¼ teaspoon of the salt, and set aside.

When ready to roast the capon, preheat the oven to 375°F. Crumble the corn bread into a bowl, and stir in the caramelized onions, the ham and chicken stock. Pour off any juices from the cavity of the bird, and sprinkle the inside of the breast with the remaining ¼ teaspoon of salt. Fill the capon loosely with the stuffing, and cover the opening with a small piece of aluminum foil. Place any excess stuffing in a small ovenproof dish, moisten it with a little chicken stock, cover it with foil and bake it along with the capon during the last 20 minutes of roasting time.

Put the bird, breast side up, on a rack in a roasting pan. Roast the capon for about one hour and 10 minutes or until the skin is crisp and golden and the juices run clear when a thigh is pierced with the tip of a sharp knife. A meat thermometer inserted into the thigh will register 180°F. when the capon is done.

■ FRESH WAYS WITH POULTRY

CHICKEN KIEV

## Roast Chicken with Apples and Turnips

**To serve 4**

| | |
|---|---|
| 1 tablespoon paprika | 3 small white turnips, |
| Salt |   peeled, quartered |
| Freshly ground black pepper |   and sliced thin |
| One 4-pound roasting chicken | 6 garlic cloves, peeled |
| 2 or 3 Golden Delicious | 2 tablespoons fresh |
|   apples, peeled, cored |   lemon juice |
|   and cut into 8 wedges | |

Preheat the oven to 325°F. Mix the paprika with ⅛ teaspoon of salt and ½ teaspoon of pepper, and rub the seasonings onto the chicken, inside and out. With a pastry brush, lightly coat a small roasting pan with melted or softened butter. Put the chicken in the pan and arrange the apples, turnips and garlic around the bird. Sprinkle the lemon juice over the apples and turnips.

Basting the chicken with pan juices from time to time, roast it for one to one and one-quarter hours, until it is golden brown all over and the juices run clear when a thigh is pierced with the tip of a sharp knife. A meat thermometer inserted in the thigh should register 180°F.

Transfer the chicken to a platter. Let the chicken rest for 10 minutes or so to make carving easier. Meanwhile, skim the fat from the pan juices, and mash the apples, turnips and garlic together with the juices. Serve as an accompaniment to the chicken.

■ FRESH WAYS WITH POULTRY

CHICKEN BREASTS STUFFED WITH PERSIAN RICE

## Chicken Breasts Stuffed with Persian Rice

**To serve 4**

Two whole 1-pound chicken
   breasts, boned but
   not skinned
2 teaspoons butter
2 teaspoons olive oil

PERSIAN RICE STUFFING
½ cup long-grain white rice
⅔ cup water
¼ cup butter
1 cup pecans, chopped
⅓ cup finely chopped shallots
¼ cup golden raisins, soaked
   in 2 tablespoons Madeira
   wine for 15 minutes
6 strips orange peel, cut into
   thin julienne strips
¼ teaspoon salt

Freshly ground white pepper
Freshly grated nutmeg
1 egg yolk

ORANGE BUTTER SAUCE
2 tablespoons finely chopped
   shallots
⅓ cup fresh orange juice
1½ tablespoons white-wine
   vinegar
1 tablespoon dry white wine
5 tablespoons butter, cut into
   5 pieces and chilled
2 strips orange peel, cut into
   thin julienne strips
Salt
Freshly ground white pepper
Freshly grated nutmeg

First prepare the stuffing: In a small, heavy saucepan, bring the rice, water and 1 tablespoon of the butter to a boil. Stir, scraping, so that the rice does not stick. Reduce the heat to low, cover, and cook for 20 minutes, until the rice is just tender. Stir once during this time, scraping the sides of the pan; add more water if needed. Set the rice aside.

Melt the remaining 3 tablespoons of butter in a 6- to 8-inch skillet. Add the pecans and stir until lightly browned. Add the ⅓ cup of shallots and, stirring frequently, cook until soft but not brown—about two minutes. Stir in the raisins with the Madeira, and the julienne strips made from six pieces of orange peel. Remove the pan from the heat and stir its contents into the rice. Cool, then season to taste with salt, white pepper and nutmeg. Stir in the egg yolk, cover the skillet, and set it aside.

With a small, sharp knife, trim away the fat, sinew and cartilage from the chicken breasts, keeping the skin intact. To form pockets for stuffing, use your fingers to gently separate the skin from the meat where the breastbone was, keeping skin and meat intact around the remaining edges. If necessary, use a knife to cut out along the center of each breast, but do not split it. Fill the pockets with the rice stuffing. Smooth the skin over the rice so that it is completely covered, and pull the skin down around the filling, tucking the edges under the meat, and using small metal skewers, if necessary.

In a heavy 10- to 12-inch skillet, melt the 2 teaspoons of butter in the oil. Add the breasts, skin side up, and brown them over high heat for two minutes. Turn them and brown the skin for two minutes. Holding one breast at a time with tongs, brown the raw edges. Place the breasts skin side up, reduce the heat to moderate, and cook the breasts for 10 minutes. Turn them and cook them, skin side down, for five minutes.

Place the breasts on a heated platter, and let them rest while you prepare the orange butter sauce. Combine the 2 tablespoons of shallots, the orange juice, vinegar and wine in a small nonreac-

tive pan. Cook over high heat until the liquid is reduced to about 2 teaspoonfuls. Set the heat very low and whisk in the butter bits, a few at a time. The finished sauce should look opaque. Do not overheat it or the butter will separate.

Remove the pan from the heat, stir in the julienne strips made from 2 pieces of orange peel and season the sauce to taste with salt, white pepper and nutmeg. To serve, slice each breast into four pieces and pour the sauce over the chicken.
■ CHICKEN AND GAME HEN MENUS

## Chicken Potpie

*In Pennsylvania Dutch cooking, potpies are pieces of noodle or baking-powder dough that are boiled with meat and often potatoes to make rib-sticking stews. Thus, this recipe for chicken and noodle stew is called "chicken potpie" although it bears no resemblance to the kind of pastry-encased potpie familiar in other parts of the United States. To make fresh potpie noodles, use the recipe for homemade pasta (Index/Glossary), but omit the olive oil; cut the rolled dough into 2-inch squares.* ❖●

**To serve 6 to 8**

One 5- to 6-pound roasting
   chicken, cut into pieces
4 quarts water
2 celery ribs, including leaves,
   cut into 3-inch pieces,
   plus ½ cup coarsely
   chopped celery
¼ teaspoon crumbled dried
   saffron threads
2 teaspoons salt

6 black peppercorns
2 boiling potatoes, peeled and
   chopped coarse
½ pound 2-inch potpie
   squares, preferably
   homemade
2 tablespoons finely chopped
   fresh parsley leaves
Freshly ground black pepper

Combine the chicken and water in a heavy 6- to 8-quart casserole, and bring to a boil over high heat, meanwhile skimming off the foam and scum that rise to the surface. Add the celery pieces, the saffron, 1 teaspoon of the salt and the peppercorns, and reduce the heat to low. Simmer, partially covered, for about 1 hour or until the chicken shows no resistance when a thigh is pierced deeply with a small, sharp knife.

With a slotted spoon, transfer the chicken to a plate. Strain the stock through a fine sieve, and return 2 quarts to the casserole. (Reserve the remaining stock for another use.) With a small, sharp knife, remove the skin from the chicken, and cut the meat from the bones. Discard the skin and bones; slice the meat into 1-inch pieces and set aside.

Add the chopped celery, potatoes and the remaining teaspoon of salt to the stock in the casserole, and bring it to a boil over high heat. Cook for five minutes or so, then drop in the potpie squares and stir briefly. Cook the potpies for two or three minutes if fresh, for up to 15 minutes if dried. The noodles are done when they are tender but still resistant to the bite. Stir in the reserved chicken and the parsley, and cook for a minute or so to heat them through. Taste and season with more salt if desired and some pepper. To serve, ladle the chicken potpie into heated individual bowls.
■ AMERICAN COOKING: THE EASTERN HEARTLAND

# Chicken Tetrazzini

*This voluptuous chicken casserole, believed to have been invented by a New York restaurateur in the early 1900s, was named in honor of Luisa Tetrazzini, a famous coloratura of the period.* ❧

**To serve 8**

| | |
|---|---|
| One 3-pound chicken, cut into 6 or 8 pieces | 1 pound broad egg noodles |
| 1 small onion, halved | |
| 1 carrot | CREAM AND SHERRY SAUCE |
| 2 celery ribs with leaves | 6 tablespoons butter |
| 2 cloves | 6 tablespoons flour |
| 1 small bay leaf | ½ cup heavy cream |
| 1 teaspoon salt | ½ cup sherry wine |
| 6 cups water | 2 egg yolks |
| 6 tablespoons butter | ⅛ teaspoon Tabasco sauce |
| ½ pound mushrooms, sliced thin | 1 cup freshly grated Parmesan cheese |

Combine the chicken, onion, carrot, celery, cloves, bay leaf, salt and water in a 3- to 4-quart casserole, and bring to a boil over high heat. Reduce the heat to low, cover partially, and simmer for 30 minutes or until the chicken is tender but not falling apart.

With tongs, transfer the chicken to a cutting board. Strain the cooking liquid through a fine sieve set over a large bowl, pressing down hard on the vegetables with the back of a spoon before discarding them. With a large spoon, skim off and discard the fat from the stock. Set the stock aside. Remove the skin and bones from the chicken, and discard them. Cut the chicken into 1-inch pieces and place them in a bowl.

Preheat the oven to 350°F. With a pastry brush, lightly coat the bottom and sides of a 9-by-13-by-2-inch baking dish with melted or softened butter.

In a heavy 8- to 10-inch skillet, melt 6 tablespoons of butter over moderate heat. Stir in the mushrooms and cook, stirring frequently, for about five minutes or until they are soft and lightly colored. Set aside off the heat.

For the sauce, melt 6 tablespoons of butter in a 1½- to 2-quart enameled or stainless-steel saucepan over moderate heat. Stir in the flour with a whisk and mix together thoroughly. Whisking constantly, gradually pour in 2 cups of the reserved chicken stock, the cream and the sherry. Bring to a boil over high heat, then reduce the heat to moderate.

In a small bowl, beat the egg yolks with a whisk until smooth. Whisking constantly, slowly pour in about ½ cup of the hot liquid, then stir this egg mixture into the saucepan. Cook for one or two minutes more, then stir in the Tabasco and remove the pan from the heat.

Bring 3 to 4 quarts of lightly salted water to a boil in a 6- to 8-quart pot. Add a splash of oil to prevent the water from foaming over, then drop in the noodles. Stir to separate them, then boil them—stirring from time to time—for eight to 10 minutes, until tender but still slightly resistant to the bite. Drain the noodles in a colander.

To assemble the tetrazzini, pour 1 cup of the sauce into the pre-pared baking dish, and arrange half of the noodles over it. Spread the noodles with half of the mushrooms, and top these with half of the chicken. Repeat the layers—using 1 cup of sauce and the remaining noodles, mushrooms and chicken—and top with the remaining sauce. Sprinkle with the grated Parmesan and bake in the center of the oven for 30 minutes. Serve at once, directly from the baking dish.

■ AMERICAN COOKING: THE MELTING POT

# Chicken en Papillote

**To serve 4**

| | |
|---|---|
| 2 tablespoons butter | basil leaves or 1 teaspoon crumbled dried basil, plus basil sprigs for garnish |
| 1 onion, chopped fine | |
| ½ pound mushrooms, trimmed, 12 left whole, the rest chopped fine | Salt |
| | Freshly ground black pepper |
| 3 dried morels, soaked in hot water for 10 minutes, stems discarded and caps chopped fine | ¼ cup Madeira wine |
| | ¼ cup heavy cream |
| | Two 1½-pound whole chicken breasts, skinned, boned and halved |
| 3 large garlic cloves, chopped fine | |
| ¼ cup chopped fresh parsley leaves | 2 small tomatoes, cored and sliced thin |
| 1 tablespoon chopped fresh | ½ cup shredded Jarlsberg or Emmentaler cheese |

In a heavy 8- to 10-inch skillet, melt the butter over moderate heat and in it cook the onion, stirring occasionally, for five minutes or until it is soft. Add the fresh and dried mushrooms, the garlic, parsley, basil, 1 teaspoon of salt and a few grindings of pepper. Stirring occasionally, cook the mixture until it is almost dry—about 7 minutes. Add the Madeira and cook for about four minutes, until the wine evaporates. Remove the skillet from the heat and stir in the heavy cream. Taste for seasoning and add more salt and pepper if necessary.

Preheat the oven to 475°F. Cut each chicken breast half horizontally into two thin slices. Cut four pieces of parchment paper into 12-inch squares, fold each piece in half and cut it into the shape of half of a heart. Open each heart and spoon one-quarter of the chopped mushrooms onto the centerfold. Place a chicken-breast slice lengthwise on top, and season it with salt and pepper. Place three or four overlapping tomato slices and three whole mushrooms over the chicken. Top with another chicken slice. Sprinkle with the cheese.

Fold the edges of each heart together, then roll and crimp the edges together tightly, starting from the center top. Twist the tip of the heart to seal it. Place the packages, side by side, on a baking sheet. Bake the chicken for 10 to 12 minutes; the paper should be puffed and lightly browned. Place each package on a heated individual plate and, with scissors, cut an X in the top of each package. Fold back the corners, garnish each serving with a basil sprig, and serve at once.

■ VEGETABLE MENUS

CHICKEN EN PAPILLOTE

# Chicken Breasts with Spring Vegetables

**To serve 4**

| | |
|---|---|
| 12 to 16 small new potatoes | lettuce leaves |
| 8 small carrots with tops | 1 tablespoon chopped fresh |
| 1 bunch scallions | parsley leaves for garnish |
| 8 large mushrooms | |
| 2 lemons | GARLIC SAUCE |
| 1 pound asparagus | ½ cup butter |
| Two ¾-pound whole chicken | 4 egg yolks |
| breasts, skinned, boned | 1 tablespoon tarragon vinegar |
| and halved | 4 teaspoons fresh lemon |
| Salt | juice |
| Freshly ground black pepper | 2 garlic cloves |
| 2 tablespoons chopped fresh | ½ teaspoon salt |
| tarragon leaves or | 1 tablespoon chopped fresh |
| 2 teaspoons crumbled | parsley leaves |
| dried tarragon | Freshly ground white pepper |
| Savoy cabbage leaves or | |

Bring several quarts of lightly salted water to a boil in a 3- to 4-quart saucepan. Peel a ring around each potato. Cut off all but 2 inches from the green carrot tops, then peel the carrots and trim them to 3 or 4 inches in length. Trim the scallions, leaving 2 inches of green. Put the potatoes in the boiling water and cook them for five minutes. Add the carrots and scallions, and cook for another five minutes. Drain the potatoes, carrots and scallions.

Trim the ends of the mushroom stems; gently rub the mushroom caps with the cut half of a lemon. Snap or cut off the tough end of each asparagus stalk; then peel the stalk from the base upward with a small knife or vegetable parer.

Fill a large vegetable steamer with water to just below the steamer rack. The steamer must be large enough to hold the chicken and vegetables in one layer without crowding them; if not, steam the food in two batches or on a rack in a pot filled with water to a depth of 1 inch. Place the chicken, asparagus and mushrooms in the center of the steamer rack; arrange the carrots, scallions and potatoes around them. Sprinkle the chicken and vegetables with salt, pepper and tarragon. Cover the steamer, bring the water to a boil over moderate heat, and steam the food for 15 minutes or until the juices of the chicken run clear when a breast is pierced with a knife, and the vegetables are tender.

Meanwhile, to prepare the sauce, first melt the butter in a small saucepan. Place the egg yolks, tarragon vinegar, lemon juice, garlic and the ½ teaspoon of salt in a blender or food processor, and mix to incorporate all of the ingredients. With the motor on, slowly pour in the melted butter. When the sauce thickens, stir in 1 teaspoon of chopped parsley. Add salt and white pepper to taste.

Arrange cabbage or lettuce leaves on a serving platter. Place the chicken breasts in the center, and group the vegetables around them. Sprinkle the potatoes and mushrooms lightly with chopped parsley, if you like, and garnish the platter with lemon wedges. Serve the garlic sauce separately.

■ CHICKEN AND GAME HEN MENUS

# Yakitori

*In Japan, the pepper in this recipe would be replaced by ground prickly-ash leaf, or kona sansho. Sake and mirin are rice wines; mirin is sweeter. Both are available at liquor stores.* ✜●

**To serve 4**

| | |
|---|---|
| 3 tablespoons sake | 3 inches of green tops, |
| 1 tablespoon Japanese soy | cut into 1½-inch pieces |
| sauce | Freshly ground black |
| 2 teaspoons sugar | pepper |
| One 1-inch piece fresh ginger | |
| root, sliced thin | TERIYAKI SAUCE |
| 8 chicken livers, trimmed | ½ cup *mirin* or 1 cup |
| Two ½-pound whole chicken | less 2 tablespoons pale |
| breasts or four ¼-pound | dry sherry wine |
| legs, skinned, boned and | ½ cup Japanese soy sauce |
| cut into 1-inch pieces | ½ cup chicken stock |
| 8 scallions, including | |

To marinate the chicken livers, first combine the sake, 1 tablespoon of soy sauce, the sugar and sliced ginger in a small mixing bowl. Add the chicken livers, stir to moisten them well, and marinate at room temperature for at least six hours or overnight in the refrigerator. Remove the livers from the marinade and cut each one in half. Reserve the marinade.

For the teriyaki sauce, warm the *mirin* briefly in a small nonreactive saucepan over moderate heat. Turn off the heat. If the *mirin* does not ignite spontaneously, ignite it with a match, and slide the pan back and forth until the flames die. Stir in the soy sauce and chicken stock, and bring the mixture to a boil. Pour this sauce into a shallow bowl, and cool it to room temperature.

Preheat the broiler, or light coals in a hibachi or charcoal grill and let them burn until white ash forms on the top.

On each of four small skewers, string four halved chicken livers. On each of eight skewers, alternate four chunks of chicken with three strips of scallion. Broil the livers about 3 inches from the heat for four minutes. Then roll them in the teriyaki sauce and broil for four to five minutes on the other side. Set the livers aside on a plate.

Quickly dip the chicken-and-scallion skewers into the teriyaki sauce, and broil one side for two or three minutes. Dip the skewers again into the sauce, and broil for two minutes, dip once more and broil the other side for two minutes. The entire process should take six to seven minutes.

To serve, place one skewer of chicken livers and two skewers of chicken and scallions on each of four heated plates. Sprinkle them with a little pepper and moisten each skewer with some of the marinade.

■ THE COOKING OF JAPAN

# Poule-au-pot

**To serve 6**

One 5-pound stewing chicken, rinsed and dried, neck, gizzard and heart reserved
1 teaspoon salt
2 tablespoons butter
2 tablespoons vegetable oil
2 onions, cut in half
3 celery ribs, cut up
1 veal knuckle, sawed into 2-inch pieces
1 leek, white part plus 2 inches of green
4 parsley sprigs
1 bay leaf
8 cups chicken stock
8 cups water

SAUSAGE STUFFING
2 tablespoons butter
½ cup finely chopped onions
¾ cup long-grain white rice
1½ cups chicken stock

½ pound breakfast-sausage meat
2 chicken livers, trimmed
¼ cup chopped fresh parsley leaves
½ teaspoon crumbled dried thyme
¼ cup heavy cream
Salt
Freshly ground black pepper

VEGETABLE GARNISH
6 carrots, cut into 2-inch ovals
4 white turnips, quartered
3 parsnips, quartered
6 leeks, including 2 inches of green tops, tied in a bunch
6 small potatoes, unpeeled if new

For the stuffing, first melt 2 tablespoons of butter in a heavy 8- to 10-inch skillet over moderate heat. Add the chopped onions and cook, stirring frequently, for five to 10 minutes, or until they are soft and transparent. Add the rice and stir for two or three minutes without browning it. Pour 1½ cups of stock over the mixture, cover, reduce the heat, and simmer for 12 minutes or until the rice is barely tender and the liquid has been absorbed; transfer to a bowl and set aside.

In the same skillet, fry the sausage meat over moderate heat, mashing it with a fork to break it up, until it is lightly browned. Drain the sausage, saving the fat, and add the meat to the rice. Heat 2 tablespoons of the sausage fat in the skillet, and cook the chicken livers for two or three minutes, until they stiffen and brown. Remove them from the pan and chop them coarse; stir them into the rice and sausage mixture along with the parsley, thyme and cream. Season the stuffing with salt and pepper.

Rub the main cavity of the chicken with a little salt, and spoon in the stuffing loosely; don't overfill it, or the stuffing will pop out in the cooking. Neatly sew the openings and truss the chicken.

In a heavy 10- to 12-inch skillet, melt 2 tablespoons of butter and the oil over moderately high heat, and in it brown the chicken lightly on all sides. Transfer the chicken to a heavy 6- to 8-quart soup pot or casserole, and arrange the giblets, onion halves, celery chunks, veal knuckle, 1 leek, parsley sprigs and bay leaf around it. Pour in 8 cups of chicken stock and the water. If the liquid does not cover the bird, add more stock or water. Over high heat, bring the liquid to a boil, skimming the surface of scum as it appears. When the scum is gone, reduce the heat to low and partially cover the pot.

Simmer the chicken for two hours, then lift it out onto a plate; strain the stock through a fine sieve or double layer of cheese-cloth into a large saucepan or bowl, and discard the stewing vegetables. Skim off as much surface fat as possible from the stock. Return the chicken and stock to the pot.

Bring the chicken and stock to a simmer, add the carrots, turnips, parsnips and the bunch of leeks, and cook slowly for about 30 minutes or until tender. Meanwhile boil the potatoes in a small covered saucepan for 20 to 30 minutes; when they are done, drain them, cover, and set aside.

To serve, transfer the bird to a carving board, cut off the trussing strings, and let it rest for five to 10 minutes. With a slotted spoon, remove the vegetables from the stock to a heated platter, and arrange them attractively with the potatoes. Carve the chicken and serve it arranged on a heated platter, surrounded with the stuffing. Serve the vegetables separately. Save the stock to serve at another meal.

■ THE COOKING OF PROVINCIAL FRANCE

# Stir-fried Chicken with Hot Chilies

**To serve 4**

Two ¾-pound whole chicken breasts, skinned, boned, halved and cut lengthwise into julienne strips
2 teaspoons cornstarch, plus 1 teaspoon cornstarch, dissolved in 1 tablespoon cold chicken stock or water
1 egg white
1½ teaspoons salt
1 tablespoon Chinese rice wine or pale dry sherry
½ teaspoon sugar

¼ cup peanut oil
3 small, fresh hot red and green chilies, seeded and cut into julienne strips
1 teaspoon fresh ginger root julienne strips
12 Boston, Bibb or iceberg lettuce leaves, washed and spun or patted dry
2 to 4 snow peas, trimmed, strings removed, outside edges fringed and pods opened, for garnish

Place the julienne chicken in a small bowl, add 2 teaspoons of cornstarch, and toss the chicken about until lightly coated. Add the egg white, salt, wine and sugar, and stir with the chicken until thoroughly mixed.

Set a 12-inch wok or 10-inch skillet over high heat for 30 seconds. Pour in 1 tablespoon of the oil, swirl it about in the pan, and heat for another 30 seconds; do not let the oil smoke. Add the chilies, stir-fry them for a minute, then scoop them out with a slotted spoon and set them aside in a small dish. Pour the remaining 3 tablespoons of oil into the pan, heat for 30 seconds and add the ginger. Stir for a few seconds and drop in the chicken mixture. Stir-fry over moderate heat for one or two minutes or until the chicken turns firm and white. Stir in the chilies and cook for about 10 seconds to heat them through.

Give the cornstarch mixture a quick stir to recombine it, and pour it into the pan. Cook for a few seconds, stirring constantly, until all of the ingredients are coated with a light, clear glaze. Immediately transfer to a platter lined with a few lettuce leaves. Garnish the platter with snow peas, if you like, and serve the chicken at once, accompanied by the remaining lettuce leaves.

To eat, pick up a lettuce leaf in one hand or lay it on a plate,

STIR-FRIED CHICKEN WITH HOT CHILIES

then place about 2 tablespoonfuls of the chicken mixture on the center of the leaf and fold the leaf in half, enclosing the chicken within it. Then roll the lettuce into a loose cylinder that can be held in the fingers and eaten.

■ THE COOKING OF CHINA

## Chicken Breasts with Prosciutto and Cheese

**To serve 4**

| | |
|---|---|
| Two 1-pound whole chicken breasts, skinned, boned and halved | 8 thin 2-by-4-inch slices prosciutto ham |
| Salt | 8 thin 2-by-4-inch slices Fontina or Bel Paese cheese |
| Freshly ground black pepper | 4 teaspoons freshly grated Parmesan cheese |
| Flour | |
| 3 tablespoons butter | 2 tablespoons chicken stock |
| 2 tablespoons vegetable oil | |

Preheat the oven to 350°F. Using a pastry brush, spread a light coating of melted or softened butter inside a shallow baking-serving dish about 9 or 10 inches square. With a very sharp knife, carefully slice each breast half horizontally in two, to make eight thin slices. Lay them an inch or so apart between strips of wax paper and pound them lightly with the flat of a cleaver or a meat pounder to flatten them slightly. Strip off the paper. Season the

slices with salt and a few grindings of pepper; dip them in flour and shake off the excess.

In a heavy 10- to 12-inch skillet, melt the butter with the oil over moderate heat. Add the slices in a single layer—three or four at a time—and cook them for about two minutes on each side or until they are light golden. Do not overcook.

As they brown, transfer the chicken breasts to the buttered dish. Place a slice of prosciutto and then a slice of cheese on each one. Sprinkle them with grated Parmesan and dribble the stock over them. Bake them uncovered for about 10 minutes or until the cheese melts and browns lightly. Serve at once.

■ THE COOKING OF ITALY

## Chicken Riesling

**To serve 4**

| | |
|---|---|
| Two ½-pound whole chicken breasts, skinned, boned and halved | 1½ cups Riesling wine |
| Freshly ground black pepper | 1 tablespoon chopped fresh tarragon leaves, or 1 teaspoon crumbled dried tarragon |
| ½ teaspoon salt | 1¼ cups chicken stock |
| 1 tablespoon safflower oil | 2 teaspoons cornstarch |
| 1 tablespoon unsalted butter | ¾ cup seedless red grapes, halved |
| 2 tablespoons finely chopped shallots | |
| 1 cup thinly sliced mushrooms | |

Preheat the oven to 200°F. Sprinkle the chicken with a few grindings of pepper and ¼ teaspoon of the salt. In a heavy 8- to 10-inch skillet, heat the oil over moderately high heat. Sauté the chicken in the oil until brown—four or five minutes on each side. Transfer the chicken to an ovenproof plate, and cover it with foil to keep it warm.

Add the butter, shallots and mushrooms to the skillet, sprinkle with ⅛ teaspoon of the salt, and cook for two or three minutes or until the shallots soften. With a slotted spoon, transfer the mushrooms to the plate with the chicken, and keep it warm in the oven.

Pour 1¼ cups of the wine into the skillet, add the tarragon, and boil to reduce the wine to about ¼ cup. Add the stock and reduce the liquid to about ¾ cup.

Mix the cornstarch with the remaining ¼ cup of wine. Reduce the heat under the skillet so that the liquid simmers, and stir in the cornstarch mixture and the remaining ⅛ teaspoon of salt. Add the grapes and cook for two minutes. Arrange some of the grape mixture on each breast half, and pour the sauce over all.

■ FRESH WAYS WITH POULTRY

## Chicken and Ham in Green Paradise

**To serve 4 to 6**

| | |
|---|---|
| 2 pounds broccoli | rinsed and patted dry |
| 8 cups chicken stock | Three slices cooked |
| 1 scallion, including green | Smithfield ham, cut |
| top, cut into 2-inch pieces | into 2-by-1-inch pieces |
| 4 slices peeled fresh ginger | ¼ teaspoon salt |
| root, about 1 inch across | 1 teaspoon cornstarch |
| and ⅛ inch thick | dissolved in 1 tablespoon |
| One 4-pound roasting chicken, | cold water |

With a small, sharp knife cut off the broccoli florets. Peel the stalks by cutting ⅛ inch deep into the skin and stripping it away. Slice the stalks diagonally into 1-inch pieces; discard the woody ends.

In a heavy flameproof casserole or pot just large enough to hold the chicken snugly, bring the stock to a boil. Add the scallions and ginger, and place the chicken in the pot. The liquid should cover the chicken; add more boiling stock or water if it does not. Bring the liquid to a boil again, cover the casserole, reduce the heat to low, and simmer for 15 minutes. Then turn off the heat and leave the chicken in the covered casserole for 2 hours: The residual heat will cook the chicken through.

Transfer the chicken to a chopping board, reserving the stock. With a cleaver or knife, cut off the wings and legs, and split the chicken in half lengthwise, cutting through the breast and back bones. Cut the meat from the bones, leaving the skin in place. Then cut the meat into pieces about 2 inches long and 1 inch wide. Arrange the chicken and ham attractively in overlapped layers on a heated serving dish, and cover with foil.

Pour 2 cups of the reserved stock into a 3-quart saucepan. Bring it to a boil and drop in the broccoli. Return the stock to a boil, turn off the heat and let the broccoli stand uncovered for three minutes. Arrange the broccoli on the dish with the chicken and ham. Or garnish the meat with the florets and serve the stems separately from it.

In a small saucepan, combine ½ cup of the reserved stock with the salt and bring to a boil. Stir the cornstarch mixture and add it to the stock. When the stock thickens slightly and becomes clear, pour it over the chicken and ham. Serve at once.

■ THE COOKING OF CHINA

## Sautéed Chicken with Calvados Sauce

**To serve 4**

| | |
|---|---|
| One 2½- to 3-pound frying | shallots or scallions |
| chicken, cut into 8 serving | ¼ cup finely chopped celery |
| pieces | 1 cup chopped peeled cored |
| 6 tablespoons butter | tart apples |
| 2 tablespoons vegetable oil | ½ teaspoon crumbled dried |
| Salt | thyme |
| Freshly ground white pepper | 2 egg yolks |
| ⅓ cup Calvados | ½ cup heavy cream |
| ½ cup chicken stock | Watercress or parsley sprigs |
| 2 tablespoons finely chopped | for garnish |

Preheat the oven to 200°F. In a heavy 8- to 10-inch skillet, melt ¼ cup of the butter in the oil over moderate heat, then brown the chicken lightly on all sides. Transfer the chicken to a plate, pour off all but a thin film of fat from the skillet, then return the chicken to the skillet and season it with salt and white pepper. With the skillet off the heat, warm the Calvados slightly in a small saucepan over low heat. If the Calvados does not burst into flames spontaneously, carefully ignite it with a match and pour it flaming over the chicken, a little at a time. Slide the skillet gently back and forth until the flame dies. Then pour in the stock and, with a wooden spoon, scrape in any browned bits. Set aside.

In a separate small saucepan or skillet, melt the remaining 2 tablespoons of butter over moderate heat, and in it cook the shallots, celery, apples and thyme, stirring occasionally with a wooden spoon, for 10 minutes or until they are soft but not brown. Spread them over the chicken, return it to high heat and bring the stock to a boil. Tightly cover the skillet, reduce the heat, and simmer the chicken, basting it with pan juices every seven or eight minutes. After about 20 minutes, when the chicken is tender, remove it from the skillet and arrange the pieces on a large ovenproof platter. Cover the chicken loosely with foil and keep it warm in the oven.

Strain the contents of the skillet through a fine sieve set over a small saucepan, pressing down hard on the vegetables and the apples with the back of a spoon to squeeze out all of their juices. Let the vegetable mixture settle a minute, then skim off as much of the surface fat as possible. Stirring from time to time, boil the mixture over high heat for two or three minutes, until it is reduced to about ½ cup.

With a wire whisk, blend the egg yolks and cream in a bowl and gradually beat in all of the reduced vegetable mixture, 1 tablespoon at a time. Pour this sauce into the pan and—stirring constantly—cook over moderately low heat for two or three minutes, until it is as thick as heavy cream. Do not allow it to boil or it will curdle. Taste and correct the seasoning with salt and white pepper. To serve, mask each piece of chicken with the sauce and decorate the platter with watercress or parsley sprigs.

NOTE: The Calvados called for in this recipe is French apple brandy. American applejack will yield as delicious a sauce.

■ THE COOKING OF PROVINCIAL FRANCE

## Country Captain

*A century or more before most Americans had heard of Indian food, cooks in the South were making this delectable curried chicken. Its name, presumably, refers to the captains who brought silks and spices from Asia to ports such as Charleston.* ❦

**To serve 4**

| | |
|---|---|
| 2 tablespoons bacon fat | juices reserved |
| One 2½- to 3-pound frying chicken, cut into 8 serving pieces | 1½ teaspoons salt |
| | 1 teaspoon freshly ground black pepper |
| 2 tablespoons butter | ½ teaspoon crumbled dried thyme |
| 1 large onion, sliced thin | |
| 1 large green pepper, cut into thin strips | 2 tablespoons dried currants |
| | ¼ cup sliced almonds, toasted in a 350°F. oven for 5 minutes |
| 2 garlic cloves, chopped fine | |
| 2 teaspoons or more curry powder, to taste | 1½ tablespoons chopped fresh parsley leaves |
| One 16-ounce can whole tomatoes, chopped and | Mango chutney |

Preheat the oven to 350°F. Melt the bacon fat in a 10- to 12-inch cast-iron skillet over moderate heat, and—turning the pieces with tongs—brown the chicken on both sides. This will take about 10 minutes. Drain the chicken on a plate lined with paper towels.

Rinse out the skillet and wipe it dry. Add the butter, and in it cook the onion, green pepper, garlic and curry powder for about five minutes or until the onion is soft. Add the tomatoes and their juice, the salt, pepper and thyme. Bring to a boil, then reduce the heat, and simmer this sauce mixture, uncovered, for 10 minutes.

Return the chicken to the skillet and baste it with the sauce. Cover the skillet and place it in the oven. Bake the chicken for 20 minutes, then stir in the currants and bake for 10 minutes longer. Arrange the chicken on a heated platter, and sprinkle them with the toasted almonds and chopped parsley. Serve country captain accompanied by spicy mango chutney.

■ AMERICAN REGIONAL MENUS

## Flamed Chicken with Mushrooms

**To serve 4**

| | |
|---|---|
| 5 tablespoons butter | fresh chives |
| ¼ cup finely chopped shallots | Salt |
| ½ pound fresh mushrooms, wiped clean, trimmed and sliced | Freshly ground black pepper |
| | ¼ cup dry white wine |
| 1 tablespoon chopped fresh marjoram leaves or 1 teaspoon crumbled dried marjoram | Four 1-pound chicken breasts, skinned, boned and halved |
| | ¼ cup brandy |
| 2 tablespoons finely cut | 2 tablespoons chopped fresh parsley leaves for garnish |

Melt 3 tablespoons of the butter in a 10- to 12-inch skillet. Stir in the shallots and cook over low heat for about a minute. Add the mushrooms and continue cooking for another minute. Stir in the

COUNTRY CAPTAIN

marjoram, chives, salt to taste, a few grindings of black pepper and the wine. Cook over moderately high heat for about three minutes or until the wine is reduced to a few spoonfuls. With a rubber spatula, transfer the mushroom mixture to a plate; cover to keep it warm.

Place the chicken breasts between sheets of wax paper. Using the flat of a cleaver or a meat pounder, pound them to a thickness of about ½ inch. Season them with salt and pepper. In the original skillet, melt the remaining 2 tablespoons of butter over moderately high heat. Add the chicken breasts in one layer and sauté them for about four minutes on each side or until they are lightly browned. If all of the breasts will not fit easily, use more butter and a second skillet. After cooking, fit the second batch of breasts into the first skillet.

Turn off the heat under the chicken. Divide the mushroom topping among the breasts. Briefly warm the brandy in a small saucepan. Standing back, hold a match just above the brandy and set it aflame. Pour the flaming brandy over the chicken. Slide the

pan gently back and forth until the flames subside. Arrange the chicken on a platter and garnish it with parsley, if desired.

■ CHICKEN AND GAME HEN MENUS

## Baked Chicken Parmesan

**To serve 8**

| | |
|---|---|
| 4 cups fresh white bread crumbs | 1 garlic clove, crushed |
| 1 cup freshly grated Parmesan cheese | 1 tablespoon Dijon mustard |
| 1 tablespoon salt | 1½ teaspoons Worcestershire sauce |
| ⅓ cup chopped fresh parsley leaves | Three 2½- to 3-pound frying chickens, each cut into 6 or 8 serving pieces |
| 1½ cups butter, cut into bits | |

In a bowl, combine the crumbs, cheese, salt and parsley. Spread the mixture in a shallow pan. In a 2- to 3-quart saucepan, melt the butter over low heat without letting it brown. Stir in the garlic, mustard and Worcestershire sauce. Then let the butter mixture cool enough so that you can put your fingers in it, but do not allow it to congeal.

Preheat the oven to 350° F. Dip the chicken pieces into the butter mixture, then roll them in the bread-crumb mixture. To make sure that each piece is well coated, pat the crumbs on with your hands. Place the pieces of chicken, side by side, in a large, shallow baking pan (it is possible that two pans will be necessary). Pour the remaining butter mixture over the chicken pieces. Bake the chicken for 30 to 40 minutes or until it is golden and the juices run clear when a thigh is pierced with the tip of a sharp knife. While the chicken is baking, baste it once or twice with the pan drippings.

■ GREAT DINNERS FROM LIFE

## Chicken Thighs with Vinegar Sauce

**To serve 4**

| | |
|---|---|
| 3 pounds chicken thighs | scallions |
| ¼ cup Chinese red rice vinegar or 3 tablespoons red-wine vinegar | 3 tablespoons finely chopped garlic |
| ¼ cup light soy sauce | 4 cups peanut oil |
| ½ cup finely chopped | Curly endive or Boston lettuce for garnish |

Bring 1 inch of water to boil in a wok or large skillet. Set a metal rack or trivet in the water, place the chicken on a deep heatproof plate, and set it on the rack. Cover and steam for 20 minutes.

Meanwhile, combine the vinegar, soy sauce, scallions and garlic in a small bowl to make the vinegar sauce. Set it aside. Preheat the oven to 200°F. Pour the oil into a wok or deep saucepan and heat it to 375°F. on a deep-frying thermometer or until a scallion ring sizzles on contact.

When the chicken has been steamed, blot off any moisture with paper towels. Gently add half of the chicken pieces to the hot oil and deep-fry for 10 minutes or until crisp and brown. Remove the chicken pieces from the oil with a Chinese mesh spoon or a long-handled slotted metal spoon, and briefly hold them above the pan to drain off the excess oil. Arrange them on a large platter and set them in the oven to keep warm. Return the oil to 375°F. and cook the second batch.

Serve the chicken on a bed of curly endive or Boston lettuce, if desired, and spoon some vinegar sauce over it. Serve the remaining sauce separately.

■ CHINESE MENUS

## Chicken Fans with Basil-Tomato Sauce

**To serve 4**

| | |
|---|---|
| 2 cups chicken stock | 1 garlic clove |
| 2 cups loosely packed fresh basil leaves , plus basil leaves for garnish | ½ cup water |
| | 2 teaspoons mayonnaise, preferably homemade |
| Two 1-pound whole chicken breasts, skinned, boned and halved | 1 tomato, peeled, seeded and chopped |

In a pot large enough to hold the chicken breasts snugly, simmer the stock with ½ cup of the basil leaves over moderately low heat for five minutes. Add the breasts to the stock, cover, and poach gently for eight minutes. Turn the breasts over and poach until they feel firm but springy to the touch—about four minutes more.

Meanwhile, chop the garlic in a food processor or blender. Add the remaining 1½ cups of basil along with ½ cup of water, and purée the mixture. Pour the purée into a sieve, and lightly press it with the back of a spoon to remove excess water. To prepare the sauce, scrape the purée into a small bowl and stir in the mayon-

naise and half of the chopped tomato. There will be about ½ cup of sauce.

Lift the chicken breasts from their poaching liquid and pat them dry. Cut each piece diagonally into slices and spread them in a fan pattern on individual serving plates, setting them on large basil leaves, if you like. Spoon the sauce between the slices of each fan, dividing it equally among them. Scatter the remaining chopped tomato over the sauce.

■ FRESH WAYS WITH POULTRY

## Old-fashioned Chicken Fricassee

**To serve 4**

| | |
|---|---|
| One 2½- to 3-pound frying chicken, cut into 8 serving pieces | dried thyme |
| | 16 to 24 white onions, about 1 inch across |
| ½ cup butter | ¾ pound mushrooms, trimmed, left whole if small, sliced or quartered if large |
| Salt | |
| Freshly ground white pepper | |
| ¼ cup flour | ½ to 1 teaspoon fresh lemon juice |
| 3⅔ to 4 cups chicken stock | 2 egg yolks |
| 1 bouquet garni made of 4 parsley sprigs and 1 bay leaf, tied together | ½ cup heavy cream |
| | 2 tablespoons finely chopped fresh parsley leaves |
| ¼ teaspoon crumbled | |

Pat the chicken pieces completely dry with paper towels. In a heavy 2- to 3-quart flameproof casserole, melt 6 tablespoons of the butter over moderate heat. Using tongs, lay a few pieces of chicken at a time in the butter, and cook them—turning them once or twice—for about five minutes or until they stiffen slightly and are no longer pink. Do not let them brown. Transfer them to a plate and season the chicken with salt and white pepper.

With a wire whisk, stir the flour into the butter remaining in the casserole. Stirring constantly, cook this roux over low heat for one or two minutes without letting it brown. Slowly pour in 3 cups of the chicken stock, beating vigorously to blend the roux and stock. Whisk constantly until the sauce thickens and comes to a boil; then reduce the heat and let the sauce simmer for one or two minutes.

Return the chicken to the casserole, together with the juices that have collected on the plate, and add the bouquet garni of parsley and bay leaf, and the thyme. The sauce should almost cover the chicken; add stock if it does not. Bring the sauce to a boil over moderate heat, cover the casserole, reduce the heat to low, and simmer for 30 minutes.

Meanwhile, combine the remaining ⅔ cup of stock, 2 tablespoons of butter and the onions in an 8- to 10-inch enameled or stainless-steel skillet. Bring to a boil, cover, and simmer over low heat for 15 to 20 minutes or until the onions are tender when pierced with the tip of a sharp knife. With a slotted spoon, transfer the onions to a bowl. Stir the mushrooms and 1 teaspoon of lemon juice into the stock remaining in the skillet. Bring to a boil, cover, and simmer over low heat for five minutes. Add the mush-

**CHICKEN FANS WITH BASIL-TOMATO SAUCE**

rooms to the onions. Boil the liquid left in the skillet until it is reduced to 2 or 3 tablespoons; then pour it into the simmering casserole of chicken.

To test the chicken for doneness, pierce a thigh with the tip of a sharp knife; the juices should be clear. Alternatively, a meat thermometer inserted into a thigh should register 180°F. With tongs, transfer the chicken to a plate. Discard the bouquet garni.

Skim the fat from the surface of the sauce, which by now should be as thick as heavy cream; if it is not, boil the sauce rapidly, uncovered, to reduce it. With the whisk, blend the egg yolks and cream together in a bowl. Whisk in about ½ cup of the hot sauce, 2 tablespoonfuls at a time; then gradually whisk the egg-yolk mixture into the remaining sauce. Whisking

constantly, bring the sauce to a boil, then cook over low heat for 30 seconds. Taste and correct the seasoning with salt, white pepper and lemon juice. Strain the sauce through a fine sieve into a large bowl.

Wash the casserole, arrange the chicken pieces, onions and mushrooms in it, and pour the sauce over them. Do not use any juices that have accumulated under the chicken unless the sauce needs thinning. Before serving, cover the casserole and simmer it over moderate heat for five to 10 minutes or until the chicken is hot. Do not let the sauce come to a boil again. Serve the chicken from the casserole or arranged on a heated platter, masked with sauce and sprinkled with parsley.

■ THE COOKING OF PROVINCIAL FRANCE

# Coq au Vin

*The extra effort that makes this version of chicken with wine so special includes adding flaming brandy and, most crucial, removing the finished chicken and vegetables from the sauce while boiling it to reduce it to about half its original quantity. This intensifies the flavor of the sauce immeasurably. Although an exquisite vintage would be wasted, the wine chosen for this recipe should be one that deserves to be drunk; so-called cooking wines may contain salt and flavorings.* ❧

**To serve 4**

| | |
|---|---|
| 6 chicken breast halves, with wings left on | 24 mushrooms, trimmed |
| 6 chicken legs | 1 clove garlic, chopped fine |
| Salt | ¼ cup brandy |
| Freshly ground black pepper | 2 cups dry red wine |
| ¼ cup butter, cut into bits, plus 1 tablespoon butter, softened | 2 cups chicken stock |
| | ½ teaspoon crumbled dried thyme leaves |
| 3 thick bacon slices, cut into ½-inch pieces | 1 bay leaf |
| 24 white onions, 1 inch across | 1 tablespoon chopped fresh parsley leaves |
| 1 teaspoon sugar | 1 tablespoon flour |

Pat the chicken pieces completely dry with paper towels and sprinkle them with salt and pepper. In a heavy 5- to 6-quart casserole or Dutch oven, melt ¼ cup of butter over moderate heat and in it cook the bacon for three minutes or until lightly browned. Remove the bacon and drain it on paper towels.

Pour half of the accumulated fat into a second large casserole or a heavy skillet in order to have two pans for browning the chicken. Add the chicken to the fat, skin side down. Do not crowd the pieces; even with two pans it may be necessary to brown the chicken in batches. Cook the chicken over moderate heat for four to five minutes on each side or until they are lightly browned. Transfer the chicken pieces to a platter and set them aside.

Drop the onions into the fat remaining in the original casserole, add the sugar, and cook the onions over moderate heat, stirring constantly until they brown. Add the mushrooms and garlic to the onions, and stir for two or three minutes or until they brown. Return the chicken and bacon to the casserole. Warm the brandy slightly in a pan over low heat. If it does not ignite spontaneously, ignite it with a match and pour it flaming over the chicken.

When the flame dies, add the wine, stock, thyme, bay leaf and parsley. Cover the casserole, reduce the heat to low, and simmer the chicken for 30 minutes or until it is tender. Arrange the chicken with the onions, mushrooms and bacon on a heated serving dish, and drape them with foil to keep them warm.

Skim the fat off the stock left in the casserole and bring the stock to a boil. Boil it over high heat for five minutes or until it is reduced to about 2 cups. Mix the tablespoon of softened butter and the flour in a small bowl and stir this *beurre manié* into the sauce. Cook until the sauce thickens. Strain the sauce and pour it over the chicken.

■ **GREAT DINNERS FROM LIFE**

# Curried Chicken Croquettes

*The garam masala used to curry these croquettes is a mixture of spices, ground together and sieved. It may be homemade, as it would be in India, or purchased where Indian foods are sold. The ingredients vary but usually consist of equal parts of cardamom seeds, cinnamon, cloves, black cumin seeds, nutmeg and mace.* ❧

**To make eight 3-inch croquettes**

| | |
|---|---|
| One 3-pound chicken | fresh ginger root |
| 2¼ cups fresh white-bread crumbs | ½ teaspoon finely chopped garlic |
| 1 cup finely chopped onions | 1 teaspoon *garam masala* |
| ½ cup coarsely chopped tomato | 1 teaspoon ground cumin |
| ¼ cup finely chopped fresh coriander leaves | ⅛ teaspoon cayenne pepper |
| | 1 tablespoon salt |
| 1 tablespoon finely chopped | 1 whole egg |
| | ¼ cup *ghee* or clarified butter |

Ask the butcher to skin, bone and grind the chicken. Or, do it yourself: With a large, sharp knife, cut off the wings; discard them, or reserve for another use. Remove the skin from the body, legs and thighs, and bone the chicken roughly, cutting as close to the bones as you can. Discard skin and bones. Put the chicken meat through a meat grinder, using the finest disk. Or, use the knife to chop it as fine as possible.

Combine the chicken, 1 cup of the bread crumbs, the onions, tomato, coriander, ginger, garlic, *garam masala,* cumin, cayenne, salt and the egg in a deep bowl. Knead vigorously with both hands or beat with a wooden spoon until the mixture is smooth. Divide it into eight equal portions, then shape these into flattened rounds about 3 inches across and ¾ inch thick. Dip both sides of each round into the remaining 1¼ cups of bread crumbs, and arrange these cutlets, side by side, on wax paper.

In a heavy 10- to 12-inch skillet, heat the *ghee* over moderate heat until a drop of water flicked into it splutters instantly. Reduce the heat to low, add the chicken croquettes and—turning them gently with a wide metal spatula—fry them for seven or eight minutes on each side. The croquettes are done when the outside surfaces are crisp and brown and no trace of pink shows when a small knife is inserted into the center of one of them. Serve them at once from a warmed platter.

■ THE COOKING OF INDIA

## Sautéed Chicken Breasts with Carrot Purée

**To serve 4**

| | |
|---|---|
| ¼ cup unsalted butter, cut into bits | halved and pounded ½ inch thick |
| 2 tablespoons chopped shallots | 1 teaspoon fresh lemon juice |
| 8 carrots, chopped coarse | Salt |
| 1 cup heavy cream | Freshly ground black pepper |
| Two 1-pound whole chicken breasts, skinned, boned, | Watercress sprigs for garnish |

In a 2- to 3-quart nonreactive saucepan, heat half of the butter bits over moderate heat. Add the shallots and, stirring occasionally, cook them for two minutes. Add the carrots and stir until evenly coated with butter. Cover the pan and cook, sliding the pan back and forth occasionally to prevent scorching, for five minutes, until the carrots are very tender.

Remove the pan from the heat, uncover it, and set the carrots aside to cool for a few minutes. Transfer the carrots to a food processor or blender, and purée them. Add the cream and blend again. With a rubber spatula, scrape the carrot purée into the original saucepan and let it simmer, uncovered, over low heat for 20 to 25 minutes or until it is very thick.

Heat the remaining butter bits in a heavy 10- to 12-inch skillet over moderately high heat until very hot but not brown. Add the chicken breasts and sauté them for three to four minutes on each side, until lightly browned. Add lemon juice, and salt and pepper to taste to the carrot purée. Divide the purée among four warmed dinner plates, top each serving with two chicken breast halves and garnish with sprigs of watercress.

■ LATE-NIGHT SUPPER MENUS

## Virginia Fried Chicken with Cream Gravy

**To serve 4**

| | |
|---|---|
| ½ teaspoon salt | and skinned |
| ¼ teaspoon freshly ground black pepper | ½ to ¾ cup butter |
| ⅛ teaspoon freshly grated nutmeg | 1 to 2 tablespoons vegetable oil |
| Ground allspice | 1 cup chicken stock |
| ½ cup plus 2 tablespoons flour | 1 cup heavy cream |
| One 4-pound frying chicken, cut into 8 serving pieces | 1 teaspoon bourbon |
| | Parsley sprigs and chopped parsley for garnish |

Combine the salt, pepper, nutmeg, a pinch of allspice and ½ cup of the flour in a paper bag. Place a few pieces of chicken at a time in the bag, and shake to coat them with flour.

In a heavy 10- to 12-inch skillet, melt ½ cup of the butter with 1 tablespoon oil over moderately low heat. Do not let the butter burn. When the butter stops foaming, place the chicken in the skillet in one layer. Fry the chicken until golden brown—about five minutes a side—adding butter and oil if necessary.

Meanwhile, preheat the oven to 375°F. Remove the chicken

VIRGINIA FRIED CHICKEN WITH CREAM GRAVY

from the skillet, drain it on paper towels, and place it in one layer in a baking dish. Bake the chicken, uncovered, for 20 to 25 minutes or until the juices run clear when a thigh is pierced with a knife. A meat thermometer inserted in a thigh will register 180°F. when the chicken is done.

Meanwhile, drain all but 2 tablespoons of the fat from the skillet. Set the skillet over low heat and, stirring constantly with a wire whisk, add the remaining 2 tablespoons of flour. Still stirring, cook this roux for two minutes. Whisk in the chicken stock and scrape into this gravy mixture any browned bits clinging to the bottom and sides of the skillet. Stir in the cream and, stirring occasionally, cook the gravy for 15 minutes. Season it to taste with salt and pepper, then stir in the bourbon.

Serve the chicken from the baking dish or arrange it on a heated platter. Spoon some gravy over the chicken and pass the rest separately. If you like, garnish the chicken with parsley sprigs, and sprinkle chopped parsley over the gravy.

■ CHICKEN AND GAME HEN MENUS

## Lime-marinated Fried Chicken

*In the Dominican Republic, where this dish originated, hot boiled rice
usually accompanies it.* ❧

**To serve 4**

| | |
|---|---|
| ¼ cup dark rum | **wings, thighs, drumsticks** |
| ¼ cup fresh lime juice | **and breasts** |
| ¼ cup soy sauce | **2 cups vegetable oil** |
| One 3½- to 4-pound chicken, | **1 cup flour** |
| cut into 16 pieces by halving | |

Warm the rum in a small pan over low heat. Off the heat, ignite
the rum with a match and gently slide the pan back and forth
until the flame dies. Stir in the lime juice and soy sauce; pour the
mixture into a deep bowl. Add the chicken and turn the pieces
with a spoon to coat them. Marinate at room temperature for
about two hours or in the refrigerator for at least four hours, turning the pieces occasionally.

Preheat the oven to 200°F. and line a large, shallow baking dish
with paper towels. In a heavy 10- to 12-inch skillet, heat the oil
over high heat. Pat the chicken pieces dry with paper towels, dip
them in the flour, and tap off any excess. Fry five or six pieces of
chicken at a time for about five minutes on each side, or until
richly browned. Transfer them to the lined dish and keep them
warm in the oven.

Serve from a heated platter as soon as all the pieces are fried.

■ THE COOKING OF THE CARIBBEAN ISLANDS

## Blanquette of Chicken with Morels

**To serve 4**

| | |
|---|---|
| 2 pounds skinned, boned chicken breasts | well, or 2 ounces dried morels, soaked in water for 2 hours |
| 2½ cups chicken stock | ¼ cup unsalted butter |
| 1 rosemary sprig or ½ teaspoon crumbled dried rosemary, plus 4 rosemary sprigs for garnish | 1 tablespoon flour |
| | ½ cup heavy cream |
| | Salt |
| 6 ounces fresh morels, washed | Freshly ground white pepper |

Cut the chicken into 1-inch pieces and drop them into boiling water. Blanch the pieces for one minute or until they become opaque. Drain the chicken in a colander.

In a 4-quart stockpot, combine the stock and one rosemary sprig. Bring to a boil over moderate heat, and simmer for five minutes. Add the chicken, reduce the heat to low, and poach the chicken, uncovered, for 10 minutes or until barely tender.

Meanwhile, pat the morels completely dry. Melt 2 tablespoons of the butter in a 3- to 4-quart saucepan over moderate heat. When the foam subsides, add the morels and stir to coat them with butter. Remove the cover, increase the heat to moderate, and sauté the morels for a minute, stirring frequently. Add the morels and their pan juices to the chicken, and simmer the mixture for five minutes. With a slotted spoon, transfer the chicken and morels to a plate.

Boil the liquid left in the pan until it is reduced to about 1¼ cups. With a wire whisk, stir in the heavy cream. Blend the remaining 2 tablespoons of butter and the flour together with your fingers, and add this *beurre manié* to the simmering cream mixture. Whisk for about a minute until the sauce thickens. Then add the chicken and morels, and stir to combine them well with the sauce. Season to taste with salt and white pepper.

Serve the blanquette from a large heated bowl, garnishing it with the remaining rosemary sprigs if you like.

■ SOUP AND STEW MENUS

## Vermont Chicken Pie

**To serve 4 to 6**

| | |
|---|---|
| One 4½- to 5-pound roasting chicken rinsed, patted dry, cavity fat reserved and bird trussed | water |
| | 2 tablespoons butter |
| | 6 tablespoons flour |
| | ½ teaspoon freshly ground white pepper |
| 3 large onions, cut into ¼-inch slices | |
| 1 cup coarsely chopped celery, including green leaves | BISCUIT TOPPING |
| 1 bouquet garni made of 4 sprigs fresh parsley and 1 small bay leaf, tied together | 2 to 2¼ cups flour |
| | 1 tablespoon baking powder |
| | 1 teaspoon salt |
| ¼ teaspoon crumbled dried thyme | 2 tablespoons butter, cut into bits, plus ½ cup butter, melted |
| 1½ teaspoons salt | 2 tablespoons lard, cut into bits |
| Freshly ground black pepper | |
| 4 cups plus 2 tablespoons | ½ cup cold milk |

Place the bird in a heavy 6- to 8-quart flameproof casserole. Scatter the onions, celery, the bouquet garni, the thyme, 1 teaspoon of the salt and a few grindings of pepper around the chicken, and pour in 4 cups of the water.

Bring the water to a boil over high heat, reduce the heat to low, and cover the casserole. Poach the chicken for about one and one-quarter hours. The chicken is done when the juices run clear if a thigh is pierced with the tip of a sharp knife.

Transfer the chicken to a platter, and strain the cooking stock through a fine sieve into a bowl, pressing down on the vegetables and herbs with the back of a spoon to extract their juices before discarding them. Measure and reserve 2½ cups of stock. When the bird is cool enough to handle, remove the skin and pull the meat from the bones with your fingers or a small knife. Cut the meat into 1-inch pieces.

Drop the reserved chicken fat into a heavy 10- to 12-inch skillet, add 2 tablespoons of water, and cook over moderate heat, stirring frequently. When the bits render all of their fat, remove the residue with a slotted spoon and discard it.

Add 2 tablespoons of butter to the chicken fat, and melt it over moderate heat. When the foam begins to subside, stir in the flour and mix to a smooth paste with a whisk. Pour in the reserved chicken stock and, stirring constantly with the whisk, cook over high heat until the sauce comes to a boil, thickens heavily and is smooth. Reduce the heat to low and simmer, uncovered, for about five minutes.

Stir in ½ teaspoon of salt and the white pepper and taste for seasoning. Take the sauce off the heat, add the chicken pieces and stir gently but thoroughly. Pour the contents of the skillet into a 7-by-7-by-2-inch baking-serving dish, and spread the chicken pieces evenly.

To prepare the biscuits to top the pie, first preheat the oven to 450° F. Combine 2 cups of flour, the baking powder and 1 teaspoon of salt, and sift them into a large chilled bowl. Add the butter bits and lard and, with your fingertips, rub the flour and fat together until they look like flakes of coarse meal. Pour in the

milk and beat with a wooden spoon until the dough is smooth and can be gathered into a fairly dry, compact ball. If the dough remains moist and sticky, beat in up to ¼ cup more flour by the tablespoonful.

Place the dough on a lightly floured surface, and roll it out into a rough rectangle about ⅓ inch thick. With a biscuit cutter or the rim of a glass, cut the dough into 2-inch rounds. Gather up the scraps, roll them, and cut as many more rounds as you can. Ideally you should have 12 biscuits.

Place the biscuits, side by side, over the chicken in the baking dish, arranging them so that they cover the top completely. Brush the biscuits with the melted butter and bake in the middle of the oven for about 25 minutes, or until the biscuits have puffed and are golden brown. Serve at once, directly from the baking dish.

■ AMERICAN COOKING: NEW ENGLAND

## Chicken and Shrimp Basque Style

**To serve 4**

| | |
|---|---|
| One 2½- to 3-pound chicken, cut into 8 serving pieces | ½ pound boiled ham, cut into ¼-inch dice (about 1 cup) |
| ½ teaspoon salt | ¼ teaspoon paprika |
| ¼ teaspoon freshly ground black pepper | 1 cup dry white wine |
| ½ cup olive oil | ½ pound medium-sized shrimp, shelled and deveined |
| ¾ cup finely chopped onions | |
| 1½ teaspoons finely chopped garlic | 2 tablespoons chopped parsley leaves |
| 3 tablespoons flour | |

Season the pieces of chicken with the salt and pepper. In a heavy 10- to 12-inch nonreactive skillet, heat the olive oil over moderate heat. Add the chicken and cook the pieces for four or five minutes on each side, or until golden brown. Transfer the chicken to a 2½- to 3-quart flameproof casserole and set aside.

Drop the onions and garlic into the skillet, and cook over moderate heat until the onions are golden brown. Mix in the flour and, stirring constantly, cook for another minute or two. Stir in the ham and paprika, pour in the wine, and bring to a boil over high heat. Pour the mixture over the chicken, and set the casserole on high heat. Bring to a boil, tightly cover the casserole, reduce the heat, and simmer for 20 minutes or until the chicken is done: The juices will be a clear yellow when a thigh is pierced with the tip of a knife.

Place the shrimp on top of the chicken, cover the casserole, and cook for five minutes or until the shrimp are firm and opaque. Arrange the pieces of chicken and the shrimp attractively on a heated serving platter, and ladle the sauce in the casserole over them. Sprinkle with parsley and serve at once.

■ AMERICAN COOKING: THE MELTING POT

## Sautéed Chicken Breasts with Apricots

**To serve 4**

| | |
|---|---|
| ½ pound dried apricots | 1 shallot, chopped fine |
| ⅓ cup bourbon | 1 teaspoon tomato paste |
| ¾ cup chicken stock | 2 teaspoons grainy mustard |
| 1 teaspoon butter | ¼ cup pecans, toasted in a |
| 1 teaspoon safflower oil | 350°F. oven for 5 minutes, |
| 2 whole 1-pound chicken | then coarsely crushed with |
| breasts, skinned, boned and | a rolling pin |
| halved | 1 scallion, cut into 2-inch |
| ¼ teaspoon salt | pieces and sliced thin |
| Freshly ground black pepper | lengthwise |

Marinate the apricots in the bourbon and ¼ cup of the stock for eight hours or overnight. Or, bring the bourbon and ¼ cup of the stock to a boil, turn off the heat, and steep the apricots in the liquid until they soften—about 10 minutes.

Heat the butter and oil in a heavy 10- to 12-inch skillet over moderately high heat. Sauté the chicken breasts on one side for four minutes or until lightly colored. Turn them over and sprinkle with the salt and pepper. Sauté them on the second side for four minutes. Drain the apricots and pour the marinade over the chicken. Add the remaining ½ cup of stock, reduce the heat to low, and cook until the chicken feels firm but springy to the touch —about five minutes. Transfer the chicken to a plate, and cover it with aluminum foil to keep it warm.

Add the apricots and shallot to the skillet, and simmer for two minutes. Stir in the tomato paste and mustard, and simmer the sauce for three minutes, stirring occasionally. Return the breasts to the skillet for a minute, to heat them through.

Arrange the chicken and apricots on a warmed serving platter. Spoon the sauce over the chicken, and sprinkle with the pecans and scallion.

■ FRESH WAYS WITH POULTRY

## Arroz con Pollo

*In Spain, rice with chicken requires saffron—the stigma of a kind of crocus—which gives the rice a glorious golden hue and a unique musky taste. Although priced above all other spices, saffron is not expensive to use, because a few threads are all that are needed for most recipes.* ❦

**To serve 4**

| | |
|---|---|
| One 2½- to 3-pound chicken, | 1 tablespoon paprika |
| cut into 6 to 8 serving pieces | 1 cup finely chopped tomatoes |
| Salt | 1½ cups long-grain white rice |
| Freshly ground black pepper | 1 cup green peas |
| 1 tablespoon lard | 3 cups boiling water |
| ¼ pound salt pork, diced fine | ⅛ teaspoon crushed saffron |
| 1 cup finely chopped onions | threads |
| 1 teaspoon finely chopped | 2 tablespoons chopped fresh |
| garlic | parsley leaves |

Pat the chicken pieces dry with paper towels and sprinkle them with salt and a few grindings of pepper. In a heavy 4-quart casse-

role, melt the lard over moderate heat. Add the salt pork and, stirring frequently, cook until it has rendered all its fat and become crisp and golden brown; then, with a slotted spoon, transfer the dice to paper towels to drain. Add the chicken to the fat in the casserole and brown it quickly and evenly without burning. Set the chicken aside on a platter.

Pour off all but a thin film of fat from the casserole. Stir in the onions and garlic, and cook for about five minutes or until the onions are soft and transparent but not brown. Stir in the paprika, then the tomatoes, and bring to a boil, stirring frequently. Cook briskly, uncovered, for about five minutes or until most of the liquid in the pan evaporates and the mixture is thick enough to hold its shape in a spoon.

Return the chicken and pork dice to the casserole, and add the rice, peas, boiling water, saffron and 1 teaspoon of salt. Stir together gently but thoroughly. Bring to a boil over high heat, then reduce the heat to low, cover tight, and simmer for 20 to 30 minutes or until the chicken is tender and the rice has absorbed all of the liquid. Stir in the parsley, and taste for seasoning. Cover and let stand off the heat for five minutes before serving directly from the casserole.

■ THE COOKING OF SPAIN AND PORTUGAL

the chicken stock, and boil for one or two minutes, stirring constantly and scraping in any browned bits that cling to the pan.

Return the browned chicken to the skillet, add the oregano and bay leaf, and bring to a boil. Cover the skillet, reduce the heat, and simmer, basting occasionally. In about 30 minutes, the chicken should be done and its juice run clear when a thigh is pierced with the tip of a knife.

To serve, arrange the pieces of chicken on a heated platter. Discard the bay leaf, and boil the stock left in the skillet until it thickens slightly and has the intensity of flavor desired. Stir in the olives and anchovies, and cook for a minute or so longer. Pour the sauce over the chicken.

■ THE COOKING OF ITALY

## Red Pepper and Chicken Rolls

**To serve 4**

| | |
|---|---|
| 2 whole 1-pound chicken breasts, skinned, boned and halved | deribbed, cut into ¹/₂-inch strips and blanched for 2 minutes |
| ¹/₄ teaspoon salt | 2 tablespoons safflower oil |
| ¹/₂ teaspoon crushed Szechwan peppercorns or ¹/₄ teaspoon crushed black pepper | MIRIN SAUCE |
| 3 scallions, trimmed, blanched 30 seconds and halved lengthwise | 2 tablespoons *mirin* or dry sherry wine |
| | 3 tablespoons soy sauce |
| | 1 tablespoon sugar |
| 1 cucumber, peeled, halved lengthwise, seeded, cut into ¹/₄-inch-wide strips and blanched 30 seconds | 2 teaspoons rice vinegar |
| | ¹/₂ teaspoon crushed Szechwan peppercorns or ¹/₄ teaspoon crushed black pepper |
| 1 sweet red pepper, seeded, | 3 tablespoons water |

For the sauce, combine the *mirin*, soy sauce, sugar, vinegar, ¹/₂ teaspoon crushed Szechwan peppercorns and the water in a small bowl. Set aside.

Remove the long triangular fillet from each chicken breast half and set it aside for another use. Place the breast halves between sheets of wax paper and gently pound them about ¹/₄ inch thick with the flat of a cleaver or a meat pounder. Sprinkle the chicken with the salt and ¹/₂ teaspoon of crushed Szechwan peppercorns. Cut the scallions, cucumber strips, and pepper strips to fit across the grain of the meat of the breasts at the wide edge of each cutlet. Divide the scallions, cucumber strips, and pepper strips among the breasts. Roll the chicken around the vegetables, and fasten each roll lengthwise with a small skewer.

Heat the oil in a heavy 8- to 10-inch skillet over moderate heat and sauté the rolls—turning them frequently—for about four minutes or until they are golden. Transfer the chicken to a plate and stir the sauce into the skillet, scraping up brown bits from the bottom. Return the rolls to the skillet, cover it partially and simmer for eight minutes, turning the rolls once.

Transfer the chicken to a heated platter and remove the skewers. Pour the sauce over the rolls and serve immediately.

■ FRESH WAYS WITH POULTRY

RED PEPPER AND CHICKEN ROLLS

## Chicken with Anchovies and Olives

**To serve 4**

| | |
|---|---|
| One 2¹/₂- to 3-pound frying chicken, cut into 8 serving pieces | 2 tablespoons white-wine vinegar |
| Salt | ¹/₂ cup chicken stock |
| Freshly ground black pepper | ¹/₂ teaspoon crumbled dried oregano |
| 2 tablespoons olive oil | 1 bay leaf |
| ¹/₄ cup finely chopped onion | 1 tablespoon slivered black olives, preferably Mediterranean-style olives |
| 1 teaspoon finely chopped garlic | |
| ¹/₂ cup dry white wine | 3 flat anchovy fillets, chopped |

Pat the pieces of chicken completely dry with paper towels. Season the pieces with salt and a few grindings of pepper. In a heavy 10- to 12-inch skillet, heat the olive oil over moderate heat and brown the chicken on all sides. Transfer the pieces to a plate.

Pour off almost all of the fat from the skillet, leaving just a thin film on the bottom. Add the onions and garlic, and cook them over moderate heat, stirring frequently, for eight to 10 minutes or until they are lightly colored. Add the wine and vinegar, and boil briskly until the liquid is reduced to about ¹/₄ cup. Then pour in

## Oven-braised Chicken with Kumquats

**To serve 4**

| | |
|---|---|
| One 3-pound chicken, cut into 8 serving pieces<br>Salt<br>1 cup fresh orange juice<br>2 tablespoons fresh lemon juice<br>¼ cup honey | 2 tablespoons finely chopped seeded canned hot chilies<br>10 preserved kumquats<br>Orange or lemon slices for garnish |

Preheat the oven to 375°F. Sprinkle the chicken pieces with salt, and place them in a baking dish large enough to hold them in one layer. Mix the orange juice, lemon juice and honey, and pour them over the chicken, turning the pieces until they are well moistened. Arrange the chicken pieces skin side down, and scatter the chilies over them.

Bake the chicken, uncovered and undisturbed, for 15 minutes, then turn the pieces over and add the kumquats. Baste thoroughly with the pan liquid. Basting occasionally, bake the chicken for 15 minutes longer or until its juices run clear when a thigh is pierced with the tip of a knife. Serve from the baking dish or a heated platter, garnished with orange or lemon slices.
■ MIDDLE EASTERN COOKING

## Rock Cornish Hens in Herb Sauce

*The exotic-sounding pepitas that flavor and garnish this sauce are nothing but squash or pumpkin seeds. The tomatillos—sometimes called "tomates verdes"—look like little green tomatoes but belong to a different species and are often grown as ornamental garden plants under the name "husk tomato" or "ground cherry." The pepitas taste sweet, the tomatillos tart. Like the chilies, both of these ingredients are available wherever Latin American foods are sold.* ❧

**To serve 4**

| | |
|---|---|
| 1²/₃ cups chicken stock<br>Two 1½-pound Rock Cornish hens, quartered<br>½ cup unsalted hulled *pepitas*<br>14 to 18 fresh tomatillos, peeled, rinsed and patted dry, or one 13-ounce can tomatillos, rinsed and patted dry<br>2 slices homemade-style white bread, cubed | 3 large medium-hot green chilies, roasted, peeled, and seeded, or 3 canned chilies, rinsed<br>4 scallions, green tops only<br>1 cup coarsely chopped, packed fresh coriander leaves<br>1 cup packed chopped fresh mint leaves |

In a heavy 10- to 12-inch skillet, bring the stock to a boil over moderate heat. Add the hens to the stock, reduce the heat to low, cover, and simmer—turning the quarters once—for about 15 minutes. The hens are done when their juices run clear when a thigh is pierced with the tip of a knife.

Meanwhile, for the sauce, first toast 6 tablespoons of the *pepitas* in a small skillet over moderate heat, stirring them frequently for two to three minutes or until they puff up. (Some may "explode" like popcorn.) Set them aside to cool.

Place the tomatillos in a small saucepan with enough water to cover them. Bring to a boil, reduce the heat to low, and simmer for eight to 10 minutes or until they are soft but not falling apart. Drain and cool them.

In a food processor fitted with a metal blade or in a blender, grind the cubed bread to crumbs. Add the toasted *pepitas* and blend the mixture. One ingredient at a time, add the tomatillos, chilies, scallion tops, coriander and mint.

Remove the hens from the stock, and set them aside on a plate. Add the stock in which they have cooked to the mixture in the processor or blender. Return the hens to the skillet and pour the sauce over them. Bring the sauce to a boil over moderate heat, reduce the heat to low, and simmer the hens in the sauce for 10 minutes, turning them once.

To serve, arrange two hen quarters on each of four heated plates, and spoon some sauce over them. Garnish with the remaining *pepitas,* and present the remaining sauce separately.
■ MEXICAN MENUS

## Barbecued Rock Cornish Hens

**To serve 6**

| | |
|---|---|
| 6 Rock Cornish hens, rinsed and patted dry<br>6 small onions<br>Celery leaves<br>1½ cups butter<br>2 teaspoons crumbled dried tarragon leaves<br>1 teaspoon crumbled | dried thyme leaves<br>¼ cup fresh lemon juice<br>1 teaspoon paprika<br>1 teaspoon salt<br>Freshly ground black pepper |

Light charcoal in an outdoor grill equipped with a spit. Stuff the cavity of each hen with an onion and a few celery leaves. Tuck the wings behind the bird, and tie them together with kitchen string; tie the feet together. Impale the hens snugly, side by side, on the spit of the grill.

Put the butter in a small skillet or saucepan and sprinkle it with tarragon and thyme, rubbing the leaves between your fingers to release their flavor. Melt the butter over low heat, stirring to blend the herb flavors. Remove from the stove, and stir in the lemon juice, paprika, salt and several grindings of pepper.

Brush the hens liberally with the butter, set the spit in place on the grill, and start it rotating. Using a long-handled pastry brush, baste the hens frequently with the butter. Roast them for about 45 minutes or until the skin is well browned and the juices run clear when a thigh is pricked with the tip of a knife. Slide the hens off the spit and cut off any trussing string that has not burned away.
■ GREAT DINNERS FROM LIFE

# Honey-glazed Roast Turkey

**To serve 12**

**Salt**
**Freshly ground black pepper**
**One 12-pound turkey, rinsed and patted dry, neck, gizzard and heart reserved**
**1 cup water**
**2 tablespoons honey**

ORANGE AND SWEET POTATO
STUFFING

**Peel of 1 lemon, cut into julienne strips, plus ¼ cup fresh lemon juice**
**4 navel oranges, peeled, segments separated and halved, and peel of 2 cut into julienne strips**
**6 sweet potatoes, peeled and cut into ½-inch cubes**
**6 tablespoons unsalted butter**
**3 large onions, chopped**
**½ cup turkey or chicken stock**
**⅛ teaspoon salt**
**Freshly ground black pepper**
**½ teaspoon ground cloves**
**¾ teaspoon dry mustard**
**6 slices cracked-wheat bread,**

**cubed and lightly toasted in a 350°F. oven**
**2 tablespoons brandy**

PORT AND ORANGE GRAVY

**Turkey neck, gizzard and heart**
**1 tablespoon safflower oil**
**1 carrot, chopped**
**1 celery rib, chopped**
**2 onions, chopped**
**1 garlic clove, cut up**
**1 cup dry white wine**
**1 bay leaf**
**1 teaspoon chopped fresh thyme leaves or ¼ teaspoon crumbled dried thyme**
**3 cups water**
**1 cup turkey roasting juices, degreased**
**1 orange, peel grated and juice squeezed**
**1 tablespoon red-wine vinegar**
**2 tablespoons cornstarch**
**⅓ cup port wine**
**½ teaspoon salt**
**Freshly ground black pepper**

To prepare the stuffing, blanch the julienne strips of one lemon and two oranges in a cup of boiling water for one minute; drain. In a 4- to 5-quart pot, bring 8 cups of water to a boil. Drop in the sweet-potato cubes and blanch them for three minutes; drain and set aside with the julienne strips.

In a heavy 4- to 5-quart flameproof casserole, melt ¼ cup of the butter over moderately low heat. Add the onions and, stirring occasionally, cook until translucent—about 10 minutes. Add the lemon and orange strips, sweet potatoes, orange segments, lemon juice, stock, ⅛ teaspoon of salt and a few grindings of pepper. Cook for seven to 10 minutes, or until the sweet potato cubes are tender. Remove the casserole from the heat and add the

cloves, mustard, the remaining 2 tablespoons of butter, the bread cubes and the brandy. Mix thoroughly. Allow the stuffing to cool before using it.

To make a stock for the gravy, chop the turkey neck into pieces. Heat the oil in a heavy 3- to 4-quart saucepan over moderately high heat. Add the neck, gizzard, heart, carrot, celery, onions and garlic. Stirring frequently, cook the mixture for about five minutes, until the vegetables begin to brown. Add the white wine, bay leaf, thyme and 3 cups of water. Reduce the heat to low and simmer for one hour, skimming off scum and foam as necessary. Strain the stock through a fine sieve set over a deep bowl, pushing down on the meat and vegetables with the back of a spoon to extract all of the liquid. There should be 2 to 2½ cups; set aside.

Preheat the oven to 350°F. Rub ¾ teaspoon of salt and a few grindings of pepper inside the body and neck cavities of the turkey and over its skin. To stuff the turkey, loosely fill both cavities. Tie the drumsticks together with kitchen string, and tuck the wing tips under the bird. Put the turkey on a rack in a shallow roasting pan. Pour 1 cup of water into the pan.

To keep the turkey moist and prevent it from overbrowning, make a tent of aluminum foil. Use an extrawide sheet of foil (or two sheets of regular foil crimped together) that measures about 18 inches longer than the pan. Lay the foil, shiny side down, over the turkey, and tuck it loosely around the inside edges of the pan. Roast the turkey in the oven for two and one-half hours.

Take the turkey from the oven and carefully remove the foil tent. Brush the turkey all over with the honey. Reduce the heat to 325°F., then return the turkey to the oven. Roast it, uncovered, for one hour or until a meat thermometer inserted in the thickest part of the thigh reads 180°F. or the juices run clear when the tip of a knife pierces the thigh. There should be about 1 cup of roasting juices in the pan.

Let the turkey rest for at least 20 minutes to make carving easier. In the meantime, transfer the stuffing from the cavities to a bowl. Drape it with foil to keep it warm.

For the gravy, combine the reserved stock, roasting juices, the juice and peel of one orange, and the vinegar in a saucepan. Bring the mixture to a boil. Mix the cornstarch and the port, and whisk them into the saucepan; return the gravy to a boil. Reduce the heat to low and simmer for five minutes. Add ½ teaspoon of salt and a few grindings of pepper, and serve piping hot with the carved bird and the stuffing.

NOTE: To roast a larger turkey, increase the cooking time by 20 to 25 minutes per pound, and leave the foil tent on until one hour of cooking time remains. To cook the turkey unstuffed, rub orange peel and ¼ teaspoon of ground cloves inside the cavity for extra flavor, and subtract five minutes a pound from the total cooking time.

If you wish to cook the stuffing separately, put it in a buttered baking dish with an additional ¼ cup of stock. Cover the dish with foil and bake the stuffing in a preheated 325°F. oven for 45 minutes. Uncover the dish and return it to the oven to bake for another 45 minutes.

ROAST BREAST OF TURKEY WITH FRUIT STUFFING

## Roast Breast of Turkey with Fruit Stuffing

**To serve 8**

| | |
|---|---|
| One 4-pound turkey breast half, boned but not skinned | ¼ teaspoon ground cloves |
| ⅛ teaspoon salt | ¼ pound dried apricots, cut into small pieces |
| 1 tablespoon safflower oil | ⅓ cup seedless raisins |
| Curly-leaf kale, chopped fresh sage or parsley leaves for garnish | 3 tablespoons turkey or chicken stock |
| | ¼ cup sweet apple cider |

| FRUIT STUFFING | CIDER SAUCE |
|---|---|
| 2 tablespoons butter | 1 tablespoon finely chopped onion |
| ⅓ cup finely chopped onion | 2 tablespoons dry white wine |
| 1 large tart green apple, peeled, cored and diced | 1 cup sweet apple cider |
| 1 teaspoon sugar | ½ cup turkey or chicken stock |
| 1 teaspoon chopped fresh sage leaves or ¼ teaspoon rubbed dried sage | 1 teaspoon red-wine vinegar |

For the stuffing, melt the butter in a heavy 1- to 2-quart saucepan over moderate heat. Add the onion and cook, stirring occasionally, for five minutes, until translucent. Add the apple and sugar, and cook, stirring occasionally, for five minutes, until the apple is tender but not mushy. Stir in the sage, cloves, apricots, raisins, stock and cider. Reduce the heat, cover tight and cook until all of the liquid is absorbed by the dried fruit—about five minutes. Transfer the stuffing to a bowl and let it cool.

Preheat the oven to 350°F. Put the turkey breast, skin side down, on a working surface. With a sharp knife, cut a flap in the breast to make a pocket by slicing from the long, thin side toward the thicker side; do not cut all they way through. Open the flap and place the turkey between two pieces of wax paper. Pound lightly with the flat of a cleaver or a meat pounder to flatten the breast to a thickness of ½ inch; sprinkle with the salt, and mound the stuffing in the center. Wrap the flap around the stuffing and roll the breast snugly, skin side out, to form a cylinder. Tuck in the ends and tie securely with kitchen string.

Heat the oil in a roasting pan over moderate heat and brown the skin side of the roll for three to four minutes. Turn the turkey skin side up, and put the pan in the oven. Roast for 20 to 25 minutes or until the juices run clear when the roll is pierced deeply with the tip of a sharp knife. A meat thermometer inserted into the meat should register 180°F. Remove the turkey from the pan, and set it on a plate to rest for 10 minutes or so.

Meanwhile, for the sauce, pour off any fat left in the pan. Add the onion and wine, and cook over moderately high heat, stirring to scrape in any brown bits clinging to the pan. Add the cider, stock and vinegar, and cook for 10 minutes, until the sauce is reduced to 1 cup.

To serve, remove the kitchen string and slice the turkey. Arrange the slices on a heated serving platter and garnish them with curly-leaf kale. Pass the sauce separately.

■ FRESH WAYS WITH POULTRY

## Oyster Stuffing

**To stuff one 12-pound turkey**

| | |
|---|---|
| Two 1-pound loaves day-old homemade-type white bread, trimmed of crusts and torn into ½-inch pieces (about 10 cups) | 1 teaspoon salt |
| | ½ teaspoon freshly ground black pepper |
| ¾ cup chopped fresh parsley leaves | ½ pound butter, cut into bits |
| 2 tablespoons grated lemon peel | 3 cups finely chopped onions |
| | 3 cups finely chopped celery |
| 1 tablespoon crumbled dried sage leaves | 1½ pints shucked oysters, drained |
| | 1 egg, lightly beaten |

Combine the bread, chopped parsley, lemon peel, sage, salt and pepper in a large, deep bowl, and toss with a spoon or your hands until well mixed.

In a heavy 10- to 12-inch skillet, melt the ½ pound of butter over moderate heat. When the foam begins to subside, add the onions. Stirring frequently, cook for five minutes or until they are soft and translucent but not brown.

Stir in the celery and cook for a minute or so. Then, with a rubber spatula, scrape the contents of the skillet into the bread mixture. Add the oysters and egg, and mix the ingredients gently but thoroughly. Taste, and correct the seasoning.

■ AMERICAN COOKING: NEW ENGLAND

# Roast Duck with Cashew Stuffing

**To serve 4**

| | |
|---|---|
| ½ cup unsalted cashew nuts | 1 tablespoon vegetable oil |
| One 4½- to 5-pound duck, rinsed and patted dry; the liver, heart and gizzard chopped fine | ½ teaspoon ground cumin |
| | ½ teaspoon anise seeds |
| | 1 cup finely chopped onions |
| 3 teaspoons salt | 1 tablespoon finely chopped garlic |
| 1½ cups ½-inch bread cubes, made from homemade-type white bread with crusts removed | One 1-inch piece fresh ginger root, slivered thin |
| | ½ teaspoon ground turmeric |
| 2 hard-boiled eggs, quartered lengthwise | ½ teaspoon cardamom seeds, pulverized, or ½ teaspoon ground cardamom |
| 1 tablespoon seedless raisins | |
| 1 tablespoon finely chopped fresh coriander leaves | 1 cup chopped peeled, seeded tomatoes |
| 1 tablespoon sugar | 1 fresh hot 3-inch green chili, cut into ½-inch rounds |
| 2 tablespoons distilled white vinegar | ½ teaspoon cayenne pepper |
| 1 teaspoon coarsely ground black pepper | 2 tablespoons melted *ghee* or clarified butter |

In a small bowl or pan, soak the cashews in 2 cups of boiling water for at least 15 minutes. Rub the duck breast and neck cavity and the skin with 2 teaspoons of the salt; set aside.

Combine the bread, eggs, raisins, coriander, sugar, vinegar and black pepper in a deep bowl, and toss them about gently with a spoon or your hands until they are well mixed.

In a heavy 10- to 12-inch skillet, heat the vegetable oil over moderate heat. Stir in the cumin, anise, onions, garlic, ginger and 1 teaspoon of the salt. Stirring often, fry for seven or eight minutes, until the onions are soft and golden. Stirring after each addition, add the chopped duck liver, heart and gizzard, the turmeric, cardamom, tomatoes and green chili. Cook for three minutes, stirring, until the meats brown lightly.

With a rubber spatula, scrape the contents of the skillet over the bread and egg mixture. Stir gently to blend them.

Preheat the oven to 450°F. Drain the cashews in a sieve or colander and chop them fine. Stir the nuts and cayenne into the bread mixture. With a small skewer, gently prick the duck skin at 1-inch intervals all over its surface. Spoon the stuffing mixture loosely into the breast and neck cavities, and sew the openings securely.

Truss the bird securely and place it on its side on a rack in a shallow roasting pan. Roast in the middle of the oven for 10 minutes, then turn the duck onto its other side and roast for 10 minutes longer. Reduce the heat to 350°F., turn the duck breast side up, and roast it for about one hour and 40 minutes, basting the bird occasionally with the *ghee*.

The duck is done when its juices run clear if a thigh is pierced with the tip of a knife. Transfer the duck to a heated platter and let it rest for 10 minutes before carving.

■ THE COOKING OF INDIA

# Duck Breasts with Raspberries

*Some butchers sell halves of the breast—where most of a duck's meat lies—but it also is simple to cut them from the body. With a sharp boning knife, first remove the wings and legs close to the breast. Then make a deep incision along one side of the breastbone at a time. Keeping the knife blade against the ribs, use short strokes to cut a breast half away from the breastbone and rib cage in one piece. Set the wings, legs and bodies aside for another use.* ❧

**To serve 4**

| | |
|---|---|
| 4 boneless duck breast halves, with fat removed and skin left on | ½ cup heavy cream or crème fraîche (Index/Glossary) |
| 2 tablespoons vegetable oil | Cayenne pepper |
| Salt | 2 tablespoons unsalted butter, cut into bits |
| Freshly ground white pepper | |
| 1 tablespoon sugar | Curly-leaf kale, or chopped fresh chervil or thyme leaves, for garnish |
| 2 cups raspberries | |
| ½ cup bourbon | |

Lightly score a crosshatch pattern into the skin of each breast half, and pat the duck dry with paper towels. Preheat the oven to 200°F. Heat the vegetable oil over moderately high heat in a heavy 10- to 12-inch skillet or sauté pan. Add the duck breasts, skin side down. Without turning the breasts, cook them for seven to eight minutes, or until they are medium rare. (Cooking them skin side down the entire time will render the maximum amount of fat from the skin and at the same time prevent the flesh from becoming dry.) Place the breasts on a heatproof platter. Sprinkle them with salt and white pepper to taste, and keep them warm in the oven.

Pour off all but about a tablespoonful of the fat from the pan. Add the sugar and cook over moderate heat, stirring and scraping with a wooden spoon, until the sugar is lightly caramelized—two to three minutes. Add the raspberries and cook them just until they are coated with caramel and warmed through. Transfer the caramelized raspberries to a heatproof bowl, and keep them warm in the oven.

Add the bourbon to the pan. Over low heat, deglaze the pan by scraping up the brown bits from the bottom with the wooden spoon. If the bourbon bursts into flames, immediately cover the pan with its lid to extinguish them. Cook the bourbon until it is reduced by half. Add the cream and a pinch of cayenne, and simmer the sauce for two to three minutes. Correct the seasonings with more salt and white pepper if necessary. Add half of the raspberries, remove the sauce from the heat, and swirl the butter bits into it, a few at a time.

Spoon some of the sauce onto warmed individual dinner plates, and pour the remaining sauce into a warmed bowl or sauceboat. Slice each duck breast across the grain into five or six medallions, and arrange them on one of the plates. Garnish with the remaining raspberries and, if you like, curly-leaf kale, or chopped fresh chervil or thyme. Present the raspberry sauce separately.

■ AMERICAN REGIONAL MENUS

# Goose with Apple and Red Cabbage Stuffing

**To serve 6**

| | |
|---|---|
| One 10-pound goose, trimmed of fat, rinsed and patted dry; gizzard, heart and neck reserved | peeled, cored and cut into 8 wedges |
| ½ lemon | 2 tablespoons grated fresh ginger root |
| 1 teaspoon salt | 2 cups dry red wine |
| 3 red onions, sliced thin | ¼ cup red-wine vinegar |
| 7 cups water | ¼ cup sugar |
| 2 cups dry white wine | Freshly ground black pepper |
| 2 pounds red cabbage, quartered, cored and sliced thin | 12 small shallots |
| | 1 teaspoon cornstarch dissolved in 1 tablespoon water |
| 2 tart green apples, | |

Prick the skin of the goose all over with a trussing needle or small skewer, taking care not to penetrate the meat so that the juices do not seep out. Rub the goose inside and out with the lemon half, squeezing the lemon as you proceed. Rub the inside with ¼ teaspoon of the salt. Place half of the onion slices in the cavity of the goose. Tie the legs together with kitchen string, and tuck the wing tips under the back.

Pour 2 cups of the water and the white wine into a large, deep turkey roaster with a lid. Put a flat perforated rack in the pan and place a large plate on it. Set the goose, breast side down, on the plate. Cover, bring the liquid to a boil over high heat, and steam the goose for 10 minutes.

Reduce the heat to moderate so that the liquid bubbles gently but still steams, and cook the goose for 40 minutes more. Uncover the goose and prick its skin again. Steam it for one and a half hours more.

Transfer the goose to a platter. Pour the cooking liquid into a bowl. To cool the liquid, set the bowl in a larger bowl partially filled with ice cubes. When the liquid reaches room temperature, place the bowl in the freezer so that the fat congeals quickly.

While the goose is steaming, combine the gizzard, heart and neck, the remaining onion slices and 4 cups of the water in a 3- to 4-quart saucepan. Bring to a boil, reduce the heat, and simmer, uncovered, for about two hours. Strain this stock into another saucepan, and boil it over moderately high heat to reduce it to about 1 cup. Refrigerate the stock.

Meanwhile, make the stuffing: In a nonreactive 4- to 5-quart saucepan, first mix the cabbage, apples, ginger, 1 cup of the red wine, the remaining cup of water, the vinegar, sugar, ½ teaspoon of the salt and some pepper. Bring the liquid to a boil over moderately high heat, reduce the heat and simmer the mixture, uncovered, for 30 minutes. Add the shallots and cook for 30 minutes more. Drain all of the liquid from the stuffing and reserve it for preparing the sauce.

Preheat the oven to 325°F. Loosely fill the goose's breast and neck cavities with stuffing; close the openings with metal skewers. Sprinkle the remaining ¼ teaspoon of salt over the bird. Place the goose, breast side down, on a rack set in a large roasting pan,

ROAST SQUAB ON PÂTÉ CANAPÉS

and roast for 25 minutes. Turn the goose breast side up, and roast for 35 minutes more or until it browns richly and the juices run clear when a thigh is pierced with the tip of a knife. Place the goose on a heated platter and let it rest for 10 minutes before you carve it.

When the goose is roasting, prepare the sauce. Take the cooled cooking liquid from the freezer. Remove the fat from the top and spoon the liquid into a heavy 1- to 2-quart nonreactive saucepan. Remove any fat from the giblet stock and add the stock to the saucepan along with the drained stuffing liquid. Pour in the remaining cup of red wine, and cook the sauce over moderately high heat for about 35 minutes or until it is reduced to about 2 cups. Add the cornstarch mixture and whisk the sauce until it thickens. Spoon a little sauce around the goose and serve the rest in a gravy boat.

■ FRESH WAYS WITH POULTRY

# Roast Squab on Pâté Canapés

**To serve 6**

1 teaspoon crumbled dried
   tarragon leaves
1½ teaspoons salt
Freshly ground black pepper
2 tablespoons butter, cut into
   6 pieces, plus 6 tablespoons
   butter, softened
Six 12- to 16-ounce squabs,
   rinsed and patted dry
6 bacon slices, blanched in
   boiling water for 10 minutes
   and cut in half crosswise
¾ pound seedless green
   grapes, cut into
   6 clusters

PÂTÉ CANAPÉS
6 slices homemade-type

white bread
½ cup clarified butter
6 squab livers
¼ cup canned liver
   pâté
1 tablespoon Madeira wine
Salt
Freshly ground black
   pepper

MADEIRA SAUCE
1¾ cup beef stock
⅓ cup Madeira wine
1 tablespoon brandy
1 tablespoon butter,
   softened
1 tablespoon flour

Preheat the oven to 400°F. Mix the tarragon with the 1½ teaspoons salt and a few grindings of pepper, and put some of the tarragon mixture and one of the pieces of butter into the cavity of each squab. Truss the birds and rub each one with 1 tablespoon of the remaining butter. Tie two pieces of bacon over the breast of each bird. Place the squabs in a roasting pan, and roast them in the middle of the oven for 45 minutes to an hour, until they are browned and the juices run clear when a thigh is pierced with the tip of a knife. Baste them frequently with the pan drippings.

Meanwhile, for the canapés, first cut the bread into 2-by-3-inch rectangles. Heat the clarified butter in a skillet, add the bread, and fry it until golden on both sides. Drain the bread on paper towels. Then set the pieces on foil. Add the livers to the butter in the skillet, and cook over moderate heat for about two minutes or until they are firm and lightly browned. Transfer the livers and pan drippings to a small bowl; mash the livers well with a fork. Blend in the pâté, Madeira, and salt and pepper to taste. Spread the mixture on the bread pieces. Cover these canapés loosely with the foil and set them aside.

During the final 10 minutes of roasting time, open the foil wrapped canapés and set them in the oven. Place the grapes around the birds and baste them with the pan juices. When the squabs are done, take the birds and canapés out of the oven. Remove the bacon and cut off the trussing strings. Transfer the birds and grapes to a plate; cover to keep them warm. Cover the canapés again with foil.

Make a sauce in the roasting pan by first pouring off the fat. Add the stock, Madeira and brandy to the pan, and bring to a boil over moderate heat, stirring with a wooden spoon and scraping up the browned bits clinging to the pan. Boil until the liquid is reduced to about a cup. Work the 1 tablespoon of softened butter and 1 tablespoon of flour together with your fingers, add this *beurre manié* to the liquid, and stir for two minutes, or until the sauce thickens lightly.

To serve the squabs, place the hot pâté canapés on a warmed platter, set the birds on the canapés, and garnish the platter with the grapes. Spoon the sauce over all.
■ GREAT DINNERS FROM LIFE

# Duck Breasts with Red Wine and Juniper Berries

**To serve 6**

1 teaspoon safflower oil
6 boneless duck breast
   halves, skin and fat
   removed
¼ teaspoon salt

RED-WINE AND JUNIPER SAUCE
4 cups dry red wine
2 cups chicken stock
⅔ cup thinly sliced shallots
   or 1 cup sliced onion
½ teaspoon fennel seeds
1 tablespoon juniper berries,
   crushed with a mortar
   and pestle

8 black peppercorns
½ teaspoon chopped
   fresh thyme leaves or
   ¼ teaspoon crumbled dried
   thyme
1 bay leaf
2 tablespoons sugar
¼ cup balsamic vinegar
   or 3 tablespoons
   red-wine vinegar
2 garlic cloves, crushed
1 teaspoon honey
½ teaspoon cornstarch
   dissolved in 2 teaspoons
   water

First prepare the sauce: Combine the wine, stock, shallots, fennel, juniper, peppercorns, thyme and bay leaf in a nonreactive 2- to 3-quart saucepan, and cook over moderate heat for about 25 minutes or until the liquid is reduced by half.

Melt the sugar in a small heavy saucepan over low heat, stirring constantly with a wooden spoon until the sugar turns golden brown. Standing well back to avoid being splattered, add the vinegar all at once. Stir to dissolve the sugar, then add this mixture to the reduced wine mixture. Stir in the garlic and honey, and simmer the sauce for 10 minutes. Strain it, then return it to the pan. Cook the sauce, skimming occasionally, until it is reduced to about 1¼ cups. Stir in the cornstarch mixture, and cook until the sauce is thick and shiny—about one minute.

Heat the oil in a heavy 10- to 12-inch skillet over moderately high heat and sauté the duck breasts for five minutes. Turn them over, sprinkle with the salt, and cook for three minutes more. Remove the breasts from the skillet, set them aside, and keep them warm. Pour ¼ cup of water and ¼ cup of the sauce into the skillet—over moderate heat—and use a wooden spoon to scrape in the brown bits clinging to the bottom of the pan. Stir the deglazed pan juices into the sauce.

To serve, carve each breast half diagonally across the grain into about 10 slices and arrange them on heated individual plates or a heated platter. Spoon the hot sauce over the duck and present it immediately
■ FRESH WAYS WITH POULTRY

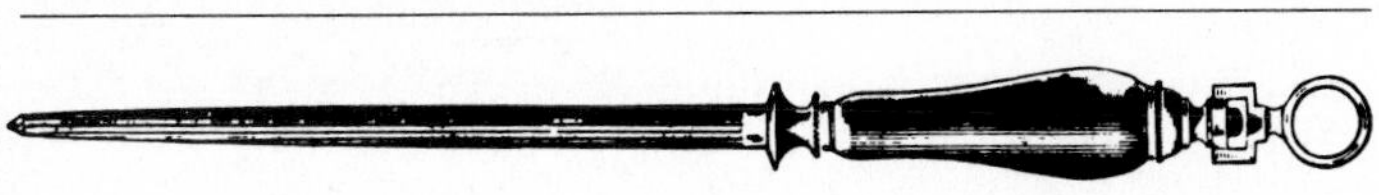

## Braised Stuffed Quail on Polenta Rounds

*An ancient Italian food, polenta is a type of porridge that cools into a firm mass suitable for cutting into rounds or other shapes. The Roman legions made it of wheat or millet; after about 1650, cornmeal became the grain of choice. In Venice and eastward, white cornmeal is used; elsewhere, polenta is made with yellow cornmeal.* ❧

**To serve 4**

| | |
|---|---|
| **Four 4- to 5-ounce quail, rinsed and patted dry** | **1 cup yellow or white cornmeal** |
| **Salt** | **2 tablespoons butter** |
| **Freshly ground black pepper** | **1 tablespoon vegetable oil** |
| **½ cup vegetable oil** | |
| **1 large onion, sliced thin** | PORK STUFFING |
| **2 tablespoons flour** | **3 tablespoons butter** |
| **½ cup Marsala wine** | **½ cup finely chopped onions** |
| **1½ cups chicken stock** | **1 teaspoon finely chopped garlic** |
| **Parsley sprigs for garnish** | **¾ pound ground pork** |
| POLENTA ROUNDS | **¼ cup chopped fresh parsley leaves** |
| **4 cups water** | **½ teaspoon salt** |
| **1 teaspoon salt** | |

First, prepare the *polenta*. Bring the water with 1 teaspoon of salt to a boil in a heavy 3- to 4-quart saucepan. Stirring constantly with a whisk, pour in the cornmeal in a slow, steady stream. Reduce the heat and simmer the *polenta,* stirring frequently, for 20 to 30 minutes, or until it is so thick that the whisk stands unsupported in the pan. Spoon the *polenta* evenly into an ungreased jelly-roll pan, and refrigerate it for about two hours, or until it is very firm.

For the stuffing, melt 3 tablespoons of butter in a 10- to 12-inch skillet over moderate heat. Drop in the chopped onions and garlic and, stirring frequently, cook for 10 minutes or until the onions are golden brown. Stir in the pork and cook until it shows no trace of pink. Add the parsley and ½ teaspoon of salt, and transfer to a large mixing bowl to cool.

Sprinkle the birds inside and out with a little salt and pepper, and stuff them with the cooled pork mixture. Close the cavities by sewing them with a large needle and heavy white thread, and truss the birds securely.

In a heavy 10- to 12-inch skillet, heat ½ cup of oil over moderate heat. Add the birds and, turning them with tongs or a spoon, brown them delicately on all sides. As they brown, transfer the birds to a 3- to 4-quart casserole. Drop the onion slices into the skillet and, stirring frequently, cook over moderate heat until they are soft and golden brown. Mix in the flour and—stirring constantly—pour in the Marsala and chicken stock. Bring to a boil over high heat, scraping in the brown particles that cling to the bottom and sides of the pan. Pour the contents of the skillet over the quail. Bring to a boil over high heat, then cover the casserole tight, reduce the heat to low, and simmer for 45 minutes.

Meanwhile, preheat the oven to 200°F. With a 3½- to 4-inch biscuit cutter or the rim of a glass, cut out four rounds from the chilled polenta. If you like, cut the edges of the rounds decoratively. In a 10- to 12-inch skillet, melt 2 tablespoons of butter with 1 tablespoon of oil over moderate heat. When the butter foam

subsides, add the *polenta* rounds and brown them delicately on both sides. Transfer them to an ovenproof platter and keep them warm in the oven.

To test the quail for doneness, pierce a thigh with the tip of a sharp knife. The juice that trickles out should be clear. Place each quail on a *polenta* round, pour the sauce in the casserole over the birds, garnish with parsley, and serve at once.

■ THE COOKING OF ITALY

## Hazelnut Turkey Cutlets

**To serve 4**

| | |
|---|---|
| **¾ cup hazelnuts, chopped fine** | **4 turkey cutlets, ½ inch thick, sliced from the breast** |
| **¾ cup dry bread crumbs** | **¼ cup olive or vegetable oil** |
| **½ cup flour** | **¼ cup butter** |
| **Salt** | **½ cup dry white wine** |
| **Freshly ground black pepper** | **¼ cup chopped fresh parsley leaves** |
| **2 eggs** | |
| **1 tablespoon water** | |

Combine the nuts with the bread crumbs on a sheet of wax paper. On a second sheet of wax paper, combine the flour with salt and pepper to taste. Break the eggs into a pie pan and, using a fork, beat them with the water until blended.

Arrange the turkey cutlets several inches apart between two sheets of wax paper and, with a meat pounder or the flat of a cleaver, pound them ¼ inch thick. If the cutlets are large, cut each one in half.

Dip one turkey cutlet at a time into the flour, and gently shake off the excess. Dip each cutlet into the eggs, then into the nut mixture, pressing gently to help the nut coating adhere. Arrange the cutlets in a single layer on a baking sheet, cover with plastic wrap, and refrigerate for at least 20 minutes to set the coating.

Preheat the oven to 200°F. In a heavy 10- to 12-inch skillet, heat the oil and butter over moderately high heat. When the butter's foam begins to subside, add as many cutlets to the skillet as will fit without crowding. Sauté them for three or four minutes on each side, or until they are lightly browned. As they brown, transfer the cutlets to an ovenproof serving platter and keep them warm in the oven. Repeat until all of the cutlets are sautéed.

Pour the wine into the skillet and cook it over high heat, using a wooden spoon to scrape up any brown bits clinging to the bottom of the pan. In three minutes or so, this sauce should be reduced to about ¼ cup. Stir the parsley into the sauce, pour it over the cutlets and serve them at once.

■ TURKEY AND DUCK MENUS

## Pheasant Breasts with Pears en Papillote

*The breasts of pheasants are removed by the technique used for ducks in duck breasts with raspberries (page 98). Cooking them in parchment paper—en papillote—gives an extra flourish to their presentation, and is practical besides. The parchment holds in all of the juices—and keeps the breasts warm for a while when dinner must wait.* ❧

**To serve 4**

| | |
|---|---|
| 1 tablespoon safflower oil | 1 shallot, chopped fine |
| 1 garlic clove, crushed | ½ cup pear-flavored liqueur |
| 4 boneless pheasant breast halves, skinned | 2 pears, quartered, cored and cut lengthwise into ¼-inch wedges |
| ¼ teaspoon salt | ½ cup chicken stock |
| Freshly ground black pepper | 2 teaspoons chopped fresh parsley leaves |
| 1 tablespoon finely chopped fresh ginger root | |

Heat the oil in a heavy 10- to 12-inch skillet over moderately high heat. Rub the garlic clove over both sides of the pheasant breasts, then brown them for one minute. Turn them over and sprinkle with the salt and some pepper. Brown the breasts for one minute, then set them aside on a plate.

Preheat the oven to 375° F. Add the ginger and shallot to the skillet, and cook them over low heat, stirring frequently, until the shallot is translucent—about two minutes. Take the skillet off the heat and stir in the pear liqueur. Return the skillet to the heat and simmer, stirring often, for three or four minutes, to reduce the liquid to about 3 tablespoons. Add the pear wedges, and toss gently to coat them with liqueur. Pour in the stock and simmer for three minutes or until the liquid is reduced by half. Remove the pan from the heat.

Cut four sheets of baking parchment or aluminum foil into 12-inch squares. Place a breast diagonally in the center of each square; spoon one-fourth of the pears and sauce over each breast. Sprinkle ½ teaspoon of the parsley over each. Lift one corner of a square and fold it over to the opposite corner, forming a triangular *papillote*. To seal the meat within, crimp the two open sides of the triangle by making overlapping folds in the paper. Repeat the process to enclose the other breasts.

Bake the *papillotes* on a baking sheet for eight to 10 minutes. Put the *papillotes* on individual plates and let each diner open his or her own to savor the aroma.

■ FRESH WAYS WITH POULTRY

## Roast Pheasant with Hazelnut Stuffing

**To serve 4**

| | |
|---|---|
| One 3- to 3½-pound pheasant, rinsed and patted dry | 6 tablespoons butter, softened |
| 2 tablespoons julienne strips orange peel | 5 slices homemade-type white bread, crusts trimmed, cut into dice |
| 1 tablespoon julienne strips lemon peel | ½ cup finely chopped celery |
| 1¼ cups chicken stock | 1 cup finely chopped onions |
| 2 tablespoons currant jelly | ½ cup hazelnuts, ground in nut grinder or food processor |
| 2 tablespoons port wine | ¼ teaspoon rubbed dried sage |
| 1 tablespoon cornstarch | 1 teaspoon salt |
| Curly-leaf lettuce | Freshly ground black pepper |
| Limequats or kumquats | |
| HAZELNUT STUFFING | |
| 9 tablespoons butter, plus | |

Preheat the oven to 400° F. To make the stuffing, melt ½ cup of the butter over moderate heat in a heavy 8- to 10-inch skillet and in it brown the bread cubes. With a slotted spoon, transfer the cubes to a deep bowl.

ROAST PHEASANT WITH HAZELNUT STUFFING

When the pheasant is done, transfer it to a heated platter. Remove the trussing strings, and drape the platter loosely with foil to keep the bird warm. With a large spoon, skim as much fat as possible from the pan juices. Add 1 cup of the stock, the remaining onion, the currant jelly and the port. Bring this sauce mixture to a boil, scraping in the brown bits that cling to the bottom and sides of the pan. Reduce the heat to low and simmer uncovered for five minutes.

Dissolve the cornstarch in the remaining chicken stock, and stir it into the simmering sauce. Stir until the sauce comes to a boil, thickens, and becomes clear. Strain the sauce through a fine sieve into a sauceboat or gravy bowl, and stir in the reserved orange and lemon peel. Taste for seasoning and add more salt and pepper if necessary.

Serve the pheasant at once, garnished if you like with curly-leaf lettuce and limequats, and accompanied by the sauce.

■ AMERICAN COOKING: THE EASTERN HEARTLAND

## Twice-cooked Quail

**To serve 4**

| | |
|---|---|
| Eight 4- to 5-ounce quail, rinsed and patted dry | crumbled dried rosemary |
| ½ teaspoon salt | 2 garlic cloves, sliced thin |
| Freshly ground black pepper | 1½ tablespoons safflower oil |
| 8 small sprigs fresh rosemary or ½ teaspoon | 2 cups chicken stock, reduced by boiling to 1 cup |
| | 1 tablespoon Madeira wine |

Preheat the oven to 450° F. Season the cavity of each quail with salt and pepper; divide among them the rosemary and garlic. Truss one bird at a time by placing it on its back lengthwise over a 9- or 10-inch piece of kitchen string. Pull the ends of the string over the center of the breast and knot them. Push the drumsticks under the string.

With a pastry brush, spread ½ tablespoon of the oil over the bottom of a flameproof roasting pan large enough to hold the quail snugly. Brush the remaining oil over the quail, and place them in the pan, breast side up. Roast them for 20 minutes without basting.

Combine the stock with the Madeira, and pour this mixture over the birds. Place the pan on the stove top over moderate heat. Simmer the stock for two to three minutes, at the same time turning the birds over and over in the liquid. Cut the strings and remove them from the birds.

Place two quail on each of four heated plates, and moisten each bird with about 2 tablespoons of the sauce from the pan. Rotate each plate to distribute the sauce evenly around the quail. Serve the birds immediately.

■ **FRESH WAYS WITH POULTRY**

Add 1 tablespoon of butter to the skillet with the celery and ½ cup of the onions. Stirring frequently, cook over moderate heat for five minutes, or until the vegetables are soft but not brown. With a rubber spatula, scrape them over the bread cubes. Add the hazelnuts, sage, salt and a little pepper, and toss together gently but thoroughly.

Fill the cavity of the pheasant loosely with the stuffing, and close the opening by lacing it with small skewers and cord or sewing it with heavy white thread. Fasten the neck skin to the back of the pheasant with a skewer and truss the bird neatly. With a pastry brush, spread ¼ cup of the softened butter evenly over the skin.

Lay the bird on its side on a rack set in a shallow roasting pan. Roast the pheasant for 10 minutes. Turn it over, brush it with the remaining softened butter, and roast it for 10 minutes. Then turn the bird breast side up and baste it with the pan juices. Continue roasting for 20 to 30 minutes or until the juices run clear when a thigh is pierced with the tip of a knife. Baste the bird with pan juices every 10 minutes.

Meanwhile, blanch the orange and lemon peel in boiling water for five minutes. Drain in a sieve and run cold water over the peel to set the color; reserve the peel.

# Meats

# Meats

FRONTISPIECE: CROWN PORK ROAST WITH SAUSAGE-APPLE STUFFING,
SWEET POTATOES IN ORANGE BASKETS (RECIPE, PAGE 237)

**W**ith premium cuts of meat, the cook's greatest challenge is to roast, sauté or grill them *au point*—just to the instant when they are perfectly done. For beef, lamb and venison, that instant comes when they are a rich mahogany color outside, but still crimson or pink inside; liver and kidney, too, are juiciest when a stroke of the knife reveals rosy meat. For veal, pork and rabbit, the meat is best when cooked until the interior is white and piercing it with a knife tip draws clear liquid untinged by pink.

Creative cooking is never out of order, and a sauce or stuffing endows a loin or leg with an especially rich finish or an unexpected flavor. And a friendly butcher makes it possible to transform even chops into a presentation as memorable as a crown roast.

Lesser cuts benefit from more complicated treatments designed to bring out their taste and to tenderize them. Browning followed by simmering in liquid kept at a bare ripple, or "smile," as the French chef Louis Diat once put it, flavors and softens tough beef chuck and lamb shoulder. The same effect can be achieved by steeping meat in a marinade for hours before cooking; sauerbraten reaches its peak after days of marination. A marinade can be any acidic liquid such as wine, vinegar or citrus juice—or a fermented dairy product such as yogurt or buttermilk. Augmented by seasonings, the marinade then provides the basis for a splendid sauce.

## Monterey Beef Roast

**To serve 4**

| | |
|---|---|
| **One 2- to 3-pound rib-eye beef roast** | **2 to 3 cups coarse (kosher) salt** |
| **½ cup Dijon mustard** | |

In a grill, light a mound of charcoal that you can later spread into a layer about 2 inches deep and an inch or so larger all around than the roast. An electric starter is convenient, but avoid petroleum-based liquid or jelly fire starters that may flavor the beef. Let the charcoal burn for 20 to 30 minutes or until a white ash appears on the surface, then spread the coals.

Meanwhile, using a metal spatula, coat the beef evenly with a thick layer of mustard. Pat on as much salt as will cling to the mustard. When the coals are ready, gently place the roast directly on top of them. Using tongs, turn the beef 90 degrees every 10 minutes; spread the coals each time so that the meal always rests on fresh coals. Cook the beef for 25 to 30 minutes for rare (an internal temperature of 130°F.), 30 to 35 minutes for medium rare (140°F.), and 35 to 40 minutes for well done (150°F.). Transfer the beef to a platter and break off the now-hardened salt layer. Let the beef rest for 10 minutes before carving it.

■ PICNIC AND OUTDOOR MENUS

## Poached Beef Tenderloin

*This French technique for poaching tenderloin on a string, or "à la ficelle," ensures the flavor and succulence of this costly cut providing it is poached briefly and served rare.* ◆●

**To serve 4**

| | |
|---|---|
| **5 cups beef stock** | **thyme leaves or ½ teaspoon crumbled dried thyme** |
| **5 cups water** | |
| **1 large shallot** | **½ small bay leaf, crumbled** |
| **1 small garlic clove** | **1½ to 2 pounds beef** |
| **1 celery rib, trimmed** | **tenderloin, in one piece,** |
| **1 large carrot, quartered** | **tied, with one end of string** |
| **Leaves of 6 fresh** | **left loose as a handle** |
| **parsley sprigs** | **1 cup Béarnaise sauce** |
| **1 teaspoon chopped fresh** | **(Index/Glossary)** |

In a heavy 4- to 5-quart casserole or saucepan, combine the stock, water, shallot, garlic, celery, carrot, parsley, thyme and bay leaf. Bring the liquid to a boil over high heat. Immerse the tenderloin in the poaching liquid and tie the loose string to a handle of the casserole or to a wooden spoon long enough to suspend over the top so that the meat does not touch the bottom of the casserole. If the meat is not covered by 1 inch, add boiling stock or water.

Over high heat, bring the liquid to a boil again, and boil the tenderloin for three minutes, until it loses its raw pink color. Reduce the heat to a simmer, and poach the tenderloin, uncovered, for 15 minutes. With the string, lift the beef out of the liquid and set it on a heated platter. Untie the string and let the tender-

loin rest for 10 minutes. (Let the cooking liquid cool, strain and save it for another use.)

To serve, slice the meat crosswise into four medallions. Present the Béarnaise sauce separately in a bowl.

■ BEEF AND VEAL MENUS

## Curried Boneless Beef Roast

**To serve 6 to 8**

| | |
|---|---|
| **¼ cup fresh lemon juice** | **pomegranate seeds** |
| **3 tablespoons coarse (kosher) salt or 2 tablespoons table salt** | **1 tablespoon chopped garlic** |
| | **1 tablespoon coarsely chopped scraped fresh ginger root** |
| **½ teaspoon coarsely ground black pepper** | |
| **¼ teaspoon cayenne pepper** | **1 tablespoon black mustard seeds** |
| **One 5- to 5½-pound boneless sirloin roast about 5½ inches in diameter, tied securely at 1-inch intervals** | **8 cloves** |
| | **One 1-inch piece stick cinnamon, crushed** |
| | **1 teaspoon fennel seeds** |
| **6 tablespoons *ghee* or clarified butter, melted** | **¼ teaspoon cardamom seeds** |
| | **½ teaspoon coriander seeds** |
| SPICE MARINADE | **½ teaspoon cumin seeds** |
| **¼ cup coarsely chopped onions** | **1 teaspoon crumbled saffron threads soaked in ¼ cup boiling water for 10 minutes** |
| **¼ cup plain yogurt** | |
| **1 tablespoon dried** | |

Mix the lemon juice, coarse salt, black pepper and cayenne together. Rub the mixture evenly over the surface of the beef and place it in a large bowl. With a long needlelike skewer, make perforations completely through the roast at ¼-inch intervals all over its surface. Then rub the beef with 2 tablespoons of the melted *ghee*, and set it aside.

To prepare the spice marinade, or *masala*, first combine the onions, yogurt, pomegranate seeds, garlic, ginger, mustard seeds, cloves, cinnamon, fennel, cardamom, coriander and cumin in a food processor or blender. Purée the mixture until smooth, stopping the machine once or twice to scrape down the sides of the bowl with a rubber spatula. Stir in the saffron and the water it has soaked in.

With your fingers, rub the mixture over the roast, and again perforate it. Cover the bowl with plastic wrap, and marinate the roast at room temperature for at least 12 hours or in the refrigerator overnight.

Preheat the oven to 450°F. Place the beef, fat side up, on a rack in a shallow roasting pan, and place it in the middle of the oven. After 15 minutes reduce the heat to 350°F. Basting the beef occasionally with the remaining melted *ghee,* roast it for 30 minutes a pound, or until it is well done and registers 150°F. on a meat thermometer.

Transfer the roast to a heated platter, carve it into slices ¼-inch thick, and serve at once.

■ THE COOKING OF INDIA

## Beef and Onions Braised in Beer

**To serve 6 to 8**

| | |
|---|---|
| 5 tablespoons butter | 1½ cups meat stock |
| 7 cups thinly sliced onions | 1½ teaspoons brown sugar |
| ¼ pound salt pork with rind removed, diced | 1 tablespoon vinegar |
| 3 pounds lean boneless beef chuck or rump, cut into 2-inch chunks | 1 teaspoon finely chopped garlic |
| | 1 teaspoon crumbled dried thyme |
| Bouquet garni made of 4 parsley sprigs and 1 bay leaf, tied together | Salt |
| | Freshly ground black pepper |
| 3 tablespoons flour | 2 tablespoons finely chopped fresh parsley leaves |
| 2 to 3 cups light beer | |

In a heavy 10- to 12-inch skillet, melt ¼ cup of the butter over moderate heat. Add the onions and cook them over very low heat, turning them frequently with a wooden spoon, for about 30 minutes or until they are limp and lightly colored. Set aside.

Meanwhile, to remove excess saltiness, blanch the pork dice in boiling water for five minutes. Drain them on paper towels and pat them dry. In another 10- to 12-inch skillet, melt the remaining tablespoon of butter over moderate heat, and in it brown the pork dice, stirring them frequently, until they are crisp. Remove them with a slotted spoon; drain the dice on paper towels. Pour off into a small bowl all but a few tablespoonfuls of the fat.

Pat the chunks of beef dry with paper towels, then brown them in the rendered fat—a handful at a time to avoid crowding the skillet. Add more pork fat to the skillet as needed. When the chunks are a rich brown on all sides, use the slotted spoon to transfer them to a heavy, flameproof 3- to 4-quart casserole. Bury the bouquet garni in the meat.

Preheat the oven to 350° F. After all of the meat is browned, stir the flour into the fat remaining in the skillet. Over very low heat, stirring constantly with a wire whisk, cook this roux until it is amber colored, being careful not to let it burn. Slowly pour in the beer and beef stock, and beat vigorously with the whisk until the roux and liquid blend.

Bring this sauce to a boil over moderate heat, whisking constantly as it thickens. Boil for one minute, then mix in the brown sugar, vinegar, garlic and thyme, and simmer over low heat for two or three minutes. Taste the sauce and season it with salt and pepper if needed.

When the onions are done, add them to the casserole, and pour the sauce over the onions and meat, stirring the mixture gently. The sauce should nearly cover the meat; add more beer if needed. Bring the sauce to a boil over moderate heat, cover the casserole, and set it in the oven. Cook for one and one-half hours or until the meat is tender.

Before serving, let the stew cool for a few minutes. Then skim off the surface fat, discard the bouquet garni, and taste the sauce for seasoning. Sprinkle the stew with the crisp pork bits and garnish with chopped parsley.

■ THE COOKING OF PROVINCIAL FRANCE

## Steak au Poivre

**To serve 4**

| | |
|---|---|
| **Four 6-ounce boneless shell steaks, 1 inch thick** | **Salt** |
| **3 tablespoons black peppercorns, coarsely crushed** | **¼ cup Cognac** |
| | **1½ cups beef stock** |
| **3 tablespoons clarified butter** | **2 tablespoons unsalted butter, chilled and cut into bits** |

Pat the steaks dry with paper towels. One at a time, sprinkle both sides of the steaks with about 2 teaspoons of the crushed pepper-corns, pushing them firmly into the meat with your hands. In a 12-inch sauté pan or heavy skillet, warm the clarified butter over high heat for 10 seconds. Place the steaks in the pan and sauté them for two or three minutes. Turn them with a metal spatula, sprinkle salt on each, and sauté for two minutes longer, or until the steaks are done to your taste. If you undercook the steaks slightly, they will continue to cook while you prepare the sauce.) Transfer the steaks to a heated platter and set them aside.

Pour the Cognac down the side of the pan into the remaining fat. Let the Cognac warm for a few seconds and—if it does not flame spontaneously—ignite it with a match. Slide the pan gently back and forth until the flames die. Pour in the stock and bring it to a boil over high heat, scraping in the brown particles that cling to the bottom of the pan. Taste for seasoning, strain the sauce into a small saucepan, and reheat. Remove the sauce from the heat and beat in the chilled butter bits.

Pour the sauce over the steaks and serve at once.

■ CLASSIC FRENCH COOKING

## Sukiyaki

*The distinctive ingredients of this famed Japanese recipe sound more exotic than they are—and all can be obtained at most supermarkets as well as in stores specializing in Asian foods. Shirataki are long noodles made from a tuber somewhat like a yam; tofu is soybean curd; sake is rice wine, which is sold at liquor stores.* ❖●

**To serve 4**

| | |
|---|---|
| **1 pound boneless lean beef, preferably tenderloin or sirloin** | **2 cakes tofu, cut into 1-inch cubes** |
| **One 8-ounce can *shirataki*** | **½ cup watercress leaves or thinly sliced Chinese cabbage** |
| **1 whole canned bamboo shoot** | |
| **6 scallions, including 3 inches of green top, cut into 1½-inch pieces** | **One 2-by-1- inch strip of beef fat, folded into a square packet** |
| **1 onion, sliced ½ inch thick** | **¾ cup Japanese all-purpose soy sauce** |
| **4 to 6 small white mushrooms, trimmed and sliced ¼ inch thick** | **1 tablespoon sugar** |
| | **¾ cup sake** |

Freeze the beef for about 30 minutes to stiffen it slightly for easier slicing. With a heavy, sharp knife, cut the beef against the grain into ⅛-inch slices. Cut the slices in half crosswise.

**TOURNEDOS WITH ROQUEFORT BUTTER**

Bring 1 cup of water to a boil and drop in the *shirataki;* return the water to a boil. Immediately drain the noodles, then cut them into thirds. Scrape the base of the bamboo shoot, halve the shoot lengthwise, and cut it crosswise into thin slices. Rinse the slices under cold running water.

Arrange the beef, *shirataki,* bamboo shoot, scallions, onion, mushrooms, tofu, and watercress leaves attractively in separate rows on a large platter.

Set the heating unit you will use in the center of the dining table. If it is an electric skillet, preheat it to 425°F. If you will use a 10- to 12-inch skillet set over a table burner, preheat the skillet in the kitchen for several minutes.

To start the sukiyaki, hold the folded strip of fat with chop-sticks or tongs and rub it over the bottom of the hot skillet. Add six to eight slices of the meat to the skillet, pour in ¼ cup of the soy sauce, and sprinkle the meat with 1 teaspoon of the sugar. Cook for a minute, stir, and turn the meat over. Push the meat to one side of the skillet. Add about one-third each of the *shirataki,* bamboo shoot, scallions, onion, mushrooms, tofu and greens, sprinkle them with ¼ cup of the sake and cook for an additional four to five minutes.

With chopsticks or a serving spoon, divide the contents of the pan among four heated individual plates and serve them. Cook the remaining sukiyaki in two batches, checking the temperature of the pan from time to time. If it gets too hot and food begins to stick or burn, reduce the heat or cool the pan more quickly by adding a little cold water to the sauce.

■ THE COOKING OF JAPAN

## Tournedos with Roquefort Butter

*The nomenclature for different cuts of the beef tenderloin is complex. The widest section, or butt, often provides a small roast; next to it is the châteaubriand section, also often reserved as a small roast; the section following produces tenderloin steaks also known as "filets mignons," "tournedos," and "medallions"; the narrow end is the tip.* ❧

**To serve 4**

| | |
|---|---|
| 3 ounces Roquefort cheese | CROÛTES WITH SHALLOT- |
| 6½ tablespoons butter | PARSLEY TOPPING |
| ⅛ teaspoon finely | **2 tablespoons finely chopped** |
| chopped garlic | **shallots** |
| Freshly ground allspice | ½ teaspoon finely chopped |
| Cayenne pepper (optional) | garlic |
| 2 teaspoons finely cut | 3 tablespoons dry white |
| fresh chives | wine |
| 1 teaspoon chopped fresh | ¼ cup butter, cut into bits |
| thyme leaves or ¼ teaspoon | ¼ cup coarsely chopped fresh |
| crumbled dried thyme, plus | parsley leaves |
| 4 thyme sprigs for garnish | 1 tablespoon Dijon mustard |
| 1½ tablespoons olive oil | Freshly ground allspice |
| Four 8-ounce tournedos, | Freshly ground white pepper |
| 1½ inches thick | 1 cup olive oil |
| Salt | Eight ¾-inch-thick slices |
| Freshly ground black pepper | French or Italian white |
| ½ sweet red pepper, seeded, | bread, cut diagonally |
| deribbed and cut into | from loaf |
| ¼-inch rings, for garnish | |

Ahead of time, prepare the topping for the croûtes. In a small nonreactive saucepan, combine the shallots, ½ teaspoon of garlic and the wine. Bring to a boil over moderate heat and simmer over low heat until the wine evaporates—four or five minutes. With a rubber spatula, scrape the shallot mixture into a food processor or blender. Let the shallots cool briefly, then add the butter bits, parsley, mustard, a pinch of allspice and white pepper to taste. Blend until smooth, then scrape the mixture into a small bowl and refrigerate it.

To prepare the Roquefort butter, combine the cheese, 5 tablespoons of the butter, ⅛ teaspoon of garlic, a pinch of allspice and, if you are using it, a pinch of cayenne in the processor or blender. Blend until smooth, stopping once to scrape down the sides of the bowl with the rubber spatula. Using the spatula, transfer the mixture to a small bowl and blend in the chives and thyme. Refrigerate the butter.

With a large, sharp knife, butterfly each steak by slicing horizontally through the middle, leaving a ½-inch uncut hinge on one side of each steak.

In a 10- to 12-inch sauté pan or heavy skillet, melt the remaining 1½ tablespoons of butter with 1½ tablespoons of oil over moder-

ate heat. Increase the heat to high and sear each tournedos on both sides, opening it at the hinges to sear the inside. Using two metal spatulas, tilt each tournedos to sear any raw edges. Be careful not to pierce the meat or its juices might escape.

Close all of the tournedos, reduce the heat to moderate, and cook the steaks for one to two minutes per side for rare, three minutes for medium, and four to five minutes for well done. Working quickly, open the tournedos and spoon a portion of Roquefort butter into the center of each. Close the steak and season it with salt and pepper.

Meanwhile, prepare the croûtes. Heat 1 cup of olive oil in a large skillet until it is very hot but not smoking—325°F. on a deep-frying thermometer. Fry four bread slices at a time for about 20 seconds on each side or until they are golden. With a slotted spoon, transfer the slices to a wire rack lined with paper towels to drain. Then spread the croûtes with the shallot-parsley topping.

Serve the tournedos on heated individual plates, accompanied by the croûtes. Garnish each steak with a slice of red pepper and a sprig of thyme, if you like.

■ BEEF AND VEAL MENUS

## Pan-broiled Steak with Tomatoes and Garlic

**To serve 4**

| | |
|---|---|
| ¼ cup olive oil | Salt |
| 1 teaspoon finely | Freshly ground black |
| chopped garlic | pepper |
| 2 cups peeled, seeded and | One 3-pound beef T-bone, |
| coarsely chopped tomatoes | porterhouse or sirloin |
| 1 teaspoon crumbled | steak, 1 inch thick |
| dried oregano | |

Heat 2 tablespoons of the olive oil in a heavy 8- to 10-inch skillet or saucepan over moderate heat. Remove the pan from the heat, add the garlic and, with a wooden spoon, stir it for about 30 seconds. Add the tomatoes, oregano, ½ teaspoon of salt and a few grindings of pepper, and cook over moderate heat, stirring frequently. In about five minutes most of the tomato liquid will have boiled away. Remove the pan from the heat.

In a heavy 10- to 12-inch skillet, heat the remaining 2 tablespoons of olive oil. Over high heat, brown the steak in the oil for one to two minutes on each side, turning it with kitchen tongs. Reduce the heat to moderate and spoon the tomato sauce over and around the meat. Cover and cook for three or four minutes or until the steak is done to your taste. (You can make a small incision near the bone with the tip of a sharp knife and judge by the redness of the meat.)

To serve, scrape off the tomato sauce and transfer the steak to a carving board. Simmer the sauce for one to two minutes, scraping in any browned bits of meat clinging to the bottom of the skillet. Taste for seasoning. Carve the steak, arrange the slices on a heated platter and moisten each slice with a little sauce.

■ THE COOKING OF ITALY

## New England Boiled Dinner

*Vegetables to complement the corned beef of this old-fashioned American favorite can also include rutabaga, turnips or parsnips, and green beans or dried ones such as cranberry or navy beans. Some vegetables should always be cooked separately: beets, because they exude color as they cook; cabbage, because it requires careful timing; and dried beans, because they cook so long. Other vegetables may be added to the beef during the last half hour or so of its cooking. However, for some tastes, the briny flavor imparted by the corned beef detracts from the vegetables' natural flavors.* ❧

**To serve 6**

| | |
|---|---|
| One 4- to 4½-pound corned-beef brisket or corned round | 12 small white onions, trimmed |
| 6 small beets, scrubbed and tops cut away leaving 1 inch of green | 1 small green cabbage, cut into 6 wedges |
| 12 to 16 small new potatoes | 2 tablespoons chopped fresh parsley leaves |
| 6 small carrots | |

Place the corned beef in a 5- or 6-quart pot, and add enough cold water to cover it by at least 2 inches. Bring the water to a boil over moderate heat, at the same time skimming off any scum that rises to the surface.

Half cover the pot, turn the heat to its lowest point, and simmer the beef for about three and a half hours, or until it is tender and shows no resistance when pierced deeply with the tip of a sharp knife. Add boiling water to the pot as necessary to keep the meat constantly covered with water while it cooks.

When the beef has simmered for several hours, place the beets in a heavy nonreactive pot, and pour in enough cold water to cover them by 2 inches. Bring the water to a boil, and simmer the beets for 30 to 40 minutes, until they are tender when pierced with a knife. Drain the beets and, when they are cool enough to handle comfortably, slip off their skins. Cover the beets with foil to keep them warm.

The potatoes, carrots and onions may be cooked together. Bring a large pot filled with lightly salted water to a boil. Drop the potatoes, carrots and onions into the water. When it returns to a boil, cook the vegetables, uncovered, for about 20 minutes or until they are tender but not falling apart. Drain the vegetables and cover them with foil to keep them warm.

Cook the cabbage separately by dropping the wedges into enough lightly salted boiling water to cover them completely. Reduce the heat to low and simmer for 10 to 15 minutes or until the cabbage is barely tender. Drain the cabbage and cover it to keep it warm.

To serve the dinner in the traditional manner, carve the corned beef and arrange the slices, slightly overlapping, along the center of a large heated platter. Surround the meat with the beets, potatoes, carrots, onions and cabbage, and sprinkle with chopped parsley.

Horseradish, mustard and a variety of pickles make excellent accompaniments to this hearty meal.

■ AMERICAN COOKING

NEW ENGLAND BOILED DINNER

## Stir-fried Beef Tenderloin with Vegetables

**To serve 2 to 4**

| | |
|---|---|
| ¼ cup snow peas, trimmed and strings removed | 1½ inches in diameter, soaked in warm water for 30 minutes, stems discarded and caps quartered |
| 1 teaspoon sugar | |
| 2 tablespoons soy sauce | |
| 1 tablespoon Chinese rice wine or pale dry sherry | 6 fresh water chestnuts, peeled, or 6 canned water chestnuts, rinsed and sliced ¼ inch thick |
| 2 teaspoons cornstarch | |
| 1 pound beef tenderloin, trimmed and cut into 1-inch cubes | |
| | ½ teaspoon salt |
| 3 tablespoons peanut oil | 4 slices peeled fresh ginger root, about ⅛ inch thick and 1 inch across |
| 4 Chinese dried mushrooms, | |

Blanch the peas in a quart of boiling water for one minute. Immediately drain them and run cold water over them to stop the cooking and set the color.

In a large nonreactive bowl, mix the sugar, soy sauce, wine and

## Beef and Chicken Pie with Corn

**To serve 6**

| | |
|---|---|
| 5 tablespoons olive oil | 1 teaspoon paprika |
| 2 pounds lean ground beef | 1 teaspoon salt |
| 4 cups coarsely chopped onions | ¼ teaspoon freshly ground black pepper |
| ¼ teaspoon finely chopped garlic | ½ cup pitted black olives |
| ¼ cup seedless raisins, soaked in hot water for 10 minutes | One 3-pound chicken, cut into 6 serving pieces |
| 1 tablespoon hot-red-pepper flakes | 2 cups fresh or defrosted corn kernels |
| 2 teaspoons ground cumin | 1 tablespoon milk |
| | 1 tablespoon sugar |

In a heavy 10- to 12-inch skillet, heat 2 tablespoons of the olive oil over high heat. Add the ground beef and brown it, stirring with a fork to break up lumps that may form and adjusting the heat if necessary. Stir in the onions, garlic, raisins, pepper flakes, cumin, paprika, salt and black pepper, and reduce the heat to low. Stirring occasionally, cook, uncovered, for 15 minutes. Transfer the contents of the skillet to a 4-quart casserole. Spread the olives evenly over the meat.

In the same skillet, heat 2 tablespoons of the remaining oil over high heat. In it brown the chicken pieces on all sides. Arrange them on top of the meat mixture.

Preheat the oven to 350°F. Place the corn and milk in a food processor or blender, and purée them, stopping the machine once or twice to scrape down the sides of the bowl with a rubber spatula. Heat the remaining tablespoon of oil in a small, heavy skillet and cook the corn over moderate heat for five minutes, stirring constantly. The finished purée should have the consistency of thick cereal.

Pour the corn purée over the chicken in the casserole and, with a spoon or rubber spatula, spread it evenly to the sides of the dish. Sprinkle the top with the sugar. Bake in the middle of the oven for 30 minutes, then increase the heat to 450°F. and bake for 10 minutes longer, until the top is golden brown. Serve hot, from the casserole.

■ THE COOKING OF LATIN AMERICA

cornstarch together thoroughly. Add the beef cubes and toss them in the bowl with a large spoon until they are coated with the soy-sauce mixture.

Set a 12-inch wok or 10-inch skillet over high heat for 30 seconds. Pour in 1 tablespoon of oil, swirl it about in the pan and heat it over moderate heat for 30 seconds. Add the mushrooms, snow peas and water chestnuts, and stir-fry them for about two minutes or until all of the ingredients are coated with the oil. Stir in the salt, then transfer the vegetables to a plate with a slotted spoon.

Pour the remaining 2 tablespoons of oil into the pan, add the ginger and turn the heat to high. Drop in the beef cubes and stir-fry for two to three minutes or until they are lightly browned on all sides. Pick out and discard the ginger, and return the vegetables to the pan. Stir-fry for about 10 seconds more to heat the vegetables through. Transfer the contents of the pan to a heated platter and serve at once.

■ THE COOKING OF CHINA

## Pot-au-feu

*The hearty "pot on the fire" provides both a soup and a main course. The vegetables can be varied to your taste.* ❧

**To serve 6**

| | |
|---|---|
| **One 3-pound boneless beef rump, bottom-round, brisket or chuck roast, tied** | **6 peppercorns** |
| **3 pounds beef marrow bones, sawed into 3-inch pieces** | **1 teaspoon salt** |
| | **2 tablespoons finely chopped fresh parsley leaves** |
| **1 veal knuckle, sawed into pieces** | VEGETABLE GARNISH |
| **6 to 8 cups beef stock** | **6 carrots, cut into cylinders or oval shapes 1½-inches long** |
| **2 tablespoons butter** | |
| **2 onions** | **3 or 4 white turnips, cut into chunks or quartered** |
| **2 carrots, halved** | **3 parsnips, quartered** |
| **1 tomato, peeled, seeded and chopped coarse** | **6 leeks, white part plus 2 inches of green, tied in a bundle** |
| **Bouquet garni made of 4 parsley sprigs, 1 bay leaf and 1 leek (white part plus 2 inches of green top), tied together** | **1 small green cabbage, cut into 6 wedges** |
| | **6 boiling potatoes, unpeeled if new** |
| **½ teaspoon crumbled dried thyme** | **½ cup butter, melted** |

In a 10- to 12-quart saucepan or stockpot, combine the beef, marrow bones, knuckle and beef stock. The stock should cover the meat by about 4 inches; add more stock or water if needed. Bring the stock to a boil over moderate heat while skimming off the scum that rises to the surface.

Meanwhile, melt 2 tablespoons of butter in a heavy 6- to 8-inch skillet, and cook the whole onions and halved carrots over moderate heat, turning them often, until they are lightly browned.

When the stock comes to a boil, reduce the heat to low, and add the browned onions and carrots, chopped tomato, bouquet garni, thyme, peppercorns and salt. Partially cover the pot and simmer slowly, undisturbed, for two and a half hours, until the beef is almost tender when pierced with the tip of a sharp knife.

Transfer the beef to a plate. Remove the bones from the stock, and scoop out their marrow with the point of a knife before discarding them. Set the marrow aside in a bowl.

Strain the stock into a bowl through a fine sieve lined with a double layer of dampened cheesecloth. Discard the vegetables and skim the surface fat from the stock. Wash and dry the pot, then return the stock and meat to the pot, and add the garnish of carrots, turnips, parsnips, and the leeks if you are using them. Bring the stock to a boil and simmer, uncovered, over low heat for 30 minutes, or until the meat and vegetables are tender. If the vegetables cook faster than the meat, remove them from the pot and cook the meat until it is tender; then return the vegetables to the pot and heat them through.

If you plan to serve cabbage, blanch it by plunging it into boiling salted water and cooking it over high heat for eight minutes. Drain the cabbage and add it to the meat and vegetables in the pot after they have cooked for 20 minutes. If you plan to serve potatoes, boil them separately.

When the meat and vegetables are done, transfer the meat to a carving board, remove the strings, and carve the roast into ¼-inch slices. Arrange the slices attractively, overlapping slightly, on a heated platter, surrounded by the vegetables and potatoes. Sprinkle melted butter over the vegetables and potatoes, cover the platter loosely with foil, and set aside. With a spoon, skim as much fat as possible from the surface of the stock. Chop the marrow into fine dice and add it to the pot. Serve the stock, sprinkled with chopped fresh parsley, as a first course, then present the meat and vegetables.

■ THE COOKING OF PROVINCIAL FRANCE

## Rolled Flank Steak with Chili Sauce

**To serve 6**

| | |
|---|---|
| **Two 2-pound beef flank steaks** | **1 celery rib, sliced** |
| **1 cup frozen mixed vegetables, defrosted** | **1 carrot, sliced** |
| | **Parsley sprigs for garnish** |
| **½ cup finely chopped onion, plus 1 onion, sliced** | |
| **¼ cup finely chopped green pepper** | CHILI SAUCE |
| | **¼ cup butter** |
| **¼ cup finely chopped pimiento** | **1 onion, chopped fine** |
| | **1 green pepper, chopped fine** |
| **2 teaspoons finely chopped hot chili** | **1 clove garlic, chopped fine** |
| | **2 tablespoons flour** |
| **2 garlic cloves, 1 chopped fine and 1 chopped coarse** | **1 tablespoon chili powder** |
| | **1 teaspoon salt** |
| **1 teaspoon salt** | **Freshly ground black pepper** |
| | **1 cup tomato juice** |
| **1 cup beef stock** | **1 cup beef stock** |

Preheat the oven to 350°F. Butterfly each steak by slicing it horizontally from one side to within an inch of the other side. With a meat pounder or kitchen mallet, pound the steaks as thin as possible. Trim off any excess fat and cut the edges straight so that each finished steak is roughly 12 inches square. Lay the steaks side by side, overlapping them by 1 or 2 inches so that when you roll them they hold together as if they were one piece of meat.

In a bowl, blend together the mixed vegetables, ½ cup of chopped onion, ¼ cup of green pepper, the pimiento, chopped chili, 1 clove of finely chopped garlic and 1 teaspoon of salt. Spread this mixture evenly over the steaks, covering the entire surface. Starting at one 12-inch end, roll the two steaks tightly together, jelly-roll fashion. With five lengths of kitchen string, tie the roll at 2-inch intervals.

Place the roll in a casserole just large enough to hold it easily, and add 1 cup of beef stock, the sliced celery, carrot and onion, and the coarsely chopped garlic. Cover and cook for two hours, basting the roll several times.

Meanwhile, prepare the sauce by first melting the butter in an 8- to 10-inch nonreactive heavy skillet. Add one chopped onion, one chopped pepper and one finely chopped garlic clove. Stirring frequently with a wooden spoon, cook the sauce over moderate heat for five minutes or until the vegetables are soft but not brown. Blend in the flour, chili powder, 1 teaspoon of salt and a

**ROLLED FLANK STEAK WITH CHILI SAUCE**

# Sauerbraten

**To serve 6**

| | |
|---|---|
| 2 cups dry white wine | 1 teaspoon mustard seeds |
| 2 cups white vinegar | 6 parsley sprigs |
| 2 cups water | One 5-pound beef top- |
| 3 large onions, sliced | round or bottom-round |
| 6 carrots, sliced | roast |
| 4 shallots, sliced | 5 tablespoons flour |
| 8 black peppercorns plus | ¼ cup vegetable oil |
| freshly ground black | 2 tablespoons butter |
| pepper | 2 tablespoons sugar |
| 12 cloves | ⅓ cup gingersnap |
| 4 bay leaves | crumbs |
| Salt | |

Combine the wine, vinegar, water, two-thirds of the sliced onions, the carrots, shallots, peppercorns, six of the cloves, three of the bay leaves, 1 teaspoon of salt, the mustard seeds and parsley sprigs in a nonreactive saucepan. Bring to a boil, reduce the heat, and simmer for five minutes. Cool this marinade. Place the beef in a large nonreactive bowl, pour the marinade over the beef, then cover the bowl with plastic wrap and marinate the roast in the refrigerator for four days. Turn the beef once a day to be sure the roast marinates evenly.

Remove the roast from the marinade and pat it dry with paper towels. Strain the marinade through a sieve into a bowl, pressing the vegetables with the back of a spoon to extract all of their liquid before discarding them. Set the marinade aside.

With a sieve, dust 2 tablespoons of the flour over the roast, coating all sides. Heat the oil in a heavy 5- to 6-quart casserole. Add the beef and cook over moderate heat for about 20 minutes or until it is well browned on all sides. Remove the roast from the casserole and pour off all of the fat. Return the roast to the casserole, add the remaining sliced onion, six cloves, one bay leaf and 3 cups of the marinade. Bring the marinade to a boil over moderate heat, reduce the heat to low, cover the casserole, and simmer the beef for three hours.

In a small skillet, melt the butter over moderate heat. Stir in the sugar and the remaining 3 tablespoons of flour, and cook over low heat, stirring constantly, until this mixture is a rich brown color. Pour the cooking liquid from the casserole; strain it and return it to the casserole. Stir the sugar-flour mixture into the cooking liquid. Cover the casserole and continue cooking over low heat until the roast is very tender—about one hour more.

To serve, transfer the roast to a heated platter. Stir the gingersnap crumbs into the gravy remaining in the casserole. Using a whisk, cook and stir for two or three minutes, until the gravy is smooth and thick. Taste it and add more salt and a few grindings of pepper if necessary.

Carve the meat into fairly thick slices and arrange them, overlapping the slices, on a heated platter. Spoon some of the gravy over the beef, and present the rest in a sauceboat.

few grindings of pepper. Stir over low heat for two minutes. Stir in the tomato juice and 1 cup of beef stock, and continue cooking, stirring occasionally, for five minutes or until the sauce thickens slightly. Set it aside, covered to keep it warm.

Transfer the roll to a platter and let it rest for about 10 minutes. Garnish with parsley sprigs. Serve carved into thick slices. Present the chili sauce separately in a bowl.

# Steak and Kidney Pie

**To serve 4 to 6**

| | |
|---|---|
| 1½ pounds lean boneless beef round or rump, cut into 1-inch cubes | fresh mushrooms |
| | ½ cup chopped onions |
| | 1½ cups water |
| 1 pound veal kidneys, halved, peeled, trimmed of fat and cut into 1-inch cubes | ¼ cup pale dry sherry or dry red wine |
| | 1 tablespoon chopped fresh parsley leaves |
| 1 teaspoon salt | |
| ½ teaspoon freshly ground black pepper | ¼ teaspoon crumbled dried thyme |
| ¼ cup flour | ¼ teaspoon Worcestershire sauce |
| ¼ cup rendered beef suet or lard, or 3 tablespoons butter plus 1 tablespoon vegetable oil | Short-crust pastry dough for a 1-crust pie (Index/Glossary) |
| 1 cup thinly sliced | 1 egg yolk lightly beaten with 1 tablespoon heavy cream |

Preheat the oven to 425°F. Pat the cubes of steak and kidney dry with paper towels. Season them with the salt and pepper. Put the flour in a large bowl, drop in the cubes, and stir to coat them evenly. Tap off the excess flour.

In a heavy 10- to 12-inch skillet, heat the suet over high heat until it splutters. Brown a handful of the cubes at a time, turning them frequently and regulating the heat so that the meat colors quickly and evenly without burning. Add more fat, if necessary. With a slotted spoon, transfer the cubes to a heavy 2-quart casserole about 4 inches deep.

Add the mushrooms and onions to the fat in the skillet and cook over moderate heat, stirring constantly, for two or three minutes. With a slotted spoon, transfer the mushrooms and onions to the casserole. Pour the water into the skillet and bring it to a boil over high heat, scraping in any brown particles clinging to the bottom of the pan. Pour it over the meat in the casserole, and add the sherry, parsley, thyme and Worcestershire sauce. Stir together gently.

On a lightly floured surface, roll the dough into a rough oval about ¼ inch thick, and cut two strips about 12 inches long and ½ inch wide. Lay the strips end to end around the rim of the casserole and press them firmly into place. Moisten them lightly with a pastry brush dipped in cold water. Then drape the remaining pastry over the rolling pin, lift it, and carefully unroll it over the casserole. With a small knife or scissors, trim off the excess dough, and secure the edges to the rim by crimping them tightly with your fingers or the tines of a fork. Make two parallel cuts each about 1 inch long in the center of the pie.

Reroll the scraps of dough and cut them into simple flower and leaf shapes. Moisten their bottom sides with the egg-yolk-and-cream mixture, and arrange them attractively on top of the pie. With a pastry brush, paint the surface with the yolk mixture.

Bake for 30 minutes, then reduce the heat to 350°F. and bake for another 30 minutes or until the crust is golden brown. Serve at once, directly from the baking dish.

■ THE COOKING OF THE BRITISH ISLES

# Steaks Esterhazy

*The Esterhazys were Hungarian aristocrats and patrons of the arts, especially music. Composer Joseph Haydn spent much of his life in their service.* ❧

**To serve 6**

| | |
|---|---|
| 2 pounds beef top-round steak, ½ inch thick, cut into 6 equal portions | dried thyme |
| | One ⅛-inch-wide strip lemon peel |
| Salt | 4 lean bacon slices, chopped coarse |
| Freshly ground black pepper | |
| 7 tablespoons flour | 2 tablespoons finely chopped fresh parsley leaves |
| 3 tablespoons lard | |
| 1½ cups finely chopped onions | ¼ cup white-wine vinegar |
| | 2 parsnips, cut into 3-by-½-inch julienne strips |
| ½ teaspoon finely chopped garlic | |
| ½ cup finely chopped carrots | 1 carrot, cut into 3-by-½-inch julienne strips |
| 3 cups beef stock | ¾ cup heavy cream |
| 3 whole allspice or ⅛ teaspoon ground allspice | 1 teaspoon fresh lemon juice |
| 3 bay leaves | 4 sour gherkins, cut into 3-by-½-inch julienne strips |
| 4 peppercorns | |
| ⅛ teaspoon crumbled | |

Sprinkle the steaks with a little salt and some pepper, dip them in a dish containing ¼ cup of the flour, and tap off the excess. Melt the lard in a heavy 10- to 12-inch skillet, and brown the steaks over high heat for about three minutes on each side. Transfer them to a platter and reduce the heat to moderate.

Add the onions, garlic and chopped carrots to the fat remaining in the skillet and cook, stirring frequently with a wooden spoon, for about eight minutes or until the vegetables are lightly colored. Stir in the remaining 3 tablespoons of flour. When all of the flour has been absorbed, pour in the stock and bring it to a boil, stirring constantly until the sauce thickens. Add the allspice, bay leaves, peppercorns, thyme, lemon peel, bacon, parsley and vinegar.

Return the meat to the skillet and bring the stock to a boil again. Reduce the heat to low, partially cover the skillet, and simmer the steaks for 50 to 60 minutes or until they are tender and show no resistance when pierced with the tip of a knife. Arrange the steaks on an ovenproof platter, and keep them warm in an oven that has been heated to 200°F.

Strain the contents of the skillet into a small saucepan, pressing hard on the vegetables before discarding them. Skim off the surface fat from this sauce.

Drop the parsnip and carrot strips into lightly salted boiling water. Boil, uncovered, for two to three minutes, until the vegetables are slightly tender. Drain them in a colander.

Whisk the cream and lemon juice into the sauce and add the carrot, parsnip and gherkin strips. Simmer for two or three minutes. Taste for seasoning. Pour the vegetables and the sauce over the steaks and serve at once.

■ THE COOKING OF VIENNA'S EMPIRE

**TEXAS CHILI CON CARNE**

## Beef Stroganoff

*A simple but elegant Russian dish, beef stroganoff has become an American favorite, served with either noodles or rice. Along the way, it also has been altered somewhat: Scallions, tomato paste and Worcestershire sauce are New World additions.* ❧

**To serve 4 to 6**

| | |
|---|---|
| 5 to 7 tablespoons butter | ½ cup dry white wine |
| 1 tablespoon oil | ½ cup sour cream |
| 2 pounds beef tenderloin, trimmed and cut into ¼-inch slices | 1 tablespoon tomato paste |
| | 2 or 3 drops Worcestershire sauce |
| ½ cup thinly sliced scallions | 1 teaspoon salt |
| ¼ pound mushrooms, trimmed and sliced thin | Freshly ground black pepper |
| 1 tablespoon flour | 1 tablespoon chopped fresh parsley leaves for garnish |

Melt 3 tablespoons of the butter in the oil in a heavy 10- to 12-inch skillet over moderate heat. Add a few of the beef slices, and fry them for two minutes on each side or until lightly browned. With tongs or a slotted spoon, transfer the slices to a plate. Fry the remaining slices in batches that do not crowd the skillet, adding more butter if necessary.

Melt two tablespoons of butter in the skillet and stir in the scallions and mushrooms. Stirring frequently, cook for five or six minutes or until they are soft and lightly browned. Add the flour and mix thoroughly with the vegetables, then pour in the white wine and add the sour cream, 1 tablespoon at a time. Stir in the tomato paste, Worcestershire sauce, salt and a few grindings of black pepper.

Return the beef to the pan, together with the juices that have accumulated on the plate. Coat the meat thoroughly with the sauce, cover the pan, and cook over very low heat for two to three minutes or until the beef is heated through. Taste for seasoning and transfer the beef stroganoff to a large heated platter. Sprinkle with the parsley and serve at once.

■ AMERICAN COOKING: THE MELTING POT

# Texas Chili con Carne

*Before they are dried, the anchos that give chili con carne its characteristic, mahogany-red color are called "poblanos." These triangular chilies are about 4½ inches long and 2½ inches wide at the top. They range from mild in taste to medium hot. Anchos are available wherever Mexican foods are sold.* ❦

### To serve 6 to 8

| | |
|---|---|
| 6 dried *ancho* chilies | dried oregano |
| 8 dried hot red chilies, each about 2 inches long | 3 tablespoons paprika |
| | 1 tablespoon sugar |
| 3½ cups boiling water | 1 tablespoon salt |
| ½ pound beef kidney suet, cut into ½-inch bits | 3 tablespoons corn flour or yellow corn meal |
| 3 pounds lean boneless beef chuck, trimmed and cut into 1½-inch cubes | 1 teaspoon cayenne pepper (optional) |
| | 6 cups freshly cooked pinto beans |
| 3 bay leaves | |
| 1 tablespoon cumin seeds | 9 cups freshly cooked long-grain white rice |
| 2 tablespoons chopped garlic | |
| 4 teaspoons crumbled | |

Under cold running water, carefully pull the stems off the chilies. Tear the chilies in half and brush out their seeds. Then cut away any large ribs in the chilies. Chop up the chilies and drop them into a bowl. Pour the boiling water over them, and let them soak for at least 30 minutes, then strain the chili soaking liquid through a sieve set over a bowl and reserve it; also set the chilies aside.

In a heavy 5- to 6-quart casserole, cook the kidney suet over moderate heat, stirring frequently until it renders all of its fat. With a slotted spoon, remove and discard the suet bits. Pour off all but about ¼ cup of the fat.

Add the beef cubes and, stirring constantly, cook over moderate heat until the pieces of meat are firm but not brown. Add 2½ cups of the reserved chili-soaking liquid, and bring it to a boil over high heat. Drop in the bay leaves and reduce the heat to low. Simmer, partially covered, for one hour, stirring the mixture from time to time.

Meanwhile, put the cumin seeds in a small ungreased skillet and, sliding the pan back and forth often, toast the seeds over low heat for 10 minutes. Place the seeds, the *ancho* and red chilies, the remaining soaking liquid, the garlic, oregano, paprika, sugar and salt in a blender or food processor, and purée them, stopping once or twice to scrape down the sides of the jar or bowl with a rubber spatula.

When the meat has cooked its allotted time, stir in the chili purée. Simmer, partially covered, for 30 minutes. Then, stirring constantly, pour in the corn flour in a slow stream, and cook over high heat until the chili comes to a boil and thickens lightly. Taste the chili for seasoning and add cayenne pepper if desired.

Serve the chili con carne directly from the casserole or from a heated serving bowl. Mound the pinto beans and the rice in separate bowls, and present them with the chili.

■ AMERICAN COOKING: THE GREAT WEST

# Joe Booker Stew

*Nobody remembers the man, but Joe Booker's stew still is favored around Boothbay Harbor, Maine.* ❦

### To serve 6

| | |
|---|---|
| ½ pound lean salt pork with rind removed, diced | into ½-inch cubes |
| | 12 carrots, cut into ½-inch pieces |
| 4 onions, sliced thin | |
| 2 pounds lean beef chuck, cut into 1-inch cubes | 1 rutabaga, cut into ½-inch cubes |
| Salt | |
| Freshly ground black pepper | PARSLEY DUMPLINGS |
| ¼ cup flour | 2 cups flour |
| 6 cups water | 1 tablespoon baking powder |
| Bouquet garni made of 4 parsley sprigs and 1 small bay leaf, tied together | ½ teaspoon salt |
| | 2 tablespoons butter, cut into bits |
| ⅛ teaspoon crumbled dried thyme | 1⅓ cups milk |
| | ¼ cup chopped fresh parsley leaves |
| 2 potatoes, peeled and cut | |

In a heavy 12-inch skillet at least 3 inches deep, fry the salt pork dice over moderate heat, turning them frequently with a slotted spoon until they brown and render all of their fat. Remove and discard the pork bits. Add the onions to the fat in the skillet and, stirring frequently, cook for eight to 10 minutes or until they are soft and light brown. With the slotted spoon, transfer the onions to a bowl and set aside.

Pat the beef cubes dry with paper towels, season them with salt and pepper, and drop them into a bowl containing ¼ cup of flour. Coat the cubes on all sides; tap off excess flour. Brown a handful of cubes at a time evenly in the remaining hot fat. As they brown, add them to the onions.

Pour 1 cup of the water into the skillet, and bring it to a boil over high heat, stirring and scraping in the brown particles from the bottom of the pan. Return the onions and beef with the liquid that has accumulated around them to the skillet. Add the remaining 5 cups of water, the bouquet garni, thyme, 1 teaspoon of salt and a liberal grinding of pepper. Bring to a boil over high heat, reduce the heat to low, cover the skillet, and simmer for one hour. Stir in the potatoes, carrots and rutabaga; cover and simmer the stew for 30 minutes.

Meanwhile, prepare the parsley dumplings by first combining the 2 cups of flour, the baking powder and ½ teaspoon of salt and sifting them into a deep bowl. Add the butter bits and, with your fingers, rub the flour and fat together until they resemble coarse meal. Add the milk and chopped parsley, and stir vigorously until the mixture is smooth.

Remove the bouquet garni from the stew, and drop in the dumplings by the heaping tablespoon. Cover and simmer, undisturbed, for 10 minutes, until the dumplings puff and are fluffy, and a cake tester inserted in the center comes out clean.

Remove the dumplings and transfer the stew to a heated bowl. Arrange the dumplings on top and serve at once.

■ AMERICAN COOKING: NEW ENGLAND

# Japanese Hot Pot

*At the dinner table, each guest cooks his own choice of beef and vegetables in bubbling broth, then dips them in sauce before eating them. The Japanese name for this dish—"shabu shabu"—comes from the sound the food makes as it is moved back and forth in the broth. The Chinese cabbage, shiitake mushrooms, daikon radish and fresh tofu shown in the photograph at right are available at many supermarkets. The chrysanthemum leaves, enoki mushrooms, kuzukiri (arrowroot noodles), yuba (dried soybean milk skin), and kombu (dried kelp) are available at stores selling Asian foods. Any combination of these ingredients is suitable depending on what you are able to obtain. According to your taste, minced scallions or grated daikon mixed with grated hot pepper can be added to either dipping sauce at the table.* ❧

**To serve 6**

1½ pounds beef eye-of-round roast in one piece
2 pounds Chinese cabbage, cut crosswise into broad strips
12 to 14 young spinach leaves, washed and stemmed
¼ pound Chinese chrysanthemum leaves, washed and trimmed
8 scallions, including 3 inches of green tops, cut into narrow strips
2 cakes fresh tofu, cut into 1-inch cubes
3 sheets *yuba*, cut into 1½-inch strips, boiled for 20 to 30 minutes, and rolled into cylinders
12 small shiitake or button mushrooms, trimmed and halved

½ pound enoki mushrooms, trimmed
3 ounces *kuzukiri*
Daikon radish and carrot slices, cut decoratively, for garnish
6 cups chicken stock
One 4-inch square *kombu*, washed well

SESAME DIPPING SAUCE
½ cup sesame seeds, ground to a paste in food processor or with mortar and pestle
3 tablespoons sake (rice wine)
2 teaspoons sugar
2 tablespoons Japanese soy sauce

LEMON DIPPING SAUCE
½ cup fresh lemon juice
½ cup Japanese soy sauce

Freeze the beef for about 30 minutes to stiffen it slightly for easier slicing. With a heavy, sharp knife, cut the beef across the grain into ⅛-inch slices. Fold each slice in half crosswise. Then arrange the beef on a platter.

Lay out the cabbage, spinach, chrysanthemum leaves, scallions, tofu, *yuba,* shiitake mushrooms, enoki mushrooms and the noodles on another platter. Garnish with the daikon and carrot slices. Mix the ingredients for each dipping sauce.

Set a heating unit and its cooking pot in the center of the dining table. Pour the chicken stock into the cooking pot and add the *kombu.* Bring the stock to a boil, then adjust the heat so that the stock simmers throughout the meal. Let each guest select a piece of food from the platter with chopsticks or a fork, and stir it in the stock to cook it. The practice is first to add beef to the stock and let it cook for two or three seconds, then add vegetables. Simmer for a minute or until the food is cooked to taste, then remove it with chopsticks. Dip it in one sauce or the other before eating.

When all of the food has been cooked, the kelp is removed and the broth is ladled into bowls and drunk as soup.

■ THE COOKING OF JAPAN

## Swedish Hamburgers

*In Sweden, these hamburgers often are made 2 or 3 inches wide, in which case the recipe yields about a dozen, and the finished product is served without fried eggs.* ✷

**To serve 4**

| | |
|---|---|
| 3 tablespoons butter | Freshly ground black pepper |
| 2 tablespoons finely chopped onion | 2 teaspoons white vinegar |
| 1 pound lean ground beef | 1/2 cup heavy cream |
| 4 egg yolks | 1/4 cup finely chopped drained beets, freshly cooked or canned |
| 1 tablespoon capers, drained and chopped fine | 2 tablespoons vegetable oil |
| 1 1/2 teaspoons salt | 4 eggs, fried |

In a small pan, melt 1 tablespoon of the butter over moderate heat. When the foam subsides, add the onion and cook for two or three minutes or until it is soft but not brown. Scrape into a large bowl, and add the beef, egg yolks, capers, salt, a few grindings of pepper and the vinegar. Mix together and moisten with the heavy cream. Then stir in the beets.

Shape the mixture into four round patties, about 2 inches thick if you want the hamburgers to be rare but only 1 to 1 1/2 inches thick for well-cooked beef.

In a heavy 10- to 12-inch skillet, heat the remaining 2 tablespoons of butter and the oil over high heat. Add the patties and cook for three to five minutes. Then turn them over, sear the second side and reduce the heat to moderate. Cook the hamburgers until they are done to your taste. Serve the hamburgers on heated individual plates with a fried egg set atop each one.

■ THE COOKING OF SCANDINAVIA

## Beef Goulash with Gherkins

**To serve 6 to 8**

| | |
|---|---|
| 3 tablespoons lard | 1 cup beef stock |
| 2 cups finely chopped onions | Salt |
| 1 tablespoon paprika | Freshly ground black pepper |
| 3 pounds lean boneless beef chuck, cut into 1 1/2-inch cubes | 2 tablespoons flour |
| | 1/2 cup sweet gherkins, cut into julienne strips |
| 1 cup dry red wine | |

Preheat the oven to 350°F. Heat the lard in a 5-quart flameproof casserole over moderate heat, then add the onions and cook for eight to 10 minutes, until they are lightly colored. Off the heat, stir in the paprika, continuing to stir until the onions are well coated. Add the beef and pour the wine and beef stock over it. Stir in 1/2 teaspoon of salt and a few grindings of pepper. Bring to a boil, then cover tightly and bake in the middle of the oven for one hour.

Remove the casserole from the oven and, with a spoon, skim off about 2 tablespoons of the surface fat. Blend this with the flour, then stir the mixture into the casserole. Return the casserole

to the oven, and cook for 30 to 40 minutes longer, or until the beef shows no resistance when pierced with the tip of a small knife. Arrange the beef on a platter. Skim the surface fat from the casserole, add the gherkins, and heat for two to three minutes longer. Taste for seasoning. Pour the sauce over the beef and serve immediately.

■ THE COOKING OF VIENNA'S EMPIRE

## Deviled Short Ribs

**To serve 4**

| | |
|---|---|
| 1/4 cup finely chopped onion | garlic |
| 1/4 cup fresh lemon juice | 1 teaspoon salt |
| 1/4 cup vegetable oil | Freshly ground black pepper |
| 3 tablespoons prepared mustard | 3 pounds lean beef short ribs, each 4 to 5 inches long |
| 1 teaspoon finely chopped | |

Combine the onion, lemon juice, oil, mustard, garlic, salt and a liberal grinding of pepper in a deep bowl, and mix them well. Add the short ribs and turn them about with a spoon until they are evenly coated. Let the ribs marinate at room temperature for two hours, turning them from time to time.

Preheat the oven to 400°F. Arrange the ribs, fat side up, in a single layer on a rack set in a shallow roasting pan. (Discard the remaining marinade.) Roast the ribs for 20 minutes. Then reduce the heat to 350°F. and continue to roast for one hour and 15 minutes longer or until the meat is tender and shows no resistance when pierced with the tip of a knife. Arrange the ribs on a heated platter and serve at once.

■ AMERICAN COOKING: THE EASTERN HEARTLAND

## Finnish Meat Loaf in Sour-Cream Pastry

**To serve 6 to 8**

| | |
|---|---|
| 1/4 cup butter | 1 egg lightly beaten with 2 tablespoons milk |
| 3/4 cup finely chopped mushrooms | Sour cream |
| 3 pounds finely ground beef, veal, pork, ham or lamb or any combination of these | Lingonberry preserves or cranberry sauce |
| 1/3 cup finely chopped onions | SOUR-CREAM PASTRY DOUGH |
| 1/4 cup finely chopped fresh parsley leaves, plus parsley sprigs for garnish | 2 1/4 cups flour |
| 1 cup grated Jarlsberg cheese | 3/4 cup butter, chilled and cut into 1/4-inch bits |
| 1/2 cup milk | 1 egg |
| | 1/2 cup sour cream |

Prepare the dough at least an hour before you plan to assemble the meat loaf. Combine the flour and butter bits in a food processor, and process until the mixture resembles coarse meal. Add the egg and sour cream, and process until the mixture forms a soft, pliable dough. Divide it in half, wrap each half in wax paper, and refrigerate for one hour.

FINNISH MEAT LOAF IN SOUR-CREAM PASTRY

Melt ¼ cup of butter in a heavy, 10- to 12-inch skillet over moderate heat. Add the mushrooms and, stirring frequently, cook for six to eight minutes or until lightly colored. Add the meat and cook, stirring occasionally, for eight to 10 minutes or until the meat loses its red color and the liquid that accumulates in the skillet cooks completely away. Transfer the contents of the skillet to a large mixing bowl, and stir in the onions, the chopped parsley, cheese and milk.

Preheat the oven to 375° F. On a lightly floured surface, using a floured rolling pin, roll each half of the pastry dough into a rough rectangle 6 inches wide and 14 inches long. With a ruler and pastry wheel, trim the rectangles. Gather the scraps into a ball and refrigerate. With a pastry brush, spread a light coating of melted or softened butter onto the bottom of a jelly-roll pan. Lift one sheet of the pastry over the rolling pin and unroll it into the pan.

Gather the meat mixture into a ball, and place it in the center of the dough. With your hands, pat the meat into a narrow loaf extending from one end of the sheet to the other. Lift the second sheet of pastry over the pin, and drape it on top of the meat loaf; press the edges of the sheets together.

Dip a pastry brush into the combined egg and milk, and moisten the edges of the dough. Seal the edges all around by pressing down on them with the tines of a fork. Use the fork to prick the top of the loaf in several places to allow steam to escape while the meat loaf is baking.

Roll the ball made from scraps of dough into a rectangle. With a pastry wheel or small, sharp knife, cut this dough into long, narrow strips. Brush the loaf with more of the egg and milk, and crisscross the pastry strips over the top of the loaf in an attractive pattern. Then brush the strips with the egg and milk. Set the loaf in the center of the oven. Bake for 45 minutes or until the pastry has turned golden brown. With the aid of a wide metal spatula, slide the meat loaf onto a heated platter. Garnish it with parsley sprigs, and serve at once, cut into thick slices and accompanied by bowls of sour cream and lingonberries.

■ THE COOKING OF SCANDINAVIA

**VEAL CHOPS WITH TARRAGON SAUCE**

## Veal Chops with Tarragon Sauce

**To serve 4**

| | |
|---|---|
| **4 boned veal rib chops, 1 inch thick** | **1½ teaspoons chopped fresh tarragon leaves or ½ teaspoon crumbled dried tarragon** |
| **Freshly ground pepper** | |
| **3 tablespoons clarified butter** | |
| **1 large garlic clove, halved** | **½ cup heavy cream** |
| **¾ cup chicken stock** | **Salt** |
| **¼ cup Cognac** | |

Preheat the oven to 200°F. Wrap the fatty tail of each chop around the lean eye section, and attach it with two rounded wooden toothpicks inserted horizontally through the meat. (Do not stretch the meat.) Score the fatty edge at ½-inch intervals to prevent the chops from curling while cooking. Sprinkle both sides of the meat with pepper.

In a heavy 10- to 12-inch skillet, melt the clarified butter over moderate heat. Add the garlic, reduce the heat to low, and cook for two minutes, stirring the garlic from time to time; do not let it brown. Discard the garlic.

Increase the heat to high, add the chops, and brown them quickly on both sides. Reduce the heat to moderate and cook, turning the chops once, for 15 minutes. Transfer them to a platter, cover loosely with foil, and keep them warm in the oven. Pour off any accumulated juices from the skillet.

For the sauce, add the stock, Cognac and tarragon to the skillet. Over high heat, deglaze the pan by scraping up the browned bits clinging to the bottom. Reduce the heat to moderate, add the cream and cook for five minutes or until the sauce is reduced to about ¾ cup. Add salt and pepper to taste, then strain the sauce through a fine sieve.

To serve, remove the toothpicks and set the chops on four heated plates. Spoon the sauce over them.

■ BEEF AND VEAL MENUS

126

## Sautéed Veal Croquettes with Onion Sauce

**To serve 4**

| | |
|---|---|
| 3/4 pound lean veal, chopped very fine or ground coarse | plus 2 tablespoons butter, chilled and cut into 1/4-inch bits |
| 2 cups heavy cream | 1/3 cup finely chopped onions |
| 1 1/2 cups fresh white-bread crumbs | 1 small bay leaf |
| Freshly grated nutmeg | 1/4 cup white-wine vinegar |
| 1 teaspoon salt | *Beurre manié* made by rubbing 1 teaspoon of butter, softened, and 1 teaspoon flour to a paste |
| 1/4 teaspoon freshly ground white pepper | |
| 6 tablespoons clarified butter, | |

Place the veal in a deep mixing bowl, and set the bowl in a large pot half filled with ice cubes and water. Beating constantly with a wooden spoon, add 2/3 cup of the cream, a tablespoonful at a time. Combine 1/3 cup of the remaining cream with 1/2 cup of bread crumbs, and beat the mixture into the veal by spoonfuls. Beat in a pinch of nutmeg, 1/2 teaspoon of the salt and 1/8 teaspoon of the white pepper.

Divide the veal mixture into four equal portions, and shape each one into a croquette about 4 1/2 inches across and no more than 1/2 inch thick. Dip both sides of each croquette into the remaining cup of bread crumbs to coat it lightly. With the dull edge of a knife, score both sides of each croquette with criss-crossing diagonal lines about 1/2 inch apart. Place the croquettes, side by side, on wax paper and refrigerate them to firm the coating while you prepare the onion sauce.

In a heavy 1- to 2-quart saucepan, melt 1 tablespoon of the clarified butter over moderate heat. Add the onions, the remaining 1/8 teaspoon of pepper and the bay leaf and, stirring constantly, cook for six to eight minutes, until the onions are soft and light gold.

Stir the vinegar into the onions, and simmer until most of the liquid in the pan evaporates. Then pour in the remaining cup of cream and, stirring from time to time with a wire whisk, cook over moderate heat until the sauce is reduced to about 2/3 cup. Whisk in the *beurre manié* and the remaining 1/2 teaspoon of salt.

When the sauce thickens lightly, taste it for seasoning and strain it through a fine sieve into another small pan, pressing the onions with the back of a spoon to extract all of their juices before discarding them. Swirl in the butter bits, and cover the pan to keep the sauce warm.

To cook the croquettes, first preheat the oven to 450°F. In a heavy 10- to 12-inch skillet, melt the remaining 5 tablespoons of clarified butter over high heat. Add the veal croquettes and sauté them for about three minutes on each side or until they are richly and evenly browned. Then transfer them to a baking sheet and bake them for five minutes.

Serve the croquettes at once, arranged on a heated platter and accompanied by the sauce in a sauceboat.

■ CLASSIC FRENCH COOKING

## Veal with Tuna Sauce

*This unlikely-sounding combination of veal and tuna is said to have come from the kitchen of the Marchese Casati of Milan. Her cook, faced with the perennial problem of unexpected guests, put together the only foods left in the kitchen and called it "vitello tonnato." The result is a summer beneficence.* ❖●

**To serve 8**

| | |
|---|---|
| Two 7-ounce cans tuna, preferably packed in olive oil | 2 bay leaves |
| 3 tablespoons olive oil | 1/2 teaspoon crumbled dried thyme |
| One 5-pound veal leg, boned and tied | 2 teaspoons salt |
| 2 onions, chopped coarse | Freshly ground black pepper |
| 2 carrots, chopped coarse | 2 cups chicken stock |
| 2 celery ribs, cut up | 6 tablespoons fresh lemon juice |
| 2 garlic cloves, chopped | 2 cups mayonnaise, preferably homemade |
| One 2-ounce can flat anchovy fillets, drained | 1/4 cup capers |
| 1/4 cup chopped fresh parsley leaves | 1 lemon, sliced thin, for garnish |

Drain the oil from the cans of tuna into a heavy 8- to 10-quart casserole or pot. Add the olive oil and heat it over moderate heat, until it is hot but not smoking. Brown the veal in the oil, turning it frequently with a pair of wooden spoons, until it is lightly colored on all sides—15 to 20 minutes. Remove the veal and set it aside.

Add the onions, carrots, celery and garlic to the oil and, stirring frequently, cook for five minutes or until the onions are soft. Add the tuna, anchovies, parsley, bay leaves, thyme, salt, a generous grinding of pepper, the chicken stock and 2 tablespoons of the lemon juice. Stir well to dissolve any browned particles that may cling to the bottom of the casserole. Bring the mixture to a boil, then add the veal. Reduce the heat, cover the casserole, and simmer the meat and tuna-vegetable mixture for three hours. Using two forks to lift the veal by the strings, transfer it to a plate and allow it to cool to room temperature. Then wrap the veal in plastic wrap and refrigerate it.

Meanwhile, let the tuna-vegetable mixture—there should be about 5 or 6 cups of it—simmer, uncovered, until it is reduced to about 4 cups; stir it from time to time to prevent it from burning. Remove the casserole from the heat and allow the reduced mixture to cool to room temperature. Then purée it through a food mill or in a blender, or in batches in a food processor. Add 2 cups of the purée to the mayonnaise along with the remaining 4 tablespoons of lemon juice. Blend in 2 tablespoons of capers. Refrigerate this sauce until you are ready to serve.

Before serving, cut the strings off the veal and slice the roast thin. Arrange the slices on a large platter. Spoon half of the tuna-mayonnaise sauce over them and garnish the platter with the lemon slices and the remaining capers. Present the rest of the sauce in a bowl.

■ GREAT DINNERS FROM LIFE

## Veal in Gougère

*The word "gougère" applies to pâte à choux—the pastry basis of cream puffs—that incorporates cheese. Usually, the paste is formed into a circle and served as an hors d'oeuvre. Here it is used to border individual gratin dishes and encircle veal stew. If necessary, the gougère can be baked several hours in advance and kept at room temperature.* ◆●

**To serve 4**

| | |
|---|---|
| **5 tablespoons butter** | **½ pound mushrooms, wiped** |
| **1 cup water** | **clean, trimmed and halved** |
| **½ cup flour, plus 2** | **1 tablespoon tomato paste** |
| **tablespooons flour** | **1 garlic clove, chopped** |
| **combined with ¼ cup water** | **fine** |
| **1 tablespoon freshly grated** | **1½ teaspoons chopped fresh** |
| **Parmesan cheese** | **thyme leaves or ½ teaspoon** |
| **2 eggs** | **crumbled dried thyme** |
| **2 bacon slices, diced** | **¾ cup dry red wine** |
| **1½ pounds boneless veal** | **Salt** |
| **round or rump, cut into** | **Freshly ground black pepper** |
| **1-inch cubes** | **4 teaspoons chopped fresh** |
| **1 cup whole small onions,** | **parsley leaves** |
| **parboiled for 10 minutes** | |

Preheat the oven to 400°F. In a heavy 2- to 3-quart saucepan, combine ¼ cup of the butter with ½ cup of the water, and bring to a boil over moderate heat. When the butter melts, add ½ cup of flour and the grated cheese all at once. Beat vigorously with a wooden spoon until a ball forms that moves freely with the spoon and comes away from the sides of the pan.

Immediately take the pan off the heat and use the spoon to make a well in the center of the ball of paste. Break one egg into the well and beat it into the paste. When the egg is absorbed, add the second and beat it in vigorously.

Using a flexible-blade spatula, spread a quarter of the mixture about ½ inch thick around the side—not on the bottom—of each of four individual gratin dishes, 5½ inches in diameter. (The dishes should not be buttered or oiled.) Bake for 18 to 20 minutes, until the pastry is a rich gold. Set the dishes aside on wire racks.

Meanwhile, in a heavy 10- to 12-inch skillet, fry the bacon in the remaining butter over moderate heat until the dice are crisp. Transfer the dice to paper towels to drain. Add half of the veal cubes and—stirring frequently—cook them over moderately high heat for about two minutes, until browned but still pink inside. Transfer them to a plate, and set them aside while you brown the remaining cubes.

When all of the veal is browned, add to the skillet the onions, mushrooms, tomato paste, garlic, thyme, wine, the remaining ½ cup of water, and salt and pepper to taste. Bring to a boil over high heat, then reduce the heat to low and simmer, uncovered, for five minutes. Add the veal and bacon to this sauce; stir in the flour paste. Stirring constantly, cook over moderately high heat for two minutes or until the sauce thickens lightly. Spoon the hot veal mixture into the pastry-bordered dishes, and sprinkle with parsley. Serve at once.

■ BEEF AND VEAL MENUS

## Veal Scallopini with Lemon and Parsley

**To serve 4**

| | |
|---|---|
| **¼ cup butter** | **Freshly ground black pepper** |
| **3 tablespoons vegetable oil** | **3 tablespoons fresh lemon** |
| **1 pound veal scallops, cut** | **juice, plus 1 lemon,** |
| **⅜ inch thick and pounded** | **sliced thin** |
| **to ¼ inch** | **3 tablespoons chopped fresh** |
| **½ cup flour** | **parsley leaves** |
| **½ teaspoon salt** | |

Preheat the oven to 200°F. In a heavy 10- to 12-inch skillet, melt 3 tablespoons of the butter in the oil over moderate heat. Pat the scallops dry. With a sharp knife, make slashes ½ inch deep across the edges all around to prevent the veal from curling as it cooks. Spread the flour on wax paper, and dip both sides of each scallop

## Hungarian Veal Paprikash

**To serve 6**

| | |
|---|---|
| ¹/₄ to ¹/₂ cup lard | Hungarian paprika |
| 3 pounds boneless veal round or rump, cut into 1¹/₂-inch cubes | 1 teaspoon salt |
| | Freshly ground black pepper |
| | 1 pound mushrooms, trimmed |
| 2 cups finely chopped onions | and sliced |
| 2 tablespoons sweet | 1 cup sour cream |

Preheat the oven to 350° F. In a heavy 4- to 5-quart casserole, melt ¹/₄ cup of the lard over high heat. Add a handful of veal cubes, and cook them for two or three minutes, tossing them constantly with a wooden spoon. When they brown lightly on all sides, transfer them to a plate and replace with more veal cubes. Add lard by the tablespoonful as needed.

When all of the veal has been browned, add the onions to the casserole, and cook over moderate heat for six to eight minutes or until soft and light gold. Return the veal to the casserole. Stir in the paprika, salt and a few grindings of pepper, and toss to coat the cubes. Cover the casserole tightly, bake for 30 minutes, then add the mushrooms, re-cover, and cook the veal and mushrooms for 30 minutes more. Remove the casserole from the oven, and stir in the sour cream. Transfer the veal *paprikash* to a heated platter and serve it at once, accompanied by noodles or rice.

■ AMERICAN COOKING: THE MELTING POT

## Veal Scallopini Marsala

**To serve 4**

| | |
|---|---|
| 1¹/₂ pounds veal scallops, cut ³/₈ inch thick and pounded to ¹/₄ inch | 2 tablespoons butter, cut into bits, plus 2 tablespoons butter, softened |
| Salt | 3 tablespoons olive oil |
| Freshly ground black pepper | ¹/₂ cup dry Marsala wine |
| ¹/₄ cup flour | ¹/₂ cup chicken or beef stock |

Season the veal scallops with salt and pepper, then dip them in the flour to coat both sides, and tap off the excess. In a heavy 10- to 12-inch skillet, melt the butter bits with the oil over moderate heat. Add the scallops, a few at a time to avoid crowding the skillet, and brown them for about one minute on each side. After they have browned, transfer them from the skillet to a plate.

Pour off all but a film of fat. Add the Marsala and ¹/₄ cup of the stock, and boil over high heat for one or two minutes, stirring in any brown bits. Return the veal to the skillet and simmer over low heat for two or three minutes, basting with the pan juices.

When the veal is fork tender, tranfer the scallops to a heated platter. Add the remaining stock to the pan juices in the skillet, and boil until this sauce has the consistency of a syrupy glaze; taste it for seasoning. Remove the skillet from the heat, stir in the softened butter, and pour the sauce over the scallops.

■ THE COOKING OF ITALY

into it, one at a time; tap off the excess. Immediately, place the scallop in the hot fat. Flour only as many scallops as will fit in the skillet without crowding.

Fry the scallops for about one minute or until lightly browned; then turn them and brown the other side for a minute or so. When they are done, sprinkle the scallops with the salt and some pepper, and transfer them to an ovenproof platter. Set them in the oven to keep them warm. Repeat the flouring and frying process with the remaining scallops. If the fat burns, pour it off and add more butter.

Take the skillet off the heat and add the lemon juice, stirring and scraping up the brown particles that cling to the bottom of the pan. Swirl in the remaining tablespoon of butter and stir in the parsley. Pour the sauce over the veal; top with lemon slices.

■ PASTA MENUS

## Osso Buco

*Milan claims credit for this rich braise of veal shanks cooked in wine and stock with vegetables. The shanks are usually served on rice—often risotto milanese—and garnished with gremolata, which is composed of lemon peel, garlic and parsley. At the table, each diner extracts the delicious marrow from the shank to create the osso buco, which translates as "hollow bone."* ❧

**To serve 6 to 8**

| | |
|---|---|
| ¼ cup butter | 3 cups drained canned whole |
| 1½ cups finely chopped | tomatoes, chopped coarse |
| onions | ½ teaspoon crumbled dried |
| ½ cup finely chopped carrots | basil |
| ½ cup finely chopped celery | ½ teaspoon crumbled dried |
| 1 teaspoon finely chopped | thyme |
| garlic | 6 parsley sprigs |
| 6 to 7 pounds veal shank or | 2 bay leaves |
| shin, sawed into eight | |
| 2½-inch pieces, each with | GREMOLATA |
| string tied around it | 1 tablespoon grated lemon |
| Salt | peel |
| Freshly ground black pepper | 1 teaspoon finely chopped |
| ½ cup flour | garlic |
| ½ cup olive oil | 3 tablespoons finely chopped |
| 1 cup dry white wine | fresh parsley leaves |
| ¾ to 1½ cups meat stock | |

Choose a heavy, shallow casserole or Dutch oven that has a tight cover and is just large enough to hold the pieces of veal standing up in one layer. Melt the butter in the casserole over moderate heat, and in it cook the chopped onions, carrots, celery and 1 teaspoon garlic, stirring the vegetables frequently with a wooden spoon for 10 to 15 minutes, or until they are lightly colored. Remove the casserole from the heat.

Season the shanks with salt and pepper, then roll them in flour and tap off the excess. In a heavy nonreactive 10- to 12-inch skillet, heat 6 tablespoons of the olive oil over moderately high heat. Brown the shanks, four or five at a time, adding more oil as needed. Put the browned pieces in the casserole, and stand them, side by side, on top of the vegetables.

Preheat the oven to 350°F. Discard all but a film of fat from the skillet. Pour in the wine, and boil it over high heat until it is reduced to about ½ cup, scraping in the browned bits clinging to the pan. Stir in ¾ cup of stock, tomatoes, basil, thyme, parsley sprigs and bay leaves, and bring to a boil, then pour this sauce mixture over the veal. The liquid should half cover the shanks; if it does not, add more stock. Bring the liquid to a boil over moderate heat. Cover the casserole and bake in the lower third of the oven, basting occasionally, for about one hour and 15 minutes or until the veal shows no resistance when pierced with the tip of a knife. Remove the casserole from the oven and increase the oven temperature to 450°F.

Transfer the veal shanks to a large ovenproof serving dish, being careful not to lose the marrow in the bones. Cut off the string. Place the dish in the oven and bake the shanks for five to 10 minutes, until deep brown and brightly glazed.

Meanwhile, strain the contents of the casserole through a fine sieve into a 2- to 3-quart nonreactive saucepan, pressing the vegetables with the back of a spoon to extract their juice before discarding them. Boil over high heat, stirring frequently, until the liquid is reduced by half. Taste for seasoning. Pour the reduced sauce over the glazed veal, and sprinkle the top with *gremolata*.

■ THE COOKING OF ITALY

## Beef Tongue in Sweet-and-Sour Sauce

*As with all tongue recipes, it is essential to peel the tongue when it is still very hot. At that stage, the thin layer of fat under the skin is melted—freeing the skin from the meat so that it slips off easily. When the tongue cools, the fat hardens and peeling is difficult.* ❧

**To serve 4 to 6**

| | |
|---|---|
| One 4- to 5-pound fresh | 5 tablespoons brown |
| beef tongue | sugar |
| ¼ cup vegetable oil | ¼ cup seedless raisins |
| 2 cups finely chopped | 2 tablespoons slivered |
| onions | blanched almonds |
| 10 gingersnaps, crushed | 1 teaspoon salt |
| (about ½ cup) | ½ lemon, sliced thin |
| 7 tablespoons cider vinegar | |

Soak the tongue in cold water for about two hours. Then put the tongue in a large pot, pour in enough fresh cold water to cover it by at least an inch, and bring the water to a boil over high heat. Reduce the heat to low and simmer the tongue for 10 minutes. Drain the tongue and rinse both tongue and pot. Put the tongue back in the pot, cover it with water by 1 inch, and bring the water to a boil. Reduce the heat to low, then simmer for two to three hours or until the tongue is tender and shows no resistance when pierced with a knife tip.

Drain the tongue in a sieve set over a pot or bowl, and reserve 4 cups of its cooking liquid. Transfer the tongue to a cutting board and allow it to cool just enough so that you can handle it. Turn the tongue upside down and use a small, sharp knife to slit the skin from the tip to the base. With the tip of the knife, loosen the skin along the slit; then use your fingers to peel away the skin. Cut off the fat, bones and gristle at the base of the tongue. Cut the tongue crosswise into slices ½ inch thick.

In a heavy 10- to 12-inch nonreactive skillet, heat the oil over moderate heat. Stir in the onions and cook, stirring frequently, for six to eight minutes or until they are soft and lightly colored. Then stir in the gingersnaps, the reserved cooking liquid, the vinegar, brown sugar, raisins, almonds and salt, and bring this sauce mixture to a boil.

Place the tongue slices in the sauce and turn them to coat them well. Top with the lemon slices, cover the skillet, and simmer for 15 minutes or until the tongue is heated through and the sauce is thick and smooth. Taste for seasoning, then transfer to a heated deep platter and serve at once.

■ AMERICAN COOKING: THE MELTING POT

## Calf's Liver with Onions

**To serve 4**

| | |
|---|---|
| 4 tablespoons olive oil | Salt |
| 1 cup thinly sliced onions | Freshly ground black pepper |
| ½ teaspoon crumbled dried sage | 2 tablespoons white-wine vinegar |
| 1 pound calf's liver, cut into ¼-inch strips | 2 tablespoons chopped fresh parsley leaves for garnish |

Heat 2 tablespoons of the oil in a heavy 8- to 10-inch skillet. Add the onions and cook over moderate heat, stirring frequently, for five minutes, until the onions are soft but not brown. Stir in the sage, and cook for two minutes longer, until the onions color lightly; transfer to a bowl.

Pat the liver dry with paper towels and season with salt and pepper. Pour the remaining oil into the skillet and heat it until hot but not smoking. Drop in the liver strips and sauté them, turning frequently, for one or two minutes or until they are lightly browned on all sides. Stir in the onions and cook them with the liver for a minute. Transfer the liver and onions to a heated platter and set aside.

Immediately pour the vinegar into the skillet and boil for a few minutes, scraping in any brown particles clinging to the pan. Pour the sauce over the liver and onions, and sprinkle with the chopped parsley. Serve at once.

■ THE COOKING OF ITALY

## Sweetbreads with Baby Vegetables

**To serve 4**

| | |
|---|---|
| 1½ pounds veal sweetbreads | 2 tablespoons butter plus ¼ cup clarified butter |
| 1 onion, stuck with 2 cloves | |
| 1 cup milk | LEMON-CREAM SAUCE |
| 16 baby carrots, trimmed | 1 teaspoon finely chopped lemon peel |
| 16 baby yellow squash, trimmed | 2 tablespoons fresh lemon juice |
| 1 cup Sugar Snap peas, trimmed and strings removed | ¼ cup dry white wine |
| ½ cup flour | ¾ cup chicken stock |
| Salt | ⅓ cup heavy cream |
| Freshly ground white pepper | Salt |
| | Freshly ground white pepper |

Soak the sweetbreads in several changes of cold water until the water stays clear. Place them in a saucepan, and add the onion, milk and enough water to cover. Bring to a boil over moderate heat, reduce the heat to low, and simmer for five to six minutes. Drain and put the sweetbreads in cold water; set aside.

Pour 1 inch of water into a large saucepan. Set a vegetable steamer in the pan and put in the carrots. Cover and steam the carrots for eight minutes, until barely tender. Transfer them to a colander, and run cold water over them to stop their cooking. Set the carrots aside on a plate and cover with foil to keep them

warm. Similarly, steam the squash for six minutes, the peas for four minutes.

Meanwhile, for the sauce, combine the peel, juice and wine in a heavy 1- to 1½-quart nonreactive saucepan. Bring to a boil over high heat and boil for one minute. Reduce the heat to low, stir in the stock and heavy cream, and season to taste with salt and white pepper. Stirring frequently, simmer the sauce for 20 minutes, until it is thick.

When the vegetables are cooked, drain the sweetbreads and pat them dry. With your fingers remove the thin surface membrane, fat and tubes that cover them. Cut the sweetbreads into four equal pieces. Place the flour on a sheet of wax paper. Then season the sweetbreads with salt and white pepper and coat them on both sides with flour; tap off excess flour.

In an 8- to 10-inch skillet, melt the plain and clarified butter over moderate heat. When hot, add the sweetbreads; sauté for about five minutes a side, until lightly browned.

To serve, slice the sweetbreads thin and place on heated individual plates. If necessary, reheat the vegetables in the sauce briefly over low heat; spoon over the sweetbreads.

■ FRENCH REGIONAL MENUS

## Veal Kidneys with Juniper Berries

**To serve 4**

| | |
|---|---|
| Four 6- to 8-ounce veal kidneys, peeled and trimmed of fat | softened |
| | 2 tablespoons vegetable oil |
| Salt | 16 juniper berries, slightly bruised with the flat of a cleaver or kitchen mallet |
| Freshly ground black pepper | |
| ¼ cup butter, cut into bits, plus 1 tablespoon butter, | ½ cup gin |
| | ¼ cup chicken stock |

With a sharp knife, cut through each kidney horizontally to within ½ inch of the edge. Open the kidneys gently and spread them flat. To hold them in shape, thread two short metal skewers diagonally crosswise through each kidney. Sprinkle the kidneys on both sides with salt and pepper.

In a heavy 12-inch skillet, melt the butter bits with the oil over high heat. Drop in the juniper berries and add the kidneys, cut side down. Sauté the kidneys for four to five minutes on each side or until they are lightly browned.

Warm the gin in a small pan over low heat, ignite it, and pour it flaming over the kidneys, while sliding the skillet back and forth over the burner. When the flames die, transfer the kidneys to a heated platter and cover with foil.

Add the stock to the liquid remaining in the skillet and bring it to a boil over high heat, stirring and scraping in the brown particles clinging to the pan. Cook, uncovered, until the sauce is reduced to a syrupy glaze. Take the pan off the heat and swirl in the softened butter. Carefully remove the skewers, pour the sauce over the kidneys, and serve at once.

■ A QUINTET OF CUISINES

## Moussaka

*Two indispensable Middle Eastern foods—lamb and eggplant—come together in moussaka. The sheep was domesticated in Kurdistan tens of thousands of years ago; Arabs brought the eggplant from India more than 1,500 years ago. Whereas Middle Eastern cooks prefer small eggplants—including the oval ones 2 or 3 inches long from which the vegetable is probably named—Americans prefer plump, pear-shaped specimens.* ❖●

**To serve 6 to 8**

| | |
|---|---|
| **Three 1-pound eggplants, peeled and cut lengthwise into ½-inch slices** | **1 teaspoon crumbled dried oregano** |
| **Salt** | **½ teaspoon ground cinnamon** |
| **1 cup flour** | **Freshly ground black pepper** |
| **1 to 2 cups olive oil** | **6 tablespoons freshly grated *kefalotiri* or Parmesan cheese** |
| **1 cup finely chopped onions** | |
| **2 pounds lean ground lamb** | |
| **3 tomatoes, peeled, seeded and chopped fine, or 1 cup chopped drained canned tomatoes** | RICH CREAM SAUCE |
| | **2 cups milk** |
| | **1 tablespoon butter** |
| **1 cup canned tomato purée** | **3 eggs** |
| **1 teaspoon finely chopped garlic** | **¼ cup flour** |
| | **½ teaspoon salt** |

Sprinkle the eggplant slices lightly with salt, place them, side by side, on paper towels, and weight them with heavy platters or casseroles. Let the juices drain for 20 to 30 minutes, then dry the slices with fresh towels. Spread the flour on wax paper, dip the slices in flour and tap off the excess.

In a heavy 12-inch skillet, heat ½ cup of the olive oil over high heat until it is very hot but not smoking. Add a few eggplant slices at a time, and brown them for a minute or two on each side, regulating the heat so that they color quickly without burning. As they finish cooking, transfer them to paper towels to drain. Add more oil as necessary.

Pour ½ cup more olive oil into the skillet, and heat it over moderate heat. Add the onions and, stirring frequently, cook them for eight to ten minutes or until they are soft and lightly colored. Stir in the ground lamb and, mashing it with the back of the spoon to break up any lumps, cook until no traces of pink show. Add the tomatoes, tomato purée, garlic, oregano, cinnamon, 1 teaspoon of salt and a few grindings of pepper, and bring to a boil over high heat. Stirring frequently, cook briskly until most of the liquid in the pan evaporates and the mixture is thick enough to hold its shape almost solidly in the spoon. Taste for seasoning.

Meanwhile, prepare the sauce. Heat 1½ cups of the milk and the butter in a small pan until bubbles appear around the edges.

**VINEYARD LEG OF LAMB**

Remove from the heat. In a heavy 2- to 3-quart saucepan, beat the eggs with a wire whisk until smooth. Blend in the flour, the ½ teaspoon of salt and the remaining ½ cup of milk. Place this saucepan over moderate heat and, stirring constantly with the whisk, slowly add the milk and melted butter mixture in a thin stream. Still stirring, cook until the sauce thickens heavily. Set the sauce aside off the heat.

Preheat the oven to 325°F. To assemble the *moussaka*, spread half of the eggplant slices in overlapping rows in the bottom of a 14-by-9-by-3-inch baking dish. Sprinkle the slices evenly with 2 tablespoons of the grated cheese, and pour in the lamb and tomato mixture, spreading it into the corners of the dish with a rubber spatula. Arrange the rest of the eggplant on top and sprinkle with 2 tablespoons the cheese. Pour the cream sauce evenly over the top, and sprinkle it with the remaining cheese.

Bake in the middle of the oven for 30 minutes, then increase the heat to 400°F. and bake for 15 minutes longer, to brown the top. Let the *moussaka* rest at room temperature for five to 10 minutes before serving it.

■ MIDDLE EASTERN COOKING

## Vineyard Leg of Lamb

*A favorite of California vintners, this method of roasting lamb is a bit complicated. However, the surface of the finished roast has an unusually rich chestnut-brown color and the flavor amply rewards the extra effort involved.* ❧

**To serve 6 to 8**

| | |
|---|---|
| One 5- to 6-pound leg of lamb, trimmed of excess fat, with fell (parchment-like covering) removed | 1 teaspoon ground cumin |
| | 1½ tablespoons salt |
| | 2 teaspoons freshly ground black pepper |
| 2 garlic cloves, cut lengthwise into thin slivers | ¼ cup dry sherry wine |
| | ¼ cup dry white wine |
| 1 cup brandy | Mint sprigs for garnish |

With the tip of a knife, cut a dozen slits 1 inch deep all over the surface of the lamb; insert a sliver of garlic into each slit. Cut a double thickness of cheesecloth about 16 inches wide and 20 inches long, and drench it with ½ cup of the brandy. Wrap the cloth around the lamb and cover with plastic wrap. Marinate the lamb at room temperature for about two hours.

Preheat the oven to 450°F. Mix the cumin, salt and pepper together in a small bowl, and combine the sherry and white wine in another bowl. Unwrap the lamb and place the leg, fat side up, on a rack in a shallow roasting pan. Press the cumin mixture into the surface of the lamb, coating the meat with the spices as evenly as is possible.

Roast the lamb for 20 minutes. Then reduce the heat to 350°F. and baste with a tablespoon or so of the wine mixture. Continue to roast for 40 to 60 minutes longer or until the leg is cooked to your taste, basting two or three more times with the remaining wine mixture. A meat thermometer inserted deep without touching bone should register 130°F. when the lamb is rare, 140°F. when medium and 150°F. when well done.

Transfer the lamb to a heated platter, and let the roast rest for 10 minutes so that it will be easier to carve. Just before serving, warm the remaining ½ cup of brandy in a small saucepan. Ignite the brandy with a match, and pour it flaming over the lamb. When the flame dies, garnish the leg of lamb with mint sprigs and serve it at once.

■ AMERICAN COOKING: THE GREAT WEST

# Rack of Lamb with Mint Sauce

*A rack of lamb consists of six or seven rib chops, each of which is so small that two racks are necessary to serve four. Ask the butcher to French the ribs by scraping off all of the flesh from the bony ends and to cut through the chine bone—a part of the backbone—to facilitate carving. When you serve the racks, decorate the rib ends with paper frills, which you can buy from a food specialty shop.* ◆●

**To serve 4 to 6**

| | |
|---|---|
| 1/4 cup finely chopped fresh parsley leaves | 2 tablespoons olive or safflower oil |
| 4 teaspoons finely chopped garlic | 2 racks of lamb, trimmed, chine bone sawed through but left attached, rib tips Frenched |
| 2 tablespoons chopped fresh thyme leaves or 2 teaspoons crumbled dried thyme | Salt |
| 1 tablespoon chopped rosemary leaves or 1 teaspoon crushed dried rosemary, plus rosemary sprigs for garnish | Freshly ground black pepper |
| | 1/4 cup red-wine vinegar |
| | 1 tablespoon sugar |
| | 2 tablespoons finely chopped fresh mint leaves |

Preheat the oven to 425°F. Mix the parsley, garlic, thyme, rosemary leaves and oil in a small bowl, and spread the mixture over the racks of lamb. Sprinkle the lamb with salt and a few grindings of black pepper. Stand the racks in a roasting pan. If you like, set them facing together, fat side out, and interlace the ribs. Cover the ends of the ribs with foil to hold the racks together and to keep the bone from charring. Roast the lamb for 30 minutes for medium rare.

Meanwhile, bring the vinegar to a boil in a small nonreactive saucepan; add the sugar and stir until it dissolves. Then take the pan off the heat and stir in the mint. Allow the mint to steep for 15 to 20 minutes.

When the lamb is done, transfer it to a serving platter, and cover it loosely with foil to keep it warm. Let the roast rest for 10 minutes before carving it. During this time, skim as much fat as possible from the pan juices. Add the mint and vinegar mixture to the pan juices, and boil briefly, scraping the sides and bottom of the roasting pan to incorporate any brown particles. Add whatever juice may have accumulated around the lamb, and then adjust the seasonings.

Remove the foil from the roast and cover the ends of the ribs with paper frills, if you like.. Garnish the lamb with rosemary sprigs, and present the mint sauce separately.

To carve the roast, cut between the first two ribs on one side. Then cut off a rib on the other side. Continue to alternate sides, so that the rack remains standing until all of the ribs are carved.

■ AMERICAN REGIONAL MENUS

# Lamb Chop Shish Kebab

*Precooking and marinating some ingredients ensure that everything on the skewer is at the right degree of doneness when the chops are grilled to your taste.* ◆●

**To serve 6**

| | |
|---|---|
| 12 single-rib lamb chops, 1 inch thick, long ends cut off | HERB MARINADE |
| | 1 1/2 cups vegetable oil |
| 12 white onions, 1 to 1 1/2 inches across | 1 cup fresh lemon juice |
| | 1 tablespoon finely chopped onion |
| 12 mushroom caps, wiped clean | 1 garlic clove, chopped fine |
| 2 small zucchini, ends trimmed, cut into 1/2-inch slices | 1 tablespoon crumbled dried oregano |
| | 1/2 teaspoon crumbled dried thyme |
| 2 green peppers, cut into sixths, seeded and deribbed | 1/4 teaspoon crushed dried rosemary |
| 12 cherry tomatoes, stemmed | 1 teaspoon salt |
| 12 thick lemon slices | Freshly ground black pepper |
| 2 tablespoons butter | |

Combine all of the marinade ingredients in a bowl and stir well. Arrange the chops in one layer in a shallow nonreactive baking pan and pour the marinade over them.

Drop the onions into a pan of boiling water and parboil them for five minutes. Drain the onions in a colander, rinse them under cold running water, then slip off the skins. Add the onions, mushroom caps, zucchini and peppers to the pan and coat them with marinade. Cover the pan and marinate the lamb and vegetables for about two hours at room temperature, at least four hours in the refrigerator. Turn the lamb and vegetables over once or twice while they marinate.

Light a mound of charcoal in a grill and let the coals burn until white ash appears on the surface, then spread them into a layer 2 inches deep. Set the rack 4 to 6 inches above the coals and let it heat for five minutes. Grease it with an oil-moistened cloth held in long-handled tongs. Alternatively, preheat a broiler to its highest setting. Set the top rack so that when the pan is in place its top surface will be 3 to 4 inches from the heating element.

To assemble each skewer, thread two chops lengthwise onto it and two each of the onions, mushroom caps, zucchini slices, pepper pieces, cherry tomatoes and lemon slices, alternating the foods attractively and pressing them firmly together as you put them in place. Brush the mushroom caps with the butter. Then lay the skewers over the baking pan or on a tray lined with foil so that excess marinade can drip off for a few minutes.

Grill the kabobs on the rack of the charcoal grill or broiler pan for seven or eight minutes, turning them once, for rare, 10 to 12 minutes for medium rare.

To serve, slide the vegetables and chops off each skewer onto heated individual plates—removing only a few pieces at a time to avoid breaking the vegetables.

■ GREAT DINNERS FROM LIFE

## Lamb Pot Roast with White Beans

**To serve 6**

One 6-pound lamb shoulder
  roast, boned and tied
2 garlic cloves, cut
  lengthwise into thin
  slivers
¼ cup vegetable oil
¼ cup butter
3 onions, sliced thin
3 carrots, cut into 1-inch
  chunks
1½ cups dry white wine
2 cups beef stock
2 tomatoes, peeled, seeded
  and chopped coarse
Bouquet garni made of
  4 parsley sprigs, 1 leek

(white part plus 2 inches
  of green top) and 1 bay
  leaf, tied together
1 teaspoon crumbled dried
  thyme
1½ teaspoons salt
Freshly ground black pepper
Water
2 cups dry white beans,
  such as Great Northern or
  navy, soaked overnight
  and drained
2 tablespoons finely chopped
  fresh parsley leaves, plus
  parsley sprigs for garnish

Preheat the oven to 350°F. Make incisions 1 inch deep over the surface of the lamb and insert a sliver of garlic in each one. Heat the oil in a heavy nonreactive 12-inch skillet and brown the lamb on all sides. Meanwhile, in a heavy flameproof nonreactive casserole just large enough to hold the lamb, melt the butter over moderate heat. In it cook the onions and carrots, stirring occasionally, for 10 minutes, until lightly colored. Place the browned lamb, fat side up, on the vegetables.

Pour the wine into the skillet, and boil briskly, scraping in any bits that cling to the pan. When the wine has reduced to 1 cup, add the beef stock, tomatoes, bouquet garni, thyme, ½ teaspoon of the salt and a few grindings of pepper, and return to a boil. Pour the stock over the lamb. Bring the liquid to a boil again over moderate heat, and drape foil over the lamb. Tightly cover the casserole and cook in the lower third of the oven for two to two and a half hours or until tender.

Meanwhile, place the beans in a heavy 3- to 4-quart saucepan, add the remaining salt, and cover the beans with water by 1 inch. Bring to a boil over moderate heat, skimming the foam that rises to the surface, then boil for 10 minutes. Reduce the heat to low, partially cover the pan, and simmer for one hour, until the beans are tender; drain and set aside.

When the lamb is done, transfer it to a plate and strain the contents of the casserole through a fine sieve into a nonreactive bowl; press down hard on the vegetables with the back of a spoon before discarding them. Skim as much fat as possible from the braising sauce and taste for seasoning.

Return the lamb to the casserole, add the beans and pour the strained sauce over them. Set over moderate heat and cook just until the sauce comes to a boil.

To serve, carve the lamb into ¼-inch slices, and arrange them on a heated platter; spoon on a little sauce and garnish with parsley sprigs. Drain the beans, sprinkle them with chopped parsley and serve with the lamb. Present the remaining sauce separately.

■ THE COOKING OF PROVINCIAL FRANCE

## Grilled Stuffed Lamb Chops

**To serve 4**

½ cup fresh white-bread
  crumbs
2 tablespoons chopped
  scallions
1 tablespoon chopped fresh
  parsley leaves
1 tablespoon chopped fresh
  rosemary leaves
2 mushrooms, trimmed and

chopped fine
1 garlic clove, chopped fine
2 tablespoons dry white wine
Salt
Freshly ground black pepper
4 loin lamb chops,
  1½ inches thick, with
  pockets cut for stuffing
4 teaspoons olive oil

In a barbecue grill, light a mound of charcoal that you can later spread into a layer about 2 inches deep and an inch or so larger all around than the four chops set side by side. Light the charcoal. An electric starter is convenient; avoid petroleum-based liquids or jellies that may impart an undesirable flavor to the lamb.

Let the charcoal burn until a white ash appears on the surface, then spread out the coals. Set the rack in the grill 4 to 6 inches above the coals, and let it heat for five minutes, then—using tongs to hold a cloth drenched with vegetable oil—grease the rack.

Meanwhile, in a small bowl, blend together the bread crumbs, scallions, parsley, rosemary, mushrooms, garlic and wine. Add salt and pepper to taste, and stir well. Using a teaspoon, insert about ¼ cup of this stuffing mixture into the pocket of each lamb chop. Close the pocket with a small skewer or a pair of crossed toothpicks that have been soaked in water for 10 minutes to keep them from burning. Rub both sides of the chops with olive oil and season them lightly with salt and pepper.

Place the chops on the preheated rack, and grill them for three minutes or until well browned. Using long-handled tongs, turn the chops over and brown the other side for three minutes. Brush the chops again with oil. Turning them every few minutes to ensure even color, cook them to the desired degree of doneness —about 10 minutes an inch all told for rare, 12 minutes for medium and 15 minutes for well done. Transfer the chops to a heated platter and remove the skewers before serving them.

■ PICNIC AND OUTDOOR MENUS

## Jamaican Lamb Shanks

**To serve 6**

6 meaty lamb shanks, each
  about ¾ pound
1 tablespoon salt
Freshly ground black pepper
2 tablespoons butter
2 tablespoons vegetable
  oil
3 cups fresh orange juice

1 cup chicken stock
1 tablespoon grated
  orange peel
1 tablespoon malt vinegar
¼ teaspoon Tabasco sauce
1 bay leaf
4 egg yolks

Pat the lamb shanks dry with paper towels and sprinkle them with the salt and a few grindings of pepper. In a heavy 12-inch

In a small bowl, beat the egg yolks with a whisk until well blended. Beat in 2 or 3 tablespoons of the hot liquid and then, stirring constantly, pour the egg mixture into the casserole in a slow stream. Still whisking, cook over very low heat until the sauce is smooth and thick enough to coat the whisk lightly. Do not let the sauce come to a boil or it will curdle. Taste for seasoning, then pour the sauce over the lamb shanks or, if you prefer, moisten the shanks with a few spoonfuls of the sauce and serve the rest separately in a bowl or sauceboat. Serve immediately.

■ THE COOKING OF THE CARIBBEAN ISLANDS

## Grilled Butterflied Leg of Lamb

*A butterflied leg of lamb has had the bones and fat removed. The thick parts are cut almost through so that the meat can be opened out as if it were hinged. The lamb is then pounded flat—and bears a resemblance to a butterfly's wings.* ❧

**To serve 4**

| | |
|---|---|
| 2½ pounds butterflied leg of lamb | Salt |
| 1 cup dry red wine | Freshly ground black pepper |
| 2 or 3 large shallots, chopped fine | 1 teaspoon cornstarch combined with 1 tablespoon cold water |
| 2 tablespoons chopped fresh rosemary leaves or 2 teaspoons crumbled dried rosemary | Fresh rosemary sprigs for garnish |

Place the lamb, fat side down, in a large shallow glass or ceramic dish. Pour the wine over it and sprinkle it with the shallots and rosemary. Marinate the meat at room temperature for 15 to 30 minutes, turning it once or twice.

Preheat the broiler to the highest setting. Brush a generous coating of oil onto the tray or rack of the broiler pan. Using tongs, lift the lamb and place it, fat side up, on the broiler pan tray or rack. Set the marinade aside.

Position the broiler pan so that the surface of the lamb will be about 2 to 3 inches from the heat source, and broil it for eight to 10 minutes or until well browned. Brush the lamb with marinade, turn, and brush the other side. Broil the lamb for 10 to 15 minutes or until well browned. The thick parts should be rare, the thin sections medium to well done. Transfer the lamb to a heated platter and cover it loosely with foil to keep it warm.

Skim most of the fat from the pan drippings and pour the drippings into a small nonreactive skillet. Add the reserved marinade and bring to a boil over high heat. Season with salt and black pepper to taste. Add the cornstarch paste to the marinade and cook, stirring, for three to five minutes, or until this sauce thickens lightly and is smooth.

Slice the lamb and divide it among four heated dinner plates. Spoon sauce over the lamb and serve it, if you like, garnished with rosemary sprigs.

■ FRENCH REGIONAL MENUS

**LAMB POT ROAST WITH WHITE BEANS**

skillet, melt the butter in the oil over high heat. Add the shanks, three at a time, and brown them in the hot fat, turning them often with tongs. As they brown, transfer the shanks to a heavy 6- to 8-quart nonreactive casserole.

Add the orange juice, stock, orange peel, vinegar, Tabasco and bay leaf, and stir the shanks to coat them evenly. Bring to a boil over high heat, reduce the heat to low, cover tightly, and simmer for about one and one-half hours or until the shanks are tender and the meat shows no resistance when pierced with the tip of a knife. Transfer them to a heated platter. Cover the platter loosely with foil to keep the shanks warm while you prepare the sauce.

With a large spoon, skim as much fat as possible from the liquid remaining in the casserole. Strain the liquid through a sieve into the casserole, and bring to a boil over high heat. Cook briskly, uncovered, until the liquid is reduced to about 2½ cups; then lower the heat.

## Braised Lamb with Lemon

**To serve 4**

| | |
|---|---|
| 2 pounds boneless lean lamb shoulder, cut into 1-inch cubes | ½ teaspoon finely chopped garlic |
| Salt | 1 tablespoon paprika |
| Freshly ground black pepper | 2 tablespoons chopped fresh parsley leaves |
| ¼ cup olive oil | 2 tablespoons fresh lemon juice |
| 1 cup finely chopped onions | 1 lemon, cut into wedges, for garnish |

Sprinkle the lamb with salt and a generous grinding of pepper. In a heavy 10- to 12-inch skillet, heat the olive oil over high heat until it is hot but not smoking. Brown the lamb, half a dozen or so pieces at a time, turning the pieces with tongs and regulating the heat so that the meat colors evenly without burning. Set the browned lamb on a plate.

Add the onions and garlic to the fat remaining in the skillet and, stirring frequently, cook for about five minutes or until the onions are soft but not brown. Stir in the paprika, then add the lamb and the juices that have accumulated around it. Stir in the parsley and lemon juice, and reduce the heat to low. Cover the skillet and simmer for about one hour or until the lamb is tender. Taste for seasoning and serve at once from a heated platter, garnished if you like with lemon wedges.

■ THE COOKING OF SPAIN AND PORTUGAL

## French Spring Lamb Stew

*Called "navarin printanier" in French, this stew tastes best when made with young lamb and early vegetables.* ◆●

**To serve 6**

| | |
|---|---|
| 4 pounds boneless lean lamb, trimmed and cut into 2-inch pieces | 1 garlic clove, chopped coarse |
| Salt | 4 parsley sprigs |
| Freshly ground black pepper | 1 small bay leaf, crumbled |
| ½ cup flour | 1 teaspoon crumbled dried rosemary |
| ¼ cup butter | 12 baby carrots or 6 medium-sized carrots, cut into 2- to 3-inch lengths |
| 2 tablespoons vegetable oil | |
| 1 tablespoon finely chopped onion | 24 small white onions |
| ½ cup dry white wine | 1 tablespoon sugar |
| 2 cups peeled, seeded, coarsely chopped tomatoes, or chopped drained canned tomatoes | 12 small or 6 medium-sized new potatoes, scrubbed |
| 2 cups water | ½ pound green beans, trimmed and cut into 1-inch pieces |
| 1 celery rib with leaves, cut into 3 pieces | 1 cup shelled green peas |

Preheat the oven to 350° F. Sprinkle the pieces of lamb with 1 teaspoon of salt and a few grindings of pepper. Spread the flour on a sheet of wax paper  dip the lamb pieces in the flour to coat them

FRENCH SPRING LAMB STEW

lightly on all sides and tap off the excess. In a heavy 12-inch non-reactive skillet, melt 1 tablespoon of the butter in the oil over moderately high heat. Brown the lamb pieces, a few at a time, turning them with tongs until they are richly colored on all sides. As they brown, place the lamb pieces in a 6- to 8-quart nonreactive flameproof casserole.

When the lamb is browned, add the chopped onion to the skillet and stir for about two minutes until it is golden. Add the onion to the lamb, then pour off all fat from the skillet. Pour the wine into the skillet, and cook over low heat for a few minutes, stirring in the brown particles clinging to the bottom of the skillet.

Add the wine to the casserole together with the tomatoes, water, celery, garlic, parsley, bay leaf and rosemary. Cover the casserole, and cook the lamb in the oven for one hour. Pour the contents of the casserole through a sieve into a large bowl. Lift out the lamb and set it aside on a plate. Strain the cooking liquid into a bowl, pressing the vegetables with a spoon to extract their juices before discarding them. Set the liquid aside. Wash the casserole.

Melt the remaining 3 tablespoons of butter over moderate heat in a heavy 10- to 12-inch skillet, add the carrots and the whole onions, and slide the skillet back and forth over the heat until the vegetables are coated with butter. Sprinkle them with the sugar, and continue cooking, sliding the skillet back and forth to turn them, until they are golden brown, about seven or eight minutes.

Skim the fat from the strained cooking liquid. Taste the liquid and add more salt and pepper, if necessary. Spread the carrots, onions and potatoes in the casserole; return the lamb and cooking liquid to the casserole. Bring the liquid to a boil over moderate heat. Reduce the heat to low, cover the casserole, and simmer the stew for 20 minutes.

Meanwhile, bring a large pot of lightly salted water to a boil, and in it parboil the beans and peas for five minutes. Drain well. Add them to the casserole, cover, and cook the stew for 10 minutes longer or until the potatoes are tender when pierced with a fork and the beans are just slightly resistant to the bite—*al dente*.

■ GREAT DINNERS FROM LIFE

## Curried Lamb

*In Jamaica, where this recipe originated, the curry is prepared with goat meat rather than lamb—and you may substitute kid or goat if it is available. Both of these meats will be similar in flavor to lamb—but more assertive.* ❧

**To serve 6**

| | |
|---|---|
| 3 pounds boneless lean lamb shoulder, trimmed and cut into 1½-inch cubes | Freshly ground black pepper |
| ¼ cup butter | 1 cup coarsely chopped fresh coconut |
| 2 tablespoons vegetable oil | 1 cup milk |
| 3 cups finely chopped onions | 1 cup chicken stock |
| 3 tablespoons curry powder | 1 bay leaf |
| 1 tablespoon finely chopped fresh hot chilies | 2 tablespoons fresh lime juice |
| ½ teaspoon ground allspice | Freshly cooked plain or saffron-flavored rice |
| 1 teaspoon salt | Mango chutney |

Pat the lamb cubes dry with paper towels. In a heavy 10- to 12-inch skillet, melt 2 tablespoons of the butter in the oil over moderate heat. Drop in six or seven lamb cubes, and brown them on all sides. As they color, transfer the cubes to a plate and add cubes that remain—never crowding the pan, to prevent the lamb from steaming instead of browning.

Melt the remaining butter in the skillet, add the onions and, stirring frequently, cook them for five minutes, or until they are soft. Add the curry, chilies, allspice, salt and a few grindings of pepper and, stirring constantly, simmer for two or three minutes. Combine the coconut and milk and, with the back of a spoon, press the mixture hard into a bowl through a sieve lined with cheesecloth.

Return the lamb and juices that have accumulated around it to the skillet, stir in the coconut milk, stock and bay leaf, and bring to a boil over high heat. Reduce the heat to low, cover, and simmer for one hour or until the lamb shows no resistance when pierced with the tip of a knife. Remove the bay leaf and stir in the lime juice. Taste for seasoning.

To serve, mound the lamb on a deep heated platter and pour the sauce over it. Curried lamb is traditionally accompanied by plain or saffron rice and mango chutney.

■ THE COOKING OF THE CARIBBEAN ISLANDS

## Lamb with Dill

*Dill is best known for its association with pickles, but it also adds spirit to such disparate foods as sauerkraut, carrots and apple pie. Native to the area around the Black Sea, dill turns up frequently in Middle Eastern cooking. When fresh dill is not available, either dried dill weed or dill seeds can take its place. The dried forms taste alike and can be used interchangeably.* ❧

**To serve 6**

| | |
|---|---|
| 3½ pounds boneless lean lamb, cut into 1½-inch pieces | ⅓ cup dry red wine |
| Salt | 1½ tablespoons finely cut fresh dill or 1½ teaspoons dill weed |
| Freshly ground black pepper | 1 pound mushrooms, trimmed, quartered if large and halved lengthwise if small |
| ½ cup flour | |
| 3 tablespoons butter | |
| ½ cup chopped onions | |
| 1¾ cups beef stock | ½ cup sour cream |

Dry the pieces of lamb with paper towels. Season them with salt and pepper to taste. Spread the flour on a sheet of wax paper, and dip the pieces in the flour to lightly coat all sides; tap off the excess. Melt the butter in a heavy 4- to 6-quart casserole over moderately high heat. In it brown the lamb, a few pieces at a time, turning them often, until they are lightly browned on all sides. Do not allow the lamb to get crusty. As it browns, transfer the lamb to a bowl.

Add the onions to the casserole, and cook them for a minute or two, until coated with the fat, then stir in the lamb and the juices that have accumulated around it. Add the stock, wine and dill weed. Stirring occasionally, bring the stew to a boil over moderate heat. Reduce the heat, cover, and simmer for an hour, until the meat is tender.

Cool, then cover the casserole and refrigerate the stew for several hours, or overnight. Remove the layer of fat that forms on top. Bring the stew to a boil over moderate heat, add the mushrooms, cover, and cook over low heat for 20 minutes, stirring the stew occasionally.

Add salt and pepper to taste, if necessary. Stir in the sour cream, and cook the stew for four or five minutes longer over very low heat, to heat it through.

■ GREAT DINNERS FROM LIFE

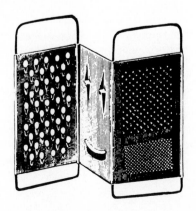

ROAST PORK CALYPSO

## Barbecued Spareribs

**To serve 4 to 6**

| | |
|---|---|
| 1 cup finely chopped onions | ¼ teaspoon Tabasco sauce |
| 1 cup spicy ketchup | 4 pounds spareribs, in 2 or |
| ¼ cup dark-brown sugar | 3 pieces, trimmed of |
| ¼ cup distilled white | excess fat |
| vinegar | 1 teaspoon salt |
| ¼ cup Worcestershire sauce | Freshly ground black pepper |
| 1 teaspoon dry mustard | |

Preheat the oven to 400°F. For the basting saucè, combine the onions, ketchup, brown sugar, vinegar, Worcestershire, mustard and Tabasco in a 1- to 1½-quart nonreactive saucepan. Stirring with a wooden spoon, bring the sauce to a boil over high heat.

Reduce the heat to low and simmer for five minutes, until the onions are soft.

Arrange the spareribs, meat side up, on a rack set in a large shallow roasting pan, and sprinkle them with the salt and a few grindings of pepper. With a pastry brush, spread about ½ cup of the basting sauce evenly over the ribs.

Bake the spareribs uncovered for an hour to an hour and a half, brushing them several times with the sauce. The ribs are done when the meat shows no resistance when pierced with the point of a small skewer or sharp knife. Arrange the spareribs on a heated platter and serve at once.

NOTE: For a sweeter sauce, you can replace the ketchup with 1 cup of peach preserves.

■ AMERICAN COOKING: SOUTHERN STYLE

142

## Crown Pork Roast with Sausage-Apple Stuffing

**To serve 8 to 10**

| | |
|---|---|
| 3 tablespoons butter | fresh parsley leaves, plus |
| ¾ cup finely chopped | parsley sprigs for garnish |
| onions | ½ teaspoon rubbed dried |
| ¼ cup finely chopped | sage |
| celery | 1 teaspoon salt |
| ½ cup peeled, cored, | Freshly ground black pepper |
| diced tart apple | One pork crown roast, |
| ½ cup fresh white-bread | consisting of 2 racks of |
| crumbs | 9 ribs each, tied together |
| 1 pound ground pork | at the ends |
| (including crown roast | Vegetable oil |
| trimmings) | 1 long continuous strip |
| ½ pound sage-flavored | of orange peel, wound |
| sausage meat | into a rose shape, for |
| ½ cup finely chopped | garnish |

Preheat the oven to 350°F. For the stuffing, melt the butter over moderate heat in a heavy 8- to 10-inch skillet. In it cook the onions, stirring often, for five minutes, then add the celery and apple. Cook without browning for five minutes longer.

With a wooden spoon, scrape the contents of the pan into a large mixing bowl. Add the bread crumbs, ground pork, sausage meat, chopped parsley, sage, salt and a few grindings of black pepper. Mix all of the ingredients gently but thoroughly together. To taste for seasoning, fry a small ball of the stuffing in the skillet until no trace of pink shows. Then eat it, and add more herbs, salt or pepper to the uncooked stuffing, if necessary.

Fill the center of the crown with the stuffing, mounding it slightly. Cover the stuffing with a circle of foil and wrap the end of each rib bone with a piece of foil to prevent it from charring and snapping off. Place the crown on a rack in a shallow roasting pan just large enough to hold it easily. Brush the sides of the ribs with vegetable oil.

Roast the pork, undisturbed, for one and a half hours. Then remove the circle of foil to allow the stuffing to brown, and continue roasting the pork for about 30 minutes or until the juices run clear if the meat is pierced with a skewer or knife tip. A meat thermometer inserted into a fleshy part without touching bone should register 170°F.

Carefully transfer the crown to a large, heated platter, strip the foil from the ends of the chops and replace it with paper frills. Garnish the top of the stuffing with the orange rose and parsley sprigs, if desired. Let the crown rest for about 10 minutes before you carve it.

To carve the crown, press down on the stuffing with the back of a large fork to steady it. With a large, sharp knife, cut between pairs of ribs, starting from the center of the crown and slicing down to the base so that a portion of stuffing is carved out with the two chops. Hold the fork and knife on either side of the chops to transfer them to a heated individual serving plate.

■ AMERICAN COOKING

## Roast Pork Calypso

*A popular accompaniment to the pork is the tropical squash known in Jamaica, where this recipe originated, as "chocho," but called "chayote," "mirliton" or "christophene" elsewhere. The squash is round or pear-shaped, white to dark green in color, from 3 to 8 inches long. To prepare it, halve the squash and cook it in lightly salted water to cover for about 30 minutes, until tender. Turn the squash into ¼-inch shells by scooping out the flesh. Chop the flesh, combine it with sautéed onions and grated Parmesan cheese, and heap it in the shells. Bake in a 350°F. oven for 20 minutes, to brown the top.* ◆●

**To serve 6 to 8**

| | |
|---|---|
| One 5- to 6-pound lean pork | 1 bay leaf, crumbled |
| center-loin roast, with | 1 teaspoon salt |
| chine sawed through | ¼ teaspoon freshly ground |
| but left attached | black pepper |
| 2 cups chicken stock | ¼ cup light rum |
| 1 cup light-brown sugar | 2 teaspoons arrowroot |
| 2 tablespoons dark rum | combined with 1 tablespoon |
| 2 teaspoons finely chopped | cold water |
| garlic | 3 tablespoons fresh lime |
| 2 teaspoons ground ginger | juice |
| ½ teaspoon ground cloves | Lime slices for garnish |

Preheat the oven to 350°F. With a sharp knife, lightly score the pork loin by making crisscrossing diagonal cuts ¼ inch deep at 1-inch intervals on the fat side. Place the pork, scored side up, in a shallow roasting pan just large enough to hold it. Roast the loin for one hour or until the pork is golden brown. Take the pan out of the oven and transfer the loin to a plate. Skim the fat from the pan juices, pour in the stock, and set the pan and its liquid aside.

With a large mortar and pestle or in a small bowl with the back of a spoon, mash the brown sugar, dark rum, garlic, ginger, cloves, bay leaf, salt and pepper to a smooth paste. With a metal spatula or your fingertips, spread the paste evenly over the scored side of the pork. Return the loin to the pan, scored side up, and roast in the middle of the oven for another 30 minutes or until the juices run clear when the pork is pierced with a skewer or knife tip and the surface of the loin is crusty and brown. (A meat thermometer inserted deeply into the loin should register 170°F.)

Transfer the loin to a heated platter, and let it rest for 10 minutes for easier carving. Meanwhile, warm the ¼ cup of light rum in a small skillet over low heat. Off the heat, ignite the rum with a match; slide the skillet gently back and forth until the flames die.

Bring the liquid remaining in the baking pan to a boil over high heat. Stir in the arrowroot-and-water mixture. Stirring constantly, cook briskly until the sauce thickens enough to coat the spoon heavily. Remove the pan from the heat and stir in the flamed rum and the lime juice. Taste for seasoning, and pour the sauce into a heated bowl or sauceboat. Garnish the loin roast with lime slices, if you wish, and present the sauce separately.

■ THE COOKING OF THE CARIBBEAN ISLANDS

## Hazelnut-Mustard Pork Chops

**To serve 4**

| | |
|---|---|
| ¼ cup coarse-grained prepared mustard, such as Pommery | chopped garlic |
| | 2 tablespoons chopped fresh parsley leaves |
| ¼ cup Dijon mustard | 4 center-cut loin pork chops, 1 inch thick |
| ¼ cup dry white wine | |
| 1 cup shelled hazelnuts, coarsely ground in a nut grinder or food processor | Freshly ground black pepper |
| | 2 tablespoons peanut or olive oil |
| ¼ cup fresh white-bread crumbs | 1½ tablespoons butter, melted (optional) |
| 1½ teaspoons finely | Garden cress for garnish |

Preheat the oven to 375°F. In a broad, shallow bowl, mix the coarse mustard and Dijon mustard with the wine; set aside. In another bowl, mix the hazelnuts, bread crumbs, garlic and parsley; set aside.

Sprinkle the chops with pepper to taste. Heat the oil in a heavy 10- to 12-inch skillet over moderately high heat. Add the chops and brown them for about five minutes on each side.

With tongs, dip one chop at a time into the mustard-wine mixture, coating both sides. Then place the chop in the hazelnut-crumb mixture. Use your hand to press crumbs into the chops and make them adhere. Place the coated chops in a lightly buttered baking pan, drizzle them with the melted butter, if you like, and bake them for 20 minutes or until a crust forms on top and the chops are cooked through but still juicy. Transfer the chops to a heated platter and garnish them with garden cress, if desired.

■ PORK AND HAM MENUS

## Pork Loin Stuffed with Prunes and Apples

**To serve 6 to 8**

| | |
|---|---|
| 12 pitted prunes | lemon juice to prevent discoloring |
| One 4½- to 5-pound boned pork center-loin roast | 3 tablespoons butter |
| Salt | 3 tablespoons vegetable oil |
| Freshly ground black pepper | ¾ cup dry white wine |
| 2 small tart apples, peeled, cored and cut into 1-inch pieces and sprinkled with | ¾ cup heavy cream |
| | 1 tablespoon red-currant jelly |

In a saucepan, cover the prunes with cold water. Bring to a boil, remove the pan from the heat and let the prunes soak for 30 minutes. Drain and set them aside. With a large, sharp knife, make a

pocket in the pork by cutting a deep slit down the length of the loin on one side to within ½ inch of the ends and 1 inch of the other side. Season the pocket lightly with salt and pepper, and stuff it with the prunes and apples, sewing up the opening with kitchen string. Tie the loin with loops of kitchen string, spaced at 1-inch intervals to keep its shape while cooking.

Preheat the oven to 350°F. In a nonreactive flameproof casserole just large enough to hold the loin, melt the butter and oil over moderate heat. Add the loin and brown it evenly on all sides, turning it with two wooden spoons. It will take about 20 minutes to brown the loin. With a bulb baster or large spoon, remove all of the fat from the casserole. Stirring constantly, add the wine and then the heavy cream, and bring them to a simmer. Cover the casserole and roast the pork for one and a half hours or until the juice runs clear when the meat is pierced with a skewer or the tip of a knife. A meat thermometer inserted into the pork should register 170°F.

Remove the loin from the pan and let it rest on a heated platter for 10 minutes while you finish the sauce. Skim the fat from the liquid in the casserole, and bring the liquid to a boil. When it has reduced to about 1 cup, stir in the red-currant jelly, reduce the heat and, stirring constantly, simmer briefly until smooth.

Taste the sauce for seasoning and pour it into a heated sauceboat. Cut away the strings from the loin, then carve the pork into 1-inch slices. Each slice of pork will enclose a portion of the stuffing. Present the sauce separately.

■ THE COOKING OF SCANDINAVIA

## Ham Loaf

**To serve 4 to 6**

| | |
|---|---|
| 3 cups ground cooked smoked ham | ½ cup grated onion |
| | ½ cup milk |
| ½ pound ground lean fresh pork | ¼ cup dark-brown sugar |
| | ½ teaspoon dry mustard |
| 1 cup dry bread crumbs | 2 tablespoons cold water |
| 2 tablespoons prepared mustard | 2 tablespoons distilled white vinegar |
| 1 egg, lightly beaten | |

Preheat the oven to 350°F. With a pastry brush, spread a light coating of oil over the bottom of a shallow roasting pan. In a large mixing bowl, combine the ground ham, fresh pork, bread crumbs, mustard, egg, onion and milk. Knead briefly with your hands to mix the ingredients well, then transfer the mixture to the pan, and pat it into a loaf about 8 inches long, 4 inches wide and 3 inches high.

Beat the brown sugar, dry mustard, water and vinegar together in a small bowl. Spoon 2 tablespoons of this sauce over the loaf, then place the loaf in the oven and bake it for one hour, basting every 10 minutes or so until you have used all of the remaining sauce. Serve the ham loaf at once.

■ AMERICAN COOKING: SOUTHERN STYLE

## Ham Braised with Burgundy

**To serve 6 to 8**

| | |
|---|---|
| **Butt or shank half of a precooked smoked ham, about 5 to 6 pounds** | **chopped coarse** |
| | **½ teaspoon ground cloves** |
| | **1 small bay leaf** |
| **3 cups water** | ***Beurre manié* made by rubbing** |
| **2 cups red Burgundy or other dry red wine** | **1 tablespoon butter,** |
| | **softened, and 1 tablespoon** |
| **1 onion, sliced thin** | **flour to a paste** |
| **1 tomato, peeled, seeded and** | |

With a small, sharp knife, separate the rind from the ham and cut the rind into chunks. Put the rind into a small saucepan, pour in 3 cups of water, and bring to a boil over high heat. Reduce the heat to low and simmer, uncovered, for 20 minutes or until the liquid is reduced by half to about 1½ cups. Strain this stock into a bowl; discard the rind. (If the ham you bought does not have a rind, reduce 3 cups of chicken stock to 1½ cups.)

Meanwhile preheat the oven to 325° F. Trim the ham of all but a ¼-inch layer of fat, and discard the extra fat. Pour the stock into a shallow nonreactive roasting pan just large enough to hold the ham easily. Add 1 cup of the wine and the onion slices, tomato, cloves and bay leaf. Stir well. Place the ham, fat side up, in the pan, spoon pan liquid over it and bake the ham uncovered for about one and one-half hours. Baste the ham every 15 minutes with pan liquid. Transfer the ham to a heated platter and let it rest for 10 minutes for easier carving.

To prepare the sauce, first skim and discard all of the fat from the pan liquid, and stir in the remaining wine. Bring to a boil over high heat, while scraping in any brown bits clinging to the bottom of the pan. Boil for a minute or two. Stir in the *beurre manié*, bit by bit, and cook over low heat, stirring constantly, until the sauce is smooth and thickens lightly. Strain it through a sieve into a bowl and taste for seasoning.

To serve, carve the ham into ¼-inch slices, and arrange the slices in overlapping layers on a heated platter. Moisten the slices with a few spoonfuls of the sauce; present the rest separately.

■ THE COOKING OF GERMANY

## Fresh Ham, Mock-Boar Style

**To serve 6 to 8**

| | |
|---|---|
| 2 cups dry red wine | 1 teaspoon ground cloves |
| ½ cup red-wine vinegar | 1 teaspoon ground allspice |
| 1 cup finely grated onions | 1 teaspoon ground ginger |
| 15 juniper berries, crushed with mortar and pestle or wrapped in towel and crushed with rolling pin | Freshly ground black pepper |
| | One 5- to 6-pound fresh ham, rind and fat removed |
| 2 tablespoons grated lemon peel | Salt |
| | 2 tablespoons lard |
| 6 small bay leaves, crumbled | 2 cups water |
| 2 teaspoons crumbled dried tarragon | 3 tablespoons flour combined with 3 tablespoons cold water |

For the marinade, pour the wine and vinegar into a nonreactive bowl, and stir in the onions, juniper berries, lemon peel, bay leaves, tarragon, cloves, allspice, ginger and 1 teaspoon of black pepper. Place the ham in a deep dish just large enough to hold it, and pour the marinade over it. Cover the dish with plastic wrap and marinate the ham in the refrigerator for two days, turning it once or twice a day.

Preheat the oven to 325° F. Take the ham from the marinade and dry it with paper towels, brushing off any particles clinging to it. Rub 1 teaspoon of salt evenly into its surface. Strain the marinade into a nonreactive bowl or saucepan, pressing the solid ingredients with the back of a spoon to extract all their liquid before discarding them.

In a heavy nonreactive flameproof casserole or Dutch oven just large enough to hold the ham, melt the lard over high heat. Add the ham and, using two wooden spoons to hold it, brown it well on all sides. Transfer the ham to a plate. Pour the marinade and water into the casserole. Bring them to a boil over high heat, meanwhile scraping in the brown bits that cling to the bottom of the casserole.

Return the ham to the casserole, cover tightly, and bake for about two hours, basting the ham every 30 minutes or so with the cooking liquid. The ham is done if its juices run clear when it is pierced with a skewer or the tip of a sharp knife or a thermometer inserted deep into the meat but not touching the bone registers 170° F.

Transfer the ham to a heated platter, and set it aside to rest for 10 minutes to make it easier to carve. Meanwhile, measure the cooking liquid, strain it into a small nonreactive saucepan, and skim off as much of the fat on the surface as possible. Boil the liquid until it is reduced to 2 cups. Reduce the heat to low. With a whisk or spoon, stir in the flour-water mixture gradually. Stirring frequently, cook for 10 minutes or until the sauce thickens lightly. Taste for seasoning, and add salt and pepper if needed.

To serve, carve the ham into ¼-inch slices, and arrange the slices attractively in overlapping layers on a large heated platter. Pour the sauce into a sauceboat or bowl, and serve it separately.

■ THE COOKING OF GERMANY

SPICY RABBIT IN WINE SAUCE

## Rabbit in Tarragon Cream Gravy

**To serve 4 to 6**

| | |
|---|---|
| One 3- to 3½-pound rabbit, cut into serving pieces, rinsed and patted dry | ¾ cup flour |
| | ½ cup vegetable oil |
| | 1¾ cups chicken stock |
| Salt | 1 cup heavy cream |
| Freshly ground white pepper | 1 teaspoon crumbled dried tarragon |

Season the pieces of rabbit with 1 teaspoon of salt and ¼ teaspoon of white pepper. Spread ½ cup of the flour on a sheet of wax paper, dip the rabbit pieces in the flour and tap off the excess.

In a heavy 6- to 8-quart casserole, heat the oil over high heat. Brown four or five pieces of rabbit at a time, starting them skin side down and turning them frequently with tongs and regulating the heat so that they brown evenly. As the pieces brown, transfer them to a plate.

Pour off all but about ¼ cup of the fat remaining in the casserole, then add the remaining ¼ cup of flour and mix well. Stirring constantly with a whisk, pour in the stock in a slow stream and cook over high heat until the sauce comes to a boil, thickens and is smooth. Whisk in the cream and tarragon, and return the rabbit and the juices that have accumulated around it to the casserole. Reduce the heat to low, cover, and simmer for about 45 minutes or until the rabbit is tender but not falling apart.

Taste for seasoning and add more salt and white pepper if needed. Serve the rabbit at once, directly from the casserole. Or arrange the rabbit pieces on a heated platter, and ladle the gravy over them.

■ AMERICAN COOKING: THE GREAT WEST

## Hasenpfeffer

*The name translates literally as "hare in pepper" ("Hasz im Pfeffer" in old German), and the stew is as old as German cooking itself. Rabbits replace the hare in America, where they are raised commercially and are available from butchers and supermarkets.* ◆●

**To serve 6**

| | |
|---|---|
| ½ pound lean bacon, chopped fine | 1 cup dry red wine |
| One 5- to 6-pound rabbit or two 2½- to 3-pound rabbits, cut into serving pieces, rinsed and patted dry | 1 cup chicken stock |
| | 2 tablespoons brandy |
| | 1 teaspoon red-currant jelly |
| | 1 small bay leaf |
| Salt | ⅛ teaspoon crumbled dried rosemary |
| Freshly ground black pepper | |
| ½ cup flour | ⅛ teaspoon crumbled dried thyme |
| ½ cup finely chopped shallots or scallions | 2 teaspoons fresh lemon juice |
| ½ teaspoon chopped garlic | |

In a heavy 5-quart flameproof casserole, cook the bacon over moderate heat, stirring until it is crisp. Drain the bacon bits on paper towels.

Sprinkle the rabbit pieces with ½ teaspoon each of salt and pepper, then dip them in the flour and tap off the excess. Heat the bacon fat over high heat and in it brown the rabbit, a few pieces at a time, for four or five minutes on each side. As they brown, transfer the rabbit pieces to a plate.

Pour off all but a film of fat from the casserole, and add the shallots and garlic. Stirring frequently, cook over moderate heat for five minutes or until the shallots are soft. Pour in the wine and stock, and bring to a boil over high heat, meanwhile scraping in any brown bits clinging to the bottom of the casserole.

Stir in the brandy, currant jelly, bay leaf, rosemary and thyme, and return the rabbit and any juices that have accumulated around it to the casserole. Add the drained bacon, cover the casserole, and simmer over low heat for one and a half hours or until the rabbit is tender but not falling apart. (If you are using small rabbits, start testing them after about 45 minutes.)

When the rabbit has finished cooking, discard the bay leaf, and stir in the lemon juice. Taste for seasoning, and add more salt and pepper if necessary. The sauce should be quite peppery.

Serve the rabbit from the casserole, or arrange the pieces on a deep heated platter and pour the sauce over them.

■ THE COOKING OF GERMANY

## Spicy Rabbit in Wine Sauce

**To serve 4 to 6**

| | |
|---|---|
| ⅓ cup olive oil | 2 tablespoons capers, rinsed |
| 3 garlic cloves, crushed | |
| One 2½- to 3-pound rabbit, cut into serving pieces, rinsed and patted dry | 1 to 1½ teaspoons crushed hot-red-pepper flakes |
| | Salt |
| 1½ cups dry white wine | Freshly ground black pepper |
| 3 sweet peppers—1 red, 1 yellow and 1 green— seeded, deribbed and cut into ½-inch strips | 1 lemon, cut into wedges, for garnish |

Preheat the oven to 400°F. With a pastry brush, spread a light coating of oil inside a nonreactive baking-serving dish just large enough to hold the rabbit pieces in one layer.

In a heavy 10- to 12-inch skillet, heat the olive oil over moderately high heat. Add the garlic cloves and sauté them for about two minutes or until they are golden brown; discard the garlic. Add the rabbit pieces to the skillet, and brown them for four or five minutes on each side, regulating the heat so the pieces color richly and evenly.

When the rabbit is browned, transfer it, using a pair of tongs, to the roasting pan. Add the wine to the skillet, bring it to a boil, and cook, stirring and scraping up any brown bits clinging to the bottom and sides of the skillet, for three minutes or until the wine is reduced by half. Stir in the sweet-pepper strips and the capers. Add the hot-pepper flakes, and salt and black pepper to taste.

Spoon the pepper mixture over and around the rabbit. Place the rabbit in the oven and roast it uncovered, for 30 minutes or until the juices run clear when the meat is pierced with the tip of a knife.

Serve the rabbit directly from the baking dish, garnished, if you like, with lemon wedges.

■ MEDITERRANEAN MENUS

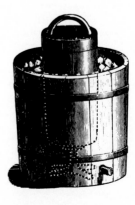

## Venison Meat Loaf

**To serve 8 to 10**

| | |
|---|---|
| ¼ cup butter | ¼ cup chopped fresh |
| 2 cups finely chopped onions | parsley leaves |
| 1½ teaspoons finely | 1 egg, lightly beaten |
| chopped garlic | ½ teaspoon crumbled |
| 2 pounds ground lean venison | dried thyme |
| 1 pound ground lean pork | 1 teaspoon salt |
| ½ pound ground fresh | ½ teaspoon freshly ground |
| pork fat | black pepper |
| 2 carrots, grated fine | |

Preheat the oven to 350°F. With a pastry brush, spread a generous coating of oil on the bottom of a large, shallow roasting pan.

In a heavy 10- to 12-inch skillet, melt the butter over moderate heat. Add the onions and garlic and, stirring often, cook for five minutes, until they are soft. With a rubber spatula, scrape them into a deep bowl. Add the venison, pork, pork fat, carrots, parsley, egg, thyme, salt and pepper, and knead the mixture with both hands; beat with a wooden spoon until smooth and fluffy.

Transfer the mixture to the roasting pan and shape it into a loaf about 12 inches long, 5 inches wide and 3 inches high. Bake for one and a half hours or until the juices run clear when the loaf is pierced deeply with a small skewer or knife. Serve the loaf at once, from a heated platter. Or, if you prefer, let it cool to room temperature, cover with foil or plastic wrap, and refrigerate it for two or three hours before serving.

■ AMERICAN COOKING: NEW ENGLAND

## Venison Tenderloin with Brandy Sauce

**To serve 4**

| | |
|---|---|
| ½ cup dry red wine | dried thyme |
| ½ cup water | Salt |
| 1 onion, sliced thin | Freshly ground black pepper |
| 2 tablespoons finely chopped | 4 venison tenderloin steaks, |
| shallots or scallions | 1 inch thick |
| One 2-inch piece cinnamon | 2 tablespoons butter |
| stick | 1 tablespoon vegetable oil |
| 1 small bay leaf | 1 tablespoon flour |
| 1 clove | ½ cup meat stock |
| 3 parsley sprigs | 2 tablespoons brandy |
| ⅛ teaspoon crumbled | |

In a small nonreactive bowl, combine the wine, water, onion, shallots, cinnamon, bay leaf, clove, parsley, thyme, ½ teaspoon of salt and a few grindings of pepper. Lay the steaks in a shallow nonreactive dish and pour the wine marinade over them; turn

the steaks to coat them well. Marinate at room temperature for about two hours, turning the steaks once or twice.

Remove the steaks from the marinade and pat them dry. Set the marinade aside. In a heavy 10- to 12-inch skillet, melt the butter in the oil over moderate heat. Add the steaks and, turning them once with a spatula, cook them for eight to 10 minutes or until they are richly browned outside but still pink inside. Transfer them to a platter and cover them loosely with foil to keep them warm.

Strain the marinade through a sieve into a bowl, pressing the vegetables with the back of a spoon before discarding them. Add the flour to the fat in the skillet, and cook over moderate heat, stirring constantly, until the flour browns lightly. Slowly pour in the marinade, stock and brandy. Stirring with a whisk, bring this sauce to a boil, and stir until it is smooth and thickens lightly. Taste for seasoning, and add more salt and pepper if necessary. Pour the sauce over the venison and serve the steaks at once.

■ THE COOKING OF GERMANY

## Barbecued Venison Chops

**To serve 6**

| | |
|---|---|
| ¼ cup vegetable oil | 1 cup beer |
| Six 6-ounce venison loin | ¼ cup fresh lemon juice |
| chops, about 1 inch thick | ¼ cup Worcestershire sauce |
| ½ cup finely chopped | 1 teaspoon crumbled dried |
| onions | basil |
| 1 teaspoon finely chopped | Salt |
| garlic | Freshly ground black pepper |
| 3 tomatoes, chopped coarse | Curly-leaf kale for garnish |
| and puréed through a food | 2 shiitake mushrooms for |
| mill or in a food processor | garnish |

Preheat the oven to 400°F. In a heavy 10- to 12-inch skillet, heat the oil over high heat. Pat the chops completely dry with paper towels. Then brown them in the oil, two or three at a time, for about a minute on each side, turning the chops with tongs. As they brown, lay the chops side by side in a baking dish just large enough to hold them in one layer.

To prepare the barbecue sauce, add the onions and garlic to the fat remaining in the skillet. Stirring frequently, cook over moderate heat for five minutes, until the onions are soft but not brown. Stir in the tomatoes, beer, lemon juice, Worcestershire, basil, 1 teaspoon of salt and a few grindings of pepper. Bring the sauce to a boil over high heat, stirring constantly. Taste for seasoning, and more salt and pepper if needed.

Pour the sauce over the chops, coating them evenly. Then bake the chops, uncovered, for eight to 10 minutes, or until they are still pink inside and show no resistance when pierced deeply with the tip of a small, sharp knife. Transfer the chops to a heated platter, garnish with kale and mushrooms, if you like, and serve at once.

■ AMERICAN COOKING: THE EASTERN HEARTLAND

# Fish & Shellfish

# Fish & Shellfish

FRONTISPIECE: ELEMENTS OF MESQUITE MIXED SHELLFISH GRILL
AND RED SNAPPER WITH VEGETABLES

Fish are naturally tender, whether denizens of ocean, lake, river or brook. Thus in cooking fish, less is always more. Apply just enough heat just long enough to render the flesh firm and opaque. The path to perfection is 10 minutes for each inch of thickness, measured at the thickest part. This simple rule holds for every species and size, whole or filleted or otherwise cut up, stuffed or plain, and every cookery method from steaming to frying.

Shellfish are slightly more complicated, but cooking times are generally brief. Live bivalves—clams and mussels—should be steamed with minimum liquid or baked or grilled only until their shells open; otherwise, their flesh will dry as the savory juices are lost. Shucked bivalves—usually the only form in which scallops are sold—need only two or three minutes of cooking to lose their translucency and be ready for the table.

Small crustaceans like shrimp, prawns and crayfish may cook in as little as three minutes. Crabs and lobsters, however, can take up to 20 or 25 minutes. All crustaceans have pigments that turn them pink, sometimes within seconds of being heated. For this reason, firmness is better than pinkness as a test for shrimp. Live lobsters are cooked when a leg can be jerked out easily; typically, lobsters require about 10 minutes per pound. With crabs, visual tests are less reliable, although some fishermen say that the apron, a narrow flap on the underside of the body, lifts slightly when the meat is cooked.

## Fried Catfish

*The catfish raised commercially in ponds have a consistent diet and, therefore, a sweet flavor that is predictable.* ❧

**To serve 4**

| | |
|---|---|
| **Four 8-ounce catfish fillets, with skin intact, rinsed and patted dry** | **Freshly ground black pepper** |
| | **Cayenne pepper** |
| **Salt** | **1 to 1½ cups white cornmeal** |
| | **Vegetable oil for frying** |

Sprinkle the fillets with salt, black pepper and cayenne to taste. If you are unsure about how much seasoning to use, go lightly. Put about 1 cup of cornmeal on a large, flat plate. Dredge the catfish in the cornmeal and shake off any excess. Set the fish aside for a few minutes so that the coating will adhere. Fill a heavy 12-inch skillet with oil to a depth of ½ inch and heat until the oil is very hot. Gently add the fillets and fry them for about five minutes on each side, or until they are golden brown. Remove the fillets with a perforated metal spatula and drain them. Serve on a heated platter.

■ AMERICAN REGIONAL MENUS

## Salt Cod with Potatoes and Onions

**To serve 4 to 6**

| | |
|---|---|
| **1½ pounds salt cod** | **2 tablespoons chopped fresh parsley leaves** |
| **6 potatoes** | |
| **1 cup olive oil** | **18 to 20 black olives, preferably Mediterranean-style, pitted** |
| **4 onions, sliced ⅛ inch thick and separated into rings** | |
| **½ teaspoon finely chopped garlic** | **5 hard-boiled eggs, cut into ¼-inch slices** |

Starting a day ahead, place the cod in a nonreactive bowl. Add enough cold water to submerge the cod, then cover the bowl and refrigerate it. Let the cod soak until it has just about doubled in volume—at least 12 hours. Change the water three or four times to reduce the saltiness of the fish. (If you like, you can soak the cod for as long as 48 hours.)

Drain the cod, and rinse it under cold running water. Place the cod in a saucepan and add enough fresh water to cover the fish by at least 1 inch. Bring the water to a boil over high heat. (Taste the water. If it seems excessively salty, drain the fish, cover it with

154

fresh water, and bring it to a boil again.) Reduce the heat to low and simmer, uncovered, for about 10 minutes or until the fish flakes apart when prodded gently with a fork. Drain the cod thoroughly. With a small knife, remove and discard any skin and bones, and separate the cod into large flakes.

Meanwhile, drop the potatoes into a pot with enough lightly salted boiling water to cover them completely. Boil until they are tender but not falling apart. Drain, peel, and cut the potatoes into ¼-inch slices.

Preheat the oven to 200° F. With a pastry brush, oil the inside of a 2½- to 3-quart casserole.

In a heavy 10- to 12-inch skillet, heat ½ cup of the oil over moderate heat. Add the onion rings. Stirring often, cook for five minutes or until they are soft but not brown. Stir in the garlic and remove the skillet from the heat.

To assemble, spread half of the potatoes in the casserole, cover them with half of the cod and then half of the onions. Then add the rest of the cod, onions and potatoes, and pour the remaining ½ cup of oil over the top. Bake for 20 minutes or until the top is lightly browned. Sprinkle with parsley and garnish with the olives and egg slices. Serve the cod from the casserole, accompanied by cruets of oil and vinegar, and a dish of freshly ground pepper or a pepper mill.

■ THE COOKING OF SPAIN AND PORTUGAL

## Batter-fried Bluegills

*Bluegills are a kind of sunfish, native to the Mississippi Valley states, but now used for stocking lakes and ponds nationwide. A much-favored sport and food fish, sunfish are known as "bream" in the South.* ❧

**To serve 4**

| | |
|---|---|
| Vegetable oil for deep frying | 1 egg, separated |
| ½ cup cake or all-purpose flour | ½ cup water |
| 2 tablespoons cornstarch | 1 pound bluegill or other sunfish fillets, skinned, rinsed and patted dry |
| ½ teaspoon salt | |
| ½ teaspoon freshly ground black pepper | 1 lemon, quartered |

Pour vegetable oil into a deep fryer or large, heavy saucepan to a depth of 2 to 3 inches and heat the oil until it reaches a temperature of 375° F. on a deep-frying thermometer.

Meanwhile, prepare the batter for the fish by first combining the flour, cornstarch, salt and pepper, and sifting them onto a plate or a sheet of wax paper. With a whisk, beat the egg yolk and water to a smooth cream, then add the flour mixture, a few spoonfuls at a time. Just before using the batter, beat the egg white with a whisk or a rotary or electric beater until it forms unwavering peaks when the beater is lifted. Scoop the egg white over the batter and fold it in gently with a rubber spatula.

Using tongs, pick up one fillet at a time, immerse it in the batter and drop it into the oil. Deep-fry four or five fillets at a time, turning them with a slotted spoon for three minutes or until

golden brown. As they brown, transfer the fillets to paper towels to drain.

Arrange the fillets attractively on a heated platter and serve them at once, accompanied by the lemon quarters.

■ AMERICAN COOKING: THE EASTERN HEARTLAND

## Bluefish with Hazelnuts

**To serve 4**

| | |
|---|---|
| ⅓ cup hazelnuts | 2 scallions, sliced thin |
| 1 pound bluefish fillets, skinned, rinsed and patted dry | 2 garlic cloves, chopped fine |
| | ¼ cup balsamic vinegar |
| | 1 tablespoon fresh lime or lemon juice |
| Flour | |
| 1 tablespoon safflower oil | 1 tomato, cored and cut into thin wedges |
| ¼ teaspoon salt | |
| Freshly ground black pepper | ¼ cup chopped fresh basil or flatleaf parsley leaves |
| 1 tablespoon butter | |

Preheat the oven to 350° F. Spread the hazelnuts in one layer in a shallow pan, and toast them in the oven for 10 minutes. Rub the nuts with a dish towel to remove most of their papery skins. Chop the nuts coarse; set them aside.

Cut the fillets into serving pieces and dust them with flour; tap off any excess flour. Heat the oil in a heavy-bottomed 10- to 12-inch skillet over moderately high heat. Add the fillets and sauté them on one side for four minutes. Turn them over and sprinkle them with the salt and some pepper. Cook the fish on the second side until they are firm to the touch—three to four minutes more. Transfer the fillets to a serving platter and keep them warm.

Melt the butter in the skillet. Add the hazelnuts and sauté them for two minutes. Stir in the scallions, garlic, vinegar and lime or lemon juice. Cook the mixture for one minute, stirring all the while. Add the tomato, the basil and some pepper. Cook for one minute more, still stirring; spread the mixture evenly over the fish. Serve immediately.

NOTE: Sea trout or halibut can be substituted for bluefish.

■ FRESH WAYS WITH FISH

155

## Trout Amandine

**To serve 6**

| | |
|---|---|
| **¹⁄₄ cup flour** | **patted dry** |
| **1 teaspoon salt** | **1 cup butter** |
| **Freshly ground black pepper** | **1 cup sliced blanched almonds** |
| **Six ³⁄₄- to 1-pound whole brook** | **1 tablespoon fresh lemon** |
| **trout, cleaned with heads** | **juice, plus 2 lemons, cut** |
| **and tails left on, rinsed and** | **into wedges, for garnish** |

Combine the flour, salt and pepper on a sheet of wax paper, and roll the trout in the flour until they are thoroughly but lightly coated. Tap off the excess flour.

Melt ¹⁄₄ cup of the butter in a 12-inch skillet over moderate heat, and in it sauté three trout for five minutes on each side or until they are golden brown and firm to the touch. With two spatulas, transfer the sautéed trout to a warmed platter, and cover them to keep them warm while you sauté the remaining trout in another ¹⁄₄ cup of the butter.

When the trout are cooked, discard the browned butter from the skillet and wipe out the skillet. Melt the remaining ¹⁄₂ cup of butter over low heat and in it cook the almonds, stirring frequently. When they are pale gold in color, remove them from the heat and add the lemon juice. Pour the almonds and butter over the trout, garnish the platter with lemon wedges, and serve the trout at once.

■ GREAT DINNERS FROM LIFE

## Soused Mackerel

**To serve 6**

| | |
|---|---|
| **Three 1-pound mackerel,** | **¹⁄₈ teaspoon crumbled** |
| **cleaned, with heads** | **dried thyme** |
| **removed but tails left intact,** | **12 black peppercorns** |
| **rinsed and patted dry** | **1 teaspoon salt** |
| **2 onions, sliced thin and** | **1 cup malt or white-wine** |
| **separated into rings** | **vinegar** |
| **¹⁄₄ cup chopped fresh parsley** | **1 cup water** |
| **leaves, plus parsley** | **2 tablespoons fresh** |
| **sprigs for garnish** | **lemon juice** |
| **2 small bay leaves, crumbled** | |

Preheat the oven to 325° F. Lay the fish, side by side, in a shallow, nonreactive, flameproof baking pan just large enough to hold them. Strew the onion rings, chopped parsley and bay leaves evenly over the fish and sprinkle them with the thyme, peppercorns and salt. Pour in the vinegar, water and lemon juice, and bring to a boil over high heat. Then bake, uncovered, for 12 to 15 minutes or until the fish are firm to the touch. While they are baking, baste them two or three times with the cooking liquid.

Let the mackerel cool to room temperature, then cover the pan tightly with foil or plastic wrap. Marinate in the refrigerator for at least six hours. Brush the onions and the seasonings off the fish and, with a slotted spatula, carefully transfer the mackerel to a platter.

To debone each mackerel, use a fish server or long-bladed knife to first cut down the center of the fish's side, just to the depth of the backbone. Then insert the blade in the incision; turn the blade outward so that it is almost flat. Work down the length of the fish, easing one-half of the upper fillet from the bones. Lift the fillet onto a serving dish. Repeat the process to remove the other half of the upper fillet. Then pull the tail forward to free the attached backbone from the lower fillet. Divide the lower fillet also into two segments, and lift these onto the serving dish. Garnish the dish with parsley sprigs.

■ THE COOKING OF THE BRITISH ISLES

## Prosciutto-stuffed Flounder Fillets

*Depending on where you live, you can make this dish with various members of the flounder family. On the West Coast, choose petrale or rex sole, sand dab or Pacific halibut; on the East Coast, the choices are winter and summer flounder, lemon sole and fluke. All have a fine texture and delicate taste.* ◆●

**To serve 4**

| | |
|---|---|
| **Four 4- to 6-ounce flounder or sole fillets, rinsed and patted dry** | HOT-AND-SOUR SAUCE |
| **2 tablespoons rice wine or dry white wine** | **1 lemon** |
| **4 scallions, trimmed, bottom 3 inches quartered lengthwise, tops sliced thin diagonally** | **1 tablespoon rice vinegar** |
| | **1 tablespoon soy sauce** |
| | **1 teaspoon sweet chili sauce, or ½ teaspoon crushed red pepper mixed with 1 teaspoon honey** |
| **½ cup snow peas** | |
| **½ sweet red pepper, seeded, deribbed and cut lengthwise into thin strips** | **¼ teaspoon dark sesame oil** |
| | **1 teaspoon cornstarch** |
| | **2 teaspoons water** |
| **1 thin slice prosciutto or other dry-cured ham, cut into 8 strips** | **1 teaspoon safflower oil** |
| | **1 tablespoon grated fresh ginger root** |
| | **1 garlic clove, chopped fine** |

Put the fillets in a shallow dish and sprinkle them with the wine; let them marinate at room temperature for 30 minutes.

Blanch the scallion bottoms and snow peas in boiling water for 10 seconds. Drain and refresh the vegetables under cold running water. Drain the fillets and pat them dry. Lay one-quarter of the scallions, snow peas, red peppers and two strips of prosciutto across the center of each fillet. Roll up the fillets from end to end and place them, seam side down, on a plate set inside a steamer. Set the steamer over a wok or large skillet filled with 1 inch of

water. Cover the steamer, bring to a boil over high heat, and steam the fillets until their flesh is opaque—about six minutes.

Meanwhile, make the sauce. Grate the lemon peel into a small bowl; squeeze the lemon juice into the bowl and blend in the vinegar, soy sauce, sweet chili sauce, sesame oil, cornstarch and 2 teaspoons of water. Heat the safflower oil in a small nonreactive skillet over moderate heat. Add the ginger and garlic, and cook them for two minutes—stirring so that the garlic does not brown. Stir in the vinegar mixture and cook this sauce for one minute to thicken it.

When the fish fillets are done, tip the plate in the steamer and spoon the accumulated liquid into the sauce; stir the sauce well to incorporate the fish liquid. Carefully transfer the fish rolls from the steamer to a serving plate. Pour the sauce over the fillets and garnish them with the sliced scallion tops. Serve immediately.

■ FRESH WAYS WITH FISH

## Pompano Stuffed with Shrimp

**To serve 4**

| | |
|---|---|
| **¼ cup butter, cut into bits, plus ¼ cup butter, softened** | **¼ cup finely chopped fresh parsley leaves** |
| **½ cup sliced scallions, including 2 inches of green** | **¼ cup pale dry sherry** |
| **1 cup fresh white-bread crumbs** | **Four 1½-pound pompano, cleaned but with heads and tails left on, rinsed and patted dry** |
| **1 pound shrimp, shelled, deveined, poached in water to cover until firm, drained and chopped coarse** | **Salt** |
| | **Freshly ground black pepper** |

In a heavy 8- to 10-inch skillet, melt half of the butter bits over moderate heat. Add the scallions and, stirring frequently, cook for two or three minutes, until they are soft but not brown. With a slotted spoon, transfer the scallions to a bowl.

Melt the remaining butter bits in the same skillet, add the bread crumbs and, stirring constantly, fry over moderate heat until the crumbs are crisp and golden brown. Scrape the entire contents of the skillet over the scallions with a rubber spatula. Add the shrimp, parsley and sherry, and toss all of the stuffing ingredients together gently but thoroughly. Taste for seasoning.

Preheat the oven to 400° F. Using a pastry brush, coat the bottom of a large jelly-roll pan with melted or softened butter. Season the cavities and skin of the pompano with salt and a few grindings of pepper. Spoon the shrimp stuffing into the cavities, dividing it evenly among them. Press the edges of the flaps together with your fingers.

Arrange the pompano side by side on the buttered pan and brush the tops of the fish with the ¼ cup of softened butter. Bake in the middle of the oven for 10 minutes per inch of thickness—measured after stuffing—or until a skewer inserted behind the gills of the pompano meets no resistance. Transfer the fish to a heated platter and serve at once.

■ AMERICAN COOKING: SOUTHERN STYLE

## Pan-blackened Red Snapper

*The cooks who named this dish took a bit of poetic license. In fact, the fillets are browned—not blackened. To make them crisp outside while keeping them moist inside, fry the fillets in clarified butter that has no milk-solid particles, which often stick to a pan and cause burning. Also necessary is a heavy skillet, preferably one of cast iron, because it will heat evenly and retain heat well.* ✒

**To serve 4**

| | |
|---|---|
| 2 cups peeled, seeded and coarsely chopped tomatoes | Freshly ground black pepper |
| ¹/₂ cup dry white wine | ³/₄ cup beef stock |
| ¹/₄ cup fresh lime juice | 3 tablespoons finely cut fresh chives |
| Four red snapper fillets, ¹/₃ to ¹/₂ inch thick, with skin left on | ¹/₄ cup butter, cut into bits and chilled, plus ¹/₄ cup clarified butter, melted |
| Salt | |

Combine the tomatoes, wine and lime juice in a medium-sized nonreactive bowl. Place the fish fillets, flesh side down, in this marinade. Let them stand at room temperature for 20 to 30 minutes. Remove the fillets from the marinade and pat them dry with paper towels; sprinkle with salt and pepper.

For the sauce, pour the marinade into a 2- to 3-quart nonreactive saucepan, and bring it to a boil over moderate heat. Boil the marinade for about 10 minutes or until it is reduced by half. Stir in the stock and 2 tablespoons of the chives, and boil for another 15 minutes or until the mixture is reduced to about 1 cup of syrupy sauce. Lower the heat and stir in the chilled butter bits, a spoonful at a time. The sauce will thicken as the butter melts. Taste and season with salt and pepper if necessary. Keep the sauce warm over very low heat.

Set a 12-inch cast-iron skillet over high heat; when it is very hot, pour in the clarified butter. Gently place the fillets, flesh side down, in the skillet, and sauté them for about three minutes. When the edges of the fillets are very brown—almost black—turn the fish and cook the other side for three to five minutes or until the edges are well browned and the fillets feel firm when prodded with a finger.

Place the fillets on four heated individual plates, top them with the sauce, and sprinkle on the remaining chives.

■ FRENCH REGIONAL MENUS

## Grilled Stuffed Coho Salmon

**To serve 6 to 8**

| | |
|---|---|
| 1¹/₂ cups dry white wine | ¹/₄ teaspoon Tabasco sauce |
| ¹/₂ cup fresh lemon juice, plus the peel of ¹/₂ lemon, cut into julienne strips, plus lemon slices cut thin and halved for garnish | 1 teaspoon salt |
| | ¹/₄ teaspoon freshly ground black pepper |
| | One 5- to 5¹/₂-pound coho salmon, cleaned, with head and tail left on, rinsed and patted dry |
| ¹/₂ cup vegetable oil | |
| 1 onion, sliced thin | 1 cup cooked rice |
| 3 garlic cloves, crushed with the side of a cleaver or heavy knife | ¹/₄ cup finely chopped scallions, including 2 inches of green tops |
| ¹/₂ cup chopped fresh parsley leaves | Julienne strips of sweet red and green peppers for garnish |
| 1 teaspoon ground ginger | |
| ¹/₂ teaspoon crumbled dried thyme | |

First prepare the marinade by combining the wine, lemon juice, oil, onion, garlic, ¹/₄ cup of the parsley, the ginger, thyme,

Tabasco, salt and pepper in a small enameled or stainless-steel saucepan. Stirring occasionally, bring to a boil over high heat. Pour the marinade into a nonreactive fish poacher or casserole large enough to hold the salmon. Set it aside and allow it to cool to room temperature.

With a sharp knife, score both sides of the fish by making three or four evenly spaced diagonal slits about 4 inches long and ¼ inch deep. Place the salmon in the cool marinade and turn it over to moisten it evenly. Cover the pan and marinate at room temperature for about three hours, or in the refrigerator for about six hours, turning the fish occasionally.

In a grill, light a mound of charcoal that you can later spread into a layer about 2 inches deep and an inch or so larger all around than the salmon. Light the charcoal; an electric starter is convenient. Do not start the fire with petroleum-based liquids or jellies that may impart undesirable flavor to the salmon. Let the charcoal burn until a white ash appears on the surface, then spread out the coals. Set the rack in the grill 4 to 6 inches above the coals and let it heat for five minutes, then hold an oily cloth in tongs and grease the rack. If you plan to use a fish-shaped grill basket to hold the

fish while it cooks, omit the rack and brush the basket with oil.

Meanwhile, transfer the salmon to paper towels and pat it dry. Pour the marinade into a pitcher or bowl. To prepare the stuffing, combine the rice, scallions, the remaining parsley and the julienne lemon peel in a small bowl. Blend in ¼ cup of marinade. Set the remaining marinade aside.

Loosely fill the salmon with the stuffing, then close the opening with small skewers and kitchen cord. Place the salmon on the rack or in the basket and brush it with a few spoonfuls of the reserved marinade. Basting the salmon frequently with the remaining marinade, grill it for about 15 minutes on each side, or until it is delicately browned and feels firm when prodded gently with a finger.

Transfer the salmon from the grill to a heated platter and serve at once, garnished if you like with lemon slices, and red and green pepper strips.

NOTE: Any kind of salmon or other round fish—such as blue-fish, red snapper or cod—of suitable size can replace the coho, or silver, salmon.

■ AMERICAN COOKING: THE EASTERN HEARTLAND

PLANKED SHAD WITH PURÉED POTATOES

## Indian Spiced Monkfish

**To serve 4**

| | |
|---|---|
| **4 garlic cloves, chopped** | **¼ teaspoon mustard seeds** |
| **1 tablespoon chopped fresh** | **¼ teaspoon salt** |
| **ginger root** | **⅓ cup fresh lemon juice** |
| **2 tablespoons chopped fresh** | **2 tablespoons safflower oil** |
| **coriander leaves** | **1 onion, chopped fine** |
| **1 teaspoon coriander seeds** | **Four 4-ounce monkfish fillets,** |
| **1 teaspoon ground turmeric** | **rinsed and patted dry** |
| **1 teaspoon dark-brown sugar** | **1 cup plain yogurt** |
| **½ teaspoon cumin seeds** | **1 cup dry bread crumbs** |

In a blender, purée the garlic, ginger, coriander leaves and seeds, turmeric, brown sugar, cumin, mustard seeds and salt with the lemon juice. Heat 1 tablespoon of the oil in a 6- to 8-inch heavy-bottomed skillet. Add the onion and cook it until soft—about five minutes. Add the puréed seasonings and cook for three minutes.

Preheat the broiler to its highest setting and the oven, if it is separate, to 450°F. Slice the fillets into pieces 2 inches thick. Transfer the contents of the skillet to a bowl and mix in the yogurt; transfer half of the yogurt mixture to a small serving bowl; set aside. Place the bread crumbs on a sheet of wax paper. Using the other half of the yogurt mixture, dip one slice of fish at a time first into yogurt, then into the bread crumbs, covering it completely; put the piece in a flameproof baking dish. Coat the remaining slices similarly and set them, side by side, in the dish.

Drizzle the remaining tablespoon of oil over the fish. Brown the fish slices 3 inches from the heat source for about three minutes on each side. Set the oven temperature at 450°F. Transfer the dish to the oven, and bake the fish until it is firm to the touch—about 10 minutes. With a spatula, carefully remove the pieces from the baking dish. Serve the fish at once, accompanied by the reserved yogurt.

■ FRESH WAYS WITH FISH

## Sole Fillets with Herb Butter

**To serve 4**

| | |
|---|---|
| **Four 8-ounce sole fillets, skinned, rinsed and patted dry** | **fresh tarragon leaves or ½ teaspoon crumbled dried tarragon** |
| **1 lemon** | **1 cup heavy cream** |
| **1 egg yolk** | **1 cup dry white wine** |
| **¼ cup unsalted butter** | **Salt** |
| **1 tablespoon chopped scallion** | **Freshly ground black pepper** |
| **1 tablespoon chopped fresh parsley leaves** | **½ cup fresh white-bread crumbs** |
| **1½ teaspoons chopped** | |

Arrange the fillets in a single layer in a large baking dish. Squeeze lemon juice over them and set them aside. Drop the egg yolk into a food processor or blender, add the butter, and blend until smooth. Blend in the scallion, parsley and tarragon. With a rubber spatula, scrape this herb butter into a small bowl; set aside.

In a 1- to 1½-quart nonreactive saucepan, cook the cream over moderately high heat for 10 to 15 minutes, stirring occasionally, to reduce it by half. Add the wine and boil the mixture for one minute. Season it with salt and pepper to taste. Then set it aside.

Preheat the oven to 450° F. Fold over each end of the fillet to make a packet three layers thick. Place the packets, flat side down, in an 8-inch square baking pan. Spread herb butter evenly over the fillets, and sprinkle them with the bread crumbs. Carefully pour the cream-wine mixture into the pan—down one side so that the liquid does not disturb the topping on the fillets. Bake until the crumbs are golden brown and the fish is firm to the touch, about 15 minutes. Using a spatula, transfer the fillets to heated dinner plates, and serve them at once.

■ FISH AND SHELLFISH MENUS

## Planked Shad with Puréed Potatoes

**To serve 6**

| | |
|---|---|
| **9 potatoes, peeled and quartered** | **white pepper** |
| **3 egg yolks, lightly beaten** | **One 2½- to 3-pound shad fillet, with skin left on, rinsed and patted dry** |
| **¾ cup butter, melted** | **Parsley sprigs for garnish** |
| **1½ teaspoons salt** | **2 lemons, sliced** |
| **½ teaspoon freshly ground** | |

Drop the potatoes into enough lightly salted boiling water to cover them by at least 1 inch. Boil briskly, uncovered, until a potato quarter is soft enough to be easily mashed against the sides of the pan with the back of a spoon. Drain the potatoes in a sieve or colander, and return them to the pan. Slide the pan back and forth over low heat for a few moments to dry the potatoes.

Pound the potatoes to a smooth purée with a potato masher, or whip them with a portable electric beater; then transfer them to a deep bowl. Or you can purée the potatoes through a food mill or ricer set in a deep bowl. Beat in the egg yolks and, when they are

completely incorporated, add 6 tablespoons of the melted butter, the salt and white pepper. Tightly cover the bowl with foil to keep the purée warm.

Meanwhile, set the broiler pan and its rack in the oven with the top of the rack 4 inches from the heat, and preheat the broiler to its highest setting. With a pastry brush, spread a generous coating of vegetable oil over the broiler pan rack, and place the fish on top of it, skin side down. Brush the shad with 2 tablespoons of the remaining melted butter, and broil it for six minutes, basting the fish once or twice with 2 more tablespoons of the butter. The shad is done when its flesh is delicately browned and firm.

With the aid of two large metal spatulas, carefully transfer the shad to the center of an oak plank large enough to hold it easily. Using a pastry bag fitted with a large star tube, pipe the potato purée around the shad. (You can spoon a ring of potatoes around the fish, but the effect will not be so grand.) Brush the shad with the remaining melted butter, and place the plank under the broiler for two or three minutes to brown the potatoes lightly.

Garnish the planked shad with parsley sprigs and two or three lemon slices, and serve it at once. Present the remaining lemon slices separately.

■ AMERICAN COOKING: THE EASTERN HEARTLAND

## Rolled Flounder Fillets in Tomato Cream Sauce

**To serve 4**

| | |
|---|---|
| **Four 6-ounce flounder fillets, skinned, rinsed and patted dry** | **¼ teaspoon crushed saffron threads** |
| **2 tablespoons butter, softened, plus 1 tablespoon butter, cut into bits** | **1 small bay leaf** |
| | **1 tablespoon chopped fresh parsley leaves** |
| **⅓ cup fish stock (Index/Glossary)** | **1 large tomato, peeled, seeded and chopped** |
| **⅓ cup dry white wine** | **Freshly ground white pepper** |
| **¼ teaspoon finely chopped garlic** | **Salt (optional)** |
| | **½ cup heavy cream** |

Preheat the oven to 200° F. Cut each fillet in half lengthwise, discarding any bones. Starting with the wider end, roll up each half.

Rub the bottom of a 10-inch nonreactive skillet with the softened butter. Add the stock, white wine, garlic, saffron, bay leaf, parsley, tomato and white pepper. Bring the sauce mixture to a boil. Stand the fish rolls upright on their cut edges in the sauce, and simmer them for about six minutes, basting the fish occasionally. The fish is fully cooked when it is opaque and somewhat firm to the touch. Using a perforated spoon, transfer the fish rolls to a heatproof serving platter and keep them warm in the oven.

Taste the sauce remaining in the skillet and add salt, if needed. Stirring constantly with a wooden spoon, pour in the cream, and simmer over moderate heat for about three minutes or until the sauce thickens and coats the spoon. Remove the skillet from the heat, and swirl in the butter bits. Pour the sauce over the fish.

■ AMERICAN REGIONAL MENUS

## Fourth-of-July Poached Salmon

**To serve 8 to 10**

| | |
|---|---|
| **One 6- to 7-pound salmon, cleaned, with head and tail left on** | EGG SAUCE |
| **4 quarts fish stock (Index/ Glossary), at room temperature** | **6 tablespoons butter, cut into bits** |
| | **½ cup flour** |
| **Fresh dill sprigs for garnish** | **4 cups milk** |
| | **Salt** |
| | **Freshly ground white pepper** |
| | **8 hard-boiled eggs, chopped coarse** |

Wash the salmon inside and out under cold running water. Without drying it, wrap the salmon in a long double thickness of dampened cheesecloth, leaving at least 6 inches of cloth at both ends to serve as handles for lowering and lifting it. Twist the ends of the cloth close to the fish and tie them tight with string, then place the salmon on the rack of a fish poacher or roasting pan long enough to hold the salmon flat. Lower the rack into the pan, then pour in the stock. Tie the ends of the cheesecloth to the handles of the poacher rack or roasting pan. The stock should cover the salmon by at least 2 inches; add water to the pan if necessary.

Place the lid on the poacher or pan, bring the liquid to a boil over moderate heat, and immediately reduce the heat to low. Simmer the salmon for 10 minutes per inch of thickness. The internal temperature of a perfectly cooked fish is 140°F.; check with an instant reading or meat thermometer inserted into the thickest part of the fish. When done, a skewer inserted into the thick flesh will meet almost no resistance.

Meanwhile, prepare the egg sauce by first melting the butter in a heavy 2- to 3-quart saucepan over moderate heat. Stir in the flour with a whisk and stir for a minute or so. Pour in the milk and, stirring constantly with the whisk, cook over high heat until the sauce comes to a boil and thickens heavily. Reduce the heat to low, whisk in 1 teaspoon of salt and ¼ teaspoon of white pepper, and simmer for 10 to 15 minutes, stirring occasionally. Remove the pan from the heat, taste the sauce for seasoning and gently stir in the hard-boiled eggs. Cover to keep the egg sauce warm.

When the salmon is poached, lift it off the rack, using the cheesecloth ends as handles. Lay the salmon on a large cutting board, and open the cheesecloth. With a small, sharp knife, slit the skin from head to tail along the back and belly. Then use your fingers to pull away the skin from the exposed upper half of the fish. Scrape off any gray fat clinging to the salmon. Holding both ends of the cheesecloth, carefully lift the salmon and turn it over onto a large heated serving platter. Peel the skin from the upturned side and scrape off the fat.

To present the salmon, garnish the platter with sprigs of dill and serve the egg sauce in a bowl or sauceboat. Or pour half of the egg sauce over the salmon, masking it completely, and serve the remaining sauce separately.

For serving, cut down the center of the fish's side just to the depth of the backbone. Then insert the blade in the incision near the head, turning the blade outward so that it is almost flat. Work

**FRIED SMELTS WITH CUCUMBER SAUCE**

down the length of the salmon, easing one-half of the upper fillet from the bones. Divide the fillet into serving portions and lift them onto plates. Detach and serve the second half of the upper fillet similarly. Pull the tail forward to free the attached backbone and head from the lower fillet. Divide the lower fillet into two segments and lift them onto plates.

■ AMERICAN COOKING: NEW ENGLAND

## Grilled Tuna Steaks

**To serve 4**

| | |
|---|---|
| **¼ cup olive oil** | **fresh rosemary or** |
| **2 tablespoons fresh lemon juice, plus lemon wedges for garnish** | **½ teaspoon crumbled dried rosemary** |
| | **½ teaspoon salt** |
| **1 tablespoon capers, rinsed** | **Freshly ground black pepper** |
| **1 teaspoon finely chopped garlic** | **Four ½- to ¾-inch-thick tuna steaks, rinsed and** |
| **1 teaspoon finely chopped** | **patted dry** |

In a nonreactive dish just large enough to hold the steaks side by side, combine the olive oil, lemon juice, capers, garlic, rosemary, salt and a few grindings of pepper. Place the steaks in the dish, and allow them to marinate at room temperature for about 30 minutes, turning the steaks every 10 minutes.

With a pastry brush, spread vegetable oil evenly on a cast-iron griddle or skillet and place the griddle over moderately high heat. When the griddle is hot but not smoking, place the steaks on it, reserving their marinade. Grill the steaks for about four minutes, or until they pale at the edges and are seared on the bottom. With a metal spatula, turn them over. Pour the marinade on the steaks, and cook them for four minutes or until they are firm to the touch.

Place the steaks on four heated dinner plates and spoon the pan drippings over them. Garnish the plates, if you like, with lemon wedges.

■ MEDITERRANEAN MENUS

## Fried Smelts with Cucumber Sauce

**To serve 2 to 4**

| | |
|---|---|
| 12 smelts, cleaned, opened flat and boned, with heads and tails left on, rinsed and patted dry | cheesecloth |
| | Parsley sprigs for garnish |
| 1 teaspoon salt | |
| Freshly ground black pepper | CUCUMBER SAUCE |
| 1 cup flour | 1 cucumber, peeled, halved, |
| 1½ cups fresh white-bread crumbs | seeded and sliced thin |
| | 1 teaspoon salt |
| 2 eggs | 1 small onion, sliced thin and separated into rings |
| Vegetable oil for deep frying | 1 cup sour cream |
| | 1 tablespoon finely cut fresh dill |
| 2 to 4 lemon halves, tied in | Cayenne pepper |

Sprinkle the fish with the salt and a few grindings of pepper. Spread the flour and bread crumbs on two separate plates, and use a fork to beat the eggs to a froth in a shallow bowl. Dip the smelts, one at a time, in the flour to coat both sides; tap off the excess flour. Then immerse each smelt in the beaten eggs and roll it in the bread crumbs. Arrange the smelts side by side on wax paper, and refrigerate them for at least 15 minutes, to allow the coating to become firm.

Meanwhile, place the cucumber in a colander and sprinkle it with salt, stirring the slices to coat them evenly. Let the cucumber drain for at least 15 minutes, then rinse it under cold running water and pat it completely dry with paper towels. Drop the cucumber into a mixing bowl and add the onion rings, sour cream, dill and a sprinkling of cayenne. Mix well. Taste the sauce for seasoning.

Pour vegetable oil into a deep fryer or large, heavy saucepan to a depth of 2 to 3 inches, and heat the oil until it registers 375°F. on a deep-frying thermometer.

Fry the smelts, three or four at a time, turning them gently about in the hot oil for about three minutes, until they are crisp and golden on all sides. As they brown, transfer the fish to paper towels to drain.

Serve the deep-fried smelts while they are still hot, arranging them on a heated platter or individual plates, accompanied by the lemon halves and garnished with parsley sprigs. Present the cucumber sauce in a bowl.

■ AMERICAN COOKING: THE NORTHWEST

## Halibut Steaks with Papaya Sauce

**To serve 4**

| | |
|---|---|
| 1 tablespoon safflower oil | ¼ cup heavy cream |
| 1 underripe papaya, peeled, seeded and cut into 1-inch pieces | ¾ teaspoon hot-red-pepper flakes |
| | Four 6-ounce halibut steaks, rinsed and patted dry |
| 1 small onion, chopped coarse | |
| ¼ teaspoon salt | 2 scallions, trimmed and sliced diagonally into ½-inch pieces |
| ½ cup fish stock (Index/Glossary) | |
| ⅓ cup fresh lime juice | |

Heat the oil in a 10- to 12-inch nonreactive skillet over moderate heat. Add the papaya, onion and ⅛ teaspoon of the salt. Cook the mixture, stirring frequently, for seven minutes. Pour in the stock and all but 1 tablespoon of the lime juice. Bring the liquid to a boil, reduce the heat to low, and simmer the mixture for about 10 minutes.

Preheat the broiler to its highest setting. Transfer the papaya mixture to a food processor or blender. Purée the mixture until it is smooth, stopping once to scrape down the sides. Put the cream and the chili strips in a heavy nonreactive 2- to 3-quart saucepan over moderate heat. Simmer the cream for three minutes, whisking often. Whisk the papaya purée into the cream a spoonful at a time. Set this sauce aside over low heat.

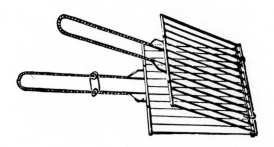

Sprinkle the halibut steaks with the remaining ⅛ teaspoon of salt and the remaining tablespoonful of lime juice. Put the fish in a shallow, heatproof dish, and set it about 4 inches below the heat source. Broil the fish for four minutes. Turn the fish over, sprinkle it with the diagonally sliced scallions, and continue broiling until the flesh is firm to the touch and the scallions are brown—about three minutes.

Transfer the steaks to a warmed serving platter and spoon the papaya sauce around them. Serve immediately.

■ FRESH WAYS WITH FISH

## Grouper with Shiitake Mushrooms

### To serve 4

| | |
|---|---|
| ½ ounce dried shiitake or other Asian mushrooms, soaked in ¾ cup hot water for 20 minutes, stems discarded and caps sliced thin, soaking water reserved | rinsed and patted dry with paper towels |
| ¼ cup dry sherry | 1½ teaspoons cornstarch |
| 2 tablespoons soy sauce | 2 tablespoons safflower oil |
| 2 tablespoons fresh lime juice | 2 scallions, trimmed and sliced thin |
| 1 teaspoon sugar | 1 tablespoon julienne strips of fresh ginger root |
| One 1½-pound grouper fillet, | 2 garlic cloves, sliced thin |
| | ½ teaspoon freshly ground black pepper |

Pour ¼ cup of the mushroom soaking liquid into a mixing bowl, being careful to leave any grit from the mushrooms behind. Stir in the sherry, soy sauce, 1 tablespoon of the lime juice and the sugar. Set the mixture aside. Rub the fillet with the remaining tablespoon of lime juice, then rub the cornstarch evenly over both sides of the fish. Heat the oil in a large, heavy skillet (preferably nonstick) over high heat. When the oil is hot, add the fish and sear it on one side for two minutes. Turn the fillet and sear the second side for two minutes. Transfer the fish to a plate.

Add the mushrooms, scallions, ginger, garlic and pepper to the hot skillet. Cook the mixture over high heat for one minute. Reduce the heat to low, pour in the sherry mixture, replace the fillet, and cover the skillet. Steam the fish until it is opaque—about five minutes. Transfer the fish to a warmed serving platter and spoon the sauce around it.

NOTE: Red snapper or monkfish can be substituted for grouper.

■ FRESH WAYS WITH FISH

## Trout Baked in Coarse Salt

*In this recipe, whole trout are baked surrounded by salt. Encasing food for cooking is an ancient technique, and a splendid one. The wrapper holds in the food's own juices, dispensing with the need for adding liquid or basting. In Spain, the wrapper is wet clay and the food cooks buried in the embers of a fire. In Senegal, wet baobab leaves encase foods; in the Caribbean, banana leaves are used. This method is said to come from China. It applies to any small fish.* ❧

### To serve 4

| | |
|---|---|
| 5 pounds coarse (kosher) salt for encasing the fish | rinsed and patted dry |
| Four 8-ounce trout, cleaned, | ¼ cup olive oil |
| | Parsley sprigs for garnish |

Preheat the oven to 500° F. Cover the bottom of a shallow baking pan about 15 by 17 inches with 3½ pounds of the coarse salt. Place the pan in the oven and heat the salt for five minutes or so. Remove the pan from the oven and arrange the trout on the hot salt. Do not let the fish touch one another. Cover the fish completely with the remaining salt.

Bake the trout for 15 minutes. Remove them from the oven and crack off the top layer of salt, which will have solidified. With two metal spatulas, gently lift the fish out of the pan and set them on a warmed jelly-roll pan. With a dry pastry brush, whisk any discolored salt from the top and belly cavity of each fish.

Discard any discolored salt from the baking pan, then transfer the rest to a platter. With the spatulas, lift the fish onto this bed of salt. Drizzle olive oil over the fish and, if you like, garnish them with parsley sprigs.

■ FISH AND SHELLFISH MENUS

## Red Snapper with Vegetables

### To serve 4 to 6

| | |
|---|---|
| ⅓ cup vegetable oil | tomatoes, drained and 1 cup of juice reserved |
| 1 cup finely chopped onions | 1 cup dry white wine |
| 1 teaspoon finely chopped garlic | One 5½- to 6-pound red snapper, cleaned and scaled but with head and tail left on, rinsed and patted dry |
| ½ cup finely chopped celery | |
| ½ cup finely chopped green pepper | |
| ½ cup thinly sliced carrots | ¼ cup fresh lemon juice |
| 2 tablespoons finely cut fresh dill | 1 teaspoon salt |
| 1 tablespoon finely chopped fresh parsley leaves | Freshly ground black pepper |
| Two 1-pound cans solid-pack | 1 tablespoon butter, softened |

Heat the oil in a heavy 10- to 12-inch nonreactive skillet over moderate heat. Drop in the onions and garlic and, stirring frequently with a wooden spoon, cook for five minutes, until the onions are soft but not brown. Stir in the celery, green pepper, carrots, dill and parsley, and cook for three to five minutes or until the vegetables are soft. Add the tomatoes, the reserved tomato juice and the wine, and bring to a boil over high heat. Cover partially, reduce the heat to low, and simmer for 15 minutes or until this sauce thickens lightly. Pour the sauce into a nonreactive baking dish just large enough to hold the fish. Set it aside.

Preheat the oven to 400° F. Rub the fish inside and out with the lemon juice, then season it with the salt and several grindings of black pepper. Lay the fish on the vegetable sauce. Cut a piece of wax paper just large enough to fit the baking dish, and coat it with the softened butter. Set it buttered side down on top of the fish.

Bake the snapper in the center of the oven for 10 minutes per inch of thickness—about 25 to 30 minutes in all—or until it feels firm when prodded gently with a finger. Transfer the fish to a heated serving platter and cover the fish loosely with foil to keep it warm.

Set the baking dish on top of the stove if it is flameproof; otherwise, pour the sauce into a small, nonreactive pan. Bring the sauce to a boil over high heat. Boil briskly, uncovered, until the sauce thickens to the consistency of heavy cream. Uncover the fish and take off the wax paper. Spoon the sauce over the fish or serve it separately in a heated bowl or sauceboat.

■ AMERICAN COOKING: THE MELTING POT

# Rex Sole en Papillote

**To serve 4**

| | |
|---|---|
| **3 tablespoons butter, cut into bits, plus ¼ cup butter, softened** | **Eight 4-ounce rex sole fillets, skinned** |
| **12 mushroom caps, each 1 inch across, wiped clean** | **1 teaspoon salt** |
| | **½ teaspoon freshly ground white pepper** |
| **One 6-by-8-inch slice prosciutto or Smithfield ham, ¼ inch thick, cut into sixteen 6-inch strips ½ inch wide** | **2 teaspoons finely cut fresh chives** |
| | **2 teaspoons chopped fresh parsley leaves** |

Preheat the oven to 450°F. In a heavy 8- to 10-inch skillet, melt the butter bits over moderate heat. Add the mushroom caps and prosciutto and, stirring frequently, cook them for about three minutes, until they are delicately browned. Remove the skillet from the heat and set the mushroom caps aside.

With scissors, cut four large hearts about 11 inches long and 15 inches wide out of parchment paper. Then, with a pastry brush, spread 1 tablespoon of the softened butter evenly over one side of each of the four paper hearts.

Season the fish with the salt and white pepper. To assemble each *papillote,* place two fillets on the buttered side of a paper heart, and arrange four ham strips side by side over the fish. Sprinkle ½ teaspoon each of the chives and parsley on the ham, and top with three mushroom caps. Fold the paper over the fish so that the edges of the heart meet. Starting at the upper end of the fold, seal the edges by crimping them together at ½-inch intervals. Before crimping the point of the heart, open the seam slightly and insert a drinking straw. Blow through the straw to inflate the *papillote,* then quickly crimp the bottom point closed.

Arrange the *papillotes* side by side on a baking sheet and bake in the middle of the oven for 12 minutes. The paper should turn a golden brown. Serve at once, opening the paper at the table.

NOTE: Any firm white-fleshed fish with 4-ounce fillets can replace the rex sole. The most likely alternatives are other members of the flounder family.

■ AMERICAN COOKING: THE GREAT WEST

## Shad Roe on a Bed of Sorrel

**To serve 4**

| | |
|---|---|
| 1 pound sorrel | Sugar |
| ¼ cup unsalted butter, cut into bits, plus 6 tablespoons butter | Salt |
| | Freshly ground black pepper |
| | 2 pairs shad roe |
| 3 egg yolks | ½ cup flour |
| ¼ cup heavy cream | Lemon wedges for garnish |

Wash the sorrel under cold running water. With a sharp knife, trim away blemished spots and cut off the white stems. Stack a handful of leaves together at a time, roll them into a tight cylinder and cut it crosswise into fine shreds. Drop the sorrel into enough lightly salted boiling water to cover the sorrel by at least 1 inch, and boil for two minutes, until the shreds wilt. Drain the sorrel.

Melt the butter bits over moderate heat in a heavy 8- to 10-inch skillet. Add the sorrel and stir with a wooden spoon to coat the shreds evenly. Then reduce the heat to low. Beat the egg yolks and cream together with a wire whisk, and pour the mixture slowly over the sorrel, stirring continuously. Add a pinch of sugar, 1 teaspoon of salt and a liberal grinding of pepper. Stir for one to two minutes. Do not let the mixture come close to boiling or the egg yolks will curdle. Remove the pan from the heat and cover it to keep the sorrel warm; set aside.

With scissors or a small knife, slit the membrane connecting each pair of roe. Sprinkle the roe with salt and pepper, dip them in the flour to coat both sides and tap off the excess. Melt the 6 tablespoons of butter in a heavy 8- to 10-inch skillet. When the foam subsides, add the roe and fry them for five to six minutes on each side, regulating the heat so that they brown evenly without burning.

Spoon the sorrel onto four heated plates and place one roe on each portion. Garnish, if you like, with lemon wedges.

■ AMERICAN COOKING: THE EAST HEARTLAND

## Grilled Skewered Swordfish

**To serve 4**

| | |
|---|---|
| 1 small onion, cut into ¼-inch slices and separated into rings | black pepper |
| | 1½ pounds swordfish steaks, cut 1 inch thick, skinned, boned and cut into 1-inch cubes |
| ¼ cup fresh lemon juice | |
| 4 teaspoons olive oil | |
| 1 teaspoon salt | |
| ½ teaspoon freshly ground | 20 large bay leaves |

In a deep bowl, combine the onion, 2 tablespoons of the lemon juice, 2 teaspoons of the oil, the salt and pepper. Add the swordfish, turning it with a spoon to coat it well. Marinate the fish at room temperature for two hours or in the refrigerator for four hours, turning it occasionally. Put the bay leaves in a bowl, pour in 2 cups of boiling water, and soak them for one hour so they will not burn when grilled.

GRILLED SKEWERED SWORDFISH

Light a mound of charcoal in a grill and let the coals burn until white ash appears on the surface, then spread them into a layer 2 inches deep. Set the rack 4 inches from the coals and let it heat for five minutes. Grease it with an oil-moistened cloth held in long-handled tongs. Alternatively, preheat the broiler to its highest setting.

Drain the bay leaves and remove the fish from the marinade. String the fish cubes and bay leaves alternately on three or four skewers, pressing them firmly together. Combine the remaining 2 tablespoons of lemon juice and 2 teaspoons of oil and brush the mixture evenly over the fish.

If you are grilling the fish over charcoal, place the skewers on the rack and grill them for six or seven minutes, turning them every minute or so to color them evenly.

If you are grilling the fish in the stove, suspend the skewers side by side across the length of a roasting pan deep enough to allow a 1-inch space below the fish. Broil 4 inches from the heat, turning the skewers occasionally, for eight to 10 minutes or until the cubes feel firm when pressed lightly with a finger.

To serve, use a kitchen fork to push the fish cubes and bay leaves off the skewers onto heated individual plates.

■ MIDDLE EASTERN COOKING

## Fish Croquettes

**To serve 4**

| | |
|---|---|
| 2 slices homemade-type white bread | 3 egg yolks plus 3 whole eggs |
| ½ cup milk | Salt |
| 5 tablespoons unsalted butter | Freshly ground black pepper |
| ½ cup finely chopped onion | 1 cup flour |
| 1½ pounds fillets of white-fleshed fish, such as flounder, cod, haddock or whiting, rinsed and patted dry | 1 cup dry bread crumbs |
| | ½ cup sour cream |
| | 1½ tablespoons prepared horseradish with beets |
| | 1 cup vegetable oil |
| | Lemon wedges for garnish |

Place the bread in a small, shallow bowl and pour in the milk. Let the bread soak for five minutes, then drain off the milk and squeeze the bread dry. Set the bread aside.

Melt 2 tablespoons of the butter in a small skillet over moderate heat. Add the onion and cook, stirring often, for about four minutes or until the onion is soft but not brown.

Cut the fish into large pieces, and put it in a food processor equipped with a metal blade. Add the bread, three egg yolks and the onion, and season the mixture with salt and pepper. Process, a few seconds at a time, until the mixture is coarsely chopped and thoroughly blended. Do not purée it.

Break the three whole eggs into a shallow bowl, and beat them with the flat of a table fork until well blended. Place the flour and bread crumbs in separate shallow bowls.

Divide the fish mixture into eight equal parts. Shape each part into an oval croquette about ¾ inch thick. One at a time, dip a croquette in the flour, turning it to lightly coat both sides; tap off any excess. Next dip the croquette into the beaten eggs and—when it is coated completely—press both sides into the bread crumbs. Finally, place it on a wire rack set in a jelly-roll pan or on a baking sheet. Cover the pan with plastic wrap and refrigerate the croquettes until about 10 minutes before serving time.

Meanwhile, in a small bowl, stir together the sour cream and horseradish. Cover and refrigerate the bowl.

To cook the croquettes, heat the remaining 3 tablespoons of butter with the oil over moderately high heat in one 12-inch or two 8- to 10-inch heavy skillets. When the fat is hot but not smoking, add the croquettes and fry them for about eight minutes, turning them once. Reduce the heat, if necessary, so that they do not brown too quickly. Drain the croquettes on a double thickness of paper towels, and divide them among four heated dinner plates. Top each serving with a generous tablespoonful of horseradish sauce and a lemon wedge.

■ MAKE-AHEAD MENUS

## Frogs' Legs Roadhouse Style

*The roadhouse—a combination restaurant, night club and social club —is an American institution. The food is hearty and, in the South or Midwest, likely to include frogs' legs, produced commercially nearby. Fresh frogs legs are available, where fish and shellfish are sold, from April to October. Frozen frogs' legs are sold year round. Frogs' legs are picked up in the fingers for eating; no forks and knives are necessary— or even desirable.* ◆●

**To serve 4**

| | |
|---|---|
| 2 cups milk | homemade |
| ½ teaspoon salt | 2 tablespoons finely chopped onion |
| ¼ cup paprika | 1 tablespoon fresh lemon juice |
| 24 pairs frogs' legs, defrosted if frozen, rinsed and patted dry | ¼ cup finely cut fresh dill or 1 tablespoon dried dill weed |
| 1½ cups flour | 2 tablespoons finely chopped fresh parsley leaves |
| Vegetable oil for deep frying | Salt |
| | Freshly ground black pepper |
| HERB MAYONNAISE | |
| 1 cup mayonnaise, preferably | |

First prepare the herb mayonnaise by combining the mayonnaise, onion, lemon juice, dill and parsley. Add salt and pepper to taste. Set the sauce aside.

In a large shallow bowl, mix the milk, salt and 2 tablespoons of the paprika. Soak the frogs' legs in the mixture for about an hour. Stir the flour and remaining paprika together and place them on a sheet of wax paper.

In a heavy 12-inch skillet, heat 2 inches of oil over high heat. Fry the frogs' legs in two or three batches, by first dipping them in the flour, tapping off any excess and placing them in the oil in one layer. Let the frogs' legs cook for about five minutes, turning them once or twice with tongs and regulating the heat so that they brown evenly. When they are golden, transfer them to paper towels to drain.

Serve the frogs' legs hot, with the herb mayonnaise.

■ AMERICAN COOKING

# Steamed Fish with Black Mushrooms and Ham

**To serve 4**

| | |
|---|---|
| 6 to 8 Chinese dried black mushrooms | 2 teaspoons dark sesame oil |
| One 3-pound whole fish, such as sea bass, flounder, wall-eyed pike, pompano or porgy, cleaned, with head and tail left on, rinsed and patted dry | 2 garlic cloves, chopped fine |
| | 1½ teaspoons finely chopped fresh ginger root |
| | 1 ounce thinly sliced prosciutto or Smithfield ham, fat chopped fine and 1 tablespoon reserved, lean cut into 1-inch squares |
| 2 teaspoons coarse (kosher) salt | |
| ¼ teaspoon sugar | |
| 2 tablespoons rice wine or dry sherry | ½ teaspoon dried hot-red-pepper flakes |
| 2 tablespoon light soy sauce | 3 tablespoons thinly sliced scallions, separated into rings |

Place the dried mushrooms in a bowl and pour in enough boiling water to cover them completely. Set the mushrooms aside to soak for 20 to 30 minutes.

With a cleaver or large knife held diagonally, score the fish at 1-inch intervals from neck to tail on both sides. Follow the natural curve of the body, and extend each cut from the dorsal to the ventral sides of the fish (that is, from top to belly), cutting down nearly to the bone. Sprinkle the coarse salt evenly outside and inside the fish, rubbing it gently into the score marks. Put the fish on a heatproof platter that will fit easily into the steamer, sauté pan or Chinese steamer tray in which you plan to cook the fish.

In a small nonreactive bowl, stir the wine, soy sauce, sesame oil and sugar together. Blend in the garlic and ginger. Pour the mixture over the fish.

In another bowl, combine the ham fat, hot-pepper flakes and scallion rings. Sprinkle them over the fish.

Drain the mushrooms and, using scissors, snip off the stems and cut the caps in half. Rinse the caps. Arrange the mushrooms and ham on the fish. Bring water about 2 inches deep to a boil in a lidded steamer or large sauté pan with a rack or trivet inside, or in a wok if you are using a Chinese steaming tray. The water should not be deep enough to touch the bottom of the platter on which the fish will steam.

Place the platter with the fish on the steaming rack, trivet or tray, and cover the pan. Steam the fish for 10 minutes per inch of thickness or until the flesh visible in the score marks is opaque and the fish feels firm to the touch.

If the fish was cooked in a Chinese steamer, bring the steamer to the table on a tray. Otherwise, lift out the platter and set it on a trivet at the table for serving.

■ CHINESE MENUS

# Clam Pie

**To serve 6**

| | |
|---|---|
| 6 dozen small live hard-shell clams, shucked and drained, with liquor reserved | ¼ teaspoon salt |
| | ¼ cup flour |
| | ¼ cup dry white wine |
| 3 tablespoons butter, softened, plus 3 tablespoons butter, cut into bits | ½ cup heavy cream |
| | ½ cup milk |
| | 2 tablespoons dry sherry |
| 1 pound mushrooms, wiped clean, trimmed and quartered lengthwise, including stems | ⅛ teaspoon freshly ground white pepper |
| | Short-crust pastry dough (Index/Glossary) for a 1-crust pie |
| 3 tablespoons fresh lemon juice | 1 egg lightly beaten with 1 tablespoon milk |

Preheat the oven to 400°F. With a sharp knife, cut the soft centers out of the clams and set them aside on a plate. Coarsely chop the remaining tougher clam meat and add it to the clam centers. Strain the clam liquor through a fine sieve lined with a double thickness of dampened cheesecloth. Measure and set aside 1 cup of the liquor.

With a pastry brush, spread the 3 tablespoons of softened butter evenly over the bottom and sides of a small, heavy casserole. Add the mushrooms, 2 tablespoons of the lemon juice and the salt. Cover the casserole tightly and cook over moderate heat for about 10 minutes or until the mushrooms release most of their liquid. Uncover and set the mushrooms aside until you are ready to assemble the pie.

In a heavy 1½- to 2-quart saucepan, melt the 3 tablespoons of butter bits over moderate heat. With a whisk, stir in the flour to make a paste, or roux. Continue to whisk while you slowly pour in the 1 cup of clam liquor, wine, cream and milk. Cook over high heat, still stirring, until this sauce comes to a boil, thickens heavily and is smooth. Reduce the heat to low and simmer for five minutes, then mix in the sherry, the remaining tablespoon of lemon juice and the white pepper.

With a slotted spoon, remove the clams and mushrooms from their liquid and stir them into the sauce. Taste for seasoning. Then pour the mixture into a shallow, round baking dish about 9½ inches in diameter and 2 inches deep.

Roll the pastry dough into a circle 12 inches across and ⅛ inch thick. Drape the dough over the rolling pin, lift it, and unroll it over the baking dish. With scissors or a knife, trim off excess dough, leaving a 1-inch margin around the rim. Turn the margin under the edge and secure the dough to the rim by crimping it tightly with fingers or a fork.

Cut a 1-inch round hole in the center of the pie and brush the pastry surface with the egg-and-milk mixture. Bake for 15 minutes, then reduce the oven temperature to 325°F. and bake for 45 minutes longer or until the crust is golden brown. Serve at once from the baking dish.

■ AMERICAN COOKING: NEW ENGLAND

## Crawfish Étouffée

*In Louisiana, crayfish are known as "crawfish"—and are considered a great treat. "Étouffée" literally means "smothered." In fact, this recipe blankets the crayfish with a rich, thick sauce.* ❧

**To serve 4**

| | |
|---|---|
| 5 pounds live crayfish | tomatoes, drained and |
| 3 tablespoons vegetable oil | chopped fine, with |
| 3 tablespoons flour | juice reserved |
| 1 cup finely chopped onions | 1 tablespoon Worcestershire |
| 1 cup finely chopped scallions | sauce |
| ½ cup finely chopped celery | ¼ teaspoon cayenne pepper |
| 1 teaspoon finely | 1 teaspoon freshly ground |
| chopped garlic | black pepper |
| 2 cups fish stock | 2 teaspoons salt |
| (Index/Glossary) | 4 cups freshly cooked long- |
| One 1-pound can whole | grain white rice |

In a heavy 8- to 10-quart pot, bring 4 quarts of water to a boil over high heat. Using tongs, drop in the crayfish and boil them, uncovered, for five minutes.

Drain the crayfish into a large colander. When they are cool enough to handle, break off the tails, snap them in half lengthwise, and lift out the tail meat in one piece. If you like, snap off the large claws, break them with a nutcracker, and pick out the bits of claw meat.

Some or all of the yellow fat or "butter" from the body of the crayfish may slide out when you break off the tail. If it does not, scoop the shell clean with the tip of one thumb and pick out the yellow fat. Reserve the crayfish meat and fat (there will be about 2 cups). Discard the shells and heads.

In a heavy 5- to 6-quart casserole, heat the oil over high heat. Add the flour and stir for five minutes or until this roux browns richly. Add the onions, scallions, celery and garlic. Stirring frequently, cook over moderate heat for five minutes or until the vegetables are soft. Stirring constantly, pour in the fish stock in a slow, thin stream, and cook over high heat until the mixture comes to a boil and thickens lightly.

Add the tomatoes, Worcestershire, cayenne, black pepper and salt, and reduce the heat to low. Simmer partially covered for 30 minutes, then stir in the crayfish meat and fat, and heat them through. Taste for seasoning and ladle the crawfish étouffée into a heated bowl; mound the rice in a separate bowl and serve it immediately.

■ AMERICAN COOKING: CREOLE AND ACADIAN

## Lobster Fra Diavolo

*The name for this dish memorializes an otherwise forgotten opera written by Daniel Auber and introduced in Paris in 1830. In the opera, Fra Diavolo is a sort of highwayman—a Neapolitan Robin Hood.* ❧

**To serve 4**

| | |
|---|---|
| Two 1½ to 2-pound live | seeded and chopped |
| lobsters, split in half | 1 tablespoon chopped fresh |
| lengthwise | flatleaf parsley leaves |
| ¼ cup olive oil | 1 teaspoon crumbled, |
| ¼ cup finely chopped onion | dried oregano |
| 1 teaspoon finely chopped | ¼ teaspoon crushed dried |
| garlic | hot-red-pepper flakes |
| 1 cup dry white wine | ½ teaspoon salt |
| 4 large tomatoes, peeled, | |

Discard the gelatinous sac (or stomach) near the head of each lobster and the long intestine attached to it. Remove and set aside the greenish tomalley (or liver) and the black caviarlike coral (or eggs), if there are any. With a heavy, sharp knife or kitchen scissors, cut off the claws and gash the flat underside of each large

NEW YORK OYSTER STEW

## New York Oyster Stew

*The Oyster Bar in the labyrinths of New York's Grand Central Station has made this stew a paradigm of simple cooking.* ❖●

**To serve 4**

| | |
|---|---|
| 1 cup butter, cut into bits, plus 4 teaspoons butter | 2 dozen live oysters, shucked and drained, with 1 cup of liquor strained and reserved |
| 2 teaspoons Worcestershire sauce | ½ cup light cream |
| Paprika | ½ cup milk |
| ½ teaspoon celery salt | Oyster crackers (optional) |
| 1 teaspoon salt | |

In a heavy 2- to 3-quart saucepan, melt the butter bits over moderate heat and stir in the Worcestershire, 1 teaspoon of paprika, the celery salt and salt. Add the oysters and oyster liquor, and bring to a boil over high heat. Reduce the heat to low, then stir in the cream and milk. Stirring gently, cook for two or three minutes longer, until the oysters plump up and their edges begin to curl. Taste for seasoning. Place a teaspoon of the remaining butter in each of four heated bowls. Ladle in the oyster stew, sprinkle with paprika, and serve at once. Traditionally the stew is accompanied by oyster crackers.

■ AMERICAN COOKING: THE EASTERN HEARTLAND

## Crab Cakes

**To serve 4**

| | |
|---|---|
| 1 egg | over to remove all cartilage |
| 2 tablespoons mayonnaise | 3 tablespoons finely chopped fresh parsley leaves |
| ½ teaspoon dry mustard | |
| ⅛ teaspoon cayenne pepper | 1½ tablespoons crumbs made from unsalted soda crackers |
| ½ teaspoon salt | |
| ½ teaspoon freshly ground white pepper | Vegetable oil for deep frying |
| | 1 lemon, cut into 8 wedges |
| 1 pound crab meat, picked | Tartar sauce (Index/Glossary) |

In a deep bowl, beat the egg lightly with a wire whisk. Add the mayonnaise, mustard, cayenne, salt and white pepper, and whisk until the mixture is smooth. Then use a fork to blend in the crabmeat, parsley and cracker crumbs.

Divide the mixture into eight parts, and shape each part into a ball about 2 inches across. Wrap these cakes in wax paper, and chill them for 30 minutes.

Pour oil into a deep fryer or large, heavy saucepan to a depth of about 2 inches, and heat the oil to a temperature of 375°F. on a deep-frying thermometer. Deep-fry four crab cakes at a time, turning them with a slotted spoon for two or three minutes, until they are golden on all sides. As they brown, transfer them to paper towels to drain. Arrange the crab cakes with the lemon wedges on a heated platter. Serve at once, accompanied by the tartar sauce in a separate bowl.

■ AMERICAN COOKING: SOUTHERN STYLE

claw with the flat of a knife. Discard the lobsters' small claws and the antennae.

In a heavy 12-inch skillet, heat the olive oil until it is hot but not smoking. Add the lobster bodies and claws, and cook them over high heat for three minutes, turning them once or twice with tongs. Transfer them to a plate.

Pour off all but a film of fat from the skillet. Add the onion and garlic and, stirring frequently with a wooden spoon, cook them over moderate heat for five minutes or until the onion is soft. Add the wine and boil it, stirring constantly, until it is reduced by half. Add the tomatoes, parsley, oregano, hot pepper and salt, and bring the mixture to a boil, stirring constantly. Return the lobster to the skillet, cover, and cook over moderate heat for five minutes, basting once or twice. Just before serving, reduce the heat to low. Press the tomalley and coral through a fine sieve into the sauce. Let the sauce simmer for a minute or two. Taste the sauce and season it.

To serve, arrange the lobster pieces on a deep heated platter and spoon the sauce over them.

■ THE COOKING OF ITALY

# Shrimp and Ham Jambalaya

**To serve 6 to 8**

| | |
|---|---|
| 2 cups water | ¼ cup finely chopped |
| 2 teaspoons salt | green pepper |
| 1 cup short-grain white rice | 1 tablespoon finely chopped |
| 2 pounds medium-sized | fresh parsley leaves |
| shrimp, shelled, deveined, | 3 whole cloves, pulverized |
| rinsed and patted dry | with a mortar and pestle |
| 6 tablespoons butter | or finely crushed with a |
| 1½ cups finely chopped | kitchen mallet or the flat |
| onions | of a heavy cleaver |
| 2 tablespoons finely | ½ teaspoon crumbled dried |
| chopped garlic | thyme |
| One 1-pound can tomatoes, | ½ teaspoon cayenne pepper |
| drained and chopped fine, | ¼ teaspoon freshly ground |
| with juice reserved | black pepper |
| 3 tablespoons canned | 1 pound cooked lean smoked |
| tomato paste | ham, trimmed of excess fat |
| ½ cup finely chopped celery | and cut into ½-inch cubes |

Bring the water and 1 teaspoon of the salt to a boil in a 1- to 1½-quart saucepan set over high heat. Add the rice, stir once or twice, and immediately cover the pan. Reduce the heat to low and simmer for about 20 minutes or until the rice is tender and has absorbed all of the liquid in the pan. Fluff the rice with a fork, cover, and set aside.

Meanwhile, fill a 3- to 4-quart saucepan halfway with water, and bring the water to a boil, then reduce the heat. When the water is barely simmering, drop in the shrimp. Poach the shrimp for about three minutes or until they are firm and opaque. Drain the shrimp thoroughly, put them in a bowl, and cover with plastic wrap; set them aside.

In a heavy 5- to 6-quart casserole, melt the butter over moderate heat. Add the onions and garlic and, stirring frequently, cook for about five minutes or until they are soft but not brown. Add the tomatoes, the tomato juice and tomato paste, and stir over moderate heat for five minutes. Then add the celery, green pepper, parsley, cloves, thyme, cayenne, black pepper and the remaining teaspoon of salt. Stirring frequently, cook, uncovered, over moderate heat until the vegetables are tender and the mixture is thick enough to hold its shape lightly in the spoon.

Add the ham and, still stirring frequently, cook for five minutes. Then stir in the shrimp and the reserved rice. Stir over moderate heat until the mixture is hot and the rice has absorbed any liquid in the pan.

Taste for seasoning and serve the jambalaya at once, from the casserole or mounded in a heated bowl.

■ AMERICAN COOKING: CREOLE AND ACADIAN

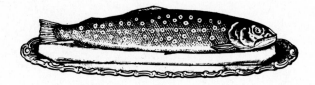

# Scallops with White-Wine Sauce

*For display, present the scallops atop spinach leaves that have been lightly sautéed in olive oil to give them a sheen.* ◆●

**To serve 4**

| | WHITE-WINE SAUCE |
|---|---|
| 3 egg yolks | ¼ cup dry white wine |
| 2 tablespoons cold water | 1 tablespoon dry sherry |
| ½ cup flour | wine |
| 1½ pounds sea scallops, | 1 tablespoon sherry vinegar |
| rinsed and patted dry | ¼ cup fresh orange juice |
| ½ cup clarified butter | 2 teaspoons finely chopped |
| ½ cup olive oil | shallot |
| 6 dried hot chilies | ½ cup unsalted butter, cut |
| ¼ cup fresh lemon juice | into bits and chilled |
| 1 tablespoon julienne strips of | Salt |
| orange peel for garnish | Freshly ground white pepper |

Preheat the oven to 200°F. Line an ovenproof platter with a double thickness of paper towels and set it aside. For starting the sauce, combine the wine, sherry, vinegar, orange juice and shallots in a 2- to 3-quart nonreactive saucepan. Bring to a boil over moderately high heat and, stirring frequently with a wooden spoon, cook for three or four minutes to reduce the mixture to about 2 tablespoons of syrupy liquid. Set this mixture aside over the lowest possible heat.

In a small bowl, beat the egg yolks with the water until they are smooth. Place the flour on a large flat plate. Dip each scallop in the yolks, let the excess drip off, then roll it in the flour to coat it evenly. Tap off excess flour. Set the coated scallops on wax paper.

In a 10- to 12-inch sauté pan or heavy skillet, heat ¼ cup of the clarified butter and ¼ cup of the olive oil over moderately high heat. When the butter mixture is hot but not smoking, add three of the hot chilies to the pan. Stirring constantly with a wooden spoon, cook them for three or four minutes or until the chilies begin to brown. Using a slotted spoon, remove the chilies from the pan and discard them.

Add half of the scallops to the pan, and sauté them for about three minutes on each side or until they are golden. With the slotted spoon, transfer the scallops to the lined platter and set them in the oven to keep them warm.

Brown the remaining chilies, adding more butter and oil to the pan as necessary; then sauté the second batch of scallops. Drain them on the platter with the first batch.

Finish the sauce by whisking the chilled unsalted butter bits into the syrupy wine and orange mixture. Add the butter about a tablespoonful at a time, and whisk the mixture well after each addition. Pour the sauce through a sieve to remove the bits of shallot. Season the finished sauce with salt and white pepper to taste.

To serve, place the scallops on a heated platter and sprinkle them with the lemon juice. Pour sauce over them and garnish the platter with orange peel, if you like.

■ FISH AND SHELLFISH MENUS

**SCALLOPS WITH WHITE-WINE SAUCE**

## Lobster Newburg

*Newburg sauce can be used with any shellfish, but it was especially conceived to complement lobster by Pascal, a chef at Delmonico's—the poshest restaurant in New York City at the turn of the century.* ❖❖

### To serve 4 to 6

| | |
|---|---|
| 6 tablespoons butter | ³/₄ teaspoon salt |
| 3 cups cooked lobster meat, cut into 2-inch pieces | ¹/₈ teaspoon cayenne pepper |
| ¹/₄ cup Madeira or dry sherry wine | ¹/₂ teaspoon fresh lemon juice |
| 2 tablespoons brandy | 6 patty shells, heated, or 4 to 6 slices homemade-type white bread, freshly toasted and cut into triangles |
| 1¹/₂ cups heavy cream | Paprika for garnish |
| 5 egg yolks | |

In a heavy, nonreactive 10- to 12-inch skillet, melt the butter over moderate heat. When the foam subsides, add the lobster meat and, stirring constantly, cook for about one minute. Pour in the Madeira and brandy. When they boil up, add 1 cup of the cream. Still stirring, bring the cream to a boil. Reduce the heat to its lowest point and cook, stirring frequently, for about two minutes.

In a small bowl, beat the egg yolks and the remaining ¹/₂ cup of cream with a wire whisk until the mixture is smooth. Gradually whisk in about four spoonfuls of the simmering lobster sauce.

Then, in a slow stream, pour the mixture into the skillet, whisking constantly. Cook over moderate heat until the sauce thickens, but do not let it come to a boil or it will curdle. Season with the salt, cayenne and lemon juice. Serve immediately in heated patty shells or on hot toast points. Sprinkle the lobster Newburg lightly with paprika.

■ AMERICAN COOKING

## Scampi with Garlic Butter

*True scampi are Adriatic shellfish that resemble miniature lobsters. Away from Venice, jumbo shrimp take their place nicely.* ❖❖

### To serve 6

| | |
|---|---|
| 2 pounds jumbo shrimp | or scallions |
| ¹/₂ cup butter, cut into bits | 1 tablespoon finely chopped garlic |
| ¹/₂ cup olive oil | 1 teaspoon salt |
| 1 tablespoon fresh lemon juice, plus 3 lemons, quartered, for garnish | Freshly ground black pepper |
| | ¹/₄ cup finely chopped fresh flatleaf parsley leaves |
| ¹/₄ cup finely chopped shallots | |

Shell the shrimp, leaving the last small segment of shell and the tail intact. Slit each shrimp down the back and lift out the black or

174

white intestinal vein. Rinse the shrimp under cold running water and pat dry with paper towels.

In a shallow flameproof baking dish or pan just large enough to hold the shrimp in one layer, melt the butter over low heat. Do not let it brown. Remove the dish from the heat. Stir in the olive oil, lemon juice, shallots, garlic, salt and a few grindings of pepper; add the shrimp and use tongs to turn them in the butter and oil until they glisten on all sides. Let the shrimp marinate for 15 to 30 minutes.

Preheat the broiler to its highest setting. Broil the shrimp 4 inches from the heat for three minutes, then turn them over and broil for about three minutes longer, or until they brown lightly and are firm to the touch.

Transfer the shrimp to a heated platter, pour the sauce from the pan over them, and sprinkle them with the chopped parsley. Garnish with lemon quarters, and serve.

■ THE COOKING OF ITALY

## Twice-fried Scallops

To serve 4

| | |
|---|---|
| ½ cup dry sherry wine | ginger root |
| 1 teaspoon plus 1 tablespoon cornstarch | 3 scallions, white parts sliced thin and separated into rings, green tops cut into julienne strips |
| 1 teaspoon salt | |
| ¼ teaspoon freshly ground white pepper | |
| 1 pound bay scallops, left whole, or sea scallops, halved crosswise, rinsed and patted dry | 2 teaspoons chopped fresh coriander leaves |
| | 2 tablespoons dark sesame oil |
| 3 cups vegetable oil | 1 small carrot, cut into julienne strips, for garnish |
| 2 teaspoons chopped fresh | |

First prepare the cooking sauce by combining the sherry, 1 teaspoon of the cornstarch, the salt and white pepper in a small bowl. Stir until the cornstarch dissolves. Set the sauce aside. In a large bowl, combine the scallops with 1 tablespoon of cornstarch, and stir to coat them evenly.

Heat the vegetable oil in a 12-inch wok or heavy 8-inch skillet over high heat until it is hot but not smoking. Add the scallops to the oil, stirring to separate them, and cook for three to four minutes, until they float to the top of the oil. Remove the scallops with a skimmer or slotted spoon and set them on a double thickness of paper towels to drain. Let the oil cool, then pour off all but a thin coating.

Heat the wok or skillet over high heat and add the ginger, scallion rings and coriander. Stirring constantly, cook these seasonings for 30 seconds, then add the scallops and the sauce. Cook until the scallops are evenly coated and heated through. Swirl in the sesame oil.

To serve, mound the scallops on a heated serving plate, and garnish the edges with the carrots and green scallion strips.

■ CHINESE MENUS

## Tempura

*This recipe for tempura includes only a few of the many ingredients that the Japanese dip in batter and deep-fry. Substitutions or additions might be 1-inch pieces of scallions, snow peas, ¼-inch-wide strips of carrot, blanched and quartered bamboo shoots, small asparagus spears or ¼-inch-thick slices of fish fillets.* ❧

To serve 4

| | |
|---|---|
| 2 pounds shrimp, shelled and deveined, with tails left on | BATTER |
| | 2 cups flour |
| ¼ pound green beans, trimmed | 1 egg |
| 2 baby eggplants, unpeeled and sliced thin | 2 to 2½ cups ice water |
| 1 sweet potato, peeled and sliced thin | DIPPING SAUCE |
| ¼ pound small mushrooms, wiped clean and trimmed | ¼ cup dry sherry wine |
| | ¼ cup Japanese soy sauce |
| Vegetable oil for deep frying | ¼ cup chicken stock |

Prepare the dipping sauce in advance, by first heating the sherry in a small nonreactive skillet over moderate heat until it is lukewarm. Ignite the sherry with a match, turn off the heat, and slide the pan gently back and forth until the flames die. Add the soy sauce and chicken stock, and bring to a boil over high heat. Pour the sauce into four small bowls, and allow it to cool to room temperature.

Butterfly the shrimp by cutting them three-quarters of the way through along their inner curves and gently spreading them open. Flatten them slightly with the side of a knife. Divide the shrimp, green beans, eggplants, sweet potato and mushrooms into four portions, and set these near the stove on separate dishes or sheets of wax paper.

For the batter, place the flour in a large mixing bowl, and make a well in the center. Drop in the egg and pour in 2 cups of ice water. With a large wooden spoon, gradually stir the flour into the liquid ingredients. Then stir vigorously until the batter is very smooth; use up to ½ cup of additional ice water if necessary to make a somewhat thin batter that will coat the spoon lightly.

Preheat the oven to 200°F. Pour vegetable oil into a deep-fat fryer or heavy 3- to 4-quart saucepan to a depth of 2 or 3 inches. Heat the oil until it registers 375°F. on a deep-frying thermometer.

Using chopsticks or tongs, dip the shrimp and pieces of vegetable one at a time in the batter, twirl each piece around to coat it evenly, then drop it into the hot oil. Fry six or eight pieces at a time, turning them once with chopsticks or tongs, for three to four minutes or until they are light gold. Lift the food out with a skimmer or perforated spoon, and drain it on paper towels. Arrange a portion on an individual ovenproof plate or in a basket and set it in the oven to keep it warm. With the skimmer, remove any food particles from the surface of the oil. Check the temperature of the oil before frying the remaining portions.

Serve each portion with its own bowl of dipping sauce.

■ AMERICAN COOKING: THE MELTING POT

**MUSSELS AND SHRIMP IN COCONUT CREAM**

## Steamed Clams with Sausages and Ham

*In Portugal, the clams are cooked—most appropriately—in a cata-plana, a metal casserole shaped like a clam.* ❖●

**To serve 4**

| | |
|---|---|
| ¹⁄₂ pound *linguiça,* chorizo or other smoked garlic-seasoned pork sausage | 2 tomatoes, peeled, seeded and chopped coarse |
| ¹⁄₂ cup olive oil | ¹⁄₂ cup finely chopped fresh parsley leaves |
| 4 onions, sliced thin | ¹⁄₂ cup dry white wine |
| 1 teaspoon paprika | 1 tablespoon finely chopped garlic |
| ¹⁄₄ teaspoon dried hot-red-pepper flakes | 2 small bay leaves, crumbled |
| Freshly ground black pepper | 3 dozen small live hard-shell clams, scrubbed |
| ¹⁄₄ pound *presunto,* Smithfield or other lean smoked ham | |

With the aid of a small knife, remove the casings from the sausages. Coarsely crumble the meat into a sieve. Plunge the sieve into a pan of boiling water and boil briskly for one minute. Then spread the sausage meat out on paper towels to drain.

In a heavy 12-inch skillet, heat the olive oil over moderate heat. Add the onions and, stirring frequently, cook for five minutes or until they are soft. Add the paprika, hot red pepper and a liberal grinding of black pepper, and cook for a minute or two. Then add the sausage meat, ham, tomatoes, parsley, wine, garlic and bay leaves. Increase the heat and bring the mixture to a boil. Stirring constantly, cook until most of the liquid evaporates.

Arrange the clams hinged side down over the meat and tomato mixture, cover the skillet tightly, and cook over moderate heat for about five minutes or until the clams open. Discard any that remain closed. To serve, transfer the clams to heated soup plates and ladle the sauce over them.

■ THE COOKING OF SPAIN AND PORTUGAL

## Mussels and Shrimp in Coconut Cream

**To serve 4**

| | |
|---|---|
| 1¹⁄₂ cups dry vermouth | 2 large or 4 small shallots, sliced thin |
| ³⁄₄ cup water | 1 tablespoon chopped fresh mint leaves, plus mint sprigs for garnish |
| 2 dozen live mussels, scrubbed and debearded | |
| 2 to 3 tablespoons coconut cream, preferably homemade | Freshly ground white pepper |
| 1 cup heavy cream | Salt |
| 1 pound shrimp, shelled and deveined | ¹⁄₂ pound snow peas, trimmed and strings removed |

In a nonreactive stockpot, bring the vermouth and water to a boil. Add the mussels, cover the pot, and cook, sliding the pot back and forth occasionally, for five minutes or until the mussels open. With a slotted spoon, transfer the mussels to a large bowl; discard any that have not opened. Shell the mussels, reserving two or three shells per serving for garnish. Set the mussels aside.

In a colander lined with a double thickness of dampened cheesecloth, strain the mussel poaching liquid into a deep skillet. Over high heat, boil the liquid to reduce it by half. Reduce the heat to moderately high. Stirring with a wooden spoon, pour in the coconut cream and heavy cream, and cook for 10 to 15 minutes or until the sauce is reduced to about ²⁄₃ cup. Add the shrimp and poach them for three minutes or until they are firm.

Add the mussels to the sauce. Stir in the shallots, chopped mint and white pepper to taste. Remove the skillet from the heat, and cover it to keep the shellfish warm.

In a 3- to 4-quart saucepan, bring about 4 cups of lightly salted water to a boil. Add the snow peas, return the water to a boil, and immediately pour the snow peas into a colander to drain. Refresh the snow peas under cold running water for an instant only.

With a slotted spoon, divide the mussels and shrimp among four heated dinner plates. Top each portion with sauce and surround it with a pinwheel of snow peas. Arrange a few reserved mussel shells, open side down, next to the shrimp and mussels. Garnish the plates with mint sprigs, if you like.

NOTE: Coconut cream is available canned where Asian food is sold. Or you can make your own: Soak ¹⁄₂ cup packaged, shredded coconut in ¹⁄₂ cup milk for 30 minutes. Purée the mixture in a blender or food processor, then strain it through a fine sieve, squeezing the pulp to extract as much liquid as possible.

■ FISH AND SHELLFISH MENUS

## Mussels in Herb Sauce

**To serve 4**

| | |
|---|---|
| 10 tablespoons unsalted butter | fresh chervil leaves or 2 teaspoons crumbled dried chervil |
| ¹⁄₂ cup finely chopped onions | |
| ¹⁄₂ cup finely chopped shallots | 2 cups dry white wine |
| ¹⁄₄ cup plus 2 tablespoons finely chopped fresh parsley leaves | Freshly ground black pepper |
| | 2 dozen live mussels, scrubbed and debearded |
| 2 tablespoons finely chopped | |

In a 6- to 8-quart heavy, nonreactive pot, melt the butter over moderate heat. When the foam begins to subside, add the onions, shallots, ¹⁄₄ cup of the parsley and the chervil. Stirring frequently, cook for about five minutes or until the onions and shallots are soft but not brown.

Stir in the wine and a few grindings of pepper, then add the mussels. Tightly cover the casserole and bring the wine to a boil over high heat. Steam the mussels for five to seven minutes or until they open. To ensure that they cook evenly, hold the lid in place and slide the pot back and forth from time to time.

With a slotted spoon, transfer the mussels to a heated tureen or individual serving bowls. Discard any mussels that have not opened. Strain the cooking liquid into a bowl through a fine sieve lined with a double thickness of dampened cheesecloth. Pour the strained liquid over the mussels, and sprinkle them with the remaining 2 tablespoons of parsley. Serve at once.

■ A QUINTET OF CUISINES

# Cioppino

*A century ago, San Francisco's Italian fishermen concocted this distinctly Mediterranean-sounding but American-tasting seafood stew. The choice of fish and shellfish can be varied to fit the local catch or the fishmonger's stock.* 

### To serve 8

| | |
|---|---|
| Two 1½-pound Dungeness crabs or four ¾-pound blue crabs | 1 cup dry white wine |
| ¼ cup olive oil or vegetable oil | 2 tablespoons chopped fresh flatleaf parsley leaves |
| 1 cup chopped onions | 2 dozen large live mussels, scrubbed and debearded |
| 1 tablespoon finely chopped garlic | 2 dozen small live hard-shell clams, scrubbed |
| 4 cups fish stock (Index/Glossary) | 1 pound large shrimp, shelled and deveined |
| 3 tomatoes, chopped coarse and put through a food mill, or 1 cup canned puréed tomatoes | 2 pounds firm white-fleshed fish such as cod, cut into serving pieces |
| | ½ teaspoon salt |

Half-fill a large pot with liquid—plain water, water plus beer, seasonings if you wish—and bring it to a boil. Reduce the heat to moderate so the water just simmers. Using tongs, plunge the crabs headfirst into the pot. Simmer, uncovered, for about 30 minutes for Dungeness crabs, 20 minutes for blue crabs. Remove the crabs and drain them.

Meanwhile, heat the oil over moderate heat in a heavy nonreactive 3- to 4-quart saucepan. Add the onions and garlic and, stirring frequently with a wooden spoon, cook for five minutes or until the onions are soft but not brown. Stir in the stock, tomato purée, wine and parsley, and bring to a boil over high heat. Reduce the heat, cover partially, and simmer for 15 minutes.

When the crabs are cool enough to handle, grasp one tightly in one hand and lift off the top shell. Pull out the spongy gray lungs, or "deadman's fingers," from each side, and scrape out the intestines in the center. Place the crab on its back and, with the tip of a knife, pry off the pointed flap or apron. Cut away the head just behind the eyes. Cut Dungeness crabs into quarters with a cleaver or heavy knife; leave blue crabs whole.

To assemble the cioppino, arrange the mussels and clams in the bottom of a 10- to 12-quart nonreactive pot, and pour in the tomato mixture. Bring to a boil over high heat, reduce the heat to low, cover tightly, and cook for five minutes. Add the shrimp and fish, arrange the crabs on top, cover the casserole again, and continue to cook for three to five minutes longer. The cioppino is done when the shrimp and fish are firm and opaque.

Serve at once, directly from the casserole, or spoon the fish and shellfish into a heated tureen and pour the broth over them. Discard any mussels or clams that remain closed.

■ AMERICAN COOKING: THE GREAT WEST

# Shrimp Curry

### To serve 4 to 6

| | |
|---|---|
| 1 pound jumbo shrimp, shelled with tails left on, deveined, rinsed and dried | fresh ginger root |
| 1 tablespoon finely chopped garlic | 1 tablespoon finely chopped garlic |
| 1 tablespoon distilled white or cider vinegar | ½ cup finely chopped onions |
| 2 teaspoons salt | 1 teaspoon turmeric |
| 1 cup peeled, coarsely chopped fresh coconut | ½ teaspoon ground cumin |
| ¼ cup coriander seeds | ¼ teaspoon cayenne pepper |
| 1¼ cups warm water | ¼ teaspoon freshly ground black pepper |
| 5 tablespoons vegetable oil | 3 tablespoons finely chopped fresh coriander leaves |
| 1 tablespoon finely chopped | |

In a small bowl, combine the shrimp with the vinegar and salt, and toss thoroughly. Turning occasionally, marinate the shrimp at room temperature for 15 to 20 minutes.

Combine the coconut, coriander seeds and water in a blender or food processor, and purée them, stopping once to scrape down the sides of the jar or bowl.

Pour the purée into a fine sieve lined with a double thickness of dampened cheesecloth and set over a deep bowl. With a large spoon, press down hard on the coconut mixture to extract as much liquid as possible. Then gather the ends of the cheesecloth together and wring vigorously to squeeze out any remaining liquid. Discard the pulp and set the coconut milk aside; there should be about 1½ cups.

In a heavy 8- to 10-inch skillet, heat 3 tablespoons of the oil over moderate heat until a drop of water flicked in splutters instantly. Drain the shrimp and reserve the marinade. Drop the shrimp into the skillet, cover tightly, and cook for 30 seconds; turn the shrimp over, cover again, and cook for 30 seconds, until the shrimp are pink and firm. With a perforated spoon, return the shrimp to the marinade.

Pour the remaining oil into the skillet, heat it, and add the ginger root. Stirring constantly, fry for 30 seconds; add the garlic and continue stirring for one minute.

Still stirring, add the onions and fry for seven to eight minutes, until they are soft and golden brown. Add the turmeric, cumin, cayenne pepper and black pepper, and stir for one minute. Then pour the shrimp marinade into the skillet and bring it to a boil immediately, scraping in any brown particles clinging to the bottom and sides of the pan.

Return the shrimp to the skillet, stirring to coat them evenly. Pour in the reserved coconut milk and, stirring constantly, bring to a boil over high heat. Reduce the heat to moderate, sprinkle in 2 tablespoons of the coriander, cover, and cook for three minutes. Taste for seasoning.

To serve, transfer the shrimp to a serving dish and pour the sauce remaining in the pan over them. Sprinkle the shrimp with the remaining tablespoon of coriander, and serve at once with boiled rice and a chutney.

■ THE COOKING OF INDIA

## Paella

*In Spain, a paella can be deliciously simple or splendidly elaborate. Vary the combination of chicken, meats and shellfish to your taste. Cubed pork, smoked ham, beef or veal might be added. A rabbit might replace the chicken legs. Squid, even snails, are appropriate. Green beans can replace the peas, and artichoke hearts are welcome.* ✦●

**To serve 6 to 8**

| | |
|---|---|
| 4 cups chicken stock | deveined, rinsed |
| ½ teaspoon crumbled | and patted dry |
| saffron threads | 2 dozen live mussels, |
| ½ cup olive oil | scrubbed and debearded |
| 6 to 8 chicken legs | 2 dozen live hard-shell |
| 1 large onion, chopped | clams, scrubbed |
| 2 garlic cloves, chopped fine | 1 pound chorizo or other |
| 2 cups long-grain white rice | garlic-seasoned smoked |
| 1 teaspoon salt | pork sausage, sliced |
| Freshly ground black pepper | 4 tomatoes, peeled, seeded |
| Three 1-pound live lobsters, | and quartered |
| cut into serving pieces | 1½ cups green peas |
| 1½ pounds shrimp, shelled | 4 ounces pimientos, sliced |
| with tails left on, | |

Preheat the oven to 325°F. Bring the chicken stock to a boil in a nonreactive pan, and in it dissolve the saffron. Set the pan aside.

In a heavy 10- to 12-inch skillet, heat the olive oil over moderate heat until it is very hot but not smoking. Add the chicken legs and brown them evenly. With tongs or a perforated spoon, transfer the legs to a bowl and cover to keep them warm. Add the onions and garlic to the oil in the skillet and cook, stirring frequently with a wooden spoon, for five minutes, until the onion is soft but not brown. Add the rice and cook it for two minutes or until it is translucent and faintly golden. Pour in the chicken stock, add the salt and a generous grinding of pepper, cover the skillet, and cook over low heat for 10 minutes so the rice absorbs some stock.

With a pastry brush, spread a generous coating of olive oil inside one 10- to 12-quart or two 6- to 8-quart casseroles. Place half of the lobsters, shrimp, mussels, clams, chorizo slices, tomatoes, peas and pimiento in the casserole. Top this with about three-quarters of the rice mixture. Arrange the chicken legs and the rest of the shellfish, chorizo, tomatoes, peas and pimiento on top, and spoon the remaining rice and broth around them.

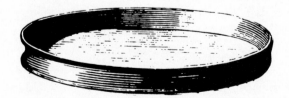

Cover the casserole and bake for 30 minutes. Check once or twice and, if it seems too dry, add boiling liquid—either stock or water. Remove the cover from the casserole and bake for 10 minutes more, until the rice is fluffy. Serve from the casserole.

■ GREAT DINNERS FROM LIFE

PAELLA

## Mesquite Mixed Shellfish Grill

**To serve 4**

| | |
|---|---|
| Two 1- to 1¼-pound live | shallots |
| lobsters, split in half | 1 dozen live hard-shell clams, |
| lengthwise | scrubbed |
| 16 large or jumbo shrimp | 2 or 3 saffron threads |
| 1 dozen live oysters, shucked, | 1 cup unsalted butter, cut into |
| liquor reserved and | bits and chilled |
| deeper shells scrubbed | 6 fresh basil leaves, |
| and reserved | chopped fine |
| 1 cup dry white wine | Salt |
| 1 tablespoon finely chopped | Freshly ground white pepper |

In a charcoal grill, stack mesquite kindling and split wood in a tepee around crumpled newspapers. Use enough wood to provide a layer of coals an inch or two larger all around than the space the seafood will occupy. Let the fire burn down to glowing

the clams open and the edges of the oyster meat curl, 10 to 12 minutes in all.

When the lobsters have cooked seven to eight minutes, turn them and cook them on the other side until the meat is firm and opaque—from four to seven minutes. Add the shrimp when you turn the lobsters; grill them for about five minutes, until firm.

Rub the saffron threads between your thumb and forefinger and add them to the sauce. Place the pan over low heat. With a whisk, incorporate the butter, about a tablespoonful at a time. Whisk in the basil, then add salt and white pepper to taste.

Arrange the grilled shellfish on serving trays or a platter and crack the claws of the lobsters with a nutcracker. Divide the sauce among four individual ramekins and present it with the shellfish.
■ PICNIC AND OUTDOOR MENUS

## Chili Shrimp

**To serve 4**

| | |
|---|---|
| 16 large shrimp | 1 teaspoon water chestnut |
| 1 garlic clove, chopped fine | powder or cornstarch |
| 2¹/₂ tablespoons plus 2 | 2 tablespoons dry sherry |
| teaspoons peanut oil | wine |
| 2 scallions, chopped | 1 tablespoon sugar |
| 2 teaspoons finely chopped | 1 teaspoon red rice vinegar or |
| fresh ginger root | red-wine vinegar |
| 1 teaspoon dark sesame oil | 1 tablespoon dark soy sauce |
| | 1¹/₂ teaspoons light soy |
| CHILI SEASONING SAUCE | sauce |
| 1 teaspoon chili paste | 2 tablespoons chicken stock |

Combine all of the seasoning sauce ingredients in a small nonreactive bowl. Stir to dissolve the water chestnut powder or cornstarch. Then set the bowl aside.

Using a pair of small scissors, cut the shell along the back of each shrimp, cutting about halfway into the meat of the shrimp. Do not remove the shell, but take out the dark or white vein with the nose of the scissors and pull off the legs. Rinse the shrimp under cold running water, drain them in a colander, and pat them dry with paper towels.

Heat a 12-inch wok or heavy 12-inch skillet over high heat for about one minute. Add 2¹/₂ tablespoons of the peanut oil and heat it until it is hot but not smoking. Add the shrimp and stir-fry them for about five minutes or until they are almost cooked through. The shrimp will be charred and deep orange in color. Empty the shrimp onto a heated serving platter.

Return the pan to high heat and add the remaining 2 teaspoons of peanut oil. Stir-fry the scallions, ginger and garlic for 30 seconds. Stir the seasoning sauce to recombine its ingredients and add it all at once to the wok or skillet. Stir until the sauce thickens lightly. Return the shrimp to the pan and stir for a minute to coat the shrimp evenly with sauce. Turn off the heat and swirl in the sesame oil. Empty the contents of the pan onto a warmed platter, and serve it at once.
■ CHINESE MENUS

gray coals—this may take 30 minutes. Then spread out the coals and set the rack in the grill 4 to 6 inches above them to heat for five minutes.

Meanwhile, prepare the lobsters and shrimp, and start the sauce. With each lobster, discard the gelatinous sac (stomach) in the head and the long white intestine attached to it. Leave the greenish tomalley (liver) and black caviarlike coral (eggs). Thread the shrimp four at a time onto pairs of short metal skewers so that they will lie flat when grilled.

For the sauce, strain the oyster liquor through a fine sieve into a small nonreactive saucepan. Add the wine and shallots and bring the mixture to a boil over high heat. Stirring occasionally, cook for 15 minutes or until about 3 tablespoons remain. Cover and set the sauce aside.

When the grill is ready for cooking, set the lobsters on the rack, meat side up. After about five minutes, add the clams and the oysters, restored to their half shells. Grill the clams and oysters until

# Pasta

# Pasta

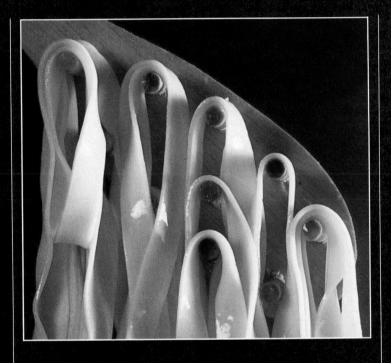

FRONTISPIECE: STRAW AND HAY PASTA WITH BUTTER SAUCE

Quickly prepared and easily sauced, pasta is the cook's delight. Fresh noodles or spaghetti can be ready after scarcely a minute of boiling; dried pasta takes only a bit longer. The sauce might be no more than a gloss of garlic morsels lightly browned in olive oil, or the butter and grated cheeses adorning the golden and green "straw and hay" on the preceding pages. With more time, the sauce may become a splendid pesto, redolent of basil, or a velvety tomato sauce.

Pasta's own repertory encompasses such beguiling forms as butterflies (farfalle), corkscrews (fusilli) and cartwheels (ruote), any of which can be tinted and delicately flavored with juice from spinach, carrots, tomatoes, even artichokes. North Africa's contribution is couscous, and Asia—where some say noodles were born—contributes sweet rice sticks, hearty soba based on buckwheat and delicate cellophane noodles produced from mung-bean starch.

Dumplings qualify as pasta, as do gnocchi. Both are traditionally home-made—and pasta can easily be produced at home. Flour, eggs and a soupçon of oil are transformed into fresh pasta in a matter of minutes with a home-style wringer or a pasta machine. Hand-mixed dough should rest for an hour after kneading; this allows the flour's gluten to relax, making the dough tender so it can be rolled wafer thin before being cut into whatever shapes the cook happens to fancy.

## Pasta with Stir-fried Vegetables

**To serve 4**

| | |
|---|---|
| 1 to 4 ounces feta cheese | and peeled |
| ¾ cup oil-cured black olives, pitted and halved lengthwise | 1 pound asparagus, ends trimmed and bottom ⅓ of stalks peeled, cut into 1-inch lengths |
| ¼ cup coarsely chopped oil-packed sun-dried tomatoes (about 6) with 2 tablespoons of the oil | 1 small red onion, cut into ¼-inch slices and separated into rings |
| ¼ teaspoon crumbled dried basil | ¼ cup pecan pieces |
| 3 tablespoons fresh lemon juice | ¾ pound egg-enriched rigatoni, linguini or tagliarini |
| 2 garlic cloves, crushed | 2 eggs, lightly beaten |

Crumble as much feta as desired into a large serving dish or bowl. Add the olives, tomatoes, basil and lemon juice, and set the dish aside.

In a wok or a heavy-bottomed 10- to 12-inch skillet, heat the reserved oil from the tomatoes over moderately high heat. Add the garlic and stir-fry it for a minute or until it browns; discard the garlic. Add the asparagus and stir-fry it for four minutes. Add the onion and stir-fry for two minutes. Add the pecans and stir-fry a minute longer. Remove the wok from the heat.

Bring 3 to 4 quarts of lightly salted water to a boil in a large, covered pot over high heat. Add a dollop of oil, which will keep the water from foaming over during cooking and help prevent the strands of pasta from sticking together. Stir in the pasta and boil it for five to seven minutes or until it is slightly resistant to the bite—*al dente.*

Drain the pasta in a colander and return it to the pot. Quickly stir in the beaten eggs and, when the strands of pasta are well coated, add the stir-fried vegetables. Then add the pasta mixture to the tomato mixture in the serving dish, and toss all of the ingredients well to combine them.

■ MEATLESS MENUS

## Spaghettini Primavera

**To serve 4**

| | |
|---|---|
| ¾ pound spaghettini | and coarsely chopped |
| ¼ cup loosely packed fresh basil leaves | 1½ tablespoons chopped fresh flatleaf parsley leaves |
| 1½ teaspoons coarsely chopped garlic | Salt |
| 3 tablespoons olive oil | Freshly ground black pepper |
| 4 tomatoes, peeled, seeded | |

Bring 3 to 4 quarts of lightly salted water to a boil in a large pot. Add a splash of oil, which will prevent foaming over and help keep the pasta from sticking together. Add the spaghettini and, stirring often, cook it for about five minutes or until slightly resistant to the bite—*al dente.*

Meanwhile, purée the basil and garlic with the olive oil in a blender or food processor. With a rubber spatula, transfer the purée to a large bowl, then fold in the tomatoes and parsley. Or, if you prefer, purée all of the ingredients together for a smoother sauce. Season the sauce to taste with salt and pepper.

When the pasta is cooked, drain it in a colander; then place it in a warmed serving bowl. Add the sauce and blend well. Or put the pasta in individual bowls and spoon the sauce over it; let each person mix at the table.

■ PASTA MENUS

## Angel-Hair Pasta with Onions and Pepper Strips

*The flat strands of angel-hair pasta, or "capelli d'angelo," are so narrow that the pasta cooks almost as soon as you immerse it in boiling water. If capelli d'angelo is not available, you can substitute capellini, which is a cylindrical pasta but just as narrow.* ◆●

**To serve 4**

| | |
|---|---|
| 1 lemon | thin and separated into rings |
| ¼ cup olive oil | 1 sweet red pepper, halved, seeded, deribbed and cut into julienne strips ⅛ inch wide |
| 4 white or yellow onions, quartered and cut into thin slivers | |
| ¾ teaspoon salt | 2 to 4 tablespoons butter |
| ¼ teaspoon freshly ground black pepper | 2 tablespoons chopped fresh parsley leaves |
| Sugar | ½ cup freshly grated Parmesan cheese |
| ½ pound angel-hair pasta | |
| 1 small red onion, sliced | |

With a small, sharp knife or a vegetable peeler, remove the peel from half of the lemon, avoiding the bitter white pith between the peel and the flesh. Reserve the remaining lemon for another use.

Over low heat warm the oil in a heavy 3- to 4-quart flameproof casserole. Add the lemon peel and, stirring constantly, cook it for two minutes. Stir in the slivered onions, salt, black pepper and a pinch of sugar. Remove the lemon and discard it. Increase the heat to moderate, cover the casserole and, stirring occasionally, cook the onions for 20 to 30 minutes, until they are browned.

Bring 3 quarts of lightly salted water to a boil over high heat in a large covered pot. Pour in a dollop of oil, which will keep the water from foaming over and help prevent the strands from sticking together. Add the pasta, stir it with a wooden spoon, and cook it for 30 seconds after the water returns to a boil. Pour the entire contents of the pot into a colander set in a sink.

As soon as the pasta drains, add it to the onions in the casserole, and toss them together gently. Add the red onion rings, pepper strips, butter to taste, parsley and ¼ cup of the Parmesan cheese. Toss the pasta again. Divide the pasta among four individual warmed bowls and serve it accompanied by the remaining Parmesan cheese.

■ ITALIAN MENUS

PASTA WITH STIR-FRIED VEGETABLES

## Straw and Hay Pasta with Butter Sauce

*The combination of colors gives this simple pasta dish its unusual name "straw"—for creamy white—and "hay"—for green.* ❧

**To serve 4**

| | |
|---|---|
| ¹/₂ cup unsalted butter, cut into small bits | Freshly ground black pepper |
| 6 ounces plain fettucini | 1 cup freshly grated Parmesan cheese |
| 6 ounces green fettucini | |

Bring 3 to 4 quarts of lightly salted water to a boil over high heat in a large, covered pot. Preheat the oven to 200° F. Drop the butter pieces into a large ovenproof bowl or casserole, and place it in the oven.

Add a dollop of oil to the boiling water to act as a foam breaker and to help keep the pasta from sticking together. Place the plain and the green fettucini in the water, and stir with a wooden spoon to blend the colors. Cook the fettucini for eight to 12 minutes or until *al dente*—slightly resistant to the bite. When the pasta is almost cooked, remove ¹/₄ cup of the pasta water and reserve it. Drain the pasta thoroughly in a colander.

Transfer the pasta to the large bowl in which the butter has melted and toss it until the strands are well coated. Add a few grindings of pepper and ¹/₂ cup of the Parmesan cheese, and toss again. If the pasta seems dry, add a little reserved pasta water and toss to mix it in. Divide the pasta among warmed bowls, and add a few grindings of black pepper. Serve the remaining cheese separately.

■ ITALIAN MENUS

## Pasta with Tomato, Anchovy and Olive Sauce

*Fedelini, capellini and spaghettini are all thin cylindrical strands of pasta. The thinnest is the fedelini, usually sold twisted into circular "nests."* ❧

**To serve 4**

| | |
|---|---|
| ¹/₄ cup unsalted butter | Kalamata olives, pitted and sliced |
| 1 garlic clove, chopped fine | 8 pimiento-stuffed green olives, sliced |
| 1 shallot, chopped fine | ¹/₄ teaspoon hot-red-pepper flakes |
| One 2-ounce can rolled anchovies, drained | 1 teaspoon crumbled dried oregano |
| One 28-ounce can plum tomatoes, drained and chopped with the liquid reserved | ³/₄ pound fedelini, capellini or spaghettini |
| 8 black olives, preferably | |

In a 3- to 4-quart nonreactive saucepan, heat 2 tablespoons of the butter over moderate heat. Add the garlic and shallot. Stirring occasionally, cook them for three minutes, or until they are soft. Do not let them brown. Add the anchovies and, still stirring occasionally, cook them for about two minutes or until they disintegrate. Stir in the tomatoes, tomato liquid, the black and green olives, the pepper flakes and oregano. Stirring occasionally, simmer for about 20 minutes, or until this sauce thickens. Do not overcook it.

Meanwhile, bring 3 to 4 quarts of lightly salted water to a boil in a large, covered pot over high heat. Pour in a little oil, which will keep the water from foaming over and help prevent the pasta from sticking together. Add the pasta, stir well and cook it for two to five minutes, depending on the thickness of the strands; cook it only until it is slightly resistant to the bite—*al dente.*

Drain the pasta in a colander, then return it to the pot together with the 2 remaining tablespoons of butter. Gently toss the pasta with two wooden spoons until it is coated. Add about one-third of the sauce to the pasta and toss it again. Divide the pasta among four individual bowls, top each serving with the remaining sauce, and serve it.

■ ITALIAN MENUS

## Sweet-and-Sour Cabbage Manicotti

**To serve 4 to 6**

| | |
|---|---|
| 2 tablespoons unsalted butter | 7 or 8 ripe tomatoes, cored |
| 1 small onion, chopped fine | and quartered |
| 1 pound green cabbage, | 1 tablespoon dark-brown |
| halved, cored and | sugar |
| sliced thin | 2 tablespoons white-wine |
| 1 carrot, peeled and grated | vinegar |
| 1 apple, peeled, cored | ¼ cup raisins |
| and grated | 12 manicotti tubes |
| ¼ teaspoon salt | 1 cup chicken stock |

To prepare the stuffing for the manicotti, first melt the butter in a 10- to 12-inch heavy-bottomed skillet over moderate heat. Add the onion and sauté it until it is translucent—about five minutes. Pour water into the skillet to a depth of ¼ inch. Stir in the cabbage, carrot, apple and ⅛ teaspoon of the salt. Cover the skillet and steam the vegetables and apple, adding more water as necessary, until they are soft—about 30 minutes. Set the stuffing aside.

Meanwhile, pour ¼ cup of water into a 3- to 4-quart nonreactive saucepan. Add the tomatoes. Stirring frequently, cook the tomatoes over moderately high heat for 20 minutes or until they are quite soft. Pour the tomatoes into a large sieve set over a bowl; drain them and discard the liquid. Purée the tomatoes into the bowl with a food mill or by pressing them through the sieve with the back of a wooden spoon. Stir in the brown sugar, vinegar, raisins and the remaining ⅛ teaspoon of salt. Set this sauce aside.

To prepare the manicotti, bring 4 quarts of lightly salted water to a boil in a large pot. Pour in a splash of oil to prevent foaming over and help keep the tubes from sticking together, then add the tubes. Stir them well to prevent sticking. Start testing the manicotti after 15 minutes and cook them until they are slightly resistant to the bite—*al dente*. With a slotted spoon, transfer the tubes to a large bowl of cold water.

Preheat the oven to 400° F. Thoroughly drain the manicotti tubes and fill each one with about ⅔ cup of the cabbage stuffing. Arrange the tubes in a single layer in a large baking-serving dish. Pour the stock over the tubes and cover the dish tightly with aluminum foil. Bake for 30 minutes. Ten minutes before serving time, transfer the sauce from the bowl to a saucepan and bring it to a boil. Reduce the heat to low and let the sauce simmer gently while the manicotti finish cooking. Serve the manicotti as soon as they are done. Spoon a little sauce over the manicotti, and pass the remaining sauce separately.

■ FRESH WAYS WITH PASTA

## Cartwheels with Mixed Vegetables

**To serve 4**

| | |
|---|---|
| 1 pound cartwheels | wiped clean and sliced thin |
| ¼ cup butter | 1 large tomato, cored and |
| 2 leeks, trimmed to 2 inches | chopped, or 6 cherry |
| above the white part, | tomatoes, chopped |
| washed thoroughly and | 1 to 1½ cups light cream |
| chopped fine | 1 cup freshly grated Parmesan |
| 1 zucchini, washed and | cheese |
| sliced thin | Salt |
| ¼ pound fresh mushrooms, | Freshly ground black pepper |

In a large covered pot, bring 3 to 4 quarts of lightly salted water to a boil. Add a dollop of oil, which will keep the water from foaming over and will help prevent sticking. Then add the cartwheels, stir well, and cook them, uncovered, for about 15 minutes or until they are slightly resistant to the bite—*al dente*.

Melt the butter in an 8- to 10-inch skillet. Add the chopped leeks and sauté them over moderate heat for about 10 minutes, stirring several times. Add the zucchini, mushrooms and tomato to the leeks, and stir-fry them over fairly high heat for two to three minutes, until the zucchini is barely tender; it should remain bright green. Add 1 cup of the cream, ½ cup of the grated cheese, and salt and pepper to taste. Heat the mixture through without

SWEET-AND-SOUR CABBAGE MANICOTTI

letting it come to a boil, then take it off the stove and set aside.

When the pasta is done, drain it in a colander and return it to the pot. Pour half of the sauce over the pasta and stir well; cover until ready to serve. Then add the remaining sauce to the pasta and toss well. Heat the pasta briefly over high heat, stirring constantly. If the pasta absorbs most of the liquid and looks dry, add an extra ½ cup of cream. Serve the remaining cheese separately.

■ PASTA MENUS

## Tortellini Stuffed with Chicken and Cheese

**To serve 8 to 10**

| | |
|---|---|
| 1½ pounds chicken breasts, boned, skinned, poached in chicken stock or water for 15 minutes, and chopped fine | lemon peel<br>Freshly grated nutmeg<br>Salt<br>Freshly ground black pepper |
| Freshly grated Parmesan cheese | Homemade pasta dough (Index/Glossary) |
| 2 egg yolks, lightly beaten | Bolognese meat sauce |
| ⅛ teaspoon freshly grated | (Index/Glossary) |

Mix the chicken, ½ cup of cheese, the egg yolks, lemon peel and a few gratings of nutmeg in a large bowl until they are thoroughly combined. Season to taste with salt and pepper. Break off one-

quarter of the pasta dough at a time, and keep the rest covered with foil or a cloth so that it stays moist.

On a floured surface, using a floured pastry pin, roll the dough paper thin; then use a 2-inch biscuit cutter to cut the roll into circles. One circle at a time, place ¼ teaspoon of the chicken mixture in the center, moisten the edges, and fold the circle in half. Press the edges firmly together and shape the semicircle around your index finger to form a little ring. Gently press the tips together. (The tortellini are best if cooked at once, but they may be covered with plastic wrap and refrigerated for a day or so.)

Bring 6 to 8 quarts of lightly salted water to a boil in a covered pot over high heat. Pour in a dollop of oil to keep the water from foaming over and to help keep the tortellini from sticking together. Drop in the tortellini, and stir gently with a wooden spoon for a moment to separate them. Stirring occasionally, boil for five minutes, or until the tortellini are barely tender; drain them in a large colander. Serve the tortellini with Bolognese meat sauce and grated Parmesan cheese.

■ THE COOKING OF ITALY

## Pasta Shells Stuffed with Cheese

**To serve 4**

| | |
|---|---|
| 24 jumbo pasta shells | chopped fine |
| 1 pound ricotta cheese | 2 teaspoons chopped fresh basil or parsley leaves |
| ¼ pound mozzarella cheese, diced | Freshly grated nutmeg |
| ¼ cup freshly grated Parmesan cheese | Salt<br>Freshly ground black pepper |
| 1 egg, beaten | 2 cups tomato sauce |
| 3 slices prosciutto, | |

Bring 3 to 4 quarts of lightly salted water to a boil in a large, covered pot over high heat. Add a dollop of oil, which will help keep the pasta from sticking together or foaming over while it cooks. Drop in the pasta shells, stir them briefly, then, stirring occasionally, boil them for about nine minutes or until they are *al dente*. Drain the shells in a colander; using potholders to protect your hands from steam, shake the colander vigorously to drain off all water.

Meanwhile, preheat the oven to 350° F. In a large bowl, mix the ricotta, mozzarella and Parmesan cheese together. Stir in the beaten egg and chopped prosciutto. Add the basil, a few gratings of nutmeg, and salt and pepper to taste.

Pour half of the tomato sauce into a shallow baking dish just large enough to hold the shells in one layer. Tip the dish until the sauce covers the bottom. When the pasta shells are drained but still hot, hold one at a time in a folded cloth towel to protect your hand, and use a teaspoon to fill it with the cheese mixture. Arrange the stuffed shells in the baking dish, and pour the remaining sauce over them. Bake the shells for 30 minutes. Serve them hot.

■ PASTA MENUS

SPICY COLD NOODLES WITH SESAME SAUCE AND TOASTED SESAME SEEDS

# Spicy Cold Noodles with Sesame Sauce and Toasted Sesame Seeds

*To the Chinese, the noodles in this dish are emblematic of long life and therefore should not be broken.* ❖●

**To serve 4**

| | |
|---|---|
| 6 tablespoons sesame paste, drained of oil | 2 to 3 tablespoons finely chopped fresh coriander leaves and upper stems (optional) |
| 5 tablespoons dark sesame oil | |
| 3 tablespoons light soy sauce | |
| 2 tablespoons sesame chili oil | 3 to 4 tablespoons water |
| 2 tablespoons unseasoned Oriental rice vinegar | 2 tablespoons sesame seeds |
| 1 tablespoon plus 2 teaspoons sugar | ³/₄ pound ¹/₁₆-inch-wide Chinese egg noodles, preferably fresh noodles |

In a food processor fitted with a metal blade or in a blender, combine the sesame paste, dark sesame oil, soy sauce, sesame chili oil, vinegar, sugar, the coriander if you are using it and 3 tablespoons of water. Blend the ingredients until the sauce is smooth. Then add more water, a teaspoonful at a time, until the mixture falls from a spoon in wide, silky ribbons. Adjust the seasoning to taste.

Pour the sauce into a bowl, and cover it with foil or plastic wrap. The sauce can be set aside at room temperature for several hours. (If you plan to keep it overnight, refrigerate it; bring it to room temperature before using it.)

Toast the sesame seeds in a small, heavy skillet over medium heat, stirring them until they are golden—about three minutes. Transfer them to a plate to cool.

Bring 3 to 4 quarts of unsalted water to a boil in a large, covered pot over high heat. If you are using fresh noodles, fluff them to separate the strands, then add them to the pot. Using wooden chopsticks or two long-handled wooden spoons, stir the noodles gently several times to separate the strands. Cook fresh noodles for one to two minutes or until they are barely resistant to the bite. Cook dried noodles for five to 10 minutes.

Drain the noodles immediately in a colander and set them under cold running water to chill them quickly and evenly and to remove surface starch, which might make them stick together. Shake the colander to dry the noodles thoroughly. Dry the pot and return the noodles to it.

Stir the sauce. If it has thickened, blend in a little more water, but do not thin the sauce too much—it should cling to the noodles. Pour half of the sauce over the noodles and, with your hands or wooden spoons, toss them gently to coat and separate each strand.

Transfer the noodles to a serving bowl, and sprinkle toasted sesame seeds on top. Serve the noodles on individual plates or in shallow bowls. Pour the remaining sauce into a small bowl and pass it separately.

NOTE: Italian noodles can take the place of the Chinese noodles if the Chinese variety are unavailable.

■ CHINESE MENUS

# Lasagne with Pesto Sauce

**To serve 4**

| | |
|---|---|
| ¹/₂ pound fresh or dried lasagne | 3 large garlic cloves, cut up |
| 1¹/₂ cups white sauce (Index/Glossary) | 1 tablespoon pine nuts |
| | 1 tablespoon blanched almonds |
| ³/₄ cup ricotta cheese | 12 pecan or walnut halves |
| ¹/₂ cup freshly grated Parmesan cheese | ¹/₃ cup olive oil |
| | ¹/₂ teaspoon salt |
| PESTO SAUCE | ¹/₂ teaspoon freshly ground white pepper |
| 10 ounces spinach, trimmed and washed | ¹/₄ cup freshly grated Parmesan cheese |
| 1 bunch basil, or 1 bunch flatleaf parsley plus 1 tablespoon dried basil | ¹/₄ cup freshly grated Romano cheese |

Bring 3 to 4 quarts of lightly salted water to a boil in a large, covered pot. Add a dollop of oil, which will keep the water from foaming over during cooking and help prevent the strips from sticking together. Add the lasagne, stir it gently and cook it, if it is fresh, for 45 seconds after it returns to a boil or, if dried, according to package directions. Cook the lasagne only until it is *al dente*, or slightly resistant to the bite. Drain the lasagne. Fill a large baking pan with cold water, and place the lasagne in it to cool, separating the noodles. Put the cooled strips in a single layer on damp kitchen towels away from your work area until you are ready to assemble the lasagne.

Pour ¹/₄ cup of the white sauce into a mixing cup. In a medium-sized mixing bowl, combine the remaining sauce with the ricotta. Cover the surface of the sauce in both the cup and bowl with plastic wrap to prevent a skin from forming.

For the pesto, combine the spinach and fresh basil in a food processor or blender, and coarsely chop them, turning the machine on and off. With the machine running, add the garlic, pine nuts, almonds and pecans, and process until blended. Add the olive oil, salt and white pepper, and process until smooth. Add the ¹/₄ cup of grated Parmesan and the Romano; process until smooth again. If the pesto seems dry, add olive oil by the teaspoonful.

Preheat the oven to 450° F. Butter an 11-by-7-inch glass baking dish. Arrange one-third of the lasagne in the bottom of the dish. Spread half of the white sauce-ricotta mixture over the lasagne, and top it with half of the pesto. Sprinkle with 1 tablespoon of grated Parmesan. Add another layer of lasagne and cover it with the remaining ricotta, the remaining pesto, and 1 tablespoon of Parmesan. Place the remaining lasagne on top and spread it with the reserved ¹/₄ cup of white sauce. Sprinkle it with the remaining Parmesan.

Bake the lasagne for 15 to 20 minutes, or until the top is golden and the pasta heated through. Remove the lasagne from the oven and let it stand for five to 10 minutes. Cut the lasagne into four portions and serve it.

■ MEATLESS MENUS

## Noodle Casserole with Apples, Raisins and Apricots

**To serve 6 to 8**

| | |
|---|---|
| ½ pound broad egg noodles | 6 tablespoons sugar |
| 4 eggs | Vegetable oil or melted |
| 2 apples, peeled, cored, and | shortening |
| cut into ¼-inch dice | Salt |
| ½ cup dried apricots, cut into | ¼ teaspoon ground cinnamon |
| ¼-inch dice | combined with ¾ teaspoon |
| ⅓ cup seedless white | sugar |
| raisins | |

In a large, covered pot, bring 3 or 4 quarts of lightly salted water to a boil over high heat. Add a dollop of oil, to prevent foaming over. Drop in the noodles, stir them briefly with a wooden spoon or fork, and boil for 15 minutes, or until they are tender. Drain the noodles in a colander, and place them in a large bowl.

Preheat the oven to 350°F. Beat the eggs lightly in a small bowl, and add them to the noodles with the apples, apricots, raisins, sugar, the ½ cup of oil and salt to taste. Lightly coat the bottom and sides of a 2-quart casserole with oil; pour in the noodle mixture. Sprinkle the top with the cinnamon-sugar mixture and bake the casserole in the center of the oven for 40 minutes. Serve hot as an accompaniment to meat or poultry.

■ AMERICAN COOKING: THE MELTING POT

## Baked Orzo with Peppers and Cheese

*Translated literally, "orzo" means barley, and the tiny pasta resembles grains of barley or perhaps rice.* ❖●

**To serve 4**

| | |
|---|---|
| 1 cup orzo | 1 cup sour cream |
| ½ cup diced roasted sweet | ½ cup freshly grated |
| red peppers | Parmesan cheese |
| ⅓ cup diced green chili peppers | 2 tablespoons butter, cut into |
| 1 cup diced Monterey Jack | small bits |
| cheese | |

Preheat the oven to 450°F. Lightly butter a medium-sized gratin dish or baking pan and set it aside. Bring 3 quarts of lightly salted water to a boil in a large covered pot. Add a dollop of oil, which will keep the water from foaming over during cooking. Sprinkle in the orzo; stir well. After the boiling resumes, cook for 10 to 12 minutes, or until the orzo is just tender—*al dente*. Drain the orzo in a colander.

Combine the orzo with the sweet peppers, chili peppers and Monterey Jack cheese, and spread the mixture in the buttered dish. Smooth sour cream evenly over the top, sprinkle on the Parmesan, and dot with the butter. Bake on the upper shelf of the oven for 15 minutes, or until the top is golden and puffy and the mixture bubbles around the edges. Serve hot.

■ PASTA MENUS

## Macaroni, Ham and Cheese Casserole

**To serve 4 to 6**

| | |
|---|---|
| 2 cups elbow macaroni | cut into ¼-inch dice |
| 6 tablespoons butter, melted | 1¾ cups grated Cheddar |
| ¼ cup flour | cheese |
| 2 cups milk | 1 tablespoon grated onion |
| ⅛ teaspoon cayenne pepper | 2 tablespoons dry bread |
| Salt | crumbs |
| 2 cups cooked smoked ham, | |

In a large, covered pot, bring 3 to 4 quarts of lightly salted water to a boil over high heat. Add a dollop of oil to prevent foaming over and to help keep the pasta from sticking together. Stirring with a wooden spoon, pour the macaroni in slowly so that the water never stops boiling. Cook it, uncovered, for about 20 minutes or until the macaroni is tender but still slightly resistant to the bite. Then drain the macaroni thoroughly in a colander.

Heat ¼ cup of the melted butter over moderate heat in a 1-quart saucepan. Add the flour and cook, stirring with a wire whisk, until the mixture froths and foams. Add the milk all at once and whisk until the sauce thickens and is smooth. Add the cayenne and salt to taste, and simmer over very low heat for about two minutes. Pour the sauce into a large mixing bowl, and stir in the macaroni, diced ham, 1½ cups of the cheese and the grated onion. Taste for seasoning.

Preheat the oven to 375°F. Lightly butter a 2½- or 3-quart casserole. Spoon in the macaroni mixture. Mix the bread crumbs with the remaining cheese and melted butter, and spread this mixture evenly over the top. Bake in the middle of the oven for 30 to 40 minutes or until the topping is lightly browned. Serve directly from the casserole.

■ AMERICAN COOKING

## Greek Macaroni and Lamb Casserole

**To serve 8 to 10**

| | |
|---|---|
| 1 pound elbow macaroni or ziti | Salt |
| 7 tablespoons olive oil | Freshly ground black pepper |
| 1 cup finely chopped onions | ½ cup fresh white-bread |
| 1½ pounds lean ground lamb | crumbs |
| 6 tomatoes, peeled, seeded | 1 egg, lightly beaten |
| and chopped fine, or 2 cups | ¾ cup freshly grated *kefalotiri* |
| chopped, drained, canned | or Parmesan cheese |
| tomatoes | |
| 1 cup tomato purée | RICH WHITE SAUCE |
| 1 teaspoon finely chopped | 4 cups milk |
| garlic | 2 tablespoons butter |
| 1 teaspoon crumbled dried | 6 eggs |
| oregano | 1 teaspoon salt |
| ¼ teaspoon ground cinnamon | ½ cup flour |

In a large, covered pot bring 4 quarts of lightly salted water to a boil over high heat. Pour in a little oil to prevent the water from foaming over and to help keep the pasta from sticking together.

NOODLE CASSEROLE WITH APPLES, RAISINS AND APRICOTS

With a wooden spoon, stir in the macaroni. Stirring occasionally, cook the pasta for 10 to 15 minutes, or until it is tender but still somewhat resistant to the bite. Immediately, drain the pasta thoroughly in a large colander and set it aside.

Meanwhile, prepare the lamb and sauce. In a heavy 10- to 12-inch skillet, heat 6 tablespoons of the olive oil over moderate heat. Add the onions. Stirring frequently, cook for five minutes or until they are soft and translucent but not brown. Add the lamb and, mashing it frequently with the back of a spoon or fork to break up any lumps, cook until all traces of pink disappear. Stir in the tomatoes, tomato purée, garlic, oregano, cinnamon, and salt and pepper to taste, then bring to a boil over high heat. Reduce the heat to low, cover tightly, and simmer for 15 minutes. Taste and adjust the seasoning. Remove the pan from the heat, stir in ¼ cup of the bread crumbs and the beaten egg, and set aside.

To make the white sauce, cook 3 cups of the milk and the butter in a small pan over low heat until bubbles appear around the rim of the pan. Remove from the heat. In a heavy 2- to 3-quart saucepan, beat the six eggs with a whisk or rotary beater until they are frothy. Add the remaining cup of milk and 1 teaspoon of salt. Beating constantly, add the flour, a tablespoon at a time. Stirring constantly, slowly pour in the heated milk and butter mixture in a thin stream and, still stirring, bring to a boil over moderate heat. Continue to boil until the sauce is thick and smooth. Then set it aside.

Preheat the oven to 350°F. With a pastry brush coat the bottom and sides of a 15-by-9-by-2½-inch baking dish with the remaining tablespoon of olive oil. Sprinkle the bottom with the remaining ¼ cup of bread crumbs and spread half of the pasta on top. Cover with meat, smoothing it into the corners. Then pour 2 cups of the white sauce evenly on top. Sprinkle with half of the grated cheese. Spread on the remaining macaroni, pour over it the rest of the white sauce, and sprinkle with the remaining cheese. Bake in the middle of the oven for 45 minutes, or until the top is a delicate golden brown. Cut into squares and serve.

■ MIDDLE EASTERN COOKING

## Lasagne with Meat Sauce

**To serve 6 to 8**

| | |
|---|---|
| ½ pound lasagne<br>3 cups white sauce (Index/<br>    Glossary), made with 2 cups<br>    milk and 1 cup heavy cream | 3½ cups Bolognese meat<br>    sauce (Index/Glossary)<br>Freshly grated Parmesan<br>    cheese |

In a large, covered pot, bring 3 to 4 quarts of lightly salted water to a boil over high heat. Pour in a spoonful of oil to keep the water from foaming over and help prevent the strips from sticking. Add the lasagne, stirring gently to separate the strips. Stirring occasionally, boil until the lasagne is tender, but still *al dente,* 10 to 25 minutes. Drain the pasta in a colander. Fill a large pan with cold water and cool the lasagne in it, separating the strips so that they do not stick together. Lay the cooled lasagne in a single layer on dampened paper towels.

Meanwhile, preheat the oven to 350°F. Generously butter the bottom and sides of a 12-by-9-by-3-inch serving casserole or baking dish. Spread a layer of Bolognese meat sauce about ¼ inch deep evenly over the bottom of the casserole. Spread over it about 1 cup of white sauce. Lay one-third of the lasagne on the white sauce, overlapping the strips slightly. Repeat the layers of meat sauce, white sauce and lasagne two more times, then top with the rest of the meat sauce and a cover of white sauce.

Sprinkle the top with ½ cup of grated Parmesan. Bake for 30 minutes, or until the sauce is bubbling hot. Serve accompanied by additional grated Parmesan.

■ THE COOKING OF ITALY

## Spaghetti al Caruso

*The Italian tenor Enrico Caruso, who reigned supreme at New York City's Metropolitan Opera House in the first decades of the 20th century, had an appetite almost as prodigious as his voice. Pasta was irresistible to him, and one of his favorite dishes—spaghetti with chicken-liver sauce—was named after him.* ❧

**To serve 4**

| | |
|---|---|
| 7 tablespoons olive oil<br>1½ cup finely chopped onions<br>2 teaspoons finely chopped<br>    garlic<br>Two 2-pound cans solid-pack<br>    tomatoes<br>¼ cup tomato paste<br>½ teaspoon basil | 1 small bay leaf<br>Salt<br>½ teaspoon sugar<br>1 pound chicken livers,<br>    trimmed<br>Freshly ground black pepper<br>Flour<br>1 pound spaghetti |

In a heavy 10- to 12-inch skillet, heat ¼ cup of the olive oil over medium heat. Drop in the onions and garlic, and cook, stirring frequently, for six to eight minutes, or until the onions are soft and translucent. Stir in the tomatoes and their liquid, then add the tomato paste, basil, bay leaf, 1 teaspoon of salt and the sugar. Bring to a boil over high heat; reduce the heat and simmer, partially covered, for 35 minutes. Stir occasionally to prevent sticking.

Season the chicken livers with salt and pepper, then dredge them in flour and shake off the excess. In a heavy skillet, heat the remaining 3 tablespoons of olive oil over moderate heat. Brown the livers in the hot oil for five minutes, or until golden brown on both sides; do not overcook them. Set the livers aside.

In a large, covered pot, bring 4 quarts of lightly salted water to a boil. Pour in a bit of oil to prevent foaming over and to help keep the pasta strands from sticking together. Drop in the spaghetti and stir it gently to separate the strands. Boil over high heat, stirring occasionally, for seven to nine minutes, or until tender. Test by tasting a strand; the spaghetti should be *al dente*—slightly resistant to the bite. Immediately drain the spaghetti.

Stir the chicken livers into the hot tomato sauce and cook for a minute or two more, until they are heated through. Transfer the spaghetti to a large, warmed serving bowl and toss it with the chicken-liver sauce. Taste it for seasoning and serve at once.

■ AMERICAN COOKING: THE MELTING POT

## Noodles with Sausage Meat and Mushrooms

**To serve 4**

| | |
|---|---|
| ½ pound Italian-style<br>    hot sausage<br>6 tablespoons butter<br>2 tablespoons vegetable oil<br>2 onions, chopped fine<br>¾ pound mushrooms, wiped<br>    clean and sliced thin,<br>    including the stems | ¼ teaspoon salt<br>Freshly ground black pepper<br>1 cup heavy cream<br>1 pound pappardelle or other<br>    wide egg noodles<br>1 cup freshly grated<br>    Parmesan cheese |

Remove the sausage meat from its casings and chop it roughly. In an 8- to 10-inch sauté pan or skillet, melt 2 tablespoons of the butter with the oil. Add the sausage meat and onions. Stirring often to break up the pieces of sausage, sauté over moderate heat for about five minutes, until the onions are translucent and the sausage loses its red color.

Turn the heat to moderately high. Add the mushrooms and continue sautéing, stirring often, for another five minutes. Reduce the heat to low, add the salt, a generous grinding of pepper and ½ cup of the cream. Cook, uncovered, until the liquid thickens slightly, about five minutes. Cover and set aside.

Bring 4 quarts of lightly salted water to a boil in a large, covered pot. Add a dollop of oil to prevent the water from foaming over and help keep the pasta from sticking. Add the pasta, stir and boil it for five to seven minutes or until it is tender but slightly resistant to the bite—*al dente.*

Meanwhile, melt the remaining 4 tablespoons of butter in the remaining ½ cup of cream. When the cream is just at a simmer, turn off the heat; set the butter-cream mixture aside.

Drain the pasta thoroughly in a colander, then transfer it to a large, warmed serving bowl. Toss the pasta with the butter-cream mixture, then the sauce, then ½ cup of the cheese. Pass the remaining cheese at the table.

■ PASTA MENUS

LASAGNE WITH MEAT SAUCE

## Spaghetti with Meatballs

*Steaming hot spaghetti smothered in meatball-laden tomato sauce has become a classic of Italian-American cooking. Although spaghetti, meatballs and tomato sauce are essential ingredients of authentic Italian cooking, they are rarely served together as a one-dish meal in Italy itself. There the spaghetti usually appears as a first course or side dish, followed by meatballs in tomato sauce.* ✦●

**To serve 8**

| | |
|---|---|
| 1½ pounds ground beef chuck | cheese |
| 1½ cups bread crumbs | 1 egg |
| ½ cup finely chopped onions | Salt |
| ½ cup finely chopped green | ¼ teaspoon freshly ground |
|    pepper |    black pepper |
| 1½ teaspoons finely chopped | ½ cup olive oil |
|    garlic | 6 cups tomato and meat sauce |
| ¼ cup finely chopped fresh |    (Index/Glossary) |
|    parsley leaves | 2 pounds spaghetti |
| Freshly grated Parmesan | |

Place the ground chuck in a large mixing bowl and add the bread crumbs, onions, green pepper, garlic, parsley, ¼ cup of Parmesan cheese, the egg, 1½ teaspoons of salt and the pepper. Knead with both hands until the ingredients are well combined, then beat vigorously with a wooden spoon until the mixture is smooth and fluffy. Shape the mixture into small meatballs about 1½ inches in diameter—there should be about 32—and lay them in one layer on a baking sheet.

Heat the olive oil in a heavy 10- to 12-inch skillet until a light haze forms above it. Fry the meatballs, five or six at a time, over moderately high heat, shaking the pan constantly to roll the meatballs and help keep their shape. When they are browned on all sides, transfer then to a 3- to 4-quart saucepan. Pour in the tomato sauce, bring to a boil, then cover the pan and simmer over low heat for 30 minutes.

Bring about 8 quarts of lightly salted water to a boil in a large, covered pot. Add a dollop of oil to prevent foaming over and to keep the spaghetti from sticking together. Drop in the spaghetti. Stir it gently with a wooden fork or spoon for a few minutes to separate the strands, then boil it briskly, stirring occasionally, for seven to nine minutes, or until the pasta is tender but still *al dente* —slightly resistant to the bite. Immediately drain the spaghetti in a large colander, lifting the strands with a fork to be sure it is thoroughly drained.

Transfer the spaghetti to a large warmed serving bowl, and toss it with the meatballs and tomato and meat sauce. Serve at once, accompanied by a small bowl of grated Parmesan cheese.
■ AMERICAN COOKING: THE MELTING POT

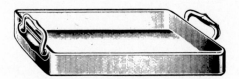

SPAGHETTINI IN CREAM WITH RED CAVIAR

## Spaghettini in Cream with Red Caviar

**To serve 4**

| | |
|---|---|
| 1 pound spaghettini | 8 ounces red salmon caviar |
| ¼ cup butter | 4 hard-boiled eggs, whites |
| 1½ cups heavy cream |    chopped fine and yolks |
| Freshly ground black pepper |    pressed through a sieve |
| 2 tablespoons fresh | 4 to 6 tablespoons finely cut |
|    lemon juice |    fresh chives |

Bring 3 to 4 quarts of lightly salted water to a boil in a large, covered pot over high heat. Add a little oil to prevent foaming over and to help keep the strands of pasta from sticking together. Add the spaghettini, stirring, and cook for eight to 10 minutes or until barely tender.

Meanwhile, melt the butter in a 1-quart saucepan. Stir in the cream and a generous grinding of pepper. Heat this mixture just to simmering, take it off the stove, add the lemon juice, and cover the pan to keep the mixture warm.

Drain the pasta in a colander, shaking it to remove as much moisture as possible. Tip the pasta into a warmed serving bowl. Add the cream mixture and toss thoroughly. Place the red caviar on the center of the spaghettini. Sprinkle sieved egg yolk in a

ring around the caviar. Sprinkle chopped egg white around the egg yolk; surround it with a ring of chives. Toss the caviar, eggs and chives with the spaghettini just before serving it on warmed plates.

■ PASTA MENUS

## Spaghetti alla Carbonara

**To serve 4**

| | |
|---|---|
| ¼ cup butter, softened | into ¼-inch strips |
| 2 eggs plus 2 egg yolks | 1 teaspoon dried hot-red- |
| 1 cup freshly grated | pepper flakes (optional) |
|    Parmesan cheese | ½ cup heavy cream |
| 1 pound spaghetti | Salt |
| 8 slices bacon, cut cross-wise | Freshly ground black pepper |

In a small bowl, cream the butter by beating it against the sides of the bowl with a wooden spoon until it is soft and fluffy. In another bowl, beat the eggs and egg yolks with a fork or whisk until they blend, then stir in ½ cup of the grated cheese. Set both bowls aside.

Heat a large ovenproof serving bowl or casserole in a 200°F. oven. At the same time, bring 4 quarts of lightly salted water to a boil in a large, covered pot. Pour a dollop of oil into the water to act as a foam breaker and help keep the pasta strands from sticking together. Drop the spaghetti into the water, and stir it for a moment or two with a wooden spoon to separate the strands. Cook the spaghetti over high heat, stirring occasionally, for seven to 12 minutes or until it is tender.

Meanwhile, fry the pieces of bacon in an 8- to 10-inch skillet over moderate heat until crisp. Pour off about half of the bacon fat and stir into the skillet the red pepper, if you are using it, then the cream. Bring the cream to a simmer and keep it warm until the spaghetti is done.

When the spaghetti is cooked, drain it thoroughly in a large colander, lifting the strands with two forks to make certain all of the water runs off. Transfer the spaghetti to the warmed serving bowl and stir in the creamed butter, tossing the spaghetti with two forks to coat every strand. Then stir in the hot bacon-and-cream mixture and finally the beaten eggs and cheese, mixing everything thoroughly. The heat of the pasta and other ingredients should cook the raw eggs on contact. Taste and season with salt and a few grindings of pepper.

Serve the *carbonara* at once with the remaining ½ cup of the grated cheese passed at the table.

■ THE COOKING OF ITALY

LINGUINI WITH MUSSELS IN SAFFRON SAUCE

## Linguini with Mussels in Saffron Sauce

**To serve 4**

| | |
|---|---|
| ¾ **pound linguini** | ⅛ **teaspoon saffron threads,** |
| **2 pounds large mussels,** | **steeped in ¾ cup hot water** |
| **scrubbed and debearded** | ¼ **cup freshly grated Romano** |
| **1 tablespoon safflower oil** | **cheese** |
| **1 shallot, chopped fine** | ¼ **teaspoon salt** |
| **2 tablespoons flour** | **Freshly ground black pepper** |
| ½ **cup dry vermouth** | **1 tablespoon finely cut chives** |

Put the mussels and ½ cup of cold water in a 3- to 4- quart pot; cover and steam the mussels over high heat until they open—about five minutes. Remove the mussels from the pot with a slotted spoon and set aside; discard any that do not open.

When the mussels are cool enough to handle, remove the meat from the shells, working over the pot to catch any liquid; set the meat aside and discard the shells. Strain the liquid from the pot through a very fine sieve. Set the liquid aside.

Heat the safflower oil in a heavy-bottomed 8- to 10-inch skillet over moderately high heat. Add the shallot and sauté it for 30 seconds. Remove the skillet from the heat. Using a wire whisk to prevent lumps from forming, add the flour, then the vermouth and saffron liquid. Return the skillet to the heat and cook the sauce over moderately low heat for two or three minutes or until it thickens. Stir in ¼ cup of the strained cooking liquid, the cheese, salt, a few grindings of pepper, the chives and mussels. Simmer for three or four minutes more to heat the mussels through.

Meanwhile, bring 3 to 4 quarts of lightly salted water to a boil in a large, covered pot. Add a bit of oil to prevent foaming over and to help keep the strands from sticking together; then drop in the linguini and stir it for a few moments. Start testing the linguini after 10 minutes, and cook it until it is *al dente*. Drain it thoroughly in a colander. Transfer it to a warmed bowl, and toss the linguini with a few spoonfuls of the sauce. Serve immediately in bowls, accompanied by the rest of the sauce.

■ FRESH WAYS WITH PASTA

## Lobster and Collard Greens with Malfalde

**To serve 2**

| | |
|---|---|
| **One 1¼-pound live lobster** | **washed, stemmed and cut** |
| **1 lemon or lime, halved** | **into strips ½ inch wide** |
| ¼ **pound malfalde or other** | **2 tablespoons unsalted butter** |
| **curly-edged ribbon pasta** | **Freshly ground black pepper** |
| ½ **pound collard greens,** | |

Pour enough water into a large pot to fill it to a depth of about 1 inch. Bring the water to a boil and add the lobster. Cover the pot tightly and steam the lobster until it turns a bright reddish orange—about 10 minutes. Remove the lobster from the pot and set it on a dish to catch the juices; do not discard the cooking liquid. Pour 2 quarts of water into the pot and bring the liquid to a boil.

Holding the lobster over the dish, remove the tail by twisting it away from the body. Twist the claws off the body, then crack the shell of the tail and claws. Remove the meat and slice it thin. Add the shells and lobster juices to the pot with the boiling liquid. Allow the shells to boil for 10 minutes. With a slotted spoon, remove the shells and discard them. Squeeze the juice of one lemon half into the liquid. Add the malfalde and cover the pot. When the liquid returns to a boil, remove the lid. Start testing the pasta after 11 minutes, and cook until it is *al dente*.

Meanwhile, transfer ⅓ cup of the cooking liquid to a heavy-bottomed 8- to 10-inch skillet, and bring it to a simmer. Stirring occasionally, add the collard greens and cook them over low heat until all of the liquid evaporates and the greens wilt.

Melt the butter in a small, heavy-bottomed saucepan over moderate heat, and cook it just until it turns nut brown; watch the butter carefully after it stops bubbling so that it does not burn. Scatter the lobster meat over the collard greens in the skillet. Squeeze the juice of the remaining lemon half over the lobster.

When the pasta is done, drain it and add it to the skillet. Add some pepper and the butter, and toss well. Serve immediately.

■ FRESH WAY WITH PASTA

## Spaghetti with Clam Sauce

**To serve 4 to 6**

| | |
|---|---|
| **6 tablespoons olive oil** | ¼ **cup dry white wine** |
| **1 teaspoon finely chopped** | **1 pound spaghetti** |
| **garlic** | **2 tablespoons butter, softened** |
| **36 small hardshell clams,** | **2 tablespoons chopped fresh** |
| **shucked, plus their strained** | **parsley, preferably flatleaf** |
| **juices and enough bottled** | **parsley** |
| **clam juice added to make** | **Salt** |
| **1 cup** | **Freshly ground white pepper** |

In a heavy 8- to 10-inch skillet, heat the olive oil over moderate heat. Stir in the garlic and, stirring constantly, cook it for about 30 seconds. Pour in the clam juice and wine; boil over high heat until the foam disappears and the liquid has reduced to about ¾ cup. Remove from the heat and set aside.

In a large, covered pot, bring 3 to 4 quarts of lightly salted water to a boil over high heat. Add a dollop of oil, which will prevent foaming over and will help keep the pasta from sticking together. Drop in the spaghetti, and stir it gently with a wooden fork or spoon for a few moments. Boil over high heat, stirring occasionally, for seven to 12 minutes, or until the pasta is *al dente*—that is, slightly resistant to the bite. Immediately drain the spaghetti in a colander, lifting the strands with a fork to be sure it is drained.

Transfer the spaghetti to a large warmed serving bowl, and toss it with the soft butter. Bring the sauce in the skillet to a boil over high heat and add the clams. Cook the clams, turning them constantly, for one or two minutes. Then pour the clams and sauce over the spaghetti, sprinkle with parsley, and toss together with two large forks until all the ingredients are well mixed. Taste and season with salt and white pepper. Serve at once.

■ THE COOKING OF ITALY

# Cannelloni

**To serve 6**

Homemade pasta dough
(Index/Glossary), made with
2¼ cups sifted all-purpose
flour, 3 eggs, ¼ cup water
and 2 tablespoons
vegetable oil
3 cups mornay sauce (Index/
Glossary)
2 cups tomato sauce (Index/
Glossary)

MEAT STUFFING
2 tablespoons olive oil

1 onion, chopped
1 carrot, chopped
1 pound boneless veal, cubed
1 pound boneless beef, cubed
1 cup dry white wine
3 egg yolks
¼ cup chopped fresh parsley
leaves
7 tablespoons grated
Parmesan cheese
Salt
Freshly ground black pepper

Divide the dough in half, leaving one part covered to stay moist. Using a floured pastry pin on a well-floured work surface, roll one-half at a time as thin as possible. Cut the dough into 4-inch squares—there may be 22 or more altogether—and save the 18 best ones.

In a large covered pot, bring about 6 quarts of lightly salted water to a boil over high heat. Pour in a little oil to prevent foaming over and to help keep the pasta from sticking together. Drop in nine of the pasta squares, stir gently, and let them cook for five minutes or until they are tender but not soft. Lift them out of the pot one at a time with a slotted spoon and place them in a large bowl or pan of cold water to chill them; then arrange them in a single layer on dampened towels. Drop the remaining nine squares into the pot, stir, cook and cool them similarly.

To prepare the stuffing, first heat the olive oil in a 10- to 12-inch skillet. Add the onion and carrot; stirring frequently, cook over moderate heat until the onion is soft, about five minutes. Pat the veal and beef cubes dry with paper towels. Add them to the vegetables, and brown them on all sides over moderate heat. Add the wine, cover, reduce the heat, and simmer for one hour. Put a little of the meat mixture at a time into a blender or processor and blend it until smooth. Place the blended mixture in a bowl and add the egg yolks, parsley, 3 tablespoons of the Parmesan and ½ cup of the mornay sauce. Mix the ingredients together thoroughly. Taste and add salt and pepper if needed.

Preheat the oven to 350°F. To assemble the cannelloni, first place 3 tablespoons of meat stuffing on the center of each pasta square, spreading the mixture out to make a center strip down the length of the square. Roll up the square and place it, seam side down, in a buttered 12-by-9-inch baking dish, which will hold all of the cannelloni in one layer. Pour the remaining mornay sauce over the cannelloni, spreading it evenly. Then spoon the tomato sauce over the top. Sprinkle with the remaining 4 tablespoons of grated Parmesan.

Bake the cannelloni for 25 minutes or until the sauce is bubbly. Put the cannelloni under a preheated broiler for a minute or two to brown the top, and serve immediately.

■ GREAT DINNERS FROM LIFE

# Spinach Gnocchi

**To serve 4**

1 onion, chopped fine
1 tablespoon olive oil
⅓ cup chopped smoked ham
1 pound fresh spinach,
washed, stemmed,
blanched in boiling water for
1 minute and drained, or 10
ounces frozen spinach,
defrosted

½ cup ricotta cheese
½ cup cottage cheese
6 tablespoons freshly grated
Parmesan cheese
2 egg whites
½ cup flour
Freshly grated nutmeg
1 tablespoon unsalted
butter

In a 6- to 8-inch skillet over moderately high heat, sauté the onion in the oil until the onion is translucent—about five minutes. Add the ham and sauté for two minutes more, then transfer the contents of the skillet to a mixing bowl. Use your hands to squeeze the spinach dry. Then chop it fine and put it in the bowl with the onion and ham.

With the back of a large spoon, press the ricotta and cottage cheeses through a sieve into the bowl. Add 4 tablespoons of the Parmesan cheese, the egg whites, flour and nutmeg. Stir this gnocchi mixture well and put it into a piping bag fitted with a ½-inch plain tip.

Preheat the oven to 400°F. In a large pot, bring 4 quarts of lightly salted water to a boil. Meanwhile, pipe 1-inch strips of the gnocchi mixture onto large sheets of wax paper, putting about 20 gnocchi in the center of each sheet. Pick up one of the wax-paper sheets by its edges and dip the gnocchi and paper together into the boiling water; the gnocchi will immediately separate from the paper. Discard the paper. Cook the gnocchi for about two minutes or until they rise to the surface of the water and stay there. With a slotted spoon, transfer this batch to a baking dish that will hold all of the gnocchi in two or three layers. Cook the remaining batches of gnocchi the same way.

Dust the gnocchi with the remaining 2 tablespoons of Parmesan cheese and dot them with the butter. Bake them until they are sizzling, about 20 minutes. Transfer the gnocchi to a warmed serving bowl, and serve them immediately.

■ FRESH WAYS WITH PASTA

# Potato Gnocchi

**To serve 6**

3 pounds potatoes, peeled
1¼ cups freshly grated
Parmesan cheese
1½ cups flour

3 egg yolks, lightly beaten
2 teaspoons salt
Freshly ground black pepper
9½ tablespoons butter, melted

Boil the potatoes in a large pot of boiling water for 20 minutes or until they are tender. Drain off the water, then put the pot back on the stove over low heat; shake the pot vigorously for about two minutes to dry the potatoes. Mash the potatoes or put them through a food mill. Stir in ¾ cup of the cheese, the flour, egg

yolks, salt, pepper to taste and 1½ tablespoons of the butter.

Pick up a small amount of the potato dough at a time in one hand and put it on a lightly floured work surface. With your palms, roll the dough into a rope about ½ inch thick. Using a sharp knife, cut the rope into 1-inch lengths. Line up these gnocchi on baking sheets or wax paper until all the dough has been rolled out and cut. Then poach small batches of the gnocchi in a skillet with 2 inches of simmering water for about five minutes, or until they rise to the surface. Lift the poached gnocchi out of the water with a slotted spoon and stack them two or three deep in a shallow buttered baking dish.

Preheat the oven to 325°F. Sprinkle the gnocchi with the remaining ½ cup of cheese and pour ½ cup of melted butter over all. Bake the gnocchi for 30 minutes. Brown the top quickly under a preheated broiler.

■ GREAT DINNERS FROM LIFE

## Chinese Egg Noodles with Meat Sauce

**To serve 4**

| | |
|---|---|
| 3 tablespoons peanut oil | lengthwise, for garnish |
| 1 pound boneless pork shoulder, freshly ground | 1 teaspoon sugar |
| | ½ cup chicken stock |
| 2 tablespoons Chinese rice wine, or pale dry sherry | 1 pound Chinese egg noodles or other narrow egg noodles |
| ¼ cup brown-bean sauce | 1 cucumber, peeled, halved, |
| 2 scallions, including green tops, chopped fine, plus 3 scallions, including green tops, cut into 2-inch pieces and finely shredded | seeded and cut into ⅛-inch slices, for garnish |
| | 1 tablespoon finely chopped garlic for garnish |

Set a 12-inch wok or 10-inch skillet over high heat for 30 seconds. Pour in 2 tablespoons of the oil, swirl it about in the pan, and heat it for another 30 seconds, turning the burner to moderate if the oil begins to smoke. Add the ground pork and stir-fry it for two to three minutes, or until it browns lightly. Add the wine, brown-bean sauce, chopped scallions and sugar; mix well and pour in the chicken stock. Bring to a boil and cook, stirring frequently, over moderate heat for eight to 10 minutes, until all of the stock has evaporated. Turn off the heat and cover the wok or skillet to keep the meat sauce warm.

Bring 3 or 4 quarts of lightly salted water to a boil over high heat in a large covered pot. Add a splash of oil to prevent foaming over and to keep the noodles from sticking together. Drop in the noodles, stir them with a large fork, and boil them, uncovered, for five minutes or until they are barely tender, stirring them occasionally. Drain the noodles in a colander.

Place the noodles on a warmed, deep platter or in a serving bowl and toss them with the remaining tablespoon of oil. Ladle the meat sauce into a serving bowl and arrange the cucumber, garlic and shredded scallions as a garnish on a small serving plate. Serve the noodles accompanied by the sauce and the garnish.

■ THE COOKING OF CHINA

SPINACH GNOCCHI

## Steamed Couscous with Chicken and Vegetables

*This Algerian recipe for couscous handles the tiny pasta pellets in the traditional North African way and calls for a special pot: a couscoussier, which is a kind of double boiler with holes in both the base and lid of the top section to allow steam from the bottom section to pass through it. Couscoussiers are available at kitchen supply stores, but can be simulated by a deep pot for the base and a cheesecloth-lined colander for the top; cover the colander with foil pierced with holes. The hrisa seasoning is a peppery spice you can make by combining ¼ cup cayenne pepper, 2 tablespoons ground cumin and 1 teaspoon salt.* ❖❖

**To serve 6**

| | |
|---|---|
| 2 pounds couscous | 1 tablespoon salt |
| 2½ teaspoons salt dissolved in 2½ cups cold water | 1 teaspoon freshly ground black pepper |
| 1 tablespoon olive oil | 4 carrots. cut into 2-inch lengths |
| One 3-pound chicken, cut into 12 pieces and patted dry | 6 turnips, quartered lengthwise |
| ¼ cup olive oil | **Boiling water** |
| 1 cup dried chickpeas, soaked overnight, drained and simmered in water for 1 hour, or 2 cups drained canned chickpeas | ¼ cup unsalted butter, cut into bits |
| 1 red onion, grated fine | ¼ teaspoon ground cinnamon |
| ½ teaspoon ground cinnamon | 6 small zucchini, unpeeled, quartered lengthwise |
| | 1 teaspoon *hrisa* (optional) |

Spread the couscous evenly in a large, shallow pan. Sprinkle it with 2 cups of the salt water, then dribble the tablespoon of olive oil over the top. Rub the moistened grains gently between your palms, lifting and dropping the couscous back into the pan, until the water and oil have been absorbed. Cover the pan with foil or plastic wrap, and set the couscous aside at room temperature for 15 to 20 minutes; the pellets will swell slightly.

Meanwhile, in the lower part of a 4-quart *couscoussier* or in a deep 6-quart pot, sauté the chicken in the ¼ cup of olive oil, turning the pieces with tongs frequently, until they are golden brown on all sides. Stir in the chickpeas, onion, ½ teaspoon of cinnamon, 1 tablespoon of salt and the black pepper. Add enough cold water to cover the chicken and the chickpeas; stir until the water comes to a boil. Reduce the heat to moderate.

Set the top part of the *couscoussier* in place. Or set a colander lined with cheesecloth in the pot; it should not touch the food below it. Twist damp paper towels or kitchen towels into long narrow strips and wrap them around the rim of the *couscoussier* to seal the joint between the upper and lower parts.

Slowly add about 2 cups of the couscous to the upper pot, rubbing the pellets between your palms as you drop them in, and letting them mound naturally. When steam begins to rise through the pellets, add another cup or so of couscous in the same manner. Repeat, letting steam appear after each addition. When all of the couscous has been rubbed into the pot, steam it, uncovered and undisturbed, for 20 minutes. Remove the top part of the *couscoussier*, return the couscous to the shallow pan, spread it out with a wooden spoon, and set it aside.

When the chicken is tender but not falling apart, transfer it with tongs to a platter, and drape foil over it to keep it warm. Add the carrots and turnips to the stew, and pour in enough boiling water to cover the vegetables completely. Stirring occasionally, bring the liquid to a boil over high heat. Reduce the heat to moderate, set the top pot in place again, and let the vegetables cook while you complete the couscous.

Sprinkle the remaining ½ cup of salt water, the butter bits and ¼ teaspoon of cinnamon over the couscous, and rub the grains gently between your palms as before until the water and butter are completely absorbed.

Again seal the joint at the rim of the pot with towel strips. Slowly add 2 cups of the couscous to the upper pot as you did before, rubbing the pellets between your palms as you drop them in, letting them mound naturally, and waiting for steam to appear before adding more. Steam, uncovered and undisturbed, for about 15 minutes, or until the carrots and turnips are tender but not falling apart. Transfer them with a slotted spoon to the platter containing the chicken, add the zucchini to the pot, and replace the top. Steam the couscous undisturbed for 10 to 15 minutes, or until it is soft but still somewhat resistant to the bite.

To serve, mound the couscous on a large heated platter. Return the chicken and vegetables to the stew and heat them through. Taste for seasoning and add *hrisa* to the stew if desired. Moisten the couscous with about 1 cup of the sauce, and arrange the chicken attractively on top. Place the vegetables in a ring around the couscous. Pour the remaining sauce into a bowl and present it separately. Serve at once.

■ A QUINTET OF CUISINES

## Couscous with Browned Onions

**To serve 4**

| | |
|---|---|
| 2 tablespoons unsalted butter | ¼ cup sliced almonds |
| 2 tablespoons olive oil | Salt |
| 2 onions, coarsely chopped | Freshly ground black pepper |
| 1 cup chicken stock | 1 teaspoon finely chopped fresh parsley leaves |
| 1 cup couscous | |

In a heavy 8- to 10-inch skillet, melt the butter in 1 tablespoon of the oil over moderate heat. Add the onions, reduce the heat to low, and cook, stirring frequently, for 10 to 15 minutes or until the onions are golden brown.

Add the stock and ½ cup water, and bring them to a boil. Stir in the couscous, cover the skillet, and remove it from the heat. Let the couscous stand for five minutes. Meanwhile, in a 6- to 8-inch skillet, toast the almonds in the remaining oil over moderate heat for two to three minutes or until golden brown. Stir the almonds into the couscous. Add salt and pepper to taste, sprinkle with the parsley, and present the couscous in a warmed serving bowl.

■ MAKE-AHEAD MENUS

# Eggs & Cheese

# Eggs & Cheese

FRONTISPIECE: FILLED OMELETS

In the drama of dining well, eggs and cheese are essential elements, both as featured players and as part of the supporting cast. English novelist Samuel Butler went so far as to declare that the hen was just an egg's way of making another egg. Cheese lovers are similarly prone to overstate their enthusiasm for a food that represents "milk's leap toward immortality," as American writer Clifton Fadiman described cheese.

The ways of presenting eggs vary endlessly. Eggs may be fried, scrambled, poached, boiled hard or soft, or lightly beaten for omelets—and these may be served plain or filled and rolled like the one at left. As cooking components, eggs supply everything from a coating for fried foods to the leavening that makes many cakes rise. Cheese marries happily with eggs to create such sublime custards as that of quiche Lorraine, hearty puddings and featherlight soufflés. By itself, cheese forms the base of those molten delights Swiss fondue and Welsh rabbit.

Made from the milk of goats and sheep as well as cows, cheese comes in thousands upon thousands of variations, ranging from bland to pungent, from soft to hard and brittle. Nonetheless, the basic fresh cheeses—farmer, cottage and cream cheese—are simple enough in formulation and technique to be produced at home. The Indian version spikes the cheese with coriander and scallions. Or, the cheese might be sweetened with grated chocolate or chopped, preserved fruits and cinnamon or nutmeg.

## Broccoli Roll with Tomato Sauce

**To serve 4**

| | |
|---|---|
| **2 or 3 broccoli stalks** | TOMATO SAUCE |
| **5 eggs, separated, with yolks lightly beaten** | **1 tablespoon plus 1 teaspoon olive oil** |
| **2 teaspoons flour** | **1/4 cup finely chopped onion** |
| **3/4 teaspoon salt** | **1 small garlic clove, chopped fine** |
| **1/4 teaspoon freshly ground black pepper** | **One 28-ounce can peeled plum tomatoes in tomato purée** |
| **1/4 teaspoon freshly grated nutmeg** | **1/2 teaspoon crumbled dried thyme** |
| **1 cup whole-milk ricotta cheese** | **Salt** |
| **1/2 cup freshly grated Parmesan cheese** | **Freshly ground black pepper** |
| **1 1/2 tablespoons butter** | |

Begin by preparing the tomato sauce: First heat the oil in a heavy nonreactive 3- to 4-quart saucepan over moderate heat. Add the onion and garlic, and cook, stirring occasionally, for about five minutes or until the onion is soft but not brown. Drain the tomatoes in a sieve set over a nonreactive mixing bowl, and add the tomatoes and the thyme to the saucepan, crushing the tomatoes with the back of a wooden spoon. Using a rubber spatula, scrape the tomato purée off the sieve and add it to the pan. Reserve the tomato juices for another use.

Set the sauce over high heat and bring it to a simmer, stirring frequently. Reduce the heat to moderate, and cook the sauce, stirring occasionally and using the spoon to crush the tomatoes into smaller pieces. When the sauce is thick and the flavors well blended—10 to 15 minutes—remove it from the heat; add salt and pepper to taste.

To prepare the broccoli roll, wash the broccoli and shake it dry. Remove the florets, trim the stalks, and peel and cut them into 1-inch chunks. Add enough stem pieces to the florets to measure about 4 cups. With a large, sharp knife or in a food processor with a steel blade, chop the broccoli fine.

Bring 1/2 cup of water to a boil in a heavy 8- to 10-inch skillet. Add the broccoli, stir, cover the skillet, and cook the broccoli until tender but still crisp—about three minutes; drain in a colander and gently pat dry. Set aside.

Butter a 12-inch round plate or flat baking dish.

Place the egg whites in a medium-sized bowl. Stir the flour, 1/4 teaspoon of the salt, 1/8 teaspoon pepper and 1/8 teaspoon nutmeg into the egg whites. With a whisk or a rotary or electric beater, beat the whites until they form soft peaks when the beater is raised. Add the yolks and beat until all traces of white disappear and the mixture is a uniform yellow.

Using the skillet in which the broccoli was cooked, combine the ricotta, Parmesan cheese, 1/2 teaspoon salt, and the remaining pepper and nutmeg. Set the skillet over the lowest possible heat, and warm the mixture, stirring occasionally. Do not permit this mixture to become hot or it might turn watery.

In a 12-inch skillet—preferably one with a nonstick coating—

melt the 1 1/2 tablespoons of butter over very low heat. Meanwhile, add the broccoli to the ricotta mixture, and warm them over very low heat, stirring occasionally.

Increase the heat under the nonstick skillet to moderately low, and carefully add the egg mixture, using a rubber spatula to spread it evenly out to the sides of the skillet. Cook until the mixture starts to bubble and heave slightly and the eggs begin to set—one or two minutes. Using a metal spatula, ease this egg pancake out onto the buttered plate.

Invert the empty skillet over the pancake. Using oven mitts or potholders to protect your hands, hold the skillet and plate firmly together and turn them over so that the pancake falls back into the skillet, uncooked side down. Return the skillet to the heat for about 30 seconds. Again cover the skillet with the plate and invert them so that the pancake falls onto the plate. Scoop the warmed cheese and broccoli filling onto the pancake, distributing the filling evenly and leaving a 1-inch margin so that the filling does not ooze out when the pancake is rolled. Roll the pancake around the filling, jelly-roll fashion.

To serve, spoon about 1/2 cup of tomato sauce onto each of four heated plates. Cut the roulade into eight slices, and place two slices on top of the sauce on each plate.

■ **EGG AND CHEESE MENUS**

## Filled Omelets

**To serve 4**

| | |
|---|---|
| **12 eggs** | **4 bacon slices** |
| **1/4 cup cold water** | **1/4 pound Gruyère cheese, shredded (about 1 cup)** |
| **8 drops Tabasco sauce** | **1/4 cup sour cream** |
| **Salt** | **Parsley sprigs for garnish** |
| **4 tablespoons butter** | |
| | |
| SAUTÉED POTATO FILLING | SMOKED SALMON FILLING |
| **8 small red potatoes** | **1/2 pound cream cheese, softened** |
| **1/4 cup butter** | **1/4 cup sour cream** |
| **1/4 cup corn oil** | **8 drops Tabasco sauce** |
| **1/2 cup finely chopped scallions** | **1/2 pound smoked salmon, sliced and cut into 1/4-inch strips** |
| | **Dill sprigs for garnish** |
| TOASTED WALNUT AND CHEESE FILLING | |
| **3/4 cup shelled walnuts** | |

To make the potato filling, first bring 2 quarts water to a boil in a large saucepan. Drop in the potatoes and cook for 15 minutes or until they have almost no resistance when pierced with the tines of a fork. Drain them in a colander.

When the potatoes are cool enough to handle, cut them into 1/2-inch cubes. In an 8- to 10-inch skillet or sauté pan, melt 1/4 cup of butter in the corn oil over moderate heat. Add the scallions and potatoes. Stirring frequently, cook until the potatoes are crisp and lightly browned. Cover loosely with foil to keep them warm.

To make the walnut and cheese filling, toast the walnuts in a shallow baking dish in a 350°F. oven for five to 10 minutes, stir-

**BROCCOLI ROLL WITH TOMATO SAUCE**

ring them frequently until they brown. Remove the nuts from the dish and put them on a cutting surface to cool. Meanwhile, fry the bacon in a 10- to 12-inch skillet until it is brown and crisp. Drain the bacon on paper towels. When the nuts cool, chop them and put them in a bowl. Crumble in the bacon and add the cheese.

To make the smoked salmon filling, blend the cream cheese, sour cream and Tabasco together in a food processor or mix them in a bowl with an electric beater.

For each omelet, break three eggs into a shallow bowl and add 1 tablespoon of water, 2 drops of Tabasco and salt to taste. Using a whisk, beat the eggs lightly until blended. Do not over beat.

In a well-seasoned 8-inch omelet pan, melt 1 tablespoon of butter over moderately high heat. When the foam subsides, pour in

one portion of the egg mixture. Keeping the pan close to the burner, swirl the mixture in a circular motion for 30 to 60 seconds, until the bottom of the omelet is set and the top is somewhat creamy. For a drier omelet, cook for 30 seconds longer.

Remove the pan from the heat. To use the walnut filling, spread 2 tablespoons of sour cream on a quarter of the omelet, top with half of the walnut mixture, and spoon a fourth of the potato mixture beside it. Using a metal spatula, fold the omelet in half over the filling, slide it out onto a heated individual plate, and garnish with a parsley sprig. Serve immediately.

To use the smoked salmon filling, spoon half of the cream cheese mixture onto one-quarter of the omelet, top the cheese with strips of salmon, and put a fourth of the potato filling beside it. Fold the omelet in half, slide it onto a plate, and garnish with a dill sprig. Serve immediately.

Repeat the process for the remaining omelets.

■ BRUNCH MENUS

## Avocado and Coriander Omelet

*Classified as a frittata, this kind of omelet is thicker than most—and flat, like a pancake, to be cut into wedges for serving.* ❧

**To serve 4**

| | |
|---|---|
| 8 large eggs | coriander leaves or 2 |
| ½ cup plain yogurt | teaspoons crumbled |
| ½ teaspoon salt | dried coriander |
| ¼ teaspoon freshly ground | 2 tablespoons unsalted butter |
|    black pepper | 1 firm avocado, peeled, |
| ½ to 1 teaspoon ground cumin |    halved, pitted and cut |
| 2 tablespoons chopped fresh |    into ½-inch chunks |

Break the eggs into a medium-sized bowl, and beat them with a whisk just until blended. Add the yogurt, salt, pepper and cumin to taste, and beat thoroughly. Stir in the coriander.

In a well-seasoned or nonstick omelet pan or skillet, melt the butter over moderate heat. When the foam begins to subside, pour in the egg mixture; cover, increase the heat to moderately high, and cook the eggs, without stirring, for five minutes, or until they are almost set but still creamy.

Sprinkle the avocado over the *frittata*, cover the pan, and cook for three minutes. Without removing the lid, take the pan off the heat. Let the *frittata* rest until the top is set but not dry—two or three minutes. Serve cut into wedges.

■ EGG AND CHEESE MENUS

## Ranch-Style Eggs and Tortillas

**To serve 6**

| | |
|---|---|
| ⅓ cup vegetable oil | chopped garlic |
| 12 fresh tortillas | 5 tomatoes, peeled, seeded |
| 6 tablespoons butter |    and chopped fine |
| 12 eggs | 3 canned serrano chilies, |
| 1 large ripe avocado, peeled, |    rinsed and chopped fine |
|    halved, pitted and sliced thin | ½ teaspoon sugar |
| | 1 teaspoon salt |
| CHILI-TOMATO SAUCE | Freshly ground black pepper |
| 3 tablespoons vegetable oil | 2 tablespoons finely chopped |
| 1 cup finely chopped onions |    fresh coriander leaves |
| ½ teaspoon finely | |

Begin with the sauce. In a heavy 2- to 3-quart saucepan, heat 3 tablespoons of vegetable oil over moderate heat. Add the onions and garlic, and cook, stirring frequently, for five minutes, until they are soft. Add the tomatoes, chilies, sugar, salt and a few grindings of pepper. When the mixture boils, reduce the heat and simmer, uncovered, stirring occasionally, for 15 minutes, until the sauce becomes a thick purée. Add the coriander; turn off the heat. Keep the sauce warm.

In a heavy 8-inch skillet, heat 2 tablespoons of the oil. One at a time, fry the tortillas for one or two minutes on each side, until they brown lightly. Add more oil, 1 or 2 teaspoons at a time, when necessary. As you proceed, transfer the fried tortillas to a double thickness of paper towels to drain.

Place two tortillas side by side on each of six individual heated plates. Over moderate heat, melt 2 tablespoons of the butter in a heavy 10- to 12-inch skillet. When the foam subsides, break four eggs into the skillet. Baste the eggs several times with the butter in the pan. Cover the skillet with a lid for one minute to set the egg whites. Separate the eggs with the edge of a metal spatula and slide or lift each one onto a tortilla. Melt more butter in the skillet and fry the remaining eggs, four at a time.

Spoon a ring of hot tomato sauce 1 inch wide around each egg, garnish the plates with avocado slices and serve at once. Present the extra sauce in a small serving bowl.

■ LATIN AMERICAN COOKING

## Egg Foo Yung

*Before starting this recipe, measure the capacity of your ladles. This recipe calls for a ladle that will hold about ¼ cup.* ❧

**To make 12 pancakes**
**(to serve 4)**

| | |
|---|---|
| Vegetable oil for deep frying | black pepper |
| 1½ cups bean sprouts | 4 scallions for garnish |
| 1 onion, halved and cut | |
|    lengthwise into ¹⁄₁₆-inch- | MUSHROOM SAUCE |
|    wide strips | 2 tablespoons vegetable oil |
| 1 celery rib, trimmed, cut into | ¼ pound mushrooms, wiped |
|    2-inch pieces, then into |    clean, trimmed and |
|    ¹⁄₁₆-inch-wide strips |    sliced thin |
| ½ pound thinly sliced | 2 cups boiling chicken stock |
|    boiled ham, cut into 2-by- | 1 tablespoon soy sauce |
|    ¹⁄₁₆-inch strips | 1 tablespoon tomato ketchup |
| 8 eggs | 2 tablespoons cornstarch, |
| ¾ teaspoon salt |    dissolved in 2 tablespoons |
| ½ teaspoon freshly ground |    cold water |

For the sauce, heat 2 tablespoons of oil in an 8- to 10-inch skillet over moderate heat. Stir in the mushrooms, and cook for five minutes or until they are soft and lightly colored. Blend in the chicken stock, soy sauce and ketchup, and bring to a boil over high heat. Stir the cornstarch and water mixture into the boiling sauce. Reduce the heat and simmer the sauce for two or three minutes, until it is clear and thick enough to coat a spoon lightly. Cover the pan partially and keep the sauce warm over the lowest possible heat.

Pour 2 inches of vegetable oil into a heavy 12-inch skillet; heat the oil until it registers 350°F. on a deep-frying thermometer. Combine the bean sprouts with the strips of onion, celery and ham in a bowl. In another mixing bowl, beat the eggs lightly and stir in the salt and pepper. Stir the bean sprouts, onions, celery and ham into the beaten eggs. Using a ¼-cup ladleful of this mixture for each pancake, cook four pancakes at a time over high heat. Turn the pancakes with a slotted spatula after 30 seconds, and fry for about 30 seconds longer, or until they puff and are golden brown. Serve at once, garnished with a scallion and accompanied by the hot mushroom sauce.

■ AMERICAN COOKING: THE MELTING POT

EGG FOO YUNG

## Portuguese Eggs with Peas

**To serve 2 to 4**

2 tablespoons butter
½ cup finely chopped onions
¾ cup chicken stock
3 cups freshly cooked
   green peas
¼ cup finely chopped fresh
   parsley leaves
¼ cup finely chopped fresh
   coriander leaves

½ teaspoon sugar
Salt
Freshly ground black pepper
¼ pound *linquiça, chorizo* or
   other garlic-seasoned
   smoked pork sausage,
   cut into ¼-inch slices
4 eggs

In a heavy 10-inch skillet or shallow flameproof casserole, melt the butter over moderate heat. When the foam has almost sub-sided, add the onions and, stirring frequently, cook for eight to 10 minutes or until they are lightly colored. Stir in the stock, peas, parsley, coriander, sugar, ¼ teaspoon of salt and a few grindings of pepper, and overlap the sausage slices around the edge of the skillet. Bring to a boil over high heat, then reduce the heat to low, cover, and simmer the contents for five minutes.

Break the eggs into the skillet, keeping them well apart. Or, more cautiously, break one egg at a time into a saucer and, holding the dish at the edge, slide the egg into the skillet. Sprinkle the eggs lightly with salt and pepper. Cover the skillet and cook for three or four minutes, until the egg yolks are covered with an opaque film and the whites are set. Serve at once, directly from the skillet.

■ THE COOKING OF SPAIN AND PORTUGAL

## Scotch Woodcock

*In fact, this is a recipe for scrambled eggs on anchovy toast—not for any bird. The name is a sly dig at the hunting abilities of the Scots.* ◆●

**To serve 4**

| | |
|---|---|
| 4 eggs | 4 slices hot buttered toast |
| 3 tablespoons heavy cream | 2 tablespoons anchovy |
| 1/8 teaspoon salt | paste |
| Freshly ground black pepper | 8 flat anchovy fillets, drained |
| 3 tablespoons butter | |

In a small bowl, beat the eggs with a fork or whisk until well blended, then beat in the cream, salt and a few grindings of pepper. In a heavy 6- to 8-inch skillet over low heat, melt the 3 tablespoons of butter; do not let the butter brown. Pour in the eggs and cook them over the lowest possible heat, stirring with the flat of a table fork, until they form soft, creamy curds. Do not overcook them; the finished eggs should be moist. Quickly spread the toast with anchovy paste, arrange the slices on individual serving plates, and spread a layer of the scrambled eggs on top. Crisscross two anchovy fillets over each portion, and serve at once.

■ THE COOKING OF THE BRITISH ISLES

## French Omelet

*To season a new omelet pan, pour in 1/4 inch of vegetable oil, and set the pan over low heat until the oil darkens and smokes. Take the pan off the heat, let it cool, then wipe it dry with a paper towel. Never wash the pan: Just wipe it clean. To prevent rusting during storage, wipe the pan lightly with oil.* ◆●

**To serve 1 or 2**

| | |
|---|---|
| 3 eggs | Gruyère cheese or |
| Salt | Gruyère and Parmesan |
| Freshly ground black pepper | cheeses combined |
| 1 tablespoon butter, cut into | 1 tablespoon chopped fresh |
| bits, plus 1/2 teaspoon | parsley, chervil, tarragon |
| butter, softened | or chives |
| | 1/4 cup chopped mushrooms, |
| FILLINGS (OPTIONAL) | sautéed in butter until |
| 2 tablespoons freshly grated | tender |

Break the eggs into a small bowl, season with salt and pepper, and stir briskly with a fork for 20 to 30 seconds or until the whites and yolks blend together. Heat an ungreased well-seasoned 7- to 8-inch omelet pan until very hot, drop in the butter bits, and swirl them in the pan so that they melt quickly and coat the bottom and sides. When the foam subsides, but before the butter browns, pour in the eggs.

Working quickly, stir the eggs with the flat of the fork, at the same time sliding the pan back and forth vigorously to prevent the eggs from sticking. In a few seconds, the eggs will form a film on the bottom of the pan and the top will thicken to a light, curded custard. Still moving the pan with one hand, gently stir through the top custard with the fork to spread the still-liquid eggs into the firmer areas; try not to pierce the bottom film. Add one of the fillings, if you like, sprinkling it onto the half of the omelet farthest from you.

Lift the nearest edge of the omelet with the fork and roll the omelet up lightly over to the far side of the pan. Let it rest for a moment on the lip of the pan, then tilt the pan and roll the omelet out onto a heated plate. Brush the top with softened butter and serve at once.

■ THE COOKING OF PROVINCIAL FRANCE

## Cheese Soufflé

**To serve 4**

| | |
|---|---|
| 1 cup freshly grated Gruyère | 3 tablespoons flour |
| cheese or Gruyère and | 1 cup milk |
| Parmesan cheeses | 1/2 teaspoon salt |
| combined | Freshly ground white pepper |
| 3 tablespoons butter, cut | 4 eggs, separated, plus |
| into bits | 2 egg whites |

Preheat the oven to 400°F. With a pastry brush, coat the bottom and sides of a 2-quart soufflé dish or charlotte mold with melted or softened butter. Sprinkle in a spoonful of the grated cheese, and tip the dish to spread it. Invert the dish to tap out the excess.

In a 2- to 3-quart saucepan, melt the 3 tablespoons of butter over moderate heat. When the foam subsides, stir in the flour with a wooden spoon and cook over low heat, stirring constantly, for one or two minutes. Do not let this roux brown. Slowly pour in the milk and beat vigorously with a whisk until the roux and liquid blend. Add the salt and pepper, and cook, whisking constantly, over low heat for about five minutes, until the sauce is smooth and thick. Remove the pan from the heat and beat in the egg yolks, one at a time, whisking each one until thoroughly blended before adding the next. Set aside.

With a large balloon whisk or a rotary or electric beater, beat the egg whites in a large bowl until they form unwavering peaks when the beater is lifted from the bowl. Stir a big spoonful of beaten egg white into the waiting sauce to lighten it; then stir in all but 1 tablespoon of the remaining grated cheese. With a rubber spatula, lightly fold in the rest of the egg whites until no trace of white appears.

Gently pour the soufflé mixture into the prepared dish; the dish should be about three-quarters full. Smooth the surface with the rubber spatula, and sprinkle the remaining spoonful of cheese on top. For a decorative effect, make a "cap" on the soufflé with a spatula by cutting a trench 1 inch deep about 1 inch from the rim all around the dish.

Place the soufflé in the middle of the oven and immediately reduce the heat to 375°F. Bake for about 35 minutes, or until the soufflé puffs up about 2 inches above the rim of the dish and the top is lightly browned. Serve at once.

■ THE COOKING OF PROVINCIAL FRANCE

## Swiss Fondue

**To serve 4 to 6**

| | |
|---|---|
| **½ pound Gruyère cheese, grated coarse** | **2 tablespoons kirsch** |
| | **Freshly grated nutmeg** |
| **½ pound Emmentaler cheese, grated coarse** | **Freshly ground white pepper** |
| | **Salt** |
| **1 tablespoon cornstarch** | **1 large loaf French or Italian** |
| **2 cups dry white wine, preferably Neuchâtel** | **bread, crust left on, cut into 1-inch cubes** |
| **1 garlic clove, crushed** | |

In a large bowl, toss together the cheeses and cornstarch until thoroughly combined. Pour the wine into a 2-quart fondue dish or other 2-quart flameproof casserole, drop in the garlic, and bring to a boil over high heat. Let the wine boil briskly for one or two minutes, then use a slotted spoon to remove the garlic. Reduce the heat so that the wine barely simmers. Stirring constantly with a table fork, add the cheese mixture a handful at a time. Let each handful melt before adding another. When the fondue is smooth and creamy, stir in the kirsch, ⅛ teaspoon nutmeg and a few grindings of white pepper. Taste for seasoning and add salt and more white pepper if necessary.

To serve, place the fondue dish or casserole over an alcohol or gas table burner in the center of the dining table. Regulate the heat under the dish so that the fondue barely simmers. Set a basketful of bread cubes beside the fondue. Traditionally, each diner spears a cube of bread on a fork—preferably a long-handled fondue fork—swirls the bread in the fondue until the bread is coated, then eats it immediately.

■ A QUINTET OF CUISINES

## Soufflé-filled Baked Peppers

**To serve 4**

| | |
|---|---|
| **4 large sweet red peppers** | **2 tablespoons finely cut fresh dill or 2 teaspoons dried dill weed** |
| **¼ cup butter** | |
| **1 small onion, chopped fine** | |
| **1¾ cups freshly grated Parmesan cheese** | **½ teaspoon Tabasco sauce** |
| | **Freshly grated nutmeg** |
| **1¼ cups fresh white bread crumbs** | **Salt** |
| | **4 large eggs** |
| **¾ cup heavy cream** | |

Preheat the oven to 400° F. With a pastry brush, spread a light coating of melted or softened butter on the bottom of a baking dish that is just large enough to hold all the peppers upright, side by side.

Slice off the tops of the peppers and pull out the seeds and core with the stem. Remove any remaining seeds and trim the ribs. Set the peppers, open end upward, in the buttered dish, cutting small slices off the bottoms if it is necessary, to make the peppers stand straight.

Melt the butter in an 8- to 10-inch skillet over moderate heat.

Add the onion and cook, stirring occasionally, for about five minutes, or until the onion is soft. Take the skillet off the heat and stir in the cheese, bread crumbs, cream, dill, Tabasco, a pinch of nutmeg and salt to taste.

Separate the eggs, dropping the whites into a medium-sized mixing bowl and blending the yolks, one by one, into the onion mixture. With a wire whisk or a rotary or electric beater, beat the whites until they are stiff enough to form unwavering peaks when the beater is lifted from the bowl. Using a rubber spatula, fold half of the whites into the onion mixture to lighten it, then gently but thoroughly fold in the remaining egg whites. Carefully spoon about 1 cup of the soufflé mixture into each pepper, mounding the top slightly.

Bake the peppers for 20 to 25 minutes, or until the soufflés are puffed and lightly browned. Gently transfer the peppers to a heated platter and serve at once.

■ EGG AND CHEESE MENUS

eggs, egg yolks, cream, salt and a few grindings of white pepper together in a large mixing bowl. Stir in the grated cheese.

Place the cooled pastry shell still in its baking dish or pan on a baking sheet. Scatter the bacon over the bottom of the shell and ladle the egg-cheese custard into it, being sure the custard does not come within ⅛ inch of the rim of the shell. Sprinkle the top with the butter bits, and bake in the upper third of the oven for 25 minutes, until the custard has puffed and browned and a knife inserted in the center comes out clean. Serve the quiche hot or let it cool for 20 minutes and serve it warm.

■ THE COOKING OF PROVINCIAL FRANCE

## Glamorgan Sausages

*These tiny croquettes, or "sausages," of cheese and bread crumbs are customarily served as a light lunch or supper.* ✺

**To make about 10 sausages**

| | |
|---|---|
| ⅔ cup freshly grated Cheddar cheese | ½ teaspoon English dry mustard |
| 2 cups soft white bread crumbs | ½ teaspoon salt |
| 2 tablespoons finely chopped scallions | Freshly ground black pepper |
| 1 tablespoon finely chopped fresh parsley leaves | 2 eggs, separated |
| | 2 tablespoons water |
| | ¼ cup vegetable oil |

In a large bowl, mix the grated cheese, 1 cup of the bread crumbs, the scallions, parsley, mustard, salt and a few grindings of pepper. Add the egg yolks and water, and stir until the mixture can be gathered into a compact ball. If it crumbles, add more water, a few drops at a time, until the ingredients cohere. Divide into 10 equal portions, and roll each into a cylinder about 2½ inches long and ¾ inch across.

In a shallow bowl, beat the egg whites with a fork until frothy. Place the remaining crumbs on a plate. One at a time, roll the cylinders in the egg whites and then in the crumbs, lining them up side by side on a baking sheet covered by a strip of wax paper as you proceed. Put the sausages aside for a few minutes, long enough to set the coating.

In a heavy 10- to 12-inch skillet, heat the oil over high heat until it sputters. Add the sausages and cook them until they brown evenly—three or four minutes. Turn them gently with a spatula, and regulate the heat so that they cook quickly without burning.

■ THE COOKING OF THE BRITISH ISLES

**QUICHE LORRAINE**

## Quiche Lorraine

**To make one 8- to 9-inch quiche**

| | |
|---|---|
| 1 teaspoon butter, plus 2 tablespoons butter, cut into bits | Freshly ground white pepper |
| 6 lean bacon slices, cut into ¼-inch pieces | ¾ cup freshly grated Gruyère cheese or Gruyère and Parmesan cheeses combined |
| 2 eggs plus 2 egg yolks | One 8- to 9-inch shortcrust pastry shell, baked partially and cooled (Index/Glossary) |
| 1½ cups heavy cream | |
| ½ teaspoon salt | |

Preheat the oven to 375°F. In a heavy 8- to 10-inch skillet, melt 1 teaspoon of butter over moderate heat. When the foam subsides, cook the bacon until it is lightly browned and crisp. Remove the bacon from the skillet with a slotted spoon and drain it on paper towels. With a wire whisk or a rotary or electric beater, beat the

## Fresh Indian Cheese

**To serve 4**

| | |
|---|---|
| 1 sweet green pepper | coriander leaves, chopped, |
| 1 sweet red pepper | plus 4 coriander sprigs |
| 1 sweet yellow pepper | for garnish |
| 3 quarts milk | 2 scallions, white parts only, |
| Salt | cut into ¼-inch slices |
| ¾ cup fresh lemon juice, plus | ¼ teaspoon freshly ground |
| 8 lemon slices for garnish | black pepper |
| 1 tablespoon vegetable oil | 4 fresh hot green chilies, |
| 1 teaspoon ground coriander | stemmed, seeded and |
| ¼ cup loosely packed fresh | chopped fine (optional) |

Line a colander with a double thickness of dampened cheese-cloth and set it aside. Core, halve, and derib the peppers; then cut them lengthwise into strips ½ inch wide. Set aside.

Combine the milk and 1 teaspoon of salt in a heavy 5- to 6-quart nonreactive saucepan. Stirring occasionally to prevent sticking, cook over moderate heat for 12 to 15 minutes or until the milk comes to a rolling boil. Add the lemon juice and stir gently. Almost immediately, the milk will curdle and milky white curds will float to the surface; the liquid whey will become greenish yellow. Set the lined colander in the sink and pour the milk mixture into the colander to drain off the whey for five minutes. Pour 2 cups cold water over the cheese, and allow it to drain for about 30 seconds.

Gather up the corners of the cheesecloth and squeeze gently to remove as much water as possible. Return the cheese, still wrapped in cheesecloth, to the colander. Weight the cheese by setting an inverted plate over it and putting a 1-pound can on top. Let the cheese drain for 10 to 15 minutes.

Meanwhile, heat an ungreased heavy 8- to 10-inch skillet over high heat for two minutes. Add the vegetable oil and ground coriander; immediately add all of the sweet pepper strips. Sprinkle with salt to taste, and toss the peppers quickly to coat them evenly with spice. Let the peppers cook, undisturbed, for one minute. Toss the peppers again, reduce the heat to very low, and cook for another two minutes. Set the skillet off the heat.

Unwrap the cheese and place it in a large bowl. Add the fresh coriander, scallions and black pepper, and mix thoroughly with your hands or a large wooden spoon. The cheese should be silky-soft without being pasty. With a pastry brush, lightly oil four 4-ounce custard cups. Pack the cheese into the cups and set it aside for 10 minutes or so.

To serve, run a knife around the edge of each cup to loosen the cheese and unmold it onto four salad plates. Divide the pepper strips among the plates. If you like, sprinkle each serving with finely chopped chilies. Garnish each with a coriander sprig and two lemon slices.

■ **MEATLESS MENUS**

## Blintzes

*These wafer-thin pancakes rolled around a creamy, delicately sweet-ened cottage cheese filling are a triumph of Middle European cuisine—welcome at brunch, lunch or supper.* ❧

**To make 10 blintzes**

| | COTTAGE-CHEESE FILLING |
|---|---|
| 3 eggs | |
| ½ cup water | 1 pound dry cottage cheese, |
| ¾ cup sifted flour | or 1 pound creamed cottage |
| ¼ teaspoon salt | or farmer cheese, wrapped |
| 2 tablespoons butter, | in cheesecloth and |
| melted and cooled, plus | squeezed dry |
| ¼ cup melted butter | 2 tablespoons sour cream |
| combined with 1 tablespoon | 1 egg yolk |
| flavorless vegetable | 2 tablespoons sugar |
| oil | ½ teaspoon vanilla extract |
| 1 cup sour cream | ¼ teaspoon salt |
| Fruit preserves or jam | |

To prepare the filling, first use the back of a wooden spoon to force the cottage cheese through a fine sieve into a deep bowl. Add 2 tablespoons of sour cream, the egg yolk, sugar, vanilla extract and ¼ teaspoon of salt. Stirring and mashing vigorously, beat with a large spoon until the ingredients are well blended and the mixture is smooth. Set it aside.

For the blintzes, combine the eggs, water, flour, ¼ teaspoon of salt and 2 tablespoons of cooled melted butter in a blender or food processor. Blend them, then turn off the machine and scrape down the sides of the jar or bowl with a rubber spatula; blend again for 40 seconds.

To make the batter by hand, stir the flour and eggs together in a mixing bowl and gradually stir in the water and ¼ teaspoon of salt. Beat with a whisk or a rotary or electric beater until the flour lumps disappear, then force the batter through a fine sieve into another bowl, and stir in the cooled melted butter.

The finished batter should have the consistency of heavy cream; dilute it if necessary by adding cold water by the tea-spoonful. Let the batter rest for an hour to ensure tender blintzes.

To cook the blintzes, heat a 6-inch crepe pan or skillet over high heat until a drop of water flicked into it evaporates instantly. With a pastry brush or crumpled paper towels, lightly grease the bottom and sides of the pan with a little of the combined melted butter and oil.

Using a ladle that holds 3 tablespoons, pour batter into the pan. Tip the pan so that the batter quickly covers the bottom; the batter should cling to the pan and begin to firm up almost immediately. Cook the blintz for a minute or so, until a rim of brown shows around the edge. Then, without turning it over, slide the blintz onto a plate. Brush the combined butter and oil on the skillet again and proceed with the rest of the blintzes. As they are cooked, stack the blintzes one on top of the other.

When all of the blintzes have been browned on one side, fill each one by first placing about 3 tablespoons of filling on the cooked side of the blintz an inch or two from the top edge. With a knife or metal spatula, smooth the filling into a strip about 3

## Cheese Pudding

*Beaten whole eggs make this substantial brunch main course similar to a bread pudding.* ❧

**To serve 4**

| | |
|---|---|
| ½ cup unsalted butter, softened | Freshly ground black pepper |
| 8 slices homemade-type white bread | Freshly grated nutmeg (optional) |
| 3 eggs, lightly beaten | 3 cups freshly grated Emmentaler, Gruyère, or Jarlsberg cheese |
| 1½ cups milk | |
| Salt | |

Preheat the oven to 350°F. With a pastry brush, spread a generous coat of the butter over the bottom and sides of a 2-quart soufflé dish or other deep baking dish. Spread the remaining butter on the bread, then cut it into cubes.

In a large mixing bowl, blend the eggs and milk with salt and pepper to taste. Add a sprinkling of nutmeg, if you wish. Stir in the bread and cheese, and mix thoroughly. Pour the mixture into the soufflé dish. Bake for about 45 minutes or until top of pudding is brown, bubbly and nicely puffed.

NOTE: For pudding with a more delicate texture, separate the eggs and beat the whites until they form stiff peaks. Fold the beaten egg whites into the pudding mixture with a rubber spatula after the rest of the ingredients are well combined.

■ BRUNCH MENUS

## Dunvegan Welsh Rabbit

*This peppery Welsh rabbit comes from Cape Breton, an island northeast of Nova Scotia, where cold winters make hearty fare essential.* ❧

**To serve 4**

| | |
|---|---|
| 3 tablespoons butter | ¼ teaspoon cayenne pepper |
| 4 cups grated sharp Cheddar cheese | ¼ teaspoon salt |
| ½ cup ale | 2 eggs, lightly beaten |
| 1 teaspoon Worcestershire sauce | 4 slices homemade-type white bread, trimmed of crusts, toasted and each cut into 4 triangles |
| 1 teaspoon dry mustard | |
| ½ teaspoon paprika | |

In a heavy 2- to 3-quart saucepan, melt the butter over moderate heat. When the foam begins to subside, add the cheese, ale, Worcestershire sauce, mustard, paprika, cayenne and salt. Stirring constantly with a fork, cook until the cheese melts completely and the mixture is smooth.

Remove the pan from the heat and beat in the eggs. Then return the pan to low heat and stir for about five minutes, until the mixture is thick and creamy. Taste for seasoning.

Arrange the toast triangles on four heated individual serving plates, ladle the Welsh rabbit over them; serve at once.

■ AMERICAN COOKING: NEW ENGLAND

**FRESH INDIAN CHEESE**

inches long and 1 inch deep down the center of the blintz.

Fold the sides of the blintz toward the center, covering the ends of the filling. Turn the top edge over the filling and roll the blintz into a cylinder 3 inches long and 1 inch wide.

Pour the remaining butter-and-oil mixture into a heavy 10- to 12-inch skillet and set it over moderate heat. Place four or five blintzes, seam side down, in the pan, and fry them for three to five minutes on each side, turning them with a metal spatula and regulating the heat so they color quickly and evenly without burning. As they brown, transfer them to a heated serving platter.

Serve the blintzes hot, accompanied by sour cream and fruit preserves or jam, presented separately in bowls.

■ AMERICAN COOKING: THE MELTING POT

The gardens of the world yield a prodigious variety of vegetables a cook now can savor fresh year round. Chile sends asparagus, Mexico tomatoes and green peas. Green beans come from the Dominican Republic, sweet peppers from the Netherlands and—of course—endive from Belgium.

Autumn and harvest seem endless, and frozen and canned vegetables have a strong second place in the larder. But the fresher vegetables are, the brighter they look at the table and the richer they taste. Just-picked carrots are the orangest, and string beans straight from the field are the greenest. Newly cut lettuce is the crispest, and the sweetest ears of corn are those snapped from stalks just before cooking.

As the seasons for fresh vegetables have broadened, so has the selection. Yellow tomatoes provide a low-acid alternative to red ones; Sugar Snap peas can be eaten pod and all. English cucumbers are about a foot long and virtually seedless. The tubers sunchoke, or Jerusalem artichoke, and jícama—both indigenous to North America—have finally found their places in vegetable bins. And other extraordinary vegetables have recommended themselves to American truck farmers. Shiitake mushrooms from Japan are cultivated here these days. So too are Chinese cabbage and Italian broccoli—vegetables so familiar that it is hard to remember they were considered exotic only a few decades ago.

## Asparagus with Lemon Cream Sauce

**To serve 4**

| | |
|---|---|
| 2 pounds asparagus | ¼ teaspoon salt |
| 1 cup light cream | 1 egg yolk, lightly beaten |
| 2 tablespoons butter | 1 teaspoon fresh lemon juice |
| 1 teaspoon finely chopped | ½ teaspoon freshly grated |
|    fresh mint leaves |    nutmeg |

Line up the asparagus tips on a cutting board and cut off the ends so that the spears are the same length. With a small sharp knife, peel off the tough outer skin of each spear. At the end, the peel may be as thick as ¹/₁₆ inch but it will become paper-thin toward the tip. Divide the spears into four equal bundles, and tie each bundle with kitchen string, looped around it several times.

Fill halfway with water a nonreactive casserole large enough to hold the asparagus flat. Salt the water lightly and bring it to a boil over high heat. Slip a kitchen fork through the string of one bundle at a time and lay the bundle in the casserole. After the water returns to a boil, cook the asparagus, uncovered, for eight to 10 minutes, or until the stalks are barely tender and show slight resistance when pierced with the point of a small, sharp knife.

With the fork, lift the bundles out of the water by their strings. Cut off the strings, spread the asparagus on paper towels to drain, then transfer them to a heated platter. Drape the platter loosely with foil to keep the asparagus warm.

In a heavy 6- to 8-inch skillet, combine the cream, butter, mint and ¼ teaspoon of salt. Bring to a boil over high heat and, stirring frequently, boil for five minutes or until the cream mixture has reduced to about ¾ cup.

Turn the heat to low. Mix about 2 tablespoons of the cream mixture with the egg yolk. Stirring constantly, slowly pour the egg-yolk mixture into the cream mixture and simmer it for one or two minutes. Do not allow the sauce to come close to a boil or it will curdle. Stir in the lemon juice, taste for seasoning, adding more salt if necessary, and sprinkle with nutmeg. Serve at once, presenting the sauce separately.

■ AMERICAN COOKING: THE EASTERN HEARTLAND

## Sautéed Green Beans with Radishes

**To serve 6**

| | |
|---|---|
| 1 pound green beans, | 3 scallions, sliced thin |
|    trimmed | ¼ teaspoon salt |
| 1 tablespoon butter | Freshly ground black pepper |
| 1 tablespoon olive oil | 1 tablespoon fresh lime or |
| 2 teaspoons fennel seeds |    lemon juice |
| 1 cup thinly sliced radishes | |

In a large saucepan, bring 8 cups of water to a boil. Add the beans and, after the water returns to a boil, cook them for four minutes. Drain them in a colander, refresh them under cold running water to stop the cooking, and drain them again.

In a heavy 10- to 12-inch skillet, melt the butter in the olive oil over moderately high heat. Add the beans and the fennel seeds and, stirring frequently, sauté the beans for three minutes. Add the radishes, scallions, salt, a generous grinding of pepper and the lime or lemon juice. Sauté, stirring constantly, until the beans are tender but still crisp—about three minutes more. Serve at once.

■ FRESH WAYS WITH VEGETABLES

## Beets and Greens with Vinegar and Caraway

**To serve 4**

| | |
|---|---|
| 1 bunch beets with greens | ¼ teaspoon caraway seeds |
| ¼ cup cider vinegar | ⅛ teaspoon salt |
| 1 garlic clove, chopped fine | |

Preheat the oven to 400° F. Wash and trim the beets, leaving 2 inches of stem attached to each one. Remove the stems from the greens, then cut the leaves crosswise into strips 1 inch wide and set them aside. Wrap the beets in aluminum foil in one package, and bake them until tender, about one hour. Unwrap the beets, let them cool, then peel them and cut them into ¼-inch slices.

Put the vinegar, garlic, caraway seeds and salt into a small non-reactive saucepan and bring the liquid to a boil. Reduce the liquid by half and set it aside.

Pour 2 tablespoons of water into a large skillet and add the beet greens. Cover the pan and bring the water to a boil, then uncover the pan and cook the greens until they are wilted—about one minute. Pour out any remaining liquid. Add the vinegar mixture and the baked beets, and toss the beets until they are heated through. Serve immediately.

■ FRESH WAYS WITH VEGETABLES

## Brussels Sprouts with Walnuts

*After the base of a Brussels sprout has been shaved off and any yellow or wilted leaves have been removed, cut a shallow cross in the base so that it will cook as quickly as the tender leaves.* ◆●

**To serve 4 to 6**

| | |
|---|---|
| 1 pound Brussels sprouts, | Freshly ground black pepper |
|    trimmed | 1 cup coarsely chopped |
| ¼ cup butter |    walnuts |
| 1 tablespoon flour | ½ cup fresh white-bread |
| ¾ cup chicken stock |    crumbs |
| 2 teaspoons salt | |

Fill a heavy 2- to 3-quart saucepan halfway with water, add a little salt, and bring the water to a boil over high heat. Drop in the Brussels sprouts and boil, uncovered, for five minutes, or until they are barely tender when tested with the tip of a knife. Drain the sprouts in a colander, pouring off the water from the pan, refresh them under cold running water for a few moments to stop the cooking and set their color, and drain them again.

Melt 2 tablespoons of the butter in the saucepan over moderate

heat, and stir in the flour. Slowly pour in the stock and bring to a boil, stirring constantly with a whisk or a wooden spoon until this sauce thickens slightly. Sprinkle with the salt and a few grindings of pepper; taste for seasoning. Stir in the sprouts and walnuts, reduce the heat to low, cover the pan partway, and simmer for 10 minutes.

In a small skillet, melt the remaining 2 tablespoons of butter over moderate heat. Sprinkle in the crumbs and stir for three or four minutes, until they are golden brown.

Transfer the Brussels sprouts and walnuts with their sauce to a heated serving bowl, and sprinkle with the browned bread crumbs. Serve the sprouts at once.

■ AMERICAN COOKING: THE MELTING POT

## Red Cabbage Tart

**To serve 6**

| | |
|---|---|
| 6 tablespoons red-wine vinegar | 6 prunes, pitted and chopped coarse |
| One 2-pound red cabbage | 1/8 teaspoon ground cloves |
| 2 tablespoons safflower oil | 1 tablespoon butter, cut into bits |
| 1 large onion, chopped fine | |
| 1/4 teaspoon salt | 6 lemon slices for garnish |

Pour 6 quarts of water and 1/4 cup of the vinegar into a large nonreactive pot; bring the liquid to a boil. Remove 10 outer leaves from the cabbage, and put them in the boiling water. When the water returns to a boil, reduce the heat to moderate, and simmer the leaves until they are tender—10 to 15 minutes. Drain the leaves and refresh them in a colander by running cold water over them until they are cool.

While the leaves are simmering, quarter, core and slice thin— or shred—the remaining cabbage. In a heavy nonreactive 6- to 8-quart flameproof casserole, heat the oil over moderate heat. Add the onion and cook, stirring frequently, for about five minutes or until it is soft. Stir in the sliced cabbage and the salt. Reduce the heat to low, cover, and simmer for about 15 minutes. Stir in the prunes and cloves. Continue cooking, still covered, until the cabbage and prunes are very soft—about 15 minutes more. Stir in the remaining 2 tablespoons of vinegar.

Preheat the oven to 350° F. With a pastry brush, lightly coat the inside of an 8- or 9-inch earthenware or glass pie dish with melted or softened butter. Arrange all but two or three of the cabbage leaves in the bottom of the dish, with their stem ends pointing outward; allow the stem ends to hang over the edge of the dish somewhat. Mound the cabbage-and-prune mixture in the center, and fold the stem ends securely over the top. Cover the top with the remaining leaves. Dot the top with the butter bits.

Cover the dish with foil and bake the tart until it is tender and all of the moisture has been absorbed—45 minutes to one hour. Cut each lemon slice halfway through, and twist to form a spiral. Serve the tart cut into wedges, garnished with the lemon spirals.

■ FRESH WAYS WITH VEGETABLES

RED CABBAGE TART

## Gingered Carrots

**To serve 6**

| | |
|---|---|
| 2 pounds carrots, sliced | 1 teaspoon ground ginger |
| 6 tablespoons butter, cut into bits | ½ teaspoon salt |
| | Freshly ground black pepper |

In a heavy 2- to 3-quart saucepan, combine the carrots with 2 cups of lightly salted water. Bring the water to a boil over moderately high heat, then cover, reduce the heat, and simmer the carrots for 15 minutes, until they are soft. Drain the carrots well, and purée them in a food mill, blender or food processor. Return the purée to the saucepan. Add the butter, ginger, salt and a grinding of pepper. Stirring frequently, cook over low heat until the carrots are piping hot.

■ GREAT DINNERS FROM LIFE

## Marbled Carrot and Zucchini Soufflé

**To serve 12 as a side dish, 6 as a main dish**

| | |
|---|---|
| 2 pounds large carrots, cut into ¼-inch slices | 1 cup freshly grated Romano cheese |
| 2 onions, chopped coarse, plus ¼ cup finely chopped onion | ½ cup milk |
| | Freshly ground black pepper |
| 1 tablespoon butter | 1 teaspoon sugar |
| 1½ pounds zucchini, halved lengthwise, seeded and grated | 1 egg, separated, plus 4 egg whites |

With a pastry brush, lightly coat the bottom and sides of a 2-quart soufflé dish with melted or softened butter. Sprinkle in a little flour and shake the dish to distribute it evenly; tap out the excess. Put the dish in the refrigerator.

Pour enough water into a saucepan to fill it to a depth of about 1 inch. Put in a vegetable steamer and place the carrots in it, with the coarsely chopped onions over them. Cover the pan, bring the water to a boil, and steam the vegetables until the carrots are very soft, about 20 minutes.

Meanwhile, melt the butter in a heavy 8- to 10-inch skillet over high heat. Add the finely chopped onion, then the zucchini. Cook the mixture, stirring frequently, until all of the liquid evapo-

rates—five to seven minutes. Transfer the mixture to a bowl. Stir in ⅓ cup of the cheese, ¼ cup of the milk and a generous grinding of pepper. Set the bowl aside.

Transfer the carrot mixture to a food processor, and process it for 30 seconds, stopping once to scrape down the sides with a rubber spatula. Pour in the remaining ¼ cup of milk and the sugar, and process for one minute to form a smooth purée. Scrape the purée into a large bowl; add the egg yolk, ½ cup of the cheese and some pepper, and mix well.

Preheat the oven to 450° F. In a large mixing bowl, beat the egg whites with a wire whisk or a rotary or electric beater just until soft peaks form on the beater when it is lifted from the bowl. Do not overbeat the egg whites.

With a clean rubber spatula, scoop ½ cup or so of the whites over the carrots, and fold in the whites and thus lighten the carrot mixture. Fold another scoop of the whites into the zucchini mixture and blend well. Gently fold half of the remaining whites into the carrot mixture; the whites should not be completely incorporated. Repeat the process with the remaining egg whites and the zucchini mixture.

Remove the soufflé dish from the refrigerator. Pour the two vegetable mixtures simultaneously into opposite sides of the dish. Place a spoon in the middle of the zucchini mixture, and draw the spoon three-quarters of the way around the soufflé to achieve a marbled effect. Sprinkle the remaining cheese over the top. Bake the soufflé for 45 minutes; the top should be golden brown and puffed. Serve immediately.

■ FRESH WAYS WITH VEGETABLES

## Cauliflower with Garlic and Sesame Seeds

**To serve 4**

| | |
|---|---|
| 1 cauliflower, broken into small florets | seeds in their husks |
| | Cayenne pepper |
| ¼ cup vegetable oil | Freshly ground black pepper |
| 4 garlic cloves, chopped fine | Salt |
| 1½ tablespoons sesame | |

In a large, heavy saucepan, bring 3 quarts of lightly salted water to a boil over high heat. Add the cauliflower, return the water to a boil, then boil the cauliflower for one to one and a half minutes or until it is tender but still somewhat crisp. Drain the cauliflower in a colander and run cold water over it for a few moments to stop the cooking. Drain the florets again, then pat them dry with paper towels.

In a 10- to 12-inch skillet, heat the oil over moderate heat. Add the garlic and stir until it turns light brown. Add the sesame seeds and continue stirring until they begin to pop, then add the cauliflower. Stir the florets gently until they are evenly coated with sesame seeds. Add a pinch of cayenne, a generous grinding of black pepper and about ¼ teaspoon salt, and stir once more. Serve the cauliflower hot.

■ VEGETABLE MENUS

MARBLED CARROT AND ZUCCHINI SOUFFLÉ

## Braised Celery with Almonds

**To serve 6 to 8**

| | |
|---|---|
| 2 bunches celery | 3 tablespoons butter |
| 4 parsley sprigs | 3 tablespoons flour |
| 1 small bay leaf | ½ cup heavy cream |
| 2 cups chicken stock | ¼ cup slivered blanched |
| Salt | almonds, toasted in a 350°F. |
| Freshly ground white pepper | oven for 5 minutes |

Remove the green leaves from the celery and wrap them in cheesecloth with the parsley and bay leaf to make a bouquet garni. Cut the celery ribs in half lengthwise, then crosswise into 1-inch lengths. Drop them into a 2- to 3-quart saucepan, add the bouquet garni, chicken stock, 1 teaspoon of salt and ⅛ teaspoon of white pepper, and bring to a boil over high heat. Cover the pan, reduce the heat to low, and simmer for 15 minutes, until the celery is tender but still crisp. With a slotted spoon, transfer the celery to a heated platter and drape with foil to keep it warm.

Pour the contents of the pan through a fine sieve, discarding the bouquet garni and reserving 1 cup of cooking liquid. In a 1- tc 1½-quart saucepan, melt the butter over moderate heat, stir in the flour and, stirring constantly with a wire whisk, pour in the cooking liquid and the cream in a slow, thin stream. Cook over high heat until the sauce comes to a boil and thickens heavily. Reduce the heat, and simmer for three minutes. Taste for seasoning, and pour over the celery. Scatter the almonds on top.

■ AMERICAN COOKING: SOUTHERN STYLE

## Summer Succotash

**To serve 6**

| | |
|---|---|
| 2 cups fresh corn kernels or | ¼ cup butter |
| frozen corn kernels, defrosted | 1 teaspoon sugar |
| 1 pound green beans, trimmed | Salt |
| and cut diagonally into | Freshly ground black pepper |
| 1-inch lengths | 1 cup heavy cream |

In a heavy 3- to 4-quart saucepan, bring 1 quart of lightly salted water to a boil over high heat. Drop in the corn and beans, and cook, uncovered, for three or four minutes, until they are tender but still crisp. Drain, then run cold water over the vegetables to stop their cooking and set their color. Drain again and spread the vegetables on paper towels to dry.

In a heavy 10-inch skillet, melt the butter over moderate heat. When the foam begins to subside, add the corn and beans and, stirring constantly, cook for one minute to heat them through. Add the sugar, ½ teaspoon of salt and ¼ teaspoon of pepper, then pour in ¼ cup of the cream and stir over moderate heat until the cream has almost but not quite cooked away. Pour in and boil down the remaining cream, ¼ cup at a time. Taste for seasoning and serve the succotash from a heated bowl.

■ AMERICAN COOKING: NEW ENGLAND

## Corn Pudding with Chilies and Cheese

**To serve 4**

| | |
|---|---|
| ¾ pound Monterey Jack or | defrosted |
| Danish Havarti cheese | 3 fresh serrano chilies, |
| 1 cup yellow cornmeal | roasted, peeled, seeded |
| ½ teaspoon baking powder | and diced |
| ¾ teaspoon baking soda | 4 scallions, trimmed and |
| ½ teaspoon salt | sliced thin |
| 2 eggs | 2¼ cups buttermilk |
| 2 cups fresh corn kernels | 2 tablespoons butter |
| or frozen corn kernels, | |

Place an 8-inch square baking dish in a cold oven, and set the temperature to 425°F. Cut enough cheese into ¼-inch dice to measure 1 cup, and grate the rest of the cheese; set aside.

In a large mixing bowl, combine the cornmeal, baking powder, baking soda and salt. Place the eggs in a medium-sized bowl, beat them lightly, then add the diced cheese, corn, chilies, scallions and buttermilk. Remove the baking dish from the oven, and melt the butter in it, rotating it until evenly coated. Immediately, pour the egg mixture into the cornmeal mixture, stirring just until combined. (Do not beat.) Scrape this mixture into the hot baking dish. Strew the grated cheese on top, then bake in the upper third of the oven for about 25 minutes or until golden on top, but slightly soft in the center. Serve the pudding hot.

■ MEXICAN MENUS

## Eggplant Fans with Tomatoes

**To serve 4**

| | |
|---|---|
| 2 small eggplants, 4 to 5 | 1 teaspoon crumbled |
| inches long, stems | dried oregano |
| removed, halved lengthwise | Salt |
| 4 small tomatoes, sliced thin | Freshly ground black pepper |
| ¼ cup olive oil | 4 watercress sprigs for |
| 1 tablespoon chopped fresh | garnish |
| oregano leaves or | |

Preheat the oven to 450°F. Cut two sheets of aluminum foil about 15 inches long. Generously oil each of them on one side.

Place the eggplant halves cut side down. Leaving an inch at the stem end whole and uncut, slice each half lengthwise into six to eight thin strips. Place two halves, cut side down, on each sheet of oiled foil. Insert slices of tomato into the slits in the eggplant halves and fan out the strips at the base. Sprinkle ¼ cup olive oil over the eggplant fans, and season them with the oregano and salt and pepper to taste. Fold the foil over the eggplant, twisting the edges of the foil together. Place the packages on a baking sheet, set them on the lowest rack of the oven and bake them for 35 to 45 minutes or until tender and cooked through.

To serve, set the eggplant fans on heated dinner plates and garnish with watercress sprigs, if you like.

■ CHICKEN AND GAME HEN MENUS

## Eggplant Parmesan

**To serve 4**

| | |
|---|---|
| 1½ pounds eggplant, peeled and cut crosswise into ½-inch slices | 2 cups tomato sauce (Index/Glossary) |
| Salt | ½ pound mozzarella cheese, sliced thin |
| ½ cup flour | ½ cup freshly grated Parmesan cheese |
| ¼ to ½ cup olive oil | |

Preheat the oven to 400° F. With a pastry brush, coat the inside of a shallow 1½- to 2-quart baking-serving dish with some olive oil.

Sprinkle both sides of the eggplant slices with salt to draw out their bitter juices, and put them in one layer between paper towels; weight them with a heavy casserole or a cutting board with canned food on top. After 20 to 30 minutes, pat the eggplant dry with paper towels.

Spread the flour on wax paper. In a heavy 10- to 12-inch skillet, heat ¼ cup of olive oil. Dip a few eggplant slices at a time into the flour to coat both sides; tap off the excess. Brown the slices, working quickly to prevent them from absorbing too much oil. If the oil cooks away, add more by the spoonful. As they brown, transfer the slices to paper towels to drain.

Pour a layer of tomato sauce ¼ inch deep into the prepared dish. Spread drained eggplant slices over the sauce, top them with a layer of mozzarella cheese, and sprinkle part of the grated Parmesan cheese over it. Repeat with one or two more layers, being sure to finish with layers of tomato sauce, mozzarella and Parmesan. Cover the dish snugly with aluminum foil and bake for 20 minutes. Remove the foil and bake, uncovered, for 10 minutes longer. If you like, put the dish under a hot broiler for about 30 seconds to brown the cheese on top. Serve the eggplant directly from the baking dish.

■ THE COOKING OF ITALY

## Ratatouille

**To serve 6 to 8**

| | |
|---|---|
| 3 pounds tomatoes | 1-inch squares |
| Salt | 2½ cups thinly sliced onions |
| 1½ to 2 pounds eggplant, peeled and cut crosswise into ¾-inch slices | ½ cup finely chopped fresh parsley leaves |
| 1½ pounds zucchini, unpeeled, cut into ½-inch slices | 1 tablespoon finely chopped fresh basil leaves or 2 teaspoons crumbled dried basil |
| ¼ to ½ cup olive oil | 2 teaspoons finely chopped garlic |
| 2 green peppers, seeded, deribbed and cut into | Freshly ground black pepper |

Drop a few tomatoes at a time into boiling water to blanch them for 30 seconds or so, and thus facilitate peeling them. Peel the tomatoes, cut them into quarters, and cut away the pulp and seeds, leaving only the shells. Cut the shells into ½-inch-wide strips and drain on paper towels. Lightly salt the eggplant and zucchini slices, spread them in one layer between paper towels, and weight them with heavy platters or a cutting board with canned food on top of it. After 20 to 30 minutes, dry the eggplant and zucchini with fresh paper towels.

In a heavy 10- to 12-inch skillet, heat ¼ cup of olive oil over moderately high heat, and brown the eggplant slices for a minute or two on each side, working quickly to prevent them from soaking up too much oil. Do not worry if they brown unevenly. As they brown, drain them on paper towels.

In the same skillet, lightly brown first the zucchini, then the peppers and finally the onions, adding more oil whenever necessary. Drain the zucchini and peppers on paper towels, but transfer the onions to a plate.

With a fork, stir the parsley, basil and garlic together in a small bowl. Pour 1 tablespoon of the oil remaining in the skillet into a heavy 4- to 5-quart casserole. Spread one third of the eggplant slices on the bottom, sprinkle with 1 teaspoon of the herb and garlic mixture, and season with salt and pepper. Arrange successive layers with half of the zucchini, half of the peppers, half of the onions and half of the tomatoes—sprinkling herbs, salt and pepper on each layer. Repeat the layers. Finish with a layer of the remaining eggplant. Sprinkle with the remaining parsley mixture, salt and pepper, and pour in the oil remaining in the skillet.

Over moderately high heat, bring the casserole to a boil. Cover it and reduce the heat to low. Every seven or eight minutes, use a bulb baster to draw up the liquid that accumulates in the casserole and transfer it to a small saucepan. In 20 to 30 minutes, when the vegetables are barely tender, remove the casserole from the heat. Boil the liquid in the saucepan for a few minutes to reduce it to about 2 tablespoons of glaze, and pour it into the casserole. Serve the *ratatouille* directly from the casserole, either hot or cold.

■ THE COOKING OF PROVINCIAL FRANCE

## Braised Endive

**To serve 6**

| | |
|---|---|
| 6 Belgian endives, trimmed and halved lengthwise | white pepper |
| ¼ cup butter | 1 tablespoon fresh lemon juice |
| 1 teaspoon salt | 2 tablespoons water |
| ⅛ teaspoon freshly ground | |

In a heavy 10- to 12-inch skillet, bring 1 inch of water to a boil. Add the endive halves and reduce the heat to low. Parboil the endives for 10 minutes, then drain them and pat them dry.

Dry the skillet and in it melt the butter. Add the endives, cut side down, and brown them for about two minutes. Sprinkle in the salt, white pepper, lemon juice and 2 tablespoons of water. Cover the skillet and cook the endives over very low heat for about 15 minutes or until tender, adding more water if needed.

■ GREAT DINNERS FROM LIFE

water. Bring the liquid to a boil, reduce the heat to low, and simmer for 10 minutes. Put the fennel quarters, cut side down, into the skillet. Turning the quarters once or twice with a slotted spoon, cook them for about 15 minutes or until tender. Lift them onto a deep platter, and cover them with foil to keep them warm.

To make the sauce, first strain the cooking liquid into a saucepan; discard the solids. Boil over high heat until the liquid is reduced to 1 cup—about 10 minutes. Drain off the liquid that has accumulated around the fennel. Arrange the fennel on the orange slices, and pour the reduced sauce over the quarters. Garnish the dish with feathery fennel tops.

■ FRESH WAYS WITH VEGETABLES

## Fiddlehead Greens with Creamy Hollandaise

*Although the mature plant—called "ostrich fern"—is poisonous, the tightly curled young fronds known as fiddleheads are edible and are counted a delicacy. During a brief spring season, they are available fresh; gourmet markets sell frozen fiddleheads year-round. The taste of these greens is slightly bitter—a wonderful foil for either sweet butter or creamy hollandaise.* ❧

**To serve 4**

| | |
|---|---|
| ³/₄ cup unsalted butter, cut into ¹/₂-inch bits, plus 1 tablespoon butter | lemon juice |
| | ¹/₂ teaspoon salt |
| 3 egg yolks | ¹/₈ teaspoon freshly ground white pepper |
| 1 tablespoon heavy cream | 1 pound fiddlehead greens, trimmed and washed well |
| 2 tablespoons fresh | |

Prepare the sauce by first melting the butter bits over moderate heat in a heavy small skillet, stirring so that the butter melts without browning. Set the butter aside.

Working quickly, drop the egg yolks into a 1¹/₂- to 2-quart nonreactive saucepan. Beat the yolks with a wire whisk until they are so thick that the bottom of the pan shows through when the whisk is drawn across it. Place the pan over very low heat, add the 1 tablespoon of butter, and beat until the mixture clings lightly to the whisk.

Remove the pan from the heat and beat in the cream at once. Still stirring constantly with the whisk, add the melted butter by the teaspoonful. After you have added about ¹/₄ cup of the butter and the sauce begins to thicken, pour in the remaining melted butter in a slow, thin stream, whisking constantly. The finished sauce should be thick and glossy. Beat in the lemon juice, taste and season with the salt and pepper. Set aside off the heat.

Meanwhile bring a large pot of lightly salted water to a boil. Add the greens and boil them for five minutes or until they are barely tender and show only slight resistance when pierced with the point of a small, sharp knife. Drain the greens and pat them dry with paper towels.

To serve, mound the greens on a heated platter. Pour the hollandaise into a sauceboat and present it separately.

■ AMERICAN COOKING: NEW ENGLAND

FENNEL WITH ORANGE SLICES

## Fennel with Orange Slices

**To serve 6**

| | |
|---|---|
| 1 orange | 1 onion, sliced |
| 3 fennel heads, stems cut into 2-inch pieces, bulbs quartered lengthwise, feathery green tops reserved for garnish | 1 bay leaf |
| | ¹/₄ teaspoon salt |
| | Freshly ground black pepper |
| | 4 cups water |

With a small, sharp knife, cut the colored peel, or zest, from the orange; set aside. Remove the white pith and cut the flesh crosswise into rounds ¹/₄ inch thick.

In an 8- to 10-inch skillet, combine the orange peel, fennel stems, onion, bay leaf, salt, a generous grinding of pepper and the

BATTER-FRIED MUSHROOMS

## Jícama with Green Beans

*The kitchen tool called a "lemon zester" was specially designed to pare off the colored peel, or zest, of the lemon without including any of the bitter white pith beneath it. You can, of course, also accomplish that feat by careful use of a sharp knife or a vegetable parer.* ❧

**To serve 4**

| | |
|---|---|
| ¾ **pound jícama, peeled and cut into julienne strips matching the size of the beans** | **trimmed** |
| | **3 tablespoons butter** |
| | **Salt** |
| ¾ **pound green beans,** | **Long lemon peel strips, cut into thin strands** |

Bring 1½ to 2 quarts of lightly salted water to a boil in a large saucepan over high heat. Drop in the jícama and—after the water returns to the boil—cook, uncovered, for one minute. Lift out the strips of jícama with a slotted spoon. Drain them in a colander, run cold water over them for a few seconds to stop the cooking, and drain them again.

Plunge the beans into the same pan of boiling water. Boil until they are barely tender—three to four minutes if they are young, otherwise up to 10 minutes. Drain them and refresh them under running cold water for a few seconds to stop the cooking and set their color. Drain them again.

Melt the butter in a 10- to 12-inch skillet over moderate heat, and sauté the beans and the jícama until they are heated through —about five minutes. Add salt to taste and the lemon zest, and toss the ingredients together. Serve at once from a heated bowl.

■ **AMERICAN REGIONAL MENUS**

## Batter-fried Mushrooms

*A sheath of batter protects mushrooms—like other foods—from the high temperatures used for deep frying. The range of batter coatings is broad indeed. Most are based on flour and liquid, which can be water, milk, wine, citrus juice, or the beer used in this recipe. Beer imparts a faintly bitter tang and aerates the batter by making it ferment slightly; stir it together with the flour only long enough to eliminate lumps. Excessive stirring of a beer-based batter will break down its bubbles. Letting the batter rest before using it allows fermentation to take place and also ensures the batter's tenderness by allowing the gluten in the flour to relax.* ❧

**To serve 4**

| | |
|---|---|
| **1 cup flour** | **2 dozen mushrooms, each about 2 inches across, trimmed** |
| **Vegetable oil** | |
| **1 cup beer, at room temperature** | |
| | **Curly-leaf lettuce for garnish** |
| **2 egg whites** | **Salt** |

Sift the flour into a deep bowl, and make a well in the center. Pour 1 tablespoon of oil into the well. Slowly pour the beer into the well. Stirring gently, gradually incorporate the flour into the beer. Keep stirring until the mixture is smooth, but do not beat or over-mix or the leavening effect of the beer will be lost. Set the batter

aside, uncovered, to rest at room temperature for three hours before using.

Preheat the oven to the lowest possible setting. Line a large shallow baking dish or a jelly-roll pan with a double thickness of paper towels, and place the dish in the oven. Pour vegetable oil into a deep fryer or large heavy saucepan to a depth of 2 to 3 inches. Heat the oil until it registers 375°F. on a deep-frying thermometer.

With a wire whisk or a rotary or electric beater, beat the egg whites until they form soft peaks when the beater is lifted. Gently fold the egg whites into the batter.

One at a time, pick up the mushrooms with tongs or a slotted spoon, immerse them in the batter and, when they are well coated on all sides, drop them into the hot oil. Deep-fry four or five mushrooms at a time for about four minutes, turning them occasionally until they are delicately and evenly browned. As they brown, transfer the mushrooms to the lined pan and keep them warm in the oven while you fry the rest.

Arrange the fried mushrooms on a heated platter, garnish them with lettuce, if you like, and sprinkle them lightly with salt just before serving.

■ **AMERICAN COOKING: THE EASTERN HEARTLAND**

## Mushrooms with Madeira

*Although shiitake mushrooms are specified in this recipe, any dried wild mushrooms—cèpes or morels, for example—can be substituted. Instead of Madeira, you might prefer to use sherry.* ❧

**Serves 4**

| | |
|---|---|
| **1 tablespoon safflower oil** | **½ cup Madeira wine** |
| **1 pound fresh button mushrooms, trimmed and quartered** | **2 tomatoes, peeled, seeded and chopped** |
| **1 shallot, chopped fine** | **½ teaspoon crumbled dried thyme** |
| **1 ounce dried shiitake mushrooms, soaked in warm water for 1 hour, squeezed dry, stems discarded, caps chopped fine and 1 tablespoon of the soaking liquid reserved** | **½ teaspoon salt** |
| | **Freshly ground black pepper** |
| | **1 teaspoon cornstarch, dissolved in the reserved mushroom-soaking liquid** |
| | **1 tablespoon chopped fresh parsley leaves for garnish** |
| **1 garlic clove, chopped fine** | |

Heat the oil in a heavy 10- to 12-inch skillet over moderately high heat. Sauté the mushroom quarters for one minute, then add the shallot and cook, stirring constantly, for 30 seconds. Add the shiitake mushrooms and garlic, and cook for one minute. Stir in the Madeira, tomatoes, thyme, salt and a generous grinding of pepper. Cook until the mushroom quarters have softened—three to four minutes. Stir in the cornstarch mixture, and cook this stew until it thickens slightly—one to two minutes. Transfer the stew to a heated serving dish and sprinkle it with parsley. Serve at once.

■ **FRESH WAYS WITH VEGETABLES**

## Spiced Steamed Okra

*An African plant, brought to the United States by slaves in the 18th century, okra has a tapered, dark-green seed pod with a tangy taste and blends well with other vegetables. When okra is cooked, it exudes a dense liquid that thickens stews such as this one and Louisiana's famous Creole gumbos. When buying okra, look for young, firm pods that will snap when bent.* ❖●

**To serve 6**

| | |
|---|---|
| ½ **pound bacon slices, halved crosswise** | **into ½-inch slices** |
| 1½ **cups coarsely chopped onions** | 3 **large tomatoes, peeled, seeded and chopped** |
| 1 **cup coarsely chopped green peppers** | 3 **small dried hot red chilies, stemmed, seeded and crumbled** |
| 1½ **pounds okra, scraped lightly, stems removed, cut** | 1 **teaspoon salt** |

Fry the bacon in a heavy 12-inch skillet set over moderate heat, turning the pieces frequently with tongs until they are crisp and brown and render all of their fat. Transfer the bacon to paper towels to drain.

Pour off all but about ¼ cup of fat from the skillet and discard; add the onions and green peppers. Stirring frequently, cook them for about five minutes or until soft but not browned.

Add the okra and, still stirring from time to time, cook uncovered for about 15 minutes. When the okra is tender, add the tomatoes, chilies and salt; reduce the heat to low, cover, and simmer the mixture for 10 minutes. Taste for seasoning, then mound the okra in a heated serving bowl and sprinkle the bacon pieces on top. Serve at once.

■ AMERICAN COOKING: CREOLE AND ACADIAN COOKING

## Parsnip Purée

**To serve 4**

| | |
|---|---|
| 2 **tablespoons unsalted butter** | 1 **cup chicken or vegetable stock** |
| 1¾ **pounds parsnips, cut into ¼-inch slices** | 1 **tablespoon prepared horseradish** |
| 1 **large tart green apple, peeled, cored and cut into ¼-inch wedges** | **Freshly ground white pepper** |

In a heavy 8- to 10-inch skillet, melt 1 tablespoon of the butter over moderately low heat. Add the parsnips and apple, and pour the stock over them. Cover the pan and cook until the parsnips are soft—30 to 35 minutes.

Purée the parsnips, apple and any remaining cooking liquid in a food processor or food mill. Place the mixture in a saucepan and warm it over moderately low heat. Add the remaining tablespoon of butter, the horseradish and a generous grinding of pepper, and stir the purée vigorously. Transfer to a warmed serving bowl, and serve the dish immediately.

■ FRESH WAY WITH VEGETABLES

## Minted Green Peas with Cucumbers

**To serve 6**

| | |
|---|---|
| 2 **cups freshly shelled peas, or 2 cups frozen peas, defrosted** | 2 **tablespoons finely chopped fresh mint leaves or 2 teaspoons crumbled dried mint** |
| 2 **cucumbers** | ¼ **teaspoon salt** |
| ½ **cup chicken or vegetable stock** | **Freshly ground black pepper** |

Parboil fresh peas for three or four minutes, until they are barely tender. Drain them, then refresh them under cold running water for a few moments to stop the cooking and set their color. Drain the peas again and set them aside. (Frozen peas do not need parboiling.)

If the cucumbers have been waxed, peel them; if they have not, leave the skins on. Slice the cucumbers in half lengthwise, and remove the seeds with a spoon or a melon baller. Cut the cucumbers on the diagonal into ¼-inch-thick slices. Bring a large saucepan full of water to a boil, and plunge the cucumbers into it. Bring the water back to a boil, and cook the cucumbers until they are barely tender—about two minutes. Drain the cucumbers and set them aside.

Bring the stock to a boil in a 2- to 3-quart saucepan. Reduce the heat to moderate, then add the peas and cucumbers. Cook, stirring occasionally, until both vegetables are heated through—about five minutes. Stir in the mint, salt and a generous grinding of pepper. Transfer the vegetables to a warmed dish and serve them immediately.

■ FRESH WAYS WITH VEGETABLES

## Snow Peas and Jícama

**To serve 4**

| | |
|---|---|
| 1 **tablespoon olive oil** | ¼- **inch julienne strips** |
| ¾ **pound snow peas, trimmed and strings removed** | **Salt** |
| ¼ **pound jícama, cut into** | **Freshly ground black pepper** |
| | 1 **teaspoon fresh lime juice** |

In a 10-inch wok or 8- to 10-inch skillet, heat the oil over high heat. When it is very hot but not smoking, add the snow peas and jícama. Stirring constantly with a wooden spatula, cook for five or six minutes, until the peas and jícama strips are just tender to the bite. Taste for seasoning and add salt and pepper to taste. Transfer the vegetables to a heated bowl, pour the lime juice over them and toss well before serving.

■ FISH AND SHELLFISH MENUS

## Onions Stuffed with Spinach and Pine Nuts

**To serve 6**

| | |
|---|---|
| 6 large sweet onions | 1/2 cup plain yogurt |
| 1/2 teaspoon safflower oil | 1/4 cup pine nuts, toasted in a |
| 1 garlic clove, chopped fine | 350°F. oven for 5 minutes |
| 1 pound spinach, stemmed, | 1 tablespoon grated |
| washed and chopped | orange peel |
| coarse | 1/8 teaspoon freshly |
| 1/4 teaspoon salt | grated nutmeg |
| 1/4 cup dried currants, soaked | 2 tablespoons fresh whole- |
| in hot water for 10 minutes | wheat bread crumbs |
| and drained | |

Level the bottoms of the onions by trimming the root ends, taking care not to remove too much, so that the onions do not lose their shape while cooking. Discard the ends and peel the onions. Cut a slice 1/2 inch thick off the top of each onion and set the tops aside. With a melon baller or a grapefruit spoon, hollow the onions, forming shells with walls about 1/2 inch thick. Reserve the scooped-out centers.

Pour enough water into a saucepan to come about 1 inch up the side of the pan. Set a vegetable steamer in the pan, and place the onion shells in the steamer. Bring the water to a boil, cover the pan, and steam the onions until the shells are tender when pierced with the tip of a sharp knife—10 to 15 minutes. Set the shells aside.

Chop the onion tops and centers fine. In a heavy 10- to 12-inch skillet, heat the oil over moderately low heat. Add the chopped onion and garlic, and cook, stirring occasionally, for five minutes or until the onion is soft but not brown.

Add the spinach, cover the skillet, and cook until the spinach wilts—about one minute. Uncover the skillet, add the salt, and cook the mixture, stirring occasionally, for five minutes, until all of the liquid evaporates. Transfer the onion-spinach mixture to a large bowl and let it cool.

Preheat the oven to 350°F. Add the currants to the onion-spinach mixture. Mix in the yogurt, pine nuts, orange peel and nutmeg. Pour out any liquid that has accumulated in the onion shells, and spoon the stuffing into them.

Spread the remaining stuffing on the bottom of a small baking dish; set the filled onion shells on the stuffing. Sprinkle the bread crumbs over the stuffed onions, and bake for 20 to 25 minutes.

Set the onions under the broiler turned to its highest setting for just long enough to crisp the bread crumbs. Serve the onions with stuffing from the bottom of the dish spooned alongside each portion, if you like.

■ FRESH WAYS WITH VEGETABLES

## Peas à la Française

**To serve 8**

| | |
|---|---|
| 3 cups freshly shelled small | 1/4 teaspoon crumbled dried |
| peas, or 3 cups frozen | chervil |
| peas, defrosted | 1/4 teaspoon crumbled dried |
| 24 tiny white onions, peeled | thyme |
| to about 1/2 inch across | 1 1/2 teaspoons salt |
| 1/4 cup butter, cut into bits | Freshly ground black pepper |
| 1 tablespoon sugar | 2 cups thinly sliced lettuce |

Parboil fresh peas, if you are using them, for three to four minutes or until they are barely tender to the bite. Drain the peas, then refresh them by running cold water over them to stop the cooking and set their color. Drain the peas again and set them aside. (Frozen peas do not need parboiling.)

Meanwhile, parboil the onions for three or four minutes or until they are tender when pierced deeply with the tip of a sharp knife. Drain them, reserving 1/4 cup of their cooking liquid.

In a heavy 3- to 4-quart saucepan, melt the butter bits over moderate heat. Add the peas, onions, reserved onion-cooking liquid, sugar, chervil, thyme, salt and a few grindings of pepper. Toss the vegetables to blend them with the seasonings. Add the lettuce and stir it in gently. Cover the pan and cook over moderate heat for five minutes, until the peas and onions are heated through. Serve from a heated bowl.

■ GREAT DINNERS FROM LIFE

## Mashed Potatoes with Cabbage

*Both the Irish and the Scots claim this concoction as native fare, both calling it "colcannon," which translates from the Gaelic literally as "white-headed kale" or "cabbage."* ◆■

**To serve 4 to 6**

| | |
|---|---|
| 4 cups thinly sliced green | lengthwise into halves |
| cabbage | and crosswise into |
| 4 tablespoons butter | 1/8-inch slices |
| 6 boiling potatoes, peeled and | Salt |
| quartered | Freshly ground black pepper |
| 3/4 to 1 cup tepid milk (100°F.) | 1 tablespoon finely chopped |
| 6 scallions, including 2 inches | fresh parsley leaves |
| of green tops, cut | |

Place the cabbage in a saucepan, pour in enough water to cover it completely, and bring to a boil. Boil rapidly, uncovered, for 10 minutes, then drain it well in a colander. In a heavy 8- to 10-inch skillet, melt 2 tablespoons of the butter over moderate heat. When the foam begins to subside, add the cabbage, and stir constantly for a minute or two. Cover and set aside off the heat.

Meanwhile, drop the quartered potatoes into enough lightly salted boiling water to cover them by 2 inches, and boil briskly, uncovered, until they are tender but not falling apart—about 10 minutes. Drain the potatoes and return them to the pan. Slide the pan back and forth over low heat until they are dry and mealy.

Then mash them to a smooth purée with a fork, a potato ricer or an electric mixer. Beat the remaining 2 tablespoons of butter into them. Then beat in up to 1 cup of milk, 2 tablespoons at a time, using as much as necessary to make a purée still thick enough to hold its shape in a spoon.

Stir in the cabbage and the scallions, and add salt and pepper to taste. Transfer the mixture to a heated serving bowl, sprinkle with parsley, and serve at once.

■ THE COOKING OF THE BRITISH ISLES

## Crock-roasted Potatoes

**To serve 4**

| | |
|---|---|
| 8 to 12 small russet potatoes, scrubbed but not peeled | (optional) |
| 2 garlic cloves, unpeeled | ¼ cup butter, cut into bits |

Arrange the potatoes in a single layer in a very heavy casserole or skillet equipped with a tight-fitting lid. Add the garlic, if you are using it. Fit a sheet of aluminum foil or baking parchment over the potatoes, extending it slightly beyond the rim of the casserole all around, then set the lid in place. Put the casserole over low heat, using a heat diffuser on the burner to ensure slow, even heat. Roast the potatoes for 15 minutes. Lift the lid and the foil or baking parchment, and use metal tongs to turn the potatoes. Do not puncture them. Cover and cook until the potatoes are very tender, about 30 minutes. Divide the potatoes among individual plates and dot them with butter before serving them.

■ FRENCH REGIONAL MENUS

## Danish Caramelized Potatoes

**To serve 8**

| | |
|---|---|
| 24 small new potatoes | ½ cup unsalted butter, melted |
| ½ cup sugar | |

Drop the potatoes, unpeeled, into a pan of boiling water and cook for 15 to 20 minutes, or until they offer no resistance when pierced with a knife. Let them cool slightly; then peel them.

Melt the sugar in a heavy 10- to 12-inch skillet over low heat. Cook slowly for three to five minutes, until the sugar turns to a light-brown caramel. Stir constantly with a wooden spoon and watch the sugar closely; the syrup changes color very rapidly and burns easily. It must not become too dark or it will be bitter. (The sugar is also very hot; be careful not to burn your fingers.)

Stir in the melted butter, and add as many potatoes as possible without crowding the skillet. Slide the skillet back and forth constantly to roll the potatoes and coat them on all sides with the caramel. Remove the hot caramelized potatoes to a heated serving bowl and repeat the procedure until all of the potatoes are coated. Serve at once.

■ THE COOKING OF SCANDINAVIA

ONIONS STUFFED WITH SPINACH AND PINE NUTS

## Potato Cake

*New potatoes have the waxy flesh that helps the shreds stick together in a cake. Use them if you can.* ❖●

**To serve 4**

| | |
|---|---|
| 1½ pounds potatoes | 3 tablespoons butter |
| ⅛ teaspoon freshly grated nutmeg | 2 tablespoons olive or vegetable oil |
| 1 teaspoon salt | Carrot curls, cut with a vegetable peeler, for garnish |
| Freshly ground black pepper | |

Peel the potatoes, dropping each one into a bowl of cold water as you finish. One by one, pat the potatoes dry with paper towels and grate them in a food processor fitted with a shredding disk, or on the coarse side of a box grater. You should have about 4 cups of shredded potatoes. Squeeze the shredded potatoes dry in kitchen towels, place them in a dry bowl, and add the nutmeg, salt and a few grindings of pepper.

In a 10-inch skillet, preferably one with a nonstick surface, heat 1½ tablespoons of the butter and 1 tablespoon of the oil over moderately high heat. When the foam subsides, add the potatoes, pressing them down with the back of a spoon to make an even layer, and cook for 2 minutes, sliding the pan back and forth to help prevent sticking. Then reduce the heat to moderately low, and cook the potato cake for 10 to 15 minutes or until the under-side browns around the edge.

Set an inverted plate or lid on top of the cake and turn plate and skillet over together to remove the cake. Add the remaining butter and oil to the skillet. When the butter melts, slide the cake back into the skillet, browned side up. Cook the cake for five to 10 min-utes or until the potatoes are tender and the second side has browned lightly. Slide the cake onto a heated platter, garnish it with carrot curls and serve it hot.

■ MEDITERRANEAN MENUS

## Mushroom-stuffed Potatoes

**To serve 6**

| | |
|---|---|
| 2 tablespoons butter, softened | 2 egg yolks, lightly beaten |
| Six 8-ounce potatoes | 1 tablespoon finely cut fresh chives |
| 6 lean bacon slices, halved crosswise | 6 tablespoons freshly grated Gruyère or Emmentaler cheese |
| 1 cup finely chopped mushrooms | |
| ¾ cup light cream | |

Preheat the oven to 425° F. With a pastry brush, spread melted or softened butter generously over the bottom of a baking dish large enough to hold the potatoes side by side.

Brush 2 tablespoons of softened butter evenly over the skins of the potatoes. Lay the potatoes on a wire rack set in a jelly-roll pan, and bake them for about 1 hour. The potatoes are done if they feel soft when squeezed gently between your thumb and forefinger.

POTATO CAKE

Remove the potatoes and reduce the oven temperature to 375° F.

In a heavy 8- to 10-inch skillet, fry the bacon, a few pieces at a time, over moderate heat, turning it with tongs until it is crisp and brown and renders all of its fat. Drain the bacon on paper towels, and coarsely crumble it.

Pour off all but ¼ cup of the fat remaining in the skillet. Add the mushrooms and, stirring from time to time, cook for five to 10 minutes, but do not let them brown. When the moisture in the pan has evaporated, transfer the mushrooms to a bowl and set them aside.

Cut a ¼-inch-thick slice lengthwise off the top of each potato and discard. With a spoon, scoop out the potato pulp, creating a boatlike shell about ¼ inch thick.

Purée the potato pulp through a ricer or food mill into a deep bowl, or place the pulp in a bowl and mash it to a smooth purée with the back of a table fork. Beat in the cream and egg yolks and, when they are completely incorporated, stir in the chives, the reserved bacon bits and the mushrooms. Taste for seasoning.

Spoon the potato mixture into the shells, mounding it in the center. Arrange the shells in the buttered dish and sprinkle the cheese on top. Bake for three minutes or until the potatoes are golden brown and crusty. Serve at once.

■ AMERICAN COOKING: THE EASTERN HEARTLAND

## Sweet Potatoes in Orange Baskets

**To serve 4**

| | |
|---|---|
| 4 large navel oranges | 1 egg |
| 2 tablespoons butter, softened, plus 2 teaspoons butter, cut into bits | 1 teaspoon salt |
| | ½ teaspoon freshly ground white pepper |
| 4 sweet potatoes, boiled, peeled and puréed (about 1½ cups) | ¼ teaspoon grated lemon peel |
| | ¼ cup chopped almonds |

Preheat the oven to 350°F. With a heavy, sharp knife, cut off and discard a 1-inch-deep slice from the stem end of each orange. Gently squeeze the oranges, being careful not to injure the skin, and reserve the juice for another purpose. With a small, sharp knife, scrape and cut away the pulp and membranes from the orange shells, keeping the shells intact and as regular in shape as possible. Set the shells side by side in a baking dish just large enough to hold them.

In a large mixing bowl, beat the softened butter into the puréed sweet potatoes, then beat in the egg, salt, white pepper and lemon peel. Taste for seasoning. Fill each orange basket with the potato mixture, swirling the top attractively with a rubber spatula. Sprinkle the filling with the almonds, and dot with the butter bits. Bake for 45 minutes, until the potatoes are hot and the tops lightly browned. Serve at once, as an accompaniment to roast meat or poultry.

■ AMERICAN COOKING: SOUTHERN STYLE

## Sweet Potato and Pear Mousse

**To serve 8**

| | |
|---|---|
| 2 pounds sweet potatoes | 1 tablespoon butter |
| 2 large pears, peeled, cored and cut into 1-inch chunks | 1½ cups chopped onions |
| | 1 cup apple juice |
| 3 tablespoons fresh lemon juice | Freshly ground black pepper |
| | 1 egg, separated, plus 1 egg white |
| ½ teaspoon curry powder | |
| ½ teaspoon ground cinnamon | |

Preheat the oven to 450°F. Prick the sweet potatoes and bake them for 30 minutes or until they begin to soften. Set them aside to cool. In a large bowl, combine the pear chunks, lemon juice, curry powder and cinnamon. When the sweet potatoes are cool enough to handle, peel them, cut them into 1-inch chunks, and add them to the bowl.

Melt the butter in a heavy 10- to 12-inch skillet over moderate heat. Add the onions and cook, stirring frequently, for five minutes, then stir in the apple juice, the sweet potato mixture and a few grindings of pepper. Cover the skillet partially and cook for 15 minutes, stirring occasionally.

Preheat the oven to 350°F. With a pastry brush, spread a light coating of melted or softened butter inside a 2-quart gratin dish and set it aside.

Transfer the contents of the skillet to a food processor or blender. Purée the mixture, stopping two or three times to scrape down the bowl. Transfer to a bowl and stir in the egg yolk.

In a separate bowl, beat the egg whites with a whisk or a rotary or electric beater until soft peaks form when the beater is lifted from the bowl. Fold the beaten whites into the purée, and pour the mixture into the gratin dish. Bake the mousse for 30 minutes. Serve it immediately.

■ FRESH WAYS WITH VEGETABLES

## Spinach Pancakes

**To serve 6 to 8**

| | |
|---|---|
| 1 cup flour | 2 eggs, lightly beaten |
| 1 teaspoon salt | ½ pound fresh spinach, cooked, squeezed dry and chopped fine, or one 10-ounce package frozen chopped spinach, defrosted and chopped fine |
| ½ teaspoon sugar | |
| ⅛ teaspoon freshly grated nutmeg | |
| 1½ cups milk | |
| 2 tablespoons butter, melted and cooled, plus 2 to 4 tablespoons butter, softened | Preserved lingonberries or cranberries |

In a large bowl, mix the flour, salt, sugar, nutmeg and milk. Stir in the melted butter, then the eggs and finally the spinach. Or mix the ingredients in a food processor or blender.

With a pastry brush, coat the bottom of a heavy 10- to 12-inch skillet with about a tablespoon of softened butter. Set the skillet over moderately high heat. When the pan is very hot, form a pancake by ladling 2 tablespoons of the batter into the skillet. Use the back of the ladle or a spatula to spread the batter to form a 3-inch disk. Cook three or four pancakes at a time for about two minutes on each side or until they brown lightly.

As they cook, transfer the pancakes to a platter, and cover them with foil to keep them warm. Add more butter to the skillet as needed. Serve the spinach pancakes as a vegetable course, accompanied, if you like, by lingonberries or cranberries.

■ THE COOKING OF SCANDINAVIA

## Zucchini Noodles with Pesto

**To serve 4**

| | |
|---|---|
| 4 small zucchini, trimmed but not peeled | ½ cup olive oil |
| 2 teaspoons salt | ½ to 1 teaspoon fresh lemon juice |
| 1 cup packed fresh basil leaves, plus 1 basil sprig for garnish | Freshly ground black pepper |
| | 2 tablespoons unsalted butter |
| ½ cup freshly grated Parmesan cheese | 3 plum tomatoes, diced |
| 2 garlic cloves, chopped coarse | ½ cup small Mediterranean-style black olives |

To make noodles out of the zucchini, first cut them lengthwise into slices ¼ inch thick. Stack half a dozen slices at a time and cut them lengthwise into thin strands. Place the zucchini noodles in a colander, sprinkle them with 2 teaspoons of salt, and toss until evenly coated. Set them aside to drain for 20 minutes.

To prepare the sauce, first combine the basil leaves, Parmesan, garlic and ¼ cup of the olive oil in a food processor or blender, and purée the mixture. With the motor running, add the remaining oil in a slow, steady stream, and process until the sauce is smooth. Sprinkle in lemon juice, a drop at a time, to taste. Add a few grindings of pepper, then transfer the sauce to a large serving bowl.

Squeeze the zucchini dry in paper towels. In a heavy 10- to 12-inch skillet, melt the butter over moderately high heat. When the foam subsides, add the zucchini and sauté for three to five minutes or just until tender. Add the zucchini to the bowl with the sauce and toss together gently but thoroughly. Taste and adjust the seasonings. Cool the zucchini and serve surrounded by the tomatoes and olives and garnished with a basil sprig.

■ MEDITERRANEAN MENUS

## Spinach Ring with Cheese Sauce

**To serve 6**

| | |
|---|---|
| 2 tablespoons fresh white-bread crumbs | cooked, drained, squeezed dry and chopped fine, or two 10-ounce packages frozen chopped spinach, defrosted, squeezed dry and chopped finer by hand or in a processor |
| 3 tablespoons butter | |
| ¼ cup flour | |
| 2 cups milk | |
| 1 cup heavy cream | |
| 1 teaspoon salt | |
| ¼ teaspoon freshly ground white pepper | Freshly ground black pepper |
| Freshly grated nutmeg | 3 eggs, separated |
| ¼ pound sliced bacon | ¼ cup freshly grated Parmesan or Gruyère cheese |
| ½ cup finely chopped onions | |
| 2 pounds spinach, washed, | |

Preheat the oven to 375°F. With a pastry brush, coat all the inner surfaces of a 1-quart ring mold with melted or softened butter. Add the bread crumbs and tip the pan from side to side to spread them evenly. Then invert the pan and tap out any excess crumbs. Set the pan aside.

In a 2- to 3-quart saucepan, melt the 3 tablespoons of butter but do not let it brown. Remove the pan from the heat, and stir in the flour. Then pour in the milk and cream, and stir with a whisk until the flour mixture is smooth. Return the pan to moderate heat and cook, whisking constantly, until the sauce comes to a boil and is thick and smooth. Stir in ½ teaspoon of the salt, the white pepper and a generous pinch of nutmeg. Set the sauce aside.

In a 10-inch skillet, fry the bacon over moderate heat, turning the slices until they render all of their fat and are golden brown and crisp. Transfer them to paper towels to drain, then crumble the bacon into small bits and set aside. Meanwhile, pour off and discard all but about ¼ cup of the bacon fat from the skillet and add the onions. Stirring occasionally, cook over moderate heat for about five minutes, until the onions are soft but not brown.

Add the spinach to the skillet and raise the heat to high. Stirring constantly, fry the mixture until all of the moisture has evaporated and the spinach begins to stick lightly to the pan. Watch carefully for any sign of burning and regulate the heat accordingly. With a rubber spatula, scrape the contents of the skillet into a large mixing bowl, and stir in the remaining ½ teaspoon of salt, a pinch of nutmeg and as much black pepper as you like. Pour in about half of the reserved sauce, and stir vigorously with a wooden spoon until the ingredients are mixed. Beat in the egg yolks, one at a time, and the crumbled bacon.

Beat the egg whites with a wire whisk or rotary beater—in an unlined copper bowl, if possible—until they are firm enough to form unwavering peaks on the beater when it is lifted from the bowl. Stir two or three large spoonfuls of the whites into the spinach mixture to lighten it, then use a rubber spatula to gently fold in the remaining whites. Ladle the mixture into the prepared mold, and smooth the top with the rubber spatula. Bake for about 30 minutes or until the ring has puffed and the top is lightly browned.

While the spinach ring is baking, bring the reserved sauce to a simmer over moderate heat. Stir in the cheese and simmer for two or three minutes, until the cheese melts. Taste for seasoning. Cover the pan to keep the sauce warm, and set it aside off the heat while you unmold the ring.

Place a large heated serving plate upside down over the top of the mold. Firmly grasping plate and mold together, invert the two. Rap them sharply on a table and the spinach ring should slide out easily onto the plate. Pour the hot cheese sauce over the ring, and serve at once.

■ AMERICAN COOKING: THE NORTHWEST

STUFFED ACORN SQUASH

## Zucchini with Cherry Tomatoes

**To serve 6**

| | |
|---|---|
| 1½ pounds small zucchini, trimmed and cut into ½-inch slices | 2 teaspoons fresh lemon juice |
| 1 pint cherry tomatoes, each halved | 1 teaspoon salt |
| 3 tablespoons butter | ¼ teaspoon sugar |
| | ⅛ teaspoon freshly ground black pepper |

Place the zucchini in a heavy 12-inch skillet, add boiling water to cover the slices, and set a lid on the pan. Cook over moderate heat for seven to 10 minutes or until the zucchini is barely tender. Drain it well in a colander. Return the zucchini to the skillet and add the tomatoes, butter, lemon juice, salt, sugar and pepper. Toss them gently together to mix. Cover and simmer for about three minutes or until the tomatoes are heated through. Taste and correct the seasoning. Serve from a heated bowl.

■ GREAT DINNERS FROM LIFE

## Squash Soufflé

**To serve 4 to 6**

| | |
|---|---|
| 2½ pounds acorn, Hubbard or butternut squash, peeled, seeded and cut into 2-inch chunks | ¼ cup heavy cream |
| | 4 eggs, separated, plus 1 egg white |
| 3 tablespoons butter | 2 teaspoons sugar |
| 1 tablespoon vegetable oil | ½ teaspoon freshly grated nutmeg |
| ¼ cup flour | Salt |
| ¾ cup milk | Freshly ground white pepper |

Pour enough water into a large pot to come about 1 inch up the side. Set a vegetable steamer in the pot, and put the squash chunks into the steamer. Cover the pot, bring the water to a boil over moderately high heat, and steam the squash for 25 to 30 minutes or until it is tender and shows no resistance when pierced with the tip of a small knife.

Purée the squash through a food mill or fine sieve set over a bowl lined with dampened cheesecloth. Wrap the cloth around the squash and, holding the ends in both hands, squeeze vigorously to remove as much of the moisture from the squash as possible. There should be about 2 cups of purée. Set it aside in a bowl.

Meanwhile, preheat the oven to 375°F. With a pastry brush, spread a light coating of melted or softened butter evenly over the bottom and sides of a 2-quart soufflé dish.

In a heavy 2- to 3-quart saucepan, melt the 3 tablespoons of butter in the oil over moderate heat. Stir in the flour and mix to a paste. Stirring constantly with a wire whisk, pour in the milk and cream, and cook over high heat until the mixture comes to a boil, thickens heavily and is smooth. Reduce the heat to low and simmer for two or three minutes. Remove the pan from the heat and stir in the squash. Then beat in the egg yolks, one at a time. Stir in

the sugar, nutmeg, 1½ teaspoons of salt and ¼ teaspoon of white pepper, and taste for seasoning.

With a whisk or a rotary or electric beater—and in an unlined copper bowl, if possible—beat the egg whites until they are firm enough to stand in peaks on the beater when it is lifted from the bowl. Stir two or three large spoonfuls of the egg whites into the squash mixture to lighten it, then gently but thoroughly fold in the remaining whites.

Pour the soufflé mixture into the buttered dish, and smooth the top with a rubber spatula. Bake in the middle of the oven for 40 minutes or until the soufflé puffs up well above the rim and the top is lightly browned. Serve at once.

■ AMERICAN COOKING: NEW ENGLAND

## Stuffed Acorn Squash

**To serve 4**

| | |
|---|---|
| 4 small acorn squash | Parmesan cheese |
| 1 zucchini, grated coarse | 1 tablespoon finely chopped fresh tarragon leaves or |
| 1 carrot, grated coarse | 1 teaspoon crumbled dried tarragon |
| 1 small apple, peeled, cored and diced | |
| 1 small onion, chopped fine | ⅛ teaspoon salt |
| ¼ cup freshly grated | Freshly ground black pepper |

Cut about 1 inch off the stem end of each acorn squash, and trim the bottom so the squash will stand upright. Scoop out the seeds and fibers from inside the squash. In a bowl, combine the zucchini, carrot, apple, onion, cheese, tarragon, salt and a few gridings of pepper. Pour enough water into a large pot to come about 1 inch up the side. Set a vegetable steamer in the pot. Stuff the acorn squash with the vegetable mixture, and put them in the steamer. Cover the pot, bring the water to a boil over moderately high heat, and steam the squash until tender—about 20 minutes. Transfer the squash to a warmed platter and serve immediately.

Alternatively, the squash can be baked. Preheat the oven to 400°F. Pour 1 inch of water into a baking dish large enough to hold the acorn squash upright. Stuff the squash with the vegetable mixture and set them in the dish. Cover the dish with foil and bake the squash until tender—about 45 minutes.

■ FRESH WAYS WITH VEGETABLES

## Savory Tofu Stew

*As "tofu" or "dou fu," bean curd serves as a staple of the diet in many Asian countries. The curd is made from soybeans that have been soaked, cooked, puréed, coagulated and pressed into white, silky-textured, mild-flavored cakes. Once available only in Asian markets, tofu now is sold at most supermarkets, and it is easily made at home (Index/Glossary).*  ❧

**To serve 4**

| | |
|---|---|
| 6 squares tofu, preferably homemade (about 1½ pounds) | 3 tablespoons dark soy sauce |
| 1 pound young carrots, peeled | 1 tablespoon brown sugar |
| 5 to 6 cups corn or peanut oil | Chinese dark vinegar or balsamic vinegar |
| 4 scallions, cut diagonally into 1- to 2-inch pieces and crushed | 8 medium-sized or 6 large Chinese dried black mushrooms soaked in hot water for 20 minutes, drained and halved if large |
| 4 thin slices fresh ginger root, crushed | ⅓ pound button mushrooms, trimmed and halved |
| 4 large garlic cloves, peeled and crushed | Salt |
| 1¾ cups chicken stock | Freshly ground black pepper |

Cut each square of tofu into four triangles. Place the tofu on a baking sheet lined with a triple thickness of paper towels, and set it aside. Cut one carrot at a time diagonally at 1-inch intervals, rolling the carrot a third of a turn away from you after each cut.

Set a 10-inch wok or deep 12-inch skillet over high heat. Add 1½ inches of oil. Meanwhile, in a small bowl, combine the scallions, ginger and garlic. In another small bowl, combine the stock, soy sauce, brown sugar and 1½ tablespoons of vinegar. Line a second baking sheet with a double thickness of paper towels, and set it beside the stove.

When the oil registers 375°F. on a deep-frying thermometer or is hot enough so that a small scrap of tofu bobs to the surface within two seconds, carefully add half of the tofu triangles to the oil, one by one. Immerse each triangle by sliding it into the oil from the side of the wok or skillet to avoid splatters. With chopsticks or a wooden spoon, gently separate the triangles. Adjust the heat to maintain the oil's temperature: It should create a crown of white bubbles around each triangle.

Fry the tofu until the triangles are golden brown about four minutes, turning them with chopsticks or wooden tongs. With a Chinese mesh strainer or a slotted spoon, transfer them to paper towels to drain. Readjust the heat of the oil before frying the remaining tofu.

Pour the stock mixture into a heavy 3- to 4-quart casserole. Stirring, bring to a boil over high heat. Add the black mushrooms and the scallion mixture, cover, reduce the heat to low, and simmer for five minutes. Add the tofu, carrots, and fresh mushrooms. Stir gently but thoroughly, cover, and simmer for 20 minutes or until the carrots are tender, stirring after 10 minutes.

Taste the stew and adjust the seasonings with vinegar or sugar. Add salt and pepper if you like.

■ VEGETABLE MENUS

## Stewed Tomatoes with Cubed Pumpernickel

**To serve 6**

| | |
|---|---|
| 1 tablespoon olive oil | parsley leaves for garnish |
| 1 onion, chopped fine | ¼ teaspoon salt |
| 2 celery ribs, chopped fine | Freshly ground black pepper |
| 2 garlic cloves, chopped fine | 6 tomatoes, peeled, seeded and chopped coarse |
| 1½ tablespoons chopped fresh basil leaves or 2 teaspoons crumbled dried basil, plus 1½ teaspoons chopped fresh basil or | 2 tablespoons dark-brown sugar |
| | 1 cup ¾-inch pumpernickel-bread cubes |

Preheat the oven to 350°F. In a heavy 8- to 10-inch skillet, heat the oil over moderately low heat. Add the onion, celery, garlic, 1½ tablespoons of fresh basil or the 2 teaspoons of dried basil, the salt and a little pepper. Stirring occasionally, cook the mixture until the celery is limp—about four minutes. Stir in the tomatoes and cook them, stirring occasionally, until they soften—about five minutes. Add the brown sugar and the bread cubes. Transfer the mixture to a shallow baking dish, and bake until the top has nicely dried—35 to 40 minutes. Serve garnished with the remaining fresh basil or the chopped parsley.

■ FRESH WAYS WITH VEGETABLES

## Green Tomato Pie

**To make one 9-inch pie**

| | |
|---|---|
| Short-crust dough for double-crust pie (Index/Glossary) | 2 tablespoons flour |
| 8 green tomatoes, cored and cut into ¼-inch slices | 1 cup fresh white-bread crumbs |
| 1 tablespoon salt | ½ teaspoon ground cinnamon |
| 1 cup sugar | 2 tablespoons cider vinegar |
| | 2 tablespoons butter, cut into bits |

Preheat the oven to 375°F. With a pastry brush, spread a light coating of melted or softened butter inside a 9-inch pie pan. Roll out half of the pastry dough and fit it into the pan.

Place the tomatoes in a deep bowl, sprinkle the salt over them, and turn the slices with a spoon until they are evenly coated. Set aside for about 15 minutes. Spread them on paper towels to drain, and pat them dry with fresh towels.

Mix the sugar, flour, bread crumbs and cinnamon in a deep bowl. Add the tomatoes and toss together gently. Arrange the tomato slices in the lined pie pan, dribble the vinegar over them, and dot with the butter bits.

Roll out the remaining dough and lay it over the pie. With scissors or a knife, trim off the excess and crimp the dough to the rim of the pan with the tines of a fork or your fingers. Cut a hole 1 inch across in the top crust. Bake the pie for 45 minutes or until the crust is delicately browned. Serve the pie at once or at room temperature.

■ AMERICAN COOKING: THE NORTHWEST

SAVORY TOFU STEW

FRIED TOMATOES

## Fried Tomatoes

*Traditionally, this Pennsylvania Dutch dish is made with green toma-*
*toes, which are not easy to buy. If you can get them, cook them over*
*lower heat and for a few minutes longer on each side.* ❧

**To serve 4 to 6**

| | |
|---|---|
| **4 or 5 large tomatoes, cut into thick slices** | **4 to 6 tablespoons butter** |
| **Salt** | **2 tablespoons brown sugar** |
| **Freshly ground black pepper** | **1 cup heavy cream** |
| **½ cup flour** | **1 tablespoon finely chopped fresh parsley leaves** |

Sprinkle the tomatoes on both sides with salt and a few grindings of black pepper. Spread the flour on a sheet of wax paper. Then dip the tomato slices in the flour, coating each side thoroughly; gently tap off any excess. In a heavy 12-inch skillet, preferably with a nonstick lining, melt ¼ cup of butter over moderate heat.

When the foam subsides, add the tomato slices and cook them for about five minutes or until they are lightly browned. Sprinkle the tops with half of the brown sugar, carefully turn the tomatoes over with a spatula, and sprinkle with the rest of the brown sugar. Add 1 or more tablespoons of butter to the skillet if necessary. Cook the tomatoes for three to four minutes, then transfer the slices to a heated serving platter.

Pour the cream into the skillet, increase the heat to high, and bring the cream to a boil, stirring constantly. Boil briskly for two to three minutes or until the cream thickens. Taste for seasoning, then pour the cream over the tomatoes. Sprinkle with the finely chopped parsley.

■ AMERICAN COOKING: THE EASTERN HEARTLAND

## Tomatoes Stuffed with Rice and Pine Nuts

**To serve 4**

| | |
|---|---|
| ⅓ cup long-grain white rice | ¼ teaspoon crumbled dried thyme |
| ¾ cup water | ¼ teaspoon crumbled dried oregano |
| 4 tomatoes | 1 tablespoon finely cut fresh chives for garnish |
| Salt | |
| 2 tablespoons pine nuts | |
| 2 tablespoons olive oil | |
| 1 garlic clove, chopped fine | |

Preheat the oven to 375°F. With a pastry brush, spread a light coating of oil inside a shallow 1-quart baking dish.

In a 1- to 1½-quart saucepan, bring the water to a boil over high heat. Add the rice, stir, cover, and cook over low heat for 20 minutes or until all the water has been absorbed and the rice is tender.

Meanwhile, slice about ¼ inch off the top of each tomato. With your index finger or a teaspoon, scoop out all of the pulp and seeds from the tomatoes, leaving hollow shells about ¼ inch thick. Reserve the pulp, but discard the seeds. Lightly salt the insides of the tomato shells, and invert them on paper towels to drain.

In a small ungreased skillet, toast the pine nuts over moderate heat, for three or four minutes, stirring constantly until they are browned. Transfer the nuts to a small bowl and set them aside.

In a heavy 6- to 8-inch skillet, heat the 2 tablespoons of olive oil over moderate heat until it is hot but not smoking. Add the tomato pulp, garlic, thyme and oregano, and cook for three or four minutes or until the excess liquid has evaporated. Remove the skillet from the heat and stir in the pine nuts and rice.

Place the tomato shells upright in the prepared baking dish, and spoon the stuffing into them. Bake the tomatoes for 15 to 20 minutes or until the stuffing is lightly browned. Serve the tomatoes hot or at room temperature, sprinkled with chives.

■ MAKE-AHEAD MENUS

## Sweet-and-Sour Turnips

**To serve 4**

| | |
|---|---|
| 3 tablespoons butter | ¼ to ½ cup chicken stock |
| 8 white turnips, cut into ¾-inch cubes | 3 tablespoons dark-brown sugar |
| Salt | ¼ cup sherry vinegar or red-wine vinegar |
| Freshly ground white pepper | |
| 1 teaspoon sugar | |

In a heavy 10- to 12-inch skillet, melt the butter over moderate heat. Add the turnips and season them with salt, a few grindings of white pepper and the 1 teaspoon of sugar. Stirring frequently, cook the turnips for four or five minutes, until they are glazed and nicely browned. Then add ¼ cup of chicken stock, cover the skillet, reduce the heat to low, and cook the turnips for 15 minutes or until they are just tender when pierced with the tip of a knife.

Check the turnips from time to time and add more chicken stock if necessary.

Combine the brown sugar with the vinegar in a small bowl. Blend well and add the mixture to the turnips. Increase the heat to moderately high, and cook until the turnips are well glazed and the pan juices are reduced to about 2 tablespoons. Transfer the turnips to a heated serving dish, and pour the pan juices over them. Serve at once.

■ CHICKEN AND GAME HEN MENUS

## Rutabaga Casserole

*The hardy rutabaga is believed to be the result of a natural hybridization of turnip with cabbage somewhere in Europe in the late Middle Ages. To add confusion, rutabagas usually are yellow and turnips are white, but there are white rutabagas and yellow turnips. The rutabaga's name comes from the Swedish "rotabagge"—and the vegetable is often called a Swede or Swede turnip. As this recipe suggests, the assertive-flavored rutabaga is popular in Scandinavia. Parsnips or turnips might take their place in this recipe, if you like.* ❧

**To serve 8**

| | |
|---|---|
| 2 rutabagas, peeled and cut into ¼-inch dice (about 8 cups) | 1 teaspoon salt |
| | 2 eggs, lightly beaten |
| ¼ cup dry bread crumbs | 2 tablespoons butter, softened, plus 2 tablespoons butter, cut into bits |
| ¼ cup heavy cream | |
| ½ teaspoon freshly grated nutmeg | |

Preheat the oven to 350°F. With a pastry brush, spread a light coating of melted or softened butter inside a 2- to 2½-quart baking dish. Set it aside.

Drop the diced rutabagas into a large pot half filled with lightly salted boiling water. Bring the water back to a boil, then reduce the heat somewhat and boil the rutabagas for about 15 minutes or until they are tender when tested with the tip of a knife.

Drain the rutabagas and purée them with a food mill or potato masher or, with the back of a spoon, rub them through a sieve into a mixing bowl. In another bowl, soak the bread crumbs in the heavy cream for a few minutes. Stir in the nutmeg, salt and the lightly beaten eggs, then add the puréed rutabagas and mix together thoroughly. Stir in the 2 tablespoons of softened butter. Transfer the rutabaga mixture to the baking dish. Dot it with the butter bits and bake, uncovered, for 45 minutes to an hour or until the top is lightly browned.

■ THE COOKING OF SCANDINAVIA

## Madras Vegetable Stew

*Fresh or dried, hot chilies are an ingredient to be handled carefully. Kitchen gloves are good protection from their powerful oils.* ❧

**To serve 4**

| | |
|---|---|
| 1 cup plain yogurt | 2 teaspoons curry powder |
| One 1-inch piece fresh ginger root, chopped coarse | 1 bunch broccoli, stalks cut off 2 inches below florets and discarded |
| ¼ cup loosely packed fresh coriander leaves | ¾ pound yellow summer squash, trimmed and cut into ½-inch slices |
| 4 fresh hot green chilies, stemmed, halved and seeded | Salt |
| 1½ teaspoons ground cumin plus ½ teaspoon cumin seeds | 1 cup water |
| | 1 teaspoon mustard seeds |
| 1½ teaspoons cornstarch | 1 red onion, halved lengthwise and cut crosswise into ¼-inch slices |
| 5 tablespoons light vegetable oil | |

Combine the yogurt, ginger, coriander, chilies, ground cumin and cornstarch in a blender or food processor, and process this yogurt sauce until smooth. Set it aside.

Heat 2 tablespoons of the oil in a heavy 3- to 4-quart saucepan over moderately high heat. When the oil is hot, add the curry powder, and slide the pan back and forth for about 10 seconds to release the fragrance of the curry powder. Add the broccoli and squash, and stir with a wooden spoon to coat them with the spice. Cook for one minute.

Add the yogurt sauce, stir thoroughly but gently, and season with salt to taste. Pour the water into the blender or food processor, shake the container to rinse out the remaining sauce, then stir this water with the vegetables. Increase the heat to high and bring the mixture to a boil. Then cover the pan, reduce the heat to moderately low, and simmer the stew for five minutes. Uncover the pan, increase the heat to high, and boil the stew rapidly for one minute to evaporate excess liquid. Set it off the heat.

In a 6- to 8-inch skillet equipped with a lid, heat the remaining 3 tablespoons of oil over high heat. When the oil is hot, add the cumin seeds and mustard seeds. Cover the skillet with its lid—the seeds will sputter and pop as they heat—and slide the pan back and forth for one to two minutes or until the sputtering subsides and the cumin seeds darken. Add the onion, and stir it rapidly for about two minutes or until it begins to brown.

To serve, transfer the stew to a large heated serving dish, and top it with the onion mixture.

■ MEATLESS MENUS

## Three-Layer Vegetable Terrine

**To serve 12**

| | |
|---|---|
| 1¼ pounds carrots, cut into ¼-inch slices | Freshly ground black pepper |
| 2 onions, chopped | 3 tablespoons freshly grated Romano or Parmesan cheese |
| One 2-pound cauliflower, cored and cut into large florets | 3 tablespoons finely chopped shallots |
| 3 eggs plus 4 egg whites, 2 whites to be used together and 2 separately | 2 pounds spinach, washed and stemmed, or two 10-ounce packages frozen spinach, defrosted |
| ¾ teaspoon salt | 2 tablespoons unsalted butter |
| ⅛ teaspoon freshly grated nutmeg | 2 garlic cloves, chopped |

With a pastry brush, spread a coating of melted or softened butter inside a 2-quart rectangular terrine mold or loaf pan. To facilitate unmolding the cooked terrine, fit a piece of wax paper in the bottom of the mold and butter it also. Put the mold in the refrigerator. Pour enough water into a large nonreactive pot to come about 1 inch up the side. Put in a vegetable steamer, add the carrots, and set a third of the onions on top of them. Cover the pot, bring the water to a boil, and steam the vegetables until very tender—about 15 minutes. Drain them briefly on paper towels; reserve.

Replenish the water in the pot. Put the cauliflower in the steamer; lay half of the remaining onions on top. Cover the pot, bring the water to a boil, and steam the vegetables until the cauliflower is tender—about 20 minutes. Drain the vegetables on paper towels for one minute; set them aside in a separate bowl.

Put one of the whole eggs and two of the egg whites into a food processor or blender. Process the eggs for 30 seconds. Add the carrots and onions, along with ¼ teaspoon of the salt, the nutmeg and some pepper. Process for a minute, stopping after 30 seconds to scrape down the sides with a rubber spatula. Transfer the carrot purée to the chilled mold, smoothing the top with the spatula. Take care not to leave any carrot on the sides of the mold so that no orange spots will blemish the finished terrine.

Put another whole egg and one egg white in the food processor and blend them for 30 seconds. Add the steamed cauliflower and onions, the cheese, shallots, ¼ teaspoon of the salt and some pepper; process for about one minute, stopping after 30 seconds to scrape down the sides.

Transfer the cauliflower purée to the mold, spreading it in an even layer over the carrot purée.

Preheat the oven to 350° F. Prepare a bain-marie, or water bath, for the terrine by first placing the mold in a large baking dish—preferably one that is at least 2 inches larger than the mold all around. Pour enough hot water into the dish to come two-thirds of the way up the sides of the mold. Remove the mold and set the dish in the oven.

Pour out any water remaining in the pot used for steaming. Then pour in just enough fresh water to cover the bottom. Set the pot over high heat, add the spinach, and cover. After three minutes, remove the pot from the heat, and stir the spinach until it is stopping after 30 seconds to scrape down the sides.

Distribute spoonfuls of the spinach mixture over the layer of cauliflower in the mold, then smooth the top with the rubber spatula. To keep the top from drying out, cover it with a piece of buttered wax paper. Set the mold in the water bath and bake it for one hour and 10 minutes.

Remove the terrine from the oven and let it stand for 20 minutes. To unmold it, first run a knife around the inside of the mold to loosen the terrine. Then remove the wax paper from the top and invert a platter larger than the mold over the terrine. Turn mold and plate over together, carefully lift away the mold and peel off the other piece of wax paper.

Allow the terrine to cool slightly—about five minutes. Serve it cut into thick slices, catching each slice on a spatula as you cut it to keep it from breaking.

■ FRESH WAYS WITH VEGETABLES

## Leek and Mushroom Tart

**To serve 4**

| | |
|---|---|
| 8 leeks, trimmed, washed, halved lengthwise and cut into 1-inch slices, including about 3 inches of green tops | Emmentaler cheese |
| | 3 tablespoons chopped fresh parsley leaves |
| 3 tablespoons butter | ½ cup milk plus ½ cup heavy cream, or 1 cup milk |
| 1 tablespoon cold water | |
| Salt | 2 egg yolks |
| 1½ cups quartered mushrooms | Cayenne pepper |
| | Freshly grated nutmeg |
| 1 cup julienne strips smoked ham | Freshly ground black pepper |
| | 1 partially baked 9-inch short-crust pastry tart shell |
| ½ cup grated Gruyère or | (Index/Glossary) |

Preheat the oven to 400° F. In a heavy 10- to 12-inch skillet, combine the leeks with 1 tablespoon of the butter, the water and a little salt. Bring to a boil over moderate heat, cover the skillet and simmer until the leeks are just limp—about 10 minutes. Uncover the skillet and stir over high heat until the liquid evaporates. Transfer the leeks to a large mixing bowl.

In the same skillet, melt the remaining 2 tablespoons of butter, and in it sauté the mushrooms, stirring over moderate heat for three or four minutes, until they are delicately browned. Add the mushrooms, ham, cheese and parsley to the leeks and mix them well.

In a separate bowl, make a custard mixture by whisking together the milk and cream, egg yolks, and a pinch each of cayenne and nutmeg. Add salt and black pepper to taste.

Spread the leek mixture in the tart shell, place it in the oven, and pour the custard mixture over the leeks. Bake for eight minutes, then reduce the heat to 375° F. Bake for 25 to 30 minutes, until the custard is set and lightly golden. A knife inserted into the custard will come out clean.

To serve, let the tart rest for five minutes; cut it into wedges.

■ VEGETABLE MENUS

THREE-LAYER VEGETABLE TERRINE

wilted. Drain the spinach and refresh it under cold running water to stop the cooking. (Frozen spinach does not need this treatment.) Form part of the spinach into a ball and firmly squeeze out the liquid with your hands; set the squeezed spinach aside. Repeat the process with the remaining spinach.

Melt the butter in a heavy large skillet over moderate heat. Add the remaining onions and the garlic, and cook for three minutes. Stir in the spinach and sprinkle with the remaining ¼ teaspoon of salt and a dash of pepper. Remove the skillet from the heat.

Place the remaining whole egg and egg white in the food processor and blend them for 30 seconds. Transfer the contents of the skillet to the food processor, and process for about one minute,

# Rice & Beans

# Rice & Beans

The oldest staples in mankind's larder are dried seeds—grains and pulses—that can be transformed into tender morsels with liquid. Rice is preeminent among grains, although wheat, corn, barley, oats and rye are all widely used. And the grass seed called "crazy oats" or "wild rice" is prized as a great delicacy in the Western world. Pulses—dried legumes such as beans, peas and lentils—as varied as grains, from tiny green mung beans and pink lentils through mottled cranberry beans to large red and white kidney and golden brown fava beans.

Lentils, because of their minute size and thin skins, cook quickly in water, stock or vegetable juice. So, too, do split peas. Other pulses have impermeable skins, and water can enter them only at the hilium, the point where the bean or pea joined its pod; rehydrating them can be slow. Soaking helps and, traditionally, peas and beans are left overnight in water to soften, but the soaking period can be reduced to one hour by first boiling the beans or peas in copious amounts of water for two minutes or so.

Grains are less demanding. Soaking is not required—some recipes for wild rice excepted—and the husked groats or kernels need only be boiled or simmered, usually for less than half an hour.

Because they are simple to cook, grains and pulses lend themselves admirably to the role of foundations for such elaborate assemblies of seafoods and meats as Spain's paella and France's cassoulet.

## Risotto Milanese

*Risottos are Italian rice dishes, made by sautéing the rice in fat or oil, then cooking it in copious liquid. Instead of containing fluffy separate grains, the dish consists of a creamy homogenous mass.* ❧

**To serve 6 to 8**

| | |
|---|---|
| 7 cups chicken stock | 2 cups long-grain white rice |
| ¼ cup butter, plus ¼ cup butter, softened | ½ cup dry white wine |
| ½ cup finely chopped onions | ⅛ teaspoon crushed saffron threads |
| ⅓ to ½ cup chopped beef marrow (optional) | ½ cup freshly grated Parmesan cheese |

Bring the chicken stock to a boil in a heavy 3- to 4-quart saucepan, then reduce the heat so the stock barely simmers.

In a heavy 3-quart casserole, melt ¼ cup of butter over moderate heat. Add the onions and cook, stirring frequently, for five minutes, until they are soft but not brown. Stir in the marrow, if you are using it, then the rice, and stir for one or two minutes, until the grains glisten and are somewhat opaque.

Pour in the wine and boil it until the rice absorbs it. Then add 2 cups of the simmering stock to the rice, and cook, uncovered, stirring occasionally, until almost all of the liquid is absorbed. Add 2 more cups of stock and cook, stirring occasionally. Meanwhile, stir the saffron into 2 cups of stock and let it steep for a few minutes. Then pour it over the rice. Cook until the stock is completely absorbed. By now the rice should be tender; if still firm, add the remaining stock—½ cup at a time—and continue cooking and stirring until the rice is soft. With a fork, stir in the softened butter and the cheese; do not mash the rice. Serve at once.

■ THE COOKING OF ITALY

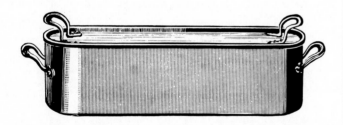

## Creamy Lemon Pilaf

**To serve 4**

| | |
|---|---|
| 2 tablespoons butter | Freshly ground black pepper |
| 1½ cups long-grain white rice | |
| 3 cups chicken stock | LEMON-CREAM SAUCE |
| Salt | 1 tablespoon fresh lemon juice |
| 3 tablespoons freshly grated Parmesan cheese | 1 teaspoon grated lemon peel |
| 3 tablespoons chopped fresh parsley leaves | 2 yolks from extra-large eggs |
| | ¼ cup heavy cream |

In a heavy 1- to 1½-quart saucepan, melt the butter over moderate heat. Add the rice and cook it for one minute, until opaque. Stir in the chicken broth and salt to taste. Bring the stock to a boil, cover the pan, reduce the heat, and simmer the rice for 20 minutes or until it is barely tender and has absorbed all of the stock. Meanwhile, combine the lemon juice, lemon peel, yolks and cream in a small bowl. Whisk them until well blended; set this sauce mixture aside.

Add the lemon-cream sauce to the rice and use a fork to mix them gently but thoroughly. Add the Parmesan cheese and parsley. Taste, and season with salt and pepper. Serve immediately from a heated bowl or mounded on a heated platter.

■ CHICKEN AND GAME HEN MENUS

## Yellow Rice with Curry Sauce and Fruit

**To serve 6**

| | |
|---|---|
| 2 tablespoons butter | 2 tablespoons cornstarch |
| 2 cups long-grain white rice | 2 tablespoons cold water |
| 4 cups boiling water | ¼ cup seedless raisins |
| ¼ teaspoon crumbled saffron threads | |
| 12 almonds, toasted in a 350°F. oven for 5 minutes | FRUIT GARNISH |
| | 1 pint strawberries, hulled and halved |
| CURRY SAUCE | 1 pint blueberries, stemmed |
| 1 cup dry white wine | 4 kiwis, peeled and sliced |
| 2½ cups chicken stock | 2 cups honeydew melon balls |
| 2 tablespoons curry powder | 6 plums, quartered and pitted |

Melt the butter over moderate heat in a heavy 2- to 3-quart saucepan. Add the rice and stir for two or three minutes, until the grains glisten with butter. Do not let the rice brown. Stir in the boiling water and saffron, and bring the mixture to a boil over high heat. Cover tight, reduce the heat to low, and simmer the rice for about 20 minutes, until it is tender and has absorbed all of the liquid.

Meanwhile, make the sauce: First combine the wine, chicken stock and curry powder in a small nonreactive saucepan. Stirring frequently, bring to a boil over high heat, then reduce the heat to low and simmer for two or three minutes. In a cup, stir the cornstarch and cold water together to make a smooth paste. Stirring the curry mixture constantly, pour in the cornstarch in a slow, thin stream, and simmer until the sauce thickens lightly and is smooth. Stir in the raisins. Set the sauce off the heat.

In a mixing bowl, gently combine the strawberries, blueberries, kiwis, melon balls and plums. Spoon the rice into a 1-quart mold or deep bowl, packing it in firmly. Place an inverted serving plate over the mold and, grasping plate and mold together firmly, turn them over. Rap the plate sharply on a table and the rice will slide out. Arrange the fruit around the rice and the toasted almonds attractively on top of the rice. Pour the sauce into a heated bowl or sauceboat, and serve it with the rice and fruit.

■ AMERICAN COOKING: THE NORTHWEST

RICE WITH LIMA BEANS AND DILL

## Pilaf with Pine Nuts and Pistachios

*Pilaf, or pilau, is a method Asian cooks devised for cooking grains in oil or fat, then in a minimum of liquid, to keep grains separate. The method was introduced to the United States by early China traders. Variations of the dish are especially popular in the Carolinas. The following version was favored by Thomas Jefferson.* ❧

**To serve 4**

| | |
|---|---|
| 2 cups chicken stock | ½ cup pine nuts |
| ¼ cup butter | ¼ cup unsalted shelled |
| ½ teaspoon salt | pistachios |
| 1 cup long-grain white rice | ¼ teaspoon ground mace |

In a heavy 1- to 2-quart saucepan, bring the chicken stock, 1 tablespoon of the butter and the salt to a boil over high heat. Pour in the rice, stir well, and reduce the heat to low. Cover the pan tight, and simmer the rice for 20 minutes, or until it is tender and absorbs all of the stock.

Meanwhile, in a heavy 8- to 10-inch skillet, melt the remaining butter over moderate heat. When the foam begins to subside, add the nuts and, stirring frequently, fry until they are a delicate golden color. Take them off the heat. Transfer the rice to a heated serving bowl, and fluff it with a fork. With a rubber spatula, scrape the contents of the skillet over the rice, and toss the rice and nuts gently together. Sprinkle with the mace and serve the pilaf at once.

■ AMERICAN COOKING: SOUTHERN STYLE

## Rice with Lima Beans and Dill

**To serve 4 to 6**

| | |
|---|---|
| 2 cups long-grain white rice | fresh dill, plus dill sprigs for |
| One 10-ounce package frozen | garnish |
| baby lima beans | 1½ teaspoons chopped fresh |
| 1¼ teaspoons salt | thyme leaves or ½ teaspoon |
| ¼ cup vegetable oil | crumbled dried thyme |
| 1 small onion, sliced thin | leaves |
| ¾ cup firmly packed chopped | 2⅔ cups water |

In a large bowl, wash the rice in several changes of water; drain in a colander. Return the rice to the bowl, and cover it with 5 cups of water; set aside for 25 minutes. Meanwhile, cook the lima beans in a small saucepan, following the package directions, except add ¼ teaspoon of salt and cook the beans for eight minutes. Drain the beans and the rice.

In a heavy 2- to 3-quart saucepan, heat the oil over moderate heat. Add the onion and, stirring frequently, cook for about two minutes, until the onion browns lightly. Add the rice, lima beans, chopped dill, thyme and the remaining salt. Stir gently and cook for two minutes. If the rice starts to stick, lower the heat.

Pour in 2⅔ cups of water and bring it to a boil. Cover the pan tight, first with aluminum foil, then with its lid. Reduce the heat to very low and cook the rice for 25 minutes. Transfer the rice to a warmed serving dish and garnish with dill sprigs.

■ VEGETABLE MENUS

## Wild Rice with Mushrooms and Almonds

**To serve 4 to 6**

| | |
|---|---|
| 5 tablespoons butter | almonds |
| 4 tablespoons finely chopped onion | ½ pound mushrooms, wiped clean, trimmed, and cut lengthwise into ⅛-inch slices |
| 1 cup wild rice | |
| 2 cups chicken stock | |
| 1 teaspoon salt | Freshly ground black pepper |
| ¼ cup slivered blanched | |

Preheat the oven to 350°F. In a heavy 2-quart casserole, melt 2 tablespoons of the butter over moderate heat. When the foam subsides, add 2 tablespoons of the onions. Stirring often, cook for five minutes, or until the onions are soft but not brown. Add the wild rice and stir until the grains glisten. Pour in the chicken stock and add ½ teaspoon of the salt. Stir until the mixture comes to a boil. Cover the casserole with a double thickness of aluminum foil, and set its lid in place. Bake for one hour, then let the rice rest at room temperature for 15 minutes before removing the lid and foil.

Meanwhile, melt 1 tablespoon of butter in a heavy 10-inch skillet, and brown the almonds for a minute or so, stirring constantly so that they color delicately and evenly. With a slotted spoon, transfer them to paper towels to drain.

Add the remaining 2 tablespoons of butter to the skillet and melt over moderate heat. In it cook the remaining 2 tablespoons of onions for about five minutes, until soft. Add the mushrooms and, stirring frequently, cook for 10 minutes, until the moisture they give off evaporates. Do not let the mushrooms brown. Season them with the remaining ½ teaspoon of salt and a few grindings of pepper; set them aside.

Add the mushrooms to the wild rice in the casserole or combine them in a heated bowl, and toss them together gently but thoroughly. Scatter the almonds on top and serve at once.

■ AMERICAN COOKING: THE NORTHWEST

## Deep-fried Rice and Cheese Croquettes

*When these croquettes are cut open, the melted cheese inside stretches in strings between the pieces, which explains their Italian name—"suppli al telefono," or telephone-wire croquettes.* ❧

**To serve 4 to 6**

| | |
|---|---|
| 2 eggs | ¼ pound mozzarella cheese, cut into ½-inch cubes |
| 2 cups leftover risotto or freshly cooked long-grain white rice | ¾ cup dry white bread crumbs |
| | Vegetable oil for deep frying |

In a mixing bowl, beat the eggs lightly with a fork until they are just combined. Then blend in the rice. Scoop up 1 tablespoonful of the mixture in a spoon, place a cube of mozzarella in the middle, and top with another spoonful of rice. Use your hands to press the rice-covered cheese into a small ball. Roll the ball in

bread crumbs and place it on wax paper. Similarly, shape other balls. Refrigerate for at least 30 minutes to set the coating.

Preheat the oven to 200°F. Line a heatproof platter with paper towels and set it in the oven.

Pour oil into a heavy saucepan or deep-fat fryer to a depth of 3 inches. Heat the oil over high heat until it registers 375°F. on a deep-frying thermometer. With a slotted spoon or a skimmer, lower four or five croquettes at a time into the hot oil. Fry them for about two minutes or until they are golden brown. Lift the croquettes out and set them on the paper-lined platter to keep warm in the oven. They may be kept warm for 10 minutes or so, if need be.

Serve the croquettes mounded on a heated serving platter. Eat them with knife and fork.

■ THE COOKING OF ITALY

## Dirty Rice

*Chicken livers and gizzards may make this rice look somewhat "dirty," but they give it a delicious flavor.* ❧

**To serve 6 to 8**

| | |
|---|---|
| ½ pound chicken livers, trimmed and cut up | 2 tablespoons olive oil |
| ½ pound chicken gizzards, trimmed and cut up | 1 teaspoon salt |
| | ½ teaspoon freshly ground black pepper |
| 2 onions, chopped coarse | 1 cup long-grain white rice |
| 1 large green pepper, seeded, deribbed and coarsely chopped | 2 cups water |
| | ½ cup chopped fresh parsley leaves |
| ½ cup coarsely chopped celery | |

Put the chicken livers, gizzards, onions, green pepper and celery through the finest disk of a food grinder. Or grind them fine in a food processor, a batch at a time, being sure not to purée them. The foods should have texture.

In a heavy 3- to 4-quart casserole, heat the olive oil over moderate heat. Add the ground chicken mixture, stir in the salt and black pepper, and reduce the heat to low. Stirring occasionally, cook uncovered for about 10 minutes, or until the bits of chicken are richly browned.

Meanwhile, place the rice in a heavy 1-quart pot, stir in the water and bring to a boil over high heat. Reduce the heat to low, cover tight, and simmer for 20 minutes or until the rice has absorbed all the liquid in the pot and the grains are tender. Remove the pot from the heat and let the rice rest, tightly covered, for 10 minutes or so.

When the chicken mixture has cooked, fluff the rice with a fork and add it to the casserole. With the fork, toss the rice and chicken mixture together gently but thoroughly. Taste for seasoning and stir in the parsley. Mound the dirty rice on a heated platter or in a heated bowl, and serve at once.

■ AMERICAN COOKING: CREOLE AND ACADIAN

## Pasta and Beans in Peppery Tomato Sauce

*Whether pasta complements beans or beans complement pasta, pasta e fagioli is a favorite with Italian Americans—and a real treat for anyone lucky enough to sample this hearty blend of two staple foods.* ❧

**To serve 6**

| | |
|---|---|
| 1 cup dried pinto beans, soaked overnight and drained | garlic |
| | 1 teaspoon crushed hot-red-pepper flakes |
| 2 cups water | 3 tomatoes, peeled, seeded and chopped |
| 1 teaspoon salt | |
| 4 bacon slices | 1 cup egg pastina |
| 1 cup finely chopped onions | 1 cup freshly grated Parmesan cheese |
| 2 teaspoons finely chopped | |

Place the beans in a heavy pot and add enough water to cover them by 1 inch. Bring the water to a boil over moderate heat. Add the salt and boil the beans for 10 minutes, then reduce the heat to low, cover the pot, and simmer the beans for about one and a half hours, or until they are tender. Drain the beans in a sieve or colander and set them aside.

For the sauce, fry the bacon in a heavy 10- to 12-inch skillet over moderate heat. Turn the slices frequently with tongs until they are crisp and brown. Transfer the bacon to paper towels to drain and pour the fat into a heatproof measuring cup. Return 1/4 cup of the fat to the skillet, and stir in the onions, garlic and hot-pepper flakes. Stirring frequently, cook for five minutes or until the onions are soft and translucent. Add the chopped tomatoes, cover the skillet, and simmer for five minutes or so.

Meanwhile, bring 2 to 3 quarts of lightly salted water to a boil in a large pot. Pour in a splash of vegetable oil to prevent foaming, then drop in the pastina and boil it for about three minutes, until it is just slightly resistant to the bite—*al dente*. Drain the pastina in a sieve and stir into the tomato sauce. Add the beans and grated cheese. Crumble the bacon over the top, stir, and taste for seasoning. Simmer over low heat for three or four minutes or until the beans are heated through. Transfer the pasta and beans to a large heated bowl and serve at once.

■ AMERICAN COOKING: THE MELTING POT

## Bulgur with Aromatic Vegetables

**To serve 4**

| | |
|---|---|
| 3 tablespoons butter | 2 cups chicken stock |
| 1/4 cup chopped carrots | 1/4 teaspoon salt |
| 1/4 cup chopped celery | 2 tablespoons chopped fresh parsley leaves |
| 1/4 cup chopped onion | |
| 1 cup bulgur | |

In a heavy 1- to 1 1/2-quart saucepan, melt the butter over moderate heat. Add the chopped vegetables and cook, stirring, for one minute. Add the bulgur and stir for four or five minutes, until the vegetables are soft and the bulgur is golden brown. Add the chicken stock and salt, and bring to a boil. Reduce the heat to low, cover

the pan, and simmer for 30 to 40 minutes or until all of the liquid has been absorbed. Stir in the parsley, and serve the bulgur from a heated bowl.

■ CHICKEN AND GAME HEN MENUS

## Harlow House Baked Beans

*Built in 1677 as the Harlow family home in Plymouth, Massachusetts, Harlow House is now a museum where—upon occasion—local women dressed in Pilgrim costumes prepare such traditional breakfast fare as baked beans and fish cakes.* ❧

**To make about 3 quarts**

| | |
|---|---|
| 4 cups (2 pounds) dried pea or Great Northern beans, soaked overnight and drained | 1/2 cup dark-brown sugar |
| | 1 tablespoon dry mustard |
| | 1 teaspoon freshly ground black pepper |
| 3 large onions, peeled, 2 each pierced with 2 whole cloves | 1/2 pound salt pork in 1 piece, with rind left on |
| 2 teaspoons salt | |
| 3/4 cup dark molasses | |

Place the beans in a heavy 4- to 5-quart casserole with the plain onion and 1 teaspoon of salt. Add enough water to cover them by 1 inch. Bring the water to a boil over moderate heat, meanwhile skimming the foam that rises to the surface. Boil the beans for 10 minutes. Reduce the heat to low, partially cover the casserole, and simmer for about one hour, until the beans are tender. Add boiling water to the pot if necessary to keep the beans covered; drain in a fine sieve set over a bowl. Discard the onion, but reserve the cooking liquid. There should be about 8 cups of liquid; add water if necessary.

In a deep bowl, mix the molasses, 1/4 cup of the brown sugar, the mustard, 1 teaspoon of salt and the pepper. Pour in about 1/2 cup of the bean liquid, and stir to blend the ingredients well. Stir in 4 1/2 cups of the bean liquid, then add the beans, and turn them about gently with a spoon until they are evenly coated. The beans should be covered by 1/2 inch. Add more bean liquid if necessary, and stir gently to mix.

Preheat the oven to 250°F. Place the clove-pierced onions in the bottom of a 4- to 5-quart bean pot, and ladle the bean mixture over them. Score the fatty side of the salt pork by making crisscrossing diagonal cuts about 1/2 inch deep and 1/2 inch apart over the entire surface. With a spoon, push the salt pork down into the beans, letting only the top edge protrude above them. Cover the pot with a piece of foil and set the lid securely in place.

Bake the beans in the middle of the oven for 5 hours, adding more bean liquid if they become dry. Then remove the lid and the foil, spread the remaining 1/4 cup of brown sugar over the beans, and bake for one hour longer. Serve the beans directly from the pot. Leftover beans can be refrigerated in the same pot; if tightly covered, they can safely be kept for up to 10 days. Add a little more water before reheating the beans in the oven.

■ AMERICAN COOKING: NEW ENGLAND

the fat in the skillet. Stirring frequently, cook for about five minutes, until the vegetables are soft but not brown. Stir in the bean paste, then add the beans and pork bits, reduce the heat to low, and simmer uncovered for 10 minutes.

Transfer the entire contents of the skillet to the heavy saucepan, and add the rice, salt and 2 cups of water. Stirring constantly, bring to a boil over high heat. Reduce the heat to low, cover tight, and simmer for about 20 minutes, until the rice is tender and all of the liquid has been absorbed. Taste and season with the salt and some pepper. Serve at once.

■ AMERICAN COOKING: CREOLE AND ACADIAN

## Refried Beans

*Instead of being presented as a vegetable, the beans may be served on lettuce as a topping for tostados—fried corn tortillas. In that case they can be accompanied by chopped tomatoes, chopped jalapeño peppers and sliced scallions.* ❧

**To serve 4 to 6**

| | |
|---|---|
| 2 cups (1 pound) dried pinto beans, pink beans or red kidney beans, soaked overnight and drained | 2 tomatoes, peeled, seeded and chopped coarse |
| | 1½ teaspoons finely chopped garlic |
| 6 cups cold water | ½ cup lard |
| 1 cup coarsely chopped onions | 1 teaspoon salt |
| | Sour cream (optional) |

Place the beans in a 3- to 4-quart heavy casserole, and add the water, ½ cup of the onions, ¼ cup of the tomatoes, the garlic and 1 tablespoon of the lard. Bring the water to a boil over high heat; boil the beans for 10 minutes, cover the pan partially, and reduce the heat to low. Simmer the beans for 1½ hours. Add the teaspoon of salt and, over the lowest possible heat, simmer for another 30 minutes or until the beans are very tender. If the beans look dry, add boiling water by the ¼ cup; however, when the beans are fully cooked they should have absorbed most of the cooking liquid. Drain the beans in a colander set over a bowl; reserve the cooking liquid.

In a heavy 12-inch skillet, melt 2 tablespoons of the lard over moderate heat. Add the remaining onions and cook for five minutes or until the onions are translucent but not brown. Stir in the remaining tomatoes, and simmer for two or three minutes. Reduce the heat to low.

Add about ½ cup of the beans to the skillet, mash them flat with a table fork, then stir in 1 tablespoon of the remaining lard. Repeat, alternating about 1 cup of the beans with 1 tablespoon of the lard until all of the beans and lard have been mashed together. The mixture should be moist and creamy. If it seems dry, beat in the reserved bean liquor by the tablespoonful until the beans achieve the consistency you desire.

Mound the refried beans in a heated serving bowl, and serve at once, accompanied if you like by sour cream.

■ AMERICAN COOKING: THE GREAT WEST

REFRIED BEANS

## Black Beans and Rice

**To serve 6 to 8**

| | |
|---|---|
| 1 cup dried black beans, soaked overnight and drained | garlic |
| | ½ cup finely chopped onions |
| ¼ cup vegetable oil | ¼ cup finely chopped green pepper |
| ¼ cup finely cubed lean salt pork | 1½ cups long-grain white rice |
| 1 teaspoon finely chopped | 1½ teaspoons salt |
| | Freshly ground black pepper |

Place the beans in a heavy 3- to 4-quart saucepan, and add enough water to cover them by 1 inch. Bring the water to a boil over moderate heat, meanwhile skimming the foam that rises to the surface. Boil the beans for 10 minutes. Reduce the heat to low, partially cover the pan, and simmer the beans for one hour or until they are tender but still intact. Do not stir them while they cook (the spoon might break them), but add boiling water if the beans look dry. Drain the beans in a colander. Mash 2 tablespoons of them to a smooth paste with a mortar and pestle or in a small bowl with the back of a fork. Set the beans and bean paste aside.

In a heavy 10- to 12-inch skillet, heat the oil over moderate heat. Fry the pork in the oil, turning the dice over with a wooden spoon until they become crisp and brown and render all of their fat. Remove them from the skillet with a slotted spoon, and drain them on paper towels. Add the garlic, onions and green pepper to

# Cassoulet

*Every region of France seems to have its special way of making this splendid white-bean dish. The version given here combines the beans with duck, pork, sausage and lamb; others mix in a variety of pork products—including the feet—or blend lamb with partridge or feature preserved goose. The recipe may sound intimidating. In fact, the process is simple: The duck and pork loin are roasted while the beans are cooked with sausage and salt pork. The lamb is cooked in a sauce, then assembled with the other ingredients for baking.* ❧

### To serve 12

| | |
|---|---|
| One 4- to 5-pound duck | 2½ teaspoons crumbled dried thyme |
| 2 pounds boned pork loin | |
| 6½ cups chicken stock | 2 pounds boned lamb shoulder, cut into 1-inch cubes |
| 6 cups dried white beans, preferably Great Northern, soaked overnight and drained | |
| | 3 garlic cloves, chopped fine |
| | Two 1-pound 13-ounce cans tomatoes, drained and chopped |
| 1½ pounds Polish sausage ring | |
| ¼ pound lean salt pork | 1 cup dry white wine |
| 2 whole onions plus 3 cups chopped onions | ½ cup chopped fresh parsley leaves |
| Bouquet garni, made of 4 parsley sprigs, 1 bay leaf and 1 halved garlic clove, tied in cheesecloth | 1 bay leaf |
| | Salt |
| | Freshly ground black pepper |
| | 1 or 2 dill sprigs for garnish |

Preheat the oven to 325°F. Place the duck, breast side up, in a shallow roasting pan, and set it in the oven. At the same time, place the pork loin in a small casserole, pour in ½ cup of the chicken stock, cover the casserole, and set it in the oven. Roast the pork for about an hour and a half or until the juices run clear when the loin is pierced deeply with a knife. A meat thermometer inserted into the pork will register 170°F. Roast the duck for two to two and a half hours, or until the juices of the thigh run clear when it is pierced or a meat thermometer inserted into the thigh registers 180°F. Set both meats aside.

While the meats are roasting, place the beans in a large pot. Pour in the remaining 6 cups of stock and, if necessary, add enough water to cover the beans by 1 inch. Bring the stock to a boil over moderate heat, meanwhile skimming off the foam that rises to the surface. Boil the beans for 10 minutes. Add the sausage, salt pork, two whole onions, bouquet garni and ½ teaspoon of the thyme. Reduce the heat to low, and simmer the beans uncovered for 30 minutes, adding more boiling water if necessary. Remove the sausage and set it aside. Continue cooking the beans for another 30 minutes, or until they are barely tender. Discard the bouquet garni and onions. Set the salt pork aside. Drain the beans and save the liquid.

Transfer 3 tablespoons of fat from the pan in which the duck roasted to a heavy 10- to 12-inch skillet over moderately high heat. Add enough of the lamb cubes to cover the bottom of the skillet without crowding and, stirring with a wooden spoon, brown the lamb on all sides. Add extra duck fat if needed. As the pieces brown, transfer them to a plate. When all of the lamb is browned,

set it aside. Add the chopped onions and garlic to the skillet, and cook, stirring, over moderate heat for five minutes or until the onions are soft. Add the tomatoes, wine, parsley, bay leaf and the remaining 2 teaspoons of thyme. Put the lamb back in the skillet, cover, and simmer it over low heat for 20 minutes.

Using a slotted spoon, remove the pieces of lamb from this sauce. Pour the sauce into a bowl and stir in 3 cups of bean liquid. Add salt and pepper to taste.

With a large, sharp knife, slice the pork roast, then cut each slice into bite-sized pieces. Cut the legs and wings from the duck; remove the skin and fat from the body, then cut the meat into bite-sized pieces. Slice the salt pork and sausage.

Preheat the oven to 350°F. To assemble the cassoulet, spread a thick layer of beans on the bottom of one 10- to 11-quart casserole or two 5- to 6-quart casseroles. Top with a generous layer of lamb, sausage, pork and duck, saving the legs and wings for garnish. Repeat with another layer of beans and most of the rest of the meats. Finish with the remaining beans. Garnish with the duck legs and wings—and a few pieces of the meats. Pour the sauce over all. The sauce should rise nearly to the top, but the dish should not be awash. Cover the cassoulet and bake it for two hours. If the cassoulet seems dry, add leftover bean liquor as necessary. When ready to serve, garnish the cassoulet with a sprig or two of dill.

■ GREAT DINNERS FROM LIFE

# Beans with Fruit and Vegetables

### To serve 4 to 6

| | |
|---|---|
| 1 cup dried white beans, preferably Great Northern or navy beans, soaked overnight and drained | peeled, cored and cut into ¼-inch wedges |
| | 1 pound green beans, trimmed and cut into 2-inch lengths |
| ½ pound slab lean bacon, cut lengthwise into 3 strips and crosswise into halves | 1 cup coarsely diced scraped carrots |
| | 3 boiling potatoes, peeled and cut into ½-inch dice |
| 1½ pounds cooking apples and 1½ pounds pears, peeled, cored and cut into ¼-inch wedges, or 3 pounds cooking apples, | Salt |
| | Freshly ground black pepper |

Place the dried beans in a heavy 5- to 6-quart casserole, and add enough water to cover them by 1 inch. Bring the water to a boil over moderate heat, meanwhile skimming the foam that rises to the surface. Boil for 10 minutes. Reduce the heat to very low, add the bacon, partially cover the casserole, and simmer the beans for one hour or until they are barely tender.

Add the apples, pears, green beans, carrots, potatoes, salt to taste and a few grindings of pepper. Partially cover the casserole and simmer, occasionally stirring gently, for 30 minutes, until the fruits and vegetables are tender and the beans fully cooked. Taste for seasoning and serve hot from a heated bowl.

■ THE COOKING OF GERMANY

## Basque Chickpea Stew with Sausage

**To serve 4 to 6**

| | |
|---|---|
| 1 cup dried chickpeas, soaked overnight and drained | One 1-pound can solid-pack tomatoes, drained and coarsely chopped |
| 1/2 pound *chorizo* or other garlic-seasoned smoked pork sausage | 1 teaspoon salt |
| 2 tablespoons olive oil | Freshly ground black pepper |
| 1/2 cup finely chopped onions | 2 tablespoons chopped fresh parsley leaves |

Place the chickpeas in a heavy 2- to 3-quart saucepan. Add enough cold water to cover them by at least 1 inch, and bring to a boil over moderate heat, meanwhile skimming the foam from the surface. Reduce the heat to low, cover the pan partially, and simmer the chickpeas for two to two and a half hours, until tender but still intact. Add boiling water from time to time if necessary. Drain the cooked chickpeas.

Place the sausages in an 8- to 10-inch skillet, and prick them in two or three places with the tip of a knife. Add enough water to cover, and bring to a boil over high heat. Reduce the heat to low and simmer, uncovered, for five minutes. Drain the sausages on paper towels; slice them into 1/2-inch rounds.

Heat the oil in a heavy 10- to 12-inch skillet. Add the onions and cook, stirring, for five minutes, until soft and translucent. Add the chickpeas, sausages and tomatoes; sprinkle with salt and pepper. Simmer, uncovered, over moderate heat until hot. Pour the stew into individual heated bowls, sprinkle with parsley, and serve at once.

■ AMERICAN COOKING: THE MELTING POT

## Hopping John

*In the American South, legend holds that hopping John must be eaten before noon on New Year's Day to ensure good luck in the coming year.* ◆●

**To serve 8 to 10**

| | |
|---|---|
| 2 cups (1 pound) dried black-eyed peas, rinsed | about 2 inches long and 1/2 inch wide |
| 6 cups cold water | 1 cup finely chopped onions |
| 1 pound salt pork with rind removed, cut into strips | 2 1/2 cups long-grain white rice |

Place the black-eyed peas in a 3- to 4-quart casserole, add the water, and bring to a boil over high heat. Reduce the heat, cover partially, and simmer for 30 minutes.

Meanwhile, drop the salt-pork strips into a pot of boiling water; bring the water back to a boil. Immediately drain the strips, pat them dry with paper towels, and place them in a 10- to 12-inch skillet. Fry, uncovered, over moderately high heat for 10 to 12 minutes, turning the strips frequently. When the strips are brown and crisp and have rendered all of their fat, transfer them to paper towels to drain. Add the chopped onions to the fat remaining in the skillet, and cook over moderate heat for five minutes, stirring

frequently, until the onions are soft but not brown. Remove the skillet from the heat.

After the peas have cooked, stir in the salt pork, onions and rice, and bring the liquid back to a boil. Cover the casserole tight, reduce the heat to low, and simmer for 20 to 30 minutes, or until the peas are tender and the rice is dry and fluffy. Taste for seasoning and serve at once.

■ AMERICAN COOKING: SOUTHERN STYLE

## Falafel Cutlets with Tahini Sauce

*In eastern Mediterranean countries falafel—ground, molded and fried chickpeas—in pita bread is a popular fast food sold at sidewalk stands, and is as dearly loved there as hamburgers are in the United States. In this recipe the falafel is made with canned chickpeas, to save time, and shaped into cutlets, which are served with a nutty-flavored sauce featuring tahini, a paste of ground sesame seeds. Tahini is available where Middle Eastern foods are sold.* ◆●

**To serve 4**

| | |
|---|---|
| 5 slices homemade-type white bread, torn into pieces | 1 egg |
| 1/3 cup loosely packed parsley sprigs, plus 4 parsley sprigs for garnish | 1 tablespoon *tahini* |
| | 3/4 cup dry bread crumbs |
| | 1 tablespoon dark sesame oil |
| 1/2 teaspoon dried marjoram | 2 tablespoons peanut oil, approximately |
| 3/4 teaspoon salt | 8 lemon slices for garnish |
| 1 1/4 teaspoons paprika | |
| 1/4 teaspoon dried thyme | TAHINI SAUCE |
| 1/4 teaspoon ground coriander | 1 1/4 cups sour cream |
| 1/4 teaspoon cayenne pepper | 1/3 cup *tahini* |
| 1/8 teaspoon ground cumin | 1/4 cup milk |
| 1/8 teaspoon freshly ground black pepper | 4 teaspoons fresh lemon juice |
| One 20-ounce can chickpeas, rinsed and drained | 1/2 teaspoon salt |
| | 1/4 teaspoon ground coriander |
| 1 small onion, quartered | 1/4 teaspoon ground cumin |
| 1 large garlic clove, crushed | 1/4 teaspoon dried thyme |
| | 1/4 teaspoon cayenne pepper |

In a food processor fitted with a steel blade or in a blender, combine the bread, 1/3 cup of parsley, marjoram, salt, 1/2 teaspoon of the paprika, 1/4 teaspoon of thyme, the coriander, cayenne, cumin and black pepper. Process until the bread is reduced to crumbs. Transfer the mixture to a large bowl.

In the food processor or blender, combine the chickpeas, onion and garlic, and process until chopped fine; stir into the

260

BASQUE CHICKPEA STEW WITH SAUSAGE

bread mixture. Add the egg and 1 tablespoon of *tahini*. Spoon this mixture onto aluminum foil, flatten it to a thickness of 1 inch, wrap in the foil, and freeze for 20 minutes.

Meanwhile, prepare the *tahini* sauce by first combining in a clean processor bowl or blender jar all of the sauce ingredients; process until smooth. Transfer the sauce to a mixing bowl, cover with plastic wrap, and set aside at room temperature.

Spread the dry bread crumbs on a large baking sheet. Divide the *falafel* mixture into four portions. Flatten each into an oval cutlet about 6 inches long and ¾ inch thick, and coat both sides with crumbs, pressing to help them adhere.

In a heavy 10- to 12-inch skillet over high heat, combine the sesame oil and 2 tablespoons of peanut oil, heat for one minute, until hot but not smoking. Add the cutlets and brown them for three minutes on one side, two on the other, adding more peanut oil if necessary.

Place the cutlets on four heated dinner plates. Top them with some *tahini* sauce, and sprinkle them with the remaining paprika. Garnish the plates with lemon slices and parsley sprigs. Serve the remaining sauce separately.

■ MEDITERRANEAN MENUS

## Smoked Pork Chops and Lentils

**To serve 6**

| | |
|---|---|
| ¼ cup vegetable oil | including 2 inches of the |
| 1 teaspoon finely chopped | green tops |
|   garlic | ¼ cup chopped fresh parsley |
| 2½ cups chicken stock | leaves |
| 2½ cups dried lentils | Six 6-ounce smoked pork loin |
| 1 cup finely chopped scallions | chops, about 1 inch thick |

In a heavy 4- to 5-quart casserole, heat the vegetable oil over moderate heat. Add the garlic and stir for a minute or so, then pour in the stock and bring to a boil over high heat. Stir in the lentils, scallions and parsley and, when the mixture returns to a boil, add the pork chops, turning them to moisten them evenly. Cover the casserole tight, reduce the heat to low, and simmer for about 45 minutes, until the lentils are tender but not falling apart. Taste for seasoning and serve at once, from the casserole, or mound the lentils on a heated platter and arrange the pork chops around them.

■ AMERICAN COOKING: THE EASTERN HEARTLAND

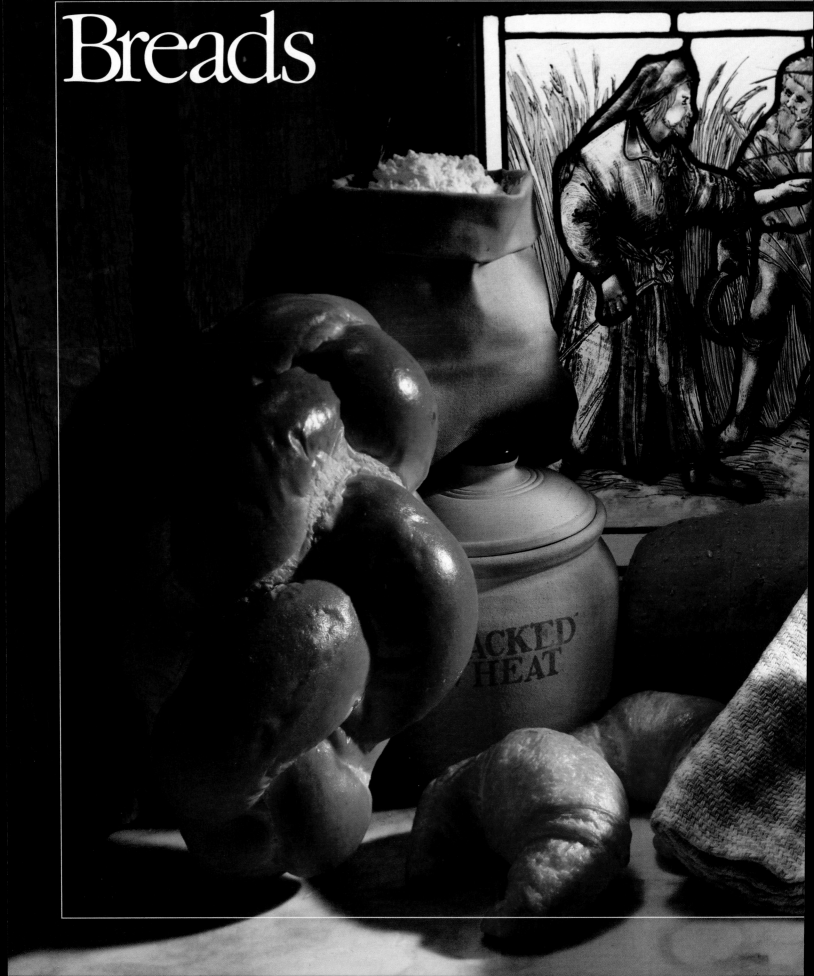

# Breads

FRONTISPIECE (LEFT TO RIGHT): BRAIDED CHALLAH, CROISSANTS,
AMERICAN WHITE BREAD (RECIPE, PAGE 342), BRIOCHE

The prophet Isaiah was the one who called bread "the staff of life." And it has been man's basic nurture from time immemorial. The earliest bread was nothing more than grain crushed to remove its chaff, moistened with water and baked by the fire. Corn tortillas are an enduring example of the sort of flatbread produced until about 4,000 years ago, when the Egyptians discovered the use of yeast and were able to leaven, or lighten, bread.

Both yeast and flours are now so highly refined that they produce breads of surpassing delicacy, as the sampling on the preceding pages gloriously demonstrates. Furthermore, today's baker enjoys the use of reliable, alternative leaveners. After centuries of experiment with ingredients as unlikely as lye—it produced carbon dioxide when combined with water and subjected to heat—a reliable baking powder was created in the 1840s. Its modern versions speed the baking of muffins, biscuits and other quick breads.

Although white wheat flour remains the fundamental ingredient, barley, buckwheat, corn, millet, oat, rice, rye and whole-wheat flours give bread unique flavors, colors, textures and aromas. Numerous recipes mix them with white flour as enhancements. A few recipes even call for them exclusively. But such flours have little or none of white flour's adhesive gluten, an essential to the rising of the dough. Therefore, do not expect these breads to rise the way white breads do.

## Oatcakes

*In Scotland, oatcakes often are buttered and served with cheese or herring, but they also taste delicious with honey or jam.* ❧

**To serve 4**

| | |
|---|---|
| 1³/₄ cups regular oatmeal<br>¹/₄ teaspoon baking powder<br>¹/₂ teaspoon salt | 1 tablespoon butter, melted<br>5 to 8 teaspoons hot water |

Preheat the oven to 350°F. Half a cup at a time, pulverize 1 cup of the oatmeal by blending it at high speed in the jar of an electric blender or by processing it in a food processor equipped with a metal blade. Combine the pulverized oatmeal, the baking powder and salt in a mixing bowl, and stir in the melted butter. When all of the butter has been absorbed, add the hot water, a teaspoonful at a time, stirring continuously until the mixture forms a smooth, firm paste.

Gather the mixture into a ball, and place it on a work surface sprinkled with ¹/₄ cup of the remaining oatmeal. Roll the ball until it is completely covered with the oatmeal flakes. Spread another ¹/₄ cup of oatmeal evenly over the board and, with a rolling pin, roll the ball out into an 8-inch circle about ¹/₈ inch thick. With a pastry wheel or sharp knife, cut the circle into eight wedges. Scatter the remaining ¹/₄ cup of oatmeal on a baking sheet and, with a large metal spatula, transfer the oatmeal wedges to the baking sheet.

Bake the cakes for about 15 minutes. When they are light brown, turn off the heat and open the oven door. Leave the oatcakes in the oven for four or five minutes or until they become firm and crisp. Serve at once.

■ THE COOKING OF THE BRITISH ISLES

## Spoon Bread

**To serve 4 to 6**

| | |
|---|---|
| 2 cups milk<br>1 cup white cornmeal<br>2 tablespoons butter, cut<br>  into bits | 1¹/₂ teaspoons baking powder<br>1 teaspoon salt<br>3 eggs, well beaten |

Preheat the oven to 375°F. With a pastry brush, spread melted or softened butter evenly inside a 1-quart baking dish.

In a heavy 1¹/₂- to 2-quart saucepan, heat the milk over moderate heat until bubbles form around the edges. Stirring constantly with a wooden spoon, pour in the cornmeal in a slow, thin stream to prevent lumps from forming. Take the pan off the heat and beat in the butter bits, baking powder and salt. When the butter is absorbed, mix in the eggs.

Pour the batter into the baking dish and bake for about 40 minutes, or until a knife inserted in the center comes out clean. Serve at once, directly from the dish.

■ AMERICAN COOKING: SOUTHERN STYLE

## Virginia Ham Biscuits

**To make sixteen 2-inch biscuits**

| | |
|---|---|
| ¹/₄ cup vegetable shortening<br>2 cups flour<br>2 teaspoons baking powder<br>¹/₄ teaspoon salt | ¹/₂ cup finely ground Smithfield<br>  or country ham<br>³/₄ cup buttermilk |

Preheat the oven to 425°F. Let the shortening warm to room temperature; it should be soft but not oily. Sift the flour, baking powder and salt together into a deep bowl. Add the ham and shortening and, with a pastry blender or two knives, cut the flour and fat together until the mixture resembles coarse crumbs. Pour in the buttermilk and stir with a fork until the ingredients cohere in a soft, loose mass.

Place the dough on a lightly floured surface and gently knead it —pressing the dough out and folding it back on itself—about 10 times. Pat the dough into a sheet about ¹/₂ inch thick. With a floured 2-inch biscuit cutter or the rim of a glass, cut the dough into biscuits. Place them an inch apart on a baking sheet. Gather the leftover scraps, pat them out as before, and cut out additional biscuits.

Bake the biscuits for 15 to 20 minutes or until they are golden brown. Serve them warm from a napkin-lined basket.

■ AMERICAN COOKING: SOUTHERN STYLE

## Popovers

**To make 8 large or 1 dozen<br>  small popovers**

| | |
|---|---|
| 1¹/₄ cups milk<br>2 tablespoons  vegetable oil<br>¹/₂ teaspoon salt | 1 cup flour<br>¹/₄ cup yellow cornmeal<br>3 eggs at room temperature |

Preheat the oven to 425°F. Heat a heavy 8-cup popover pan or 12-cup muffin pan in the oven for 10 minutes or so.

For the batter, use a wire whisk to combine the milk, oil and salt in a mixing bowl. Sift the flour and cornmeal together over the liquid ingredients. Whisk the mixture for about a minute, until it is smooth. Add the eggs, one at a time, whisking just enough after each addition to incorporate it. Do not overbeat the batter.

Take the hot pan out of the oven, and use a pastry brush to coat the cups with vegetable oil. Ladle the batter into the cups and bake the popovers for 30 minutes or until they are puffed. Do not open the oven door or the popovers might collapse. Reduce the heat to 350°F. and continue baking for five to 10 minutes to firm and brown the popovers. If you like, prick the side of each popover with the tines of a fork or cut a slit with a knife tip to let steam escape, then return the popovers to the oven for a few minutes to crisp them. Remove the popovers from the pan and serve them while they are still hot.

■ FAMILY MENUS

## Sweet Pear Bread

**To make 8 small loaves**

| | |
|---|---|
| 1 cup all-purpose flour | ¼ cup milk |
| ½ cup whole-wheat flour | 1 tablespoon grated orange |
| 2 eggs | peel |
| ⅔ cup sugar | 1 tablespoon unsalted butter |
| 2 small pears | |

Preheat the oven to 375°F. Chill eight individual 3-inch brioche molds, or 6-ounce custard cups in the freezer. Sift the all-purpose and whole-wheat flours together onto wax paper and set aside. With a wire whisk or a rotary or electric beater, beat the eggs and sugar for five to 10 minutes or until they become pale and lemon-colored, and fall from the uplifted beater in a thick ribbon. Slowly beat in the milk. Then stir in the flour mixture.

Peel and core the pears and cut them into ¼-inch dice. Add the diced pears to the batter with the orange peel, gently stirring just enough to distribute the pears and peel throughout the batter.

Melt the butter in a small pan. Remove the molds from the freezer, and brush them with the butter. Pour in the pear batter. Bake the pear bread for 30 minutes or until a tester or toothpick inserted in the center comes out clean. Unmold the bread onto heated plates and serve warm.

■ BRUNCH MENUS

## Cream Biscuits

**To make 8 biscuits**

| | |
|---|---|
| 1½ cups flour | ½ teaspoon salt |
| 2 teaspoons baking powder | 1 cup heavy cream, chilled |

Preheat the oven to 425°F. Sift the flour, baking powder and salt together onto a plate or a strip of wax paper.

In a chilled bowl, beat the cream with a wire whisk or a rotary or electric beater until stiff enough to stand in soft peaks on the beater when it is lifted from the bowl. Sprinkle the flour mixture over the cream, about ½ cup at a time, and fold them together gently but thoroughly with a rubber spatula. Do not overfold.

Place the dough on a lightly floured work surface, and pat it into a rough rectangle about ½ inch thick. Then, with a floured biscuit cutter or the rim of a glass, cut the dough into 2½-inch rounds. Gather the scraps gently, pat the dough flat, and cut as many more rounds as you can.

Arrange the biscuits about 1 inch apart on a large baking sheet, and bake in the middle of the oven for 12 to 15 minutes or until they are golden brown. Serve at once with butter and honey or jam if you like.

■ AMERICAN COOKING: THE NORTHWEST

## Cranberry Muffins

**To make 1 dozen 2½-inch muffins**

| | |
|---|---|
| 1 cup cranberries | 1 cup milk |
| 2¾ cups flour | 1 egg, lightly beaten |
| ¾ cup sugar | ¼ cup butter, melted |
| 4 teaspoons baking powder | and cooled |
| ½ teaspoon salt | |

Preheat the oven to 400°F. With a pastry brush, spread melted or softened butter over the insides of the cups of a medium-sized 12-cup muffin tin (the top of each cup should measure about 2½ inches across).

Put the cranberries through the coarse disk of a food grinder or food mill into a glass or ceramic bowl, or chop them coarse in a food processor, using the metal blade.

Combine the flour, sugar, baking powder and salt, and sift them into a deep mixing bowl. Stirring constantly with a large spoon, pour in the milk in a thin stream. When all the milk has been absorbed, add the egg and the melted, cooled butter. Stir in the cranberries.

Ladle about ⅓ cup of the batter into each muffin-tin cup, filling it about ⅔ full. Bake for 30 minutes, or until the muffins are puffed and brown on top, and a cake tester or toothpick inserted in the center comes out clean. Run a knife around the inside of each cup to loosen the muffins, then turn them out of the tin. Serve them hot or cooled.

■ AMERICAN COOKING: NEW ENGLAND

## Banana Bread

**To make one 9-by-5-inch loaf**

| | |
|---|---|
| ¾ cup unsalted shelled pecans | ½ teaspoon salt |
| ¼ cup seedless raisins | 2 large ripe bananas |
| 2 cups flour | 1 teaspoon vanilla extract |
| 1 tablespoon baking powder | ½ cup butter, softened |
| ¼ teaspoon freshly grated nutmeg | ½ cup sugar |
| | 1 egg |

Preheat the oven to 350°F. With a pastry brush, coat the inside of a 9-by-5-by-3-inch loaf pan with a little melted or softened butter.

Set ¼ cup of the most perfectly shaped pecan halves aside to be used as a garnish. Chop the rest of the nuts coarse and toss them with the raisins. Sift the flour with the baking powder, nutmeg and salt onto wax paper. Peel the bananas, cut them up, and

**CREAM BISCUITS**

put them into a small bowl. With the back of a table fork, mash the bananas to a smooth purée. Stir in the vanilla.

In a deep bowl, cream the softened butter and the sugar, beating them with a large spoon against the sides of the bowl until light and fluffy. Blend in the egg. Then beat in the flour and the bananas alternately, adding about one-third of each mixture at a time, and continue to beat until the batter is smooth. Stir in the chopped pecans and raisins.

Ladle the batter into the loaf pan and arrange the reserved pecan halves on top. Bake the bread for 50 to 60 minutes or until a cake tester or toothpick inserted into the center of the loaf comes out clean. Let the bread cool in the pan for five minutes, then turn it out on a wire cake rack. You can serve the bread either warm or cool.

■ THE COOKING OF THE CARIBBEAN ISLANDS

## Whole-Wheat Biscuits

**To make 10 biscuits**

| | |
|---|---|
| 1 cup whole-wheat flour | 1/3 cup shortening including |
| 1 cup all-purpose flour | 2 tablespoons butter |
| 1 tablespoon baking powder | 3/4 cup milk |
| 1/2 teaspoon salt | |

Preheat the oven to 425° F. Let the shortening warm to room temperature; it should be soft but not oily.

Sift the whole-wheat and all-purpose flours, baking powder and salt into a large bowl. Using a pastry blender or two knives, cut in the shortening until the mixture resembles coarse crumbs. Add the milk and stir the mixture with a fork until the ingredients cohere in a soft, loose mass.

Place the dough on a lightly floured surface, and knead it gently—pressing the dough out and folding it back on itself—about 10 times. Pat the dough into a sheet about 3/4 inch thick, and cut out biscuits with a 2-inch floured biscuit cutter. Place the biscuits an inch apart on a baking sheet. Gather the scraps, pat out the dough as before, and cut more biscuits.

Bake the biscuits for 15 to 20 minutes, or until lightly browned. Serve them warm from a napkin-lined basket.

■ PASTA MENUS

## Mexican Corn Muffins

**To make 1 dozen muffins**

| | |
|---|---|
| 2 eggs | 3/4 cup dark-brown sugar |
| 1/2 cup milk | or 1/2 cup honey |
| 1/2 cup flour | 2 teaspoons grated lime peel |
| 2/3 cup yellow cornmeal | 1/2 teaspoon ground cinnamon |
| 1 1/2 teaspoons baking powder | 1/4 teaspoon vanilla extract |
| 1/4 teaspoon baking soda | 1/3 cup dark raisins |
| 1/2 cup unsalted butter, | 1/2 cup pine nuts or slivered |
| softened | blanched almonds |

Preheat the oven to 350° F. With a pastry brush, spread melted or softened butter inside the cups of a muffin tin with 12 cups, each 2 3/4 inches across. In a small bowl, beat the eggs just until smooth. Blend in the milk. Sift the flour, cornmeal, baking powder and baking soda onto wax paper.

In a large bowl, cream the butter with the sugar or honey by beating and mashing them vigorously against the sides of the bowl until they are light and fluffy. Beat in the lime peel, cinnamon and vanilla extract. A little at a time, beat in the egg mixture alternately with the flour mixture. Stir in the raisins and nuts. Ladle the batter into the muffin tin, filling each cup about two-thirds full.

Bake the muffins for about 30 to 35 minutes or until they are golden and crusty around the edges and a cake tester inserted in the center comes out clean. Serve the hot muffins in a napkin-lined basket or bowl.

■ MEXICAN MENUS

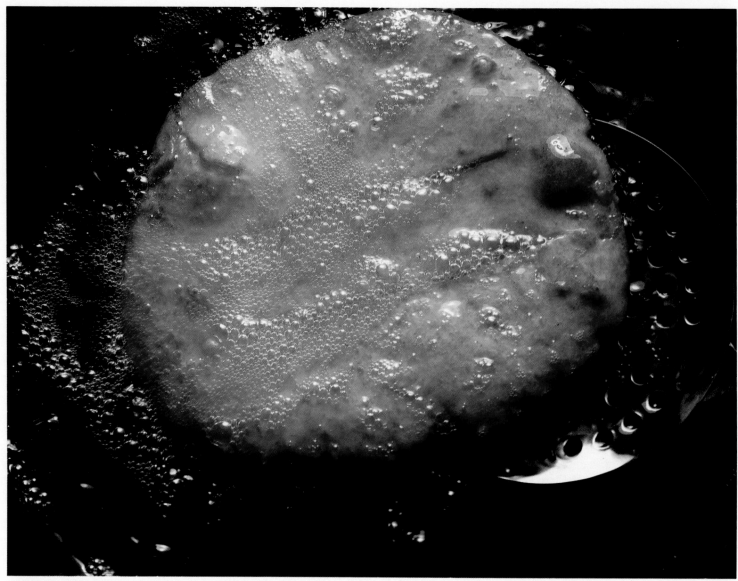

NAVAHO FRY BREAD

## Potato Flatbread

*In Norway, this bread is known as "lefse." It is rolled with a special pastry pin until it is so thin that light shines through it.* ✦●

**To make about 15 rounds**

| | |
|---|---|
| **3 large potatoes, peeled and quartered** | **¼ cup heavy cream** |
| | **½ teaspoon sugar** |
| **2 tablespoons butter, softened and cut into bits** | **1 teaspoon salt** |
| | **1 cup flour** |

Drop the potatoes into enough boiling water to cover them completely, and boil, uncovered, until they are soft but not falling apart. Drain them thoroughly and force them through a ricer or food mill, or mash them in a bowl with a fork. There should be about 2 cups of purée. Add the butter, cream, sugar and salt, and beat until the mixture is smooth. Cover the mixture with plastic wrap and refrigerate it for at least eight hours or overnight.

Gather the potato mixture into a ball, place it on a heavily floured surface, and sprinkle it with about ½ cup of the flour. Knead the mixture by pressing it down with the heel of your hand, pushing it forward, and folding it back on itself. Gradually incorporate the remaining flour into the potato dough. Knead for 10 minutes or until the dough is smooth.

Divide the dough into 15 small balls. With a rolling pin, roll one of the balls into a paper-thin round about 6 inches in diameter. Heat a large griddle or skillet until very hot, drape the round over the pin, and unroll it onto the hot surface. Cook for only a moment or two, until bubbles appear on the top and the bottom browns lightly. With a metal spatula, turn the flatbread over and brown the other side. Place the finished bread on a large plate and keep it covered with a lightly moistened kitchen towel while you roll out and cook the remaining dough.

To serve, butter the bread, roll it loosely, and cut it into diagonal slices. Or sprinkle the buttered bread with sugar and top with honey or jam.

■ AMERICAN COOKING: THE NORTHWEST

## Navaho Fry Bread

**To make three 8-inch rounds**

| | |
|---|---|
| 2 cups flour | 2 tablespoons lard, cut into |
| ½ cup powdered dry milk | ½-inch bits, plus 1 pound |
| 2 teaspoons baking powder | lard for deep-frying |
| ½ teaspoon salt | ½ cup ice water |

Combine the flour, dry milk solids, baking powder and salt, and sift them into a deep bowl. Add the 2 tablespoons of lard bits and, with your fingertips, rub the flour and fat together until the mixture resembles coarse meal. Pour in the water, and toss the ingredients together until the dough can be gathered into a ball. Cover the bowl with plastic wrap or a dampened kitchen towel, and let the dough rest at room temperature for about two hours.

Then cut the dough into three equal pieces. On a lightly floured surface, roll each piece into a round about 8 inches in diameter and ¼ inch thick. With a small, sharp knife, cut two 4- to 5-inch-long parallel slits completely through the dough down the center of each round, spacing the slits about 1 inch apart.

In a heavy 10-inch skillet, melt the pound of lard over moderate heat until it is very hot but not smoking. The melted fat should be about 1 inch deep; add more lard if necessary. Fry the bread rounds, one at a time, for about 2 minutes on each side, turning them once with tongs or a slotted spatula. The bread will puff slightly and become crisp and brown. When it is cooked, drain each round on paper towels. Serve while still warm.

■ AMERICAN COOKING: THE GREAT WEST

## Boston Brown Bread

**To make two 5½-by-3-inch cylindrical loaves**

| | |
|---|---|
| 2 cups buttermilk | 1 cup whole-wheat flour |
| ¾ cup dark molasses | 1 cup yellow corn meal |
| ¾ cup seedless raisins | ¾ teaspoon baking soda |
| 1 cup rye flour | 1 teaspoon salt |

In a deep bowl, beat the buttermilk and molasses together vigorously with a spoon. Stir in the raisins. Combine the rye flour, whole-wheat flour, corn meal, soda and salt, and sift them into the buttermilk mixture, 1 cup at a time, stirring the batter well after each addition.

Thoroughly wash and dry two empty 2½-cup (No. 2) tin cans. With a pastry brush, spread melted or softened butter inside the cans. Pour the batter into the cans. It should fill them to within about 1 inch of the tops. Cover each can loosely with a circle of

buttered wax paper and then with a larger circle of heavy-duty aluminum foil. Make the foil puff up like the top of a French chef's hat, allowing an inch of space above the can so that the batter can rise as it is steamed. Tie the wax paper and foil in place with kitchen string.

Stand the cans on a rack set in a large, deep pot, and pour in enough boiling water to come about three-quarters of the way up the sides of the cans. Return the water to a boil over high heat, cover the pot, and reduce the heat to low. Steam the bread for two and one-quarter hours. Remove the foil and paper from the cans at once, unmold the bread onto a heated platter, and serve it immediately. Or keep the bread in the cans with the foil and paper in place, and then steam it for 10 to 15 minutes to reheat the loaves just before serving. With the covers in place, the loaves can safely be kept in the refrigerator for a week to 10 days.

■ AMERICAN COOKING: NEW ENGLAND

## Pumpernickel Breadsticks

**To make 32 sticks**

| | |
|---|---|
| 1¼ cups all-purpose flour | ½ cup cold water |
| 1 cup pumpernickel rye flour | ¼ cup vegetable oil |
| One ¼-ounce package fast- | 1 tablespoon molasses |
| acting dry yeast | ¼ cup cornmeal |
| 1 tablespoon brown sugar | 1 egg white lightly beaten with |
| 1 tablespoon unsweetened | 1 teaspoon cold water |
| cocoa powder | Coarse (kosher) salt or |
| 1 teaspoon salt | caraway seeds |
| ¼ cup hot tap water | |

In a food processor fitted with a dough blade, combine the all-purpose flour, rye flour, yeast, sugar, cocoa and salt. Process for 10 seconds, or until combined. With the machine running, gradually add the hot water. Blend the cold water, oil and molasses together in a small bowl. With the processor running, slowly pour in the molasses mixture, and process until a dough forms. (To combine the ingredients by hand, mix them in a large bowl and beat with a wooden spoon until thoroughly combined.)

The dough will be quite sticky. If it is too sticky to handle, add extra flour—1 tablespoonful at a time. If it is too dry, add water by the teaspoonful. Process or stir the dough for one minute more to knead it. Then let the dough rest for 20 minutes.

Sprinkle two 17-by-11-inch baking sheets with the cornmeal. Transfer the dough to a lightly floured work surface. Halve the dough and cut each half into 16 pieces. Roll each piece into a 7-inch stick. Arrange the sticks 1 inch apart on the baking sheets. Cover the breadsticks with plastic wrap or dampened kitchen towels and let them rise in a warm—ideally, 70°F.—draft-free place for 30 minutes.

Preheat the oven to 350°F. Brush the breadsticks with the beaten egg white and sprinkle them with coarse salt or caraway seeds. Bake for 30 minutes or until the breadsticks are crisp. Transfer them to a rack to cool.

■ MAKE-AHEAD MENUS

## Dill Bread

**To make one 9-by-5-by-3-inch loaf**

| | |
|---|---|
| ¹/₄ cup tepid water (100°F.) | 1 teaspoon salt |
| One ¹/₄-ounce package active dry yeast or one ³/₅-ounce cake fresh yeast | 1 cup large-curd cottage cheese |
| 2 tablespoons plus 1 teaspoon sugar | 1 egg, lightly beaten, plus 1 egg lightly beaten with 1 tablespoon milk |
| 1 tablespoon butter | 2 tablespoons finely cut fresh dill or 2 teaspoons dried dill weed |
| 2 tablespoons finely chopped onions | |
| 2 to 2¹/₂ cups flour | Coarse (kosher) salt |
| ¹/₄ teaspoon baking soda | |

Pour the tepid water into a small bowl, and add the yeast and 1 teaspoon of the sugar. After two minutes, mix them well. Set in a warm, draft-free place for 10 minutes, until the yeast bubbles up and the mixture almost doubles in volume.

Meanwhile, melt the butter over moderate heat in a small skillet. Add the onions and, stirring frequently, cook for two or three minutes, until they are soft but not brown.

Combine 2 cups of flour, the remaining 2 tablespoons of sugar, the baking soda and salt, and sift them into a deep mixing bowl. Make a well in the center of the dry ingredients, and scrape in the onions. Add the yeast mixture, cottage cheese, egg and dill weed, and gradually incorporate the dry ingredients into the liquid ones with a wooden spoon. Continue to stir until the dough becomes smooth and can be gathered into a medium-soft ball.

Place the ball on a lightly floured surface and knead, pushing the dough down with the heels of your hands, pressing it forward, and folding it back on itself. As you knead, sprinkle flour over the ball by the tablespoonful, adding up to ¹/₂ cup flour, if necessary, to make a firm dough. Knead for 10 minutes, until the dough is smooth, shiny and elastic.

Set the ball of dough in a butter-coated bowl, and turn the ball to butter the entire surface. Cover the bowl with plastic wrap or a dampened kitchen towel, and set it in the warm, draft-free place for about 1 hour, or until it doubles in volume.

With a pastry brush, spread melted or softened butter inside a 9-by-5-by-3-inch loaf pan. Punch the dough down with a blow of your fist and, on a lightly floured surface, shape it into a loaf about 8 inches long and 4 inches wide. Place the dough in the buttered pan, and set it in the warm, draft-free place for about 45 minutes.

Preheat the oven to 375°F. Brush the top of the bread with the egg-and-milk mixture, then bake the loaf for 30 to 35 minutes, or until golden brown. To test for doneness, turn the loaf out on a flat surface, and rap the bottom sharply with your knuckles. The loaf should sound hollow; if not, put it back in the pan and bake for five to 10 minutes longer.

Place the bread on a wire rack and brush the top with melted or softened butter. Sprinkle the loaf lightly with coarse salt and let the bread cool before serving.

■ AMERICAN COOKING: THE EASTERN HEARTLAND

## Monkey Bread

*The story goes that this bread was given its name by 1930s comedienne ZaSu Pitts, who said it was the kind of loaf "you had to monkey around with."* ❦

**To make two 9-inch tube loaves**

| | |
|---|---|
| 2 cups water | 5¹/₂ to 6¹/₂ cups flour |
| 2 boiling potatoes, peeled and quartered | 2 teaspoons salt |
| One ¹/₄-ounce package active dry yeast or one ³/₅-ounce cake fresh yeast | 2 eggs, lightly beaten |
| | 1 cup tepid milk (100°F.) |
| | ¹/₂ cup vegetable shortening |
| ¹/₂ cup sugar | 1 cup butter, melted and cooled |

Bring the water to a boil in a small, heavy saucepan. Drop in the potatoes and boil, uncovered, until they are soft but not falling apart. Drain the potatoes in a sieve set over a bowl, pat them dry with paper towels, and purée them through a food mill or mash them with the back of a fork. You should have about 1 cup of purée. Measure and reserve ¹/₄ cup of the potato water.

When the potato water has cooled to tepid (100°F.), pour it into a shallow bowl. Add the yeast and 1 teaspoon of the sugar; after two minutes, mix them. Set the bowl in a warm, draft-free place for 10 minutes or until the yeast bubbles up and the mixture doubles in volume.

Combine 5¹/₂ cups of the flour, the remaining sugar and the salt in a deep mixing bowl, and make a well in the center. Add the potato purée, the yeast mixture, eggs, milk and vegetable shortening. With a large spoon, mix the dry ingredients into the liquid ones and stir until the dough is smooth and can be gathered into a soft ball. If the dough is dry, add milk or water by the spoonful; if it is sticky, stir in flour by the spoonful.

Place the ball on a lightly floured surface and knead, pushing the dough down with the heels of your hands, pressing it forward, and folding it back on itself. Knead for about 10 minutes, or until the dough is smooth, shiny and elastic.

**Monkey bread diamonds cut from a 12-by-14-inch sheet**

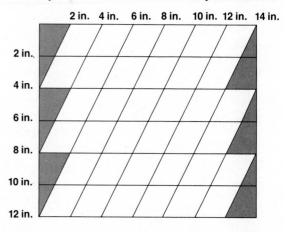

■ **Unusable as diamonds**

With a pastry brush, spread a little softened butter evenly inside a deep mixing bowl. Place the ball in the bowl, and turn it around to butter its entire surface. Cover the bowl with plastic wrap or a dampened kitchen towel and put it in the draft-free place for about one and a half hours, until the dough doubles.

With a pastry brush, spread melted or softened butter evenly over the bottom and sides of two 9-inch tube pans. Punch the dough down with a blow of your fist, and place it on a lightly floured surface. Knead it for a minute or so, then let it rest for 10 minutes. With your hands, pat the dough into a rectangle about 14 inches long, 12 inches wide and ½ inch thick.

Using a ruler and pastry wheel or sharp knife, cut out diamonds about 2 inches long and 2 inches wide. First use the tip of the knife to make tick marks at 2-inch intervals on all four edges of the rectangle. With one 14-inch side toward you, cut diagonally across the rectangle from the lower left-hand corner to the tick mark 6 inches from the upper left-hand corner on the opposite 14-inch side. Make parallel diagonal cuts across the rectangle at every tick mark along the sides of the rectangle. Cut straight across the rectangle from one end to the other at 2-inch intervals.

To assemble the monkey bread, free one diamond at a time and immerse it in the melted, cooled butter. Arrange a layer of diamonds side points touching, in a ring on the bottom of each pan. Repeat with two more layers, making each successive layer fit over spaces left in the previous ring. Cover the pans with plastic wrap, and set them aside in the draft-free place for about 1 hour, or until the loaves double in volume.

Preheat the oven to 375°F. Bake the monkey bread in the middle of the oven for 30 minutes. Turn the loaves out and rap the bottoms sharply with your knuckles. The loaves will sound hollow if the bread is done. Cool on racks before serving. Monkey bread is never sliced. Instead each diner pulls a diamond-shaped piece from the loaf.

■ AMERICAN COOKING: THE GREAT WEST

# Croissants

**To make about 32 crescents**

| | |
|---|---|
| 1¼ cups tepid milk (100°F.)<br>One ¼-ounce package active<br>    dry yeast or one ³/₅-ounce<br>    cake fresh yeast<br>1 teaspoon sugar<br>4 cups flour | 1 teaspoon salt<br>¼ cup butter, cut into pieces,<br>    plus ¾ cup butter, softened<br>1 egg yolk lightly beaten with<br>    2 tablespoons water |

Pour the tepid milk into a small bowl, and sprinkle the yeast and sugar over it. Let the yeast rest for two minutes, then mix well. Sift the flour and salt into a large, deep bowl. Make a well in the flour and pour the yeast mixture into it. Add the butter pieces, and gradually incorporate flour from the well into the liquid until all of the flour is wet and the mixture is a soft, sticky dough.

On an unfloured work surface, knead the dough for about five minutes—pushing the dough down with the heels of your hands, pressing it forward, and folding it back on itself.

Cover the dough with plastic wrap or a dampened kitchen towel, then let it rise at room temperature until doubled in volume—from one and a half to two and a half hours. Punch the dough down to expel the air. Cover the dough and let it rise again, either at room temperature for one hour and then—in a lightly buttered bowl—in the refrigerator for one hour, or place it overnight in the refrigerator.

Flatten the chilled dough on a cool, unfloured work surface. Roll out the dough into a rectangle about ½ inch thick and twice as long as it is wide. With a narrow-bladed metal spatula, spread two-thirds of the rectangle with the softened butter, leaving an unbuttered margin about ¾ inch wide. Fold the unbuttered third of the dough over half of the buttered section, then fold the other buttered section over the top. The dough will thus form three layers, with two layers of butter between them.

With a rolling pin, press the edges of the dough package to seal in the butter. Turn the dough so that a folded side faces toward you, and roll out the dough lightly: Too much pressure will force out the butter. Roll the dough until the rectangle is about twice as long as it is wide. Fold the dough into thirds again. Wrap it in plastic wrap and refrigerate it for one hour.

Place the rectangle on the work surface with a short side facing you. Roll it out lengthwise. Fold as before, wrap in plastic wrap, and return to the refrigerator. Repeat turning, rolling and folding twice more; refrigerate the dough for one hour each time.

On the work surface, roll out the dough ⅛ inch thick. Use a dough scraper or small knife and a ruler to trim the sides and create a long rectangle 12 inches wide. Cut the rectangle into two strips 6 inches wide and, with the scraper or knife, mark points on the outside edge of each strip 3 inches from one end. Then, starting from those points, make marks at 6-inch intervals along the outside edges of the strips. With the ruler as a guide, create triangles by cutting diagonal lines from the end at the center of the strips to the 3-inch marks, and then across the strips at the 6-inch marks.

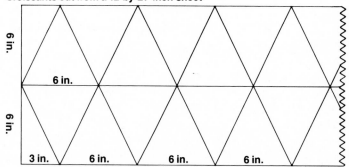

**Croissants cut from a 12-by-27-inch sheet**

To form each croissant, carefully lift one triangle away from the rest and place its base—the shortest side—toward you. Elongate the triangle slightly by rolling it away from you with a rolling pin. Gently stretch the corners of the base so they will form well-defined points on the finished croissant. Starting at the base, roll up the triangle tightly. Tuck the tip underneath—it will emerge in the baking. Curl the ends of the triangle slightly toward each other to form a crescent.

With a pastry brush, spread melted or softened butter lightly on one or more baking sheets. Place the croissants on the baking sheet, leaving at least 1 inch between them. Cover them with a dampened kitchen towel, and let them rise—about one hour at room temperature or overnight in the refrigerator—until doubled in volume.

Preheat the oven to 425°F. Brush the beaten egg-yolk mixture over the croissants, taking care not to drip it onto the baking sheet, where it would act as a glue to hold the rolls in place. Bake the croissants for two minutes, reduce the oven temperature to 375°F., and bake them for 15 to 20 minutes longer, until they turn golden brown. Cool them on a wire rack for 10 minutes or so, then serve them warm in a napkin-lined basket.

■ THE GOOD COOK: BREADS

# Braided Challah

*This Jewish bread takes its name from the challah, or tithe of dough, given to Hebrew priests in ancient times. The bread may be shaped in any form, but the four-strand braid is classic.* ◆●

**To make one 14-inch braided loaf**

| | |
|---|---|
| 1 cup tepid water (100°F.)<br>Three ¼-ounce packages<br>    active dry yeast or three<br>    ³/₅-ounces cakes fresh yeast<br>4 teaspoons sugar<br>5 cups flour | 1 tablespoon salt<br>3 eggs<br>¼ cup vegetable shortening<br>1 egg yolk lightly beaten with<br>    2 tablespoons water |

Pour ½ cup of the tepid water into a small bowl, and add the yeast and 1 teaspoon of the sugar. After two minutes, mix them well. Set the bowl in a warm, draft-free place for 10 minutes, or until the yeast bubbles up and doubles in volume.

In a deep mixing bowl, combine 4 cups of the flour, the

remaining sugar and the salt. Make a well in the center, pour in the yeast and remaining tepid water, and add the eggs and vegetable shortening. With a wooden spoon, gradually incorpte the dry ingredients into the liquid ones. Add up to 1 cup of additional flour, beating it in ¼ cup at a time, adding only enough to form a dough that can be gathered into a soft ball. If the dough becomes difficult to stir, work in the flour with your fingers.

Place the dough on a lightly floured surface and knead by pressing it down, pushing it forward several times with the heel of your hand, and folding it back on itself. Knead for 15 minutes or until the dough is smooth and elastic. To avoid sticking, sprinkle the dough occasionally with a bit of flour.

Shape the dough into a ball and place it in a lightly oiled bowl. Cover with plastic wrap and set aside in the warm, draft-free place for 45 minutes, or until the dough doubles in bulk. Punch the dough down with a single blow of your fist, and knead it again for a few minutes. Set aside to rest for 10 minutes.

With a pastry brush, spread flavorless oil or vegetable shortening lightly over a large baking sheet. Divide the dough into four equal pieces. On a lightly floured surface, roll each piece into a rope about 22 inches long. The ropes should be about 2 inches in diameter at the center and taper to about ½ inch at both ends.

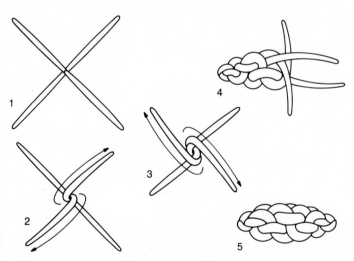

Arrange the four ropes of dough in the shape of an X with the tapered ends overlapping slightly at the center. Begin the four-part braid by lifting the ends of two opposite ropes and twisting them over the other pair to reverse their positions, still preserving the X shape. Then lift and reverse the other pair of ropes. Repeat, lifting and reversing one pair at a time to weave the four ropes into a compact braid. Tuck the loose ends under the loaf and place it on the baking sheet. Let the loaf rise in the draft-free place for about 30 minutes.

Preheat the oven to 400°F. Brush the top of the loaf with the egg yolk and water mixture, and bake in the middle of the oven for 15 minutes, then reduce the heat to 375°F. and continue baking for 15 minutes longer or until the *challah* is golden brown and crusty. Cool it on a cake rack.

■ MIDDLE EASTERN COOKING

# Brioche

| To make two 8-inch or twelve 3-inch brioches | |
|---|---|
| One ¼-ounce package active dry yeast or one ⅗-ounce cake fresh yeast | 1 teaspoon salt |
| ¼ cup tepid water (100°F.) | 6 eggs |
| 4 cups flour | 1¼ cups unsalted butter, softened |
| ¼ cup sugar | 1 egg yolk beaten with 2 teaspoons water |

Mix the yeast with the tepid water, and leave it for 10 minutes. Put the flour, sugar and salt into a bowl. Make a well in the center, and pour in the yeast mixture. Break in the eggs. With your fingers, mix the eggs and yeast, gradually pulling flour in from the sides of the well until all of the flour is moistened. The dough should be soft and sticky.

Turn the dough out onto a cool, unfloured work surface. Using your hands and a pastry scraper, knead the dough by pressing it forward with the heel of your hand and folding it back on itself; if the dough does not cohere, add a little flour. As the dough spreads, use a pastry scraper to pull it together. Knead for about 10 minutes, until smooth and elastic.

Break off walnut-sized pieces of the butter and, with the pastry scraper, fold them one at a time into the dough. Knead again until the dough is smooth; put it in a large bowl, cover with plastic wrap, and leave it in a warm, draft-free place for three to four hours, until it triples in volume.

Punch the dough down several times to expel the air, then knead it lightly in the bowl for two or three minutes. Cover the bowl with plastic wrap and let the dough rise again.

For best results, let the dough rise in the refrigerator for six to eight hours or overnight. Otherwise, let the dough rise at room temperature until doubled in bulk, three to four hours, then chill it for at least half an hour before shaping it.

With a pastry brush, spread melted or softened butter inside two 8-inch or twelve 3-inch brioche molds. Transfer the dough to a cool, lightly floured work surface, and use a pastry scraper or knife to cut it into two or 12 parts.

For each brioche, cut off about one quarter of the portion. Knead the larger piece into a ball, and put it into a mold. Shape the smaller piece into a ball, then roll it to make a tapered, teardrop shape. Indent the center of the ball with your fingertips—pressing down to the bottom of the mold. Insert the small piece, tapered end down. Its rounded top will resemble a topknot.

Cover the filled molds and let the dough rise in the draft-free place until doubled in volume, about one and a half hours.

Preheat the oven to 425°F. Brush each brioche with the beaten egg yolk without filling the seam between the small and large pieces. Bake for 10 minutes, then reduce the heat to 375°F. and bake for 30 minutes more. A brioche is done if a skewer, inserted into the topknot, comes out clean. Invert the brioches onto a wire rack to cool for 15 minutes before serving.

■ THE GOOD COOK: BREADS

## Squash Rolls

**To make about 2½ dozen rolls**

| | |
|---|---|
| One ½-pound acorn, Hubbard or butternut squash, peeled, seeded and cut into 2-inch chunks | cakes fresh yeast<br>½ cup sugar<br>5 to 6 cups flour<br>1 teaspoon salt |
| ½ cup tepid water (100°F.) | 1 cup tepid milk (100°F.) |
| Two ¼-ounce packages active dry yeast or two ⅗-ounce | ½ cup butter, softened, plus 2 tablespoons butter, melted |

Place the squash in the top part of a steamer or in a steamer basket over about 2 inches of water. The squash must be at least 1 inch above the water. Cover the pan and bring the water to a boil over high heat. Steam the squash for 20 to 30 minutes or until it is tender. Purée the squash through a food mill or mash it smooth with a fork. You should have about ½ cup of purée.

Pour the tepid water into a small bowl, and add the yeast and a pinch of the sugar. Let the yeast and sugar rest for two or three minutes, then mix well. Set in a warm, draft-free place for about 10 minutes or until the yeast bubbles up and the mixture almost doubles in volume.

Sift 5 cups of the flour, the remaining sugar and the salt into a deep mixing bowl and make a well in the center. Pour in the yeast mixture, add the squash purée, the milk and softened butter. With a large wooden spoon, gradually beat the dry ingredients into the liquid ones. Continue to beat until the dough is smooth.

Gather the dough into a ball and knead it on a lightly floured surface, pushing the dough down with the heels of your hands, pressing it forward, and folding it back on itself. As you knead, gradually incorporate up to 1 cup more flour until the dough is no longer sticky. Then continue to knead for about 10 minutes, or until the dough is smooth, shiny and elastic.

Place the ball of dough in a large buttered bowl and turn it to coat it evenly. Cover the bowl with plastic wrap or a dampened kitchen towel and put it in the draft-free place for about 1 hour, to allow the dough to double in volume. Punch the dough down with a single blow of your fist and knead it for a minute or so. Let the dough rest for 10 minutes.

With a pastry brush, spread a little melted or softened butter inside three 9-inch round cake pans. On a lightly floured surface, roll the dough into a rough rectangle about 1 inch thick. With a biscuit cutter or the rim of a glass, cut the dough into 2½-inch rounds. Gather the scraps into a ball, roll them out as before and cut out as many more rounds as you can. Using the blunt edge of a table knife, make a deep crease just off center in each round, taking care not to cut all the way through. Fold the smaller part of the round over the larger part and press the edges together securely. Place the rolls about ½ inch apart in the buttered cake pans and brush the tops with the melted butter. Set the rolls in the draft-free place to rise for about 15 minutes.

Preheat the oven to 450°F. Bake the rolls for 12 to 15 minutes, until golden brown. Serve hot from a napkin-lined basket.

■ AMERICAN COOKING: NEW ENGLAND

## Portuguese Corn Bread

*Corn flour is widely available by its Spanish name, "masa harina." If you cannot find it, pulverize yellow cornmeal in a blender or food processor until reduced to fine particles.* ✦●

**To make one 9-inch round loaf**

| | |
|---|---|
| 1 cup boiling water plus ¼ cup tepid water (100°F.) | One ¼-ounce package active dry yeast or one ⅗-ounce cake fresh yeast |
| 1½ cups corn flour | |
| 1 teaspoon salt | 1¾ to 2 cups all-purpose flour |
| 1 tablespoon olive oil | |

Pour the boiling water into a large mixing bowl and, stirring constantly with a wooden spoon, gradually add 1 cup of the corn flour and the salt. Stir vigorously until smooth. Blend in the olive oil, then let the mixture cool to lukewarm. Meanwhile, pour the tepid water into a small bowl and add the yeast. After two minutes, mix them well. Set the yeast mixture in a warm draft-free place for 10 minutes, or until it bubbles up and doubles in volume.

Stir the yeast mixture into the corn-flour mixture. Stirring constantly, gradually add the remaining ½ cup of corn flour and 1 cup of the all-purpose flour. Gather the dough into a ball, place it in an oiled bowl, and cover it with plastic wrap or a dampened kitchen towel. Set the dough aside in the warm, draft-free place for 30 minutes, or until it doubles in bulk. Place the dough on a lightly floured surface and punch it down with your fist to expel large gas bubbles. Then knead it by pressing it down with the heel of your hand, pushing it forward, and folding it back on itself repeatedly for about 5 minutes, meanwhile adding up to 1 cup more all-purpose flour to make a firm but not stiff dough.

With a pastry brush, lightly coat a 9-inch pie pan with olive oil. Using your hands, pat the dough into a round, flat loaf, and place it in the oiled pan. Cover the loaf with plastic wrap and set it in the draft-free place for 30 minutes to double in bulk again.

Preheat the oven to 350°F. Bake the bread in the middle of the oven for 40 minutes or until the top is golden. Transfer it to a rack to cool.

■ THE COOKING OF SPAIN AND PORTUGAL

# Cakes & Pies

FRONTISPIECE: BLACK FOREST CHERRY CAKE

The crown jewels of baking—cakes lavished with coconut, cherries or candied chestnuts and pies gleaming with fresh fruits—are also the delight of the kitchen. Not all cakes are fancy, of course, nor are all pies laved with glaze. The plainest batter baked with fruit on top makes an opulent dessert, as does grandmother's strawberry shortcake, which is simply biscuits with berries.

All cakes and pies, however, require attention to detail. From buttering the pan to cooling the finished product, each step must be executed with care.

Ingredients must be of the highest quality and handled with respect. Letting them come to room temperature pays high dividends. Butter beats to a creamy softness. Eggs are easier to separate straight from the refrigerator, but both whites and yolks beat to greater heights when slightly warm.

Measuring is all-important. A bit too much leavening will make a cake overflow its pans; too little shortening produces a pastry shell that cracks when the pie is cut into wedges. The means by which the ingredients are put together, and in what order, makes a world of difference: After all, both sponge cake and custard pie are based on flour, sugar, milk, eggs and butter.

Some cakes start as a single layer, some as many layers, some are rolled, and others are baked in tube pans. Similarly, many pies have one crust, others two and occasionally three. The form, as architects would say, follows the function, which always is to create the most tantalizing possible sweet.

# Black Forest Cherry Cake

**To make one 7-inch 3-layer cake**

**6 eggs, at room temperature**
**1 teaspoon vanilla extract**
**1 cup sugar**
**½ cup sifted flour**
**½ cup unsweetened cocoa**
**10 tablespoons unsalted butter, clarified and cooled**

KIRSCH SYRUP
**¾ cup sugar**
**1 cup cold water**
**⅓ cup kirsch**

CHOCOLATE CURLS
**8 ounces semisweet bar**

**chocolate, at room temperature but not soft**

CHERRY FILLING AND TOPPING
**3 cups chilled heavy cream**
**½ cup confectioners' sugar**
**¼ cup kirsch**
**1 cup canned sour red cherries, drained**
**Maraschino cherries with stems, rinsed, or fresh sweet red cherries with stems**

Preheat the oven to 350°F. With a pastry brush, spread a light coating of melted or softened butter over the bottom and sides of three 7-inch layer-cake pans. Sprinkle a spoonful of flour into each pan, and shake the pan to distribute it; tap out any excess.

With an electric mixer, beat the eggs, vanilla and 1 cup of sugar together at high speed for at least 10 minutes or until the mixture is thick and fluffy and has almost tripled in bulk. (By hand with a rotary beater, this may take as long as 20 minutes of uninterrupted beating.)

Combine the ½ cup of sifted flour and the unsweetened cocoa in a sifter. A little at a time, sift the mixture over the eggs, folding it in gently with a rubber spatula. Finaly, add the clarified butter, 2 tablespoons at a time. Do not overmix. Gently pour the batter into the prepared pans, dividing it evenly among them.

Bake the layers in the middle of the oven for 10 to 15 minutes or until a cake tester or toothpick inserted in the center of each cake comes out clean. Take the cakes from the oven and let them cool in the pans for about 10 minutes. Then run a sharp knife around the edge of each layer, and turn it out onto a rack to cool.

Meanwhile, prepare the kirsch syrup: Combine ¾ cup of sugar and 1 cup of cold water in a small saucepan, and bring to a boil over moderate heat, stirring only until the sugar dissolves. Boil, uncovered, for five minutes, then remove the pan from the heat. When the syrup cools to lukewarm, stir in the kirsch.

Transfer the cakes to a long strip of wax paper and prick each layer lightly in several places with the tines of a long fork. Sprinkle the layers evenly with the syrup and let them rest for at least five minutes.

For the decorative chocolate curls, hold the chocolate over wax paper and draw a sharp vegetable peeler along the wide surface of the bar for large curls, along the narrow side for small ones. Handle the chocolate as little as possible. Refrigerate or freeze the curls until ready to use.

In a large chilled bowl, beat the cream with a whisk or rotary or electric beater until it thickens lightly. Then sift the confectioners' sugar over the cream, and continue beating until the cream forms firm peaks on the beater when it is lifted out of the bowl. Pour in

¼ cup of kirsch in a thin stream, and beat only until the kirsch is absorbed.

To assemble the cake, place one layer on a serving plate. With a spatula, spread the top with ½ inch of whipped cream and strew the sour cherries over it, leaving a margin of about ½ inch around the edge. Gently set a second layer on top of the cherries and spread it with ½ inch of whipped cream. Then set the third layer in place. Spread the top and sides of the cake with cream. With your fingers, press chocolate curls into the cream on the sides of the cake. Arrange more curls on top, leaving a 1-inch margin around the edge. Put the remaining cream into a pastry bag fitted with a star tube, and pipe rosettes of cream on top of the cake around the edge and around the base. Place a maraschino cherry, stem up, in the center of each rosette on the top of the cake.

■ THE COOKING OF GERMANY

## Coconut Cake with Lemon Filling

*In the Florida Keys coconut cake is traditionally served during the Christmas season.* ❧

**To make one 9-inch 4-layer cake**

| | |
|---|---|
| 2 cups sifted flour | 2 tablespoons butter, cut into |
| 1 teaspoon baking powder | ¼-inch bits |
| ⅛ teaspoon salt | 2 tablespoons finely grated |
| 8 eggs, separated | fresh lemon peel |
| 2 cups sugar | ⅔ cup fresh lemon juice |
| ¼ cup fresh lemon juice | 1 cup water |
| 2 teaspoons finely grated | |
| fresh lemon peel | COCONUT ICING |
| | 4 egg whites |
| LEMON FILLING | ½ cup confectioners' sugar |
| 1½ cups sugar | 1 teaspoon vanilla extract |
| ¼ cup cornstarch | 1½ cups white corn syrup |
| ⅛ teaspoon salt | 2 cups freshly grated, peeled |
| 2 eggs, lightly beaten | coconut meat |

Preheat the oven to 350°F. With a pastry brush, spread a light coating of melted or softened butter inside two 9-inch layer-cake pans. Sprinkle a spoonful of flour into each pan and shake it to distribute the flour evenly; then tap out any excess. Sift the 2 cups of sifted flour with the baking powder and ⅛ teaspoon of salt together onto a plate or sheet of wax paper; set the mixture aside.

In a deep bowl, beat the eight egg yolks and 2 cups of sugar with a wire whisk or a rotary or electric beater for four to five minutes, or until the mixture is thick enough to fall back on itself in a slowly dissolving ribbon when the beater is lifted from the bowl. Beat in ¼ cup of lemon juice and 2 teaspoons of lemon peel. Then add the flour mixture, about ½ cup at a time, beating well after each addition.

With a clean whisk or beater, beat the eight egg whites in another bowl until they stand in unwavering peaks on the beater when it is lifted. Scoop the egg whites over the batter. With a rubber spatula, fold the egg whites gently into the batter until no trace of white shows.

Pour the batter into the pans, dividing it equally, and smooth the tops with the spatula. Bake for 20 minutes, or until a toothpick inserted in the center of the cake comes out clean. Let the cakes cool in the pans for about 10 minutes, then turn them out on wire racks to cool to room temperature.

Meanwhile, prepare the filling: First combine the 1½ cups of sugar, the cornstarch, ⅛ teaspoon of salt and the two beaten eggs in a heavy 1½- to 2-quart saucepan, and mix well with a wire whisk or wooden spoon. Stir in the butter bits, 2 tablespoons of lemon peel, ⅔ cup of lemon juice and the water; when all of the ingredients are well blended, set the pan over high heat.

Stirring the filling mixture constantly, bring it to a boil over high heat. Immediately reduce the heat to low. Continue to stir until the filling is smooth and coats the spoon heavily. Use a rubber spatula to scrape the filling into a bowl, then allow it to cool to room temperature.

When the cake and filling are cool, prepare the icing: Beat the four egg whites until they form soft peaks on the uplifted beater. Sprinkle them with the confectioners' sugar and vanilla; beat until the egg whites are stiff and glossy.

In a small saucepan, bring the corn syrup to a boil over high heat, and cook until it reaches a temperature of 235°F. on a candy thermometer or until a drop spooned into ice water immediately forms a soft ball. Beating the egg-white mixture constantly with a wooden spoon, pour in the corn syrup in a slow, thin stream. Continue beating until the icing is smooth, thick and cool.

To assemble, cut each layer in half horizontally, thus creating four thin layers. Place one layer, cut side up, on an inverted cake pan and, with a small metal spatula, spread about one-third of the lemon filling over it. Put another cake layer on top, spread with filling, and cover it with the third layer. Spread this layer with the remaining filling, and place the fourth layer on top. Smooth the icing over the top and sides of the cake. Then sprinkle the coconut generously on the top and, with your fingers, pat it into the sides of the cake.

Carefully transfer the coconut cake to a serving plate and serve it at once. If the cake must wait, drape wax paper around the top and sides to keep the icing moist.

■ AMERICAN COOKING: SOUTHERN STYLE

## Sour-Cream Poundcake

**To make one 9-by-5-inch loaf**

| | |
|---|---|
| ½ cup unsalted butter, softened | 1 teaspoon baking soda |
| | ½ teaspoon ground cinnamon |
| 1 cup sugar | 1 teaspoon ground cardamom |
| 3 eggs | 1 cup sour cream |
| 1¾ cups flour | 1 teaspoon vanilla extract |

Preheat the oven to 350°F. With a pastry brush, spread a light coating of melted or softened butter inside a 9-by-5-by-3-inch loaf pan. Sprinkle in a spoonful of dry bread crumbs or flour, and shake the pan to distribute them; tap out any excess.

Cream the butter and the sugar together by using an electric mixer set at medium speed or by beating them against the sides of the bowl with a wooden spoon until the mixture is light and fluffy. Beat in the eggs, one at a time, making sure each is thoroughly incorporated before adding another. Sift the flour with the baking soda, cinnamon and cardamom, and stir half of it into the batter. Beat in the sour cream and vanilla, then the rest of the sifted flour mixture.

With the aid of a rubber spatula, transfer the contents of the bowl to the loaf pan. Rap the pan sharply on the table once to remove any air pockets. Bake in the center of the oven for 50 to 60 minutes, or until the top of the cake is golden brown and lightly springy to the touch. A toothpick inserted in the center of the cake should come out clean.

Set the cake on a wire rack and allow it to cool in the pan for 10 minutes, then use a metal spatula to loosen the sides from the pan. Place another rack over the pan and invert the two; then place the original wire rack on top of the cake and turn them over so that the cake is right side up. Cool the cake and serve it at room temperature.

■ THE COOKING OF SCANDINAVIA

## Carrot and Almond Cake

**To make one 10-inch round cake**

| | |
|---|---|
| 1½ cups blanched almonds, pulverized in a blender or food processor, then shaken through a fine sieve | ½ teaspoon ground cinnamon |
| | 5 eggs, separated |
| | 1¼ cups sugar |
| ¾ cup finely grated carrots | 1 tablespoon baking powder |
| 1 tablespoon finely grated lemon peel | ¼ cup kirsch |
| | 5 tablespoons confectioners' sugar combined with |
| 1 teaspoon ground ginger | 2 teaspoons cold water |
| ½ teaspoon ground mace | |

Preheat the oven to 350°F. With a pastry brush, spread a light coating of butter on the bottom and sides of a 10-inch springform cake pan. Sprinkle in several spoonfuls of dry bread crumbs or flour and shake the pan to distribute the crumbs evenly; tap out the excess crumbs.

In a mixing bowl, combine the almonds, carrots, lemon peel,

SPICY CHOCOLATE BEET CAKE

ginger, mace and cinnamon, and mix well. Set it aside. In a deep bowl, beat the egg whites with a whisk or a rotary or electric beater until they are stiff enough to form unwavering peaks on the beater when it is lifted.

Using another deep bowl and the same beater, beat the egg yolks for 30 seconds or so. Then slowly sift in the sugar and continue beating for three or four minutes, until the yolks are very thick. With a wooden spoon, stir in the baking powder and kirsch, then mix in the reserved almond mixture, adding about ½ cup at a time.

Vigorously stir about a quarter of the egg whites into the batter to lighten it. Spoon the remaining egg whites over the batter and,

with a rubber spatula, fold them gently together until no streaks of white show. Do not overfold.

Ladle the batter into the cake pan, spreading and smoothing it with the spatula. Bake in the middle of the oven for one hour or until a tester inserted in the center of the cake comes out clean. Let the cake cool for 10 minutes before removing the sides of the pan. Then insert a large metal spatula under the cake to help slide it onto a rack.

While the cake is still warm, brush the top with the confectioners' sugar mixture to glaze it lightly. Let the cake cool to room temperature before serving it.

# Spicy Chocolate Beet Cake

*The surprise ingredient in this delicious cake is puréed beets. They not only tint the batter, but they add moisture as well.* ❧

**To make one 10-inch tube cake**

| | |
|---|---|
| **Four 16-ounce cans beets, drained** | **chocolate, melted and cooled** |
| **3¹/₂ cups sifted flour** | **1¹/₄ teaspoons vanilla extract** |
| **4 teaspoons baking soda** | |
| **¹/₂ teaspoon salt** | CHOCOLATE GLAZE |
| **¹/₄ teaspoon ground cloves** | **6 ounces semisweet baking chocolate** |
| **¹/₄ teaspoon ground cinnamon** | |
| **6 eggs** | **1 tablespoon unsalted butter** |
| **2¹/₂ cups granulated sugar** | **1 tablespoon light corn syrup** |
| **¹/₂ cup firmly packed dark-brown sugar** | **³/₄ cup heavy cream** |
| | **Salt** |
| **1¹/₂ cups vegetable oil** | **¹/₂ teaspoon vanilla extract** |
| **5 ounces unsweetened baking** | **Ground cinnamon** |

Preheat the oven to 350°F. With a pastry brush, spread a light coating of melted or softened butter inside a 10-inch bundt pan or angel food cake pan. Sprinkle in a few spoonfuls of flour and shake the pan to distribute it; tap out any excess. Purée the beets, a small batch at a time, in a food processor or blender. Sift the flour together with the baking soda, ¹/₂ teaspoon of salt, the cloves and ¹/₄ teaspoon of cinnamon. Set them aside.

In a large mixing bowl, beat the eggs with a wire whisk or a rotary or electric mixer until they are pale yellow and frothy. Gradually beat in both the sugars and the oil. Using a rubber spatula, fold the beet purée into the egg mixture. Gradually fold the dry ingredients into the beet mixture, making sure to combine them well. Gently but thoroughly, fold the melted unsweetened chocolate and the 1¹/₄ teaspoon of vanilla into the cake batter.

Pour the batter into the prepared pan. Bake the cake in the middle of the oven for 1¹/₂ hours, or until a toothpick inserted into the center comes out clean and dry. Invert the cake over a wire rack and let it cool completely in the pan—allow 2 hours.

To prepare the chocolate glaze, first melt the semisweet chocolate in the top of a double boiler over simmering water. Stir in the butter and corn syrup, then gradually mix in the cream. Continue stirring over simmering water for about one minute or until the mixture is well blended. Add a pinch of salt, ¹/₂ teaspoon of vanilla and a dash of cinnamon; stir again.

Turn the cake right side up and loosen it from the pan by running a knife around the inner edges. Invert the pan and tap it gently until the cake is released and falls free from the pan. Set the thoroughly cooled cake back on the rack; slide wax paper or a baking sheet under the rack. Pour the glaze over the cake, lift the rack and gently shake it to distribute the glaze evenly. Chill the cake until the glaze is set—about 20 to 30 minutes.

## Clafoutis

*Although other fruits may be used, cherries are the traditional choice for this ancient French dessert, which some call a kind of custard-topped cake and others insist is a thick pancake. Because the topping is so delicate, it will tend to fall as it cools—an excellent argument for serving it straight from the oven.* ◆●

**To make one 8-inch square cake**

| | |
|---|---|
| 1½ cups milk | extract |
| 4 eggs | 2 to 3 cups fresh black sweet |
| ½ cup flour | cherries, pitted |
| ¼ cup sugar | Confectioners' sugar |
| 2 teaspoons vanilla | |

Preheat the oven to 350°F. To make the batter in a blender, first combine the milk, eggs, flour, sugar and vanilla in the blender jar. Whirl them at high speed for a few seconds; turn off the machine and scrape down the sides of the jar with a rubber spatula, then blend again for about 40 seconds. To make the batter by hand, stir the flour and eggs together in a large bowl, and slowly stir in the milk, sugar and vanilla. Beat with a whisk or a rotary or electric beater until the batter is smooth.

With a pastry brush, lightly coat the bottom and sides of a shallow 8-inch square baking-serving dish with melted or softened butter. Spread the cherries evenly in the dish, then pour in the batter. Bake on the middle shelf of the oven for 1½ hours, or until the top is golden brown and a tester inserted in the center comes out clean. Dust the top lightly with confectioners' sugar, and serve the *clafoutis* while it is warm.

■ THE COOKING OF PROVINCIAL FRANCE

## Fresh Peach Cake

*When assembled, the batter will appear unusually thick, but the layer it forms will seem very shallow. Do not be alarmed. The batter will puff up as it bakes.* ◆●

**To make one 12-inch round cake**

| | |
|---|---|
| 1 cup sifted plus ¼ cup | ¼ cup milk |
| unsifted flour | ½ teaspoon grated lemon peel |
| 1½ teaspoons baking powder | 10 large ripe peaches, halved, |
| ½ teaspoon salt | pitted, peeled and quartered |
| ¼ cup plus 3 tablespoons | ¾ cup slivered almonds |
| granulated sugar | ¼ cup light-brown sugar |
| 7 tablespoons unsalted | ¼ cup apricot preserves |
| butter | 1 tablespoon water |
| 1 egg | |

Preheat the oven to 400°F. With a pastry brush, spread a light coating of melted or softened butter inside a 12-by-2-inch baking dish. Sprinkle in a spoonful of flour and shake the dish to distribute it; tap out any excess.

Sift 1 cup of the flour, the baking powder, salt and ¼ cup of granulated sugar into a small bowl. With your fingers or a pastry blender work in ¼ cup of butter until the mixture resembles coarse meal. Beat the egg with the milk, and add them to the flour mixture along with the lemon peel; stir just enough to blend the batter. With a rubber spatula, spread the batter evenly in the prepared dish. Arrange the peaches over the top of the batter, rounded side up. Sprinkle the fruit with the remaining 3 tablespoons of sugar. Bake the cake for 35 minutes.

While the cake is baking, whirl the almonds in a blender or food processor until they are the consistency of fine powder. Mix the almonds well with the remaining 3 tablespoons of butter, ¼ cup of flour and the brown sugar. When the cake has baked for 35 minutes, take it briefly from the oven. Border the top of the cake with the almond mixture. Put the cake back in the oven for an additional 10 minutes.

Meantime press the apricot preserves through a sieve into a small saucepan. Add the tablespoon of water and cook for a minute or two until the preserves melt. When you take the cake from the oven, brush the tops of the peaches with the preserves.

■ GREAT DINNERS FROM LIFE

## Rum Cake

**To make one 8-inch round cake**

| | |
|---|---|
| ½ cup butter, softened | lime peel |
| 1 cup sugar | 1½ cups flour |
| 4 eggs | ½ cup yellow cornmeal |
| ¼ cup dark rum | 2 teaspoons baking powder |
| 3 tablespoons fresh lime | Confectioners' sugar |
| juice | (optional) |
| 1 teaspoon finely grated | |

Preheat the oven to 350°F. With a pastry brush, spread a light coating of melted or softened butter evenly over the bottom and sides of an 8-inch springform cake pan. Sprinkle in some flour and shake the pan to distribute it; tap out the excess.

In a deep bowl, cream the butter with the sugar, beating and mashing them against the sides of the bowl with a large spoon until the mixture is light and fluffy. Beat in the eggs, one at a time, then add the rum, lime juice and lime peel, and continue beating until the batter is smooth. Combine the flour, cornmeal and baking powder, and sift the mixture into the bowl, about ½ cup at a time, beating well after each addition.

Pour the batter into the prepared pan, and bake in the middle of the oven for one hour, or until a cake tester or a toothpick inserted in the center comes out clean. Cool the cake completely before removing the sides of the pan.

Rum cake is traditionally served unfrosted in its native Curaçao, but you may sift a light dusting of confectioners' sugar over the top of the cooled cake if you prefer.

■ THE COOKING OF THE CARIBBEAN ISLANDS

MERINGUE LAYERS WITH MOCHA BUTTER CREAM

## Walnut Torte with Cocoa Icing

**To make one 9-inch round cake**

| | |
|---|---|
| 6 tablespoons fine dry bread crumbs | softened |
| 8 eggs, separated | 2 egg yolks |
| ½ cup granulated sugar | ¾ teaspoon vanilla extract |
| 2 teaspoons vanilla extract | 1¼ cups confectioners' |
| 2½ cups ground walnuts, (about ½ pound) | sugar |
| | 3 tablespoons powdered unsweetened cocoa |
| COCOA ICING | 3 tablespoons hot water |
| 6 tablespoons unsalted butter, | ¼ cup ground walnuts |

Preheat the oven to 350°F. With a pastry brush, spread a light coating of melted or softened butter over the bottom and sides of a 9-by-3-inch springform pan. Sprinkle the butter evenly with 2 tablespoons of the bread crumbs. Set the pan aside.

In a deep bowl, beat the egg whites with a wire whisk or a rotary or electric beater, until they form unwavering peaks when the beater is lifted from the bowl. In another bowl, and with the same beater, beat the eight egg yolks for one minute. Beating constantly, add the granulated sugar and 2 teaspoons of vanilla. Continue to beat for five minutes or until the mixture is thick enough to fall in a slowly dissolving ribbon from the beater.

Scoop half of the egg whites over the yolk mixture and, with a rubber spatula, gently but thoroughly fold them together. Then fold in half of the 2½ cups of walnuts. Repeat, alternating the egg whites and walnuts, then fold in the remaining bread crumbs.

Pour the batter into the prepared pan, and smooth the top with the spatula. Bake in the center of the oven for 30 minutes or until a cake tester or a toothpick inserted in the center comes out clean. Let the cake cool in the pan for 10 minutes. Remove the sides of the pan, slide a thin spatula or knife under the cake, and carefully slide it onto a wire cake rack to cool to room temperature.

Meanwhile, prepare the icing: First cream 6 tablespoons of butter in a large bowl with a wooden spoon. Beat in two egg yolks, one at a time, and then ¾ teaspoon of vanilla. Sift together the confectioners' sugar and cocoa, and alternately beat this mixture and the hot water into the creamed butter. Continue to beat until the icing is creamy and thick.

When the torte has cooled, slice it horizontally into two layers with a long, sharp knife, preferably one with a serrated blade. Place the bottom slice, cut side up, on a serving plate and, with a metal spatula or knife, spread it with ½ inch of icing. Set the second layer over it, cut side down, and spread the top and sides of the torte with the remaining icing. Sprinkle the ¼ cup of ground walnuts over the top, and refrigerate the torte until ready to serve.

■ AMERICAN COOKING: THE MELTING POT

288

## Meringue Layers with Mocha Butter Cream

*This confection goes by many names—le succès, le progrès, Dacquoise—but their origins seem lost to culinary history. Meringue, however, has a well-known ancestry: It was invented in 1720 by a Swiss pastry cook called Gasparini, who practiced his art in Mehrinyghen. France's Queen Marie Antoinette had a great fondness for meringues and is said to have made them for herself at the Trianon. Butter cream is a felicitous complement—its smooth richness setting off the crispness of meringues.* ◆●

| To make one 10-inch round cake | MOCHA BUTTER CREAM |
|---|---|
| 6 egg whites | 5 egg yolks |
| ¾ cup sugar | 1 cup unsalted butter, |
| ¾ cup blanched almonds, | softened |
| pulverized in a blender or | ⅔ cup sugar |
| with a nut grinder | ⅛ teaspoon cream of tartar |
| 1 tablespoon cornstarch | ⅓ cup water |
| 2 tablespoons confectioners' | 1 tablespoon instant powdered |
| sugar | coffee, preferably espresso |

Preheat the oven to 250°F. Cover two large baking sheets with parchment baking paper and set them aside. Or, brush each sheet with softened or melted butter, sprinkle it with flour, and tap off any excess.

In a deep bowl, beat the egg whites with a wire whisk or a rotary or electric beater until they just begin to form soft peaks on the beater when it is lifted. Beating constantly, slowly pour in 10 tablespoons of the granulated sugar. Continue to beat for at least five minutes, or until the meringue is glossy and forms unwavering peaks when the beater is lifted. Combine the almonds, cornstarch and the remaining 2 tablespoons of sugar. With a rubber spatula, fold them gently into the meringue.

Spoon half of the meringue onto the center of a baking sheet, and, with a spatula, smooth it into a round about 10 inches in diameter and ½ inch thick. Make an identical round of the remaining meringue mixture on the second sheet. Bake the meringues in the middle of the oven for 45 minutes or until they are firm and dry but not brown. Let the meringues cool to room temperature, then gently ease them off the baking sheets with a wide spatula and transfer them to separate flat plates.

To prepare the butter cream: First beat the egg yolks for two to three minutes in a large bowl with a whisk or a rotary or electric beater. Then cream the softened butter in another bowl, beating it against the sides of the bowl with a large spoon until it is light and fluffy. Place the butter in the refrigerator until ready to use; it should still be soft but not oily at that point.

Combine the ⅔ cup of sugar, the cream of tartar, water and powdered coffee in a small saucepan. Stirring constantly, bring to a boil over moderate heat. Boil briskly, without stirring, until this syrup thickens and reaches a temperature of 235°F. on a candy thermometer, until a drop spooned into ice water instantly forms a soft ball.

Immediately pour the hot syrup in a thin stream into the egg yolks, beating constantly. Continue beating for 10 to 15 minutes, until the mixture becomes a thick, smooth cream and has cooled completely. Then beat in the creamed butter, a teaspoon or so at a time. Cover the bowl and refrigerate the butter cream for about 30 minutes, or until it is firm enough to spread easily.

To assemble the meringue layer cake place one meringue round on a serving plate and—with a spatula—spread two-thirds of the butter cream to within ½ inch of the edge of the meringue. Put the remaining butter cream into a pastry bag fitted with a star tube and pipe a decorative border around the outside of the butter-cream layer. Gently place the second meringue layer on top, sprinkle with the confectioners' sugar, and serve at once. When necessary, the cake can be refrigerated for up to two hours before serving; if refrigerated longer, the meringue will soften.

■ CLASSIC FRENCH COOKING

## Three-Layer Chocolate Cake

| To make one 9-inch 3-layer cake | ¼ teaspoon salt |
|---|---|
| ¾ cup unsalted butter, | 1½ cups milk |
| softened | 12 to 15 walnut halves for |
| 2¼ cups sugar | garnish |
| 4 eggs | |
| 6 ounces unsweetened | CHOCOLATE SOUR-CREAM |
| chocolate, melted and | FROSTING |
| cooled | 18 ounces semisweet |
| 1 teaspoon vanilla extract | chocolate bits |
| 2 cups flour | 1½ cups sour cream |
| 1½ teaspoons baking powder | ¼ teaspoon salt |

Preheat the oven to 375°F. Brush a light coating of melted or softened butter on the bottom and sides of three 9-inch layer-cake pans. Sprinkle a spoonful of flour into each pan and shake the pan to distribute it; tap out any excess.

In a large mixing bowl, cream the butter and sugar together by mashing and beating them with a large spoon until they are light and fluffy. Beat in the eggs, one at a time, then beat in the melted chocolate and the vanilla. Sift the flour, baking powder and salt together into another bowl. Beat ¼ cup of the dry ingredients into the chocolate mixture, then beat in ¼ cup of milk. Continue adding the flour and milk alternately, beating until the batter is smooth.

Divide the batter equally among the prepared pans and bake the cake for 15 to 20 minutes or until the layers are firm to the touch. A toothpick inserted in the center should come out clean. Let the layers cool in the pans for about 10 minutes, then invert them onto cake racks.

While the layers are still slightly warm, melt the semisweet chocolate in the top of a double boiler over boiling water. With a whisk or spoon, stir in the sour cream and salt.

Set one cake layer on a serving plate and, with a metal spatula, spread the top with ¼ inch of chocolate sour-cream frosting. Assemble the layers one on top of another, frosting each one. Coat the sides of the cake with frosting, and add more to the top if you wish. Decorate the cake with the walnut halves.

■ AMERICAN COOKING

# Sachertorte

*This culinary legend was invented in 1832 by chef Franz Sacher for the Austrian statesman Prince Fürst von Metternich. It has a strong, somewhat bitter chocolate flavor and a slightly dry texture—balanced by the whipped cream with which it is traditionally presented.* ◆●

**To make one 9-inch round cake**

| | CHOCOLATE GLAZE |
|---|---|
| 6½ ounces semisweet chocolate, cut into chunks | 3 ounces unsweetened chocolate, broken or chopped into small chunks |
| ½ cup unsalted butter | 1 cup heavy cream |
| 8 eggs, separated, plus 2 egg whites | 1 cup sugar |
| 1 teaspoon vanilla extract | 1 teaspoon light corn syrup |
| Salt | 1 egg |
| ¾ cup sugar | 1 teaspoon vanilla extract |
| 1 cup sifted flour | 2 cups heavy cream, whipped |
| ½ cup apricot jam, rubbed through a sieve | |

Preheat the oven to 350°F. With a pastry brush, lightly coat two 9-by-1½-inch layer-cake pans with melted or softened butter. Then, line the pans with circles of wax paper, butter the paper, sprinkle it with flour and shake off the excess.

Using a small, heavy saucepan and stirring constantly, melt the chocolate and butter over low heat; allow them to cool. In a small mixing bowl, break up the egg yolks with a fork, then beat in the melted chocolate and butter and 1 teaspoon of vanilla. With a wire whisk or a rotary or electric beater, beat the 10 egg whites and a pinch of salt until they foam, then add the ¾ cup of sugar, 1 tablespoon at a time, continuing to beat until the whites form firm unwavering peaks on the beater when it is lifted.

Mix about one-third of the egg whites into the egg yolk-chocolate mixture, then reverse the process and pour the chocolate over the remaining egg whites. Sprinkle the flour over the top. With a rubber spatula, fold the whites and chocolate mixture together until no trace of the whites remains. Do not overfold.

Pour the batter into the prepared pans, dividing it evenly between them. Bake in the middle of the oven for 25 to 30 minutes or until a cake tester inserted into the center of a layer comes out clean.

Let the cake cool in the pans for 10 minutes. Loosen the sides of the layers by running a sharp knife around them. Turn them out on a wire rack to cool completely; peel off the paper.

To prepare the glaze: Combine the 3 ounces of unsweetened chocolate, the 1 cup of cream, 1 cup of sugar and the corn syrup in a small, heavy saucepan. Stirring constantly with a wooden spoon, cook over low heat until the chocolate melts, then increase the heat to moderate and cook, without stirring, for about five minutes, until the mixture registers 235°F. on a candy thermometer or a little of the mixture dropped into cold water forms a soft ball.

In a small mixing bowl, beat the egg lightly, then stir 3 tablespoons of the chocolate mixture into it. Pour this into the chocolate in the saucepan and stir it briskly. Stirring constantly, cook this glaze over low heat for three or four minutes or until it coats the spoon heavily. Remove the pan from the heat and add the vanilla. Cool the glaze to room temperature.

When the cake layers have completely cooled, spread the apricot jam on one of them and put the other layer on top. Set the rack in a jelly-roll pan and, holding the saucepan about 2 inches away from the cake, pour the glaze over the cake evenly. Smooth the glaze with a metal spatula. Let the cake stand until the glaze stops dripping. Then, using two metal spatulas, transfer the cake to a plate and refrigerate it for three hours to harden the glaze. Remove it from the refrigerator a half hour before serving it. Slice the torte into thin wedges and top with whipped cream.

■ THE COOKING OF VIENNA'S EMPIRE

# English Christmas Cake

*Putting this cake together takes a counter full of rich ingredients and the better part of a day—plus another hour's work decorating the basic assembly—but, to an Englishman, the resulting confection is as much a part of the holiday tradition as a yule log.* ◆●

**To make one 12-inch round cake**

| | |
|---|---|
| 2 cups chopped mixed candied fruit peel (about 10 ounces) | 4 eggs |
| 2 cups white raisins (about 10 ounces) | ¼ cup pale dry sherry, rum or brandy |
| 1½ cups dried currants (about 8 ounces) | MARZIPAN |
| 1 cup seedless raisins (about 5 ounces) | 2 cups almond paste |
| ½ cup candied cherries, cut in half (about 4 ounces) | 1 teaspoon almond extract |
| ½ cup chopped candied angelica (about 4 ounces) | ½ teaspoon salt |
| 2 cups flour | 1 cup light corn syrup |
| ½ teaspoon baking powder | 7 cups confectioners' sugar (2 pounds), sifted |
| ½ teaspoon salt | |
| 1 cup butter, softened | CURRANT GLAZE |
| 1 cup dark-brown sugar | ¼ cup red-currant jelly |
| 1 cup shelled almonds (about 6 ounces), pulverized in a blender or food processor or with a nut grinder | CONFECTIONERS' SUGAR ICING |
| | 6 cups confectioners' sugar, sifted |
| | 4 egg whites |
| | 1 tablespoon fresh lemon juice |
| | ⅛ teaspoon salt |

Preheat the oven to 325°F. With a pastry brush, spread a light coating of melted or softened butter over the bottom and sides of a 12-by-3-inch springform pan. Cut a round of parchment baking paper or wax paper to fit inside the pan and coat the paper with butter. Set it in the pan. Then cut a 36-by-3-inch paper strip, butter it, and fit it in around the side.

In a large bowl, combine the fruit peel, white raisins, currants, seedless raisins, cherries and angelica. Sprinkle the fruit with ½ cup of the flour, tossing it about with a spoon to coat the pieces evenly. Sift the remaining 1½ cups of flour with the baking powder and salt. Set these aside.

In another large bowl, cream the ½ pound of butter with the

brown sugar by mashing and beating them against the sides of the bowl until they are light and fluffy. Add the pulverized almonds, then beat in the eggs one at a time. Add the flour mixture, a half cup or so at a time, then beat the fruit mixture into the batter. Finally, add the sherry and pour the batter into the pan. The batter should come to no more than an inch from the top. If necessary, remove and discard any excess.

Bake the cake in the middle of the oven for 1 hour and 45 minutes or until a cake tester inserted in the center comes out clean. Let the cake cool for an hour before removing the sides of the pan, then slip the cake off the pan's bottom onto a rack and let it cool completely.

Meanwhile, prepare the marzipan, using an electric mixer, preferably one equipped with a paddle. Crumble the almond paste in small pieces into a bowl, add the almond extract and 1/2 teaspoon of salt, and beat at medium speed until well blended. Gradually add the corn syrup in a thin stream, beating constantly until the mixture is smooth. Then begin to beat in the 7 cups of confectioners' sugar, 1/2 cup at a time. As soon as the mixture becomes so stiff that it clogs the beater, place it on a cool work surface and knead in the remaining sugar with your hands: Press the ball of marzipan down, push it forward, add sugar, then fold the marzipan back on itself. Continue kneading as long as necessary to make the marzipan pliable. Set the marzipan aside.

When the fruitcake is cool, carefully peel off the paper. Heat the currant jelly in a small saucepan over moderate heat until it registers 225°F. on a candy thermometer or is thick enough to coat a wooden spoon lightly. With a small metal spatula, spread the hot glaze evenly over the top and sides of the cake.

On a clean surface, roll out half of the marzipan into a circle about 1/2 inch thick. Using a 12-inch pan or plate as a pattern, cut out a 12-inch disk with a pastry wheel or small, sharp knife. Roll and cut the remaining marzipan into a 36-by-3-inch strip. Gently set the disk of marzipan on top of the cake and press it into place. Wrap the strip of marzipan around the cake, pressing to secure it. If the strip overlaps the top, fold the rim down lightly.

Wrap the cake in foil or plastic, and let it stand at room temperature for at least 48 hours before icing. The cake may be wrapped in cheesecloth and foil and then stored in the refrigerator for several months.

Just before serving, ice the cake. Combine the 6 cups of confectioners' sugar, egg whites, lemon juice and 1/8 teaspoon salt in a large mixing bowl. With a whisk or a rotary or electric beater, beat until the mixture is fluffy but forms soft peaks on the lifted beater. With a small metal spatula, spread the icing over the sides and top of the cake. Then decorate the cake to your taste with marzipan holly or candied fruits.

■ THE COOKING OF THE BRITISH ISLES

ENGLISH CHRISTMAS CAKE

# Candied-Chestnut Roll

*This is one of the most impressive looking desserts and—with candied chestnuts, or "marrons glacés," to flavor it—one of the most delectable. Yet it takes just an hour or so to put together and is close to being foolproof.*◆●

**To make one 15-inch roll**

| | |
|---|---|
| ³/₄ cup sifted cake flour | ¹/₂ cup sugar |
| 1 teaspoon baking powder | ¹/₃ cup light corn syrup |
| ¹/₄ teaspoon salt | ¹/₄ cup dark rum |
| 4 eggs | 12 ounces *marrons glacés*, |
| ³/₄ cup sugar | 5 chestnuts reserved for |
| 1 teaspoon vanilla extract | garnish and the rest cut |
| Confectioners' sugar | into small bits |
| | |
| CHESTNUT BUTTER CREAM | Chocolate curls, shaved from |
| 3 egg yolks | unsweetened chocolate |
| ¹/₂ pound unsalted butter, | with a vegetable peeler |
| softened | |

Preheat the oven to 400°F. Use a pastry brush to coat the bottom of a 15-by-10-inch jelly-roll pan lightly with melted or softened butter. Line the pan with parchment baking paper or wax paper trimmed to fit, and butter the paper. Sift the flour, baking powder and salt together, and set them aside.

Beat the eggs with a wire whisk or a rotary or electric beater until they are light and foamy. Adding the ³/₄ cup sugar slowly, continue beating for at least 10 minutes, until the mixture thickens and almost triples in bulk. Sprinkle the sifted dry ingredients over the batter, and use a rubber spatula to fold them in gently. Fold in the vanilla. Pour the batter into the prepared pan. Bake the cake for 12 minutes or until it is springy and delicately browned.

Loosen the cake around the edges with a knife, and turn it out onto a cloth towel sprinkled evenly with confectioners' sugar. Working quickly while the cake is still warm, carefully peel away the paper. Cut off the crisp edges of the cake with a sharp knife. Starting at one long side, gently roll up the cake along with the towel, which will keep the cake from sticking to itself. Place the roll, towel and all, on a cake rack to cool.

Meanwhile, prepare the butter cream by first beating the egg yolks with a wire whisk or rotary or electric beater for two or three minutes, until they are foamy and lemon colored. In

CANDIED-CHESTNUT ROLL

another bowl, cream the butter by beating it vigorously against the sides of the bowl with a spoon until the butter is light and fluffy; refrigerate briefly.

Combine the ¹/₂ cup sugar and the corn syrup in a small heavy saucepan. Stirring constantly, cook over moderate heat until the mixture comes to a boil. Then, beating the egg yolks constantly, add the hot syrup to them in a thin stream; continue to beat for 10 to 15 minutes, until the mixture cools. Beat in the butter, a spoonful or so at a time. Stir in the rum and chestnuts. Cover the bowl and refrigerate the butter cream for about 30 minutes or until it is firm enough to spread easily.

When the cake is cool, unroll it and remove the towel. Spread the top with a half of the chestnut butter cream. Reroll the cake, place it on a serving plate and frost the outside of the roll with the rest of the cream. Cut each of the reserved chestnuts in half. Decorate the sides of the roll with the chestnuts and the top with the chocolate curls.

■ **GREAT DINNERS FROM LIFE**

# Blueberry Crumb Cake

**To make one 13-by-9-inch cake**

| | |
|---|---|
| **8 tablespoons butter, chilled and cut into small bits, plus 8 tablespoons butter, softened** | **1 tablespoon baking powder** |
| | **½ teaspoon freshly grated nutmeg** |
| **3¼ cups flour** | **¼ teaspoon ground cloves** |
| **2 cups sugar** | **1 teaspoon salt** |
| **1 teaspoon ground cinnamon** | **3 eggs** |
| **3 cups blueberries, stemmed** | **¾ cup milk** |
| | **Heavy cream (optional)** |

Preheat the oven to 375°F. With a pastry brush, coat the bottom and sides of a 13-by-9-by-3-inch baking dish with melted or softened butter. Sprinkle in a few spoonfuls of flour and shake the dish to spread it evenly; tap out the excess.

Prepare the crumb topping by first mixing the butter bits, ¾ cup of the flour, 1 cup of the sugar and the cinnamon in a deep bowl. Working quickly, rub them together with your fingertips until the mixture resembles flakes of coarse meal. Set aside.

Combine the remaining 2½ cups of flour, the baking powder, nutmeg, cloves and salt, and sift them together into a bowl. In a deep bowl, cream the softened butter and the remaining cup of sugar by beating and mashing them against the sides of the bowl with the back of a spoon until they are light and fluffy. Beat in the eggs, one at a time. Add about 1 cup of the sifted flour mixture and, when it is well incorporated, stir in ¼ cup of the milk. Repeat twice more, alternating the flour and milk, beating well after each addition. Gently stir in the blueberries.

Pour the blueberry batter into the prepared baking dish. Smooth the top with a rubber spatula. Then sprinkle the reserved crumb topping evenly over the cake. Bake in the middle of the oven for 40 or 50 minutes, or until the top is crusty and a cake tester inserted in the center of the cake comes out clean. Serve the cake warm or at room temperature, accompanied—if you like—by a pitcher of heavy cream.

■ AMERICAN COOKING: THE EASTERN HEARTLAND

## Baba au Rhum

**To make one 12-inch tube cake**

2 packages active dry yeast
¹/₃ cup sugar
1 cup tepid milk (100°F.)
1 teaspoon salt
4 cups sifted flour
8 eggs, lightly beaten
³/₄ pound unsalted butter,
    softened
¹/₂ cup dried currants
¹/₄ cup seedless raisins

RUM SYRUP

2 cups sugar
1¹/₂ cups water
1 cup dark rum

LEMON ICING

2 cups confectioners' sugar
¹/₄ cup cold water
2 teaspoons fresh lemon juice

In a small, shallow bowl, sprinkle the yeast and ¹/₂ teaspoon of the sugar over ¹/₂ cup of the tepid milk. Let the mixture stand for two to three minutes, then stir to dissolve the yeast completely. Set the bowl aside in a warm, draft-free place for five minutes or until the mixture doubles in volume.

In a deep mixing bowl, combine the rest of the ¹/₃ cup of sugar with the salt and flour. Make a well in the center and pour in the yeast mixture. Add the remaining milk, drop in the eggs and—with a large spoon—stir the flour into the liquid ingredients. Continue to stir until a fairly stiff dough forms. Knead the dough by pushing it down with the heels of your hands, pressing it forward, and folding it back on itself. Knead for about 10 minutes, or until the dough is smooth and elastic. Drape the bowl loosely with a kitchen towel and set it in the warm, draft-free place for one hour, or until the dough doubles in bulk. Then punch it down and knead in the softened butter, a tablespoon or so at a time. Knead in the currants and raisins.

With a pastry brush, coat the inside of a 12-cup kugelhof mold with melted or softened butter. Pat the dough into the mold; it should come about halfway up the sides. Drape the mold with a towel and set it aside for about one hour or until the dough doubles in volume and rises almost to the top of the pan.

Preheat the oven to 400°F. Bake the cake in the center of the oven for 10 minutes, then reduce the heat to 350°F. and bake it for another 35 minutes. Remove the mold from the oven, drape a kitchen towel loosely over it, and let the baba rest for 10 minutes. Run a knife around the inside edge of the mold and turn the cake out onto a serving plate, then carefully invert the cake on the plate.

For the syrup, combine the 2 cups of sugar and 1¹/₂ cups of water in a small saucepan, and cook, stirring constantly, until the mixture comes to a boil over high heat. Boil for five minutes, undisturbed, until the mixture forms a syrup thick enough to coat a spoon lightly. Pour the syrup into a bowl, then stir in the rum. With a large spoon, distribute the syrup evenly over the warm cake. Then baste the cake every 10 minutes or so with the syrup collecting around the cake. When all of the syrup has been absorbed, mix the confectioners' sugar, ¹/₄ cup of cold water and the lemon juice, and drizzle this icing over the top of the cake, allowing it to run down the cake in streams.

■ RUSSIAN COOKING

BABA AU RHUM

## Pineapple Upside-down Cake

**To make one 9-inch round cake**

5 tablespoons unsalted butter,
    cut into bits, plus ¹/₂ cup
    unsalted butter, softened
²/₃ cup brown sugar
6 canned unsweetened
    pineapple rings, drained
9 maraschino cherries, stemmed
¹/₂ cup plus ¹/₃ cup flour

¹/₄ teaspoon salt
1¹/₂ teaspoons baking powder
1 cup granulated sugar
2 eggs
¹/₂ teaspoon vanilla extract
¹/₃ cup milk
Whipped cream (optional)

Preheat the oven to 350°F. Melt the 5 tablespoons of butter bits over moderate heat in a 9-inch cast-iron skillet with an ovenproof handle. Sprinkle the brown sugar over the butter, place the pineapple rings on the sugar and set the cherries in the centers of the rings and between them. Remove the skillet from the heat.

Into a small bowl, sift ¹/₂ cup of the flour and the salt. Sift the

## Gingerbread with Hot Lemon Sauce

*This is not the usual gingerbread flavored with molasses, but a lighter, spicier version that uses maple syrup—the authentic kind, not so-called pancake syrup, which is usually made of maple-flavored corn syrup.* ❖●

**To make one 8-inch square cake**

| | |
|---|---|
| **1½ cups sifted flour** | **½ cup sour milk** |
| **½ cup sugar** | **1 egg , beaten** |
| **½ teaspoon baking soda** | |
| **½ teaspoon baking powder** | LEMON SAUCE |
| **½ teaspoon salt** | **¾ cup sugar** |
| **1 teaspoon ground ginger** | **1 tablespoon plus 2 teaspoons cornstarch** |
| **1 teaspoon ground cinnamon** | **Salt** |
| **¼ teaspoon ground allspice** | **1½ cups boiling water** |
| **¼ teaspoon freshly grated nutmeg** | **1 teaspoon grated lemon peel** |
| **¼ cup pure maple syrup** | **3 tablespoons fresh lemon juice** |
| **¼ cup butter, melted and cooled** | **3 tablespoons butter** |

Preheat the oven to 350°F. With a pastry brush, lightly coat the bottom and sides of an 8-inch square baking pan with melted or softened butter. Sprinkle in a spoonful of flour and shake the pan to distribute it; tap out any excess.

Sift the flour, ½ cup of sugar, baking soda, baking powder, ½ teaspoon of salt and the spices together into a large bowl. In a smaller bowl, stir the maple syrup with the ¼ cup of melted butter, the sour milk and egg until they are well blended. Add the liquid ingredients to the flour and spices, and beat until the batter is smooth and creamy, about two minutes. Spoon the batter into the prepared pan. Bake the gingerbread for 30 minutes or until the cake springs back when lightly touched and a tester inserted in the center comes out clean.

Meanwhile, in a nonreactive saucepan, mix the ¾ cup of sugar, the cornstarch and a pinch of salt together. Gradually stir in the boiling water. Bring to a boil, and cook for 10 minutes, stirring occasionally. Add the lemon peel, lemon juice and 3 tablespoons of butter. Cook for another minute or two, until the butter melts and the sauce is hot.

Serve the gingerbread while it is still warm, accompanied by the hot lemon sauce. If need be, the gingerbread and sauce can be made ahead; the cake can be reheated for 10 minutes in a preheated 350°F. oven while the sauce is reheated in a double boiler over simmering water.

NOTE: To sour the milk called for, mix 1½ teaspoons of lemon juice with ½ cup of milk; set them aside for 10 minutes or until the milk sours.

■ GREAT DINNERS FROM LIFE

remaining ⅓ cup of flour and the baking powder into another small bowl. Set both bowls aside.

In a large mixing bowl, cream the softened butter with the sugar, mashing and beating them against the sides of the bowl until they are light and fluffy. Beat in the eggs, one at a time, and the vanilla. Still beating, alternately add the flour-salt mixture and the milk. Then add the flour-baking powder mixture and beat just until blended.

Pour the batter into the skillet and, using a spatula, spread the batter gently out to the edges. Bake the cake in the middle of the oven for 45 to 50 minutes or until a cake tester inserted into the center comes out clean.

Cool the cake on a wire rack for 10 minutes, then set an inverted serving plate on top of the skillet. Grasping the plate and skillet together firmly, turn them over. The cake will slide out easily. Serve the cake warm or at room temperature, accompanied with whipped cream if you like.

■ AMERICAN REGIONAL MENUS

## Lindy's Strawberry Cheesecake

*Cheesecake comes in as many guises as it boasts ardent admirers. This version was featured for many years at Lindy's Restaurant in New York, once a Broadway landmark.* ❖

**To make one 9-inch round cake**

PASTRY SHELL
1 cup flour
¼ cup sugar
1 teaspoon finely grated
   lemon peel
¼ teaspoon vanilla extract
1 egg yolk
½ cup unsalted butter, chilled
   and cut into ¼-inch bits

CHEESE FILLING
1¼ pounds cream cheese,
   softened
¾ cup sugar
1½ tablespoons flour
1 teaspoon finely grated

lemon peel
1 teaspoon finely grated
   orange peel
½ teaspoon vanilla extract
3 eggs plus 1 egg yolk
2 tablespoons heavy cream

STRAWBERRY TOPPING
1 quart fresh strawberries,
   hulled
½ cup sugar
4 teaspoons cornstarch
   dissolved in ¼ cup
   cold water
Salt
Red food coloring (optional)

To prepare the dough for the pastry shell, first mix 1 cup of flour, ¼ cup of sugar, 1 teaspoon of lemon peel, ¼ teaspoon of vanilla, the egg yolk and butter in a large bowl. With your fingertips, rub the ingredients together until they form a dough that can be gathered into a ball. Dust the ball with a little flour, wrap in wax paper, and refrigerate for at least an hour.

Preheat the oven to 400°F. Place the chilled dough in an ungreased 9-inch springform pan. With your hands, pat and spread the dough evenly over the bottom and about 2 inches up the sides of the pan. Bake the pastry shell for 10 minutes; cool.

Reduce the oven temperature to 250°F. Place the cream cheese in a large mixing bowl, and beat it vigorously with a wooden spoon until it is creamy and smooth. Beat in ¾ cup of sugar, a few tablespoons at a time. Then beat in 1½ tablespoons of flour, 1 teaspoon of lemon peel, the orange peel, ½ teaspoon of vanilla, the eggs and egg yolk, and the heavy cream. Pour this filling into the cooled pastry shell, and bake the cheesecake in the center of the oven for one hour. Set it aside to cool in the pan.

Place the strawberries, 1 cup at a time, in a fine sieve set over a bowl. With the back of a wooden spoon, press just enough berries through the sieve to get ¾ cup of purée. Set the purée aside. With the cake still in the pan, arrange the remaining whole berries, stem side down, over the top of the cake.

Beat ½ cup of sugar, the cornstarch-and-water mixture and a dash of salt into the puréed berries. Pour this syrup mixture into a 1- to 1½-quart enameled or stainless-steel saucepan. Stirring frequently, bring the syrup to a boil over high heat, then boil it undisturbed for 2 minutes. Remove from the heat and, if you prefer a deeper red color, stir in a drop or two of food coloring. Spoon the hot glaze over the whole berries and refrigerate the cheesecake for at least 3 hours before serving.

■ AMERICAN COOKING: THE MELTING POT

## Strawberry Shortcake

*Genuine shortcake, like that your grandmother made, is really baking-powder biscuit with extra butter to make it flakier. Plan to serve the biscuits hot from the oven, with copious whipped cream. The berries will have more flavor if sweetened several hours ahead of time and kept at room temperature.* ❖

**To serve 6**

4 cups strawberries, hulled
Sugar
2 cups sifted flour
2 teaspoons baking powder
1 teaspoon salt

½ cup butter
½ cup milk
2 cups heavy cream,
   whipped

Slice 1 cup of the strawberries, but leave the rest whole. Put them into separate bowls and sweeten them to taste.

Preheat the oven to 450°F. Sift the flour, baking powder and salt into a mixing bowl. With a pastry blender or your fingers, work in 5 tablespoons of butter until the mixture is coarse and grainy. Stir in the milk.

Shape the dough into a ball, and roll it out ½ inch thick on a lightly floured surface. With a 3-inch biscuit cutter, cut out six rounds. Set them on a baking sheet and bake them for 15 minutes or until they are golden brown.

Immediately, split the biscuits and use the remaining butter to butter the bottom halves. Place them on serving plates. Put whole berries on the bottom half of each biscuit, spoon on a generous amount of whipped cream, set the top halves of the biscuits in place and top with more whole berries and whipped cream. Garnish with sliced berries and berry juice.

■ GREAT DINNERS FROM LIFE

## Decadent Brownie Bars

*These rich, moist brownies are made up of two complementary layers joined with raspberry preserves. The resemblance to an exotic European torte is unmistakable.* ❖

**To make one 8-inch square cake**

PASTRY LAYER
1¾ cups flour
½ cup sugar
½ teaspoon baking powder
¼ teaspoon salt
½ cup unsalted butter, cut into
   pieces and softened
1 egg

BROWNIE LAYER
½ cup unsalted butter

3 tablespoons unsweetened
   cocoa
1 cup sugar
2 eggs
1 tablespoon dark rum
¾ cup flour
¼ teaspoon salt

¾ cup raspberry preserves
¼ cup chopped pecans or
   hazelnuts

Preheat the oven to 350°F. For the pastry layer, combine the 1¾ cups of flour, ½ cup of sugar, the baking powder and ¼ teaspoon of salt in a mixing bowl and blend them with a fork. Add the softened butter pieces and work them into the dry ingredients until

**DECADENT BROWNIE BARS**

the mixture resembles small peas. Add one egg and stir with the fork until the pastry is well blended. Press the pastry into the bottom of an ungreased 8-inch square baking pan, and bake it for 20 minutes, or until a cake tester inserted in the center comes out clean.

Meanwhile prepare the brownie layer: First melt ½ cup of butter in a small heavy-bottomed saucepan over moderately low heat. Pour the butter into a mixing bowl. Add the cocoa to the butter and stir until blended. Stir in 1 cup of sugar. Add two eggs,

one at a time, beating well after each addition. Add the rum, ¾ cup of flour and ¼ teaspoon of salt.

Remove the pastry from the oven briefly. Using a metal spatula, spread the pastry with raspberry preserves, then with brownie batter. Sprinkle the top evenly with hazelnuts and bake the confection for another 25 to 30 minutes or until a tester inserted in the center of the brownie layer comes out clean. Set the pan on a wire rack to cool. Cut the brownies into bars before serving.

■ LATE-NIGHT SUPPER MENUS

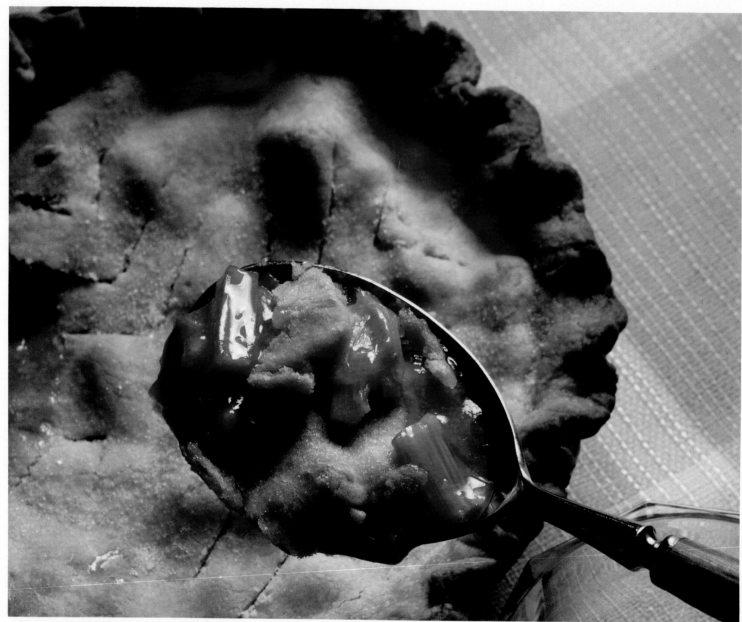

DEEP-DISH RHUBARB PIE

## Lemon-Soufflé Pie

**To make one 9-inch pie**

2 eggs, separated
¾ cup sugar
¼ cup flour
1 cup milk
¼ cup fresh lemon juice
2 teaspoons finely grated
  lemon peel

1 tablespoon butter, melted
  and cooled
One 9-inch short-crust pie
  shell (Index/Glossary),
  partially baked and
  cooled

Preheat the oven to 350°F. With a wire whisk or a rotary or electric beater, beat the egg whites until they form unwavering peaks on the beater when it is lifted.

In another bowl, with the same beater, beat the egg yolks lightly. Add the sugar and flour and, when they are completely incorporated, gradually pour in the milk and lemon juice, beating constantly. Add the lemon peel and cooled melted butter, and beat until the mixture is smooth.

With a rubber spatula, scoop the egg whites over the egg-yolk mixture and fold them together gently but thoroughly until no trace of white remains. Pour the mixture into the partially baked pie shell, smoothing the top with the spatula.

Bake in the middle of the oven for 25 to 30 minutes, or until a knife inserted in the center of the pie comes out clean. Cool the lemon-soufflé pie to room temperature before serving.
■ AMERICAN COOKING: THE EASTERN HEARTLAND

# Black-Bottom Pie

*The "black bottom" consists of chocolate custard. Above it is rum custard under lavishings of whipped cream. Making the custards takes time and attention, but a cookie-crumb crust is simplicity itself to prepare.* ❖

**To make one 9-inch pie**

| | |
|---|---|
| One 9-inch cookie-crumb pie shell (Index/Glossary), made with gingersnaps, baked and cooled | chocolate, melted |
| ¼ cup cold water | 1 teaspoon vanilla extract |
| 1 tablespoon unflavored gelatin | RUM LAYER |
| 1¾ cups milk | 4 egg whites |
| 4 egg yolks | ⅛ teaspoon cream of tartar |
| ½ cup sugar | ⅓ cup sugar |
| 1 tablespoon cornstarch | 1 tablespoon rum |
| Salt | |
| | TOPPING |
| CHOCOLATE LAYER | 1 cup heavy cream, chilled |
| 3 ounces semisweet | 2 tablespoons confectioners' sugar |
| | ¼ ounce semisweet chocolate |

Pour the cold water into a small heatproof bowl and sprinkle the gelatin over it to soften for two or three minutes. Then set the bowl in a skillet of simmering water. Stirring constantly, cook over low heat until the gelatin dissolves completely. Remove the skillet from the heat, but leave the bowl in the water to keep the gelatin fluid.

In a heavy 2- to 3-quart saucepan, scald the milk by heating it until small bubbles begin to form around the edge. Remove from the heat and cover to keep warm. With a wire whisk or a rotary or electric beater, beat the egg yolks, ½ cup of sugar, cornstarch and a pinch of salt for three or four minutes, or until the yolks thicken slightly. Beating constantly, pour in the hot milk in a thin stream, then pour the mixture into the saucepan.

Place the pan over low heat and, stirring constantly and deeply with a wooden spoon, simmer for 10 to 12 minutes, or until the custard is thick enough to coat the spoon lightly. Do not allow the mixture to come near the boiling point or it might curdle. Remove the pan from the heat and stir in the dissolved gelatin.

Measure 1 cup of the custard into a bowl and, stirring constantly, slowly pour in the melted chocolate. Add the vanilla. Pour the chocolate-custard into the cooled pie shell, smoothing the top with a rubber spatula. Set the remaining custard aside. Refrigerate the chocolate layer for at least one hour, or until it is firm to the touch.

With a whisk or beater, beat the egg whites and cream of tartar together until they begin to thicken. Add the sugar and continue to beat until the whites form unwavering peaks on the lifted beater. Set the reserved custard in a larger pan half-filled with ice and cold water. Stir it with a metal spoon until it thickens enough to flow sluggishly off the spoon. Remove from the ice. With a rubber spatula, stir the rum and 2 or 3 tablespoons of the egg whites into the custard. Spoon the remaining egg whites over the custard and, with the spatula, fold them together gently but thor-

oughly. Pour the mixture into the pie shell, and smooth with the spatula. Refrigerate for two hours, or until the top layer is firm to the touch.

Just before serving, whip the heavy cream in a chilled bowl until it stands in unwavering peaks when the beater is lifted from the bowl. Beat in the confectioners' sugar, then spread over the top of the pie with a rubber spatula. Using the finest side of a hand grater, grate the remaining chocolate evenly over the cream. Serve at once.

■ AMERICAN COOKING: SOUTHERN STYLE

# Deep-Dish Rhubarb Pie

*The pastry dough for this pie must be handled with care, but it produces a flaky crust that could never be confused with store-bought kinds.* ❖

**To make one 9-by-8-inch oval or 8-inch square pie**

| | |
|---|---|
| 2 pounds rhubarb, scrubbed clean with a brush, ends trimmed, and stalks cut into 1-inch pieces | CREAM-CHEESE PASTRY DOUGH |
| ½ cup flour | One 3-ounce package cream cheese, softened |
| 1 cup sugar | 6 tablespoons butter, softened |
| ½ cup light corn syrup | ¾ cup sifted flour |
| 1 tablespoon butter, cut into bits | |
| | 1 pint heavy cream, whipped and sweetened |

To start with, prepare the pastry dough by first combining the cream cheese and butter in a bowl and beating them against the sides of the bowl with a wooden spoon until they are light and fluffy. Add ¾ cup of sifted flour and beat until the dough is well blended. Form the dough into a ball. Wrap it in wax paper and chill it for at least two hours before rolling.

Preheat the oven to 425° F. In a large mixing bowl, toss the rhubarb with ½ cup of flour; then pour the rhubarb pieces into a 9-by-8-inch oval pan 2 inches deep. Sprinkle any leftover flour over the rhubarb. In a small saucepan, mix the sugar and corn syrup; stirring constantly, bring the mixture to a boil over moderate heat. Pour this syrup over the rhubarb and dot the top with the butter bits.

On a cool working surface, roll out the pastry between two pieces of wax paper to a size an inch larger than the baking pan. Remove the top piece of wax paper. Cut several small gashes in the center of the pastry to let steam escape while the pie bakes. Place the pastry over the rhubarb with the wax-paper side up; peel off the wax paper. Fold the edges of the pastry under and crimp them against the inside edges of the pan.

Bake the pie for 25 minutes or until the pastry is golden brown and the rhubarb tender when tested with a skewer inserted through the gashes in the crust. Allow the pie to cool slightly before serving it. Spoon portions into heated individual bowls and accompany the pie with the whipped cream.

■ GREAT DINNERS FROM LIFE

## Pear Galette

*The French word "galette" means flat pastry, like this tart.* ❦

**To make one 9-inch pie**

| | LEMON-FLAVORED SHORT-CRUST PASTRY |
|---|---|
| ¼ cup fresh lemon juice | |
| 4 cups water | 1½ cups flour |
| 8 Bosc or Anjou pears | 2 tablespoons vanilla sugar or granulated sugar |
| 1 cup sugar | |
| 2 julienne strips lemon peel | 1 teaspoon finely grated lemon peel |
| ½ cup heavy cream | ½ cup butter, chilled and cut into small bits |
| ¼ cup sour cream | |
| 3 tablespoons pear brandy or Cognac | 1 egg yolk |

For the pastry, which must be baked and cooled before the filling is made, first combine the flour, 2 tablespoons of sugar and the grated lemon peel in a food processor fitted with a steel blade. Mix them quickly. Add the butter bits and process just until the ingredients form coarse crumbs. Add the egg yolk and process for about 30 seconds, or until dough forms and pulls away from the sides of the bowl. If necessary, continue to process and add cold water, 1 teaspoon at a time, only until the dough forms a ball. Shape the dough into a flat round cake, wrap it in plastic, and refrigerate it for at least an hour, to chill the butter and relax the flour's gluten content—making it easier to roll.

Preheat the oven to 400°F. Roll out the dough between two pieces of wax paper into a circle about ⅛ inch thick. Fit the circle into a 9-inch tart pan or pie pan. Line the dough with parchment paper, wax paper or foil; weight it with pie weights or dried beans, and bake it for 10 minutes, until the pastry is set. Remove the filled paper or foil, lightly prick the bottom of the pastry, and return the pan to the oven for 10 to 15 minutes or until the pastry is crisp and golden brown. Cool the pastry in the pan for about five minutes. Then remove and cool the pastry on a wire rack before using it.

In a large bowl, combine the lemon juice with the water. Peel, halve, and core the pears, placing the halves in the lemon water to prevent discoloration. Pour 2 cups of the lemon water into a non-reactive skillet, add 1 cup of sugar and the strips of lemon peel. Bring the water to a boil over moderate heat, stirring until the sugar dissolves. Add the pears and poach them for 10 to 15 minutes, or until they are transparent and just tender. With a slotted spoon, transfer the pears to a plate.

Pour 1 cup of the cooking syrup into a small saucepan and bring it to a boil over high heat. Boil for 10 minutes, or until the syrup is very thick and reduced to ½ cup. Set it aside.

Just before serving, beat the heavy cream with a wire whisk or a rotary or electric beater in a chilled bowl until the cream forms unwavering peaks on the lifted beater. In a small bowl, combine the sour cream, pear brandy, and 2 tablespoons of the reduced syrup; beat them until blended. Gently fold the sour-cream mixture into the whipped cream.

Cut the pears lengthwise into thin slices, arrange them in a pin-

wheel pattern in the baked crust, and drizzle the syrup over them. Cut the galette into wedges and serve it, passing the brandy cream separately.

■ TURKEY AND DUCK MENUS

## Three-Crust Blueberry Pie

**To make one 9-inch pie**

| Short-crust dough (Index/Glossary) for a double-crust pie | 1½ to 2 cups sugar |
|---|---|
| 6 cups blueberries, stemmed | 2 tablespoons fresh lemon juice |

Preheat the oven to 400°F. Divide the chilled pastry dough into three pieces, one somewhat smaller than the other two. Refrigerate the smaller piece and one of the larger ones. On a lightly floured surface, roll the third piece into a rough circle about ⅛ inch thick and 12 to 13 inches in diameter.

Drape the dough over the rolling pin, lift it up, and unroll it slackly over a 9-inch pie pan. Gently press the dough against the sides of the pan, being careful not to stretch it. Cut off the excess dough from the edges, leaving a 1-inch overhang around the rim. Gather the scraps and refrigerate both the shell and the scraps.

Place the blueberries in a deep bowl, add 1½ cups of sugar and the lemon juice, and toss together gently but thoroughly. Taste the berries and add up to ½ cup more sugar if you like.

On a lightly floured surface, roll the smaller of the two reserved pieces of dough into a circle no more than 1/16 inch thick and 10 inches in diameter. With a pastry wheel or sharp knife, cut it into a circle about 8½ inches in diameter, using an inverted cake pan as a guide. Cut a ½-inch hole in the center of the circle. Gather and refrigerate the scraps.

Spread half of the blueberry mixture evenly over the bottom of the lined pie pan; gently place the 8½-inch circle of dough on top and cover it with the rest of the blueberries. Then roll the remaining piece of dough (adding the scraps to the ball if necessary) into a circle about ⅛ inch thick and 12 to 13 inches in diameter. With a pastry brush dipped in cold water, moisten the outside edge of the pastry shell. Drape the dough over the rolling pin, lift it up, and unroll it over the blueberries. Trim the excess pastry from around the rim, then crimp the top and bottom pastry together. Cut a 1-inch hole in the center of the top crust to allow steam to escape while the pie bakes. Bake it at 400°F. for 15 minutes, then reduce the oven temperature to 350°F., and continue baking for one hour or until the top is golden brown.

Serve the pie while it is still warm. The center crust, which will steam as the pie bakes, will have a dumplinglike texture and will have absorbed some of the berry juice.

■ AMERICAN COOKING: NEW ENGLAND

PEAR GALETTE

## Apple Tart with Apricot Preserves

**To make one 9-inch tart**

| | |
|---|---|
| 4 cooking apples, peeled, cored, quartered and cut lengthwise into ¼-inch slices | 1 tablespoon Cognac |
| | One 9-inch short-crust pie shell (Index/Glossary), baked in a false-bottomed tart pan and cooled |
| 5 tablespoons sugar | 1 tablespoon water |
| 1 egg | ½ cup apricot preserves |
| ½ cup heavy cream | |
| 2 tablespoons flour | |

Preheat the oven to 350° F. In a deep bowl, combine the apples and 4 tablespoons of the sugar. Turn the slices about with a spoon until they are sugar coated. For a custard topping, beat the egg and cream together with a wire whisk in another bowl for about a minute, then beat in the remaining tablespoon of sugar, the flour and Cognac.

Arrange the apple slices attractively in slightly overlapping concentric circles in the baked pastry shell and bake in the middle of the oven for 20 minutes. Then pour in the custard mixture and bake for 15 minutes longer, or until the custard puffs and browns, and a knife inserted in the center comes out clean. Set the tart aside.

In a small saucepan, combine the water and the preserves, and bring to a boil over moderate heat, stirring until the preserves dissolve. Then reduce the heat and simmer until the mixture thickens to a syrupy glaze. With the back of a spoon, rub the preserves through a fine sieve into a bowl. While the tart is still warm, brush the glaze gently over its entire top surface. Place the false-bottomed pan on a large jar or coffee can and slip down the outside rim. Let the tart cool to room temperature before serving it.

■ A QUINTET OF CUISINES

## Raspberry Pie

**To make one 9-inch pie**

| | |
|---|---|
| 1 envelope unflavored gelatin | 1 to 3 teaspoons fresh lemon juice |
| ¼ cup cold water | 1¾ cups heavy cream, 1 cup whipped and sweetened |
| 2½ cups fresh raspberries or two 10-ounce packages frozen raspberries, defrosted and drained | One 9-inch cookie-crumb pie shell (Index/Glossary), made with 1½ cups graham-cracker crumbs and ½ cup ground walnuts, baked and cooled |
| 1 teaspoon vanilla extract | |
| 6 ounces cream cheese, softened | ½ cup fresh raspberries for garnish |
| ⅓ cup confectioners' sugar | |

Sprinkle the gelatin into a heatproof measuring cup containing the cold water. When the gelatin has softened for two or three minutes, set the cup in a small pan of simmering water and stir over low heat until the gelatin dissolves. Remove the pan from the heat, but leave the cup in the water to keep the gelatin fluid.

STRAWBERRY TARTS WITH CASSIS

With the back of a large spoon, purée the raspberries through a fine sieve into a small mixing bowl. Stir in the vanilla and set aside. In a deep bowl, cream the cream cheese and confectioners' sugar together, beating and mashing them against the sides of the bowl with the back of a spoon until they are light and fluffy.

Add the raspberry purée to the cream-cheese mixture, and beat them vigorously together with a rotary or electric beater. Stir in 1 teaspoon of the lemon juice and the gelatin. Pour in ¾ cup of cream, and beat vigorously until the mixture is smooth and no

## Strawberry Tarts with Cassis

*Fresh strawberries, strawberry jam and crème de cassis—black currant liqueur—create a lively filling for simple tarts.* ❧

**To make four 4-inch tarts**

| | |
|---|---|
| ³/₄ cup strawberry jam | Four 4-inch short-crust tart |
| 2 tablespoons crème | shells (Index/Glossary), |
| de cassis | baked and cooled |
| 1 pint strawberries, hulled and | 4 hazelnuts or almonds |
| halved | ¹/₂ pint sour cream (optional) |

Stirring constantly, heat the jam in a small, heavy-bottomed saucepan over moderate heat for one or two minutes, until the jam is smooth and spreadable. Stir in the crème de cassis, then remove the pan from the heat.

Set aside 2 tablespoons of the jam mixture and about one-third of the strawberries for garnish, choosing the most perfect. Combine the remaining berries and jam mixture, stirring gently. Divide the strawberry mixture among the tart shells; smooth the filling. Garnish each tart with the reserved strawberries and top it with a hazelnut or almond. Brush each tart with some of the reserved jam mixture. Accompany the tarts with a bowl of sour cream, if desired.

■ LATE-NIGHT SUPPER MENUS

## Bourbon and Caramel Custard Pie

**To make one 9-inch pie**

| | |
|---|---|
| 1¹/₂ cups heavy cream | 1 teaspoon vanilla extract |
| 1¹/₂ cups milk | One 9-inch short-crust pie |
| 1 cup sugar | shell (Index/Glossary), |
| 5 egg yolks | partially baked and cooled |
| ¹/₄ cup bourbon | Freshly grated nutmeg |

Preheat the oven to 450°F. In a heavy 1- to 1¹/₂-quart saucepan, warm the cream and milk over moderate heat, stirring occasionally, until small bubbles appear around the edges of the pan. Cover the pan and set aside off the heat.

Caramelize the sugar in a small, heavy saucepan by stirring it over moderate heat until it melts and turns a light golden brown. Stirring the sugar constantly with a wooden spoon, pour in the warm cream-and-milk mixture in a thin stream. Continue to stir until the caramel dissolves thoroughly. Set it aside off the heat.

With a whisk or a rotary or electric beater, beat the egg yolks in a large mixing bowl until they are well blended. Stirring constantly, slowly pour in the caramel-and-cream mixture, the bourbon and the vanilla extract. Strain the mixture through a fine sieve directly into the baked, cooled pie shell. Sprinkle the top evenly with nutmeg, and place the pie in the center of the oven. Reduce the heat at once to 350°F., and bake the pie for 30 minutes. The filling will appear somewhat undercooked, but it will become firm as it cools. Cool the pie to room temperature before serving.

trace of the cream remains. Taste and add more lemon juice if desired. Pour the filling into the cooled crust, spreading it and smoothing the top with a spatula. Cover loosely with foil or plastic wrap and refrigerate for at least four hours or until the filling is firm to the touch.

Just before serving, spread the whipped cream evenly over the pie, creating decorative swirls with the tip of a knife. If you like, arrange whole fresh raspberries on top.

■ AMERICAN COOKING: THE NORTHWEST

■ AMERICAN COOKING: SOUTHERN STYLE

## Fruit in Phyllo Bundles

**To make 4 bundles**

| | |
|---|---|
| ³/₄ cup unsalted butter | ³/₄ teaspoon ground cinnamon |
| ¹/₂ cup plus 2 teaspoons sugar | Freshly grated nutmeg |
| ¹/₄ cup seedless raisins | 2 large pears |
| 2 tablespoons flour | 1 large Granny Smith or other cooking apple |
| 1 teaspoon finely grated lemon peel | 16 sheets phyllo |

With a pastry brush, lightly coat a large baking sheet with melted or softened butter. In a small, heavy-bottomed skillet, melt the ³/₄ cup of butter over low heat. Set the butter aside.

Combine ¹/₂ cup of the sugar, the raisins, flour, lemon peel, ¹/₂ teaspoon of cinnamon and a grating of nutmeg in a mixing bowl. Peel the pears and apple. Quarter them, remove the cores, and cut the fruit crosswise into slices ¹/₈ inch thick. Add the fruit to the sugar mixture and toss it to coat it well.

Place the phyllo sheets on a dampened kitchen towel covered with plastic wrap, and cover the top sheet of phyllo with plastic wrap and a second dampened towel. To make one bundle, lay one phyllo sheet flat on a work surface and brush it lightly with melted butter. Top it with a second sheet, and brush that with butter. Repeat the procedure with a third sheet. Fold a fourth sheet in half, and lay it on the center of the stack. Brush it lightly with butter and spoon one-fourth of the fruit mixture onto the center of the folded sheet.

Fold over the long sides of the phyllo stack to cover the fruit, then fold over the short sides—twisting the edges in the center to close the bundle. Brush it with butter and gently transfer the bundle to the prepared baking sheet. Make three more bundles in the same manner.

Combine the remaining 2 teaspoons of sugar and ¹/₄ teaspoon of cinnamon in a small bowl. Sprinkle this cinnamon-sugar mixture over the bundles, cover the pan, and refrigerate until 30 minutes before serving time. Preheat the oven to 400°F. Bake the bundles for 25 minutes, or until they are golden brown. Using a wide metal spatula, transfer the phyllo bundles to a napkin-lined platter, and serve them hot.

■ MAKE-AHEAD MENUS

## Paris Brest

*Impressive as it looks, this crown of cream-puff pastry goes together easily, then awaits your convenience to be served.* ❖●

**To make one 12-inch pastry ring**

| | |
|---|---|
| 1 cup water | ¹/₂ teaspoon water |
| 6 tablespoons butter, cut into bits | 3 tablespoons slivered blanched almonds |
| 1 cup flour, sifted with 1 teaspoon sugar | 2 cups heavy cream |
| | Confectioners' sugar |
| 4 eggs, plus 1 egg beaten with | 2 teaspoons vanilla extract |

Preheat the oven to 450°F. With a pastry brush, spread a light coating of melted or softened butter on a large baking sheet; the sheet must be 14 inches wide. Sprinkle a spoonful of flour over the butter, and shake the sheet to distribute it; tap off any excess. Center an inverted 8-inch plate or pan on the sheet, and press down hard to make an impression in the flour. Remove the plate or pan and set the sheet aside.

In a heavy 2- to 3-quart saucepan, bring the water and the butter to a boil over moderate heat, stirring occasionally. As soon as the butter melts, remove the pan from the heat and pour in the flour all at once. Beat the mixture vigorously with a wooden spoon for a few seconds to blend it, then return the pan to moderate heat and cook, beating vigorously, for one or two minutes, until the mixture forms a paste that moves freely with the spoon.

Immediately remove the pan from the heat, and use the spoon to make a well in the center of the paste. Break an egg into the well and beat it into the paste. When the egg is absorbed, add another —repeating the process until four eggs have been absorbed and the paste is smooth and shiny.

Using a pastry bag and a large plain tip, make a ring or crown of paste 2 inches wide and 1 inch high around the impression in the flour. If you do not have a pastry bag, place spoonfuls side by side around the pattern and smooth them with a spatula.

Paint the top of the crown with the egg-and-water mixture. Sprinkle it with almonds. Bake in the middle of the oven for 10 minutes, reduce the heat to 350°F., and bake for 10 minutes more. Then reduce the heat to 325°F., and bake for 20 minutes or until the crown has more than doubled in size and is golden brown and crusty.

Turn off the oven and make three or four tiny cuts near the bottom of the crown with the tip of a sharp knife. Let the crown stay in the oven for 5 minutes to dry out. Slice it in half horizontally with a serrated knife, and spoon out any soft dough.

Before serving, whip the cream in a large chilled bowl with a wire whisk or a rotary or electric beater until it begins to thicken. Add 1 tablespoon of confectioners' sugar and the vanilla, and beat until the cream holds its shape firmly. Using a pastry bag with a decorative tip, or a tablespoon, fill the bottom of the crown with whipped cream. The cream should rise well above the rim of the pastry. Gently replace the top so that it floats on the cream. Sprinkle the top with confectioners' sugar, if desired, and serve at once.

■ THE COOKING OF PROVINCIAL FRANCE

# Fruits & Desserts

FRONTISPIECE: LADYFINGER AND WHIPPED CREAM DESSERT

The flourish with which a meal ends might be a fancy ladyfinger construction such as that shown at left or old-fashioned baked apples presented in goblets. Desserts are limited only by the imagination. They need merely to please. Even the strait-laced Victorian cookbook writer Mrs. Isabella Beeton confessed that "if there be any poetry at all in meals, it should be in the dessert."

At their simplest, desserts might be uncooked fruits, alone or served with a complement of cheeses—blue for tanginess, Cheddar for mellowness, double-cream for sweetness. Berries invite a lavishing of cream and, when whipped cream is desired, a chilled bowl and beater speed the whipping process. With sugar and vanilla extract, the result can then be transformed into crème chantilly. Maple syrup turns it into maple cream.

A single fruit or a selection might be poached and bathed in a lush sauce. A mélange of fruit may be displayed dramatically in a jelly enlivened with wine. Or fruit may be the base for a sherbet or an Italian *granita*.

Every country has its grand display. In England, the trifle—dating from the 16th century—is far from trivial, being a veritable farrago of sponge cake drenched with sherry, berries, peaches and custard. The Sicilian cream cake is studded with candied fruits, nuts and grated chocolate. And America's baked Alaska is ice cream encased in a glorious swirl of meringue, which is broiled to golden before being presented with pride.

## Apple and Pumpernickel Crumb Dessert

*The Germans call this luscious confection "Apfelbettelmann," which translates as "beggar's apple." Certainly the basic ingredients are simple, and the end result looks deceivingly plain. The Danes make a similar dessert called "veiled country lass"—presumably because its appearance masks its delicacy.* ❧

**To serve 4**

| | |
|---|---|
| ½ cup dried currants | plus 2 tablespoons butter |
| 5 tablespoons rum | cut into small bits |
| 1½ cups fine dark-pumpernickel bread crumbs, made in the blender or food processor | 1 teaspoon finely grated lemon peel |
| | 1½ teaspoons ground cinnamon |
| ½ cup coarsely chopped almonds or hazelnuts | 4 tart cooking apples |
| ¾ cup sugar | ½ cup heavy cream, chilled and whipped (optional) |
| 5 tablespoons butter, melted, | |

In a large mixing bowl, soak the currants in the rum for 30 minutes. Preheat the oven to 350°F. With a pastry brush spread a light coating of melted or softened butter inside a 1½-quart soufflé or baking dish.

Add to the currants the bread crumbs, chopped nuts, ½ cup of the sugar, the melted butter, lemon peel and cinnamon, and stir until all the ingredients are well combined.

With a small, sharp knife, quarter, peel and core the apples and cut them lengthwise into ¼ inch slices. Drop the slices into a bowl as you proceed, and sprinkle them with the remaining ¼ cup of sugar; turn the slices with a wooden spoon to sugar-coat them evenly.

With a metal spatula, spread about one-third of the bread-crumb mixture on the bottom of the baking dish and strew about one half of the apple slices evenly over it. Repeat with another layer of crumbs, and cover with the last of the apples and remaining crumbs. Dot the top with the butter bits.

Bake the dessert in the middle of the oven for 30 to 40 minutes or until the apples are tender when tested with the tip of a knife. Serve at once, directly from the dish. If you like, you may serve the dessert with whipped cream.

■ THE COOKING OF GERMANY

## Baked Apples with Almond Topping

**To serve 6**

| | |
|---|---|
| 2 cups cold water | ½ cup unsalted butter, softened |
| ¼ lemon plus 2 teaspoons fresh lemon juice | |
| 4 large tart cooking apples | 3 eggs, separated |
| ½ cup plus ⅔ cup sugar | ½ cup ground blanched almonds |

In a 1½- to 2-quart saucepan, combine the cold water, the juice of the lemon quarter and the lemon quarter itself. Halve, peel and core each apple and, as you proceed, drop the halves into the lemon water to prevent discoloration. Then stir ½ cup of the sugar into the water. Bring it quickly to the boil, stirring occasionally, reduce the heat, and simmer, uncovered, for six to eight minutes, or until the apples are tender. Remove them from the pan and drain on a cake rack.

Preheat the oven to 350°F. With a pastry brush, spread a light coating of melted or softened butter in a shallow baking dish just large enough to hold the apple halves in one layer. Place the apples side by side in the dish, cut side down.

In a mixing bowl, cream the butter and the remaining ⅔ cup of sugar by beating them against the sides of the bowl with the back of a wooden spoon until they are light and fluffy. Beat in the egg yolks, one by one, then the ground almonds and 2 teaspoons of lemon juice.

With a whisk or a rotary or electric beater, beat the egg whites in a large bowl until they form unwavering peaks. With a rubber spatula, mix several spoonfuls of egg white into the butter mixture to lighten it, then fold the butter mixture into the remaining egg whites. Spread this almond topping over the apples and bake the dessert in the middle of the oven for 20 minutes, or until the top is golden. Serve at room temperature.

■ THE COOKING OF SCANDINAVIA

## Apple Pancakes

**To make four 8- to 9- inch pancakes**

| | |
|---|---|
| 2 cups flour | 2 tart cooking apples, peeled, quartered, cored and cut lengthwise into ¼-inch-thick slices |
| ½ teaspoon salt | |
| 4 eggs, lightly beaten | |
| 2 cups milk | |
| ¾ cup butter | Golden or maple syrup |

Combine the flour and salt in a deep bowl, make a well in the center, and pour in the eggs. With a large spoon or whisk, gradually incorporate the flour into the eggs. Then, stirring constantly, pour in the milk in a thin stream and continue to mix until the batter is smooth. Do not overmix.

In a heavy 8- to 9-inch skillet (preferably one with a nonstick cooking surface), melt 2 tablespoons of the butter over moderate heat. When the foam begins to subside, add about one-fourth of the apple slices to the pan and turn them about in the butter until

## Blueberries with Maple Cream

*Wild blueberries, or huckleberries, are a mite smaller than the culti-vated berries and not as sweet. Nonetheless their flavor is more intense. Both cultivated and wild blueberries are available commercially. The sweetener must be pure maple syrup, not pancake syrup, which is corn syrup with maple flavoring.* ◆●

**To serve 4**

| | |
|---|---|
| ½ cup heavy cream, chilled | ½ cup sour cream |
| 2 tablespoons pure maple syrup | 1 pint blueberries, stemmed |

Pour the heavy cream into a deep, chilled bowl, and beat it with a wire whisk or a rotary or electric beater until the cream forms soft peaks when the beater is lifted from the bowl. Still beating, driz-zle in the maple syrup; continue to beat until the cream forms unwavering peaks.

Gently fold the sour cream into the maple cream. To serve, divide the berries among four small goblets or bowls, and top each serving with some of the maple cream.

■ LATE-NIGHT SUPPER MENUS

## Bananas Foster

*This elegant dessert of flamed bananas and ice cream was created at Brennan's in New Orleans in the 1940s. Richard Foster, the patron for whom the dessert was named, obviously was a man of enduring taste, for bananas Foster has become one of the restaurant's most popular trademarks.* ◆●

**To serve 4**

| | |
|---|---|
| 1 pint vanilla ice cream, preferably homemade | and halved lengthwise |
| ½ cup butter, cut into bits | ½ teaspoon ground cinnamon |
| ½ cup brown sugar | ½ cup liqueur |
| 4 firm, ripe bananas, peeled | 1 cup rum |

Prepare and assemble the bananas Foster at the dinner table when you are ready to serve them. Light an alcohol burner or tabletop stove and set a 12-inch copper flambé or crepe-suzette pan over the flame. Arrange all of the ingredients conveniently beside the pan. Place a scoop of ice cream on each of four chilled individual dessert plates and set them to one side.

Combine the butter and brown sugar in the flambé pan and stir until the mixture becomes a smooth caramel syrup. Add the bananas and baste them with the syrup for three to four minutes, then sprinkle in the cinnamon.

Carefully pour the banana liqueur and the rum into one side of the pan, and let them warm for a few seconds. They may burst into flame spontaneously. If not, ignite them with a match. Slide the pan back and forth until the flames die, basting the bananas all the while. Place two banana halves around each scoop of ice cream, spoon the sauce over the top, and serve at once.

■ AMERICAN COOKING: CREOLE AND ACADIAN

BLUEBERRIES WITH MAPLE CREAM

the slices are lightly and evenly browned. Pour in 1 cup of the batter, and cook the pancake for two to three minutes. When it has browned around the edges, place an inverted plate over the pan and turn the pancake out onto the plate, browned side up. Add 1 tablespoon of butter to the pan. Slide the pancake back into the pan for two minutes longer to brown the under side. Then slide it onto a heated serving plate.

With a fork, roll the pancake into a cylinder, and drape foil over it to keep it warm. Fry the remaining pancakes in the same way, using one fourth of the apple slices and 1 cup of batter for each one. Serve the pancakes as soon as possible after they are done, accompanied by syrup in a pitcher.

■ A QUINTET OF CUISINES

## Kentucky Fried Peaches

**To serve 4**

| | |
|---|---|
| 2 large firm ripe peaches | 4 tablespoons sugar |
| 2 tablespoons unsalted butter | 2 tablespoons bourbon |

Drop the peaches into enough boiling water to cover them completely, and boil briskly for two or three minutes. Then, with a slotted spoon, transfer the peaches to a colander to drain. Peel them, halve them, and remove the pits. Pat the peaches dry.

In an 8- to 10-inch nonreactive skillet, combine the butter and sugar over moderate heat. Stir constantly with a wooden spoon until the butter melts, then add the peaches, cut side down. Cook uncovered for two to three minutes, or until the bottoms of the peaches are golden. Turn them over with a spatula, baste them with the caramel from the skillet, and cook them for an additional two minutes. Turn the peaches over again.

Warm the bourbon in a ladle or small saucepan. Stepping back, ignite it with a match and pour it into the pan of peaches. Gently slide the pan back and forth over the heat until the flames die. Serve the peaches at once.

■ AMERICAN COOKING: SOUTHERN STYLE

## Grapes Juanita

**To serve 8**

| | |
|---|---|
| 2 pounds green seedless grapes, stemmed | ½ cup brown sugar |
| 1 cup sour cream | 2 teaspoons grated orange peel |

In a serving bowl, combine the grapes with the sour cream and mix well. Sprinkle the brown sugar on top. Cover the bowl and refrigerate the grapes for at least two hours. Garnish them with the grated orange peel just before serving them.

■ GREAT DINNERS FROM LIFE

## Fresh Figs in Monks' Robes

*Select smooth-skinned figs that are medium-soft and exude a drop of liquid from the rounded blossom end. The figs are peeled, then given a cocoa-sugar coating as brown as a monk's robe.* ✦●

**To serve 4**

| | |
|---|---|
| 8 large figs | cocoa powder |
| 8 blanched almonds | ¾ cup confectioners' sugar |
| ¾ cup unsweetened | |

Peel each fig by cutting off the stem with a small, sharp knife. Then nick the skin at the stem end, grasp a corner of the skin between your thumb and the knife blade, and pull a strip of skin away from the flesh; remove the rest of the peel in the same way. Press a whole blanched almond far enough into the bottom end of each fig to enclose the nut totally.

Sift the cocoa and sugar together into a shallow dish. Roll each fig in the cocoa mixture until it is evenly coated. Place the figs on a small serving platter, cover, and refrigerate them for 15 to 20 minutes before serving them.

■ ITALIAN MENUS

## Gingered Orange Slices

**To serve 4**

| | |
|---|---|
| 3 navel oranges | 1 teaspoon slivered crystallized ginger, plus |
| 1 teaspoon cornstarch | |
| 1 tablespoon water | 2 teaspoons slivered crystallized ginger |
| ½ cup fresh orange juice | |
| 2 tablespoons ginger brandy or | |

With a small, sharp knife, peel the oranges, removing as much of the white pith as possible. Cut the oranges crosswise into ½-inch-thick slices; set the slices aside.

Stir the cornstarch and 1 tablespoon of water together in a cup until the cornstarch dissolves. Then, in a nonreactive 8- to 10-inch sauté pan or skillet, use a wooden spoon to mix the orange juice with the ginger brandy. Bring the juice to a boil over moderate heat, add the cornstarch, reduce the heat to low, and stir for one minute or until the mixture thickens. Add the orange slices to the pan. Turning the slices to coat them with sauce, cook them for one minute or until they are heated through. Divide the orange slices among four warmed dessert plates, sprinkle on the 2 teaspoons of crystallized ginger, and serve at once.

■ LATE-NIGHT SUPPER MENUS

## Flamed Peaches

**To serve 4**

| | |
|---|---|
| 1 cup sugar | and pitted |
| 1 cup water | ⅓ cup brandy, kirsch or rum |
| 1 tablespoon vanilla extract | 1 tablespoon peach liqueur or apple brandy |
| 4 peaches, peeled, halved | |

In a heavy nonreactive 3- to 4-quart saucepan, combine the sugar, water and vanilla. Bring the mixture to a boil over moderate heat and boil it for five minutes to form a syrup. Add the peach halves and poach them—turning them once with a slotted spoon—for six to eight minutes or until they are barely tender when pierced with the tip of a small knife. Using the slotted spoon, transfer the peach halves to a chafing dish and ladle hot syrup over them.

At the dinner table, pour the brandy and liqueur over the peaches. (If the peaches and syrup have cooled, first warm the brandy and liqueur in a small pan over low heat.) The brandy may ignite spontaneously; otherwise, hold a match just above it to set it aflame. Slide the dish back and forth gently until the flames die. Serve immediately.

■ AMERICAN REGIONAL MENUS

## Oranges Poached in White Wine

**To serve 4**

| | |
|---|---|
| 1 cup fruity white wine, such as Pinot Grigio, Vernaccia di San Gimignano, Chardonnay or Riesling | 1 cup sugar<br>2 cups water<br>4 navel oranges<br>Mint sprigs for garnish |

Combine the wine, sugar and water in a 2- to 3-quart nonreactive saucepan. Bring the mixture to a boil over moderate heat and, stirring constantly, boil for one minute, or until the sugar dis-

solves. Reduce the heat to low and simmer, uncovered, for 10 minutes.

Meanwhile, using a vegetable peeler, remove three 2-by-2½-inch pieces of peel from one of the oranges. Cut the strips into very thin julienne strips; set these aside. With a small, sharp knife, remove the rest of the peel and pith from the oranges and discard or save for another use.

Carefully submerge the oranges in the simmering syrup. Add the julienne peel. Cover the pan and cook the oranges over low heat for 20 minutes.

Transfer the oranges, the syrup, and the julienne peel to a

heatproof bowl, and allow them to cool to room temperature.

Refrigerate the oranges for at least three hours or until they are well chilled. To serve the dessert, cut each orange crosswise into four slices, and reassemble it in a shallow individual serving bowl. Ladle some syrup and julienne peel over each orange. Garnish the oranges with mint sprigs, if desired.

■ MAKE-AHEAD MENUS

## Poached Pears with Crème Anglaise

**To serve 6**

| | |
|---|---|
| 6 slightly underripe pears | CRÈME ANGLAISE |
| 4 cups water | 1 cup milk |
| 2 cups sugar | ½ cup heavy cream |
| 1 tablespoon fresh lemon juice | One 1-inch piece vanilla bean |
| 1 teaspoon grated lemon peel | 4 egg yolks |
| 1 cinnamon stick | 6 tablespoons sugar |
| 3 whole cloves | 2 teaspoons cornstarch |

Peel the pears, leaving the stems on if desired. If necessary, trim the bottoms so that the pears will stand upright later. As you work, drop the pears into cold water containing a little lemon juice to prevent discoloration.

In a 4- to 6-quart nonreactive pot, bring the 4 cups of water, the sugar, lemon juice and lemon peel to a boil over high heat. Add the cinnamon stick, cloves and the pears. Cover, reduce the heat to moderate, and poach the pears for 20 minutes or until they are slightly translucent and tender when tested with the tip of a sharp knife. With a slotted spoon, transfer the pears to a shallow serving plate, standing them upright. Pour a little of the cooking syrup over the pears, cover them, and chill for several hours.

For the *crème anglaise,* or pouring custard, first combine the milk, cream and vanilla bean in a heavy 1- to 2-quart saucepan. Bring the liquid just to a boil; remove the pan from the heat and let it stand for 10 minutes to absorb the flavor of the vanilla bean.

In a mixing bowl, beat the egg yolks with a whisk until they are smooth; gradually beat in the sugar, and continue beating for about three minutes, until the mixture is pale yellow and creamy. Beat in the cornstarch. Stir the milk mixture into the yolks, whisking vigorously.

Return this mixture to the saucepan and cook it over low heat, stirring, until the mixture is quite thick and coats the back of a metal spoon. This will take about 15 minutes. Do not let the sauce boil. Remove it from the heat and cool it, stirring frequently. Remove the vanilla bean, wash it, dry it, and save it to use again; cover the custard sauce and chill it.

To serve, present the pears in their dish, and accompany them with the *crème anglaise* in a separate bowl.

NOTE:   Use winter pears—Bosc or Anjou—that are slightly underripe. Pears ready for eating fall apart in the poaching. Watch the sauce attentively as it cooks. If it boils, it will curdle. To prevent this, stir steadily and keep the sauce at a low temperature.

■ GREAT DINNERS FROM LIFE

## Spiced Pears in Red-Wine Sauce

**To serve 4**

| | |
|---|---|
| 2 cups red wine | peel |
| 2 cups sugar | 4 slightly underripe Bosc or |
| 2 whole cloves | Anjou pears |
| 1 cinnamon stick, 1½ to 2 inches long | 1 tablespoon cornstarch |
| ½ teaspoon grated lemon peel | ¾ cup cold water |
| ½ teaspoon grated orange | Lime sherbet (optional) |
| | Mint leaves for garnish |

In a 3- to 4-quart nonreactive pot, combine the wine, sugar, cloves, cinnamon, and lemon and orange peels. Bring the mixture to a boil over high heat, then reduce the heat to low, cover the pot and let the mixture simmer.

Peel the pears, leaving the stems intact. Stand the pears upright in the wine; if necessary, add enough water so that the liquid almost immerses the pears. Cover the pot and poach the pears for 20 minutes or until they are tender when tested with the tip of a sharp knife. Remove the pot from the heat. Uncover it and allow the pears to cool in the wine mixture. With a slotted spoon, transfer the pears to dessert plates.

Bring the wine mixture to a boil over moderate heat and boil it for eight to 10 minutes or until it is reduced to 1 cup. Using a whisk, mix the cornstarch with the ¾ cup of water in a small bowl. When the cornstarch is completely dissolved, pour the mixture into the wine in a slow stream, whisking until the cornstarch is incorporated. Reduce the heat and stir the sauce until it is thick enough to coat the whisk—two to three minutes. Pour the sauce through a fine sieve into a heatproof bowl, and allow it to cool to room temperature.

To serve, if you wish, cut a slit partway down through one side of each pear; open the notch out somewhat, and pipe some slightly softened lime sherbet into it. Pour about ¼ cup of sauce over each pear. Garnish the pears with mint leaves and serve immediately.

NOTE: For a more intense flavor, prepare the pears a day in advance of when you plan to serve them, and let them steep in the wine overnight.

■ FISH AND SHELLFISH MENUS

## Strawberry Semifreddo

*The Italian "semifreddo" translates as "half frozen." In culinary language, it means a parfait—or a frozen dessert made with heavy cream, such as this splendid concoction.* ❧

**To serve 4**

| | |
|---|---|
| 1½ pints strawberries, hulled | ¾ cup heavy cream, chilled |
| 3 egg whites | 1 tablespoon confectioners' |
| 1½ teaspoons vanilla extract |    sugar |
| ⅓ cup sugar | 2 teaspoons fresh lemon juice |

Set about 1 cup of the strawberries aside, and purée the rest in a food processor or blender. Combine the purée, egg whites and 1 teaspoon of the vanilla in a large bowl, and beat them with an electric mixer for two minutes or until they are frothy and pale. Beating constantly, add the granulated sugar gradually.

In a deep, chilled bowl, beat the heavy cream with a whisk or a rotary or electric beater until it forms soft peaks on the beater when it is lifted from the bowl. Using a rubber spatula, fold the cream into the strawberry mixture. Cover the bowl, and chill the strawberry cream in the freezer for one hour. After one hour, beat the cream with an electric mixer until it is thoroughly blended. Cover the strawberry cream, return it to the freezer, and chill it for about three hours or until it is firm.

Meanwhile, cut the remaining strawberries into halves. In a mixing bowl, combine them with the remaining ½ teaspoon of vanilla, the confectioners' sugar and the lemon juice, and toss the berries gently to coat them completely with the sugar mixture. Cover the bowl with plastic wrap and refrigerate the berries until ready to serve.

About 10 minutes before serving, set out the frozen strawberry cream to soften at room temperature. Divide it among four individual goblets or bowls, and top each serving with some of the sweetened strawberries.

■ ITALIAN MENUS

## Summer Pudding

*Nothing more than a bread-lined mold filled with fresh berries, this pudding turns out as a glorious treat—to see and to eat.* ❧

**To serve 6 to 8**

| | |
|---|---|
| 2 quarts ripe raspberries, | 1¼ cups superfine sugar |
|    blackberries, blueberries, | 10 to 12 slices homemade- |
|    red currants or a mixture |    type white bread |
|    of these, stemmed | 1 cup heavy cream, chilled |

Place the berries in a large mixing bowl, sprinkle them with the sugar, and toss them about gently with a large spoon until the sugar dissolves completely. Taste the berries, and add more sugar if necessary. Cover the berries tightly and set them aside.

With a small, sharp knife, cut one slice of bread into a circle or octagon so that it will exactly fit the bottom of a 2-quart English pudding basin, a deep 2-quart bowl, or a charlotte mold. Set the

STRAWBERRIES WITH SABAYON

bread in place. Trim six or seven slices of the bread into wedge shapes as long as the basin is deep, 3½ to 4 inches wide across the top and about 3 inches wide across the bottom. Stand the wedges of bread, narrow ends down, around the inner surface of the mold, overlapping them by about ¼ inch.

Ladle the berry mixture into the mold, and cover the top completely with the remaining bread. Cover the mold with a flat plate, and on it set a 3- to 4-pound kitchen weight, or a heavy pan or casserole. Refrigerate the pudding for at least 12 hours, until the bread is completely saturated with the berry juices.

To remove the pudding from the mold, place a chilled serving plate upside down over it and, grasping the plate and mold firmly together, quickly invert them. The pudding should slide out easily. In a large, chilled bowl, beat the heavy cream with a whisk or a rotary or electric beater until it forms soft peaks on the beater. Serve the whipped cream separately with the pudding.

NOTE: If the berries have not fully ripened and are not soft,

combine the fruit and sugar in a heavy nonreactive 3- to 4-quart saucepan, and cook them over low heat for about five minutes, shaking the pan frequently and stirring them with a spoon.

■ THE COOKING OF THE BRITISH ISLES

## Strawberries with Sabayon

**To serve 4**

| | |
|---|---|
| 1 pint strawberries, hulled | Grand Marnier or other |
| 4 egg yolks | orange liqueur |
| ¼ cup superfine sugar | 2 to 3 tablespoons |
| Juice of ½ orange | heavy cream |
| 1½ tablespoons Triple Sec, | |

Cut four strawberries into fan shapes by slicing lengthwise through the berries four or five times to within ½ inch of the stem end and spreading the slices into fan shapes; set aside.  Arrange the remaining strawberries, pointed upward, on individual dessert plates. In the top of a double boiler set over simmering—not boiling—water, beat the egg yolks with a whisk until they are smooth. Add the sugar and continue whisking for five minutes or until the sauce mixture is pale, thick and foamy.

Add the orange juice and whisk until the mixture thickens again. Repeat this procedure with the Triple Sec and then with the cream. Cool the sauce by setting the pan in a bowl of ice, stirring the sauce with the whisk to keep it from developing lumps. Drizzle the sauce over the berries and garnish each serving with a strawberry fan. Serve at once.

■ CHICKEN AND GAME HEN MENUS

317

## Wine Jelly with Fruit

**To serve 4 to 6**

| | |
|---|---|
| 2 envelopes unflavored gelatin | peeled and cored pear |
| 1½ cups water | halves; pitted cherries, |
| 2 cups dry white wine | whole strawberries or |
| 2 tablespoons fresh | strawberry halves; whole |
|    lemon juice | grapes or grape halves; |
| ½ cup sugar | banana slices, melon cubes |
| 2 cups assorted fruit: peeled | or orange sections |
|    peach halves or slices; | Sweetened whipped cream |
|    peeled apricot halves; | (optional) |

In a small heatproof bowl, sprinkle the gelatin over 1 cup of the water. When the gelatin has softened for two or three minutes, set the bowl in a skillet of simmering water; cook over low heat, stirring, until the gelatin dissolves. Remove the skillet from the heat, leaving the bowl of gelatin in the water.

In a large bowl, combine the wine, the remaining ½ cup of water, the lemon juice and sugar, and stir until the sugar dissolves. Thoroughly stir in the gelatin. Pour a ¼-inch layer of the mixture into a 1½-quart mold, pack the mold into a bowl half filled with crushed ice, and refrigerate until firm. (Keep the remaining jelly at room temperature so that it remains liquid and ready to use.)

Spread the pieces of fruit between paper towels to dry them. Arrange a layer of one kind of fruit or various kinds on the surface of the set gelatin. Gradually pour on enough liquid wine jelly to reach almost to the top of the fruit.

Chill again until set, then pour in enough jelly to cover the fruit by ¼ inch. Chill. Repeat this process four or five more times, filling the mold with alternating layers of fruit and jelly and refrigerating the mold after each step. Finally add enough jelly to come to within ¼ inch of the top. Refrigerate the dessert for at least six hours until it is firm. (Any remaining jelly may be chilled in a flat pan and used chopped or cut into decorative shapes as a garnish.)

To serve, run a knife around the sides of the mold and dip the bottom in hot water for a few seconds. Wipe the mold dry, place an inverted serving plate over it, and, grasping plate and mold together, turn them over. Rap them on a table; the jelly should slide out easily. Chill until ready to serve. If you like, pass some whipped cream separately.

NOTE: When choosing fruits to be suspended in jelly, pick those that are firm enough to retain their shape. But do not use raw pineapple, papaya, kiwi, prickly pear or fig: These fruits contain enzymes that interfere with the jelling process.

■ THE COOKING OF GERMANY

## Chocolate Pots de Crème with Chestnuts

**To serve 4**

| | |
|---|---|
| 4 ounces sweet baking | 1½ teaspoons vanilla extract |
|    chocolate, cut into bits | ½ cup coarsely chopped |
| 1 cup heavy cream | cooked chestnuts, plus |
| 5 egg yolks | 2 whole chestnuts for |
| 2 tablespoons sugar | garnish |
| Salt | |

Combine the chocolate and cream in a small, heavy saucepan. Stirring frequently with a wooden spoon, melt the chocolate and scald the cream over moderate heat by cooking them until bubbles form around the edges of the cream. Immediately remove the pan from the stove. Set the chocolate cream aside to cool to room temperature.

In a deep bowl, beat the egg yolks with a wire whisk or a rotary or electric beater until they are smooth. Add the sugar and a pinch of salt, and continue beating until the mixture thickens. Stirring constantly, slowly beat in the chocolate cream. Stir in the vanilla and chopped chestnuts. Divide the mixture among four porcelain *pots de crème,* without lids, or small ramekins, and refrigerate the puddings for at least two hours or until they are firm to the touch. Before serving, garnish each *pot de crème* with a chestnut half, if you like.

NOTE: To cook fresh chestnuts—you will need up to a dozen—first cut a cross through the shell on the flat side of each one. Parboil the chestnuts for 10 minutes; then use a small knife to cut away the shell and peel off the brown skin. Cook the chestnuts in water to cover for about 45 minutes to tenderize them. If time is short, you can substitute water-packed canned chestnuts, available where gourmet foods are sold.

■ FRENCH REGIONAL MENUS

## Chocolate Ricotta

**To serve 4**

| | |
|---|---|
| 2 ounces semisweet | ½ cup confectioners' |
|    chocolate |    sugar |
| 1½ teaspoons freshly grated | Vanilla extract, rum or |
|    nutmeg | bourbon to taste |
| 2 cups ricotta cheese | |

Using the fine side of a box grater, grate the chocolate onto a sheet of wax paper. Without washing the grater, grate the nutmeg over a separate sheet of wax paper.

In a small serving bowl, mix the ricotta cheese, sugar, half of the chocolate and nutmeg to taste. Stir until blended. Sprinkle the remaining chocolate over the top, cover the bowl with plastic wrap, and refrigerate until ready to serve.

NOTE: Instant coffee may take the place of some or all of the chocolate. Experiment to suit your taste.

■ FAMILY MENUS

WINE JELLY WITH FRUIT

## Orange Caramel Custard

*The first step in making this dessert is to line the bottom of eight individual custard cups with caramel. Then the custard is prepared and baked in the caramel-lined cups. Lining the cups with caramel demands quick work. Because the temperature of the caramel will be over 300°F., handle it with extreme caution.* ❦

**To serve 8**

| | |
|---|---|
| **2½ cups sugar** | **Two 4-inch cinnamon sticks** |
| **¼ cup water** | **1 teaspoon vanilla extract** |
| **3 small navel oranges** | **6 eggs plus 2 egg yolks** |
| **4 cups milk** | |

In a small, heavy saucepan or skillet, bring 1 cup of the sugar and the water to a boil over high heat, stirring until the sugar dissolves. Reduce the heat to moderate, and cook, without stirring but gently sliding the pan back and forth, until the syrup becomes a deep golden brown; this may take 10 minutes or more.

The moment the syrup reaches the desired color, remove the pan from the heat, and pour about a tablespoonful of the hot syrup into the first cup. Tip and swirl the syrup around the cup's bottom, then set the cup aside. In a similar fashion, line seven more cups.

Preheat the oven to 325°F. With a small, sharp knife or vegetable peeler, remove the peel from the three oranges without cutting into the white pith underneath it. Set the peel aside. Remove and discard the pith and the outside membranes of the oranges. Then free the individual segments of orange by cutting along both sides of one segment at a time down to the center core. Carefully lift out each piece as it is loosened. Set aside.

In a 2- to 3-quart saucepan, combine the milk, reserved orange peel and cinnamon sticks, and cook over moderate heat until small bubbles appear around the edge of the milk. Remove the pan from the heat, discard the peel and the cinnamon sticks and stir in the vanilla.

With a wire whisk or a rotary or electric beater, beat the eggs and egg yolks together until well blended, then add the remaining 1½ cups of sugar gradually, and continue to beat until the mixture is thick and pale yellow. Stirring constantly, pour in the hot milk in a thin stream; strain through a fine sieve into a bowl.

Place two or three orange segments in the bottom of each caramel-lined cup, and pour in enough custard to come almost to the top. Place the cups in a large shallow baking pan, and set the pan on the middle shelf of the oven. Pour in enough boiling water to come halfway up the sides of the cups. Bake, reducing the oven temperature if the water in the pan begins to simmer, for about 40 minutes or until a knife inserted in the center of the custard comes out clean.

Remove the cups from the water, and refrigerate the custard for at least three hours or until it is thoroughly chilled.

Unmold the custards one at a time. Run a sharp knife around the sides, and dip the bottom of the cup briefly in hot water. Wipe the outside of the cup dry, place a chilled serving plate upside down over it and, grasping cup and plate together firmly, quickly turn them over. Rap the plate on a table and the custard should slide out of the cup easily. Pour any extra caramel remaining in the cup over the custard.

■ THE COOKING OF SPAIN AND PORTUGAL

## Baked Goat Cheese with Raspberry Sauce

*For this unusual dessert, scoops of goat cheese are dipped into beaten egg, then covered with a sweet nut and bread crumb mixture before being baked. This protective coating prevents the cheese from running at the high baking temperature. Some imported goat cheeses are too strong-flavored and dense-textured for this recipe; for a pleasing result, select a mild, creamy domestic cheese or a mild imported variety such as French Capricette.* ❧

### To serve 4

| | |
|---|---|
| 2 slices homemade-type white bread, crusts trimmed | 1 egg |
| 6 tablespoons sugar | ¼ cup flour |
| ½ cup pine nuts | ¾ pound mild-flavored goat cheese |
| 1½ cups raspberries | 2 tablespoons unsalted butter |
| 1 to 2 tablespoons pure maple syrup | Mint sprigs for garnish |

Tear the bread into pieces and combine it with the sugar and pine nuts in a blender or food processor. Chop the mixture into coarse crumbs. Spread the crumbs evenly in a pie pan or shallow plate. Purée 1 cup of the raspberries in the blender or processor and add maple syrup to taste. With the back of a spoon, press the purée through a fine sieve set over a small bowl to remove the raspberry seeds. Set the crumbs and purée aside.

Break the egg into a small bowl and beat it lightly with a fork or whisk until it is smooth. Place the flour on a sheet of wax paper. Using a dessert spoon, shape the goat cheese into ovals. Roll each one in the flour to coat it lightly; brush off any excess. Dip it in the egg, then roll it in the crumbs until well coated. Set the cheese ovals several inches apart on a baking sheet.

When ready to serve the dessert, preheat the oven to 400° F. Melt the butter in a small, heavy saucepan over low heat. Drizzle the cheese ovals with melted butter and bake them for eight to 10 minutes or until golden. Meanwhile, divide the puréed sauce among four small dessert bowls. Using a metal spatula, transfer the cheese ovals to the bowls with the purée. Garnish each serving with a few of the remaining berries and a mint sprig.

■ SALAD MENUS

## Chilled Chocolate Loaf

*A "cake" with no flour and no baking, this loaf has many variations, some incorporating chestnuts. The one given here comes from Turin, where it is called "dolce Torinese."* ❧

### To serve 8

| | |
|---|---|
| ½ pound semisweet chocolate, cut into bits | blanched almonds |
| ¼ cup rum | 12 butter biscuits such as Petits Beurre or Social Tea or vanilla wafers, cut into 1-by-½-inch pieces |
| 1 cup unsalted butter, softened | Confectioners' sugar |
| 2 tablespoons superfine sugar | ½ cup heavy cream, chilled and whipped (optional) |
| 2 eggs, separated | |
| 1½ cups coarsely chopped | |

With a pastry brush, spread a light coating of melted or softened butter over the bottom and sides of an 8-by-4-inch loaf pan. In a heavy 1- to 1½-quart saucepan, melt the chocolate over low heat, stirring constantly. When all the chocolate dissolves, stir in the rum and remove the pan from the heat. Cool to room temperature.

Cream the butter and sugar together by beating them vigorously against the sides of a large, heavy mixing bowl with the back of a wooden spoon until they are light and fluffy. Beat in the egg yolks, one at a time. Stir in the grated almonds and cooled chocolate. In a separate bowl, beat the egg whites with a wire whisk or rotary or electric beater until they are stiff enough to cling to the beater in soft peaks. With a rubber spatula, fold them into the chocolate mixture. When no streaks of white remain, gently fold in the cut-up biscuits, discarding the biscuit crumbs. Spoon the mixture into the loaf pan and smooth the top with a spatula to spread it evenly. Cover the loaf lightly with plastic wrap and refrigerate it for at least four hours, or until very firm.

Unmold the loaf an hour or so before serving it. Run a sharp knife around the sides of the pan, and dip the bottom into hot water for a few seconds. Place a chilled serving platter upside down over the pan and, grasping both sides, quickly invert the plate and pan. Rap the plate on the table. The loaf should slide out easily; if it does not, repeat the process. Smooth the top and sides of the unmolded loaf with a metal spatula, then return it to the refrigerator. Just before serving, sieve a little confectioners' sugar over the top. Cut the loaf into thin slices and serve it, if desired, with whipped cream.

■ THE COOKING OF ITALY

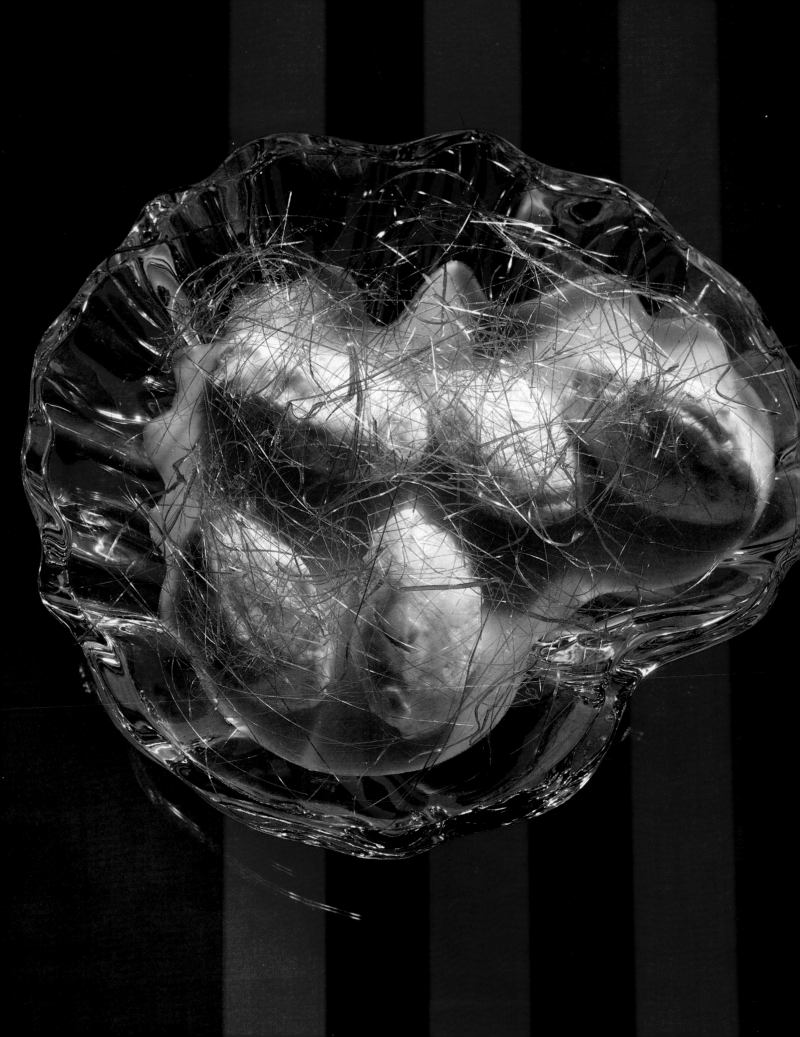

## Floating Island

*The "islands" of this dessert are meringues—beaten and sweetened egg whites—poached to create soft, fluffy ovals that "float" on the custard below them. The whiteness of the ovals inspires the dessert's French name: "oeufs à la neige," or "snow eggs." Spun sugar, which is simply threads of cooled caramel, is a traditional decoration. If a vanilla bean is not available to flavor the meringue and custard, substitute 1 teaspoon of vanilla extract—adding it when the egg yolks are beaten with sugar for the custard.* ❧

**To serve 8 to 10**

| | |
|---|---|
| 5 eggs, separated | SPUN SUGAR |
| ½ cup plus ⅔ cup sugar | ⅔ **cup sugar** |
| 2 to 2½ cups light cream | ⅓ **cup water** |
| One 2-inch piece vanilla bean | |

With a wire whisk or a rotary or electric beater, beat the egg whites. As soon as they are frothy, add the ½ cup of sugar. Then continue to beat until the meringue is stiff enough to stand in unwavering peaks on the beater when it is lifted from the bowl.

In a heavy 8- to 10-inch skillet, heat 2 cups of cream and the vanilla bean over low heat. When small bubbles begin to form around the sides of the pan, reduce the heat to the lowest setting. To form each "island" scoop up meringue in one dessert spoon and invert another dessert spoon over it to shape the meringue into an oval. Slide the meringue off the spoon onto the surface of the simmering cream. Make similar ovals of the remaining meringue. Simmer the meringues uncovered for two minutes, turn them over gently with a slotted spoon, and cook for one or two minutes, or until they are just firm to the touch. Do not overcook the meringue or they might disintegrate. Transfer the meringues to a kitchen towel to drain and cool to room temperature.

Remove the vanilla bean and strain the cream through a fine sieve. Measure it and add enough more cream to make 2 cups. Return the vanilla bean and set the cream aside.

Combine the egg yolks and ⅔ cup of sugar in a heavy 2- to 3-quart saucepan, and beat them together with a wire whisk. Whisking the mixture constantly, pour in the cream in a slow, thin stream. Add the vanilla bean once again and place the pan over low heat. Stir gently with a spoon until the custard coats the spoon heavily. Do not let the custard come anywhere near a boil or it will curdle. Strain the custard through a fine sieve into a bowl, discarding the vanilla bean. Refrigerate the custard for three to four hours to chill it thoroughly.

About half an hour before serving, prepare the caramel for the spun sugar: Combine ⅔ cup of sugar and ⅓ cup of water in a small, heavy pan and bring it to a boil over high heat, stirring until the sugar dissolves. Boil the syrup over moderate heat, gently sliding the pan back and forth until the syrup turns a tea brown. This may take 10 minutes or more. Immediately remove the pan from the heat and pour the caramel into a heatproof serving bowl.

Arrange the meringues on top of the custard and, when the caramel is lukewarm, drizzle wisps of spun sugar over them by scooping up a little liquid caramel in a small spoon and tilting the spoon while moving it back and forth above the bowl of custard. The liquid will fall in thin threads and firm as it falls. For even finer traceries, spread a small sheet of wax paper or parchment paper on a work surface. Grasp two table forks back to back, dip the tines in the liquid and then quickly move the forks over the paper from one end of the sheet to the other in a figure-eight pattern. Allow to cool and harden.

To serve, ladle the meringues onto individual dessert plates and spoon custard around them. Add spun sugar to each plate.
■ **AMERICAN COOKING: THE EASTERN HEARTLAND**

## Crème Brûlée

*In England, the name for this dessert is "burnt cream," describing the custard's sugar topping, which is broiled, or "burnt," to a crackly caramel just before serving time. The dessert is neither difficult to make nor time consuming, but it does require constant attention—especially when it is under the broiler. For a caramel with milder flavor, you can substitute white sugar for brown. To be sure everyone has some caramel with the custard, tap the glazed surface all over with the back of the serving spoon before apportioning the dessert.* ❧

**To serve 6**

| | |
|---|---|
| 2½ **cups heavy cream** | 1 **teaspoon almond extract** |
| 6 **eggs** | 1 **cup light-brown sugar,** |
| 6 **tablespoons sugar** | **sieved before measuring** |
| 1 **teaspoon cornstarch** | |

In the top of a double boiler, scald the cream over low heat by cooking it until small bubbles begin to form around the edges. Remove the cream from the heat and set it aside to cool. With a whisk or a rotary or electric beater, beat the eggs for three or four minutes or until they are pale in color and thick. Combine the sugar with the cornstarch and add the mixture gradually to the eggs, beating constantly.

Still beating, very slowly add the cream to the beaten eggs. Pour the custard into the original double boiler and cook over gently simmering, not boiling, water. Stir constantly until the custard coats a metal spoon with a light layer. Take the custard off the heat, stir in the almond extract, and strain the custard through a fine sieve into a heatproof serving dish—or strain it into a mixing bowl and divide it among six individual heatproof dishes. Gently stir it twice during the first 10 minutes of cooling to prevent a surface skin from forming.

When the custard is lukewarm, refrigerate it. A large serving dish should be chilled for at least six hours, individual dishes for three hours.

Just before serving, sprinkle the top of the custard with the sieved brown sugar. Set the dish or dishes in a pan of ice—to avoid the chance of breaking the china because of a sudden change in temperature—and place the pan, ice, custard and all, under the broiler for two or three minutes or until the sugar bubbles. Watch carefully: Sugar burns easily. Serve at once.
■ **GREAT DINNERS FROM LIFE**

## Biscuit Tortoni

*A popular Italian-American restaurant dessert, biscuit tortoni was introduced in Paris in 1798 by a Neapolitan restaurateur named Tortoni.* ❖●

**To serve 12**

2½ cups heavy cream, chilled
½ cup confectioners' sugar
1 cup macaroon crumbs, made
    from stale macaroons
    pulverized in a food
    processor or blender

¼ cup dark rum
1½ teaspoons vanilla extract
¼ cup sliced almonds, toasted
    in a 350°F. oven for 5 minutes
6 candied cherries, halved,
    for garnish

Place a pleated paper liner in each of twelve 2- to 2½-inch muffin cups; set aside. In a bowl, combine 1¼ cups of the cream, the sugar and macaroons; refrigerate for at least 30 minutes.

In a deep, chilled mixing bowl, beat the remaining heavy cream with a whisk or a rotary or electric beater until it thickens and forms soft peaks. With a rubber spatula, fold in the macaroon mixture, the rum and vanilla. Fill the cups with the mixture. Sprinkle the tops evenly with the sliced almonds and, if you like, top each one with a cherry half. Freeze the biscuit tortoni for at least two hours.

■ AMERICAN COOKING: THE MELTING POT

## Ginger Peach Ice Cream

**To make about 1½ quarts**

4 cups heavy cream
¾ cup sugar
⅛ teaspoon salt
1½ teaspoons vanilla extract

6 ripe peaches
½ cup crystallized ginger,
    coarsely chopped

In a heavy 2- to 3-quart saucepan, heat 1 cup of the cream, the sugar and salt over low heat, stirring until the sugar dissolves; do not let the mixture come to a boil. Pour the cream mixture into a deep bowl, stir in the remaining 3 cups of cream and the vanilla, and refrigerate until chilled.

Meanwhile, drop the peaches, two or three at a time, into enough boiling water to cover them completely, and boil briskly for two to three minutes. With a slotted spoon, transfer the peaches to a colander and run cold water over them. Peel the peaches with a small knife, halve them and take out the stones, then chop the fruits coarse. Cover with foil or plastic wrap and refrigerate until ready to use.

Pack a 2-quart ice-cream freezer with layers of finely crushed or cracked ice and coarse rock salt as recommended by the freezer manufacturer. Add cold water if called for. Then ladle the chilled cream mixture into the ice-cream can and place the cover on top of it.

If you have a hand ice-cream maker, fill it with the cream mixture; let it stand for three or four minutes before turning the handle. Then, slowly at first, crank continuously for about five minutes. Stir in the peaches and ginger, and crank for 10 to 15 minutes more. Do not stop turning at any time or the ice cream might become lumpy.

When the handle can barely be moved, the ice cream is ready. If you wish to keep it for an hour or two, remove the lid and dasher. Scrape the ice cream off the dasher, and pack it firmly into the container with a spoon. Cover the container securely, pour off any water in the bucket, and repack the ice and salt solidly around it.

If you have an electric ice-cream maker, fill the can with the chilled cream mixture, cover it, turn on the switch and let the mixture churn for about five minutes. Stir in the peaches and ginger, cover again, and continue to churn for 10 to 15 minutes more, until the motor slows or stops. Serve the ice cream immediately or follow the procedure above.

■ AMERICAN COOKING: SOUTHERN STYLE

## Granite

*The somewhat rough texture of these water ices suggests their Italian name and distinguishes them from sherbets. This recipe offers four variations, but you can create others with whatever fruits are in season, and with tea as well as coffee.* ❖●

**To make about 1½ pints of**
    **each flavor**

LEMON ICE

2 cups water
1 cup sugar
1 cup fresh lemon juice

ORANGE ICE

2 cups water
¾ cup sugar
1 cup fresh orange juice
3 tablespoons fresh lemon
    juice

COFFEE ICE

1 cup water
½ cup sugar
2 cups strong espresso coffee

STRAWBERRY ICE

1 cup water
½ cup sugar
2 cups strawberries, puréed
    through a sieve or food mill
2 tablespoons fresh
    lemon juice

In a 1½- to 2-quart saucepan, bring the water and sugar to a boil over moderate heat, stirring only until the sugar dissolves. From the moment the sugar and water begin to boil, cook the mixture for exactly five minutes. Immediately remove the pan from the heat and cool the syrup to room temperature.

Depending on which of the flavored ices you want to make, stir in the lemon juice, the orange and lemon juices, the espresso coffee, or the puréed strawberries and lemon juice.

For a *granita* with a coarse texture, pour the mixture into an ice-cube tray and freeze it solid: Allow about three hours. Then remove the cubes and crush them with an ice crusher.

To achieve a fine texture, pour the mixture into a metal ice-cube tray from which the divider has been removed or a small shallow baking pan. Freeze the *granita* for three to four hours, stirring it every 30 minutes and scraping into it the ice particles that form around the edges of the pan.

■ THE COOKING OF ITALY

## Brandied Orange Bombe

*A bombe—it takes its name from its traditional shape—is a layered and molded assembly of ices, sherbets and ice creams, fruits and parfaits. A bombe mold is copper, which conducts heat well to facilitate both freezing and unmolding. However, a bombe can be made in any deep metal bowl or charlotte mold; fancier molds are tempting but complicate unmolding.* ✦●

**To serve 8**

| | |
|---|---|
| ½ cup white seedless<br>  raisins<br>½ cup brandy<br>1 quart orange sherbet<br>1 quart vanilla ice cream<br>1 pint raspberry sherbet | Fresh or canned mandarin<br>  orange segments<br>  for garnish<br>Orange leaves for<br>  garnish |

At least 12 hours ahead of time, combine the raisins and brandy in a covered jar, and let them stand at room temperature.

To make the bombe, chill a 2½-quart mold in the freezer. Spread the inside of the chilled mold with orange sherbet that has been softened slightly, pressing the ice against the mold with the back of a spoon so that it will take the shape of the mold. The layer of orange ice should be about ½ inch thick. Return the mold to the freezer for one hour.

Drain the soaked raisins and stir them quickly into slightly softened vanilla ice cream without letting the ice cream melt. Then pack the ice cream into the center of the mold, forming a second ½-inch layer. Return the mold to the freezer for one hour. Fill the center of the mold with slightly softened raspberry sherbet. Cover the mold with its lid, if it has one, or with foil. Return it to the freezer and freeze it for at least six hours.

To unmold, remove the lid or foil, then place the mold on a chilled serving plate, wipe the outside of the mold several times with a cloth wrung out in hot water and lift off the mold. The bombe can be unmolded ahead of time and kept frozen. However, let the bombe soften in the refrigerator for about 30 minutes before serving it. Garnish the bombe with mandarin orange segments and orange leaves if you wish.

■ GREAT DINNERS FROM LIFE

## Grand Marnier Soufflé

**To serve 6**

| | |
|---|---|
| ⅓ cup butter<br>¾ cup flour<br>½ teaspoon salt<br>1½ cups milk<br>5 eggs, separated, plus<br>  3 egg whites | 1 cup sugar<br>2 tablespoons fresh lemon<br>  juice<br>1 teaspoon finely grated lemon<br>  peel<br>½ cup Grand Marnier |

With a pastry brush, lightly coat the bottom and sides of a 2-quart soufflé dish with melted or softened butter. Sprinkle sugar into the dish and shake to distribute it evenly.

Cut a strip of parchment paper, wax paper or foil about 30 inches long and 6 inches wide—long enough to overlap itself by at least 2 inches when placed around the outside of the dish. Fold the strip in half lengthwise, then coat one side with butter and sprinkle it with sugar.

Using string, tie the paper or foil as a collar around the soufflé dish, sugared side inward; the collar should extend at least 2 inches above the dish. Secure the ends of the collar with a paper clip so that it will hold firm when the soufflé rises in the oven, thus ensuring that the soufflé will not overflow the dish, but will rise to maximum height.

In a small, heavy saucepan, melt the butter over low heat—stirring frequently with a wire whisk to prevent browning. Remove the pan from the heat, add the flour and salt, and whisk until the roux is smooth. Add the milk, a little at a time, stirring constantly. Return the pan to low heat and, still stirring, cook the sauce for two or three minutes, until it thickens and is smooth. Take the pan off the heat.

In a mixing bowl, beat the egg yolks for a minute or so, until they are thick and lemon colored. Stirring constantly with the whisk, pour in the hot sauce a small amount at a time. Set the yolk mixture aside to cool.

Preheat the oven to 350°F. With a whisk or a rotary or electric beater, beat the eight egg whites until they form soft peaks on the beater when it is lifted. Beating constantly, gradually pour in the sugar; continue beating until the mixture becomes a firm meringue and forms unwavering peaks. Gradually beat in the lemon juice, a few drops at a time.

Stir the lemon peel and Grand Marnier into the egg yolks. Add the yolks, all at once, to the egg whites and, using a rubber spatula, fold them in gently but thoroughly until no trace of white remains.

Carefully pour the soufflé mixture into the prepared dish. Set the dish in a shallow baking pan containing an inch of hot water. Bake the soufflé for one hour or until it is well risen and lightly browned; a knife inserted through the side should come out dry. Carefully remove the paper collar and serve the soufflé at once, apportioning it with a large spoon.

NOTE: Any kind of fruit liqueur or brandy or rum can be substituted for the orange-flavored Grand Marnier.

■ GREAT DINNERS FROM LIFE

## Crepes Calvados

**To serve 8**

| | |
|---|---|
| 4 Granny Smith or other tart apples | dissolved in 2 tablespoons cold water |
| 4 tablespoons unsalted butter | Ground cinnamon |
| ¼ cup sugar | Eight 8-inch dessert crepes (Index/Glossary) |
| 1 cup Calvados or other apple brandy | Confectioners' sugar |
| 2 teaspoons fresh lemon juice | 2 cups heavy cream, chilled and whipped (optional) |
| 2 teaspoons cornstarch, | |

Peel, core and dice enough apples to measure 3 cups. In an 8- to 10-inch skillet, heat the butter over moderate heat until it sizzles. Add the apples and granulated sugar. Stirring occasionally, cook the apples for about eight minutes or until they are lightly caramelized. Remove the skillet from the heat and carefully add the Calvados, pouring it down the side of the pan. The brandy may ignite spontaneously; if not, avert your face, hold a long match just above the skillet and ignite the brandy. Gently slide the pan back and forth until the flames die.

In a small bowl, blend the lemon juice, cornstarch mixture and a pinch of cinnamon. Stir this mixture into the apples in the skillet. Top one crepe at a time with 3 to 4 tablespoons of the apple filling, roll up the crepe, and set it on a serving platter. Sprinkle the top with confectioners' sugar. Serve the crepes with whipped cream, if desired.

■ FRENCH REGIONAL MENUS

## Indian Pudding

*This is among the oldest of New England dishes. How it got its name is a puzzlement. It was certainly not an Indian invention—they lacked the necessary spices—but it was a staple with the colonists, who baked it for 10 hours, usually on Saturday, and served it with thick sweet cream, as here. The dish tastes somewhat like pumpkin pie, although there is no trace of pumpkin in it.* ◆●

**To serve 6**

| | |
|---|---|
| ½ cup corn meal | ½ teaspoon ground cinnamon |
| 4 cups milk | 1 teaspoon salt |
| 1 cup brown sugar | ½ cup dark molasses |
| 1 teaspoon ground ginger | 2 cups light cream |
| ½ teaspoon freshly grated nutmeg | 2 cups heavy cream |

Preheat the oven to 275°F. With a pastry brush spread a light coating of butter over the bottom and sides of a 2-quart baking and serving dish.

In a small bowl mix the corn meal with 1 cup of the milk. Scald the remaining 3 cups of milk in a heavy 3- to 4-quart saucepan by cooking it over moderate heat until bubbles appear all around the edge. Stirring constantly, add the corn-meal mixture to the milk, a little at a time. Still stirring frequently, cook the corn meal for about 15 minutes or until the mixture is as thick as a cooked breakfast cereal. It is important to keep stirring to prevent lumps from forming.

Remove the pan from the heat. Stir in the sugar, ginger, nutmeg, cinnamon and salt, then add the molasses and light cream. Pour this pudding mixture into the prepared baking dish and bake for two hours.

Set the pudding aside to rest for at least an hour. Serve the pudding warm, accompanied by a pitcher of heavy cream to pour over each portion at the table.

■ GREAT DINNERS FROM LIFE

## Crepes with Lemon Soufflé Filling

**To serve 4 to 6**

| | |
|---|---|
| 3 tablespoons unsalted butter | 1 tablespoon grated lemon peel, plus 1 long strip lemon peel for garnish |
| 5 tablespoons sifted flour | |
| ½ cup milk | Eight 7- to 8-inch dessert crepes (Index/Glossary) |
| 3 eggs, separated | |
| ¼ cup sugar | Confectioners' sugar |
| 3 tablespoons fresh lemon juice | |

Preheat the oven to 400°F. For the soufflé base, first melt the butter over low heat in a heavy 1- to 2-quart saucepan. Stir in the flour, then cook, stirring, for one to two minutes. Remove the pan from the heat and let this roux cool for a moment. Beat in the milk vigorously to blend the roux and liquid. Stirring constantly, cook for a few minutes, until the mixture boils and thickens. Immediately scoop it into a large bowl and beat in the egg yolks, one at a time. Add 3 tablespoons of the granulated sugar, the lemon juice and grated lemon peel, stirring thoroughly.

In a separate bowl, beat the egg whites with a whisk or a rotary or electric beater until they cling to the beater in soft peaks. Add the remaining tablespoon of granulated sugar and beat until the whites form unwavering peaks on the beater when it is lifted from the bowl. With a rubber spatula, stir a heaping tablespoonful of egg white into the lemon-soufflé base to lighten it; then fold the soufflé base into the rest of the whites.

Carefully separate the crepes and lay them, speckled side up, on wax paper. Place about 1 tablespoon of the lemon-soufflé mixture on the top half of each crepe and gently lift the lower half over it. Then lightly fold the crepes into quarters to make small triangles.

Arrange the crepes side by side on a buttered ovenproof platter. Bake them in the middle of the oven for 10 minutes or until they puff up. Sieve confectioners' sugar over the crepes, garnish with the strip of lemon peel, and serve at once.

■ THE COOKING OF PROVINCIAL FRANCE

RUSSIAN EASTER DESSERT

## Russian Easter Dessert

*In Russian "paskha" means "Easter," and paskha is what this classic dessert is called. After being decorated with the Orthodox cross and the letters XB, which are the initials of the words for "Christ is risen," a paskha was taken to the church to be blessed. Only then was it ready to be served as dessert on Easter Day.* ❧

**To serve 12 to 16**

| | |
|---|---|
| 3 pounds large-curd pot cheese | 1 cup unsalted butter, softened |
| ½ cup chopped candied fruits and peels, plus ½ to 1 cup candied fruits and peels for garnish | 1 cup heavy cream |
| | 4 egg yolks |
| | 1 cup sugar |
| 1 teaspoon vanilla extract | ½ cup finely chopped blanched almonds |

Drain the pot cheese of all its moisture by setting it in a colander, covering it with cheesecloth or a kitchen towel, and weighting it down with a heavy pot or a small, heavy board. Let the cheese drain for two or three hours. Meanwhile, stir the candied fruits and the vanilla together in a small bowl, and let the mixture rest for one hour. With the back of a wooden spoon, rub the cheese through a fine sieve set over a large bowl. Beat the softened butter thoroughly into the cheese, and set aside.

Over high heat, scald the cream in a heavy 1½- to 2-quart saucepan by heating it until small bubbles form around the edges. Set aside. In a mixing bowl, beat the egg yolks and sugar together with a wire whisk or a rotary or electric beater for about 10 minutes or until they thicken enough to run sluggishly off the beater when it is lifted from the bowl. Still beating, slowly add the hot cream in a thin stream, then pour the mixture into the pan. Stirring constantly, cook over low heat until the mixture thickens to a custardlike consistency. Do not allow it to boil or it will curdle.

Remove the custard from the heat, stir in the candied fruits, and set the pan in a large bowl partially filled with ice cubes covered with water. Stir the custard constantly with a metal spoon until it is completely cool, then mix it gently but thoroughly into the cheese, and stir in the chopped almonds.

Set a 2-quart *paskha* form—or a 2-quart clay flowerpot with an opening in the bottom—in a deep plate, and line it with a double thickness of dampened cheesecloth cut long enough so that it overhangs the rim of the *paskha* form by at least 2 inches. Pour in the batter and fold the ends of the cheesecloth lightly over the top. Set a 2- to 3-pound weight—perhaps a pan filled with two or three heavy cans of food—directly on top of the cheesecloth and chill the *paskha* in the refrigerator for at least eight hours or overnight, until the dessert is firm.

To unmold, unwrap the cheesecloth from the top, invert a flat serving plate on top of the pot and, grasping the two firmly together, turn them over. The *paskha* will slide out easily. Gently peel off the cheesecloth and decorate the top and sides as fancifully as you like. Once unmolded, the *paskha* can be safely kept refrigerated for a week before serving.

■ **RUSSIAN COOKING**

## Ladyfinger and Whipped Cream Dessert

*In Italy, this cake bears the resounding title "zuccotto mandorlo." Generally, "zuccotto" means "skullcap," which suggests that this dessert first was molded in a bowl to give it a rounded top. Now, like other ladyfinger constructions, zuccotto gets a flat top from being molded in a springform pan, soufflé dish or charlotte mold. "Mandorlo" translates simply as "almond."* ❧

**To serve 4**

| | |
|---|---|
| 30 to 36 ladyfingers, preferably homemade | toasted in a 350°F. oven for 5 minutes |
| 3 tablespoons light rum | 1½ cups heavy cream |
| 2 tablespoons Marsala wine | ¾ cup confectioners' sugar |
| 2½ ounces unsweetened chocolate, chopped coarse | 1 teaspoon vanilla extract |
| ½ cup coarsely chopped blanched almonds, | Chocolate curls, shaved from a semisweet chocolate bar with a vegetable peeler |

Line the sides of a 9-inch springform pan with a double thickness of foil, letting the foil extend 2 to 3 inches above the rim of the pan.

Stand ladyfingers upright with the curved side outward around the sides of the pan. Cover the bottom of the pan with ladyfingers, trimming them to create a daisy design. Fill in any spaces with scraps. Combine the rum and Marsala and sprinkle the mixture over the ladyfingers. Grate the chocolate and almonds in a blender or food processor. Set them aside.

In a deep, chilled bowl, whip the cream with a whisk or a rotary or electric beater until it forms soft peaks on the beater when it is lifted from the bowl. Beating constantly, add the sugar and vanilla; continue beating until the cream forms unwavering peaks. With a rubber spatula, fold in the chocolate and nuts, and transfer the mixture to the ladyfinger-lined dish.

Cover the dish tightly with plastic wrap or foil and refrigerate the dessert overnight. At serving time, set the *zuccotto* on a chilled serving plate and carefully remove the sides of the springform pan; peel off the foil. Tie a ribbon about 4 feet long around the ladyfingers. Garnish the top of the *zuccotto* with chocolate curls and serve immediately.

■ **PASTA MENUS**

## Baked Alaska

**To serve 6 to 8**

| | |
|---|---|
| 1½ quarts vanilla ice cream, preferably homemade, softened slightly<br>One 9-inch round sponge-cake layer, preferably homemade (Index/Glossary) sliced horizontally into 2 equal layers | 1 cup orange marmalade or apricot preserves<br>1 or 2 tablespoons fresh orange juice (optional)<br>8 egg whites<br>¾ cup superfine sugar<br>Crystallized violets for garnish |

Pack the softened ice cream into a 1½-quart bowl 8 to 9 inches in diameter. Cover the ice cream with foil, and freeze it until it is solid—two or three hours.

About 10 minutes before serving time, preheat the broiler to its highest setting. Spread one layer of the cake with the marmalade; if it is too thick to spread, thin it by beating into it 1 or 2 tablespoons of orange juice. Place the second cake layer on top. Set the cake on a flat, ovenproof dish.

In a deep bowl, beat the egg whites with a whisk or a rotary or electric beater until they form soft peaks on the beater when it is lifted from the bowl. Still beating, slowly pour in the sugar, and continue to beat for about five minutes or until the egg whites become a stiff and glossy meringue. Remove the ice cream from the freezer and place it on top of the cake.

Using a narrow-bladed metal spatula, encase the cake and ice cream on all sides with the meringue, swirling the surface of the meringue as decoratively as you like. Slide the dessert under the broiler for two to three minutes or until the meringue is golden brown. Watch the dessert carefully; meringue burns easily. As soon as the baked Alaska is browned, garnish it with crystallized violets if you wish, and serve it before the ice cream melts.

■ AMERICAN COOKING

## Sicilian Cream Cake

*Called "cassata alla Siciliana" in Italian, this dessert is an extravaganza. Be generous with measurements: Anything Sicilian should be done with flourishes, and desserts are no exception.* ❖●

**To serve 6**

| | |
|---|---|
| 1½ pounds ricotta cheese, or cream-style cottage cheese, pressed through a fine sieve<br>½ cup sugar<br>2 teaspoons vanilla extract<br>1 ounce unsweetened chocolate, grated<br>½ cup almonds, chopped<br>6 tablespoons diced mixed | candied fruit<br>One 8-inch sponge-cake layer, preferably homemade (Index/Glossary), sliced horizontally into three ½-inch layers<br>6 tablespoons rum<br>1½ cups heavy cream, whipped |

Combine the ricotta, sugar and vanilla in a large bowl, and beat them with a whisk or a rotary or electric beater for a minute or two, until they are light and fluffy. Mix in the chocolate, almonds and 4 tablespoons of the candied fruit.

Place the bottom layer of the sponge cake on a serving plate and sprinkle it with 2 tablespoons of rum. Spread it with half of the ricotta mixture. Set the second cake layer on top, sprinkle that with 2 tablespoons of rum and spread it with the rest of the ricotta. Add the third cake layer and sprinkle it with the remaining rum.

Wrap the cake in foil or plastic wrap and chill it for at least three hours. About one hour before serving, spread the whipped cream over the top and sides of the cake. Sprinkle the top with the remaining 2 tablespoons of fruit; chill until ready to serve.

■ GREAT DINNERS FROM LIFE

## Trifle

**To serve 8**

| | |
|---|---|
| One 9-inch sponge-cake layer, preferably homemade (Index/Glossary), sliced horizontally into three ½-inch layers<br>¾ cup dry sherry<br>2 pints raspberries, stemmed<br>4 large peaches, blanched, peeled, halved, pitted and sliced<br>2 egg whites | 1 cup heavy cream, chilled<br>1 tablespoon sugar<br>½ cup slivered, blanched almonds, toasted in a 350°F. oven for 5 minutes<br><br>CUSTARD SAUCE<br>2 cups milk<br>6 egg yolks<br>¼ cup sugar<br>1 teaspoon vanilla extract |

The custard sauce must be made in advance and chilled before the trifle is assembled. For the sauce, first scald the milk by heating it in the top of a double boiler until bubbles appear around the edge. Meanwhile, with a wire whisk, beat the egg yolks in a small bowl until they are smooth, and whisk in the ¼ cup of sugar. Continue whisking until the egg yolks are pale and creamy—about 10 minutes. Pour a little hot milk into the egg yolks, whisking, then stir the egg yolks into the pan of milk.

Set the pan over simmering, not boiling, water and cook, stirring frequently, until the mixture coats a metal spoon. Pour the custard into a bowl and stir in the vanilla. Cover and refrigerate for one hour, until the sauce thickens, before adding it to the trifle.

Place one layer of sponge cake in the bottom of flat-bottomed serving bowl about 10 inches across and 5 inches deep. Sprinkle the cake with ¼ cup of the sherry. Spread about a third of the raspberries and peach slices on top. Pour one-third of the custard over the fruit. Repeat with cake, sherry, fruit and custard for two additional layers, saving a dozen or so choice berries for garnish.

To make the topping, beat the egg whites with a wire whisk or a rotary or electric beater until they stand in unwavering peaks on the beater when it is lifted from the bowl. In a separate bowl, whip the cream until it forms soft peaks, stir 1 tablespoon of sugar into the cream, and continue beating until the cream forms stiff peaks. Gently fold the beaten egg whites into the whipped cream. Mound the cream mixture over the top of the trifle. Garnish it with raspberries and almonds. Refrigerate.

■ GREAT DINNERS FROM LIFE

# Sauces & Other Refinements

*The grace note that lends distinction to simple steamed vegetables or boiled pasta is a wonderful sauce that has been homemade rather than store-bought. The recipes for scores of particular sauces appear in preceding chapters; this chapter offers a spectrum of the fundamentals along with some of their most interesting variations. In addition, as a complement to the foods in other parts of this volume, here are recipes for such timeless basics as mayonnaise, chicken stock, béchamel, pasta, white bread and sponge cake—and the newly popular home-produced cottage cheese and tofu.*

## Vinaigrette

*This simplest of sauces is useful for many foods besides salads. It makes an excellent marinade, and marries well as a dressing for hot and cold vegetables, cold poultry and meats, and fish and shellfish. The types and proportions of vinegar and oil can be varied according to the acidity of the vinegar used and the tartness of the food to be sauced. One part vinegar to four parts oil is a good ratio. Despite its name, this dressing may be made with fresh lemon or lime juice instead of vinegar.* ✦●

**To make about ½ cup**

| | |
|---|---|
| **1 teaspoon salt** | **2 tablespoons wine vinegar** |
| **¼ teaspoon freshly ground black pepper** | **½ cup oil** |

Put the salt and pepper into a small nonreactive bowl, and add the vinegar, stirring with a fork or whisk until the salt dissolves. Stir in the oil, and continue mixing until the ingredients are amalgamated. Use at once, or stir again before using.

GREEN VINAIGRETTE: After adding the vinegar, stir in 2 tablespoons of puréed spinach made by parboiling ¼ pound of spinach for two minutes, draining it, squeezing it dry, chopping it, and then puréeing it through a food mill or in a processor. Then stir in 1 tablespoon of *fines herbes* (mixed chopped fresh herbs such as parsley, chives, tarragon and chervil) and 1 tablespoon of finely chopped fresh watercress. Finally, add the oil.

MUSTARD VINAIGRETTE: Mix 1 teaspoon of Dijon mustard with the salt and pepper. Add the vinegar and stir until the mustard is dissolved before adding the oil.

PROVENÇAL VINAIGRETTE: Rinse two salt anchovies in cold water. With your fingernail, split open the belly of each fish. Pull the anchovy apart lengthwise, leaving the bones attached to one half; slide your thumb under the backbone, which runs down the center of one half, and peel away the backbone and ribs. Put the fillets into cold water to soak for 30 minutes. Pat the fillets dry with paper towels, then, using a mortar and pestle or a spoon and small bowl, mash the anchovies with 1 garlic clove, 1 teaspoon of coarse (kosher) salt and some freshly ground black pepper. When the mixture forms a smooth paste, stir in the vinegar, then about ⅓ cup of oil. Stir in 1 tablespoon of chopped capers, 2 tablespoons of parboiled, squeezed and finely chopped spinach and 2 tablespoons of chopped mixed fresh herbs such as parsley, chives, tarragon, basil and chervil.

TOMATO VINAIGRETTE: Peel and halve one large, ripe tomato; squeeze out and discard the seeds and juice. Press the flesh through a sieve. Stir together the salt, pepper and vinegar, then mix in the puréed tomato. Gradually stir in ½ cup of oil.

VINAIGRETTE WITH EGG: Before adding the oil, stir in the yolk of a soft-boiled egg. If desired, chop the cooked part of the egg white and add it to the prepared vinaigrette. *Fines herbes* and chopped shallot may also be added to taste.

■ THE GOOD COOK: SALADS

## Mayonnaise

*Store-bought mayonnaise will do, but homemade mayonnaise will make a treat out of the simplest salad or cold food presentation. To prevent the ingredients from curdling, all of them should be at room temperature and the oil should be added very gradually at first. In a covered container, the mayonnaise can be safely refrigerated for three days; stir it before use.* ❖

**To make about 2 cups**

| | |
|---|---|
| 2 egg yolks, at room temperature | 1 tablespoon wine vinegar or fresh lemon juice |
| Salt | 2 cups oil |
| Freshly ground white pepper | |

Put the egg yolks in a bowl. Season them with salt and a few grindings of pepper, and whisk them until they are smooth. Add the vinegar or lemon juice and mix thoroughly. Whisking constantly, add the oil, drop by drop to begin with. When the sauce starts to thicken, pour the remaining oil in a thin, steady stream, whisking rhythmically. If the mayonnaise becomes too thick, thin it with a little more vinegar or lemon juice, or with some warm water.

NOTE: For an even more flavorful mayonnaise, mix 1 or 2 teaspoons of Dijon mustard with the vinegar or lemon juice.

ANDALOUSE SAUCE (*tomato-flavored mayonnaise*): Make 2 cups of mayonnaise. Stir in 2 to 3 tablespoons of tomato purée (*recipe, page 340*). Garnish the mayonnaise with a red pepper that has been roasted, seeded, peeled and cut into julienne strips. This sauce is served with cold meats or fish.

CHANTILLY SAUCE (*cream-enriched mayonnaise*): Make 2 cups of mayonnaise, using lemon juice. Beat 3 tablespoons of heavy cream until foamy but not stiff. Fold the cream into the mayonnaise just before serving. This sauce is served with poached fish and boiled vegetables.

MOUSQUÉTAIRE SAUCE (*shallot-flavored mayonnaise*): Make 2 cups of mayonnaise. Boil two or three finely chopped shallots in ½ cup of dry white wine until almost no liquid remains. Cool the shallots, then stir them into the mayonnaise. Garnish the mayonnaise with 1 tablespoon of finely cut fresh chives and a little cayenne pepper. This sauce is served with grilled meats.

RÉMOULADE SAUCE (*pickle and herb-flavored mayonnaise*): Prepare 2 cups of mayonnaise, adding 1 tablespoon of prepared mustard. Stir in 1 tablespoon each of chopped sour gherkins and whole capers; add 1 teaspoon each of chopped fresh parsley, chervil and tarragon (or ¼ teaspoon of each, if dried) and two or three finely chopped drained anchovy fillets. This sauce is served with cold lobster, meat or poultry.

TARTAR SAUCE (*pungent mayonnaise*): Make 2 cups of mayonnaise, using five hard-boiled egg yolks and one raw yolk, instead of two raw yolks. Stir in ⅓ cup of finely chopped onion and 1 tablespoon of finely cut fresh chives. This sauce is served with fish. Alternatively, make 2 cups of mayonnaise with two raw egg yolks. Stir in finely chopped sour gherkins, capers, parsley, chives and chervil—varying the proportions to taste. This sauce is also served with fish.

SAUCE VERTE (*green mayonnaise*): Make 2 cups of mayonnaise. Blanch ¼ cup each of fresh parsley, chervil, tarragon, chives and watercress and ½ cup of spinach leaves in boiling water for about two minutes. Drain and refresh them in cold water, then squeeze them dry in a towel. Pound the blanched seasonings to a paste, then pass the paste through a sieve. Stir the paste into the mayonnaise. This sauce is served with fried fish and cold vegetables.

■ THE GOOD COOK: SAUCES

## Sauce Gribiche

*This unusual version of mayonnaise may be used to accompany cold fish and cold variety meats.* ❖

**To make about 2½ cups**

| | |
|---|---|
| 5 eggs plus 1 egg yolk, at room temperature | 1 teaspoon chopped fresh parsley leaves |
| 1 teaspoon Dijon mustard | 1 teaspoon chopped fresh chervil leaves |
| 1 tablespoon fresh lemon juice | |
| 2 cups oil | ½ tablespoon chopped sour gherkins |
| 1 teaspoon chopped fresh tarragon leaves | ½ tablespoon chopped capers |

Place five eggs in a nonreactive saucepan, and add water to cover them by 1 inch. Bring the water to a boil over moderate heat and —timing from the moment that bubbles begin to rise from the bottom of the pan—cook them for 10 minutes. Adjust the heat as needed to keep the water at a barely bubbling simmer. Plunge the eggs into cold water to stop further cooking.

When the eggs are cool enough to handle, shell them and separate the yolks from the whites. Cut the whites into julienne strips and set them aside. In a nonreactive mixing bowl, mash the hard-boiled yolks with the remaining raw egg yolk and the mustard to form a smooth paste. Add the lemon juice and mix thoroughly.

Whisking constantly, add the oil, drop by drop to begin with, then in a steady stream as the sauce begins to thicken. Stir in the fresh herbs, along with the sour gherkins and capers. Garnish the sauce with the egg-white strips.

■ THE GOOD COOK: SAUCES

## Processor or Blender Mayonnaise

*To form an emulsion, the egg and oil should both be at room tempera-
ture. The basic mayonnaise may be turned into a rémoulade or green
mayonnaise, or flavored with mustard, shallots, tomatoes or herbs as
described in the basic mayonnaise recipe on page 335.* ❧

**To make about 1½ cups**

| | |
|---|---|
| **1 egg, at room temperature** | **Freshly ground white pepper** |
| **2 teaspoons vinegar or fresh** | **1 to 1½ cups oil, at room** |
| **lemon juice** | **temperature** |
| **Salt** | |

Combine the egg, vinegar or lemon juice, and a bit of salt and
pepper in the bowl of a food processor or the jar of an electric
blender. Cover and blend for a few seconds to mix the ingredients thoroughly. Without stopping the machine, pour in the oil in
a slow stream through the tube of the processor or the hole in the
lid of the blender. Add 1 cup of oil for a soft mayonnaise, up to 1½
cups for a firm one.

Turn off the machine and use a rubber spatula to transfer the
mayonnaise to a bowl. Taste and add more seasonings, vinegar or
lemon juice, if desired. Tightly covered, the mayonnaise can be
kept refrigerated for three days.

■ THE GOOD COOK: HORS D'OEUVRE

## Hollandaise Sauce

*Among the most luxurious of hot sauces are hollandaise and its varia-
tions—especially Béarnaise sauce. The classic technique for making
hollandaise is to use bits of cold butter as described below. For a silkier
sauce, use ⅔ cup of melted clarified butter instead of the specified butter bits. Pour the melted butter, a small ladleful at a time, into the
pan, whisking constantly. Do not add more butter until the previous
addition has been completely incorporated.* ❧

**To make about 1½ cups**

| | |
|---|---|
| **3 egg yolks** | **1 cup butter, cut into bits and** |
| **1 tablespoon cold water** | **chilled** |
| **Salt** | **1 tablespoon fresh lemon** |
| **Freshly ground white or black** | **juice** |
| **pepper** | |

First make a water bath to protect the pan holding the sauce by
pouring water to a depth of about 1 inch into a large pan. Place a
metal rack or trivet inside the pan. Bring the water to a simmer.

In a small, heavy, nonreactive saucepan, combine the egg
yolks, cold water, a little salt and a few grindings of pepper. Set the
saucepan in the water bath and whisk the egg yolks until the mixture is smooth. Whisk a handful of butter bits into the yolks and,
when the butter is absorbed, add more. Repeat until all of the butter is incorporated. While whisking the butter into the egg-yolk
mixture, remove the pan from the water bath if it gets too hot.
The side of the saucepan should never be too hot to be comfortably touched by the palm of your hand.

Continue whisking the sauce until it becomes thick and

creamy, then add the lemon juice and correct the seasoning. If
the finished sauce is too thick, thin it by whisking in warm water,
1 tablespoon at a time, or a little extra lemon juice. If the sauce is
too thin, add more butter.

The sauce can wait for a few minutes, if necessary, but is best
served as soon as it is finished. Serve the sauce with fish, vegetables or egg dishes; it is indispensable for eggs Benedict.

BÉARNAISE SAUCE (*tarragon-flavored hollandaise*): Combine ⅔
cup of dry white wine, ¼ cup of white-wine vinegar, two finely
chopped shallots and ¼ cup each of chopped fresh tarragon and
chervil leaves in a heavy nonreactive saucepan. Boil over moderate heat, stirring often, for 10 to 15 minutes or until about 2 tablespoons of syrupy liquid remain. Strain the reduction through a
fine sieve into a bowl, discarding the solids, let it cool, and return
it to the saucepan.

Gradually whisk in three egg yolks. Place the pan in a water
bath, and whisk the mixture until it is pale in color and thickens
slightly. Whisk in 1 cup of cold butter bits or 1 cup of oil. The
finished sauce should be thick but pourable, translucent and
shiny. Thin the sauce with water or lemon juice, if necessary.

Take the sauce out of the water bath and stir in 1 teaspoon each
of finely chopped tarragon and chervil leaves. This sauce is
served with grilled meats.

CHORON SAUCE (*tomato-flavored hollandaise*): Prepare 1½
cups of Béarnaise sauce; if you prefer, omit the final addition of
chopped tarragon and chervil. Stir in 2 tablespoons of tomato
purée (*recipe, page 340*). This sauce is served with poached or
grilled fish.

MALTAISE SAUCE (*orange-flavored hollandaise*): Make 1½ cups
of hollandaise sauce. Instead of the final addition of lemon juice,
whisk in ⅓ cup of the juice of blood oranges. If blood oranges are
not available, juice oranges may be used. The sauce will have the
same flavor but the color will be less intense. This sauce is served
with vegetables, especially asparagus.

NOISETTE SAUCE (*brown-butter-flavored hollandaise*): Make
1½ cups of hollandaise sauce. Heat 4 tablespoons of butter until it
foams. As it begins to brown, it will give off the odor of hazelnuts;
remove it from the heat. Let the melted butter stand for a while to
allow the solids to settle before pouring it into a sieve lined with
dampened cheesecloth or muslin and set over a bowl. Discard
any solids that cling to the dampened cloth. Stir the strained clarified butter into the hollandaise sauce. This sauce is usually served
with boiled fish, especially salmon and trout.

■ THE GOOD COOK: SAUCES

## Mock Hollandaise Sauce

*Called "sauce bâtarde" by French chefs, this hot egg-based sauce has much of the richness of hollandaise but is easier to prepare.* ❖●

**To make about 2 cups**

| | |
|---|---|
| 2 egg yolks | 3 tablespoons flour |
| 1 tablespoon cold water or heavy cream | 2 cups warm water, lightly salted |
| ¼ cup butter, plus ¾ cup butter, cut into bits and chilled | 1 tablespoon fresh lemon juice |
| | Salt |
| | Freshly ground white pepper |

In a bowl, beat the egg yolks with the cold water until they are smooth. Set them aside.

Over low heat, melt ¼ cup of butter in a heavy saucepan, add the flour, and stir the mixture with a whisk until it begins to bubble. Whisk in the lightly salted warm water, stirring the mixture rapidly until it boils. Remove the mixture from the heat, let it cool for one or two minutes, then gradually whisk in the beaten egg yolks. Return the pan to low heat, and whisk until the sauce thickens slightly. Do not let it boil.

Remove the pan from the heat, and whisk in the lemon juice. Add the butter bits—a handful at a time—whisking steadily until the butter is incorporated. Flavor with the lemon juice, some salt and a few grindings of pepper. Serve the sauce immediately with fish, poultry or vegetables.

CAPER SAUCE: Make 2 cups of mock hollandaise. Stir in 2 tablespoons of rinsed capers. This sauce is usually served with poached fish.

■ THE GOOD COOK: SAUCES

## Whipped Butter Sauce

*Called "beurre blanc" in French, this sauce is so creamy that it looks white. For an even more delicate product, increase the butter to 1½ cups. Use the sauce with vegetables, fish and shellfish, and poultry.* ❖●

**To make about 1½ cups**

| | |
|---|---|
| ¼ cup dry white wine | Freshly ground white pepper |
| ¼ cup white-wine vinegar | 1 cup butter, cut into bits and chilled |
| 2 shallots, chopped fine | |
| Salt | |

In a heavy nonreactive saucepan, simmer the wine and vinegar with the shallots over low heat until only enough liquid remains to moisten the shallots. Remove the pan from the heat, season the mixture with salt and pepper to taste, and allow it to cool for a few minutes. Place the pan on a heat-diffusing pad over very low heat and whisk in the butter bits, a handful at a time, adding more after the preceding batch disappears. Remove the pan from the heat as soon as all of the butter has been incorporated and the sauce has the consistency of light cream.

■ THE GOOD COOK: SAUCES

## Crème Fraîche

*This recipe produces an American version of France's naturally fermented crème fraîche. Use it as a substitute for whipped cream. To turn it into a salad dressing, whisk in 3 to 4 tablespoons of fresh lime or lemon juice, and season to taste with salt and freshly ground black or white pepper. For best results, make crème fraîche with the pasteurized —but not ultrapasteurized—heavy cream obtainable at health-food stores and specialty dairy markets.* ❖●

**To make about 2 cups**

| | |
|---|---|
| 2 cups heavy cream | 1 tablespoon cultured buttermilk |

In a small, heavy enameled saucepan, stir the cream and buttermilk together until well blended. Set the pan over low heat and insert a meat-and-yeast thermometer into the cream mixture. Stirring gently but constantly, warm the mixture until the thermometer registers 85°F.

Immediately remove the pan from the heat, and pour the cream mixture into a 1-quart jar that has been scalded by filling it with boiling water and then pouring the water out. Cover the jar loosely with foil or wax paper, and set the cream mixture aside at a room temperature of 60°F. to 85°F. for eight to 24 hours or until it reaches the consistency of whipped cream.

Cover the jar tightly. Refrigerated, the crème fraîche will keep for about a week.

■ THE GOOD COOK: SALADS

## Court Bouillon

*An all-purpose poaching liquid, this court bouillon can be used for tender white variety meats such as brains and for all kinds of fish and shellfish. The amount of wine can be increased or decreased according to taste. For brains, omit the fennel and garlic; for crayfish, substitute two sprigs of dill for the fennel.* ❖●

**To make about 8 cups**

| | |
|---|---|
| 1 large onion, sliced | 2 fresh thyme sprigs |
| 1 large carrot, sliced | 1 bay leaf |
| 1 large leek, sliced | 6 cups water |
| 1 celery rib, diced | Salt |
| 2 fennel stalks (optional) | 2 cups dry red or white wine |
| 1 garlic clove (optional) | 5 or 6 black peppercorns |
| 12 fresh parsley sprigs | |

Put the vegetables, herbs and water into a large, nonreactive pan, and season them with a pinch of salt. Bring them to a boil, then reduce the heat, cover, and simmer the mixture for about 15 minutes. Pour in the wine and simmer the court bouillon for 15 minutes longer—adding the peppercorns for the last few minutes of cooking time.

Strain the court bouillon through a sieve into a bowl or a clean pan before using it.

■ THE GOOD COOK: SAUCES

## Meat Stock

*According to your taste and recipe requirements, this stock may be made from beef, veal or pork—or a combination of these meats with chicken. For the beef, use such cuts as shank, short ribs, chuck and oxtail. For the veal, use neck, shank and rib tips; for the pork, use hocks, Boston shoulder and back ribs. For the chicken, use backs, necks, wings and carcasses. Lamb may be used alone or mixed with other meat, but its flavor will tend to dominate any combination; suitable cuts include lamb shank, ribs and neck. Adding gelatinous elements such as calf's feet, pig's feet or pork rind will make the finished stock set to a clear, firm jelly, if prepared carefully enough.* ❧

**To make about 8 cups**

| | |
|---|---|
| 4 to 5 pounds meat, bones and trimmings of beef, veal, pork and/or chicken | 1 celery rib |
| 1 pound pig's, calf's or chicken feet, pig's ears or fresh pork rind (optional) | 1 leek, split and washed, or 1 garlic bulb, unpeeled |
| Water | 1 bouquet garni, made of 4 parsley sprigs, 1 bay leaf and 1 fresh thyme sprig or ¼ teaspoon dried thyme, tied in cheesecloth |
| 4 carrots | |
| 2 large onions, 1 stuck with 3 cloves | Salt |

Place a metal rack or trivet in the bottom of a heavy stockpot to prevent the ingredients from sticking to the bottom. Starting with the largest pieces, fit all of the meat into the pot.

Add enough cold water to cover the meat by 2 inches. Bring the water to a boil very slowly over low heat; it should take at least an hour for the water to reach the boiling point. With a slotted spoon, carefully lift off the surface scum as the liquid comes to a boil. Keep skimming, occasionally adding cold water, until no more scum rises. Avoid stirring, which can cloud the stock.

Add the carrots, onions, celery, leek, bouquet garni and a little salt, and skim once more as the liquid returns to a boil. Turn the heat down as low as possible, cover the pot partially, and let the stock simmer for three and a half hours if you wish to serve the beef afterward, or for five hours if you wish to extract all of the goodness of the beef into the broth.

Strain the finished stock into a large bowl or clean pot through a colander lined with dampened cheesecloth. Degrease the surface thoroughly with paper towels or allow the stock to cool and refrigerate it until the solidified fat can be lifted off the top.

Refrigerate the stock if you do not plan to use it immediately; it will keep safely for three or four days. To preserve the stock longer, lift off the last bits of fat, then warm the stock so that you can pour it into four or five 1-pint containers. Be sure to leave room in the containers for expansion; cover them tightly. The frozen stock will keep for six months while you use it—container by container—as necessary.

■ THE GOOD COOK: SNACKS AND SANDWICHES

## Chicken Stock

**To make about 8 cups**

| | |
|---|---|
| One 5-pound stewing chicken, trussed | Bouquet garni, made of 4 parsley sprigs, 1 bay leaf and 1 fresh thyme sprig or ¼ teaspoon dried thyme, tied in cheesecloth |
| Water | |
| 1 large onion stuck with 3 cloves | |
| 2 carrots | Salt |
| 1 large garlic bulb, unpeeled | |

Place the chicken, breast up, in the bottom of a heavy pot—preferably oval-shaped—that is just large enough to hold the ingredients. Pour in water to cover the bird by about 2 inches, and slowly bring it to a boil. While the liquid heats, use a spoon to skim the surface until no more scum forms on top. As the fat from the bird melts and rises to the top, skim that off, too.

When the boiling point is reached, place the vegetables and the bouquet garni around the chicken. Add a little salt and partially cover the pot. Reduce the heat and cook undisturbed at a slow simmer for one and a half to three hours, depending on the age of the bird—the older it is the longer it takes to cook.

As soon as the thigh meat feels tender when pierced with the tines of a fork, remove the bird and the vegetables from the pot. Strain the stock through a colander lined with several layers of dampened cheesecloth and placed over a large bowl or clean pot. The stock can be kept refrigerated for three or four days, frozen for about six months.

■ THE GOOD COOK: SOUPS

## Fish Stock

**To make about 8 cups**

| | |
|---|---|
| 2 pounds fish heads, bones and trimmings, rinsed and chopped into pieces | 1 leek, sliced |
| | 1 celery rib, cut into pieces |
| | 1 bay leaf |
| Water | 2 fresh or dried thyme sprigs |
| 1 onion, sliced | 2 fresh parsley sprigs |
| 1 carrot, sliced | Salt |

Place the fish in a large nonreactive pot. Add enough water to cover the pieces by about 2 inches, and bring to a boil over low heat. As the liquid heats, use a large slotted spoon to skim off the scum that rises to the surface. Keep skimming, occasionally adding a glass of cold water, until no more scum rises. Avoid stirring, which could cloud the stock.

Add the vegetables, herbs, and a little salt, partially cover the pot, and simmer the stock for 30 minutes. Without pressing down on the solids, strain the stock through a colander lined with dampened cheesecloth or muslin and set over a bowl or clean pot. Keep the stock refrigerated for up to three days, frozen for about six months.

■ THE GOOD COOK: SOUPS

## Vegetable Stock

**To make about 6 cups**

| | |
|---|---|
| 2 leeks, sliced thin | sliced thin |
| 2 celery ribs with leaves, chopped | 4 parsley sprigs, chopped |
| 2 onions, sliced thin | 1 teaspoon crumbled dried thyme |
| 4 carrots, chopped | 1 bay leaf |
| 2 cabbage leaves, sliced thin | Salt |
| 1 head lettuce, cored and | 6 cups cold water |

Place all of the ingredients in a large saucepan and bring very slowly to a boil. Skim, then partially cover and allow the stock to simmer, undisturbed, for about 45 minutes. Strain the stock through a sieve into a bowl without pressing down on the vegetables. The stock can be safely refrigerated for three days, frozen for about six months.

■ THE GOOD COOK: SOUPS

## Béchamel

*Béchamel, or white sauce, seems to have been invented by a court chef to Louis XIV of France while the Marquis Louis de Béchamel was Lord Steward of the Royal Household. It must have been wiser for the chef to dedicate the sauce to Béchamel rather than name it for himself. Today most versions are cooked for only a few minutes, but lengthy simmering gives béchamel a finesse not possible with shortcuts. Any version can be served with vegetables, poached fish or poultry.* ❖

**To make about 1½ cups**

| | |
|---|---|
| 2 tablespoons butter | Freshly ground white pepper |
| 2 tablespoons flour | Freshly grated nutmeg |
| 2 cups milk | (optional) |
| Salt | |

In a heavy 2- to 3-quart saucepan, melt the butter over low heat. With a whisk, stir in the flour and cook—still stirring—for two or three minutes. Whisking constantly, pour in the milk. Increase the heat and whisk until the sauce comes to a boil. Reduce the heat and simmer for at least 45 minutes, stirring occasionally to prevent the sauce from sticking. When the sauce thickens to the desired consistency, add salt, a few grindings of pepper and a pinch of nutmeg, if you are using it.

MORNAY SAUCE *(cheese sauce):* Make 1½ cups of béchamel and whisk in ⅓ cup of heavy cream. Add about 3 tablespoons each of grated Gruyère and Parmesan cheeses, stirring until the cheeses melt. Remove the pan from the heat, and finish the sauce with 1 tablespoon of butter, which has been cut into tiny bits. This sauce is served with fish or cooked vegetables. If the sauce is to be used as part of a gratin, stir in an additional ⅓ cup of heavy cream in place of the butter.

SOUBISE SAUCE *(onion sauce):* Bake three unpeeled large onions in a pie pan in a 375°F. oven for one hour or until they feel soft when lightly squeezed. When the onions are cool, peel them

and, with a pestle, force them through a sieve into a bowl or purée them in a food processor. Make 1½ cups of béchamel, stir in 1½ cups of onion purée, and heat the mixture. Stir in ½ cup of heavy cream. This sauce is served with lamb.

■ THE GOOD COOK: SAUCES

## Velouté

*A velouté—meaning "velvety" in French—is a sauce of roux-thickened stock, served with meat, poultry or fish. For a very fine and concentrated velouté, a chef would simmer the sauce for several hours with occasional skimming. Two cups of such sauce would require three times the quantities of the ingredients listed here.* ❖

**To make about 2 cups**

| | |
|---|---|
| ¼ cup butter, cut into bits | fish stock |
| ¼ cup flour | Heavy cream |
| 4 cups meat, poultry or | |

In a heavy 2- to 3-quart saucepan, melt the butter over low heat. With a whisk, stir in the flour to make a roux. Still stirring, cook for a minute or two, then stir the stock slowly into the roux.

Increase the heat and whisk until the sauce comes to a boil. Reduce the heat to low and move the pan half off the heat so that the liquid simmers on only one side. A skin of impurities will form on the surface of the still side. Remove this skin periodically with a spoon.

Cook the sauce for at least 45 minutes to reduce it to about half its original volume. Stir in enough cream to give the sauce the consistency desired.

AURORE SAUCE *(tomato-flavored velouté):* Make 2 cups of velouté using veal, chicken or fish stock. Add ⅓ cup of tomato purée *(recipe, page 340).* Remove the pan from the heat and whisk in ¼ cup of butter bits, a few at a time. This sauce is served with vegetables, chicken or fish.

POULETTE SAUCE *(egg-yolk-enriched velouté):* Make 2 cups of velouté using veal or chicken stock. Mix 2 to 3 tablespoons of the velouté with four egg yolks, 3 tablespoons of heavy cream and 1½ tablespoons of lemon juice. Remove the pan from the heat and slowly stir this mixture into the velouté. Return the pan to low heat and stir until the sauce is lightly thickened, but do not allow it to boil. To finish the sauce, remove the pan from the heat and stir in ¼ cup of butter bits. This sauce is meant to be served with poached white meats.

RAVIGOTE SAUCE *(tangy wine-flavored veal velouté):* Make 2 cups of velouté using veal stock. Blanch 1 tablespoon of coarsely chopped shallot for half a minute, drain and pound to a paste. When the shallot is cool, pound in 1 tablespoon of butter. Set this shallot butter aside. Boil ½ cup of dry white wine with 2 tablespoons of white-wine vinegar until the mixture is reduced by half. Add the reduced liquid to the velouté. Off the heat, stir in the shallot butter and a little chopped fresh chervil, tarragon and chives. This sauce is served with white meats.

■ THE GOOD COOK: SAUCES

## Tomato Purée

*Every grocer sells tomato purée, but you can make your own when tomatoes are in season and then stock it in the freezer.* ✦●

**To make about 1 cup**

| | |
|---|---|
| 4 medium-sized tomatoes, peeled, | seeded and chopped |

Place the tomatoes in a heavy nonreactive saucepan. Stirring frequently, cook the tomatoes over low heat for about 10 minutes or until most of their juices have evaporated and their flesh has been reduced to a thick pulp. Purée the tomatoes through a food mill or sieve into a bowl.

Tightly covered and refrigerated, the purée will keep safely for up to five days.

■ THE GOOD COOK: DRIED BEANS AND GRAINS

## Basic Tomato Sauce

*The flavor of tomato dominates this sauce; herbs and seasonings are complements. The sauce marries well with pasta of all sorts and is useful whenever cooked tomatoes are required as an ingredient of another dish. If fresh ripe tomatoes are not available, use 3 cups of drained canned Italian-style tomatoes and, if you like, add 1 or 2 teaspoons of sugar to the sauce with the salt and pepper.* ✦●

**To make about 1½ cups**

| | |
|---|---|
| 6 tomatoes, quartered | (optional) |
| 1 bay leaf | 1 tablespoon finely chopped fresh parsley leaves |
| 1 large fresh or dried thyme sprig or 1 teaspoon crumbled dried thyme | 1 tablespoon chopped fresh basil leaves or 1 teaspoon crumbled dried basil |
| 1 onion, sliced | Salt |
| 1 garlic clove, crushed (optional) | Freshly ground black pepper |
| 1 or 2 tablespoons butter | |

Place the tomatoes in a 3- to 4-quart nonreactive saucepan with the bay leaf and thyme. Add the onion and the garlic, if you are using it. Bring the tomato mixture to a boil over moderate heat, crushing the tomatoes lightly with a wooden spoon. Stirring often, cook, uncovered, for 10 minutes or until the tomatoes have become a thick pulp. Remove and discard the bay leaf and, if you used one, the thyme sprig.

Tip the tomatoes into a plastic or stainless-steel sieve placed over a bowl and, using a wooden pestle, push them through the sieve. Discard the skins and seeds, and return the sieved tomato pulp to the pan.

Stirring occasionally, cook uncovered over low heat for 10 to 15 minutes or until the sauce is reduced to the required consistency. If you like, whisk in a little butter to enrich the sauce. Taste for seasoning and whisk in the parsley and basil, and add salt and pepper to taste.

■ THE GOOD COOK: PASTA

## Tomato and Meat Sauce

*With Italian American cooks, some variation of this recipe is the basic tomato sauce for pasta.* ✦●

**To make about 5 cups**

| | |
|---|---|
| ¼ cup olive oil | tomatoes and their liquid |
| ½ pound boneless pork in one piece | One 6-ounce can tomato paste |
| | 2 cups water |
| ½ pound beef chuck in one piece | 1 teaspoon crumbled dried oregano |
| 1 cup finely chopped onions | 1 tablespoon crumbled dried basil |
| 1½ teaspoons finely chopped garlic | 1 teaspoon salt |
| Three 1-pound cans solid-pack | Freshly ground black pepper |

In a heavy 10- to 12-inch skillet, heat the oil. Add the pork and beef, and brown them over moderate heat, turning them with tongs and regulating the heat so that the meats color richly without burning. Add the onions and garlic and, stirring frequently, cook until the onions are soft but not brown. Stir in the tomatoes and their liquid, the tomato paste, water, oregano, basil, salt and a generous grinding of pepper, and bring to a boil over high heat. Partially cover the pan, reduce the heat, and simmer for two to two and a half hours or until the meat offers no resistance when pierced with the tip of a sharp knife. Remove the meat from the sauce and set it aside; the meat may be served as a main course with pasta. Before serving the sauce, taste it for seasoning.

■ AMERICAN COOKING: THE MELTING POT

## Bolognese Sauce

**To make about 3½ cups**

| | |
|---|---|
| ¼ pound smoked ham, chopped coarse (about 1 cup) | ¼ pound lean pork, ground twice |
| 1 cup coarsely chopped onions | ½ cup dry white wine |
| | 2 cups beef stock |
| ¼ cup coarsely chopped carrot | 2 tablespoons tomato paste |
| ½ cup coarsely chopped celery | ½ pound chicken livers, trimmed |
| ¼ cup butter | 1 cup heavy cream |
| 2 tablespoons olive oil | Freshly grated nutmeg |
| ¾ pound beef round, ground twice | Salt |
| | Freshly ground black pepper |

Combine the chopped ham, onions, carrot and celery on a cutting board, and chop them together into very small pieces. (This mixture is called a *battuto,* which when cooked becomes a *soffritto.*) Melt 2 tablespoons of the butter over moderate heat in a heavy 10- to 12-inch skillet. Add the *battuto* and, stirring frequently, cook for about 10 minutes or until it is lightly browned. With a rubber spatula, transfer the *soffritto* to a heavy 3- to 4-quart saucepan.

Heat the 2 tablespoons of olive oil in the same skillet, and in it lightly brown the ground beef and ground pork over moderate heat, stirring the meat constantly to break up any lumps. Then pour in the wine, increase the heat, and boil briskly, still stirring constantly, until almost all of the liquid in the skillet has cooked away. Add the meat to the *soffritto* in the saucepan, and stir in the stock and tomato paste. Bring to a boil over high heat, then reduce the heat and simmer, partially covered, for 45 minutes, stirring occasionally.

Meanwhile, over high heat, melt 2 more tablespoons of butter in the original skillet, and in it cook the chicken livers for three or four minutes or until they are firm and lightly browned. Chop the chicken livers into small dice and add them to the sauce 10 minutes before it is done.

A few minutes before serving, stir in the cream and let it heat through. Taste the Bolognese sauce and season it with nutmeg, salt and pepper.

■ THE COOKING OF ITALY

## Homemade Pasta

*Bread flour or unbleached all-purpose flour is best for homemade pasta dough, although any type of wheat flour can be used. The exact proportion of flour to eggs depends on the type of flour and the size of the eggs, but you can estimate about ¾ cup flour to one egg.* ❖●

| To make about 1½ pounds fresh pasta or about ¾ pound dried pasta | |
| --- | --- |
| 3 to 4 cups flour<br>4 eggs<br>Salt | 2 tablespoons olive oil or other vegetable oil |

Mound 3 cups of flour on a work surface. Make a well in the center of the flour and break the eggs into it. Add a pinch of salt and the oil. With one hand, gradually incorporate the flour from around the edge of the well into the eggs, stirring with your fingers to form a batter. Use the other hand to support the outer wall of the flour well and prevent the eggs from flowing out. Continue incorporating the flour until the dough becomes fairly stiff but malleable. If it is soft or feels moist, work in more flour gradually.

*To roll out and cut the dough by hand:* First gather it into a ball. On a lightly floured surface, knead the dough by pressing it flat with the heel of your hand, folding it double and pressing it again.

Continue kneading for five to 10 minutes or until the dough is silky and elastic.

Cover the kneaded dough with plastic wrap or a cloth, and let it rest for an hour. Divide it into fist-sized portions, then roll one portion of dough at a time into a thin circle, and cut it into strips or squares with a pastry wheel.

*To knead the dough with a pasta machine:* Gather it into a ball and briefly knead it by hand. Divide it into fist-sized portions, flatten one with your hand, and set the others aside under plastic wrap or a cloth. Open smooth machine rollers fully, flour the flattened dough, and pass it between the rollers. Fold the rolled sheets into thirds, flour the package, and turn it 90 degrees before passing it between the rollers again.

Repeat the folding, flouring and rolling four or five times, until the dough is smooth. Then decrease the gap between the rollers by several notches and pass the dough through again. Decreasing the gap repeatedly, roll the dough until it is thin enough to cut into shape. Hang up the sheet of dough to dry while you knead and roll the remaining portions. Finally, cut the dough into noodles with the cutting rollers on the machine, or cut it into other shapes with a knife or pastry wheel.

After cutting, the pasta can be used immediately or left to dry at room temperature until brittle, not crumbly—about four hours. You can store the dried pasta—in a tightly covered container or well-sealed plastic bag—in a cool place such as the refrigerator for about a week, or in the freezer for at least a month.

### COLORED PASTA DOUGH

*It is simpler to amalgamate the ingredients for colored pasta dough if you mix them in a bowl, not on a flat surface. To compensate for extra moistness when coloring pasta with vegetables (especially spinach), you will need to incorporate extra flour into the dough when kneading and rolling it.* ❖●

GREEN PASTA: Parboil ½ pound of spinach for two minutes or ½ pound of chard for five minutes. Drain, rinse in cold water and squeeze the leaves as dry as possible. Chop the leaves fine or purée them with a food mill or processor. Use a fork to add them to the other pasta ingredients. Knead the dough.

SPECKLED GREEN PASTA: Trim, wash, pat dry and chop fine about 6 tablespoons of mixed fresh herbs. Parsley, sorrel, thyme, sage, tarragon, lovage, marjoram, basil, dandelion, rocket, hyssop and tender savory shoots are all suitable. However, the strong herbs—thyme, sage, savory, marjoram and tarragon—may not marry well with others, so choose your herb mixture carefully. Stir the herbs into the pasta ingredients. Knead and roll out the dough.

RED PASTA: Boil two small unpeeled beets in salted water for 40 minutes to one hour, until tender. Peel and chop the beets, then purée them with a food mill or processor. Stir the beet purée into the pasta dough ingredients before kneading them.

ORANGE PASTA: Stir about ¼ cup of puréed tomato into the pasta ingredients. Knead the dough.

YELLOW PASTA: Mix a pinch of ground saffron with the flour and salt. Stir in the eggs and oil. Knead the dough.

■ THE GOOD COOK: PASTA

## American White Bread

*Versatile is the word for this basic dough. It produces bread with a tender crumb and soft crust. Shape it into a rectangular loaf, as here, or gently pat and rotate it into a round loaf—slash the top with a razor to give it a checkerboard pattern, if you like. Or stretch and roll the dough into a French-style loaf, and top it with a decorative sprinkling of poppy seeds. Break off small pieces to form round or elongated rolls. Or join sets of three walnut-sized pieces in muffin cups for cloverleaf rolls.* ❖●

**To make two 9-by-5-inch loaves**

| | |
|---|---|
| One ¼-ounce package active dry yeast or one ⅗-ounce cake fresh yeast | bread flour |
| | 1 teaspoon salt |
| | 3 tablespoons butter, softened |
| 1½ cups tepid milk (100°F.) | 1 egg lightly beaten with |
| 4 to 6 cups all-purpose or | 1 tablespoon milk |

Sprinkle the yeast into ½ cup of the tepid milk. After two minutes, mix well. Set the yeast in a warm, draft-free place for about 10 minutes, until it bubbles up and doubles in volume.

Sift 4 cups of the flour and the salt into a large mixing bowl and make a well in the center. Into it pour the remaining cup of milk and the yeast. Add the butter to the well. Stirring with a wooden spoon, gradually incorporate the dry ingredients into the liquid ones. Beat until the mixture forms a shaggy mass that can be gathered into a ball. Carefully incorporate additional flour by the spoonful until the dough feels fairly firm and is no longer sticky.

Place the dough on a lightly floured surface, and knead it by pushing it down with the heel of your hand, pressing it forward, and folding it back on itself. Knead for 10 minutes or until the dough is smooth, shiny and elastic.

Set the ball of dough in a large bowl, and cover it with plastic wrap. Let the dough rise in the warm, draft-free place for about one and a half hours or until it doubles in bulk and springs back slowly when gently poked with a finger. Punch the dough down with one blow of your fist to expel large gas bubbles and reduce it to its original volume. Let it rise for 45 minutes or until it again doubles in bulk.

With a pastry brush, spread melted or softened butter inside two 9-by-5-inch loaf pans. Punch the dough down, place it on the work surface, and knead it for a minute or two. Then let it rest for about 10 minutes. Cut it into two pieces with a sharp knife, and cover one half with plastic wrap while you shape the other half into a rectangular loaf about 8 inches long and somewhat high and round in the center. Place the loaf in a prepared pan, then shape the other half of the dough. Cover the pans with plastic wrap or a dampened towel, and let the dough rise in the warm place for 30 minutes, until it reaches the top of the pans.

Preheat the oven to 425°F. Using a pastry brush, glaze the top of the loaves with the beaten egg and milk. Bake for 30 to 40 minutes or until the loaves are golden brown. Turn a loaf out onto the work surface and rap the bottom sharply with your knuckles. The loaf will sound hollow when the bread is fully baked. Place the bread on a wire rack to cool before slicing it.

■ **THE GOOD COOK: BREADS**

## Cottage or Pot Cheese

**To make about 1 pound**

| | |
|---|---|
| 9 cups milk | Salt |
| 1 tablespoon buttermilk | |

In a saucepan set in a larger pan of hot water, slowly heat the milk to a temperature of 80°F. on a dairy or instant-read thermometer. Add the buttermilk. Stir thoroughly, cover the milk, remove it from the water bath, and let it stand for up to 24 hours at a room temperature of 65°F. to 70°F. If the curd does not set, put the milk pan in a larger pan of tepid water, and let it stand, covered, for two hours longer.

When the curd forms a mass that is clearly separate from the surrounding clear whey, line a large colander with dry cheesecloth. Pour in the curd and drain it for five hours. Then pull up the corners of the cloth, tie them tightly, and hang up the resulting bag to allow the curd to drain thoroughly.

After six to eight hours, or longer depending on the degree of firmness you want, salt the curd to taste and flavor it, if you wish. Beating it will make the curd creamier and the cheese smoother.

■ **THE GOOD COOK: EGGS AND CHEESE**

## Tofu

*Freshness gives tofu, or soybean curd, its silky texture and subtle flavor. The surest guarantee of freshness is to produce it at home. It requires no special skill, although you may want to use a pressing sack and settling box, both sold at health-food stores, to shape the cake. For slightly sweet tofu, use nigari (magnesium chloride) from a health-food store to solidify the soybean milk. For a mild-flavored cake, substitute 2 teaspoons Epsom salts (magnesium sulfate) dissolved in 1 cup cold water for the nigari in this recipe. For tart-flavored tofu, substitute ¼ cup of lemon or lime juice or 3 tablespoons of vinegar.* ❖●

**To make one 12- to 16-ounce cake**

| | |
|---|---|
| 1½ cups soybeans, soaked overnight, drained and rinsed | 12 cups water |
| | 1½ teaspoons *nigari* dissolved in 1 cup water |

In a food processor or blender, purée about half of the beans with 2 cups of the water. Pour the purée into a heavy pot containing 8 cups of water. Blend the remaining beans with an additional 2 cups of water, and add the purée to the pot.

Bring the mixture to a boil over moderately high heat, and cook for 10 minutes, stirring occasionally with a wooden spoon. Meanwhile, set a large colander in another pot and line the colander with a double thickness of dampened cheesecloth or a dampened pressing sack with the mouth of the sack fitted around the rim of the colander.

Ladle the soybean purée into the cheesecloth or pressing sack. Let the purée cool slightly, then press it with the spoon or ladle to force the soy milk through the cloth. When the cloth is cool enough to handle, twist the ends together to enclose the purée.

Press and squeeze the cloth to extract all of the soy milk, then discard the pulp.

Bring the soy milk to a boil, stirring constantly. Remove the pot from the heat and stir in one-third of the *nigari*. Cover the pot and let the mixture sit for three minutes while the first curds form. Remove the lid and sprinkle in half of the remaining *nigari* while stirring the top of the liquid gently back and forth with the wooden spoon. Replace the lid and wait another three minutes. Repeat the process with the remaining *nigari* to form fine, white bean curds, which will be floating in an almost clear liquid.

Ladle the bean curds into a settling box lined with a pressing sack or into a cheesecloth-lined mold with drain holes on all sides. Cover the box or mold, weight it down with a 4-pound weight, and set it aside.

A soft tofu cake will develop in about 35 to 40 minutes; a firm tofu takes from one and a half to two hours. Test for doneness by removing the weight and gently prodding the curd to make sure it has reached the desired consistency. Transfer the cake to a container of water; the water should cover the cake completely. Tofu can be kept in the refrigerator for up to one week. Change the water daily.

■ THE GOOD COOK: DRIED BEANS AND GRAINS

## Homemade Ice Cream

| To make about 1 gallon | |
|---|---|
| 2½ quarts heavy cream | 1 vanilla bean |
| 2 cups sugar | |

In a heavy 4- to 5-quart saucepan, mix 1 quart of the cream with the sugar and vanilla bean. Stir over moderate heat until the sugar dissolves and the mixture is scalded, but do not allow it to boil. Remove the pan from the heat and let the cream cool to room temperature. Remove the vanilla bean. (Wash and dry the vanilla bean, and reserve it for another use.)

Stir the remaining 1½ quarts of cream into the mixture. Cover the pan and refrigerate the mixture for one hour or until the mixture is well chilled.

Pack a 1-gallon ice-cream freezer with layers of finely crushed or cracked ice and coarse rock salt, as recommended by the freezer manufacturer. Add cold water if called for. Then ladle the chilled cream mixture into the ice-cream can and cover it.

If you have a hand ice-cream maker, fill it with the cream mixture; let it stand for three or four minutes before turning the handle. Then, slowly at first, crank continuously for about 15 minutes. Do not stop turning at any time or the ice cream might become lumpy. When you can barely move the handle, the ice cream is ready to eat.

Should you want to keep it for an hour or two, remove the lid and dasher. Scrape the ice cream off the dasher and pack it firmly into the container with a spoon. Cover securely, pour off any water in the bucket, and repack the ice and salt solidly around it.

If you have an electric ice-cream maker, fill the can with the chilled cream mixture, cover it and turn on the motor. Let the mixture churn for about 15 minutes, until the motor slows or stops, indicating the ice cream is ready.

PHILADELPHIA VANILLA ICE CREAM: As soon as the cream mixture is removed from the heat, take out the vanilla bean and split it lengthwise. Scrape the seeds into the pan and discard the pod.

CHOCOLATE ICE CREAM: Melt 4 ounces of semisweet chocolate in 1 cup of the cream, and stir it into the sweetened mixture after removing the vanilla bean.

CHOCOLATE-CHIP ICE CREAM: Grate 14 ounces of semisweet baking chocolate, and stir it into the frozen ice cream while the ice cream is still soft.

BERRY ICE CREAM: While the frozen ice cream is still soft, stir into it 3 cups of crushed or sliced strawberries or 3 cups of crushed raspberries.

■ THE GOOD COOK: CLASSIC DESSERTS

## Custard Ice Cream

*All of the flavorings for homemade ice cream (recipe, above) can be added in the same way to this custard-based mixture. For an especially smooth ice cream, whip the heavy cream before adding it to the custard; in this case, chill the custard alone and add the whipped cream just before freezing the mixture.* ❖

| To make about 1 gallon | |
|---|---|
| 4 cups milk | 2 cups sugar |
| 1 vanilla bean | 4 cups heavy cream |
| 12 egg yolks | |

In a heavy 3- to 4-quart saucepan, warm the milk over moderate heat until bubbles appear around the rim of the pan. Remove the pan from the heat, add the vanilla bean, cover the pan, and let the milk infuse for 20 minutes. Remove the bean. (The bean can be rinsed, dried and saved for another use.)

Meanwhile, with a whisk or a rotary or electric beater, beat the egg yolks and sugar together in a bowl for five minutes or until the mixture is thick and pale and forms a slowly dissolving ribbon when the whisk is lifted from the bowl.

Gradually add the warm milk stirring constantly. Pour the mixture into the saucepan, and set over very low heat—or place the pan on a trivet in a larger pan partly filled with hot water. Stir and cook the custard mixture, without allowing it to come to a boil, until it coats the spoon.

Strain the custard into a bowl and stir occasionally as it cools. Blend in the cream, cover, and refrigerate for about one hour. Then freeze the mixture, preferably in an ice-cream maker.

MERINGUES: The whites from the eggs needed for this recipe can be turned into meringues. Whisk 12 egg whites until very stiff, sift and whisk in 4 to 6 cups of confectioners' sugar, fold in 1 or 2 tablespoons of cocoa, if you like, then drop the mixture by spoonfuls onto baking sheets, and bake in a 200° F. oven for two hours or until the meringues are dried but not colored.

■ THE GOOD COOK: CLASSIC DESSERTS

## Short-Crust Dough

*This basic short-crust recipe yields enough dough for an 8-inch or 9-inch two-crust pie or lattice pie, or a dozen 3-inch tart shells. For a deep-dish pie topping or open-faced tart, use half of the quantities of ingredients specified.* ❧

**To make 1 pound**

| | |
|---|---|
| 2 cups flour | butter, cut into bits |
| ½ teaspoon salt | 3 to 4 tablespoons ice water |
| 10 tablespoons unsalted | |

Into a large mixing bowl, sift together the flour and salt, and add all of the butter. With the tips of your fingers, rub together the butter and flour, or cut the butter into the flour with two knives or a pastry blender. The mixture will be coarse and mealy.

Stirring lightly with a knife or using the pastry blender, sprinkle the water over the mixture a spoonful at a time, until the dough begins to cohere. Gather the dough into a ball, pressing it together with your hands. Cover the dough with plastic wrap, and refrigerate it for one or two hours before using it.

The dough can safely be kept in the refrigerator for two days, in the freezer for one month. If frozen, let the dough defrost in the refrigerator for one day before using it.

*To roll out dough:* Unwrap the dough and put it on a cool, floured surface (a marble slab is ideal). Divide the ball, if necessary; rewrap the excess portion and return it to the refrigerator. Partially press out the dough with your hand, then give it a few gentle smacks with the rolling pin to flatten it and render it more supple. Roll out the dough from the center, turning it 90 degrees clockwise after each roll, until it forms a round, an oblong or a rectangle—depending on the shape called for in the recipe—about ⅛ inch thick.

*To line a pan:* Roll the dough onto the rolling pin, lift it up, and unroll it over a pie pan or tart pan. Press the dough firmly against the bottom and sides of the pan.

For a pie pan, use a small knife to trim off the excess dough around the rim, leaving a margin ½ inch wide. Fold this margin toward the center of the pan to create a double thickness, then crimp the edge. For a tart pan, roll the pin across the top to cut off the excess dough around the rim.

*To prebake, or "blind bake," a pastry shell:* Preheat the oven to 400° F. Cut a piece of parchment paper, wax paper or foil slightly larger than the pie pan or tart pan. Press the paper into the dough-lined pan, and fill the center with dried peas, beans or rice. Bake the shell for about 10 minutes or until the dough is set. Remove the filled paper or foil and, with a fork, lightly prick the bottom of the dough lining.

For a partially baked pastry shell, return the pan to the oven for five minutes. For a fully baked shell, return the pan to the oven for 10 to 15 minutes or until the pastry is crisp and golden brown. Cool the pastry shell in the pan for about five minutes. Then remove the shell and cool it on a wire rack before using it.

■ THE GOOD COOK: PIES AND PASTRIES

## Crumb Crust

*Among the suitable bases for this crust are graham crackers, ginger-snaps, vanilla or chocolate wafers, zwieback and stale or fresh cake or bread—including pumpernickel bread. To produce crumbs, break or tear the crackers, cookies, cake or bread into small pieces, and pulverize them, a small batch at a time, in a blender or food processor. The amount and kind of sugar and spices can be adjusted to taste.* ❧

**To make a 9-inch pie or tart shell**

| | |
|---|---|
| ½ cup unsalted butter, melted | Ground cinnamon or freshly grated nutmeg (optional) |
| 3 tablespoons granulated or brown sugar | 2 cups fine crumbs |
| Salt | |

In a mixing bowl, combine the butter and sugar with a pinch of salt and a little cinnamon or nutmeg, if you are using one of them. Stir in the crumbs. When the mixture is well blended, spoon it into a heavily buttered pie pan. With a rubber spatula, spread the crust evenly over the bottom and sides of the pan. Refrigerate the pie shell for at least 15 minutes to firm it.

Preheat the oven to 325° F. Bake the crust for about 10 minutes or until it is crisp and dry to the touch. Cool the crust in the pan before adding the filling.

NOTE: To make a chocolate-flavored crust, melt 1 to 3 ounces of semisweet baking chocolate with the butter.

■ THE GOOD COOK: PIES AND PASTRIES

## Dessert Crepes

**To make eight or nine 8-inch crepes**

| | |
|---|---|
| ½ cup milk | ½ teaspoon finely grated fresh orange peel (optional) |
| ¼ teaspoon vanilla extract | 2 to 4 tablespoons butter, melted |
| 2 eggs | |
| ½ cup flour | |
| 1 tablespoon sugar | |

To make the crepe batter in a food processor or blender, combine the milk, vanilla, eggs, flour and sugar in the bowl or jar. Blend for about a minute, stopping the machine once to scrape down the sides with a rubber spatula. Pour the batter into a bowl and stir in the orange peel.

To make the batter by hand, stir the flour, sugar and eggs together in a bowl, and gradually mix in the milk and vanilla. Beat with a whisk or a rotary or electric beater until the flour lumps disappear, then rub the batter through a fine sieve into another bowl. Stir in the orange peel.

Cover the bowl tightly with foil or plastic wrap, and let the batter rest at room temperature for at least one hour before using it.

To fry the crepes, warm an 8-inch crepe pan—or an 8-inch skillet with sloping sides—over high heat until a drop of water flicked into it splutters and evaporates instantly. Using a brush with natural-hair bristles (not meltable plastic bristles), spread a light coating of melted or softened butter on the bottom and sides of the heated pan.

Stir the crepe batter lightly with a wire whisk or a spoon. Then, using a small ladle, pour about ¼ cup of the batter into the pan. Tip the pan from side to side so that the batter quickly covers the bottom; the batter will cling to the pan and begin to firm almost immediately. At once, tilt the pan over the bowl and pour off any excess batter; the finished crepe should be paper thin.

Cook the crepe for 10 seconds or so, until a rim of brown shows around the edge and it slides easily back and forth when you gently shake the pan. With your fingers or a table knife or spatula, turn the crepe over. Fry the other side for 10 seconds longer or until golden.

Slide the crepe onto a plate. Brush melted butter on the pan again and make the remaining crepes similiarly. As you finish the crepes, stack them one upon the other. The crepes may be made ahead of time and kept, covered with plastic wrap, at room temperature for up to six hours.

■ AMERICAN COOKING: CREOLE AND ACADIAN

## Sponge Cake

*The batter for this cake is adequate for one 16-by-11-inch rectangular pan 1 inch deep, one 13-by-9-inch rectangular pan 2 inches deep, or one 9-inch round pan 3 inches deep. The pan you choose determines both baking temperature and time.* ✣

| | |
|---|---|
| **5 large eggs** | **½ teaspoon vanilla extract** |
| **½ cup plus 3 tablespoons sugar** | **1 cup sifted cake flour** |

Preheat the oven to 375°F. if you plan to make a 16-by-11-by-1-inch cake or a 13-by-9-by-2-inch cake. Preheat the oven to 350°F. if you plan to make a 9-inch round cake in a 3-inch-deep pan. With a pastry brush, spread a light coating of melted or softened butter over the bottom and sides of the pan you plan to use. Cut pieces of baking parchment paper or wax paper to fit the bottom and—in the case of the 3-inch-deep pan—the sides. Set the paper in place and butter it lightly.

In a large mixing bowl, combine the eggs and sugar. Set the bowl over a pot of simmering water—the bottom of the bowl must not touch the water—and beat with a wire whisk or a rotary or electric beater until the mixture is lukewarm. Remove the mixture from the heat and beat until it triples in volume and forms a slowly dissolving ribbon when the beater is lifted from the bowl. This will take about five minutes with an electric beater, 15 minutes with a whisk. With a rubber spatula, stir in the vanilla, then gently fold in the flour. Do not overmix the batter. Transfer the batter to the prepared pan and smooth the top with the spatula.

Bake the 16-by-11-inch cake in the middle of the preheated 375°F. oven for 10 minutes or until it begins to shrink from the sides of the pan and feels springy and firm to your fingertips. A tester inserted into the center should come out clean. Bake the 13-by-9-inch cake at 375°F. for about 15 minutes. Bake the 9-inch round cake at 350°F. for about 25 minutes to make allowance for its 3-inch thickness.

Cool the cake in the pan for five minutes, then turn it out onto a wire rack, and gently peel off the paper. Let the cake cool completely—this will take at least 30 minutes—before cutting the deeper cake horizontally into two or three layers, or cutting the shallow cakes vertically into bars.

■ AMERICAN COOKING

## Ladyfingers

*The homemade ladyfinger is a delicate cookie, quite unlike the usual grocery-store product. Although ladyfingers will keep for two to three weeks in an airtight container, it seems more likely that they would be gone within a day or two.* ✣

**To make 30 to 36 ladyfingers**

| | |
|---|---|
| **3 large eggs, separated** | **½ cup flour, sifted** |
| **⅓ cup superfine sugar** | |

Preheat the oven to 350°F. With a pastry brush, spread a light coating of melted or softened butter on the bottom and sides of three baking sheets, line them with buttered wax paper, and dust the paper with flour.

Put the egg yolks and ⅓ cup of superfine sugar in a heatproof bowl; balance the bowl in a pan partly filled with hot water and set over low heat. The bottom of the bowl should not touch the water. Beat the egg yolks and sugar together until they are very thick and very pale. This should take about five minutes if you use an electric mixer, about 15 minutes with a wire whisk.

With a rubber spatula, scrape the egg-yolk mixture into a large bowl. Carefully fold in the sifted flour. In a separate bowl, beat the egg whites with a whisk or a rotary or electric beater until they are firm enough to stand in stiff peaks when the beater is lifted from the bowl. Stir a quarter of the egg whites into the egg-yolk mixture to lighten it, then very carefully fold in the remaining egg whites.

Fit a large pastry bag with a ½-inch plain tube. Fill the bag with the ladyfinger mixture, and pipe strips about 4 inches long onto the prepared baking sheets, leaving about 2 inches between the strips. Dust the piped strips with superfine sugar and bake for about 20 minutes or until the ladyfingers are lightly browned. With a wide spatula carefully remove the ladyfingers from the paper and place them on wire racks to cool.

NOTE: To flavor the ladyfingers with chocolate, sift ½ to 1 tablespoon of cocoa with the flour. For orange flavor, add 1 tablespoon of grated peel to the egg yolk mixture along with the flour. For almond flavor, add ¼ teaspoon of almond extract to the beaten batter.

■ THE GOOD COOK: CLASSIC DESSERTS

# Index/Glossary

347

# Acknowledgments/Credits

**The editors are particularly indebted to:** Carolyn Rothery, Alexandria, Virginia; Rebecca C. Christofferson, Adam deVito, Henry Grossi, Barbara Sause, John T. Shaffer and Susan Stuck of the staff of Healthy Home Cooking; Carol Cutler, Washington, D.C.; Ann Ready, Alexandria, Virginia; and Jolene Worthington, Chicago, Illinois.

The editors also wish to thank National Wildlife Federation, Washington, D.C.; Kitchens Plus, Rochelle Park, New Jersey; Yasutaka Fujiwara, manager, and Shigeo Sato, chief chef, Hakubai Restaurant, New York.

**In New York City, the following shops, galleries and companies contributed to the production of this book:** Cover—Rosenthal, U.S.A., plate, wineglass, teapot; Vera, cloth; Henri Bendel, plastic mat; Sybaritic Industries, napkin; The Flower Service Store, flowers. 8–9—A la Vieille Russie. 13–Country Floors, tiles, plate; Vera, linen; Henri Bendel, salt and pepper shakers. 14–15—Fitz and Floyd, bowl; Mikassa, mat; Henri Bendel, napkin; Pottery Barn, ladle. 16—Fitz and Floyd, platter; Bergdorf Goodman, linen. 18—Bergdorf Goodman, terrines; Lord & Taylor, spreader; Vera, linen; Bloomingdale's, trivet, ramekin. 21—Terrafirma Ceramics, dish. 23—Iittala, Finland, plate; Vera, linen. 24—Iittala, Finland, dish; Henri Bendel, tray; Vera, linen. 26–27—Ceralene, china; Pierre Deux, pewter tureen and plate; Porthault, fabric. 30—Iittala, Finland. 32–33—Pierre Deux, bowl, plates, spoon, cloth; Wedgwood, wineglass. 35—Handblock, cloth, napkin, bowls, flatware; Flowers Unlimited, flowers. 38—Mikassa. 40–41—Villeroy & Boch, plate; Regent Sheffield, Ltd. (Farmingdale, New York), flatware. 45—Country Floors, tiles, plates, coffee pot; Vera, linen. 46–47—Waterford. 48–49—Country Floors, platter; Handblock, cloth. 50–51—Palmer-Smith, Inc. 55—Vera, napkin; Handblock, plate; Flowers Unlimited, flowers. 56—Terrafirma Ceramics, dish; Pierre Deux, cloth. 59—Handblock, plates, fabric; Wolfman-Gold and Good Company, wooden plate. 60–61—Royal Copenhagen Porcelain-Georg Jensen Silversmiths. 63—Mikassa, white bowl. 64–65—Bloomingdale's. 69—Hutschenreuther, sauceboat, plate; Palmer-Smith, cloth; Sybaritic Industries, mat. 71—Hutschenreuther, plate; Christofle, flatware. 72—Hutschenreuther, plate; Porthault, linen; Christofle, flatware. 75—Rosenthal, plate; Henri Bendel, mat; Sybaritic Industries, napkin; The Flower Service Store, flowers. 76—Country Floors, tiles; Ad Hoc Housewares, plate; Hutschenreuther, sauce dish and warmer. 81—Sointu, dish. 82–83—Corning Glass Works, skillet; Handblock, linen. 85—Rosenthal, plates, flatware; Sybaritic Industries, napkin. 86—Ad Hoc Housewares, pot; Palmer-Smith, cloth. 88–89—Country Floors, platter. 90—Corning Glass Works, baking dish and basket; Ad Hoc Housewares, serving spoon; Rosenthal, flatware; The Wilton Company, salt and pepper shakers. 92–93—Rosenthal, platter, salt and pepper shakers; Sybaritic Industries, mat. 97—Wolfman-Gold and Good, platter, serving fork; Handblock, cloth; Flowers Unlimited, flowers. 99—Hutschenreuther, plate, napkin ring; Wolfman-Gold and Good, flatware, lace; Vera, linen. 100—Ceralene, plate. 102—Mottahedeh, plates, ginger jar; Karl Mann Associates, wallpaper. 104–105—Hutschenreuther, platter, sauceboat; Vera, linen; Karl Mann, wallpaper. 106–107—Country Station Antiques (Tannersville, New York), pitcher. 112—Ceralene, china; Christofle, flatware; Christian Schlumberger, fabric. 114–115—Country Station Antiques (Tannersville, New York), platter; Handblock, napkin. 117—Laura Ashley, wallpaper; Ceralene, china. 118—Bloomingdale's, casserole, dish. 122–123—Hakubai Restaurant. 125—Pierre Deux, china, linen; Country Station Antiques (Tannersville, New York), dried flower wreath. 126—Royal Copenhagen Porcelain-Georg Jensen Silversmiths, porcelain, flatware; Laura Ashley, wallpaper; Christian Schlumberger, pleated silk; Baccarat, wineglass; George Matouk, napkin. 128–129—Christian Schlumberger, fabric; Corning Glass Works, ovenware; Sointu, flatware; Hutschenreuther, warmer. 130—Ad Hoc Housewares, bowl, spoon, cloth; Pierre Deux, vase. 133—Bernardaud Limoges, china, crystal; Elite Limoges, spoon; Christian Schlumberger, fabric. 134–135—George Matouk, cloth; Mottahedeh, china. 137—Iittala, Finland, platter. 139—Iittala, Finland. 140—Ad Hoc Housewares. 142—Handblock, cloth and napkins. 145—Elite Limoges, china, flatware; Vera, linen. 146—Corning Glass Works, dish; Taylor Woodcraft, chopping board; George Matouk, cloth. 149—Pierre Deux, fabric, platter, salt and pepper shakers. 150–151—Hutschenreuther, platter; Handblock, napkin. 154—Pratt's Place (Tannersville, New York), fish platter and small dish; Henri Bendel, napkin. 156—Hutschenreuther, plate; Sointu, marble slab, flatware; Vera, linen. 158–159—Handblock, fabric; The Wilton Company, pewter plate. 160—Royal Copenhagen Porcelain-Georg Jensen Silversmiths, fish platter. 162—Sointu, platter, bowl; Hutschenreuther, spoon. 165—Royal Copenhagen Porcelain-Georg Jensen Silversmiths, wooden dish, plate. 168—Hutschenreuther, plate. 170–171—Terrafirma Ceramics, shell bowl; The Wilton Company, spoon. 173—Henri Bendel, plate, tray, cloth; Royal Copenhagen Porcelain-Georg Jensen Silversmiths, flatware. 174—Sointu, dish, rock cup, fabric; Hutschenreuther, flower holder, Japanese chopsticks. 176—Handblock, fabric; Sointu, salt and pepper shakers, glass, plate. 179—Country Floors, tiles. 180–181—Pratt's Place (Tannersville, New York), paella dish. 182–183—Ad Hoc Housewares, pasta servers. 187—Henri Bendel, plate. 188–189—Ad Hoc Housewares, baking dish, cooling rack, salt cellar, serving spoon; Handblock, fabric. 190—Bloomingdale's, Chinese bowl and lid; The Flower Service Store, flowers and basket. 193—Ad Hoc Housewares. 196–197—Kay Strickler Interiors, antiques. 198—Palmer-Smith, plate, bowl, wineglass, linen cloth. 201—Ad Hoc Housewares, plate, bowl; Kay Strickler Interiors, white lattice bowl; Vera, linen. 202—Victor Bonomo, cloth; The Wilton Company, pewter; Henri Bendel, plate. 212—Handblock, linen. 214–215—Hutschenreuther, crystal; Corning Glass Works, quiche dish. 218–219—Mottahedeh, asparagus dishes and tureen; Fitz and Floyd, sauce holder; Laura Ashley, wallpaper. 223—Ad Hoc Housewares, yellow plate; Karl Mann, wallpaper. 225—Saint Gobain, soufflé dish, chrome holder. 229—Iittala, Finland. 230—Karl Mann, wallpaper; Hutschenreuther, leaf plate. 233—Zona, earthenware bowl and plate; Handblock, cloth. 235—Royal Copenhagen Porcelain-Georg Jensen Silversmiths, glass dishes, flatware; Laura Ashley, wallpaper. 236—Rosenthal, plate; Vera, napkin. 239—Ad Hoc Housewares, bowl, wooden board. 240—Laura Ashley, wallpaper; Pratt's Place (Tannersville, New York), pottery. 243—Karl Mann, wallpaper. 247—Hutschenreuther, terrine, plates; George Matouk, cloth; Zona, wooden planter. 248–249—Terrafirma Ceramics, dish; Handblock, runner. 254—Handblock, linen; Hutschenreuther, casserole. 261—Handblock, mat; Vera, napkin; Corning Glass Works, cookware. 262–263—George Donskoj (Kingston, New York), stained glass; Le Croissant Shop, brioche. 282—Hutschenreuther, china. 287—Corning Glass Works, glass dish. 288—KitchenAid, mixer. 291—Wedgwood, china; Vera, linen. 292–293—The Wilton Company, platter; The Flower Service Store, flowers and holder. 297—Ceralene, plate; Vera, napkin. 298—Vera, linen. 301—Hutschenreuther, plate. 302–303—Hutschenreuther, china; Vera, linen; Christofle, fork. 306–307—Cherchez, linen. 311—Porthault, linen; Baccarat, crystal glass. 316–317—Baccarat, wineglass; Hutschenreuther, glass dish. 320—Mottahedeh, china. 322—Baccarat, crystal dish. 327—Christofle, flatware.